An Introduction to Programming with
C++
Fourth Edition

Diane Zak

D1305041

THOMSON

COURSE TECHNOLOGY

Australia • Canada • Mexico • Singapore • Spain • United Kingdom • United States

An Introduction to Programming with C++, Fourth Edition,
by Diane Zak

Executive Editor:
Mac Mendelsohn

Managing Editor:
William Pitkin III

Senior Acquisitions Editor:
Drew Strawbridge

Senior Product Manager:
Tricia Boyle

Associate Product Manager:
Sarah Santoro

Marketing Manager:
Brian Berkeley

Editorial Assistant:
Jennifer Smith

Production Editor:
Pamela Elizian

Cover Designer:
Abby Scholz

Compositor:
GEX Publishing Services

Manufacturing Coordinator:
Laura Burns

COPYRIGHT © 2005 Thomson Course Technology, a division of Thomson Learning, Inc. Thomson Learning™ is a trademark used herein under license.

Printed in the United States of America

1 2 3 4 5 6 7 8 9 GLOB 07 06 05 04

For more information, contact Thomson Course Technology, 25 Thomson Place, Boston, Massachusetts, 02210.

Or find us on the World Wide Web at: www.course.com

ALL RIGHTS RESERVED. No part of this work covered by the copyright hereon may be reproduced or used in any form or by any means—graphic, electronic, or mechanical, including photocopying, recording, taping, Web distribution, or information storage and retrieval systems—without the written permission of the publisher.

For permission to use material from this text or product, submit a request online at www.thomsonrights.com.

Disclaimer
Thomson Course Technology reserves the right to revise this publication and make changes from time to time in its content without notice.

ISBN 0-619-21711-1 [Student Edition]

ISBN 0-619-21729-4 [Instructor Edition]

Contents

Chapter 2

Chapter 3

Chapter 4

Variables, Constants, and Arithmetic Operators 123

Chapter 5

The Selection Structure 169

Chapter 6

More on the Selection Structure 209

Chapter 7

The Repetition Structure 257

Chapter 8

More on the Repetition Structure 303

Chapter 9

Value-Returning Functions 333

Chapter 10

Void Functions 373

Chapter 11

Arrays 415

Chapter 12

String Manipulation 463

Chapter 13

Sequential Access Files 499

Chapter 14

Classes and Objects 539

Appendix A

Appendix B

Appendix C

Preface

An Introduction to Programming with C++, Fourth Edition is designed for a beginning programming course. This book uses the C++ programming language to teach programming concepts. Although the book assumes that students are using the Microsoft Visual C++ .NET compiler, they will be able to create the programs in the book using most C++ compilers, often with little or no modification.

Organization and Coverage

An Introduction to Programming with C++, Fourth Edition contains 14 chapters and 3 appendices. In the chapters, students with no previous programming experience learn how to plan and create well-structured programs. By the end of the book, students will have learned how to write programs using the sequence, selection, and repetition structures, as well as how to create and manipulate functions, strings, classes, objects, sequential access files, and arrays.

Approach

An Introduction to Programming with C++, Fourth Edition is distinguished from other textbooks because of its unique approach, which motivates students by demonstrating why they need to learn the concepts and skills presented. Each chapter contains a Concept Lesson that introduces one or more programming concepts. Following the Concept Lesson is an Application Lesson that contains three labs; each lab teaches students how to apply the concepts taught in the Concept Lesson. The first lab asks students to stop and analyze an existing program. In the second lab, students plan and create a program. The third lab requires students to modify an existing program.

Features

An Introduction to Programming with C++, Fourth Edition is an exceptional textbook because it also includes the following features:

- **"Read This Before You Begin" Section** This section is consistent with Thomson Course Technology's unequaled commitment to helping instructors introduce technology into the classroom. Technical considerations and assumptions about hardware, software, and default settings are listed in one place to help instructors save time and eliminate unnecessary aggravation.

New!
- **Lessons** Each chapter is divided into two lessons—Concept and Application. The Concept Lesson introduces various programming concepts, including programming syntax and code examples. The Application Lesson in each chapter now contains three labs (rather than one) that teach students how to apply the concepts taught in the Concept Lesson to real-world problems. The first lab asks students to stop and analyze an existing program. In the second lab, students plan and create a program. The third lab requires students to modify an existing program. Answers to the labs are provided in the chapters. Concepts are combined in later Application Lessons so that students have the opportunity to use multiple programming features to efficiently solve programming tasks.

New! • **Standard C++ Syntax** The book now uses the standard C++ syntax rather than the .NET syntax. For example, the standard `cout` and `cin` streams are used rather than the .NET `Console::WriteLine` and `Console::ReadLine` methods. Although the book assumes that students are using the Microsoft Visual C++ .NET compiler, they will be able to create the programs in the book using most C++ compilers, often with little or no modification.

New! • **Order of Topics** The selection and repetition structures are now covered before value-returning and void functions. Arrays are now covered before sequential access files, and both array tutorials are combined in one chapter. The book now includes a chapter on string manipulation. The Classes and Objects chapter is now the last chapter in the book. Appendix B now covers C-Strings rather than the built-in .NET mathematical methods.

New! • **Two New Chapters** In the previous edition, Tutorial 3 covered the last three steps in the problem-solving process, as well as getting started with C++. It also covered variables, constants, and arithmetic operators. In this edition, the detailed information about variables, constants, and arithmetic operators was removed from Chapter 3 and is now covered in its own chapter, Chapter 4. The book now includes a chapter (Chapter 12) on string manipulation.

New! • **Two New Appendices** Appendix B covers C-Strings. Appendix C includes an expanded coverage of pointer variables.

• **TIPs** The Tip feature provides additional information about a procedure. For example, it might offer an alternative method of performing the procedure.

• **Mini-Quizzes** Mini-quizzes are strategically placed to test students' knowledge at various points in each chapter. Answers to the quiz questions are provided in the chapters, allowing students to determine whether they have mastered the material covered thus far before continuing with the lesson.

• **Summary** Following each Concept Lesson is a Summary, which recaps the programming concepts and commands covered in the lesson.

• **Questions and Exercises** Each Concept Lesson concludes with meaningful, conceptual Questions that test the students' understanding of what they learned in the lesson. The Questions are followed by Exercises, which provide students with additional practice of the skills and concepts they learned in the lesson. Each Application Lesson also includes Exercises, many of which provide practice in applying cumulative programming knowledge or allow students to explore alternative solutions to programming tasks.

• **Discovery Exercises** These are designated by an icon in the margin and encourage students to challenge and independently develop their own programming skills.

• **Debugging Exercises** One of the most important programming skills students can learn is the ability to correct problems, called "bugs," in an existing program. The Debugging Exercises, also designated by an icon in the margin, provide an opportunity for students to detect and correct errors in an existing program.

New! ## Testing Center

Available free with this book, Thomson Course Technology's Testing Center combines challenging assessment with helpful review material to provide students with a robust, Web-based learning tool. Utilizing the virtual compiler CodeSaw, students sharpen their programming skills through hands-on exercises, self-assessment, and interactive tutorials, all fully integrated with the text. For instructors, the Testing Center provides a central location for review and detailed feedback on student performance. For more information please visit **www.course.com/testingcenter**.

Teaching Tools

The following supplemental materials are available when this book is used in a classroom setting. All of the teaching tools available with this book are provided to the instructor on a single CD-ROM. Most are also available (password protected) at the Thomson Course Technology Web site—**www.course.com**.

Electronic Instructor's Manual The Instructor's Manual that accompanies this textbook includes additional instructional material to assist in class preparation, such as Sample Syllabi, Chapter Outlines, Technical Notes, Lecture Notes, Quick Quizzes, Teaching Tips, Discussion Topics, and Key Terms.

ExamView® This textbook is accompanied by ExamView, a powerful testing software package that allows instructors to create and administer printed, computer (LAN-based), and Internet exams. ExamView includes hundreds of questions that correspond to the topics covered in this text, enabling students to generate detailed study guides that include page references for further review. The computer-based and Internet testing components allow students to take exams at their computers, and also save the instructor time by grading each exam automatically.

PowerPoint Presentations This book offers Microsoft PowerPoint slides for each chapter. These are included as a teaching aid for classroom presentation, to make available to students on the network for chapter review, or to be printed for classroom distribution. Instructors can add their own slides for additional topics they introduce to the class.

Data Files Data Files to accompany this text contain all of the data necessary for labs within the chapters and the end-of-lesson Exercises. Both students and instructors should have access to these, so they are not password protected.

Solutions Files Solutions to end-of-lesson Questions and Exercises are also provided. The solutions are password protected.

Distance Learning Thomson Course Technology is proud to present online courses in WebCT and Blackboard, to provide the most complete and dynamic learning experience possible. When you add online content to one of your courses, you're adding a lot: self-tests, links, glossaries, and, most of all, a gateway to the 21st century's most important information resource. We hope you will make the most of your course, both online and offline. For more information on how to bring distance learning to your course, contact your local Thomson Course Technology sales representative.

Acknowledgments

I would like to thank all of the people who helped to make this book a reality, especially Tricia Boyle (Senior Product Manager), Pamela Elizian (Production Editor), and the great testers in Quality Assurance. Last, but certainly not least, I want to thank the following reviewers for their invaluable ideas and comments: James Ball, Indiana State University, and Michael Danchak, Rensselaer Polytechnic Institute.

Finally, I dedicate this book to the loving memory of Mary Clare Karnick. We all loved you more.

Diane Zak

Read This Before You Begin

To the User

Data Files

To complete the steps and exercises in this book, you will need data files that have been created for this book. Your instructor will provide the data files to you. You also can obtain the files electronically from the Thomson Course Technology Web site by connecting to **www.course.com** and then searching for this book by title, author, or ISBN.

Each chapter in this book has its own set of data files, which are stored in a separate folder within the Cpp folder. For example, the files for Chapter 3 are stored in the Cpp\Chap03 folder. Similarly, the files for Chapter 4 are stored in the Cpp\Chap04 folder. Throughout this book, you will be instructed to open files from or save files to these folders.

You can use a computer in your school lab or your own computer to complete the labs and exercises in this book.

Using Your Own Computer

To use your own computer to complete the labs and exercises in this book, you will need the following:

- **A 486-level or higher personal computer running Microsoft Windows XP** This book was written and Quality Assurance tested using Microsoft Windows XP.
- **A C++ compiler.** This book was written using Microsoft Visual Studio .NET 2003 Professional Edition and Quality Assurance tested using Microsoft Visual C++ .NET 2003 Standard Edition. If you purchased a copy of the text, then you also received Microsoft Visual C++ .NET 2003 Standard Edition contained on a set of 6 CD-ROMs.
- **Data files.** You will not be able to complete the labs and exercises in this book using your own computer unless you have the data files. You can get the data files from your instructor, or you can obtain the data files electronically from the Thomson Course Technology Web site by connecting to **www.course.com** and then searching for this book title.

Visit Our World Wide Web Site

Additional materials might be available for your course on the Web. Visit the Thomson Course Technology Web site—**www.course.com**—and periodically search this site for more details.

To the Instructor

To complete the labs and exercises in this book, your students must use a set of data files. These files are included on the Teaching Tools CD-ROM. They may also be obtained electronically through the Thomson Course Technology Web site at **www.course.com**. Follow the instructions in the Help file to copy the data files to your server or standalone computer. You can view the Help file using a text editor such as WordPad or Notepad. Once the files are copied, you should instruct your users how to copy the files to their own computers or workstations.

Thomson Course Technology Data Files

You are granted a license to copy the data files to any computer or computer network used by individuals who have purchased this book.

An Overview of a Personal Computer System

After completing this overview, you will be able to:

- Describe the components of a personal computer system

- Explain the relationship between hardware and software

- Explain the history of programming languages

An Introduction to a Personal Computer System

In the 1970s, the first **microcomputers**, also called **personal computers**, appeared in the marketplace. Since then, the personal computer has become so popular that it is difficult to imagine what a person ever did without one. Imagine typing a letter on a typewriter, or keeping track of your investments manually, or drawing the blueprints for a house without the aid of a computer!

Since the introduction of the personal computer, situations and tasks that once were considered impossible are now commonplace. For example, **telecommuting**, where an employee works from home and uses a personal computer to communicate with his or her office, is now an option available to many business professionals. Personal computers also allow you to access information from around the world, via the Internet and the World Wide Web, from the comfort of your home, office, or school.

Figure 1 shows a typical personal computer system found in most businesses and homes.

Figure 1: A typical personal computer system

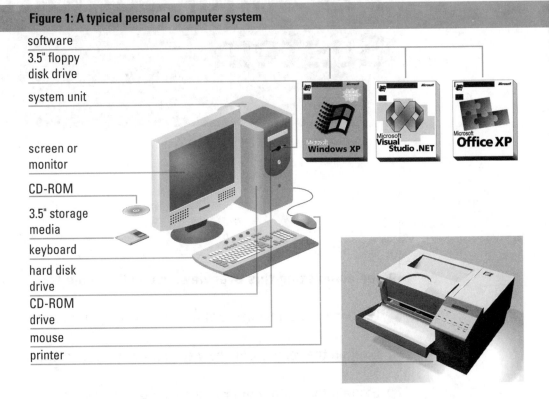

software
3.5" floppy disk drive
system unit
screen or monitor
CD-ROM
3.5" storage media
keyboard
hard disk drive
CD-ROM drive
mouse
printer

Notice that a **personal computer system** is composed of both hardware and software. **Hardware** refers to the physical components of the system. **Software** refers to the programs (step-by-step instructions) that tell the hardware how to perform a task. In the next section, you learn about the hardware and software found in a personal computer system and how they interact.

An Overview of Hardware and Software

As Figure 1 shows, the hardware in a personal computer system consists of a **system unit**, which is the case or box that contains the main circuit boards and storage devices. The hardware also includes other devices, called peripheral devices.

Peripherals

A **peripheral device** is a device that is attached to the system unit. Peripheral devices extend the capabilities of the computer system, and they provide the user a means by which he or she can communicate with the computer. The three categories of peripheral devices are input devices, output devices, and auxiliary storage devices.

An **input device** allows you to communicate with the computer by entering data into it. Examples of commonly used input devices are a keyboard, mouse, and scanner. As you are working through the lessons and exercises in this book, you will use an input device—the keyboard—to enter your C++ program instructions into the computer.

An **output device** allows the computer to communicate with you by displaying or printing information. Examples of commonly used output devices are a monitor and printer. You will use a monitor to display the C++ instructions you enter into the computer, and you will use a printer to print the instructions. You also will use a monitor and printer to display and print the results of your C++ programs.

Auxiliary storage devices, the third category of peripheral devices, allow you to permanently store information. Floppy disk drives, CD-ROM drives, DVD drives, and hard disk drives are the most common auxiliary storage devices. These storage devices use an auxiliary storage media—a floppy disk, a CD (compact disc), a DVD (digital video disc), or a hard disk—to store the information. You will use an auxiliary storage device to save your C++ program instructions. By doing so, you will be able to use the program again without having to retype it.

Internal Memory

Now look inside the system unit to see what it contains. See Figure 2.

Figure 2: The inside of the system unit

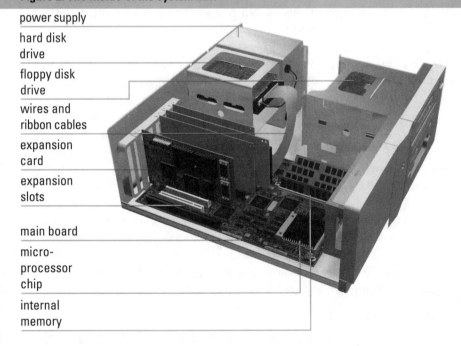

power supply

hard disk drive

floppy disk drive

wires and ribbon cables

expansion card

expansion slots

main board

microprocessor chip

internal memory

The system unit houses an area called **internal memory**, which is an ordered sequence of memory cells contained on chips—integrated circuits residing on silicon. Internal memory is like a

tip

Auxiliary (which means "additional" or "secondary") storage devices and auxiliary storage media are so named because they provide storage capability in addition to that available in the internal memory of the computer.

large post office, where each memory cell, like each post office box, has a unique address, and each can contain mail. Figure 3 illustrates this comparison.

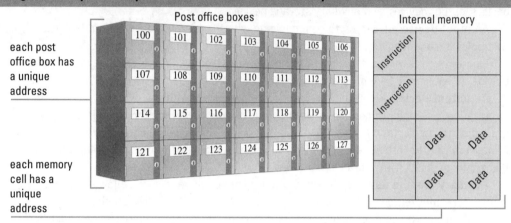

Figure 3: Comparison of post office boxes to internal memory

Post office boxes

each post office box has a unique address

each memory cell has a unique address

Internal memory

tip

The sequence of events that occur between the time that you turn on the computer and the time that it is ready for you to use is referred to as the boot process or "booting" the computer.

Unlike a post office box, which can contain many pieces of mail at the same time, a memory cell can store only one piece of mail at any time. The mail found in a memory cell is typically either a program instruction or an item of data. **Data** refers to the information processed by a program. The data may be input by the user, such as the number of hours an employee worked, or it may be the result of a calculation made by the computer, such as an employee's gross pay.

Some of the chips in internal memory are **Random-Access Memory** (**RAM**) chips; others are **Read-Only Memory** (**ROM**) chips. There are two major differences between a RAM chip and a ROM chip. First, while the computer is on, the user can both write information to and read information from the memory cells located on a RAM chip. In contrast, a user can only read information from a ROM chip's cells; he or she cannot write information to the memory cells on a ROM chip. Second, a RAM chip is volatile, which means that any information stored on the chip is temporary. The information contained on a RAM chip is lost when the computer is turned off or loses power unexpectedly. A ROM chip, on the other hand, is nonvolatile; instructions remain on a ROM chip even when the computer is off.

The memory cells located on ROM chips contain instructions written there by the manufacturer. When you turn a computer on, these instructions perform an automatic self-test of the computer. The self-test makes sure that the different components of the computer are working properly. If all is well, the instructions contained on the ROM chips search either the computer's hard drive or a floppy drive for a set of instructions known as the operating system, which is discussed in the Types of Software section later in this Overview.

The instructions on the ROM chips direct the computer to read the operating system instructions from either the hard disk or a floppy disk. As the instructions are read, they are written to the RAM chips in internal memory, where they are stored until the computer is turned off (or loses power). In addition to the operating system instructions, the RAM chips also store program instructions and data entered from the keyboard or read from a file previously saved on a disk.

The Central Processing Unit

Besides internal memory, the system unit also houses the **Central Processing Unit** (**CPU**), which is the brain of the computer. The CPU resides on a microprocessor chip, which is a single integrated circuit, and it contains two principal components—the control unit and the Arithmetic/Logic Unit (ALU). It also contains special high-speed storage locations called **registers**.

The **control unit** in the CPU directs the flow of information from one part of the computer to another. The control unit is responsible for making sure that the computer correctly processes the program instructions and data stored in internal memory.

The second component of the CPU, the **Arithmetic/Logic Unit** (**ALU**), performs the arithmetic calculations and comparison operations for the computer. If the control unit instructs the computer to add two numbers, it is the ALU that performs the addition. The ALU also would be responsible for comparing the number of hours an employee worked with the number 40 to determine whether the employee should receive overtime pay.

The ALU uses the registers in the CPU to hold the data that is being processed. It uses a special register, called an **accumulator**, to temporarily store the result of an arithmetic or comparison operation. Figure 4 illustrates how the CPU processes an instruction to add the numbers 4 and 5.

Figure 4: Diagram of how the CPU processes an instruction to add two numbers

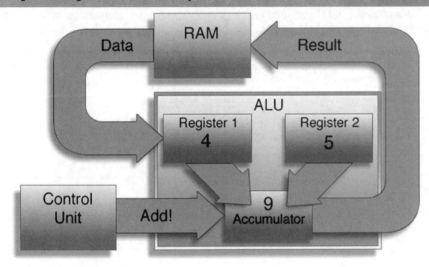

First, the control unit sends the data to be processed—in this case, the numbers 4 and 5—from RAM to the ALU, where it is held in registers. The control unit then sends a signal to the ALU, directing it to add both numbers. After performing the necessary operation, the ALU stores the result—in this case, the number 9—in the accumulator. The control unit then sends the contents of the accumulator to RAM so it can be output, saved on a disk, or used for further processing.

Types of Software

The hardware component of a computer system isn't of much use without software. Recall that the term *software* refers to the instructions that tell the computer how to perform a task. Software typically is divided into two general categories: system software and application software. Each of these categories contains various types of software, as shown in Figure 5.

The purpose of **system software** is to manage the computer and its peripheral devices. As Figure 5 indicates, included in the system software category are operating systems, device drivers, utilities, and programming languages. **Operating systems** are programs that coordinate the activities within the computer and allow both you and the computer to communicate with each other. Windows, Mac OS, UNIX, and Linux are popular operating systems. **Device drivers** are programs that help the computer control a peripheral device, and **utilities** are programs that allow the user to perform tasks such as formatting a disk, copying data from one disk to another, and protecting the computer from viruses. **Programming languages** are programs that allow a user to control how the computer processes data to produce the information that he or she wants. You learn more about programming languages in the next section.

Figure 5: Types of software included in the system and application software categories

system software	application software
operating systems device drivers utilities programming languages	productivity software entertainment software educational software

Unlike system software, **application software** allows a user to computerize a task that he or she might otherwise perform manually, such as writing a letter, preparing a budget, or playing a game. Included in the application software category are productivity software (such as word processors, spreadsheets, databases, and graphics programs), entertainment software (such as computer games), and educational software (such as math tutors and encyclopedias).

In the next section, you learn more about the programming language component of system software.

MINI-QUIZ

Mini Quiz 1

1) The two components of a personal computer system are _____ and _____.

2) The three categories of peripheral devices are _____, _____, and _____.

3) The information processed by a program is called _____.

4) When you enter a program into the computer, the program is stored on _____ chips in internal memory.

5) The CPU contains the _____, _____, and special high-speed storage locations called _____.

6) Word processors belong to a category of software called _____ software.

7) Programming languages belong to a category of software called _____ software.

8) The data to be processed is stored in _____ in the ALU.

A Brief History of Programming Languages

Although computers appear to be amazingly intelligent machines, they cannot yet think on their own. Computers still rely on human beings to give them directions. These directions are called **programs**, and the people who write the programs are called **programmers**.

Just as human beings communicate with each other through the use of languages such as English, Spanish, Hindi, or Chinese, programmers use a variety of special languages, called **programming languages**, to communicate with the computer. Some popular programming languages are C++, C#, Java, Visual Basic, Perl (Practical Extraction and Report Language), C, and COBOL (Common Business Oriented Language). In the next sections, you follow the progression of programming languages from machine languages to assembly languages, and then to high-level languages.

Machine Languages

A computer represents each character in its **character set**—the letters, numerals, and special symbols that can be entered into the computer—by a series of microscopic electronic switches. Like the light switches in your house, each electronic switch can be either on or off. Computers use the binary number system to represent the two switch states. Unlike the decimal number system, with which you are familiar, the **binary number system** uses only the digits 0 and 1, rather than the digits 0 through 9. A 0 in the binary number system indicates that the switch is off; a 1 indicates that it is on. Each character in the computer's character set is represented by a series of these off and on switches—in other words, by a series of 0s and 1s.

Each switch—each 0 or 1—is called a **bit**, which is short for *binary digit*. Most computers use eight switches—in other words, eight bits or binary digits—to represent each number, letter, or symbol. Both the character being represented and the coding scheme used by the computer determine which of the eight switches are on and which are off. Personal computers typically use a coding scheme called **ASCII** (pronounced *ASK-ee*), which stands for American Standard Code for Information Interchange. The letter X, for example, is represented in the ASCII coding scheme by the eight bits 01011000. The collection of eight bits used to represent a character is called a **byte**. Appendix A in this book shows the ASCII codes for the letters, numerals, and special symbols included in your computer's character set.

Because computers can understand only these on and off switches, the first programmers had to write the program instructions using nothing but combinations of 0s and 1s. Instructions written in 0s and 1s are called **machine language** or **machine code**. The machine languages (each type of machine has its own language) represent the only way to communicate directly with the computer. Figure 6 shows a segment of a program written in a machine language.

Figure 6: A segment of a program written in a machine language

```
0100
001101 100000 001101 110001
00101 10001 10000
01110
111001
111001 001 11000 001
11000
0011100
100010 00110
```

As you can imagine, programming in machine language is very tedious and error-prone and requires highly trained programmers.

Assembly Languages

Slightly more advanced programming languages are called **assembly languages**. Figure 7 shows a segment of a program written in an assembly language.

Figure 7: A segment of a program written in an assembly language

```
main proc pay
    mov ax, dseg
    mov ax, 0b00h
    add ax, dx
    mov a1, b1
    mul b1, ax
    mov b1, 04h
```

The assembly languages simplify the programmer's job by allowing the programmer to use mnemonics in place of the 0s and 1s in the program. **Mnemonics** are memory aids—in this case, alphabetic abbreviations for instructions. For example, most assembly languages use the mnemonic ADD to represent an add operation and the mnemonic MUL to represent a multiply operation. The mnemonic MOV is used to move data from one area to another. Programs written in an assembly language require an **assembler**, which also is a program, to convert the assembly instructions into machine code—the 0s and 1s the computer can understand. Although it is much easier to write programs in assembly language than in machine language, programming in assembly language still is tedious and requires highly trained programmers.

The next major development in programming languages was the introduction of the high-level languages.

High-Level Languages

High-level languages allow the programmer to use instructions that more closely resemble the English language. Programs written in a high-level language require a compiler to convert the English-like instructions into the 0s and 1s the computer can understand. Like assemblers, compilers are separate programs. A **compiler** translates the entire program into machine code before running the program.

Like their predecessors, the first high-level languages were used to create procedure-oriented programs. When writing a **procedure-oriented program**, the programmer concentrates on the major tasks that the program needs to perform. A payroll program, for example, typically performs several major tasks, such as inputting the employee data, calculating the gross pay, calculating the taxes, calculating the net pay, and outputting a paycheck. The programmer must instruct the computer every step of the way, from the start of the task to its completion. In a procedure-oriented program, the programmer determines and controls the order in which the computer processes the instructions. Examples of high-level languages used to create procedure-oriented programs include COBOL, BASIC (Beginner's All-Purpose Symbolic Instruction Code), and C.

Figure 8 shows a segment of a program written in BASIC. Notice how closely most of the instructions resemble the English language. Even if you do not know the BASIC language, it is easy to see that the program shown in Figure 8 tells the computer, step by step, *how* to compute and display an employee's net pay.

tip

Some high-level languages—for example, some versions of the BASIC language—use a program called an interpreter, instead of a compiler, to convert the English-like instructions into machine code. Unlike a compiler, an interpreter translates the high-level instructions into machine code, line-by-line, as the program is running.

Figure 8: A procedure-oriented program written in BASIC—a high-level language

```
input "Enter name";names$
input "Enter hours worked";hours
input "Enter pay rate";rate
grossPay = hours * rate
federalTax = .2 * grossPay
socSecTax = .07 * grossPay
stateTax = .06 * grossPay
netPay = grossPay - federalTax - socSecTax - stateTax
print names$, netPay
end
```

In all procedure-oriented programs, the order of the instructions is extremely important. For example, in the program shown in Figure 8, you could not put the instruction to display the net pay before the instruction to calculate the net pay, and then expect the computer to display the correct results. When writing a procedure-oriented program, the programmer must determine not only the proper instructions to give the computer, but the correct sequence of those instructions as well. A programmer typically uses a design methodology called **top-down design** to assist him or her in planning a procedure-oriented program.

When using top-down design to create a procedure-oriented program, the programmer begins with a statement that describes the overall purpose or goal of the program—in other words, it describes what the program is supposed to do. The purpose of the program shown in Figure 8, for example, is to determine the amount an employee should be paid. The program's purpose states *what* needs to be done, but it does not tell *how* to get it done. The programmer tells *how* to accomplish the program's purpose by dividing the solution into small, manageable tasks. The payroll program shown in Figure 8, for example, is broken up into small tasks that input the employee name, hours worked, and pay rate; calculate the gross pay, taxes, and net pay; and display the employee name and net pay. These tasks describe how to reach the program's goal—in this case, determining how much to pay the employee. You learn more about top-down design in Chapter 2.

Recently, more advanced high-level languages have emerged; these languages are used to create object-oriented programs. Examples of high-level languages used to create object-oriented programs include C++, C#, Java, Smalltalk, and Visual Basic. Different from a procedure-oriented program, which views a problem solution as a set of ordered tasks, an **object-oriented program** views a problem solution as a set of interacting objects. A programmer typically uses a design methodology called **object-oriented design (OOD)** to assist him or her in planning an object-oriented program. As with top-down design, the programmer begins with a statement that describes the purpose of the program. However, rather than breaking up the program into one or more tasks, the programmer divides the program into one or more objects, resulting in programs whose code is very different from those created using the procedure-oriented approach.

The objects in an object-oriented program can take on many different forms. For example, programs written for the Windows environment typically use objects such as check boxes, list boxes, and buttons. A payroll program, on the other hand, might utilize objects found in the real world, such as a time card object, an employee object, a check object, and a date object. The partial program shown in Figure 9 shows how you can use the C++ language to create a Date object named payDay.

tip

Because high-level languages are more machine-independent than are machine and assembly languages, programs written in a high-level language can be used on many different types of computers.

tip

Almost everyone, at one time or another, has used top-down design to create a solution to a problem. You probably used top-down design when you planned your last vacation. Your overall goal was to "take a vacation." To accomplish that goal, you divided the solution into small tasks, such as "choose vacation spot," "make hotel reservations," "make airline reservations," and "call kennel." Notice that top-down design considers a problem from the "general" to the "specific."

Figure 9: A segment of an object-oriented program written in C++—a high-level language

```
class Date //defines what a Date object looks like
{
public:
     //changes the month, day and year
     void changeDate(int month, int day, int year);
     // displays the month, day, and year
     void displayDate( );
private:
     int month;   //a Date object contains a month,
     int day;     //a day, and a year
     int year;
};


Date payDay;       //creates a Date object named payDay
```

All but the last instruction shown in Figure 9 simply describe what a Date object looks like. You describe an object by specifying its characteristics and behaviors. In this case, a Date object is composed of a month, day, and year. The Date object's month, day, and year can be both changed and displayed. The last instruction shown in Figure 9—Date payDay;—uses the object's description to create the object named payDay.

Object-oriented programming offers two advantages over procedure-oriented programming. First, object-oriented programming allows a programmer to use familiar objects to solve problems. The ability to use objects that model things found in the real world makes problem solving much easier. Assume, for example, that your task is to create a program that handles the checking account transactions for a bank. Thinking in terms of the objects used by the bank—checking accounts, withdrawal slips, deposit slips, and so on—will make this task easier to accomplish. Second, because each object is viewed as an independent unit, an object can be used in more than one application, with either little or no modification; this saves programming time and money. For example, you can use the Date object shown in Figure 9 in any program that requires a date. In a personnel program, for instance, you could use a Date object to represent a hire date. In an airline reservation program, on the other hand, a Date object might represent a departure date.

Many high-level languages, such as C++ and Visual Basic, can be used to create both procedure-oriented and object-oriented programs.

tip

Languages that can be used to create both procedure-oriented and object-oriented programs are often referred to as hybrid languages.

MINI-QUIZ

Mini Quiz 2

1) The collection of letters, numerals, and symbols that you can enter into a computer is called the computer's _____ .

2) Instructions written in 0s and 1s are called _____ language.

3) _____ languages allow a programmer to use mnemonics in place of the 0s and 1s in a program.

4) When writing a(n) _____ program, the programmer concentrates on the major tasks needed to accomplish a goal.

5) When writing a(n) _____ program, the programmer breaks up a problem into interacting objects.

6) When designing procedure-oriented programs, programmers use a design methodology called _____ .

As you can see, programming languages have come a long way since the first machine languages. What haven't changed about programming languages, however, are the three basic control structures used by programmers: sequence, selection, and repetition. These structures are referred to as **control structures** because they control the flow of the program; in other words, they control the order in which the program instructions are processed. You learn about these three structures in Chapter 1.

You now have completed the Overview. You can either take a break or complete the end-of-lesson questions and exercises.

SUMMARY

A personal computer system contains both hardware and software. Hardware refers to the physical components of the system, and consists of the system unit, input devices, output devices, and peripheral devices. The system unit houses internal memory, which is composed of both RAM and ROM chips, and the Central Processing Unit (CPU), which is the brain of the computer.

The CPU contains two principal components—the control unit and the Arithmetic/Logic Unit (ALU)—and special high-speed storage locations called registers. The control unit is responsible for making sure that the computer correctly processes the program instructions and data stored in internal memory. The ALU performs the arithmetic calculations and comparison operations for the computer. The data to be processed is stored in registers in the CPU. The result of arithmetic or comparison operations is stored in a special register, called the accumulator.

Software refers to the step-by-step instructions, called programs, that tell the hardware how to perform a task. Software typically is divided into two categories: system software and application software. System software includes operating systems, device drivers, utilities, and programming languages. Application software includes productivity software, entertainment software, and educational software.

A computer represents each character in its character set—the letters, numerals, and special symbols that can be entered into the computer—by a series of microscopic electronic switches that can be either on or off. Computers use the binary number system to represent the two switch states. The binary number system uses the digit 0 to indicate that a switch is off; it uses a 1 to indicate that the switch is on.

Each switch—each 0 or 1—is called a bit, which is short for *binary digit*. Most computers use eight bits, referred to as a byte, to represent each number, letter, or symbol. Both the character being represented and the coding scheme used by the computer determine which of the eight bits are on and which are off. Personal computers typically use a coding scheme called ASCII (pronounced ASK-ee), which stands for American Standard Code for Information Interchange.

Programs are the step-by-step instructions that tell a computer how to perform a task. Programmers, the people who write computer programs, use various programming languages to communicate with the computer. The first programming languages were machine languages, also called machine code. The assembly languages came next, followed by the high-level languages. The first high-level languages were used to create procedure-oriented programs. More recent high-level languages are used to create object-oriented programs.

ANSWERS TO MINI-QUIZZES

Mini-Quiz 1

1) hardware, software

2) input devices, output devices, auxiliary storage devices

3) data

4) RAM

5) ALU, control unit, registers

6) application (or productivity)

7) system

8) registers

Mini-Quiz 2

1) character set

2) machine

3) Assembly

4) procedure-oriented

5) object-oriented

6) top-down design

QUESTIONS

1) Which of the following is not a peripheral device?

   A. auxiliary storage device

   B. input device

   C. output device

   D. system unit

2) A computer's system unit contains _____.

    A. the ALU

    B. the control unit

    C. internal memory

    D. all of the above

3) A storage cell in the internal memory of a computer can store _____ at a time.

    A. one instruction

    B. one piece of data

    C. two or more pieces of data

    D. either a or b

4) While the computer is on, you can both write information to and read information from a storage cell located on _____.

    A. a RAM chip

    B. a ROM chip

    C. either a RAM chip or a ROM chip

5) Which of the following is responsible for making sure that the program instructions stored in internal memory are processed correctly?

    A. ALU

    B. control unit

    C. internal memory unit

    D. RAM chip

6) Which of the following performs the arithmetic calculations and logic operations for the computer?

    A. ALU

    B. control unit

    C. internal memory unit

    D. ROM chip

7) Where is the result of an arithmetic or comparison operation stored?

    A. accumulator

    B. adder

    C. compiler

    D. control unit

8) The set of step-by-step directions given to a computer is called _____.

    A. computerese

    B. a command

    C. a collection

    D. a program

9) Using the binary number system, which of the following indicates that a switch is off?

A. 0

B. 1

C. 2

D. 3

10) Which of the following is a program that translates high-level instructions into machine code?

A. assembler

B. compiler

C. source program

D. translator

Look For These Symbols

Debugging

Discovery

EXERCISES

1) Briefly explain the history of programming languages as outlined in the Overview.

2) Make a list of your computer system's input devices, output devices, and auxiliary storage devices. Which operating system is your computer using?

3) Appendix A in this book lists the ASCII codes for the letters, numerals, and special symbols included in a computer's character set. What are the ASCII codes for the ampersand (&), the letter S, and the letter s?

4) Use the ASCII codes listed in Appendix A to write your first name.

5) Explain the difference between top-down design and object-oriented design.

6) List and explain two advantages of using object-oriented languages.

Exercises 7 and 8 are Discovery Exercises, which may include topics that are not covered in the lesson. Discovery Exercises allow you to "discover" the solutions to problems on your own.

 7) Research the C++ programming language. Where did it originate? Who developed it? What is the meaning of the two plus signs in the C++ name? (You can use either the Internet or the library to do your research.)

 8) Research both the decimal number system and the binary number system. Explain how both systems work. For example, why do the digits 10100 represent a different number in each system? What number do those digits represent in each system? How can you convert a binary number to its decimal equivalent? How can you convert a decimal number to its binary equivalent?

 Please visit the Testing Center at www.course.com/testingcenter for more practice on the topics covered in this chapter.

Chapter 1

An Introduction to Control Structures

Objectives

After completing this chapter, you will be able to:

- Explain the sequence, selection, and repetition structures

- Write simple algorithms using the sequence, selection, and repetition structures

Concept Lesson

Defining Control Structures

All computer programs, no matter how simple or how complex, are written using one or more of three basic structures: sequence, repetition, and selection. These structures are called **control structures** or **logic structures**, because they control the flow of a program's logic. You will use the sequence structure in every program you write. In most programs, you also will use both the selection and repetition structures.

This chapter gives you an introduction to the three control structures used in computer programs. It also introduces you to a computerized mechanical man named Rob, who will help illustrate the control structures. More detailed information about each structure, as well as how to implement these structures using the C++ language, is provided in subsequent chapters. Begin by learning about the sequence structure.

The Sequence Structure

You already are familiar with the sequence structure—you use it each time you follow a set of directions, in order, from beginning to end. A cookie recipe, for example, provides a good example of the sequence structure. To get to the finished product—edible cookies—you need to follow each recipe instruction in order, beginning with the first instruction and ending with the last. Likewise, the **sequence structure** in a computer program directs the computer to process the program instructions, one after another, in the order listed in the program. You will find the sequence structure in every program.

You can observe how the sequence structure works by programming a mechanical man named Rob. Like a computer, Rob has a limited instruction set—in other words, Rob can understand only a specific number of instructions, also called commands. Rob's instruction set includes the following three commands: `walk`, `turn`, and `sit`. When told to `walk`, Rob takes one complete step forward. In other words, Rob moves his right foot forward one step, then moves his left foot to meet his right foot. When told to `turn`, Rob turns 180 degrees, which is half of a full turn of 360 degrees. When told to `sit`, Rob simply sits down.

For this first example, assume that Rob is facing a chair that is two steps away from him. Your task is to write the instructions, using only the commands that Rob understands, that direct Rob to sit in the chair. Figure 1-1 shows Rob, the chair, and the instructions that will get Rob seated in the chair.

Figure 1-1: An example of the sequence structure

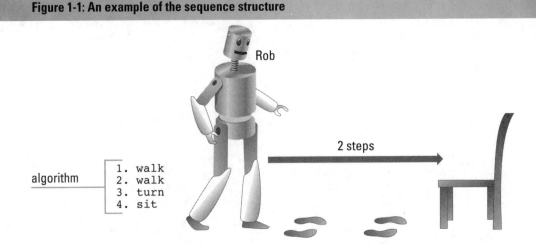

The four instructions shown in Figure 1-1 are called an algorithm. An **algorithm** is simply the set of step-by-step instructions that accomplish a task. Figure 1-1's algorithm, for example, contains the instructions that are necessary to get Rob seated in the chair. Notice that it is important that Rob follow the instructions in the list in order—in other words, in sequence. Rob first must `walk` two times, then `turn`, and then `sit`. He cannot `turn` first, then `walk` two times, and then `sit`.

You learn about the repetition structure next.

MINI-QUIZ

Mini-Quiz 1

1) The three basic control structures are _____, _____, and _____.

2) All programs contain the _____ structure.

3) When using the _____ structure, instructions are followed in the order that they appear in the program.

4) The step-by-step instructions that accomplish a task are called a(n) _____.

The Repetition Structure

As with the sequence structure, you already are familiar with the repetition structure. For example, shampoo bottles typically include the repetition structure in the directions for washing your hair. Those directions usually tell you to repeat the "apply shampoo to hair," "lather," and "rinse" steps until your hair is clean. When used in a program, the **repetition structure**, also referred to as a loop, directs the computer to repeat one or more instructions until some condition is met, at which time the computer should stop repeating the instructions.

You can observe how the repetition structure works by programming Rob, the mechanical man. In this example, Rob is facing a chair that is 50 steps away from him. Your task is to write the algorithm that directs Rob to sit in the chair. If the sequence structure were the only control structure available to you, you would need to write the `walk` instruction 50 times, followed by `turn`, then `sit`. Although that algorithm would work, it is quite cumbersome to write. Imagine if Rob were 500 steps away from the chair! The best way to write the algorithm to get Rob seated in a chair that is 50 steps away from him is to use the repetition structure. To do so, however, you need to add another instruction to Rob's instruction set: in addition to `walk`, `turn`, and `sit`, Rob now can understand the command `repeat x times:`, where x is the number of times you want him to repeat something. The illustration of Rob and the chair, along with the correct algorithm, is shown in Figure 1-2. Notice that the algorithm contains both the sequence and repetition structures.

Rather than writing the `walk` instruction 50 times, the algorithm shown in Figure 1-2 uses the `repeat 50 times:` instruction to direct Rob to walk 50 times before he turns and then sits. Notice that the instruction to be repeated—in this case, `walk`—is indented below the `repeat 50 times:` instruction. Indenting in this manner indicates that the instruction is part of the repetition structure and, therefore, needs to be repeated. Because the `turn` and `sit` instructions are not part of the repetition structure—in other words, they are to be followed only once, not 50 times—they are not indented. The algorithm shown in Figure 1-2 is both easier to write and much clearer than one containing 50 `walk` instructions.

tip
The repetition structure also is referred to as iteration.

tip

Although the repetition structure shown in Figure 1-2 includes only one instruction, a repetition structure can include many instructions.

Figure 1-2: An example of the repetition structure

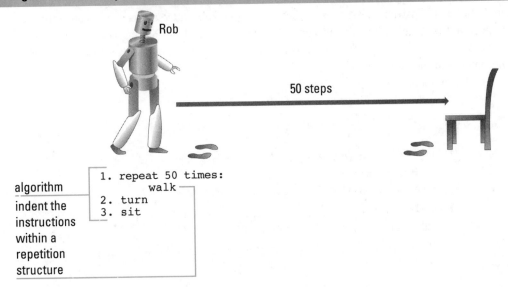

```
algorithm          1. repeat 50 times:
                        walk
indent the         2. turn
instructions       3. sit
within a
repetition
structure
```

Recall that the repetition structure repeats one or more instructions until some condition is met, at which time the repetition structure ends. In the example shown in Figure 1-2, the repetition structure ends after Rob walks 50 times. Rob is then free to continue to the next instruction in the algorithm—in this case, `turn`, followed by `sit`. But what if you don't know precisely how many steps there are between Rob and the chair? In that case, you need to change the repetition structure's condition.

In the next example, assume that Rob is facing a chair and you don't know how far away from the chair he is. As before, your task is to write the algorithm that gets Rob seated in the chair. To accomplish this task, you need to add another instruction to Rob's instruction set: Rob now can understand the instruction `repeat until you are directly in front of the chair:`. The new algorithm is shown in Figure 1-3.

Figure 1-3: Another example of the repetition structure

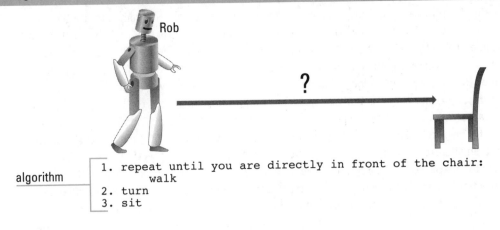

```
algorithm          1. repeat until you are directly in front of the chair:
                        walk
                   2. turn
                   3. sit
```

The repetition structure shown in Figure 1-3's algorithm ends when Rob is standing directly in front of the chair. If Rob is 10 steps away from the chair, the repetition structure directs him to walk 10 times before he turns and then sits. If Rob is 500 steps away from the chair, the repetition structure directs him to walk 500 times before he turns and then sits. If Rob is directly in front of the chair, the repetition structure is bypassed, and Rob simply turns and then sits.

The last of the three control structures is the selection structure.

The Selection Structure

Like the sequence and repetition structures, you already are familiar with the **selection structure**, also called the **decision structure**. The selection structure makes a decision, and then takes an appropriate action based on that decision. You use the selection structure every time you drive your car and approach an intersection. Your decision, as well as the appropriate action, is based on whether the intersection has a stop sign. If the intersection has a stop sign, then you stop your car; otherwise, you proceed with caution through the intersection. When used in a computer program, the selection structure alerts the computer that a decision needs to be made. The selection structure also provides the appropriate action to take based on the result of that decision.

As before, Rob can demonstrate the selection structure, although you need to add to his instruction set to do so. In this example, assume that Rob is holding either a red or yellow balloon, and that he is facing two boxes. One of the boxes is colored yellow and the other is colored red. The two boxes are located 20 steps away from Rob. Your task is to have Rob drop the balloon into the appropriate box; the yellow balloon belongs in the yellow box, and the red balloon belongs in the red box. After Rob drops the balloon, you then should return him to his original position. To write an algorithm to accomplish the current task, you need to add four additional instructions to Rob's instruction set. The new instructions allow Rob to make a decision about the color of the balloon he is holding, and then take the appropriate action based on that decision. Rob's new instruction set is shown in Figure 1-4.

Figure 1-4: Rob's new instruction set

```
              walk
              turn
              sit
              repeat x times:
              repeat until you are directly in front of the chair:
four new      if the balloon is red, do this:
instructions  otherwise, do this: (this instruction can be used only in combination with
                 an if instruction)
              drop the balloon in the red box
              drop the balloon in the yellow box
```

Figure 1-5 shows an illustration of this example, along with the correct algorithm.

Figure 1-5: An example of the selection structure

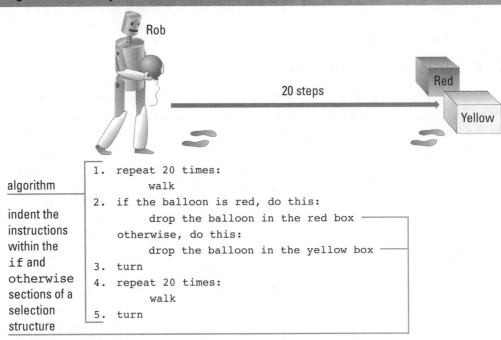

algorithm

indent the
instructions
within the
`if` and
`otherwise`
sections of a
selection
structure

```
1. repeat 20 times:
        walk
2. if the balloon is red, do this:
        drop the balloon in the red box
   otherwise, do this:
        drop the balloon in the yellow box
3. turn
4. repeat 20 times:
        walk
5. turn
```

Notice that the instruction to be followed when the balloon is red—in this case, `drop the balloon in the red box`—and the instruction to be followed when the balloon is not red—in this case, `drop the balloon in the yellow box`—are indented. As you do with the instructions contained in a repetition structure, you also indent the instructions contained within the `if` and `otherwise` sections of a selection structure. Indenting in this manner makes it clear which instructions are to be followed when the balloon is red and which should be followed when the balloon is not red. Also indented in Figure 1-5 is the `walk` instruction contained in both repetition structures.

Notice that the algorithm shown in Figure 1-5 contains all three control structures: sequence, repetition, and selection. The repetition structure, which directs Rob to walk 20 times, is processed first. After Rob walks the 20 steps, the repetition structure ends and Rob proceeds, sequentially, to the next instruction listed in the algorithm; that instruction involves a decision. If the balloon Rob is holding is red, then Rob should drop it into the red box; otherwise, he should drop it into the yellow box. Once the decision is made and the proper action is taken, the selection structure ends and Rob proceeds to the next instruction listed in the algorithm—`turn`. After turning 180 degrees, the second repetition structure (which directs Rob to walk 20 times) and the last instruction (which turns Rob 180 degrees) returns Rob to his original position.

MINI-QUIZ

Mini-Quiz 2

1) You use the _____ structure to repeat one or more instructions in a program.

2) The _____ structure ends when its condition has been met.

3) The _____ structure, also called the decision structure, instructs the computer to make a decision, and then take some action based on the result of the decision.

You now have completed Chapter 1's Concept lesson. You can either take a break or complete the end-of-lesson questions and exercises before moving on to the Application lesson.

SUMMARY

An algorithm is the set of step-by-step instructions that accomplish a task. The algorithms for all computer programs contain one or more of the following three control structures: sequence, repetition, and selection. The control structures, also called logic structures, are so named because they control the flow of a program's logic.

The sequence structure directs the computer to process the program instructions, one after another, in the order listed in the program. The repetition structure directs the computer to repeat one or more program instructions until some condition is met. The selection structure, also called the decision structure, directs the computer to make a decision, and then selects an appropriate action to take based on that decision. The sequence structure is used in all programs. Most programs also contain both the selection and repetition structures.

ANSWERS TO MINI-QUIZZES

Mini-Quiz 1

1) sequence, selection, repetition

2) sequence

3) sequence

4) algorithm

Mini-Quiz 2

1) repetition

2) repetition

3) selection

QUESTIONS

1) Which of the following is not a programming control structure?
   A. repetition
   B. selection
   C. sequence
   D. sorting

2) Which of the following control structures is used in every program?
   A. repetition
   B. selection
   C. sequence
   D. switching

3) The set of instructions for how to add two numbers is an example of the _____ structure.

A. control

B. repetition

C. selection

D. sequence

4) The set of step-by-step instructions that solve a problem is called _____.

A. an algorithm

B. a list

C. a plan

D. a sequential structure

5) The recipe instruction "Beat until smooth" is an example of the _____ structure.

A. control

B. repetition

C. selection

D. sequence

6) The instruction "If it's raining outside, then take an umbrella to work" is an example of the _____ structure.

A. control

B. repetition

C. selection

D. sequence

7) Which control structure would an algorithm use to determine whether a credit card holder is over his or her credit limit?

A. repetition

B. selection

C. both repetition and selection

8) Which control structure would an algorithm use to calculate a 5% commission for each of a company's salespeople?

A. repetition

B. selection

C. both repetition and selection

9) Assume a company pays a 3% annual bonus to employees who have been with the company more than 5 years; other employees receive a 1% bonus. Which control structure would an algorithm use to calculate each employee's bonus?

A. repetition

B. selection

C. both repetition and selection

Look For These
Symbols

Debugging

Discovery

EXERCISES

Use Rob, the mechanical man, to complete Exercises 1 and 2. Rob's instruction set is shown in Figure 1-6.

Figure 1-6

walk   (Rob moves his right foot forward one step, then moves his left foot to meet his right foot)

sit

turn   (180-degree turn)

jump   (allows Rob to jump over anything in his path)

throw the box out of the way

if the box is red, do this:

otherwise, do this: **(this instruction can be used only in combination with an `if` instruction)**

repeat x times:

1) Rob is five steps away from a box, and the box is 10 steps away from a chair, as illustrated in Figure 1-7. Create an algorithm, using only the instructions shown in Figure 1-6, that direct Rob to sit in the chair. Assume that Rob must jump over the box before he can continue toward the chair.

Figure 1-7

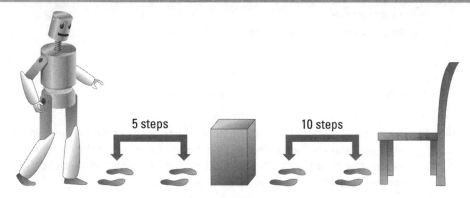

2) Rob is five steps away from a box, and the box is 10 steps away from a chair, as illustrated in Figure 1-7. Create an algorithm, using only the instructions shown in Figure 1-6, that direct Rob to sit in the chair. Assume that Rob must jump over the box if the box is red; otherwise he must throw the box out of the way.

3) Assume a company pays an annual bonus to its employees. The bonus is based on the number of years the employee has been with the company. Employees working at the company for less than 5 years receive a 1% bonus; all others receive a 2% bonus. Write two versions of an algorithm that prints each employee's bonus; use only the instructions shown in Figure 1-8 to do so. Be sure to indent the instructions appropriately.

Figure 1-8

calculate the bonus by multiplying the salary by 1%
calculate the bonus by multiplying the salary by 2%
if the years employed are greater than or equal to 5, do this:
if the years employed are less than 5, do this:
otherwise, do this:
print the bonus
read the salary and years employed
repeat for each employee:

4) Assume a store gives a 10% discount to customers who are at least 65 years old. Write two versions of an algorithm that prints the amount of money a customer owes. Use only the instructions shown in Figure 1-9 to do so. Be sure to indent the instructions appropriately.

Figure 1-9

assign 10% as the discount rate
assign 0 as the discount rate
calculate the amount due by multiplying the item price by (1 minus the discount rate)
if the customer's age is greater than or equal to 65, do this:
if the customer's age is less than 65, do this:
otherwise, do this:
print the amount due
read the customer's age and item price

Exercise 5 is a Discovery Exercise, which may include topics that are not covered in the lesson. Discovery Exercises allow you to "discover" the solutions to problems on your own.

5) Create an algorithm that tells someone how to evaluate the following expression (the / operator means division and the * operator means multiplication). (*Hint*: As you may remember from your math courses, division and multiplication are performed before addition and subtraction.)

12 / 2 + 3 * 2 − 3

A computer program is good only if it works. Errors in either an algorithm or programming code can cause a program to run incorrectly. Therefore, a programmer needs to know how to locate and fix these errors. Exercise 6 is a Debugging Exercise. Debugging Exercises allow you to practice recognizing and solving errors in a program.

6) The algorithm shown in Figure 1-10 should evaluate the expression x + y / z * 3, but it is not working correctly. Correct the algorithm.

Figure 1-10

1. add x to y
2. divide the result of step 1 by z
3. multiply the result of step 2 by 3

Application Lesson

Using the Control Structures

Lab 1.1 - Stop and Analyze The sales manager of a local business has asked you to create a program that calculates the amount of each salesperson's bonus. The program should print each salesperson's name and bonus amount. Assume that the business employs five salespeople and pays a 3% bonus on sales. Study the algorithm shown in Figure 1-11, then answer the questions.

Figure 1-11: Algorithm for Lab 1.1

repeat 5 times:
     get the salesperson's name and sales amount
     calculate the bonus amount by multiplying the sales amount by 3%
     print the salesperson's name and bonus amount

Questions

1. Which control structures does the algorithm in Figure 1-11 use?
2. What will the algorithm shown in Figure 1-11 print if the user enters Mary Smith and 2000 as the salesperson's name and sales amount, respectively?
3. How would you modify the algorithm shown in Figure 1-11 so that it also prints the salesperson's sales amount?
4. How would you modify the algorithm shown in Figure 1-11 so that it can be used for any number of salespeople?
5. How would you modify the algorithm shown in Figure 1-11 so that it allows the user to enter the bonus rate, and then uses that rate to calculate the bonus amount?

Lab 1.2 The sales manager from Lab 1.1 has asked you to modify the algorithm shown in Figure 1-11. The bonus amount now should be calculated as follows: salespeople selling more than $2,000 receive a 3.5% bonus, while all others receive a 3% bonus. Modify the algorithm appropriately.

Lab 1.3 Rob, the mechanical man, is standing in front of a flower bed that contains six flowers. Your task is to create an algorithm that directs Rob to pick the flowers as he walks to the other side of the flower bed. Rob should pick all red flowers with his right hand. Flowers that are not red should be picked with his left hand.

Activity for Lab 1.3

Before you can complete this lab, the Rob the Mechanical Man files must be installed on your computer's hard disk; the installation process is described in the following eight steps.

Important note: If you are working on a computer in your school's computer lab, the files may already be installed on the computer. If they are installed, you can skip the following eight steps. If you are unsure whether the files are installed, ask your instructor or technical support person before completing the eight steps.

To install the Rob the Mechanical Man files on your computer's hard disk:

1. Click the **Start** button on the Windows taskbar, and then click **Run** to open the Run dialog box.

2. Click the **Browse** button to open the Browse dialog box. Open the **Rob Installation Files** folder, which is located in the Cpp\Chap01 folder on your computer's hard disk.

3. Click **Setup** (Setup.exe) in the list of filenames, and then click the **Open** button to return to the Run dialog box.

4. Click the **OK** button in the Run dialog box. A message box appears and indicates that seven files are being copied to your computer's hard disk. After the files are copied, the Rob the Mechanical Man Setup dialog box opens.

5. Read the message in the dialog box. If necessary, close any open files, then click the **OK** button in the dialog box. A message concerning installation appears in the dialog box, as shown in Figure 1-12.

Figure 1-12: Installation message shown in the Rob the Mechanical Man Setup dialog box

click here to begin setup button

the files will be installed in this directory (your drive letter might be different)

As the dialog box indicates, the files will be installed in the Program Files\Rob directory (folder) on your computer's hard disk. You can use the Change Directory button to install the files in a different directory.

6. If desired, change the default installation directory to one of your choosing.

7. Click the **Click here to begin setup** button in the dialog box. The Rob the Mechanical Man – Choose Program Group dialog box opens and shows Rob the Mechanical Man selected in the list of groups.

8. Click the **Continue** button. When the message "Rob the Mechanical Man Setup was completed successfully." appears, click the **OK** button.

Figure 1-13 shows an illustration of Rob and the flower bed.

Figure 1-13: Illustration of Rob and the flower bed

Rob should end up on the other side of the flower bed

Your computer's hard disk contains an application that you can use to create the algorithm that directs Rob to pick the flowers as he walks to the other side of the flower bed.

To run the application that you will use to create Rob's algorithm:

1. Click the **Start** button on the taskbar, and then point to **All Programs** on the Start menu.

2. Point to **Rob the Mechanical Man** on the All Programs menu, and then click **Application Lesson**. The Rob the Mechanical Man application shown in Figure 1-14 appears on your screen.

Figure 1-14: Rob the Mechanical Man application

Algorithm list box

Instruction Set list box

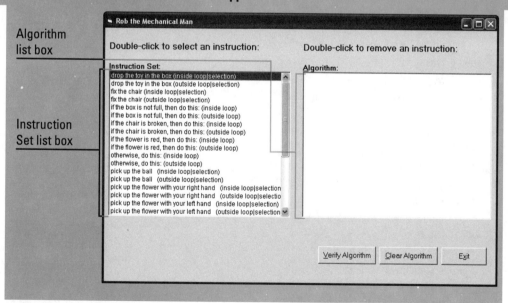

The application shown in Figure 1-14 contains two list boxes, identified by the labels Instruction Set and Algorithm. The Instruction Set list box displays the set of instructions that Rob can understand. Double-clicking an instruction in the Instruction Set list box copies the instruction to the Algorithm list box, which currently is empty. If you make a mistake and want to remove an instruction from the Algorithm list box, you do so simply by double-clicking the instruction in the Algorithm list box. When you are finished adding the appropriate instructions to the Algorithm list box, you can click the Verify Algorithm button to verify that the algorithm is correct. Clicking the Clear Algorithm button removes all of the instructions from the Algorithm list box, and clicking the Exit button ends the application.

As Figure 1-13 indicates, Rob is standing in front of a flower bed that contains six flowers. If the first flower is red, Rob should pick up the flower with his right hand; otherwise, he should pick it up with his left hand. He then should walk one step forward to position himself in front of the second flower. If the second flower is red, Rob should pick it up with his right hand; otherwise, he should use his left hand. He then should walk one step forward to position himself in front of the third flower. Rob needs to follow the same procedure for each flower in the flower bed. After picking up the last flower, Rob must walk two steps forward, rather than one step, to end up on the other side of the flower bed. Figure 1-15 shows the initial algorithm for Rob.

Figure 1-15: Initial algorithm for Rob

1. if the flower is red, then do this:
   pick up the flower with your right hand
   otherwise, do this:
   pick up the flower with your left hand
2. walk
3. if the flower is red, then do this:
   pick up the flower with your right hand
   otherwise, do this:
   pick up the flower with your left hand
4. walk
5. if the flower is red, then do this:
   pick up the flower with your right hand
   otherwise, do this:
   pick up the flower with your left hand
6. walk
7. if the flower is red, then do this:
   pick up the flower with your right hand
   otherwise, do this:
   pick up the flower with your left hand
8. walk
9. if the flower is red, then do this:
   pick up the flower with your right hand
   otherwise, do this:
   pick up the flower with your left hand
10. walk
11. if the flower is red, then do this:
   pick up the flower with your right hand
   otherwise, do this:
   pick up the flower with your left hand
12. walk
13. walk

Although the algorithm shown in Figure 1-15 works correctly, notice that it is quite long. Imagine if Rob had 50 flowers to pick—you would need to repeat the selection structure and the `walk` instruction 50 times! Figure 1-16 shows a more efficient and convenient way of writing this algorithm.

Figure 1-16: Final algorithm for Rob

1. repeat 6 times:
>> if the flower is red, then do this:
>>> pick up the flower with your right hand
>> otherwise, do this:
>>> pick up the flower with your left hand
>> walk
2. walk

Rather than listing the instructions to determine the color, pick up the flower, and then walk for each of the six flowers, the algorithm shown in Figure 1-16 uses the repetition structure to direct Rob to repeat those instructions six times.

Now use the application on your screen to enter the algorithm shown in Figure 1-16 and verify that it works correctly.

To enter the algorithm shown in Figure 1-16, and then verify that it works correctly:

1. Scroll down the Instruction Set list box until you see the `repeat 6 times:` instruction. Double-click **repeat 6 times:** in the Instruction Set list box. The instruction appears in the Algorithm list box, as shown in Figure 1-17.

Figure 1-17: First instruction shown in the Algorithm list box

the
instruction is
copied here

double-click
this
instruction

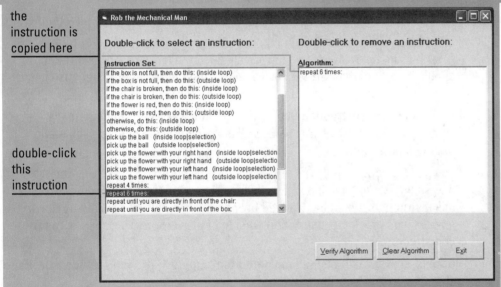

HELP? If you inadvertently selected the wrong instruction, double-click the incorrect instruction in the Algorithm list box to remove the instruction, then repeat Step 1.

According to the algorithm shown in Figure 1-16, Rob needs to use a selection structure to determine whether the color of the current flower is red. The Instruction Set list box contains two instructions that can be used to determine this: `if the flower is red, then do this: (inside loop)` and `if the flower is red, then do this: (outside loop)`. The instruction you use depends on whether you want the instruction to be part of a repetition structure (loop). If the instruction should be included in a repetition structure, you choose `if the flower is red, then do this: (inside loop)`; otherwise, you choose `if the flower is red, then do this: (outside loop)`. In this case, you want the instruction that determines the flower's color to be included in the loop.

2. Double-click **if the flower is red, then do this: (inside loop)** to copy this instruction to the Algorithm list box. Notice that the instruction appears indented below the `repeat 6 times:` instruction. The indentation indicates that the `if the flower is red, then do this: (inside loop)` instruction is included in the repetition structure.

   If the flower is red, then Rob must pick it up with his right hand. The instruction to pick up the flower should be included in the selection structure. You can do so using the `pick up the flower with your right hand (inside loop|selection)` instruction. (The `loop|selection` in an instruction means that you can use the instruction within either a loop or a selection structure.)

tip

Technically, the `pick up the flower with your right hand (inside loop| selection)` instruction also is inside the `repeat 6 times:` loop. This is because the selection structure that contains the instruction is inside the loop.

3. Double-click **pick up the flower with your right hand (inside loop|selection)** to copy this instruction to the Algorithm list box. Because this instruction is part of the selection structure, it appears indented below the **if the flower is red, then do this: (inside loop)** instruction.

   If the flower is not red, then Rob must pick it up with his left hand.

4. Double-click **otherwise, do this: (inside loop)**, then double-click **pick up the flower with your left hand (inside loop|selection).**

   After picking up a flower, Rob must walk one step forward. This instruction should be part of the `repeat 6 times:` repetition structure, because it needs to be done after picking each of the six flowers.

5. Scroll down the Instruction Set list box, if necessary, until you locate the `walk (inside loop|selection)` instruction, then double-click **walk (inside loop|selection).**

   The last instruction in the algorithm shown in Figure 1-16 is to have Rob walk one step forward, which positions him at the end of the flower bed. Because this instruction should be followed only once, after Rob has picked up the six flowers, you place the instruction outside of the `repeat 6 times:` repetition structure.

6. Double-click **walk (outside loop|selection)**. Figure 1-18 shows the completed algorithm in the Algorithm list box.

Figure 1-18: Completed algorithm shown in the Algorithm list box

completed
algorithm

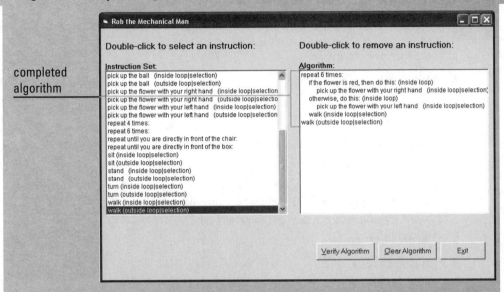

You can verify that the algorithm is correct by clicking the Verify Algorithm button.

7. Click the **Verify Algorithm** button. The Verify message box opens and displays the "Great job!" message. Click the **OK** button to close the message box.

8. Click the **Exit** button to close the application.

Important note: Rob, the mechanical man, is used only in this chapter. When you have completed this lesson's exercises, you can remove the Rob the Mechanical Man files from your computer's hard disk. However, if you are working on a computer in your school's computer lab, check with your instructor or technical support person before removing the files.

To uninstall the Rob the Mechanical Man program:

1. Click the **Start** button, and then click **Control Panel** on the Start menu.

2. Click **Add or Remove Programs** to open the Add or Remove Programs window.

3. Scroll down the list of currently installed programs, if necessary, then click **Rob the Mechanical Man** in the list. Click the **Change/Remove** button. When you are asked if you are sure you want to remove Rob the Mechanical Man and all of its components, click the **Yes** button.

4. When the "Program installation removed" message appears, click the **OK** button.

5. Click the **Close** button to close the Add or Remove Programs window, then close the Control Panel window.

You now have completed Chapter 1's Application lesson. You can either take a break or complete the end-of-lesson exercises.

ANSWERS TO LABS

Lab 1.1

1. sequence and repetition

2. Mary Smith and 60

3. change the last instruction to *print salesperson's name, sales amount, and bonus amount*

4. The modifications are shaded in the algorithm.

   repeat for each salesperson:
      get the salesperson's name and sales amount
      calculate the bonus amount by multiplying the sales amount by 3%
      print the salesperson's name and bonus amount

5. The modifications are shaded in the algorithm.

   get the bonus rate
   repeat 5 times:
      get the salesperson's name and sales amount
      calculate the bonus amount by multiplying the sales amount by the bonus rate
      print the salesperson's name and bonus amount

Lab 1.2

The modifications are shaded in the algorithm.

repeat 5 times:
   get the salesperson's name and sales amount
   if the sales amount is greater than 2000, do this:
      calculate the bonus amount by multiplying the sales amount by 3.5%
   otherwise, do this:
      calculate the bonus amount by multiplying the sales amount by 3%
   print the salesperson's name and bonus amount

Lab 1.3

No answer required.

Look For These Symbols

Debugging

Discovery

EXERCISES

1) In this exercise, you create an algorithm that directs Rob, the mechanical man, to perform a set of tasks.

   A. Click the Start button, and then point to All Programs on the Start menu. Point to Rob the Mechanical Man on the All Programs menu, and then click Application Exercises.

   B. Rob is facing a box that is located zero or more steps away from him. Rob is carrying a toy in his right hand. Create an algorithm, using only the instructions shown in the Instruction Set list box, that directs Rob to drop the toy in the box.

   C. When you have completed the algorithm, click the Exercise 1 button to verify that the algorithm is correct.

   D. When the algorithm is working correctly, click the Exit button to end the application.

2) In this exercise, you create an algorithm that directs Rob, the mechanical man, to perform a set of tasks.

A. Click the Start button, and then point to All Programs on the Start menu. Point to Rob the Mechanical Man on the All Programs menu, and then click Application Exercises.

B. Rob is seated in a chair and is four steps away from a table. A ball is resting on the top of the table, as illustrated in Figure 1-19. Create an algorithm, using only the instructions shown in the Instruction Set list box, that directs Rob to pick up the ball, and then return him to his original position.

C. When you have completed the algorithm, click the Exercise 2 button to verify that the algorithm is correct.

D. When the algorithm is working correctly, click the Exit button to end the application.

Figure 1-19

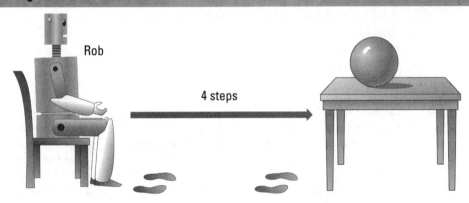

3) In this exercise, you create an algorithm that directs Rob, the mechanical man, to perform a set of tasks.

A. Click the Start button, and then point to All Programs on the Start menu. Point to Rob the Mechanical Man on the All Programs menu, and then click Application Exercises.

B. Rob is facing a chair that is located zero or more steps away from him. Create an algorithm, using only the instructions shown in the Instruction Set list box, that directs Rob to sit in the chair, but only if the chair is not broken. If the chair is broken, the algorithm should instruct Rob to fix the chair.

C. When you have completed the algorithm, click the Exercise 3 button to verify that the algorithm is correct.

D. When the algorithm is working correctly, click the Exit button to end the application.

4) In this exercise, you create an algorithm that directs Rob, the mechanical man, to perform a set of tasks.

A. Click the Start button, and then point to All Programs on the Start menu. Point to Rob the Mechanical Man on the All Programs menu, and then click Application Exercises.

B. Rob is seated in a chair, facing a box that is zero or more steps away from him. Rob is holding a toy in his left hand. Create an algorithm, using only the instructions shown in the Instruction Set list box, that directs Rob to drop the toy in the box—but only if the box is not full. The algorithm also should return Rob to his original position.

C. When you have completed the algorithm, click the Exercise 4 button to verify that the algorithm is correct.

D. When the algorithm is working correctly, click the Exit button to end the application.

5) Using only the instructions shown in Figure 1-20, create an algorithm that shows the steps an instructor takes when grading a test that contains 25 questions.

Figure 1-20

if the student's answer is not the same as the correct answer, do this:
repeat 25 times:
read the student's answer and the correct answer
mark the student's answer incorrect

6) You have just purchased a new personal computer system. Before putting the system components together, you read the instruction booklet that came with the system. The booklet contains a list of the components that you should have received. The booklet advises you to verify that you received all of the components by matching those that you received with those on the list. If a component was received, you should cross its name off the list; otherwise, you should draw a circle around the component's name in the list. Using only the instructions shown in Figure 1-21, create an algorithm that shows the steps you should take to verify that the package contains the correct components.

Figure 1-21

cross the component name off the list
read the component name from the list
circle the component's name on the list
search the package for the component
if the component was received, do this:
otherwise, do this: (this instruction can be used only in combination with an **if** instruction)
repeat for each component name on the list:

Exercises 7 and 8 are Discovery Exercises, which may include topics that are not covered in the lesson. Discovery Exercises allow you to "discover" the solutions to problems on your own.

7) Complete the algorithm shown in Figure 1-22. The algorithm should show a payroll clerk how to calculate and print the gross pay for five workers. If an employee works more than 40 hours, he or she should receive time and one-half for the hours worked over 40.

Figure 1-22

1. _____

read the employee's name, hours worked, and pay rate

_____

    calculate the gross pay by multiplying the hours worked by the pay rate

otherwise, do this:

    calculate the overtime hours by subtracting 40 from the number of hours worked

    calculate the overtime pay by multiplying the overtime hours by the pay rate divided by 2

    calculate the gross pay by _____

print the employee's name and gross pay

8) Create an algorithm that tells someone how to evaluate the following expression (the / operator means division and the * operator means multiplication):

$$12 / 2 + 3 * (4 - 2) + 1$$

A computer program is good only if it works. Errors in either an algorithm or programming code can cause a program to run incorrectly. Therefore, a programmer needs to know how to locate and fix these errors. Exercises 9 and 10 are Debugging Exercises. Debugging Exercises allow you to practice recognizing and solving errors in a program.

9) The algorithm shown in Figure 1-23 is not working correctly, because it does not get Rob seated in the chair. Correct the algorithm.

Figure 1-23

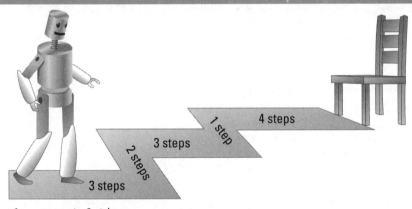

```
1.  repeat 3 times:
        walk
2.  turn left 90 degrees
3.  repeat 2 times:
        walk
4.  turn right 90 degrees
5.  repeat 2 times:
        walk
6.  turn right 90 degrees
7.  walk
8.  turn right 90 degrees
9.  repeat 4 times:
        walk
10. turn around 180 degrees
11. sit
```

10) The algorithm shown in Figure 1-24 does not get Rob through the maze. Correct the algorithm.

Figure 1-24

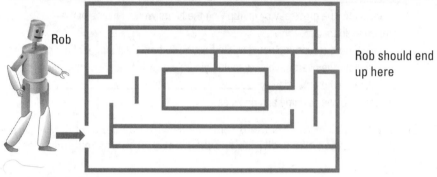

Rob should end up here

```
1.  walk into maze
2.  turn left 90 degrees
3.  repeat until you are directly in front of a wall:
        walk
4.  turn right 90 degrees
5.  repeat until you are directly in front of a wall:

        walk
6.  turn right 90 degrees
7.  repeat until you are directly in front of a wall:
        walk
8.  turn right 90 degrees
9.  repeat until you are directly in front of a wall:
        walk
10. turn right 90 degrees
11. repeat until you are directly in front of a wall:
        walk
12. turn left 90 degrees
13. repeat until you are directly in front of a wall:
        turn right 90 degrees
14. repeat until you are out of the maze:
        walk
```

 Please visit the Testing Center at www.course.com/testingcenter for more practice on the topics covered in this chapter.

Beginning the Problem-Solving Process

After completing this chapter, you will be able to:

- Explain the problem-solving process used to create a computer program

- Analyze a problem

- Complete an IPO chart

- Plan an algorithm using pseudocode and flowcharts

- Desk-check an algorithm

Concept Lesson

Problem Solving

In this chapter, you learn the process that programmers follow to solve problems using a computer. Although you may not realize it, you use a similar process to solve hundreds of small problems every day, such as how to get to school and what to do when you are hungry. Because most of these problems occur so often, however, you typically solve them almost automatically, without giving much thought to the process your brain goes through to arrive at the solutions. Unfortunately, problems that are either complex or unfamiliar usually cannot be solved so easily; most require extensive analysis and planning. Understanding the thought process involved in solving simple and familiar problems will make solving complex or unfamiliar ones easier.

First, you explore the thought process that you follow when solving common, daily problems. Then, you learn how to use a similar process to create a computer solution to a problem—in other words, to create a computer program. The computer solutions you create in this chapter contain the sequence control structure only, where each instruction is processed in order, from beginning to end.

Solving Everyday Problems

The first step in solving a familiar problem is to analyze the problem. You then plan, review, implement, evaluate, and modify (if necessary) the solution. Consider, for example, how you solve the everyday problem of being hungry. First, your mind analyzes the problem to identify its important components. One very important component of any problem is the goal of solving the problem. In this case, the goal is to stop the hunger pangs. Other important components of a problem are the things that you can use to accomplish the goal. For example, you can use the lettuce, tomato, cucumber, and salad dressing that are in your refrigerator to relieve your hunger pangs.

After analyzing the problem, your mind plans an algorithm. Recall from Chapter 1 that an algorithm is the set of step-by-step instructions that describe how to accomplish a task. In other words, an algorithm is a solution to a problem. The hunger problem's algorithm, for example, describes how to use the lettuce, tomato, cucumber, and salad dressing to stop your hunger pangs. Figure 2-1 shows a summary of the analysis and planning steps for the hunger problem.

tip

In Chapters 5 and 6, you learn how to include the selection structure in a program. Then, in Chapters 7 and 8, you learn how to include the repetition structure.

Figure 2-1: Summary of the analysis and planning steps for the hunger problem

result of
analysis step

Items used to accomplish the goal	Algorithm	Goal
lettuce tomato cucumber salad dressing	1. rinse the lettuce, tomato, and cucumber 2. cut up the lettuce, tomato, and cucumber 3. place the lettuce, tomato, and cucumber in a salad bowl 4. pour the salad dressing on the salad 5. eat the salad	stop the hunger pangs

result of
planning step

After planning the algorithm, you review it (in your mind) to verify that it works as intended. When you are satisfied that the algorithm is correct, you implement the algorithm by following each of its instructions in the order indicated. In this case, for example, you rinse the lettuce, tomato, and cucumber, and then cut them up, place them in a salad bowl, pour salad dressing on the salad, and then eat the salad.

Finally, after implementing the algorithm, you evaluate it and, if necessary, you modify it. In this case, if your hunger pangs are gone after eating the salad, then your algorithm is correct because it accomplishes its goal. If, on the other hand, you still are hungry, then you know that you need to modify the algorithm for the next time. An example of a modified algorithm for the hunger problem is shown in Figure 2-2.

Figure 2-2: Modified algorithm for the hunger problem

Items used to accomplish the goal	Algorithm	Goal
lettuce tomato cucumber salad dressing apple	1. rinse the lettuce, tomato, and cucumber 2. cut up the lettuce, tomato, and cucumber 3. place the lettuce, tomato, and cucumber in a salad bowl 4. pour the salad dressing on the salad 5. eat the salad 6. rinse the apple 7. eat the apple	stop the hunger pangs

modifications made to original algorithm

In the next section, you learn that a similar thought process is used to create computer solutions to problems.

Creating Computer Solutions to Problems

In the previous section, you learned how you create a solution to a problem that occurs every day. A similar problem-solving process is used to create a computer program. A computer program also is a solution, but one that is implemented with a computer. The problem-solving process that computer programmers use when creating a computer program is shown in Figure 2-3.

Figure 2-3: The problem-solving process for creating a computer program

1. Analyze the problem.

2. Plan the algorithm.

3. Desk-check the algorithm.

4. Code the algorithm into a program.

5. Desk-check the program.

6. Evaluate and modify (if necessary) the program.

tip

The term *desk-checking* refers to the fact that the programmer is seated at his or her desk, rather than in front of the computer, when reviewing the algorithm. The term *hand-tracing* refers to the fact that the programmer uses a pencil and paper to follow each of the steps in the algorithm by hand.

Just like you do, a computer programmer also first analyzes the problem. He or she then plans the algorithm—the steps that tell the computer how to solve the problem. Programmers use tools such as IPO (Input, Processing, Output) charts, pseudocode, and flowcharts to help them analyze problems and develop algorithms. You learn about these tools in this lesson.

After completing the analysis and planning steps, the programmer then moves on to the third step in the problem-solving process, which is to desk-check the algorithm. **Desk-checking**, also called **hand-tracing**, means that you use pencil and paper, along with sample data, to walk through each of the steps in the algorithm manually, just as if you were the computer. Programmers desk-check the algorithm to verify that it works as intended. If any errors are found in the algorithm, the errors are corrected before the programmer continues to the fourth step in the problem-solving process. Eliminating errors at this pencil and paper stage makes it much easier to produce a correct program in the later steps of the problem-solving process.

The importance of the first three steps in the problem-solving process cannot be emphasized enough. If a programmer does not take the time to analyze the problem, then plan and desk-check the algorithm, the computer program he or she creates typically will contain errors that are difficult to find and expensive to correct.

When the programmer is satisfied that the algorithm is correct, he or she then translates the algorithm into a language that the computer can understand. Programmers refer to this step as **coding** the algorithm. You begin learning how to code an algorithm in Chapter 3. A coded algorithm is called a **program**. In this book, you use the C++ programming language to code your algorithms.

After creating the program, which is the coded version of the algorithm, the programmer desk-checks the program to make sure that he or she translated each of the algorithm's steps correctly. If any errors are found in the program, the errors are corrected before the programmer continues to the final step in the problem-solving process.

The final step in the problem-solving process is to evaluate and modify (if necessary) the program. A programmer evaluates a program by running it, along with sample data, on the computer. If the program does not work as intended, then the programmer makes the necessary modifications until the program works correctly.

In this chapter, you learn how to use the first three steps in the problem-solving process for creating a computer program; you explore the last three steps in Chapter 3. Begin with the first step, which is to analyze the problem.

Analyzing the Problem

You cannot solve a problem unless you understand it, and you cannot understand a problem unless you analyze it—in other words, unless you identify its important components. The purpose of analyzing a problem is to determine the goal of solving the problem and the items that are needed to achieve that goal. Programmers refer to the goal as the **output** and the items needed to achieve the goal as the **input**. When analyzing a problem, you always search first for the output, and then for the input. Many times you will need to consult with the program's user—the person for whom you are creating the program—to determine the output and the input. This is especially true if the problem specification provided by the user is unclear or incomplete. Analyze the problem specification shown in Figure 2-4.

Figure 2-4: Problem specification

Sarah Martin has been working for Quality Builders for four years. Last year, Sarah received a 4% raise, which brought her current weekly pay to $250. Sarah is scheduled to receive a 3% raise next week. She wants you to write a program that will display, on the computer screen, the amount of her new weekly pay.

When analyzing a problem, you always determine the output first. A helpful way to identify the output is to search the problem specification for an answer to the following question: *What does the user want to see printed on paper, displayed on the screen, or stored in a file?* The answer to this question typically is stated as nouns and adjectives in the problem specification. The problem specification shown in Figure 2-4, for instance, indicates that Sarah (the program's user) wants to see her new weekly pay displayed on the screen; the output, therefore, is the new weekly pay. Notice that the words *new* and *weekly* are adjectives, and that the word *pay* is a noun.

IPO Charts

Many programmers use an **IPO (Input, Processing, Output)** chart to organize and summarize the results of a problem analysis. Figure 2-5 shows a partially completed IPO chart for Sarah's problem. Notice that you list the output items in the Output column of the IPO chart.

Figure 2-5: Partially completed IPO chart showing the output

Input	Processing	Output
	Processing items: Algorithm:	new weekly pay

After determining the output, you then determine the input. A helpful way to identify the input is to search the problem specification for an answer to the following question: *What information will the computer need to know to print, display, or store the output items?* As with the output, the input typically is stated as nouns and adjectives in the problem specification. When determining the input, it helps to think about the information that you would need to solve the problem manually, because the computer will need to know the same information. For example, to determine Sarah's new weekly pay, both you and the computer need to know Sarah's current weekly pay, as well as her raise rate; both of these items, therefore, are the input. Here again, notice that *current*, *weekly*, and *raise* are adjectives, and *pay* and *rate* are nouns. Figure 2-6 shows the partially completed IPO chart listing the problem's input and output. Notice that you list the input items in the Input column of the IPO chart.

tip

You can draw an IPO chart by hand, or you can draw one using the table feature in a word processor (such as Microsoft Word).

Figure 2-6: Partially completed IPO chart showing the input and output items

result of
analysis step

Input	Processing	Output
current weekly pay raise rate	Processing items: Algorithm:	new weekly pay

You now have completed the analysis step for the current problem. Keep in mind that analyzing real-world problems will not always be as easy as analyzing the ones found in a textbook. You will find that the analysis step is the most difficult of the problem-solving steps, primarily because most problem specifications contain either too much information or too little information.

A problem specification that contains too much information—more than is necessary to solve the problem—can be confusing to analyze. If you are not sure if an item of information is important, ask yourself this question: *If I didn't know this information, could I still solve the problem?* If your answer is "Yes," then the information is superfluous and you can ignore it. The current problem specification, for example, tells you that Sarah works for Quality Builders. Now ask yourself the following question: *If I didn't know that Sarah worked for Quality Builders, could I still solve the problem?* The answer is "Yes," so you can ignore this information.

When reading a problem specification, it helps to use a pencil to lightly cross out the information that you feel is unimportant to the solution, thereby reducing the amount of information you need to consider in your analysis. If you later find that the information is important, you can always erase the pencil line. In the current problem, for example, you can cross out the unimportant information as shown in Figure 2-7.

Figure 2-7: Problem specification with unimportant information crossed out

~~Sarah Martin has been working for Quality Builders for four years. Last year, Sarah received a 4% raise, which brought her~~ current weekly pay to $250. Sarah is scheduled to receive a 3% raise next week. ~~She wants you to~~ write a program that will display, on the computer screen, the amount of her new weekly pay.

Even worse than having too much information in a problem specification is not having enough information to solve a problem. Consider, for example, the problem specification shown in Figure 2-8.

Figure 2-8: Problem specification that does not contain enough information

Jack Osaki, one of the shipping clerks at Quality Builders, earns $7 per hour. Last week, Jack worked 40 hours. He wants you to write a program that will display his weekly net pay.

It is clear from reading the problem specification that the output is the weekly net pay. The input appears to be both the hourly pay and the number of hours worked during the week. However, is that the only information the computer needs to know to display Jack's net pay? Although you can display a person's gross pay if you know only the hours worked and the hourly pay, a net pay calculation typically involves deducting federal and state taxes, as well as insurance, from the gross pay. What taxes and insurance, if any, will you need to deduct from Jack's gross pay to calculate his net pay? You cannot tell because the problem specification does not contain enough information. Before you can solve this problem, you will need to ask Jack to be more specific about how his net pay is to be calculated.

As a programmer, it is important to distinguish between information that truly is missing in the problem specification, and information that simply is not stated, explicitly, in the problem specification—that is, information that is implied. For example, consider the problem specification shown in Figure 2-9.

Figure 2-9: Problem specification in which the input is not explicitly stated

Sharon Begay, who works for Quality Builders, needs a program that will display the area of any rectangle. The dimensions of the rectangle will be given in feet.

As you may remember from your math courses, you calculate the area of a rectangle by multiplying its length by its width. Therefore, the length and width of the rectangle are the input items for this problem. Notice, however, that the words *length* and *width* do not appear in the problem specification. Although both items are not stated explicitly in the problem specification, neither are considered missing information, because the formula for calculating the area of a rectangle is common knowledge—or, at least, the formula can be found in any math book. With practice, you will be able to "fill in the gaps" in a problem specification also.

If you are having trouble analyzing a problem, try reading the problem specification several times, as it is easy to miss information during the first reading. If the problem still is not clear to you, do not be shy about asking the user for more information. Remember, the greater your understanding of a problem, the easier it will be for you to write a correct and efficient solution to the problem.

MINI-QUIZ

Mini-Quiz 1

For each problem specification that follows, identify the output and the input. Also identify what information, if any, is missing from the problem specification.

1) Paul Eisenstein lives in a state that charges a 3% state income tax on his yearly taxable wages. He wants you to write a program that displays the amount of state income tax he must pay at the end of the year.

2) Deepa Charna belongs to a CD (compact disc) club. The club requires Deepa to purchase 10 CDs each year, at a reduced cost of $8 per CD. Deepa wants to know how much she saves each year by buying the CDs through the club rather than through a store.

3) Penny Long saves $1.25 per day. Penny would like to know the total amount she saved during the month of January.

4) If Jerry Rides saves $1.45 per day, how much will he save in one year?

After analyzing a problem, you then plan its algorithm—its solution.

Planning the Algorithm

The second step in the problem-solving process is to plan the algorithm, which is the step-by-step instructions that the computer must follow to transform the problem's input into its output. You record the algorithm in the Processing column of the IPO chart.

Most algorithms begin with an instruction that enters the input items into the computer. The input items are the items listed in the Input column of the IPO chart. To determine Sarah Martin's new weekly pay, for example, you will record the instruction "enter the current weekly pay and raise rate" as the first step in the algorithm. You will record this instruction in the Processing column of the IPO chart, below the word "Algorithm".

After the instruction to enter the input items, you usually record instructions to process those items, typically by performing some calculations on them, to achieve the problem's required results. The required results are listed in the Output column of the IPO chart. In Sarah's problem specification, consider how you can use the input items (current weekly pay and raise rate) to achieve the output item (new weekly pay).

Before you can display the new weekly pay, you must compute it. To compute the new weekly pay, you first calculate the weekly raise by multiplying the current weekly pay by the raise rate; you then add the weekly raise to the current weekly pay. You will record the instructions, "calculate the weekly raise by multiplying the current weekly pay by the raise rate" and "calculate the new weekly pay by adding the weekly raise to the current weekly pay," as Steps 2 and 3 in the IPO chart. Notice that both calculation instructions state both *what* is to be calculated and *how* to calculate it.

Unlike the current weekly pay, raise rate, and new weekly pay, the weekly raise amount calculated within the algorithm is neither an input item nor an output item; rather, it is a special item, commonly referred to as a processing item. A **processing item** represents an intermediate value that the algorithm uses when processing the input into the output. In this case, the algorithm uses the two input items (current weekly pay and raise rate) to calculate the intermediate value—weekly raise—which the algorithm then uses to compute the new weekly pay. Not all algorithms require a processing item. If one or more processing items are required, they are listed in the Processing column of the IPO chart, below the words "Processing items". You will enter "weekly raise" as a processing item used in the current algorithm.

Most algorithms end with an instruction either to print, display, or store the output items, which are listed in the Output column of the IPO chart. (*Display*, *print*, and *store* refer to the computer screen, the printer, and a file on a disk, respectively.) In this case, you need to display Sarah's new weekly pay, so you will record the instruction "display the new weekly pay" as the last step in the IPO chart. The completed IPO chart is shown in Figure 2-10. Notice that the algorithm begins by entering some data (the input items), then processing that data (the two calculations), and then displaying some data (the output item). Most algorithms follow this same format.

Figure 2-10: Completed IPO chart

Input	Processing	Output

current weekly pay
raise rate
	Processing items:
	   weekly raise
	
	Algorithm:
	1. enter the current weekly
	   pay and raise rate
	2. calculate the weekly
	   raise by multiplying the
	   current weekly pay by
	   the raise rate
	3. calculate the new weekly
	   pay by adding the weekly
	   raise to the current
	   weekly pay
	4. display the new weekly pay
		new weekly pay

Notice that the algorithm shown in Figure 2-10 is composed of short English statements. The statements represent the steps the computer must follow to display the new weekly pay. In programming terms, the list of steps shown in Figure 2-10 is called pseudocode. **Pseudocode** is a tool programmers use to help them plan an algorithm. Pseudocode is not standardized—every programmer has his or her own version—but you will find some similarities among the various versions.

Although the word *pseudocode* might be unfamiliar to you, you already have written pseudocode without even realizing it. Think about the last time you gave directions to someone. You wrote down each direction on paper, in your own words. These directions were a form of pseudocode. As you will learn in Chapter 3, a programmer uses the pseudocode as a guide when coding the algorithm.

To avoid confusion, it is important to be consistent when referring to the input, output, and processing items in the IPO chart. For example, if the input item is called "current weekly pay" in the Input column, then the algorithm should refer to the item as "current weekly pay", rather than using a different name, such as "weekly pay" or "current pay".

In addition to using pseudocode, programmers also use flowcharts to help them plan the algorithm for a problem. Unlike pseudocode, which consists of short English statements, a **flowchart** uses standardized symbols to show the steps the computer must take to accomplish the program's goal. Figure 2-11 shows the current problem's algorithm in flowchart form.

tip

You can draw the flowchart symbols by hand, or you can use the drawing feature in a word processor. You also can use a flow-charting program, such as SmartDraw.

Figure 2-11: IPO chart shown with a flowchart in the Processing column

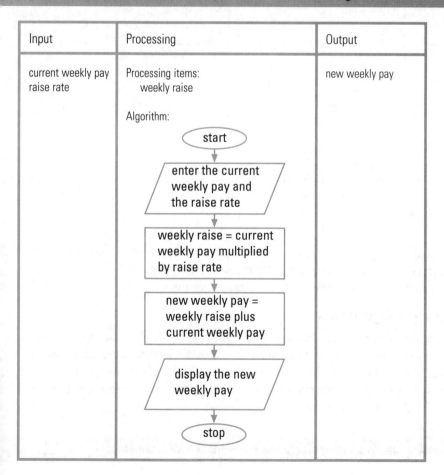

Input	Processing	Output
current weekly pay raise rate	Processing items: weekly raise Algorithm: start enter the current weekly pay and the raise rate weekly raise = current weekly pay multiplied by raise rate new weekly pay = weekly raise plus current weekly pay display the new weekly pay stop	new weekly pay

tip

Many programmers prefer flowcharts to pseudocode, because a picture is sometimes worth a thousand words.

Notice that the flowchart shown in Figure 2-11 contains three different symbols: an oval, a rectangle, and a parallelogram. The symbols are connected with lines, called **flowlines**. The oval symbol is called the **start/stop symbol**. The start oval indicates the beginning of the flowchart, and the stop oval indicates the end of the flowchart. Between the start and the stop ovals are two rectangles, called **process symbols**. You use the process symbol to represent tasks such as calculations.

The parallelogram in a flowchart is called the **input/output symbol** and is used to represent input tasks (such as getting information from the user) and output tasks (such as displaying or printing information). The first parallelogram shown in Figure 2-11 represents an input task. The last parallelogram represents an output task.

When planning the algorithm, you do not need to create both a flowchart and pseudocode; you need to use only one of these planning tools. The tool you use is really a matter of personal preference. For simple algorithms, pseudocode works just fine. When an algorithm becomes more complex, however, the program's logic may be easier to see in a flowchart. In this book, you usually will use pseudocode in planning algorithms.

Keep in mind that a problem can have more than one solution. For example, you could have solved Sarah's problem without using a processing item, as shown in Figure 2-12.

Figure 2-12: Another way of solving Sarah's problem

Input	Processing	Output
current weekly pay raise rate	Processing items: none Algorithm: 1. enter the current weekly pay and raise rate 2. calculate the new weekly pay by multiplying the current weekly pay by the raise rate, and then adding the result to the current weekly pay 3. display the new weekly pay	new weekly pay

Rather than calculating the weekly raise separately, the algorithm shown in Figure 2-12 includes the calculation in the one that computes the new weekly pay.

In the next section, you learn some hints for writing algorithms.

Hints for Writing Algorithms

It is important to remember that you don't need to "reinvent the wheel" each time you create a solution to a problem. Before you write an algorithm, consider whether the problem you are solving is similar to one you have already solved. If it is, you then can use that problem's algorithm to solve the current problem, often with very little modification. For example, consider the problem specification shown in Figure 2-13.

Figure 2-13: Problem specification similar to one you worked with in this lesson

Quality Builders is increasing each of its prices by 3%. The owner of the company wants you to write a program that will display the amount of the increase and the new price.

Although it may not be obvious at first glance, the problem specification shown in Figure 2-13 is almost identical to the one shown earlier in Figure 2-4—only the terminology is different. As you may remember, you solved the problem specified in Figure 2-4 by calculating both the increase in Sarah's pay and her new pay, and then displaying the new pay. That is not much different than calculating and displaying both an increase in an item's price and a new price, which Figure 2-13's problem specification requires you to do. The IPO chart for Figure 2-13's problem is shown in Figure 2-14. If you compare this IPO chart to the one shown earlier in Figure 2-10, you will notice the similarity between both solutions.

Figure 2-14: IPO chart for the problem specification shown in Figure 2-13

Input	Processing	Output
current price increase rate	Processing items: none Algorithm: 1. enter the current price and increase rate 2. calculate the increase amount by multiplying the current price by the increase rate 3. calculate the new price by adding the increase amount to the current price 4. display the increase amount and new price	increase amount new price

Even if the problem you are trying to solve is not identical to one that you already solved, you may be able to use a portion of a previous solution to solve the current problem. Consider, for example, the problem specification shown in Figure 2-15.

Figure 2-15: Problem specification that contains a portion that is similar to one you worked with in this lesson

At the end of every year, Quality Builders gives each of its employees a bonus. This year the bonus rate is 6% of the employee's current yearly salary. Mary Vasko wants you to write a program that will display her bonus.

Although the problem specified in Figure 2-15 is not identical to any that you solved in this lesson, you can use a part of a previous algorithm to solve it; more specifically, you can use the raise calculation part of Figure 2-10's algorithm. Calculating a bonus, which you need to do now, is no different than calculating a raise. Both calculations require you to take an amount and multiply it by a percentage rate. Recall that you calculated Sarah's raise by multiplying her current weekly pay by her raise rate. Similarly, in Figure 2-15's problem, you calculate Mary's bonus by multiplying her yearly salary by her bonus rate. The IPO chart for the current problem is shown in Figure 2-16.

Figure 2-16: IPO chart for the problem specification shown in Figure 2-15

Input	Processing	Output
current yearly salary bonus rate	Processing items: none Algorithm: 1. enter the current yearly salary and bonus rate 2. calculate the bonus by multiplying the current yearly salary by the bonus rate 3. display the bonus	bonus

If you have not solved a similar problem, and you cannot find a portion of an existing algorithm that you can use, try solving the problem manually, writing down on paper every step you take to do so. If you were to solve Figure 2-15's problem manually, for example, you would need first to read Mary's yearly salary and her bonus rate into your mind. You then would calculate her bonus by multiplying the bonus rate by the yearly salary. Lastly, you would write down the bonus amount on a piece of paper. You can use the steps that you wrote down as a guide when creating your algorithm.

Figure 2-17 summarizes what you learned in this section about planning algorithms.

Figure 2-17: Hints for planning algorithms

1. Before writing an algorithm, consider whether you have already solved a similar problem. If you have, you can use the same solution, often with little modification, to solve the current problem.

2. If you have not solved a similar problem, consider whether you can use a portion of an existing algorithm to solve the current problem.

3. If you have not solved a similar problem, and if you cannot use a portion of an existing algorithm, solve the problem manually, noting each step you take to do so.

MINI-QUIZ

Mini-Quiz 2

1) The input/output symbol in a flowchart is represented by a(n) _____.

2) Calculation tasks are placed in a processing symbol, which is represented in a flowchart by a(n) _____.

3) Paul Eisenstein lives in a state that charges a 3% state income tax on his yearly taxable wages. He wants you to create a program that displays the state income tax he must pay at the end of the year. The output is the annual state income tax. The input is the yearly taxable wages and the state income tax rate. Complete the Processing section of the IPO chart. (Use pseudocode to show the steps.)

4) Deepa Charna belongs to a CD (compact disc) club. The club requires Deepa to purchase 10 CDs each year, at a reduced cost of $8 per CD. Deepa wants to know how much she saves each year by buying the CDs through the club rather than through a store that charges $12 for each CD. The output is the annual savings. The input is the number of CDs purchased each year, the club's CD price, and the store's CD price. Complete the Processing section of the IPO chart. (Use pseudocode to show the steps.)

After analyzing a problem and planning its algorithm, you then desk-check the algorithm, using either the flowchart or the pseudocode, along with sample data.

Desk-Checking the Algorithm

A programmer reviews an algorithm by desk-checking, or hand-tracing, it—in other words, by completing each step in the algorithm manually. You desk-check an algorithm to verify that it is not missing any steps, and that the existing steps are correct and in the proper order. Before you begin the desk-check, you first choose a set of sample data for the input values, which you then use to manually compute the expected output values. For example, you will use input values of $250 and .03 (3%) as Sarah Martin's current weekly pay and raise rate, respectively. Sarah's new weekly pay should be $257.50, which is her current weekly pay of $250 plus her weekly raise of $7.50 (250 multiplied by .03); the 257.50 is the expected output value. You now use the sample input values (250 and .03) to desk-check the algorithm. If the algorithm produces the expected output value of 257.50, then the algorithm appears to be correct.

You can use a desk-check table to help you desk-check an algorithm. The table should contain one column for each input item shown in the IPO chart, as well as one column for each output item and one column for each processing item. Figure 2-18 shows a partially completed desk-check table for Sarah Martin's problem.

Figure 2-18: Desk-check table showing columns for the input, processing, and output items from the IPO chart

current weekly pay	raise rate	weekly raise	new weekly pay

You can desk-check an algorithm using either its pseudocode or its flowchart. The pseudocode for Sarah Martin's problem is shown in Figure 2-10, and the flowchart is shown in Figure 2-11. In both figures, the first step is to enter the input values—in this case, the current weekly pay of 250 and the raise rate of .03. You record the results of this step by writing 250 and .03 in the current weekly pay and raise rate columns, respectively, in the desk-check table, as shown in Figure 2-19.

Figure 2-19: Desk-check table showing input values entered in the appropriate columns

current weekly pay	raise rate	weekly raise	new weekly pay
250	.03		

The second step in the algorithm is to calculate the weekly raise by multiplying the current weekly pay by the raise rate. The desk-check table shows that the current weekly pay is 250 and the raise rate is .03. Notice that you use the table to determine the current weekly pay and raise rate values; this helps to verify the accuracy of the algorithm. If, for example, the table did not show any amount in the raise rate column, you would know that your algorithm missed a step; in this case, it would have missed entering the raise rate.

Multiplying the current weekly pay of 250 by the raise rate of .03 results in a 7.50 raise. You record the number 7.50 in the weekly raise column, as shown in Figure 2-20.

Figure 2-20: Weekly raise entry included in the desk-check table

current weekly pay	raise rate	weekly raise	new weekly pay
250	.03	7.50	

The next step in the algorithm is to calculate the new weekly pay by adding the weekly raise to the current weekly pay. According to the desk-check table, the weekly raise is 7.50 and the current weekly pay is 250. Added together, those amounts result in a new weekly pay of 257.50. You write the 257.50 in the new weekly pay column, as shown in Figure 2-21.

Figure 2-21: New weekly pay entry included in the desk-check table

current weekly pay	raise rate	weekly raise	new weekly pay
250	.03	7.50	257.50

The last instruction in the algorithm is to display the new weekly pay on the screen. In this case, 257.50 will be displayed, because that is what appears in the table's new weekly pay column. Notice that this amount agrees with the manual calculation you performed prior to desk-checking the algorithm, so the algorithm appears to be correct. The only way to know for sure, however, is to test the algorithm a few more times with different input values. For example, you will test the algorithm with a current weekly pay of $100 and a raise rate of .10 (10%). The new weekly pay should be $110, which is the current weekly pay of $100 plus the weekly raise of $10 (100 multiplied by .10).

Recall that the first instruction in the algorithm is to enter the current weekly pay and the raise rate. Therefore, you write 100 in the current weekly pay column and .10 in the raise rate column, as shown in Figure 2-22.

Figure 2-22: Desk-check table for the second set of input values

cross out the previous values

current weekly pay	raise rate	weekly raise	new weekly pay
~~250~~ 100	~~.03~~ .10	7.50	257.50

Notice that you cross out the previous values of these two items in the table before recording the new values; this is because each column should contain only one value at any time.

The next step in the algorithm is to calculate the weekly raise. Multiplying the current weekly pay, which is listed in the table as 100, by the raise rate, which is listed as .10, results in a weekly raise of 10. So you cross out the 7.50 that appears in the weekly raise column in the table and write 10 immediately below it.

The next step is to calculate the new weekly pay. Adding the raise, which is listed in the table as 10, to the current weekly pay, which is listed in the table as 100, results in a new weekly pay of 110. Therefore, you cross out the 257.50 that appears in the new weekly pay column in the table and write 110 immediately below it. The completed desk-check table is shown in Figure 2-23.

Figure 2-23: Desk-check table showing the results of the second desk-check

current weekly pay	raise rate	weekly raise	new weekly pay
~~250~~ 100	~~.03~~ .10	~~7.50~~ 10	~~257.50~~ 110

The last step in the algorithm is to display the new weekly pay. In this case, the algorithm will display 110, because that is what appears in the table's new weekly pay column. The amount in the table agrees with the manual calculation you performed earlier, so the algorithm still appears to be correct. To be sure, however, you should desk-check it a few more times.

In addition to desk-checking the algorithm using valid data, you also should desk-check it using invalid data, because users sometimes make mistakes when entering data. **Valid data** is data that the programmer is expecting the user to enter. For example, in the algorithm that you just finished desk-checking, the programmer expects the user to provide positive numbers for the input values (current weekly pay and raise rate). **Invalid data** is data that the programmer is not expecting the user to enter. In this case, the programmer is not expecting the user to enter a negative value as the current weekly pay. A negative weekly pay is obviously an input error, because an employee cannot earn a negative amount for the week. Beginning in Chapter 5, you learn how to create algorithms that correctly handle input errors. For now, however, you can assume that the user of the program will always enter valid data.

As a way of summarizing and reinforcing what you learned in this lesson, you will use the first three steps in the problem-solving process to solve another problem.

The Gas Mileage Problem

Figure 2-24 shows the problem specification for the gas mileage problem, which you solve next.

Figure 2-24: Problem specification for the gas mileage problem

When Jacob Steinberg began his trip from California to Vermont, he filled his car's tank with gas and reset its trip meter to zero. After traveling 324 miles, Jacob stopped at a gas station to refuel; the gas tank required 17 gallons. Create a program that Jacob can use to display his car's gas mileage—the number of miles his car can be driven per gallon of gas—at anytime during the trip.

First, analyze the problem, looking for nouns and adjectives that represent both the output and the input. The output should answer the question *What does the user want to see printed on paper, displayed on the screen, or stored in a file?* The input should answer the question *What information will the computer need to know to print, display, or store the output items?* In the gas mileage problem, the output is the miles per gallon, and the input is the number of miles driven and the number of gallons used.

Next, plan the algorithm. Recall that most algorithms begin with an instruction that enters the input items into the computer, followed by instructions that process the input items and then print, display, or store the output items. Figure 2-25 shows the completed IPO chart for the gas mileage problem.

Figure 2-25: Completed IPO chart for the gas mileage problem

Input	Processing	Output
number of miles driven number of gallons used	Processing items: none Algorithm: 1. enter the number of miles driven and the number of gallons used 2. calculate the miles per gallon by dividing the number of miles driven by the number of gallons used 3. display the miles per gallon	miles per gallon

After planning the algorithm, you then desk-check it, which is the third step in the problem-solving process. You will desk-check the algorithm twice, first using 324 and 17 as the miles driven and number of gallons, respectively, and then using 200 and 12. Figure 2-26 shows the completed desk-check table for the gas mileage problem.

Figure 2-26: Completed desk-check table for the gas mileage problem

number of miles driven	number of gallons used	miles per gallon
~~324~~ 200	~~17~~ 12	~~19.06~~ 16.67

MINI-QUIZ

Mini-Quiz 3

1) Desk-check the following algorithm twice. First, use a yearly taxable wage of $20,000 and a 3% state income tax rate. Then use a yearly taxable wage of $10,000 and a 2% state income tax.

Input	Processing	Output
yearly taxable wages state income tax rate	Processing items: none Algorithm: 1. enter the yearly taxable wages and the state income tax rate 2. calculate the annual state income tax by multiplying the yearly taxable wages by the state income tax rate 3. display the annual state income tax	annual state income tax

2) Desk-check the following algorithm twice. Use 5 and 7 as the first set of input values, then use 6 and 8 as the second set of input values.

Input	Processing	Output
first number second number	Processing items: sum Algorithm: 1. enter the first number and the second number 2. calculate the sum by adding together the first number and the second number 3. calculate the average by dividing the sum by 2 4. display the average	average

You now have completed Chapter 2's Concept lesson, which covered the first three of the six steps required to create a computer program. Recall that the first three steps are to analyze the problem, plan the algorithm, and desk-check the algorithm. You complete the last three steps—code the algorithm into a program, desk-check the program, and evaluate and modify (if necessary) the program—in Chapter 3. You can either take a break or complete the end-of-lesson questions and exercises before moving on to the Application lesson.

SUMMARY

If you are like most people, you probably do not pay much attention to the problem-solving process that you use when solving everyday problems. This process typically involves analyzing the problem, and then planning, reviewing, implementing, evaluating, and modifying (if necessary) the solution. You can use a similar problem-solving process to create a computer program, which also is a solution to a problem.

Programmers use tools such as IPO (Input, Processing, Output) charts, pseudocode, and flowcharts to help them analyze problems and develop algorithms. During the analysis step, the programmer first determines the output, which is the goal or purpose of solving the problem. The programmer then determines the input, which is the information he or she needs to reach the goal. During the planning step, programmers write the steps that will transform the input into the output. Most algorithms begin by entering some data (the input items), then processing that data (usually by performing some calculations), and then displaying some data (the output items).

After the analysis and planning steps, a programmer then desk-checks the algorithm to determine whether it will work as intended. Desk-checking means that the programmer follows each of the steps in the algorithm by hand, just as if he or she were the computer. When the programmer is satisfied that the algorithm is correct, he or she then codes the algorithm. Coding refers to translating the algorithm into a language that the computer can understand. A coded algorithm is called a program. After coding the algorithm, the programmer then desk-checks the program to be sure that he or she translated each of the steps in the algorithm correctly. The programmer then evaluates and modifies (if necessary) the program by executing it, along with sample data, using the computer. If the program does not work as intended, then the programmer makes the necessary modifications until it does.

Before writing an algorithm, you should consider whether you have already solved a similar problem. If you have, you can use that solution to solve the current problem, often with little modification. If you have not solved a similar problem, consider whether a portion of an existing algorithm is similar enough to use in the current problem. If no existing algorithms help, try solving the problem manually, being sure to write down every step you take to do so, because the computer will need to follow the same steps.

ANSWERS TO MINI-QUIZZES

Mini-Quiz 1

1) Output: annual state income tax
     Input: yearly taxable wages, state income tax rate
     Missing information: none

2) Output: annual savings
     Input: number of CDs purchased each year, CD cost when purchased through the club, CD cost when purchased through the store
     Missing information: CD cost when purchased through the store

3) Output: total amount saved in January
     Input: amount saved per day, number of days in January
     Missing information: none (Although the number of days in January is not specified in the problem specification, that information can be found in any calendar.)

4) Output: yearly savings
     Input: amount saved per day, number of days in the year
     Missing information: number of days in the year (Because some years are leap years, you would need to know the number of days in the year.)

Mini-Quiz 2

1) parallelogram

2) rectangle

3)

Input	Processing	Output
yearly taxable wages state income tax rate	Processing items: none Algorithm: 1. enter the yearly taxable wages and the state income tax rate 2. calculate the annual state income tax by multiplying the yearly taxable wages by the state income tax rate 3. display the annual state income tax	annual state income tax

4)

Input	Processing	Output
number of CDs purchased each year club's CD price store's CD price	Processing items: amount spent through the club amount spent at the store Algorithm: 1. enter the number of CDs purchased each year, the club's CD price, and the store's CD price 2. calculate the amount spent through the club by multiplying the number of CDs purchased each year by the club's CD price 3. calculate the amount spent at the store by multiplying the number of CDs purchased each year by the store's CD price 4. calculate the annual savings by subtracting the amount spent through the club from the amount spent at the store 5. display the annual savings	annual savings

Mini-Quiz 3

1)

yearly taxable wages	state income tax rate	annual state income tax
~~20000~~ 10000	~~.03~~ .02	~~600~~ 200

2)

first number	second number	sum	average
~~5~~ 6	~~7~~ 8	~~12~~ 14	~~6~~ 7

QUESTIONS

1) The first step in the problem-solving process is to _____.
   A. plan the algorithm
   B. analyze the problem
   C. desk-check the algorithm
   D. code the algorithm

2) Programmers refer to the goal of solving a problem as the _____.
   A. input
   B. output
   C. processing
   D. purpose

3) Programmers refer to the items needed to reach a problem's goal as the
   _____.
   A. input
   B. output
   C. processing
   D. purpose

4) A problem's _____ will answer the question *What does the user want
   to see printed on the printer, displayed on the screen, or stored in a file?*
   A. input
   B. output
   C. processing
   D. purpose

5) Programmers use _____ to organize and summarize the results of their problem analysis.

    A. input charts

    B. IPO charts

    C. output charts

    D. processing charts

6) A problem's _____ will answer the question *What information will the computer need to know to print, display, or store the output items?*

    A. input

    B. output

    C. processing

    D. purpose

7) Most algorithms begin by _____.

    A. displaying the input items

    B. entering the input items into the computer

    C. entering the output items into the computer

    D. processing the input items by doing some calculations on them

8) You record the algorithm in the _____ column of the IPO chart.

    A. Input

    B. Output

    C. Processing

    D. Purpose

9) The calculation instructions in an algorithm should state _____.

    A. only *what* is to be calculated

    B. only *how* to calculate something

    C. both *what* is to be calculated and *how* to calculate it

    D. both *what* is to be calculated and *why* it is calculated

10) Most algorithms follow the format of _____.

    A. entering the input items, then displaying, printing, or storing the input items, and then processing the output items

    B. entering the input items, then processing the output items, and then displaying, printing, or storing the output items

    C. entering the input items, then processing the input items, and then displaying, printing, or storing the output items

    D. entering the output items, then processing the output items, and then displaying, printing, or storing the output items

11) The short English statements that represent the steps the computer must follow to solve a problem are called _____.

    A. flow diagrams

    B. IPO charts

    C. pseudocharts

    D. pseudocode

12) _____ use standardized symbols to represent an algorithm.

    A. Flowcharts

    B. Flow diagrams

    C. IPO charts

    D. Pseudocharts

13) The _____ symbol is used in a flowchart to represent a calculation task.

    A. input

    B. output

    C. process

    D. start

14) The _____ symbol is used in a flowchart to represent a step that gets information from the user.

    A. input/output

    B. process

    C. selection/repetition

    D. start/stop

15) The process symbol in a flowchart is the _____.

    A. ◇

    B. ⬭

    C. ▱

    D. ▭

16) The input/output symbol in a flowchart is the _____.

    A. ◇

    B. ⬭

    C. ▱

    D. ▭

17) The start/stop symbol, which marks both the beginning and ending of a flowchart, is a(n) _____.

    A. ◇

    B. ⬭

    C. ▱

    D. ▭

18) After planning an algorithm, you should _____ to verify that it will work correctly.

    A. analyze the algorithm

    B. code the algorithm

    C. desk-check the algorithm

    D. evaluate and modify (if necessary) the program

19) When desk-checking an algorithm, you should set up a table that contains _____.

    A. one column for each input item

    B. one column for each output item

    C. one column for each processing item

    D. all of the above

Look For These
Symbols

Debugging

Discovery

EXERCISES

1) Hai Chang needs a program that calculates and displays the square of a number. Complete an IPO chart for this problem. Use pseudocode in the Processing column. Also complete a desk-check table for your algorithm. Use the number 4 for the first desk-check, then use the number 6.

2) Mingo Sales needs a program that the company can use to enter the sales made in each of two states. The program should display the commission, which is 5% of the total sales. (In other words, if you have sales totaling $3,000, your commission is $150.) The commission rate may change in the future, so you should treat it as an input item. Complete an IPO chart for this problem. Use pseudocode in the Processing column. Also complete a desk-check table for your algorithm. For the first desk-check, use 1000 and 2000 as the two state sales, and use .05 (the decimal equivalent of 5%) as the commission rate. Then use 3000 and 2500 as the two state sales, and use .06 as the commission rate.

3) Joan Brimley is the accountant at Paper Products. The salespeople at Paper Products are paid a commission, which is a percentage of the sales they make. The current commission rate is 10%, but that rate may change in the future. (In other words, if you have sales totaling $2,000, your commission is $200.) Joan wants you to create a program that displays the commission after she enters the salesperson's sales and commission rate. Complete an IPO chart for this problem. Use a flowchart in the Processing column. Also complete a desk-check table for your algorithm. Use 2000 and .1 (the decimal equivalent of 10%) as the salesperson's sales amount and commission rate, respectively, and then use 5000 and .06.

4) RM Sales divides its sales territory into three regions: 1, 2, and 3. Robert Gonzales, the sales manager, wants a program in which he can enter the current year's sales for each region and the projected increase (expressed as a percentage) in sales for each region. He then wants the program to display the following year's projected sales for each region. (For example, if Robert enters 10,000 as the current sales for region 1, and then enters a 10% projected increase, the program should display 11,000 as next year's projected sales.) Complete an IPO chart for this problem. Use pseudocode in the Processing column. Also complete a desk-check table for your algorithm.

Use the following information for the first desk-check:

Region	Sales	Increase rate
1	10000	.1
2	3000	.09
3	6000	.1

Use the following information for the second desk-check:

Region	Sales	Increase rate
1	5000	.02
2	2000	.03
3	1000	.02

5) Modify the algorithm that you created in Exercise 1 so that it calculates and displays the square of positive numbers only. If the number entered by the user is either zero or less than zero, the algorithm should display an error message. Desk-check the algorithm using the numbers 10 and −3.

6) Etola Systems wants a program that displays the ending inventory amount, given the beginning inventory amount, the amount sold, and the amount returned. The algorithm shown in Figure 2-27 is supposed to solve this problem, but it is not working correctly. First calculate the expected results using a beginning inventory of 50, an amount sold of 10, and an amount returned of 2. Then use these values to desk-check the algorithm. Rewrite the algorithm correctly, then desk-check it again.

Figure 2-27

Input	Processing	Output
beginning inventory amount sold amount returned	Processing items: none Algorithm: 1. enter the beginning inventory, amount sold, and amount returned 2. calculate the ending inventory by adding the amount sold to the beginning inventory, then subtracting the amount returned from the result 3. display the ending inventory	ending inventory

7) The algorithm shown in Figure 2-28 should calculate an employee's gross pay. Correct any errors in the algorithm. (You do not have to worry about overtime pay.)

Figure 2-28

Input	Processing	Output
hours worked rate of pay	Processing items: none Algorithm: 1. enter the hours worked and pay rate 2. calculate the gross pay by multiplying the hours by the rate of pay 3. display the gross	gross pay

Application Lesson

Using the First Steps in the Problem-Solving Process

Lab 2.1 - Stop and Analyze   The manager of a video store has asked you to create a program that calculates the amount a customer owes when he or she returns a video. Assume that a customer can return only one video at a time. The daily rental fee is $3.50. Customers are charged a late fee of $2.00 per day when the video is returned past the due date. Study the IPO chart and desk-check table shown in Figure 2-29, then answer the questions.

Figure 2-29: IPO chart and desk-check table for Lab 2.1

Input	Processing	Output
number of late days	Processing items: none Algorithm: 1. get the number of late days 2. calculate the amount due by multiplying the number of late days by 2, and then adding 3.50 to the product 3. display the amount due	amount due

number of late days	amount due
~~3~~ 0	~~9.50~~ 3.50

Questions

1. What will the algorithm shown in Figure 2-29 display if the user enters the number three as the number of late days? What will it display if the user enters the number zero as the number of late days?
2. Assume you want to include the late charge as a processing item. How would you modify the IPO chart and desk-check table shown in Figure 2-29 to do so?
3. Assume the manager also wants to display the late charge. How would you modify the IPO chart and desk-check table shown in Figure 2-29 to do so?

Lab 2.2   Last year, Mark Williams opened a new wallpaper store named The Paper Tree. Business is booming at the store, and Mark and his salesclerks are always busy. Recently, however, Mark has received several complaints from customers about the store's slow service, and he has decided to ask his salesclerks for suggestions on how the service can be improved. The overwhelming response from the salesclerks is that they need a more convenient way to calculate the number of single rolls of wallpaper required to cover a room. Currently, the salesclerks perform this calculation manually, using pencil and paper. Doing this for so many customers, however, takes a great deal of time, and service has begun to suffer. Mark has asked for your assistance in this matter. He would like you to create a program that the salesclerks can use to quickly calculate and display the required number of rolls.

The Problem Specification

Before you begin the problem-solving process, you meet with Mark to develop an appropriate problem specification—one that contains all of the information needed to solve the problem. You also ask Mark to show you how the clerks currently calculate the required number of rolls. As you learned in the Concept lesson, the computer needs to make the same calculations as you do. Figure 2-30 shows the final problem specification and a sample calculation.

Figure 2-30: Problem specification and sample calculation

Problem specification:

Create a program that calculates and displays the number of single rolls of wallpaper needed to cover a room. The salesclerk will provide the length, width, and ceiling height of the room, in feet. He or she also will provide the number of square feet a single roll will cover.

Sample calculation:

Room size: 10 feet by 12 feet, with a ceiling height of 8 feet

Single roll coverage: 30 square feet

1. Calculate the perimeter of the room by adding together its length and width, and then multiplying the sum by 2: (10 feet + 12 feet) * 2 = 44 feet
2. Calculate the wall area by multiplying the room's perimeter by its height: 44 feet * 8 feet = 352 square feet
3. Calculate the required number of single rolls by dividing the wall area by the number of square feet a single roll provides: 352 square feet / 30 square feet = 11.73 (rounded to two decimal places), or approximately 12 single rolls

Armed with this information, you now can begin the problem-solving process.

Analyze the Problem

As you learned in the Concept lesson, the first step in the problem-solving process is to analyze the problem. You do so to determine the goal of solving the problem (output) and the items that are needed to achieve the goal (input). Recall that you always search the problem specification first for the output, and then for the input. The input and output typically are stated as nouns and adjectives in the problem specification.

Asking yourself the question *What does the user want to see printed on the printer, displayed on the screen, or stored in a file?* will help you determine the output. In this case, the user wants to see the number of single rolls of wallpaper needed to cover a room, so you record "number of single rolls" in the Output column of this problem's IPO chart.

The question *What information will the computer need to know to print, display, or store the output items?* will help you determine the input. In this case, the input is the length, width, and ceiling height of the room, as well as the coverage provided by a single roll of wallpaper. Figure 2-31 shows the IPO chart with the Input and Output columns completed.

Figure 2-31: IPO chart showing input and output items

Input	Processing	Output
room length room width ceiling height single roll coverage	Processing items: Algorithm:	number of single rolls

The next step in the problem-solving process is to plan the algorithm.

Planning the Algorithm

After determining a problem's input and output, you then plan its algorithm, which is the step-by-step instructions that will transform the input into the output. Recall that most algorithms begin by entering the input items into the computer. In the current problem's algorithm, for example, the first step will be "enter the room length, room width, ceiling height, and single roll coverage". Notice that the instruction refers to the input items using the same names listed in the Input column of the IPO chart.

After the instruction to enter the input items, you usually record instructions to process those items, typically by performing some calculations on them. According to the sample calculation shown in Figure 2-30, first you calculate the room's perimeter. You do so by adding together the room's length and width, and then multiplying that sum by two. Notice that the room perimeter does not appear in either the Input or Output column in the IPO chart. This is because the room perimeter is neither an input item nor an output item; rather, it is a processing item. As you learned in the Concept lesson, a processing item represents an intermediate value that the algorithm uses when processing the input into the output. For this problem, you enter "room perimeter" in the Processing items section of the IPO chart, and "calculate the room perimeter by adding together the room length and room width, and then multiplying the sum by 2" in the Algorithm section, as shown in Figure 2-32.

Figure 2-32: IPO chart showing the partially completed algorithm

Input	Processing	Output
room length room width ceiling height single roll coverage	Processing items: room perimeter Algorithm: 1. enter the room length, room width, ceiling height, and single roll coverage 2. calculate the room perimeter by adding together the room length and room width, and then multiplying the sum by 2	number of single rolls

Next, you calculate the wall area by multiplying the room's perimeter by the height of its ceiling. This calculation gives you the total number of square feet to be covered. Like the perimeter, the wall area is a processing item. Therefore, you enter "wall area" in the Processing items section of the IPO chart and "calculate the wall area by multiplying the room perimeter by the ceiling height" in the Algorithm section.

The last calculation you make is to divide the wall area by the coverage provided by a single roll. This calculation gives you the required number of single rolls. You enter "calculate the number of single rolls by dividing the wall area by the single roll coverage" in the Algorithm section of the IPO chart.

Recall that most algorithms end with an instruction to print, display, or store the output items. In this case, you need simply to display the number of single rolls. You record "display the number of single rolls" in the Algorithm section of the IPO chart. The completed IPO chart is shown in Figure 2-33.

Figure 2-33: Completed IPO chart for the wallpaper store problem

Input	Processing	Output

room length
room width
ceiling height
single roll coverage
	Processing items:
	    room perimeter
	    wall area
	
	Algorithm:
	1. enter the room length,
	   room width, ceiling height,
	   and single roll coverage
	2. calculate the room perimeter
	   by adding together the room
	   length and room width, and
	   then multiplying the sum by 2
	3. calculate the wall area by
	   multiplying the room
	   perimeter by the ceiling
	   height
	4. calculate the number of single
	   rolls by dividing the wall area
	   by the single roll coverage
	5. display the number of
	   single rolls
		number of single rolls

After completing the IPO chart, you then move on to the third step in the problem-solving process, which is to desk-check the algorithm that appears in the chart.

Desk-Checking the Algorithm

You desk-check an algorithm to verify that it is not missing any steps and that the existing steps are correct and in the proper order. Recall that, before you begin the desk-check, you first choose a set of sample data for the input values, which you then use to manually compute the expected output values. In this case, you will use the input values shown earlier in Figure 2-30. In that figure, the values 10 feet, 12 feet, 8 feet, and 30 square feet are specified as the room length, room width, ceiling height, and single roll coverage, respectively. The sample calculation provided in Figure 2-30 shows that the required number of single rolls, using those input values, is 11.73 (rounded to two decimal places), or approximately 12 single rolls. Now see whether the algorithm shown in Figure 2-33 results in the same amount.

First, create a desk-check table that contains a column for each input, processing, and output item, as shown in Figure 2-34.

Figure 2-34: Desk-check table for the wallpaper store problem

room length	room width	ceiling height	single roll coverage	room perimeter	wall area	number of single rolls

Now you can begin desk-checking the algorithm. The first instruction in the algorithm is to enter the room length, room width, ceiling height, and single roll coverage. Figure 2-35 shows these values entered in the desk-check table.

Figure 2-35: Input values entered in the desk-check table

room length	room width	ceiling height	single roll coverage	room perimeter	wall area	number of single rolls
10	12	8	30			

The next instruction is to calculate the room perimeter by adding together the room length and room width, and then multiplying the sum by 2. The room length column in the desk-check table contains the number 10, and the room width column contains the number 12. When you add together the numbers 10 and 12, you get 22. And when you multiply the 22 by 2, you get 44, which you enter in the room perimeter column in the table, as shown in Figure 2-36.

Figure 2-36: Room perimeter value entered in the desk-check table

room length	room width	ceiling height	single roll coverage	room perimeter	wall area	number of single rolls
10	12	8	30	44		

The third instruction in the algorithm is to calculate the wall area by multiplying the room perimeter by the ceiling height. The room perimeter column in the table contains the number 44, and the ceiling height column contains the number 8. When you multiply 44 by 8, you get 352, which you enter in the wall area column in the table, as shown in Figure 2-37.

Figure 2-37: Wall area value entered in the desk-check table

room length	room width	ceiling height	single roll coverage	room perimeter	wall area	number of single rolls
10	12	8	30	44	352	

The fourth instruction in the algorithm is to calculate the number of single rolls by dividing the wall area by the single roll coverage. The wall area column in the table contains the number 352, and the single roll coverage column contains the number 30. When you divide 352 by 30, you get 11.73 (rounded to two decimal places), which you enter in the number of single rolls column in the table. The completed desk-check table is shown in Figure 2-38.

Figure 2-38: Desk-check table showing the results of the first desk-check

room length	room width	ceiling height	single roll coverage	room perimeter	wall area	number of single rolls
10	12	8	30	44	352	11.73

The last instruction in the algorithm is to display the number of single rolls. According to the desk-check table, the number of single rolls is 11.73, which agrees with the manual calculation shown earlier in Figure 2-30. Although the algorithm appears to be correct, recall that you should test it several times using different data to be sure. Figure 2-39 shows the desk-check table using input values of 12 feet, 14 feet, 10 feet, and 37 square feet as the room length, room width, ceiling height, and single roll coverage, respectively.

Figure 2-39: Desk-check table showing the results of the second desk-check

room length	room width	ceiling height	single roll coverage	room perimeter	wall area	number of single rolls
~~10~~ 12	~~12~~ 14	~~8~~ 10	~~30~~ 37	~~44~~ 52	~~352~~ 520	~~11.73~~ 14.05

Almost every problem—no matter how simple it is—can be solved in more than one way. For example, rather than using the algorithm shown in Figure 2-33 to solve the wallpaper problem, you also can use the algorithm shown in Figure 2-40.

Figure 2-40: Another correct algorithm for the wallpaper store problem

Input	Processing	Output
room length room width ceiling height single roll coverage	Processing items: room perimeter Algorithm: 1. enter the room length, room width, ceiling height, and single roll coverage 2. calculate the room perimeter by adding together the room length and room width, and then multiplying the sum by 2 3. calculate the number of single rolls by multiplying the room perimeter by the ceiling height, and then dividing the result by the single roll coverage 4. display the number of single rolls	number of single rolls

Lab 2.3 Mark Williams, the manager of The Paper Tree wallpaper store, informs you that he would like to change the problem specification shown earlier in Figure 2-30. He now wants the program to display both the number of single rolls of wallpaper and the number of double rolls of wallpaper. A double roll covers twice as much area as a single roll. Make the appropriate modifications to the algorithm shown in Figure 2-33 in Lab 2.2, then desk-check the algorithm using input values of 12 feet, 12 feet, 8 feet, and 40 square feet as the room length, room width, ceiling height, and single roll coverage.

You now have completed Chapter 2's Application lesson. You can either take a break or complete the end-of-lesson exercises.

ANSWERS TO LABS

Lab 2.1

1. 9.50, 3.50

2.

Input	Processing	Output
number of late days	Processing items: late charge Algorithm: 1. get the number of late days 2. calculate the late charge by multiplying the number of late days by 2 3. calculate the amount due by adding 3.50 to the late charge 4. display the amount due	amount due

number of late days	late charge	amount due
~~3~~ 0	~~6.00~~ 0	~~9.50~~ 3.50

3.

Input	Processing	Output
number of late days	Processing items: none Algorithm: 1. get the number of late days 2. calculate the late charge by multiplying the number of late days by 2 3. calculate the amount due by adding 3.50 to the late charge 4. display the late charge and amount due	late charge amount due

number of late days	late charge	amount due
~~3~~ 0	~~6.00~~ 0	~~9.50~~ 3.50

Lab 2.2

No answer required.

Lab 2.3

Input	Processing	Output

room length
room width
ceiling height
single roll coverage
	Processing items:
	    room perimeter
	    wall area
	
	Algorithm:
	1. enter the room length, room width, ceiling height, and single roll coverage
	2. calculate the room perimeter by adding together the room length and room width, and then multiplying the sum by 2
	3. calculate the wall area by multiplying the room perimeter by the ceiling height
	4. calculate the number of single rolls by dividing the wall area by the single roll coverage
	5. calculate the number of double rolls by dividing the number of single rolls by 2
	6. display the number of single rolls and the number of double rolls
		number of single rolls
		number of double rolls

room length	room width	ceiling height	single roll coverage	room perimeter	wall area	number of single rolls	number of double rolls
12	12	8	40	48	384	9.6	4.8

Look For These Symbols

Debugging

Discovery

EXERCISES

1) Rewrite the IPO chart shown in Figure 2-33 using a flowchart in the Algorithm section.

2) John Lee wants a program that allows him to enter the following three pieces of information: his checking account balance at the beginning of the month, the amount of money he deposited during the month, and the amount of money he withdrew during the month. He wants the program to display his balance at the end of the month. Complete an IPO chart for this problem, using pseudocode in the Processing column. Also complete a desk-check table for your algorithm.

Use the following information for the first desk-check:

checking account balance at the beginning of the month:	2000
money deposited during the month:	775
money withdrawn during the month:	1200

Use the following information for the second desk-check:

checking account balance at the beginning of the month:	500
money deposited during the month:	100
money withdrawn during the month:	610

3) Lana Jones wants a program that displays the average of any three numbers she enters. Complete an IPO chart for this problem, using pseudocode in the Processing column. Also complete a desk-check table for your algorithm. Use the following three numbers for the first desk-check: 25, 76, and 33. Use the following three numbers for the second desk-check: 10, 15, and 20.

4) Jackets Unlimited is having a sale on all of its merchandise. The store manager asks you to create a program that requires the clerk to enter the original price of a jacket and the discount rate. The program should then display both the sales discount and the new sales price. Complete an IPO chart for this problem, using pseudocode in the Processing column. Also complete a desk-check table for your algorithm. For the first desk-check, use 100 as the jacket price and .25 (the decimal equivalent of 25%) as the discount rate. For the second desk-check, use 50 as the jacket price and .1 as the discount rate.

5) Typing Salon currently charges $.10 per typed envelope and $.25 per typed page, although those prices may change in the future. The company accountant wants a program that will help her prepare the customer bills. She will enter the number of typed envelopes and the number of typed pages, as well as the current charges per typed envelope and per typed page. The program should display the total amount due from the customer. Complete an IPO chart for this problem, using pseudocode in the Processing column. Also complete a desk-check table for your algorithm.

Use the following information for the first desk-check:

number of typed envelopes:	100
number of typed pages:	100
charge per typed envelope:	.10
charge per typed page:	.25

Use the following information for the second desk-check:

number of typed envelopes:	10
number of typed pages:	15
charge per typed envelope:	.20
charge per typed page:	.30

6) Management USA, a small training center, plans to run two full-day seminars on December 1. Because each seminar lasts the entire day, a person can register for only one of the two seminars at a time. The current seminar price is $200, but that price could change in the future. Registration for the seminars will be taken by telephone. When a company calls to register its employees, the Management USA telephone representative will ask for the following two items of information: the number of employees registering for the first seminar and the number registering for the second seminar. Claire Jenkowski, the owner of Management USA, wants a program that displays the total number of employees the company is registering and the total cost. Complete an IPO chart for this problem, using pseudocode in the Processing column. Also complete a desk-check table for your algorithm.

Use the following information for the first desk-check:

number registering for the first seminar:	10
number registering for the second seminar:	10
seminar price:	200

Use the following information for the second desk-check:

number registering for the first seminar:	30
number registering for the second seminar:	10
seminar price:	100

7) Suman Gadhari, the payroll clerk at Sun Projects, wants a program that computes an employee's net pay. Suman will enter the hours worked, the hourly rate of pay, the federal withholding tax (FWT) rate, the Social Security (FICA) tax rate, and the state income tax rate. For this program, you do not have to worry about overtime, as this company does not allow anyone to work more than 40 hours. Suman wants the program to display the employee's gross pay, FWT, FICA, state income tax, and net pay. Complete an IPO chart for this problem, using pseudocode in the Processing column. Also complete a desk-check table for your algorithm.

Use the following information for the first desk-check:

hours worked:	20
hourly pay rate:	6
FWT rate:	.2
FICA rate:	.08
state income tax rate:	.02

Use the following information for the second desk-check:

hours worked:	30
hourly pay rate:	10
FWT rate:	.2
FICA rate:	.08
state income tax rate:	.04

8) Perry Brown needs a program that allows him to enter the length of four sides of a polygon. The program should display the perimeter of the polygon. Complete an IPO chart for this problem, using pseudocode in the Processing column. Also complete a desk-check table. Desk-check the algorithm twice, using your own sample data.

9) Builders Inc. needs a program that allows its salesclerks to enter the diameter of a circle and the price of railing material per foot. The program should display the circumference of the circle and the total price of the railing material. (Use 3.14 as the value of pi.) Complete an IPO chart for this problem, using a flowchart in the Processing column. Also complete a desk-check table for your algorithm. Desk-check the algorithm twice, using your own sample data.

10) Tile Limited wants a program that allows its salesclerks to enter the length and width (in feet) of a rectangle and the price of a square foot of tile. The program should display the area of the rectangle and the total price of the tile. Complete an IPO chart for this problem, using pseudocode in the Processing column. Also complete a desk-check table for your algorithm. Desk-check the algorithm twice, using your own sample data.

11) Willow Pools wants a program that allows its salespeople to enter the dimensions of a rectangular pool in feet. The program should display the volume of the rectangular pool. Complete an IPO chart for this problem, using pseudocode in the Processing column. Also complete a desk-check table for your algorithm. Desk-check the algorithm twice, using your own sample data.

12) IMY Industries needs a program that its personnel clerks can use to display the new hourly pay, given both the current hourly pay for each of three job codes (1, 2, and 3) and the raise rate (entered as a decimal). Complete an IPO chart for this problem, using pseudocode in the Processing column. Also complete a desk-check table for your algorithm.

Use the following information for the first desk-check:

current hourly pay for job code 1:	7.55
current hourly pay for job code 2:	10.00
current hourly pay for job code 3:	10.30
raise rate:	.02

Use the following information for the second desk-check:

current hourly pay for job code 1:	8.00
current hourly pay for job code 2:	6.50
current hourly pay for job code 3:	7.25
raise rate:	.02

13) Sue Chen attends Jefferson University in Kentucky. Students attending Jefferson University are considered full-time students if they are registered for at least 15 semester hours. Students registered for less than 15 hours are considered part-time students. Sue would like you to create a program that displays the total cost per semester. Tuition is $100 per semester hour. Room and board is $3,000. (Assume that all students live on campus and will have room and board charges.) Complete an IPO chart for this problem, using a flowchart in the Processing column. Also complete a desk-check table for your algorithm. Desk-check the algorithm twice. Use 20 semester hours for the first desk-check, and use 14 hours for the second desk-check.

14) George Markos, the payroll clerk at Microstep Company, wants a program that computes an employee's gross pay. George will enter the hours worked and the hourly rate of pay. Employees working more than 40 hours receive time and one-half on the hours more than 40. George wants the program to display the employee's gross pay. Complete an IPO chart for this problem, using pseudocode in the Processing column. Also complete a desk-check table for your algorithm. For the first desk-check, use 20 as the hours worked and 6 as the hourly pay rate. For the second desk-check, use 43 as the hours worked and 10 as the hourly pay rate.

15) Jean Marie wants a program that displays the cube of a number. The algorithm shown in Figure 2-41 is supposed to solve this problem, but it is not working correctly. Rewrite the algorithm correctly, then desk-check it using the number 4.

Figure 2-41

Input	Processing	Output
number	Processing items: none Algorithm: 1. calculate the cube of the number by multiplying the number by itself three times	cube of the number

16) GeeBees Clothiers is having a sale. The manager of the store wants a program that allows the clerk to enter the original price of an item and the discount rate. The program should display the discount and the sale price. The algorithm shown in Figure 2-42 is supposed to solve this problem, but it is not working correctly. Rewrite the algorithm correctly, then desk-check it using an original price of $100 and a discount rate of 25%.

Figure 2-42

Input	Processing	Output
original price discount rate	Processing items: none Algorithm: 1. enter the original price and the discount rate 2. calculate the sale price by subtracting the discount from the original price 3. display the discount and the sale price	discount sale price

Please visit the Testing Center at www.course.com/testingcenter for more practice on the topics covered in this chapter.

Chapter 3

Completing the Problem-Solving Process and Getting Started with C++

Objectives

After completing this chapter, you will be able to:

- Code an algorithm into a program

- Desk-check a program

- Evaluate and modify a program

- Differentiate among source code, object code, and executable code

- Understand the components of a C++ program

- Create a Visual C++ .NET solution, project, and source file

- Open a Visual C++ .NET solution

- Save, build, and execute a C++ program

- Locate an error in a C++ program

- Make a backup copy of a solution

Concept Lesson

More on the Problem-Solving Process

In Chapter 2, you learned how to analyze a problem, as well as how to plan and desk-check an algorithm designed to solve the problem. Recall that analyzing, planning, and desk-checking are the first three steps in the problem-solving process used to create a computer program. The entire process is shown in Figure 3-1.

Figure 3-1: The problem-solving process for creating a computer program

1. Analyze the problem.

2. Plan the algorithm.

3. Desk-check the algorithm.

4. Code the algorithm into a program.

5. Desk-check the program.

6. Evaluate and modify (if necessary) the program.

Only after the programmer is satisfied that an algorithm is correct does he or she then move on to the fourth step in the problem-solving process. As Figure 3-1 indicates, Step 4 is to code the algorithm—in other words, translate the algorithm into a language that the computer can understand. As you may remember from Chapter 2, a coded algorithm is called a program. In this book, you use the C++ programming language to translate your algorithms into programs.

After completing the coding step, the programmer then desk-checks the program to make sure that the algorithm was translated correctly—this is Step 5 in the problem-solving process. Programmers typically desk-check the program using the same sample data used to desk-check the algorithm. If the program does not produce the same results as the algorithm, the programmer corrects the errors in the program before continuing to the final step in the problem-solving process.

The final step in the problem-solving process is to evaluate and modify (if necessary) the program. A programmer evaluates a program by running (executing) it on the computer. While the program is running, the programmer enters the same sample data he or she used when desk-checking the program. If the executed program does not work as intended, the programmer makes the necessary modifications until it does.

In this chapter, you take a closer look at Steps 4 through 6 in the problem-solving process.

Coding the Algorithm into a Program

In Chapter 2, you analyzed the problem specification shown in Figure 3-2 for Sarah Martin. You then created and desk-checked an appropriate algorithm.

Figure 3-2: Problem specification for Sarah Martin

Sarah Martin has been working for Quality Builders for four years. Last year, Sarah received a 4% raise, which brought her current weekly pay to $250. Sarah is scheduled to receive a 3% raise next week. She wants you to write a program that will display, on the computer screen, the amount of her new weekly pay.

Figure 3-3 shows the IPO chart you created for this problem.

Figure 3-3: IPO chart for Sarah Martin's problem

Input	Processing	Output

current weekly pay
raise rate
	Processing items:
	    weekly raise
	
	Algorithm:
	1. enter the current weekly pay
	   and raise rate
	2. calculate the weekly raise by
	   multiplying the current weekly
	   pay by the raise rate
	3. calculate the new weekly pay
	   by adding the weekly raise to
	   the current weekly pay
	4. display the new weekly pay
		new weekly pay

Recall that the IPO chart shows the problem's input, processing, and output items, as well as the algorithm needed to solve the problem. The algorithm shown in Figure 3-3, for example, shows the steps the computer must follow to calculate and display Sarah's new weekly pay. The calculation is based on the current weekly pay and raise rate values entered by the user. Notice that the algorithm also calculates an intermediate value, weekly raise. As you learned in Chapter 2, an intermediate value, referred to as a processing item, is one that the algorithm uses when processing the input into the output.

Assigning Names, Data Types, and Initial Values to the IPO Items

Programmers use the information in the IPO chart to code the algorithm. First, the programmer assigns a descriptive name to each unique input, processing, and output item listed in the IPO chart. In most programming languages, the names can contain only letters, numbers, and the underscore; they cannot contain punctuation characters or spaces. Most C++ programmers use lowercase letters for the names. However, if a name contains more than one word, most C++ programmers capitalize the first letter in the second and subsequent words. In this case, you will assign the names `currentPay` and `raiseRate` to the two input items. You will assign the name `raise` to the processing item, and the name `newPay` to the output item.

The programmer also assigns a data type to each input, processing, and output item. The data type specifies the type of data (for example, decimal or integer) each item represents. In this case, because the input, processing, and output items could contain decimal numbers, you will assign the `double` data type to each item. You learn more about data types in Chapter 4.

In addition to assigning both a name and data type to each input, processing, and output item, the programmer also assigns an initial value. This is referred to as **initializing** the item. As you will learn in Chapter 4, items assigned the `double` data type typically are initialized to zero using the value 0.0, as shown in Figure 3-4.

tip

The practice of capitalizing only the first letter in the second and subsequent words in a name is referred to as "camel casing." Because the uppercase letters in the name are taller than the lowercase letters, the uppercase letters appear as "humps" in the name.

Figure 3-4: C++ instructions corresponding to the Sarah Martin problem's input, processing, and output items

IPO chart information	C++ instructions
Input current weekly pay raise rate	`double currentPay = 0.0;` `double raiseRate = 0.0;`
Processing weekly raise	`double raise = 0.0;`
Output new weekly pay	`double newPay = 0.0;`
Algorithm 1. enter the current weekly pay and raise rate 2. calculate the weekly raise by multiplying the current weekly pay by the raise rate 3. calculate the new weekly pay by adding the weekly raise to the current weekly pay 4. display the new weekly pay	

tip

Not all lines of code in a C++ program are statements. As you will learn later in this chapter, program comments, which are lines of code used to internally document a program, are not statements, because they do not cause the computer to perform any action.

The four C++ instructions shown in Figure 3-4 direct the computer to declare (or create) four variables, which are computer memory locations that the program will use while it is running. The word `double`, which must be typed using lowercase letters, is a keyword in C++. A **keyword** is a word that has a special meaning in a programming language. In C++, the keyword `double` indicates that the variable (memory location) can store a number with a decimal place.

Notice that each of the C++ instructions shown in Figure 3-4 ends with a semicolon (;). The instruction to declare a variable is considered a **statement**, which is simply a C++ instruction that causes the computer to perform some action after it is executed, or processed, by the computer. All C++ statements must end with a semicolon.

Translating the Algorithm Steps into C++ Code

After assigning a name, data type, and initial value to each input, processing, and output item, the programmer then translates each step in the algorithm into one or more C++ instructions. Figure 3-5 shows the C++ instructions corresponding to the Sarah Martin problem's algorithm.

Figure 3-5: C++ instructions for the Sarah Martin problem's algorithm

IPO chart information	C++ instructions
Input current weekly pay raise rate	`double currentPay = 0.0;` `double raiseRate = 0.0;`
Processing weekly raise	`double raise = 0.0;`
Output new weekly pay	`double newPay = 0.0;`

Algorithm
1. enter the current
   weekly pay and raise
   rate
	`cout << "Enter current weekly pay: ";`
	`cin >> currentPay;`
	`cout << "Enter raise rate: ";`
	`cin >> raiseRate;`

2. calculate the weekly
   raise by multiplying
   the current weekly pay
   by the raise rate
	`raise = currentPay * raiseRate;`

3. calculate the new
   weekly pay by adding
   the weekly raise to
   the current weekly pay
	`newPay = raise + currentPay;`

4. display the new weekly pay	`cout << "New pay: " << newPay << endl;`

Do not be concerned if the C++ instructions shown in Figure 3-5 look confusing to you. Each instruction is described in this lesson with a minimal amount of explanation. You will learn more detail about each instruction in the following chapters. For now, you need simply to pay attention to how each instruction corresponds to a step in the algorithm.

Step 1 in the algorithm is to enter the input items, which are the current weekly pay and raise rate. You will have the user enter the input items at the keyboard. To do so, you first use a C++ instruction that displays an appropriate message, or prompt, on the computer screen. The message should clearly indicate the information you want the user to enter. You then use a C++ instruction to accept the input items from the user.

In C++, you use **streams**, which are just sequences of characters, to perform standard input and output operations. The standard output stream is called `cout` (pronounced *see out*), which refers to the computer screen. The standard input stream is called `cin` (pronounced *see in*), which refers to the computer keyboard. To make the concept of streams easier to understand, it may help to think of the `cout` stream as a sequence of characters sent "out" to the user through the computer screen, and think of the `cin` stream as a sequence of characters sent "in" to the computer through the keyboard.

The C++ statement `cout << "Enter current weekly pay: ";` prompts the user to enter the current weekly pay by displaying an appropriate message on the computer screen. (You can tell that this line of code is a statement because it ends with a semicolon.)

tip

Like most programming languages, the C++ programming language follows a specific format, referred to as its syntax. The syntax of a language, whether it is C++ or English, is the set of rules that you must follow to use the language. The syntax of the C++ language, like the syntax of the English language, will take some time and effort to learn.

The << that follows `cout` in the statement is called the **insertion operator**. It may help to think of the insertion operator as meaning "sends to." In this case, the insertion operator (<<) sends the "Enter current weekly pay: " message to the computer screen (`cout`). Keep in mind that this statement only displays the message on the screen. The statement does not allow the user to actually enter the current weekly pay; you need to use the standard input stream `cin` and the extraction operator to do so.

The C++ statement `cin >> currentPay;` allows the user to enter the current weekly pay. The >> that follows `cin` is called the **extraction operator**. It may help to think of the extraction operator as meaning "gets from." In this case, the statement `cin >> currentPay;` gets the current weekly pay from the keyboard (`cin`), and stores that amount in the `currentPay` variable. (Recall that a variable is a computer memory location.)

After the user enters the current weekly pay, the statement `cout << "Enter raise rate: ";` prompts the user to enter the raise rate. The statement `cin >> raiseRate;` then allows the user to enter the raise rate, which the statement stores in the `raiseRate` variable.

The second step in the algorithm is to calculate the weekly raise by multiplying the current weekly pay by the raise rate. The C++ statement `raise = currentPay * raiseRate;` accomplishes this task by multiplying the value stored in the `currentPay` variable by the value stored in the `raiseRate` variable. Notice that a computer uses an asterisk to represent multiplication. The statement stores the result of the calculation in the `raise` variable. Recall that the `raise` variable represents a processing item.

The third step in the algorithm is to calculate the new weekly pay by adding the weekly raise to the current weekly pay. This task is handled by the C++ statement `newPay = raise + currentPay;`, which adds the contents of the `raise` variable to the contents of the `currentPay` variable, and then stores the result in the `newPay` variable.

The last step in the algorithm is to display the new weekly pay, which was calculated in the previous step. You can do so using the C++ statement `cout << "New pay: " << newPay << endl;`. This statement will display the message "New pay: " along with the contents of the `newPay` variable. (Notice that you can use more than one insertion operator in a statement.) The `endl` (pronounced *end of line*) text that appears at the end of the statement is one of the C++ stream manipulators. A **stream manipulator** allows the program to manipulate, or manage, the input and output stream characters in some way. When outputting information to the computer screen, for example, you can use the `endl` stream manipulator to advance the cursor to the next line on the screen.

After the programmer finishes coding the algorithm into a program, he or she then moves on to the fifth step in the problem-solving process, which is to desk-check the program.

MINI-QUIZ

Mini-Quiz 1

1) The programmer assigns a _____, _____, and _____ to each unique input, processing, and output item listed in the IPO chart.

2) A _____ is a location in the computer's memory that the program uses while it is running.

3) Write a C++ statement that declares a variable named `grossPay`. Use `double` and `0.0` as the data type and initial value, respectively.

4) Write a C++ statement that stores the value entered at the keyboard in a variable named `grossPay`.

Desk-Checking the Program

The fifth step in the problem-solving process is to desk-check the program to make sure that each step in the algorithm was translated correctly. You should desk-check the program using the same sample data that you used to desk-check the algorithm. The results obtained when desk-checking the program should be identical to the results obtained when desk-checking the algorithm. For your convenience in comparing the results of both desk-checks later in this lesson, Figure 3-6 shows the desk-check table that you completed for the Sarah Martin algorithm in Chapter 2.

Figure 3-6: Completed desk-check table for the Sarah Martin algorithm

current weekly pay	raise rate	weekly raise	new weekly pay
~~250~~ 100	~~.03~~ .10	~~7.50~~ 10	~~257.50~~ 110

As Figure 3-6 indicates, you desk-checked the algorithm twice, using two sets of data. The first set of data used 250 as the current weekly pay and .03 as the raise rate. The second set of data used 100 and .10 as the current weekly pay and raise rate, respectively. You will use both sets of data to desk-check the program.

When desk-checking the program, you first place the names of the input, processing, and output variables in a new desk-check table, along with each variable's initial value, as shown in Figure 3-7.

Figure 3-7: Variable names and initial values shown in the program's desk-check table

variable names

initial values

currentPay	raiseRate	raise	newPay
0.0	0.0	0.0	0.0

Next, you complete each of the C++ instructions in order, recording in the desk-check table any changes made to the variables. For example, the statement `cout << "Enter current weekly pay: ";` prompts the user to enter the current weekly pay. The statement does not make any changes to the program's variables, so no entry is necessary in the desk-check table as a result of the statement. However, recall that the next statement, `cin >> currentPay;`, allows the user to enter the current weekly pay, and it stores the user's response in the `currentPay` variable. If the user enters the number 250 as the current weekly pay, for example, the statement stores the number 250 in the `currentPay` variable. You record the result of the statement by crossing out the 0.0 that appears as the initial value in the `currentPay` column and entering the number 250.0 there instead. (You cross out the initial value because, as you learned in Chapter 2, each column in a desk-check table should contain only one value at any time.)

The statement `cout << "Enter raise rate: ";` prompts the user to enter the raise rate, and the statement `cin >> raiseRate;` stores the user's response in the `raiseRate` variable. Assuming the user enters the number .03, you cross out the 0.0 that appears in the desk-check table's `raiseRate` column and record the number .03 there instead, as shown in Figure 3-8.

Figure 3-8: Current status of the desk-check table

currentPay	raiseRate	raise	newPay
0.0 250.0	0.0 .03	0.0	0.0

The next statement, `raise = currentPay * raiseRate;`, first multiplies the contents of the `currentPay` variable (250.0 according to the desk-check table) by the contents of the `raiseRate` variable (.03 according to the desk-check table), giving 7.5. The statement then stores the number 7.5 in the `raise` variable. Notice that the calculation that appears on the right side of the assignment operator (the = sign) in the statement is performed first, and then the result is stored in the variable whose name appears on the left side of the assignment operator. As a result of this statement, you cross out the number 0.0 that appears in the desk-check table's `raise` column and record the number 7.5 there instead, as shown in Figure 3-9.

Figure 3-9: Desk-check table showing the results of the raise calculation

currentPay	raiseRate	raise	newPay
0.0 250.0	0.0 .03	0.0 7.5	0.0

The next statement, `newPay = raise + currentPay;`, adds the contents of the `raise` variable (7.5) to the contents of the `currentPay` variable (250.0), and then stores the result (257.5) in the `newPay` variable. In the desk-check table, you cross out the 0.0 that appears in the `newPay` column and record the number 257.5 there instead, as shown in Figure 3-10.

Figure 3-10: Desk-check table showing the results of the new weekly pay calculation

currentPay	raiseRate	raise	newPay
0.0 250.0	0.0 .03	0.0 7.5	0.0 257.5

The last statement, `cout << "New pay: " << newPay << endl;`, displays the message "New pay: ", along with the contents of the `newPay` variable (257.5), on the screen.

If you compare the second row of values shown in Figure 3-10 with the first row of values shown earlier in Figure 3-6, you will notice that the results obtained when desk-checking the program are the same as the results obtained when desk-checking the algorithm. Recall, however, that you should perform several desk-checks, using different data, to make sure that the program is correct.

Next, desk-check the program using 100 as the current weekly pay and .10 as the raise rate. (This is the same data used in the second desk-check shown in Figure 3-6.) Each time you desk-check a program, keep in mind that you must complete all of the program's instructions, beginning with the first instruction. In this case, the first instruction initializes the `currentPay` variable. The completed desk-check table is shown in Figure 3-11.

Figure 3-11: Desk-check table showing the results of the second desk-check

currentPay	raiseRate	raise	newPay
~~0.0~~	~~0.0~~	~~0.0~~	~~0.0~~
~~250.0~~	~~.03~~	~~7.5~~	~~257.5~~
~~0.0~~	~~0.0~~	~~0.0~~	~~0.0~~
100	.10	10.0	110.0

Here again, if you compare the fourth row of values shown in Figure 3-11 with the second row of values shown earlier in Figure 3-6, you will notice that the program produced the same results as did the algorithm.

After desk-checking the program, the programmer then evaluates and modifies (if necessary) the program.

Evaluating and Modifying the Program

The final step in the problem-solving process is to evaluate and modify (if necessary) the program. You do so by entering, into the computer, the C++ instructions listed in your algorithm, along with other instructions required by the C++ compiler; you then run (execute) the program.

Programmers often refer to the final step in the problem-solving process as the "testing and debugging" step. **Testing** refers to running the program, along with sample data, on the computer. The results obtained when the program is run on the computer should agree with those shown in the program's desk-check table. If the results of running the program differ from those of the desk-check, then the program contains errors that must be corrected.

Debugging refers to the process of locating and removing any errors, called **bugs**, in a program. Program errors can be either syntax errors or logic errors. You create a **syntax error** when you enter an instruction that violates the programming language's **syntax**, which is the set of rules that you must follow when using the language. Typing `ednl` rather than `endl` is an example of a syntax error. Most syntax errors occur as a result of mistyping a keyword or variable name, or forgetting to enter a semicolon at the end of a statement. In most cases, syntax errors are easy to both locate and correct, because they trigger an error message from the C++ compiler. The error message indicates the general vicinity of the error and includes a brief explanation of the error.

Unlike syntax errors, logic errors are much more difficult to find, because they can occur for a variety of reasons and usually do not trigger an error message from the compiler. You create a **logic error** when you enter an instruction that does not give you the expected results. An example of a logic error is the instruction `average = number1 + number2 / 2;`, which is supposed to calculate the average of two numbers. Although the instruction is syntactically correct, it is logically incorrect, because it tells the computer first to divide the contents of the `number2` variable by 2, then add the result to the contents of the `number1`

tip

You learn about the precedence order for the arithmetic operators in Chapter 4.

variable, and then assign the sum to the `average` variable. (Notice that the computer uses a slash [/] to represent division.) This error occurs because division is performed before addition in an arithmetic expression. The instruction to calculate the average of two numbers, written correctly, is `average = (number1 + number2) / 2;`. Adding the parentheses to this instruction tells the computer first to add the contents of the `number1` variable to the contents of the `number2` variable, then divide that sum by 2, and then assign the result to the `average` variable. Other logic errors occur typically as a result of neglecting to enter a program instruction or entering the program instructions in the wrong order.

If a program contains an error, the programmer must locate and then correct the error. The programmer's job is not finished until the program runs without errors and produces the expected results.

MINI-QUIZ

Mini-Quiz 2

1) How many values can a variable contain at any time?

2) Errors in a program are also called _____.

3) Program errors can be either _____ errors or _____ errors.

Next, you learn how to create a C++ program that can be entered into the computer.

Creating a C++ Program

C++ evolved from the procedure-oriented C programming language, which was developed in 1972 at Bell Laboratories by Dennis Ritchie. In 1985, Bjarne Stroustrup, also of Bell Laboratories, added, among other things, object-oriented features to the C language. This enhanced version of the C language was named C++.

C++ is a superset of C, which means that, with few exceptions, everything available in C also is available in C++. This means that you can use C++ as a procedural, as well as an object-oriented, language. Before using the object-oriented features of C++, you learn how to use C++ to create procedure-oriented programs. The techniques you learn from procedural programming will help you create object-oriented programs later.

To create and execute a C++ program, you need to have access to a text editor, often simply called an editor, and a C++ compiler. You use the editor to enter the C++ instructions, called **source code**, into the computer. You then save the source code in a file on a disk. Source code files created using Microsoft Visual C++ have the filename extension .cpp, which stands for *C plus plus*. The file containing the source code is called the **source file**.

As you learned in the Overview, the computer cannot understand instructions written in a high-level language. Rather, a compiler is necessary to translate the high-level instructions into machine code—the 0s and 1s that the computer *can* understand. Machine code is usually called **object code**. When you compile a Microsoft Visual C++ program, the compiler generates the appropriate object code, saving it automatically in a file whose filename extension is .obj. (The *obj* stands for *object*.) The file containing the object code is called the **object file**.

After the compiler creates the object file, it then invokes another program called a linker. The **linker** combines the object file with other machine code necessary for your C++ program to run correctly—such as machine code that allows your program to communicate with input and output devices. The linker produces an **executable file**, which is a file that contains all of the machine code necessary to run your C++ program as many times as desired without the need for translating the program again. The executable file has an extension of .exe on its filename. (The *exe* stands for *executable*.)

Figure 3-12 illustrates the process the C++ compiler follows when translating your source code into executable code.

Figure 3-12: Process by which source code is translated into executable code

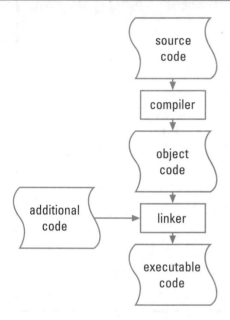

Many C++ systems, such as Microsoft Visual C++ and Borland C++ Builder, contain both the editor and compiler in one integrated environment, referred to as an **IDE (Integrated Development Environment)**. Other C++ systems, called command-line compilers, contain only the compiler and require you to use a general-purpose editor (such as Notepad, WordPad, and vi) to enter the program instructions into the computer. In this book, you use Microsoft Visual C++ .NET to enter and run your C++ programs.

Figure 3-13 shows the source code for the Sarah Martin program. The lines are numbered in the figure so that it is easier to refer to them in the text; you do not enter the line numbers in the program. (Do not be concerned if parts of the source code look confusing to you. Each new program instruction is described in this lesson with a minimal amount of explanation. You will learn more detail about the instructions in the following chapters.)

tip

The C++ syntax does not require you to align the initial values in the variable declaration statements as shown in Figure 3-13. However, doing so makes it easier to verify that each variable has been initialized.

Figure 3-13: C++ program designed to solve the Sarah Martin problem

comments

#include directive

using statements

function header

the function body is enclosed in braces

```
1   //Ch3Lab2.cpp - calculates and displays the new weekly pay
2   //Created/revised by <your name> on <current date>
3
4   #include <iostream>
5
6   using std::cout;
7   using std::cin;
8   using std::endl;
9
10  int main()
11  {
12      //declare variables
13      double currentPay = 0.0;
14      double raiseRate  = 0.0;
15      double raise      = 0.0;
16      double newPay     = 0.0;
17
18      //enter input items
19      cout << "Enter current weekly pay: ";
20      cin >> currentPay;
21      cout << "Enter raise rate: ";
22      cin >> raiseRate;
23
24      //calculate raise and new pay
25      raise = currentPay * raiseRate;
26      newPay = raise + currentPay;
27
28      //display output item
29      cout << "New pay: " << newPay << endl;
30
31      return 0;
32  } //end of main function
```

The first two lines in the program are comments. A **comment** is a message to the person reading the program and is referred to as **internal documentation**. It is a good programming practice to include comments similar to the ones shown in Figure 3-13. Notice that the comments indicate the program's name and purpose, as well as the programmer's name and the date the program was either created or revised. It also is a good programming practice to use comments to explain various sections of the program code. Comments make the program instructions more readable and easier to understand by anyone viewing the program.

You create a comment by typing two forward slashes (//) before the text you want treated as a comment, like this: //Ch3Lab2.cpp - calculates and displays the new weekly pay. The C++ compiler does not process the comments in a program; rather, the compiler ignores the comments when it translates the source code into object code. Comments do not end with a semicolon, because they are not statements in C++.

The fourth line in the program is called a directive. C++ programs typically include at least one directive, and most include many directives. The #include <iostream> directive is a special instruction that tells the compiler to include the contents of another file—in this case, the iostream file—in the current program. The iostream file must be included in any program that uses `cout` to output data to the screen or `cin` to input data from the keyboard. A **#include directive** provides a convenient way to merge the source code from one file with the source code in another file, without having to retype the code.

Lines 6 through 8 are called **using statements**; notice that each ends with a semicolon. The `using std::cout;` statement tells the compiler where it can find the definition of the keyword `cout`. In this case, the definition is located in a namespace (a special area in the computer's internal memory) named `std`, which is short for "standard." Similarly, the `using std::cin;` and `using std::endl;` statements indicate that the definitions of the keywords `cin` and `endl` are also located in the `std` namespace.

Line 10 in the program is `int main()`. The word `main()`, which must be typed using lowercase letters, is the name of a function. A **function** is a block of code that performs a task. Functions have parentheses following their names. Some functions require you to enter information between the parentheses; other functions, like `main()`, do not.

Every C++ program must have a `main()` function, because this is where the execution of a C++ program always begins. Most C++ programs contain many more functions in addition to `main()`. Some functions return a value after completing their assigned task, while others, referred to as **void functions**, do not. If a function returns a value, the data type of the value it returns appears to the left of the function name; otherwise, the keyword `void` appears to the left of the name. Notice that `int`, which stands for *integer* and is typed using lowercase letters, precedes `main()` in the code. The `int` indicates that the `main()` function returns a value of the integer data type—in other words, the function returns a number that does not contain a decimal place. The entire line of code, `int main()`, is referred to as a **function header**, because it marks the beginning of the function.

After the function header, you enter the code that directs the function on how to perform its assigned task. Examples of such code include statements that declare variables, and statements that input, calculate, and output data.

In C++, you enclose a function's code within a set of braces (`{}`). The braces mark the beginning and the end of the code block that comprises the function. You enter the opening brace (`{`) immediately below the `int main()` function header in the program, and you enter the closing brace (`}`) at the end of the function. In Figure 3-13, the opening brace appears on line 11, and the closing brace on line 32. Everything between the opening and closing braces is included, in this case, in the `main()` function, and is referred to as the **function body**. Notice that you can include a comment—in this case, `//end of main function`—on the same line with any C++ instruction. However, you must be sure to enter the comment *after* the instruction, and not before it. Only the text appearing after the `//` on a line is interpreted as a comment.

In the line immediately below the opening brace is the comment `//declare variables`, which describes the purpose of the statements entered on lines 13 through 16. The statements are the variable declaration statements from this problem's IPO chart (shown earlier in Figure 3-5).

Line 18, which contains the comment `//enter input items`, describes the purpose of the four statements that follow it. The four statements are the input instructions from the IPO chart.

Line 24 contains the comment `//calculate raise and new pay`. This comment describes the purpose of the statements entered on lines 25 and 26. The statements are the calculation instructions from the IPO chart.

Line 28 contains the comment `//display output item` and describes the purpose of the `cout << "New pay: " << newPay << endl;` statement. Recall that this statement also comes from the IPO chart.

Line 31 contains the `return 0;` statement. As mentioned earlier, the `main()` function returns an integer value. In this case, it returns the number 0 to the operating system to indicate that the program ended normally.

In Lab 3.2, you learn how to use the Visual C++ .NET editor to enter the program shown in Figure 3-13 into the computer. You also learn how to use the Visual C++ .NET compiler to run the program.

MINI-QUIZ

Mini-Quiz 3

1) The .cpp file that contains your C++ instructions is called the _____ file.

   a. executable

   b. object

   c. source

2) The compiler saves the machine code version of your C++ instructions in the _____ file.

   a. executable

   b. object

   c. source

3) The linker produces the _____ file, which is a file that contains all of the machine code necessary to run your C++ program.

   a. executable

   b. object

   c. source

You now have completed Chapter 3's Concept lesson, which covered the last three steps required to create a computer program. Recall that the steps are to code the algorithm into a program, desk-check the program, and evaluate and modify (if necessary) the program. You can either take a break or complete the end-of-lesson questions and exercises before moving on to the Application lesson.

SUMMARY

After analyzing a problem, and then planning and desk-checking an appropriate algorithm, the programmer continues to the fourth step in the problem-solving process, which is to code the algorithm into a program, using the information in the IPO chart. First the programmer assigns a name, data type, and initial value to each unique input, processing, and output item listed in the IPO chart. He or she then translates each step in the algorithm into one or more C++ instructions.

In C++, you use streams, which are sequences of characters, to perform standard input and output operations. The standard output stream is called `cout` (pronounced *see out*) and refers to the computer screen. The standard input stream is called `cin` (pronounced *see in*) and refers to the keyboard.

The << operator is called the insertion operator, and it is used to send information to the output stream. The >> operator is called the extraction operator, and it is used to get information from the input stream.

After coding the algorithm, the programmer then desk-checks the program to make sure that the algorithm was translated correctly. You should desk-check the program using the same sample data that you used to desk-check the algorithm. The results obtained when desk-checking the program should be identical to the results obtained when desk-checking the algorithm.

The final step in the problem-solving process is to evaluate and modify (if necessary) the program. A programmer evaluates, or tests, a program by running (executing) it, along with sample data, on the computer. If the executed program does not work as intended, the programmer makes the necessary modifications until it does.

Some programs have errors, called bugs. Program errors can be either syntax errors or logic errors. A syntax error occurs when you violate one of the rules of the programming language, referred to as the language's syntax. Examples of syntax errors include mistyping a keyword or variable name and forgetting to enter a semicolon at the end of a statement. A logic error can occur for a variety of reasons, such as neglecting to enter an instruction or entering the program instructions in the wrong order. Debugging refers to the process of locating and removing the errors in a program.

To create and execute a C++ program, you need to have a text editor and a C++ compiler. The C++ instructions you enter are called source code and are stored in a source file. Source files in Microsoft Visual C++ have the filename extension .cpp.

The compiler translates the source code into machine code, also called object code. The object code is saved in an object file. In Microsoft Visual C++, object files have the filename extension .obj.

The linker produces an executable file, which is a file that contains all of the machine code necessary to run your C++ program. The executable file has an extension of .exe on its filename.

A comment is a message to the person reading the program. Comments are referred to as internal documentation. You create a comment by typing two forward slashes. The compiler ignores comments when it translates the source code into object code.

C++ programs typically include at least one directive, and most include many directives. The `#include <iostream>` directive tells the compiler to include the contents of the iostream file in the current program.

C++ programs typically include `using` statements. The `using` statements tell the compiler where it can find the definition of certain keywords.

A function is a block of code that performs a task. Every C++ program must have a `main()` function, because this is where the execution of a C++ program always begins. Some functions, like `main()`, return a value; others do not and are called void functions.

The first line in a function is called the function header. After the function header, you enter the code that directs the function on how to perform its assigned task. The code is called the function body and must be enclosed in braces. The `return 0;` statement in the `main()` function returns the number 0 to the operating system to indicate that the program ended normally.

ANSWERS TO MINI-QUIZZES

Mini-Quiz 1

1) descriptive name, data type, initial value

2) variable

3) `double grossPay = 0.0;`

4) `cin >> grossPay;`

Mini-Quiz 2

1) one

2) bugs

3) syntax, logic

Mini-Quiz 3

1) c. source

2) b. object

3) a. executable

QUESTIONS

1) Which of the following is the fourth step in the problem-solving process?

A. Evaluate and modify (if necessary) the program.

B. Code the algorithm into a program.

C. Plan the algorithm.

D. Desk-check the program.

2) The rules of a programming language are called its _____.

A. guidelines

B. procedures

C. regulations

D. syntax

3) Which of the following statements declares a variable that can contain a decimal number?

A. `payRate double = 0.0`

B. `double payRate = 0.0`

C. `double payRate = 0.0;`

D. `double payRate = 0.0:`

4) A C++ statement must end with a _____.

A. : (colon)

B. , (comma)

C. ; (semicolon)

D. none of the above

5) In C++, you use _____ to perform standard input and output operations.

   A. characters

   B. sequences

   C. streams

   D. none of the above

6) The standard output stream, which refers to the computer screen, is called _____.

   A. `cin`

   B. `cout`

   C. `stdin`

   D. `stdout`

7) The standard input stream, which refers to the computer keyboard, is called _____.

   A. `cin`

   B. `cout`

   C. `stdin`

   D. `stdout`

8) Which of the following statements displays the word "Hello" on the computer screen?

   A. `cin << "Hello";`

   B. `cin >> "Hello";`

   C. `cout << "Hello";`

   D. `cout >> "Hello";`

9) Which of the following is the extraction operator?

   A. `>>`

   B. `<<`

   C. `//`

   D. `/*`

10) Which of the following statements allows the user to enter data at the keyboard?

   A. `cin << currentPay;`

   B. `cin >> currentPay;`

   C. `cout << currentPay;`

   D. `cout >> currentPay;`

11) Which of the following stream manipulators advances the cursor to the next line on the computer screen?

   A. `advln`

   B. `edlin`

   C. `endl`

   D. `lineadv`

12) The final step in the problem-solving process is to _____.

    A. evaluate and modify (if necessary) the program

    B. code the algorithm into a program

    C. desk-check the program

    D. none of the above

13) The process of locating and removing the errors in a program is called _____.

    A. analyzing

    B. correcting

    C. debugging

    D. tracking

14) Typing `cot`, rather than `cout`, in a program is an example of _____.

    A. an entry error

    B. a function error

    C. a logic error

    D. a syntax error

15) The C++ compiler cannot detect _____ errors.

    A. entry

    B. function

    C. logic

    D. syntax

16) Which of the following is a valid comment in C++?

    A. `**This program calculates a bonus.`

    B. `@@This program calculates a bonus.`

    C. `/This program calculates a bonus.`

    D. none of the above

17) Which of the following tells the compiler the location of the keyword `cout`?

    A. `#include std::cout`

    B. `include std::cout;`

    C. `using cout::std;`

    D. `using std::cout;`

18) The first line in a function is called the _____.

    A. function header

    B. function heading

    C. function top

    D. none of the above

19) Which of the following tells the compiler to merge the code contained in the iostream file with the current file's code?

    A. `#include iostream`

    B. `#include <iostream>`

    C. `#include <iostream>;`

    D. `using <iostream>;`

20) In a C++ program, the function body is enclosed in _____.

    A. braces

    B. parentheses

    C. square brackets

    D. none of the above

EXERCISES

1) Three C++ instructions are missing from the code shown in Figure 3-14. First study the algorithm, then complete the C++ code by entering the three missing instructions.

Look For These
Symbols

Debugging

Discovery

Figure 3-14

IPO chart information	C++ instructions

Input
  first number
  second number
	`double num1 = 0.0;`
	`double num2 = 0.0;`

Processing	
Output sum	`double sum = 0.0;`

Algorithm
1. enter the first number and the second number
	`cout << "Enter first number: ";`
	`cin >> num1;`
	_____
	_____

2. calculate the sum by adding the first number to the second number	_____
3. display the sum	`cout << "The sum is " << sum << endl;`

2) Desk-check the program you completed in Exercise 1 two times, using the numbers 3 and 5 first, and then using the numbers 50.5 and 31.3. Use the desk-check table shown in Figure 3-15.

Figure 3-15

num1	num2	sum

3) Study the algorithm shown in Figure 3-16, then complete the C++ code shown in the figure.

Figure 3-16

IPO chart information	C++ instructions

Input
  number of miles driven
  number of gallons used
	`double milesDriven = 0.0;`
	`double gallonsUsed = 0.0;`

Processing	
Output miles per gallon	_____

Algorithm
1. enter the number of miles driven and the number of gallons used
	`cout << "Enter miles driven: ";`
	`cin >> milesDriven;`
	_____
	_____

2. calculate the miles per gallon by dividing the number of miles driven by the number of gallons used	`milesPerGal =`_____
3. display the miles per gallon	_____

4) Create a desk-check table for the program you completed in Exercise 3. Desk-check the program twice. For the first desk-check, use 324 as the number of miles driven and 17 as the number of gallons used. For the second desk-check, use 200 and 12 as the number of miles driven and number of gallons used, respectively. When you are finished desk-checking, compare your desk-check table with the one shown in Chapter 2's Figure 2-26; the results (other than the initialization rows) should be the same.

5) Study the algorithm shown in Figure 3-17, then complete the C++ code shown in the figure.

Figure 3-17

IPO chart information	C++ instructions

Input
  yearly taxable wages
  state income tax rate
 	
Processing
 	
Output
  annual state income tax
 	
Algorithm
1. enter the yearly taxable wages
   and the state income tax rate
 	
2. calculate the annual state income
   tax by multiplying the yearly
   taxable wages by the state
   income tax rate
 	
3. display the annual state income tax
	_____
	_____
	
	_____
	
	_____
	_____
	_____
	_____
	
	_____
	
	_____

6) Create a desk-check table for the program you completed in Exercise 5. Desk-check the program twice. For the first desk-check, use 20000 as the yearly taxable wages and .03 as the state income tax rate. For the second desk-check, use 10000 and .02 as the yearly taxable wages and state income tax rate, respectively. When you are finished desk-checking, compare your desk-check table with the one shown in the answers to Mini-Quiz 3 in Chapter 2; the results (other than the initialization rows) should be the same.

7) If necessary, complete Exercise 1. Then use the information shown in Figure 3-14 to complete the C++ program shown in Figure 3-18.

Figure 3-18

```
//Ch3Ex7.cpp - calculates and displays the sum of two numbers
//Created/revised by <your name> on <current date>

_____


_____
_____
_____


_____

{
    //declare variables
    _____
    _____
    _____

    //enter input items
    _____
    _____
    _____
    _____

    //calculate sum
    _____

    //display output item
    _____

    _____
} //end of main function
```

8) Study the algorithm and C++ code shown in Figure 3-19, then desk-check the code using an original price of 100 and a discount rate of 25%. Notice that the code does not work correctly. Make the necessary corrections to the code, then desk-check the code again, using the same sample data.

Figure 3-19

IPO chart information	C++ instructions

Input
  original price
  discount rate
	```double original = 0.0;```
	```double rate = 0.0;```

Processing discount	```double discount = 0.0;```
Output sale price	```double sale = 0.0;```

Algorithm
1. enter the original
    price and the
    discount rate
	```cout << "Original price: ";```
	```cin >> original;```
	```cout << "Discount rate: ";```
	```cin >> rate;```

2. calculate the discount
    by multiplying the
    original price by the
    discount rate
	```discount = original * discRate;```

3. calculate the sale
    price by subtracting
    the discount from
    the original price
	```sale = discount - original;```

4. display the sale price	```cout << "Sale price: " << sale << endl;```

Application Lesson

Completing the Problem-Solving Process

Lab 3.1 - Stop and Analyze   In Lab 2.1 in Chapter 2, you viewed an IPO chart created for a video store program. Recall that the program calculates the amount a customer owes when he or she returns a video. Figure 3-20 shows the C++ instructions entered in the IPO chart; it also shows the desk-check table. Study the IPO chart and desk-check table shown in the figure, then answer the questions.

Figure 3-20: IPO chart and desk-check table for Lab 3.1

IPO chart information	C++ instructions
Input number of late days	`double lateDays = 0.0;`
Processing	
Output amount due	`double amountDue = 0.0;`
Algorithm 1. get the number of late days	`cout << "Late days: ";` `cin >> lateDays;`
2. calculate the amount due by multiplying the number of late days by 2, and then adding 3.50 to the product	`amountDue = lateDays * 2 + 3.50;`
3. display the amount due	`cout << "Due: " << amountDue <<` `endl;`

lateDays	amountDue
~~0.0~~ ~~3~~ ~~0.0~~ 0	~~0.0~~ ~~9.50~~ ~~0.0~~ 3.50

Questions

1. What is the purpose of the `cout << "Late days: ";` statement?
2. Assume you want to include the late charge as a processing item. How would you modify the IPO chart and desk-check table shown in Figure 3-20 to do so?
3. Assume the video store manager also wants to display the late charge. How would you modify the IPO chart and desk-check table shown in Figure 3-20 to do so?

4. What `#include` directive needs to be included in the C++ program, and why is the directive necessary?

5. What `using` statements will need to be included in the C++ program, and why are they necessary?

Lab 3.2 In this lab, you learn how to use Microsoft Visual C++ .NET to enter and run the program you created for Sarah Martin. (You created the program in this chapter's Concept lesson.)

Activity for Lab 3.2

Before you can use Visual C++ .NET, you must start Visual Studio .NET, which is Microsoft's newest integrated development environment. An integrated development environment (IDE) is an environment that contains all of the tools and features you need to create, run, and test your programs. For example, an IDE contains an editor for entering your program instructions, and a compiler for running and testing the program.

To start Visual Studio .NET 2003, which is the version of Visual Studio .NET used in this book:

1. Click the **Start** button on the Windows taskbar to open the Start menu.

2. Point to **All Programs**, point to **Microsoft Visual Studio .NET 2003**, and then click **Microsoft Visual Studio .NET 2003**. The Microsoft Visual Studio .NET copyright screen appears momentarily, and then the Microsoft Development Environment window opens.

3. If the Start Page window is not open, click **Help** on the menu bar, and then click **Show Start Page**.

   Notice that the Start Page window contains three tabs, which are labeled Projects, Online Resources, and My Profile. The Projects tab allows you to open a new or existing project, and also lists the names and dates of projects on which you have recently worked. The Online Resources tab provides online access to information about Visual Studio .NET. For example, you can use the Online Resources tab to search the MSDN (Microsoft Developer's Network) Online library or to download the latest product updates and sample code. The My Profile tab allows you to customize various program settings in the IDE, such as the keyboard scheme, window layout, and help filter. A collection of customized preferences is called a profile. Visual Studio .NET provides a set of predefined profiles for your convenience. The steps and figures in this book assume you are using the Visual Studio Developer profile.

4. Click the **My Profile** tab on the Start Page window. The My Profile pane appears in the Start Page window, as shown in Figure 3-21. (Your screen might not look identical to Figure 3-21.)

Figure 3-21: My Profile pane in the Start Page window

My Profile
tab

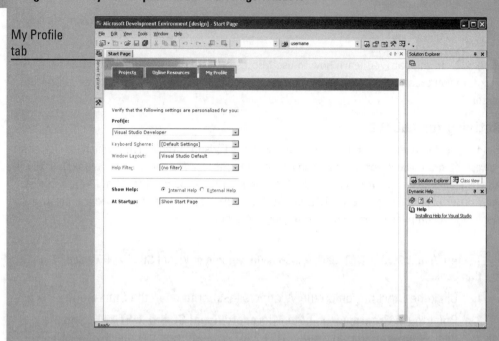

5. If necessary, click the **Profile** list arrow, and then click **Visual Studio Developer** in the list.

6. If necessary, change the Keyboard Scheme, Window Layout, Help Filter, and At Startup list box selections on your screen to match those shown in Figure 3-21.

7. If necessary, click the **Internal Help** radio button to select it. If the Changes will not take effect until Visual Studio is restarted message appears in a dialog box, click the **OK** button to close the dialog box.

8. Click the **Projects** tab on the Start Page window. The Projects pane appears in the Start Page window, as shown in Figure 3-22. (Do not be concerned if your Projects pane shows project names and dates.)

Figure 3-22: Projects pane in the Start Page window

Solution
Explorer
window

Server
Explorer
window

Toolbox
window

your Projects
pane may
show project
names and
dates

Class View
window

Dynamic
Help window

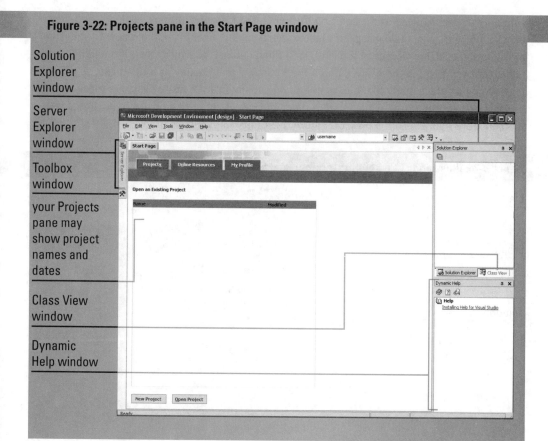

As Figure 3-22 indicates, the Visual Studio .NET IDE contains five windows in addition to the Start Page window: Solution Explorer, Server Explorer, Toolbox, Class View, and Dynamic Help. Figure 3-23 briefly describes the purpose of each window in the IDE.

Figure 3-23: Purpose of the windows included in the IDE

Window	Purpose
Class View	display the classes, methods, and properties included in a solution
Dynamic Help	display links to context-sensitive help
Server Explorer	display data connections and servers
Solution Explorer	display the names of projects and files included in a solution
Start Page	display the Projects, Online Resources, and My Profile panes
Toolbox	display items that you can use when creating a project

After starting Visual Studio .NET, you then can use Visual C++ .NET to enter your C++ program instructions into the computer. Although you can create many different types of applications in Visual C++ .NET, the applications you create in this book are console applications. A console application is a program that runs in a Command Prompt window.

Applications created in Visual Studio .NET are composed of solutions, projects, and files. You create an application by first creating a blank Visual Studio .NET solution, and then you add one or more projects to the solution. A solution is a container that stores the projects and files for an entire application. A project also is a container, but it stores files associated with only a specific piece of the solution. Although the idea of solutions, projects, and files may sound confusing, the concept of placing things in containers is nothing new to you. Think of a solution as being similar to a drawer in a filing cabinet. A project then is similar to a file folder that you store in the drawer, and a file is similar to a document that you store in the file folder. You can place many file folders in a filing cabinet drawer, just as you can place many projects in a solution. You also can store many documents in a file folder, similar to the way you can store many files in a project. Figure 3-24 illustrates this analogy.

Figure 3-24: Illustration of a solution, project, and file

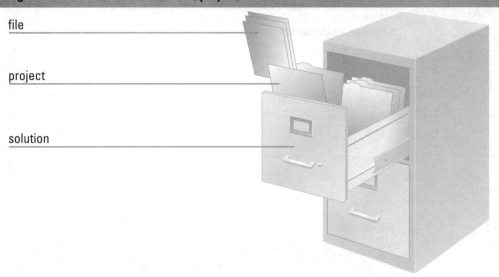

file

project

solution

You can create a blank Visual Studio .NET solution by clicking File on the menu bar, pointing to New, and then clicking Blank Solution.

To create a blank Visual Studio .NET solution:

1. Click **File** on the menu bar, point to **New**, and then click **Blank Solution**. The New Project dialog box opens with Visual Studio Solutions selected in the Project Types list box, and Blank Solution selected in the Templates list box. The message located below the Project Types list box indicates that the Blank Solution template creates an empty solution containing no projects.

   A template is simply a pattern that Visual Studio .NET uses to create solutions and projects. Each template listed in the Templates list box includes a set of standard folders and files appropriate for the solution or project. The Blank Solution template, for example, contains one folder and two files. The folder and files are automatically created on your computer's hard disk when you click the OK button in the New Project dialog box.

2. Change the name entered in the Name text box to **Ch3Lab2 Solution**. If necessary, use the Browse button, which appears to the right of the Location text box, to open the **Cpp\Chap03** folder on your computer's hard disk. Figure 3-25 shows the completed New Project dialog box.

Figure 3-25: New Project dialog box used to create a blank solution

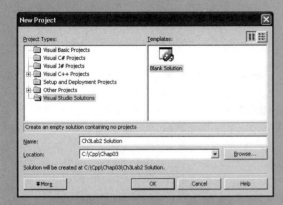

HELP? If the More button is not displayed, click the Less button.
Notice that the message "Solution will be created at C:\Cpp\Chap03\Ch3Lab2 Solution." appears above the More button in the dialog box.

3. Click the **OK** button to close the New Project dialog box. Visual Studio .NET creates a blank solution on your computer's hard disk. It also records in the Solution Explorer window the solution's name (Ch3Lab2 Solution) and the number of projects contained in the solution (0 projects). See Figure 3-26.

Figure 3-26: Solution Explorer window showing the name of a blank solution

HELP? If the Solution Explorer window does not appear in the IDE, click View on the menu bar, and then click Solution Explorer.

HELP? You might need to widen the Solution Explorer window to view its contents. To do so, position your mouse pointer ▷ on the window's left border until ▷ becomes ⟷, then drag the border to the left.

When a solution's name appears in the Solution Explorer window, it indicates that the solution is open and ready for you to add information to it. (You also can delete information from a solution.)

Recall that when you use the Blank Solution template to create a solution, Visual Studio .NET automatically creates one folder and two files on your computer's hard disk. The folder has the same name as the solution; in this case, the folder is named Ch3Lab2 Solution. The two files, which are stored in the folder, also bear the solution's name. However, one file has

tip

To view the names of hidden files, open the My Computer window, click Tools on the menu bar, and then click Folder Options. When the Folder Options dialog box appears, click the View tab, click the Show hidden files and folders radio button to select it, and then click the OK button.

.sln (which stands for "solution") as its filename extension, and the other has .suo (which stands for "solution user options"). The Ch3Lab2 Solution.sln file keeps track of the projects and files included in the solution. The Ch3Lab2 Solution.suo file, which is a hidden file, records the options associated with your solution so that each time you open the solution, it includes any customizations you made.

After you create a blank solution, you then add one or more projects to it. The number of projects in a solution depends on the application you are creating. Most simple applications require one project only, while complex applications usually involve several projects. The application you are working on is a simple application and requires just one project, which you will create using Visual C++ .NET.

You can add a new project to the current solution by clicking File on the menu bar, pointing to Add Project, and then clicking New Project. You also can right-click the solution's name in the Solution Explorer window, point to Add, and then click New Project.

To add a new Visual C++ .NET project to the current solution:

1. Right-click **Solution 'Ch3Lab2 Solution' (0 projects)** in the Solution Explorer window. Point to **Add**. then click **New Project**. The Add New Project dialog box opens.

   The Project Types list box lists the various types of projects you can add to a solution.

2. Click **Visual C++ Projects** in the Project Types list box.

   The Templates list box lists the project templates available in Visual C++ .NET.

3. Scroll down the Templates list box until you see Win32 Console Project, then click **Win32 Console Project**.

4. Change the name in the Name text box to **Ch3Lab2 Project**.

5. Verify that the Location text box contains the location of the Ch3Lab2 Solution folder. The completed Add New Project dialog box is shown in Figure 3-27. Notice that the message "Project will be created at C:\Cpp\Chap03\Ch3Lab2 Solution\Ch3Lab2 Project." appears below the Location text box in the dialog box.

Figure 3-27: Completed Add New Project dialog box

tip

Be sure to select the Win32 Console Project template and not the Console Application (.NET) template.

select this template

select this project type

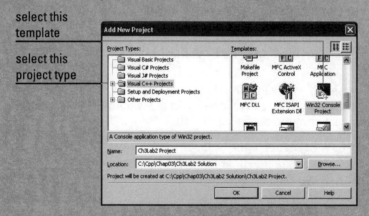

As you learned earlier, a template contains a set of standard folders and files. The folders and files included in the Win32 Console Project template are automatically created on your computer's hard disk when you click the OK button in the Add New Project dialog box.

6. Click the **OK** button to close the Add New Project dialog box. The Win32 Application Wizard – Ch3Lab2 Project dialog box opens.

7. Click **Application Settings** in the dialog box, then click the **Empty project** check box to select it. See Figure 3-28.

Figure 3-28: Application settings for the Ch3Lab2 Project

this radio button should already be selected

select this check box

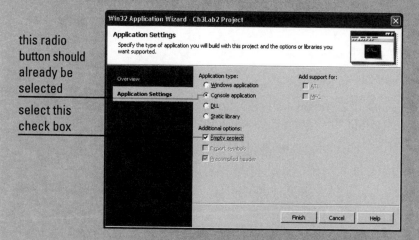

8. Click the **Finish** button. Visual Studio .NET adds a new, empty Win32 Console Project to the current solution. It also records the project's name (Ch3Lab2 Project), as well as other information pertaining to the project, in the Solution Explorer window. See Figure 3-29.

Figure 3-29: New C++ Win32 Console Project added to the solution

project name

project information

Properties window

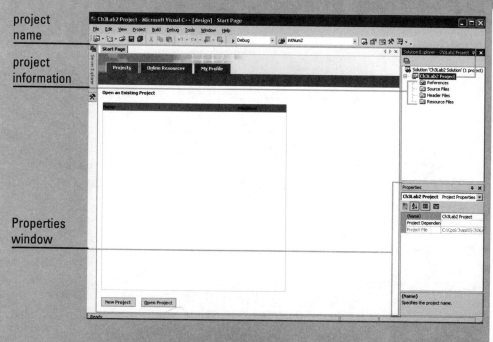

HELP? If the Properties window does not appear in the IDE, click View on the menu bar, and then click Properties Window.

Notice that, in addition to the six windows discussed earlier, a new window appears in the development environment: the Properties window. Having seven windows open at the same time can be confusing, especially when you are first learning the IDE. In most cases, you will find it easier to work in the IDE if you either close or auto-hide the windows you are not currently using. In the next section, you learn how to manage the windows in the IDE.

After adding a project to the solution, you then add a C++ source file to the project. You can do so by clicking File on the menu bar, and then clicking Add New Item. You also can right-click the project name in the Solution Explorer window, point to Add, and then click Add New Item.

To add a C++ source file to the project:

1. Right-click **Ch3Lab2 Project** in the Solution Explorer window. Point to **Add**, and then click **Add New Item**. The Add New Item dialog box opens.

2. Verify that C++ File (.cpp) is selected in the Templates list box.

3. Change the name in the Name text box to **Ch3Lab2**.

4. Verify that the Location text box contains the location of the Ch3Lab2 Project folder. The completed Add New Item dialog box is shown in Figure 3-30.

Figure 3-30: Completed Add New Item dialog box

C++ source
file

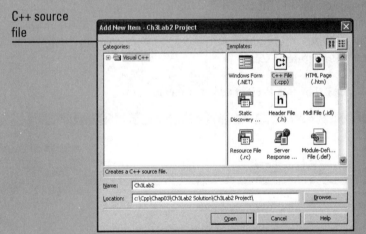

5. Click the **Open** button to close the Add New Item dialog box. Visual Studio .NET adds an empty C++ source file to the project. It also records the file's name (Ch3Lab2.cpp) in the Solution Explorer window. See Figure 3-31.

Figure 3-31: Source file added to the project

Auto Hide button

insertion point

source file name

empty C++ source file

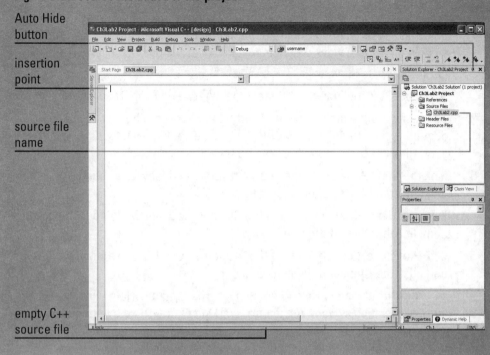

As mentioned earlier, you will find it easier to work in the Visual Studio .NET IDE if you either close or auto-hide the windows you are not currently using.

Managing the Windows in the IDE

The easiest way to close an open window in the IDE is to click the Close button on the window's title bar. In most cases, the View menu provides an appropriate option for opening a closed window. To open the Toolbox window, for instance, you click View on the menu bar, and then click Toolbox on the menu. The options for opening the Start Page and Dynamic Help windows, however, are located on the Help menu rather than on the View menu.

You can use the Auto Hide button (see Figure 3-31) on a window's title bar to auto-hide a window. When you auto-hide a window and then move the mouse pointer away from the window, the window is minimized and appears as a tab on the edge of the IDE. Additionally, the vertical pushpin on the Auto Hide button is replaced by a horizontal pushpin, which indicates that the window is auto-hidden. The Server Explorer and Toolbox windows shown in Figure 3-31 are examples of auto-hidden windows.

To temporarily display a window that has been auto-hidden, you simply place your mouse pointer on the window's tab; doing so slides the window into view. You can permanently display an auto-hidden window by clicking the Auto Hide button on the window's title bar. When you do so, the horizontal pushpin on the button is replaced by a vertical pushpin, which indicates that the window is not auto-hidden.

In the next set of steps, you close all of the windows in the IDE, except the Solution Explorer window.

To close most of the windows in the IDE:

1. Place your mouse pointer on the **Server Explorer** tab. (The Server Explorer tab is usually located on the left edge of the IDE.) When the Server Explorer window slides into view, which may take several moments, click the **Close** button ☒ on its title bar.

   Now close the Toolbox, Start Page, Class View, and Properties windows.

2. Place your mouse pointer on the **Toolbox** tab. (The Toolbox tab is usually located on the left edge of the IDE.) When the Toolbox window slides into view, click the **Close** button on its title bar.

3. Click the **Start Page** tab to make the Start Page window the active window, then click the **Close** button on its title bar.

4. Click the **Class View** tab to make the Class View window the active window, then click the **Close** button on its title bar.

5. Click the **Properties** tab to make the Properties window the active window, then click the **Close** button on its title bar.

   You close the Dynamic Help window next. The Dynamic Help window is a context-sensitive system. As you are working in the IDE, the window is constantly being updated with links pertaining to whatever is appropriate at the time. An advantage of keeping the Dynamic Help window open is that it allows you to conveniently access help as you are working in the IDE. A disadvantage is that an open Dynamic Help window consumes computer memory and processor time, both of which are required to keep the window updated.

6. Click the **Close** button on the Dynamic Help window's title bar.

Next, practice auto-hiding and displaying the Solution Explorer window.

To practice auto-hiding and displaying the Solution Explorer window:

1. Click the **Auto Hide** button (the vertical pushpin) on the Solution Explorer window's title bar, then move the mouse pointer away from the window. The Solution Explorer window is minimized and appears as a tab on the right edge of the IDE.

   HELP? If the Solution Explorer window remains on the screen when you move your mouse pointer away from the window, click another window's title bar.

   Now temporarily display the Solution Explorer window.

2. Place your mouse pointer on the **Solution Explorer** tab. The Solution Explorer window slides into view. Notice that a horizontal pushpin now appears on the Auto Hide button.

   Now hide the window.

3. Move your mouse pointer away from the Solution Explorer window. The window is minimized and appears as a tab again.

   Next, use the Auto Hide button to permanently display the Solution Explorer window on the screen.

4. Place your mouse pointer on the **Solution Explorer** tab. When the Solution Explorer window slides into view, click the **Auto Hide** button (the horizontal pushpin) on its title bar. The horizontal pushpin on the button is replaced with a vertical pushpin.

5. Move your mouse pointer away from the Solution Explorer window. The window remains displayed on the screen.

   Now auto-hide the Solution Explorer window again.

6. Click the **Auto Hide** button (the vertical pushpin) on the Solution Explorer window's title bar, then move the mouse pointer away from the window. The window appears as a tab on the edge of the IDE.

Now you can begin entering your C++ instructions.

Entering the C++ Instructions into the Source File

The insertion point in the Ch3Lab2.cpp source file (see Figure 3-31) indicates where you start entering your C++ instructions.

To begin entering the C++ instructions into the Ch3Lab2.cpp source file:

1. Type **//Ch3Lab2.cpp - calculates and displays the new weekly pay** and press **Enter**, then type **//Created/revised by <*your name*> on <*current date*>**, replacing <*your name*> and <*current date*> with your name and the current date, respectively. Press **Enter** twice.

   Next, enter the #include directive; when doing so, keep in mind that the C++ language is case sensitive. Typing #Include, rather than #include, will create a syntax error, because the compiler will not recognize the word Include. In other words, in the C++ programming language, include is not the same as Include or INCLUDE.

2. Type **#include <iostream>** and press **Enter** twice.

   The using statements are entered next.

3. Enter the following three using statements. After typing the last using statement, press **Enter** twice.

   ```
   using std::cout;
   using std::cin;
   using std::endl;
   ```

   If you are using a color monitor, you will notice that the Visual C++ .NET editor displays the comments, keywords (include and using), and symbols (#) in a different color from the rest of the code. The colors help you quickly identify the various elements in the code.

   Next, enter the main() function header.

4. Type **int main()** and press **Enter**. (Do not include a space between the opening and closing parentheses.)

   Recall that the main() function's instructions must be enclosed in a set of braces, and the last statement in the function should be return 0;. It is a good practice to type the opening and closing braces and the `return 0;` statement right away, so that you don't forget to do it.

5. Type **{** (the opening brace) and press **Enter** twice. Notice that the editor indents the next line in the Ch3Lab2.cpp window.

6. Type **return 0;** and press **Enter**, then type **}** (the closing brace). Notice that the editor enters the closing brace at the window's left margin to align it with the opening brace.

7. Press **Tab**, then type **//end of main function** and press **Enter**. Figure 3-32 shows the current status of the Ch3Lab2 program. (For readability, the font used to display the text in Figure 3-32 was changed to 14-point Courier New. It is not necessary for you to change the font.)

Figure 3-32: Current status of the Ch3Lab2 program

the asterisk
indicates that
the source
file contains
changes that
have not
been saved

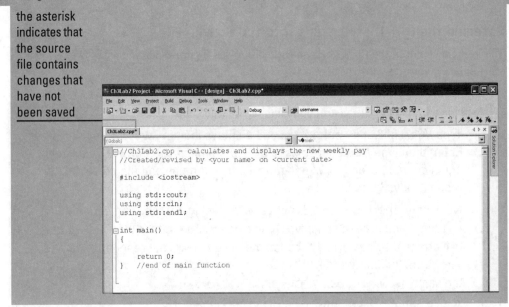

The asterisk that appears on the Ch3Lab2.cpp tab indicates that the Ch3Lab2.cpp file contains changes that have not been saved. You learn how to save the changes in the next section.

Saving a Solution

It is a good practice to save the current solution every 10 or 15 minutes so that you will not lose a lot of work if the computer loses power. The easiest way to save the solution is to click the Save All button on the Standard toolbar. Doing so saves any changes made to the files included in the solution. You also can click File on the menu bar, and then click Save All.

To save the current solution:

1. Click the **Save All** button on the Standard toolbar. The asterisk disappears from the Ch3Lab2.cpp tab, indicating that the file does not contain any unsaved changes.

tip

You can use the Options dialog box to change the font used to display text in the Code Editor window. To open the Options dialog box, click Tools on the menu bar, and then click Options. When the Options dialog box appears, open the Environment folder, then click Fonts and Colors. Select Text Editor from the Show settings for list box and Text from the Display items list box.

tip

You also can save the solution by right-clicking its name in the Solution Explorer window, and then clicking Save *<solution filename>* on the context menu. Or, you can click the solution's name in the Solution Explorer window, click File on the menu bar, and then click Save *<solution filename>* on the menu.

You also can use the Save button 🖫 on the Standard toolbar to save the solution, but you first must select the solution's name in the Solution Explorer window, because the Save button saves only the changes made to the selected item. For example, if the source filename is selected in the Solution Explorer window, then the Save button saves only the changes made to the source file. Similarly, if the project name is selected, then only changes made to the files included in the project are saved. The tooltip box that appears when you rest your mouse pointer on the Save button indicates which files will be saved. In this case, the tooltip box will say "Save Ch3Lab2.cpp" if the source file's name is selected, "Save Ch3Lab2 Project" if the project name is selected, and "Save Ch3Lab2 Solution.sln" if the solution name is selected.

Next, you learn how to close the current solution and how to open an existing solution. Both of these skills will help you complete the end-of-lesson exercises.

Closing the Current Solution

You close a solution using the Close Solution option on the File menu. When you close a solution, all projects and files contained in the solution also are closed. If unsaved changes were made to the solution, project, or source file, a dialog box opens and prompts you to save the appropriate files. The dialog box contains Yes, No, Cancel, and Help buttons. You click the Yes button to save the files before the solution is closed. You click the No button to close the solution without saving the files. You click the Cancel button to leave the solution open, and you click the Help button to display Help pertaining to the dialog box.

tip
The Close button on the Ch3Lab2.cpp window's title bar closes the window only; it does not close the solution.

To close the current solution:

1. Click **File** on the menu bar, then click **Close Solution**.

2. Temporarily display the Solution Explorer window to verify that the entire Ch3Lab2 Solution is closed.

Next, you learn how to open a solution that was saved previously.

Opening an Existing Solution

To open an existing solution, you click File on the menu bar, then click Open Solution. You then select the appropriate solution file in the Open Solution dialog box. Recall that Solution filenames have an .sln filename extension. If a solution is already open in the IDE, it is closed before another solution is opened. In other words, only one solution can be open in the IDE at any one time.

To open the Ch3Lab2 Solution:

1. Click **File** on the menu bar, then click **Open Solution**. The Open Solution dialog box opens.

2. Locate and then open the **Cpp\Chap03\Ch3Lab2 Solution** folder.

3. Click **Ch3Lab2 Solution** (Ch3Lab2 Solution.sln) in the list of filenames, then click the **Open** button.

4. If the Ch3Lab2.cpp source file is not displayed, right-click **Ch3Lab2.cpp** in the Solution Explorer window, and then click **Open**.

Now complete the Ch3Lab2 program by entering the `main()` function's instructions.

To complete the Ch3Lab2 program:

1. Enter the additional instructions shaded in Figure 3-33. Although the C++ syntax does not require you to align the assignment operators (=) in a list of declaration statements, doing so helps to make the program easier to read.

Figure 3-33: Completed Ch3Lab2 program

enter the shaded instructions

```cpp
//Ch3Lab2.cpp - calculates and displays the new weekly pay
//Created/revised by <your name> on <current date>

#include <iostream>

using std::cout;
using std::cin;
using std::endl;

int main()
{
    //declare variables
    double currentPay = 0.0;
    double raiseRate  = 0.0;
    double raise      = 0.0;
    double newPay     = 0.0;

    //enter input items
    cout << "Enter current weekly pay: ";
    cin >> currentPay;
    cout << "Enter raise rate: ";
    cin >> raiseRate;

    //calculate raise and new pay
    raise = currentPay * raiseRate;
    newPay = raise + currentPay;

    //display output item
    cout << "New pay: " << newPay << endl;

    return 0;
}   //end of main function
```

Next, you learn how to build and execute a C++ program.

Saving, Building, and Executing a C++ Program

Before you can execute a C++ program, you need to save it and then build it. Building a C++ program involves compiling the source code into object code, and then invoking the linker program to link the object code to other machine code necessary for the program to run.

To save, build, and then execute the Ch3Lab2 program:

1. Click the **Save All** button on the Standard toolbar.

2. Click **Build** on the menu bar, then click **Build Solution**. The compiler translates the source code into object code, and the linker links the object code with other machine code. The message "Build: 1 succeeded, 0 failed, 0 skipped" appears in the Output window, as shown in Figure 3-34. This message indicates that the program was built (compiled and linked) successfully.

Figure 3-34: Build message displayed in the Output window

build
message

Output
window

Other messages also are displayed in the Output window while the program is being built. It is a good practice to view those messages to be sure that the program generated no warnings. (An error in a program results in an unsuccessful build; however, a warning does not.)

3.   Scroll up the Output window, as shown in Figure 3-35.

Figure 3-35: Status messages displayed in the Output window

The messages in the Output window indicate that the program was compiled and linked, and that no errors or warnings occurred during the build process. The program is now ready to execute.

4.   Click **Debug** on the menu bar, then click **Start Without Debugging**. The "Enter current weekly pay: " prompt appears in a Command Prompt window, as shown in Figure 3-36.

tip

Be sure to click Start Without Debugging on the Debug menu rather than Start. If you use Start, the Command Prompt window will not display the "Press any key to continue" message. Instead, the window will close immediately after displaying the program output.

Figure 3-36: Prompt appears in a Command Prompt window

Command
Prompt
window

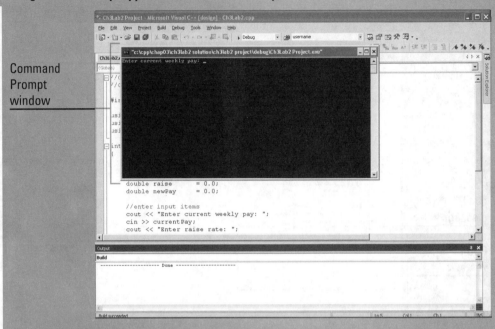

You will test the program using 250 as the current weekly pay, and .03 as the raise rate. According to the desk-check table shown in Figure 3-11 in the Concept lesson, the new weekly pay should be 257.50.

5. Type **250** as the current weekly pay, then press **Enter**. When the prompt to enter the raise rate appears, type **.03**, then press **Enter**. The new weekly pay (257.5) appears on the screen, along with the "Press any key to continue" message. The Visual C++ .NET editor automatically displays the "Press any key to continue" message on the screen when your program ends. See Figure 3-37.

Figure 3-37: Command Prompt window showing the results of executing the program

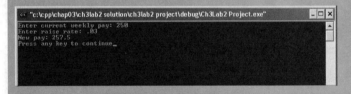

HELP? If your result is different, you probably made an error when entering the program instructions. You learn how to correct errors in C++ code in the next section.

6. Press **Enter** to close the Command Prompt window, then close the Output window by clicking the **Close** button on its title bar.

Next, you introduce a syntax error into the current program. You then learn how to locate and correct the error; in other words, you learn how to debug and modify the program.

Locating and Correcting an Error in a Program

It is extremely easy to make a typing error when entering a C++ program, thereby producing a syntax error in the program. Observe what happens when a C++ program contains a syntax error.

To introduce a syntax error, then locate and correct the error:

1. Delete the semicolon that appears at the end of the `double currentPay = 0.0;` statement in the program.

2. Click the **Save All** button on the Standard toolbar.

3. Click **Build** on the menu bar, then click **Build Solution**. The Task List window opens and indicates that line 14 in the program contains a syntax error.

4. Double-click the **error message in the Task List window**. See Figure 3-38.

Figure 3-38: Screen showing the description and location of the syntax error

location
where error
was
encountered

double-click
the error
message in
the Task List
window

The editor displays an arrow at the location where the error was encountered in the program. In this case, the arrow is pointing to the statement `double raiseRate = 0.0;`. Although that is the statement where the compiler discovered the error, it is not the statement that actually caused the error. Rather, the error occurred as a result of the previous statement: `double currentPay = 0.0`. Notice that the semicolon is missing from that statement.

5. Type a semicolon at the end of the `double currentPay = 0.0` statement.

Now save and build the solution, then execute the program to verify that it is working correctly.

6. Save and then build the solution. The message "Build: 1 succeeded, 0 failed, 0 skipped" appears in the Output window.

7. Scroll up the Output window to view all of the messages generated during the build process. Verify that the process generated no warnings.

Now use the program to display the new weekly pay using 100 and .10 as the current weekly pay and raise rate, respectively. According to the desk-check table shown in Figure 3-11 in the Concept lesson, the new weekly pay should be 110.

8. Execute the program by clicking **Debug** on the menu bar, then clicking **Start Without Debugging**. Type **100** as the current weekly pay and **.1** as the raise rate. The new weekly pay (110) appears in the Command Prompt window, along with the "Press any key to continue" message.

9. Press **Enter** to close the Command Prompt window.

Although the program is not designed currently to handle invalid data correctly, you will test it with invalid data to see the results. You will do so using a negative number as the current weekly pay. Because you did not make any changes to the program since the last time it was saved and built, you can simply execute the program; you do not need to save and build it again.

To test the program using invalid data:

1. Execute the program by clicking **Debug** on the menu bar, then clicking **Start Without Debugging**.

2. When the "Enter current weekly pay: " prompt appears, type **-10** (be sure to type the hyphen before the number 10) and press **Enter**.

   Because the current weekly pay should not be a negative number, the program should respond at this point by prompting the user to enter a positive number, rather than by prompting the user to enter the raise rate. You learn how to design such a program in a later chapter in this book.

3. Type **.05** as the raise rate. The number −10.5 appears as the new weekly pay.

4. Press **Enter** to close the Command Prompt window.

5. Close the Output and Task List windows.

When you are sure that a program works correctly, you should keep your IPO chart and a printout of the program in a safe place, so you can refer to them if you need to change the program in the future. The IPO chart and printout are referred to as **external documentation**.

Printing a C++ Program

The File menu on the menu bar contains a Print command, which you can use to print the program.

To print the current program, then close the program's solution and exit Visual Studio .NET:

1. Click **File** on the menu bar, then click **Print**. When the Print dialog box appears, click the **OK** button. The program prints on your printer.

2. Click **File** on the menu bar, then click **Close Solution** to close the current solution. This removes the solution from the computer's internal memory. You now can open either a new or an existing solution.

3. Click **File** on the menu bar, then click **Exit** to exit Visual Studio .NET.

Finally, you learn how to make a backup copy of a C++ solution.

Making a Backup Copy of a C++ Solution

It is a good idea to make a backup copy of your C++ solutions so that you don't lose a lot of work if your computer loses power.

To make a backup copy of a C++ solution:

1. Click the **Start** button on the Windows taskbar to open the Start menu, then click **My Computer** on the Start menu.

2. Right-click **the drive that contains the Cpp folder** (in most cases, this will be the C: drive), then click **Open** on the context menu.

3. Open the **Cpp** folder, then open the **Chap03** folder.

4. Open the **Ch3Lab2 Solution** folder, then delete the **Ch3Lab2 Solution.ncb** file.

5. Open the **Ch3Lab2 Project** folder, then delete the **Debug** folder.

6. Click the **Back** button twice to return to the Chap03 folder.

7. Right-click the **Ch3Lab2 Solution** folder. Point to **Send To** on the context menu, then click **3½ Floppy (A:)**.

8. When the computer has finished copying the solution, close the Cpp\Chap03 folder.

Lab 3.3   In this lab, you modify the program created in Lab 3.2 so that it doesn't use a processing item.

Activity for Lab 3.3

Before modifying the program created in Lab 3.2, copy the instructions contained in the Ch3Lab2.cpp file to a new solution.

To copy the instructions contained in the Ch3Lab2.cpp file to a new solution:

1. If necessary, start Visual Studio .NET. Create a blank solution named **Ch3Lab3 Solution**. Save the solution in the Cpp\Chap03 folder.

2. Add an empty C++ Win32 Console Project to the solution. Name the project **Ch3Lab3 Project**.

3. Add a new C++ source file to the project. Name the source file **Ch3Lab3**.

4. Click **File** on the menu bar, point to **Open**, and then click **File**. The Open File dialog box opens.

5. Open the Cpp\Chap03\Ch3Lab2 Solution\Ch3Lab2 Project folder. Click **Ch3Lab2.cpp** in the list of filenames, then click the **Open** button to open the Ch3Lab2.cpp file.

6. Click **Edit** on the menu bar, then click **Select All** to select all of the instructions in the Ch3Lab2.cpp window.

7. Click **Edit**, then click **Copy** to copy the selected instructions to the clipboard.

8. Close the Ch3Lab2.cpp window by clicking the **Close** button on its title bar.

9. Click the Ch3Lab3.cpp tab. Click **Edit**, then click **Paste** to paste the Ch3Lab2.cpp instructions in the Ch3Lab3.cpp window.

10. Change the filename in the first program comment to **Ch3Lab3.cpp**. If necessary, change the date in the second comment.

Now remove the processing item (raise) from the program.

To remove the processing item from the program:
1. Make the appropriate modifications to the program.
2. Save and then build the solution. If necessary, correct any syntax errors, then save and build the solution again.
3. Execute the program. Test the program using your own sample data, then close the Command Prompt window.
4. When the program is working correctly, close the Output window, then use the File menu to close the solution.

You now have completed Chapter 3's Application lesson. You can either take a break or complete the end-of-lesson exercises.

ANSWERS TO LABS

Lab 3.1

1. The statement displays the message "Late days: " on the screen. The message prompts the user to enter the required information.

2.

IPO chart information	C++ instructions
Input number of late days	`double lateDays = 0.0;`
Processing late charge	`double lateCharge = 0.0;`
Output amount due	`double amountDue = 0.0;`
Algorithm 1. get the number of late days	`cout << "Late days: ";` `cin >> lateDays;`
2. calculate the late charge by multiplying the number of late days by 2	`lateCharge = lateDays * 2;`
3. calculate the amount due by adding the late charge to 3.50	`amountDue = 3.50 + lateCharge;`
4. display the amount due	`cout << "Due: " << amountDue << endl;`

lateDays	lateCharge	amountDue
~~0.0~~	~~0.0~~	~~0.0~~
~~3~~	~~6.00~~	~~9.50~~
~~0.0~~	~~0.0~~	~~0.0~~
0	0	3.50

3.

IPO chart information	C++ instructions
Input number of late days	`double lateDays = 0.0;`
Processing	
Output late charge amount due	`double lateCharge = 0.0;` `double amountDue = 0.0;`
Algorithm 1. get the number of late days	`cout << "Late days: ";` `cin >> lateDays;`
2. calculate the late charge by multiplying the number of late days by 2	`lateCharge = lateDays * 2;`
3. calculate the amount due by adding the late charge to 3.50	`amountDue = 3.50 + lateCharge;`
4. display the late charge and amount due	`cout << "Late charge: " << lateCharge << endl;` `cout << "Amount due: " << amountDue << endl;`

lateDays	lateCharge	amountDue
~~0.0~~	~~0.0~~	~~0.0~~
~~3~~	~~6.00~~	~~9.50~~
~~0.0~~	~~0.0~~	~~0.0~~
0	0	3.50

4. You will need to include the `#include <iostream>` directive. The directive is necessary because the program uses `cout` to output data to the screen and `cin` to input data from the keyboard.

5. You will need to include the `using std::cout;`, `using std::cin;`, and `using std::endl;` statements. These statements indicate the location of the keywords `cout`, `cin`, and `endl`.

Lab 3.2

No answer required.

Lab 3.3

```cpp
//Ch3Lab3.cpp - calculates and displays the new weekly pay
//Created/revised by <your name> on <current date>

#include <iostream>

using std::cout;
using std::cin;
using std::endl;

int main()
{
    //declare variables
    double currentPay = 0.0;
    double raiseRate  = 0.0;
    double newPay     = 0.0;

    //enter input items
    cout << "Enter current weekly pay: ";
    cin >> currentPay;
    cout << "Enter raise rate: ";
    cin >> raiseRate;

    //calculate new pay
    newPay = currentPay * raiseRate + currentPay;

    //display output item
    cout << "New pay: " << newPay << endl;

    return 0;
}   //end of main function
```

EXERCISES

1) In this exercise, you complete an existing program that calculates and displays the sum of two numbers. The IPO chart information, C++ code, and desk-check for this problem are shown in Figures 3-14 and 3-15 in the Concept lesson.

A. If necessary, start Visual Studio .NET. Open the Ch3AppE01 Solution (Ch3AppE01 Solution.sln) file contained in the Cpp\Chap03\Ch3AppE01 Solution folder. The program calculates and displays the sum of two numbers. Review the IPO chart and code shown in Figure 3-14. Notice that three instructions are missing from the program: the instruction that prompts the user to enter the second number, the instruction that allows the user to enter the number, and the instruction that calculates the sum. Enter the missing statements in the appropriate areas of the program.

B. Save and then build the solution. If necessary, correct any syntax errors, then save and build the solution again.

C. Execute the program. Test the program twice, using the numbers 3 and 5 first, and then using the numbers 50.5 and 31.3. Compare your results to the desk-check table shown in Figure 3-15.

D. When the program is working correctly, close the Output window, then use the File menu to close the solution.

2) In this exercise, you complete an existing program that calculates and displays the number of single rolls of wallpaper required to cover a room. The IPO chart information for this problem is shown in Figure 3-39.

Figure 3-39

IPO chart information	C++ instructions
Input room length room width ceiling height single roll coverage	_____ _____ _____ _____
Processing room perimeter wall area	_____ _____
Output number of single rolls	_____
Algorithm 1. enter the room length, room width, ceiling height, and single roll coverage	_____ _____ _____ _____ _____ _____ _____ _____
2. calculate the room perimeter by adding together the room length and room width, and then multiplying the sum by 2	_____
3. calculate the wall area by multiplying the room perimeter by the ceiling height	_____
4. calculate the number of single rolls by dividing the wall area by the single roll coverage	_____
5. display the number of single rolls	_____

A. Complete the IPO chart shown in Figure 3-39 by entering the appropriate C++ instructions.

B. If necessary, start Visual Studio .NET. Open the Ch3AppE02 Solution (Ch3AppE02 Solution.sln) file contained in the Cpp\Chap03\Ch3AppE02 Solution folder. Use the C++ statements from the IPO chart to complete the program.

C. Save and then build the solution. If necessary, correct any syntax errors, then save and build the solution again.

D. Execute the program. Test the program twice. For the first test, use 10, 12, 8, and 30 for the room length, room width, ceiling height, and roll coverage. For the second test, use 12, 14, 10, and 37 for the room length, room width, ceiling height, and roll coverage. Compare your results to the desk-check table shown in Figure 2-39 in Chapter 2's Application lesson.

E. When the program is working correctly, close the Output window, then use the File menu to close the solution.

3) In this exercise, you complete an existing program that calculates and displays a commission amount based on the sales and commission rate entered by the user.

A. If necessary, start Visual Studio .NET. Open the Ch3AppE03 Solution (Ch3AppE03 Solution.sln) file contained in the Cpp\Chap03\Ch3AppE03 Solution folder. The program calculates and displays a commission amount.

B. Study the existing code. Notice that the statements to calculate and display the commission are missing from the program. Enter the missing statements in the appropriate areas of the program. The statement that displays the commission amount should display the message "Your commission is $*commission*.", where *commission* is the commission amount.

C. Create an appropriate desk-check table, then desk-check the program twice. For the first desk-check, use 2000 as the sales and .10 as the commission rate. For the second desk-check, use 5000 as the sales and .06 as the commission rate.

D. Save and then build the solution. If necessary, correct any syntax errors, then save and build the solution again.

E. Execute the program. Test the program twice, using the same data used in Step C. Compare your results to the desk-check table that you created in Step C.

F. When the program is working correctly, close the Output window, then use the File menu to close the solution.

4) In this exercise, you create a program that calculates and displays an ending balance amount based on the beginning balance, deposit, and withdrawal amounts entered by the user.

A. Complete an IPO chart and desk-check table for this problem. Or, use the IPO chart and desk-check table you created in Exercise 2 in Chapter 2's Application lesson.

B. Desk-check the algorithm twice. For the first desk-check, use 2000 as the beginning balance amount, 775 as the deposit amount, and 1200 as the withdrawal amount. For the second desk-check, use 500 as the beginning balance amount, 100 as the deposit amount, and 610 as the withdrawal amount.

C. Use the IPO chart to code the program.

D. Desk-check the program using the data supplied in Step B.

E. If necessary, start Visual Studio .NET. Create a blank solution named Ch3AppE04 Solution. Save the solution in the Cpp\Chap03 folder.

F. Add an empty C++ Win32 Console Project to the solution. Name the project Ch3AppE04 Project.

G. Add a new C++ source file to the project. Name the source file Ch3AppE04.

H. Enter the appropriate C++ instructions into the source file.

I. Save and then build the solution. If necessary, correct any syntax errors, then save and build the solution again.

J. Execute the program. Test the program using the data supplied in Step B.

K. When the program is working correctly, close the Output window, then use the File menu to close the solution.

5) In this exercise, you create a program that calculates and displays the average of three numbers.

A. Complete an IPO chart and desk-check table for this problem. Or, use the IPO chart and desk-check table you created in Exercise 3 in Chapter 2's Application lesson.

B. Desk-check the algorithm twice. For the first desk-check, use the numbers 25, 76, and 33. For the second desk-check, use the numbers 10, 15, and 20.

C. Use the IPO chart to code the program.

D. Desk-check the program using the data supplied in Step B.

E. If necessary, start Visual Studio .NET. Create a blank solution named Ch3AppE05 Solution. Save the solution in the Cpp\Chap03 folder.

F. Add an empty C++ Win32 Console Project to the solution. Name the project Ch3AppE05 Project.

G. Add a new C++ source file to the project. Name the source file Ch3AppE05.

H. Enter the appropriate C++ instructions into the source file.

I. Save and then build the solution. If necessary, correct any syntax errors, and then save and build the solution again.

J. Execute the program. Test the program using the data supplied in Step B.

K. When the program is working correctly, close the Output window, and then use the File menu to close the solution.

6) In this exercise, you practice working with the **cout** stream.

A. If necessary, start Visual Studio .NET. Open the Ch3AppE06 Solution (Ch3app06 Solution.sln) file contained in the Cpp\Chap03\Ch3AppE06 Solution folder. The program shows three different ways to display the message "C++ is a programming language." on the screen.

B. Build the solution, then execute the program. What differences (if any) do you see in the manner in which each of the three ways displays the message? What do these differences tell you about how the **cout** stream and the insertion operator handle the display of data on the screen?

C. Close the Command Prompt window, then close the Output window.

D. Use the File menu to close the solution.

7) In this exercise, you debug a C++ program.

A. If necessary, start Visual Studio .NET. Open the Ch3AppE07 Solution (Ch3AppE07 Solution.sln) file contained in the Cpp\Chap03\Ch3AppE07 Solution folder. The program should calculate and display the sales discount and the new sales price.

B. Create an appropriate desk-check table, then desk-check the program using 100 as the original price and .25 as the discount rate. Notice that the program does not give the correct results.

C. Correct any errors in the program, then desk-check the program twice. For the first desk-check, use 100 as the original price and .25 as the discount rate. For the second desk-check, use 50 as the original price and .1 as the discount rate.

D. Save and then build the solution. If necessary, correct any errors, and then save and build the solution again.

E. Execute the program. Test the program twice, using the data supplied in Step C. Compare your results to the desk-check table that you created in Step C.

F. When the program is working correctly, close the Output window, then use the File menu to close the solution.

Please visit the Testing Center at www.course.com/testingcenter for more practice on the topics covered in this chapter.

Variables, Constants, and Arithmetic Operators

Objectives

After completing this chapter, you will be able to:

- Distinguish among a variable, a named constant, and a literal constant

- Select an appropriate name, data type, and initial value for a memory location

- Explain how data is stored in memory

- Declare and initialize a memory location

- Type cast data

- Use an assignment statement to assign data to a variable

- Include arithmetic operators in an expression

- Get string input using the **getline()** function

- Ignore characters using the **ignore()** function

Concept Lesson

More on the Problem-Solving Process

In Chapter 3, you completed a C++ program for Sarah Martin. The program is shown in Figure 4-1.

Figure 4-1: C++ program for Sarah Martin

numeric
literal
constant

variable

arithmetic
operators

string literal
constant

```
//Ch3Lab2.cpp - calculates and displays the new weekly pay
//Created/revised by <your name> on <current date>

#include <iostream>

using std::cout;
using std::cin;
using std::endl;

int main()
{
    //declare variables
    double currentPay = 0.0;
    double raiseRate  = 0.0;
    double raise      = 0.0;
    double newPay     = 0.0;

    //enter input items
    cout << "Enter current weekly pay: ";
    cin >> currentPay;
    cout << "Enter raise rate: ";
    cin >> raiseRate;

    //calculate raise and new pay
    raise = currentPay * raiseRate;
    newPay = raise + currentPay;

    //display output item
    cout << "New pay: " << newPay << endl;

    return 0;
} //end of main function
```

Most programs, like the one shown in Figure 4-1, include the following components: variables, constants, and operators. You learned a little about variables and arithmetic operators in Chapter 3; you learn more about both topics in this chapter. You also learn about two types of constants: named and literal.

Variables and Named Constants

Variables and named constants are locations (within the computer's internal memory) where a program can temporarily store data. The data may be entered by the user at the keyboard, or it may be read from a file, or it may be the result of a calculation made by the computer. The program shown in Figure 4-1, for example, stores the user's input—current weekly pay and raise rate—in memory locations named `currentPay` and `raiseRate`. The program also stores the results of the raise and new pay calculations in memory locations named `raise` and `newPay`.

It may be helpful to picture a memory location as a small box inside the computer. You can enter and store data in the box, but you cannot actually see the box. Two types of memory locations (boxes) are available for your program to use: variable memory locations and named constant memory locations. The difference between the two types is that the contents of a variable memory location can change (vary) as the program is running, whereas the contents of a named constant memory location cannot.

You need to declare a memory location for each unique input, processing, and output item listed in a problem's IPO chart. But how do you determine which type of memory location to declare—variable or named constant? If you want the capability of changing an item's value each time a program is executed, you need to store the value in a variable memory location—referred to simply as a **variable**—because that is the only type of memory location whose contents can change while a program is running. In the program shown in Figure 4-1, for example, the values of the input, processing, and output items are stored in variables, giving the user the ability to change the amounts each time the program is executed. (Recall that the input items are the current weekly pay and raise rate; the processing item is the raise; and the output item is the new weekly pay.)

You use a named constant memory location, referred to simply as a **named constant**, for any item whose value will remain the same each time the program is executed. For example, if Sarah Martin always received a 3% raise, you would store the value of the raise rate (.03) in a named constant rather than in a variable, because the value will be the same each time the program is executed.

The problem specification and IPO chart shown in Figure 4-2 provide another example of using variables and named constants.

Figure 4-2: Problem specification and IPO chart for the circle area problem

Problem specification:

Mr. Johnson needs a program that he can use to calculate and display the area of a circle based on the circle radius he enters. Use 3.141593 as the value for pi.

Input	Processing	Output
radius pi (3.141593)	Processing items: radius squared Algorithm: 1. enter the radius 2. calculate the radius squared by multiplying the radius by itself 3. calculate the area by multiplying pi by the radius squared 4. display the area	area

The IPO chart indicates that the program, which calculates and displays the area of a circle, requires four memory locations: two for the input items (radius and pi), one for the processing item (radius squared), and one for the output item (area). The values of the radius, radius squared, and area items should be stored in variables, because those values will change each time the program is executed. The value of the pi item, however, will remain constant at 3.141593 and should be stored in a named constant.

The method of creating variables and named constants—in other words, the method of reserving memory locations in a program—differs in each programming language. However, most programming languages require the programmer to assign both a name and data type to each variable and named constant the program uses. The programmer also must assign a beginning value to each named constant. Although assigning a beginning value to a variable is optional in most programming languages, it is considered a good programming practice to do so and is highly recommended.

Before learning how to declare variables and named constants in a C++ program, you learn how to select an appropriate name, data type, and initial value for the memory location.

Selecting a Name for a Memory Location

You should assign a descriptive name to each variable and named constant used in a program. The name, also called the **identifier**, should help you remember the purpose of the memory location—in other words, the meaning of the value stored therein. For example, the names `length` and `width` are much more meaningful than are the names `x` and `y`, because `length` and `width` remind you that the amounts stored in the memory locations represent a length and width measurement, respectively.

In addition to being descriptive, the name that a programmer assigns to a memory location must follow several specific rules. The C++ naming rules, along with examples of valid and invalid names in C++, are listed in Figure 4-3. Figure 4-3 also lists the keywords in C++. A **keyword**— often referred to as a **reserved word**—is a word that has a special meaning in a programming language. You cannot use a keyword—for example, the word `double`—as the name of a variable or named constant in a C++ program, as indicated in the fourth rule shown in the figure.

Figure 4-3: Naming rules, examples of valid and invalid names, and C++ keywords

Rules for names (identifiers) in a C++ program
1. The name must begin with a letter.
2. The name must contain only letters, numbers, and the underscore. No punctuation characters or spaces are allowed in the name.
3. The C++ compiler you are using determines the maximum number of characters in a name. Although names can contain thousands of characters, the recommended maximum number of characters to use is 32.
4. The name cannot be a keyword, such as **double,** because a keyword has a special meaning in C++. The C++ keywords, also called reserved words, are listed below.
5. Names in C++ are case sensitive.

Valid names	Invalid names	
deposit	98deposit	(the name must begin with a letter)
end_Balance	end Balance	(the name cannot contain a space)
withdrawal	withdrawal.amt	(the name cannot contain punctuation)
privateLocation	private	(the name cannot be a keyword)

C++ Keywords

asm	else	operator	throw
auto	enum	private	true
bool	explicit	protected	try
break	extern	public	typedef
case	false	register	typeid
catch	float	reinterpret_cast	typename
char	for	return	union
class	friend	short	unsigned
const	goto	signed	using
const_cast	if	sizeof	virtual
continue	inline	static	void
default	int	static_cast	volatile
delete	long	struct	wchar_t
do	mutable	switch	while
double	namespace	template	
dynamic_cast	new	this	

Notice that a memory location's name must begin with a letter and include only letters, numbers, and the underscore; no punctuation characters or spaces are allowed in the name. Many C++ programmers use uppercase letters when naming named constants, and lowercase letters when naming variables; this allows them to distinguish between the named constants and variables in a program. If a variable's name contains two or more words, however, most C++ programmers capitalize the first letter in the second and subsequent words, as shown in the names **grossPay** and **juneInventoryAmount**. In this book, you follow the naming convention used by most C++ programmers.

Figure 4-4 lists possible names that you could use in a C++ program to identify the circle area problem's input, processing, and output items.

tip

The practice of capitalizing only the first letter in the second and subsequent words in a memory location's name is referred to as "camel casing." Because the uppercase letters in the name are taller than the lowercase letters, the uppercase letters appear as "humps" in the name.

Figure 4-4: Names of memory locations for the circle area problem

Memory location type	Name
variable	`radius`
variable	`radiusSquared`
variable	`area`
named constant	`PI`

In addition to selecting an appropriate name for each variable and named constant the program uses, you also must determine the appropriate data type for each.

Selecting a Data Type for a Memory Location

Each variable and named constant must be assigned a **data type** that controls the type of data the memory location can store. Figure 4-5 shows some of the data types available in C++.

Figure 4-5: Some of the data types available in C++

Data type	Stores	Memory required	Values
`char`	one character	1 byte	one character
`short`	integer	2 bytes	−32,768 to 32,767
`int`	integer	4 bytes	−2,147,483,648 to 2,147,483,647
`float`	single precision floating point number	4 bytes	−3.4e38 to 3.4e38
`double`	double precision floating point number	8 bytes	−1.7e308 to 1.7e308
`String`	zero or more characters	1 byte per character	zero or more characters
`bool`	Boolean value	1 byte	`true`, `false`

tip

The fundamental data types are also called primitive data types.

All of the data types listed in Figure 4-5, except the `string` data type, belong to a category of data types called fundamental data types. The **fundamental data types** are the basic data types built into the C++ language. Unlike the fundamental data types, the `string` data type is added to the C++ language through the use of a class, which is simply a group of instructions used to create an object. The `string` class (data type), for example, creates a string, which is considered an object. Some classes, like the `string` class, come with Visual C++ .NET. However, you also can create your own classes; you learn how to create a class in Chapter 14.

tip

Some programmers prefer to use C-strings rather than the `string` class. You learn about C-strings in Appendix B.

To use the `string` class in a program, the program must contain the `#include <string>` directive and the `using std::string;` statement. The statement allows the program to use the `string` class to create a `string` variable or `string` named constant, and the directive gives the program access to operators (such as `<<` and `>>`) and functions [such as `getline()`] used to manipulate `string` memory locations.

tip

In the past, the amount of storage space consumed by a program was much more of a concern than it is now. This is because computers can now store vast amounts of data.

As Figure 4-5 indicates, the C++ programming language contains one or more data types for storing **integers** (whole numbers), **floating-point numbers** (numbers with a decimal place), **characters** (letters, symbols, and numbers that will not be used in calculations), and **Boolean** values (`true` and `false`). The appropriate data type to use for a memory location depends on the values the memory location will store. For example, memory locations assigned either the `short` or `int` data type can store integers only. The differences between the two data types are in the range of integers each type can store and the amount of memory each type needs to store the integer. You can reduce the amount of internal memory that a program consumes, thereby improving the program's efficiency, by using memory locations with smaller memory requirements wherever possible. Although an `int` memory location can store numbers in the `short` range of −32,768 to 32,767, the `int` data type takes twice as much memory as the `short` data type to do so. Therefore, you can conserve internal memory by storing a person's age in a `short` variable rather than in an `int` variable.

Keep in mind, however, that memory usage is not the only important factor in determining a program's efficiency; the speed at which a program executes also is important. Although a `short` memory location uses less internal memory than does an `int` memory location, a calculation containing `int` memory locations takes less time to process than the equivalent equation containing `short` memory locations. This is because the computer must convert `short` memory locations to the `int` data type while the calculation is being performed. Similarly, the computer converts `float` memory locations to the `double` data type when performing calculations. Therefore, a calculation containing `double` variables takes less time to process than the same calculation containing `float` variables.

Important note: In most of the programs you create in this book, you will use the `int` data type to store integers and the `double` data type to store numbers with a decimal place.

As Figure 4-6 shows, the data type selected for each of the circle area problem's memory locations is `double`. The `double` data type allows each memory location to store a floating-point number.

Figure 4-6: Data type assigned to the memory locations for the circle area problem

Memory location	Name	Data type
variable	radius	double
variable	radiusSquared	double
variable	area	double
named constant	PI	double

Knowing how data is stored in the computer's internal memory will help you understand the importance of a memory location's data type.

How Data Is Stored in Internal Memory

Numeric data—data assigned to memory locations that can store only numbers—is represented in internal memory using the binary (or *base 2*) number system. Recall from the Overview that the binary number system uses only the two digits 0 and 1. Although the binary number system may not be as familiar to you as the decimal (or *base 10*) number system, which uses the ten digits 0 through 9, it is just as easy to understand. Figure 4-7 compares both number systems.

Figure 4-7: Comparison of the decimal and binary number systems

Decimal number system (base 10)		Decimal number	10^7	10^6	10^5	10^4	10^3	10^2	10^1	10^0
		110						1	1	0
		342						3	4	2
		31509				3	1	5	0	9
Binary number system (base 2)	**Binary number**	**Decimal equivalent of binary number**	2^7	2^6	2^5	2^4	2^3	2^2	2^1	2^0
	110	6						1	1	0
	11010	26				1	1	0	1	0
	1001						1	0	0	1

tip

When you raise any number to the 0th power, the result is 1. When you raise a number to the 1st power, the result is the number itself.

As Figure 4-7 illustrates, the position of each digit in the decimal number system is associated with the system's base number, 10, raised to a power. Starting with the right-most position, for example, the positions represent the number 10 raised to a power of 0, 1, 2, 3, and so on. The decimal number 110, therefore, means zero 1s (10^0), one 10 (10^1), and one 100 (10^2), and the decimal number 342 means two 1s (10^0), four 10s (10^1), and three 100s (10^2). The decimal number 31509 means nine 1s (10^0), zero 10s (10^1), five 100s (10^2), one 1000 (10^3), and three 10000s (10^4).

The position of each digit in the binary number system also is associated with the system's base number—in this case, 2—raised to a power. Starting with the right-most position, the positions represent 2 raised to a power of 0, 1, 2, 3, and so on. The binary number 110, therefore, means zero 1s (2^0), one 2 (2^1), and one 4 (2^2). The decimal equivalent of the binary number 110 is 6, which is calculated by adding together 0 + 2 + 4 (zero 1s + one 2 + one 4). The binary number 11010 means zero 1s (2^0), one 2 (2^1), zero 4s (2^2), one 8 (2^3), and one 16 (2^4). The decimal equivalent of the binary number 11010 is 26, which is calculated by adding together 0 + 2 + 0 + 8 + 16. On your own, calculate the decimal equivalent of the last binary number (1001) shown in Figure 4-7. If your answer is the decimal number 9 (one 1 + zero 2s + zero 4s + one 8), you are correct.

Unlike numeric data, character data (which is data assigned to memory locations that can store characters) is represented in internal memory using ASCII codes. ASCII (pronounced *ASK-ee*) stands for American Standard Code for Information Interchange. The ASCII coding scheme assigns a specific code to each character (letter, number, and symbol) on your keyboard. The ASCII codes for the letters, numbers, colon, and semicolon, along with the binary representation of these codes, are shown in Figure 4-8.

Figure 4-8: Partial ASCII chart

Character	ASCII	Binary	Character	ASCII	Binary	Character	ASCII	Binary
0	48	00110000	K	75	01001011	g	103	01100111
1	49	00110001	L	76	01001100	h	104	01101000
2	50	00110010	M	77	01001101	i	105	01101001
3	51	00110011	N	78	01001110	j	106	01101010
4	52	00110100	O	79	01001111	k	107	01101011
5	53	00110101	P	80	01010000	l	108	01101100
6	54	00110110	Q	81	01010001	m	109	01101101
7	55	00110111	R	82	01010010	n	110	01101110
8	56	00111000	S	83	01010011	o	111	01101111
9	57	00111001	T	84	01010100	p	112	01110000
:	58	00111010	U	85	01010101	q	113	01110001
:	59	00111011	V	86	01010110	r	114	01110010
A	65	01000001	W	87	01010111	s	115	01110011
B	66	01000010	X	88	01011000	t	116	01110100
C	67	01000011	Y	89	01011001	u	117	01110101
D	68	01000100	Z	90	01011010	v	118	01110110
E	69	01000101	a	97	01100001	w	119	01110111
F	70	01000110	b	98	01100010	x	120	01111000
G	71	01000111	c	99	01100011	y	121	01111001
H	72	01001000	d	100	01100100	z	122	01111010
I	73	01001001	e	101	01100101			
J	74	01001010	f	102	01100110			

tip
The full ASCII chart is shown in Appendix A.

As Figure 4-8 shows, the uppercase letter A is assigned the ASCII code 65, which is stored in internal memory using the eight bits ("binary digits") 01000001 (one 64 and one 1). Notice that the lowercase version of each letter on your keyboard is assigned a different ASCII code than the letter's uppercase version. The lowercase letter a, for example, is assigned the ASCII code 97, which is stored in internal memory using the eight bits 01100001. This fact indicates that the computer does not consider both cases of a letter to be equivalent. In other words, the uppercase letter A is not the same as the lowercase letter a. This concept will become important when you compare characters and strings in later chapters.

At this point, you may be wondering why the numeric characters on your keyboard are assigned an ASCII code. Aren't they supposed to be stored using the binary number system, as you learned earlier? The answer is this: The computer uses the binary number system to store the *number* 9, but it uses the ASCII coding scheme to store the *character* 9. But how does the computer know whether the 9 is a number or a character? The answer to this question is simple: by the memory location's data type. For example, assume that a program displays the message "Enter the age of your pet:" on the computer screen. Also assume that the program stores your response in a variable named **age**. When you press the 9 key on your keyboard in response to the message, the computer uses the **age** variable's data type to determine whether to store the 9 as a number (using the binary number system) or as a character (using the ASCII coding scheme). If the variable's data type is **int**, the 9 is stored as the binary number 1001 (one 1 + one 8). If the variable's data type is **char**, on the other hand, the 9 is stored as a character using the ASCII code 57, which is represented in internal memory as 00111001 (one 1 + one 8 + one 16 + one 32).

tip

Some programmers pronounce char as "care" because it is short for *character*, while others pronounce char as in the first syllable of the word *charcoal*.

The memory location's data type also determines how the computer interprets the data already stored in a memory location. For example, if a program instruction needs to access the value stored in a memory location—perhaps to display the value on the screen—the computer uses the memory location's data type to determine the value's data type. To illustrate this point, assume that a memory location named `inputItem` contains the eight bits 01000001. If the memory location's data type is `char`, the computer displays the uppercase letter A on the screen. This is because the computer interprets the 01000001 as the ASCII code 65, which is equivalent to the uppercase letter A. However, if the memory location's data type is `int`, the computer displays the number 65 on the screen, because the 01000001 is interpreted as the binary code for the decimal number 65.

As you just learned, the data type of the memory location is important, because it determines how the data is stored when first entered into the memory location. It also determines how the data is interpreted when the memory location is used in an instruction later in the program.

In addition to assigning an appropriate name and data type to each variable and named constant, recall that you also should assign an initial value to each.

Selecting an Initial Value for a Memory Location

Assigning an initial, or beginning, value to a memory location is referred to as **initializing**. You typically initialize a memory location by assigning a literal constant to it. Unlike variables and named constants, literal constants are not memory locations. Rather, a **literal constant** is an item of data that can appear in a program instruction, and that can be stored in a memory location. Literal constants can have a data type that is numeric, character, or string.

A **numeric literal constant** is simply a number. Examples of numeric literal constants include the numbers 0.0, −2.5, and 146. Numeric literal constants can consist only of numbers, the plus sign (+), the minus sign (−), the decimal point (.), and the letter e in uppercase or lowercase (for exponential notation). Numeric literal constants cannot contain a space, a comma, or a special character, such as the dollar sign ($) or the percent sign (%).

A **character literal constant** is one character enclosed in single quotation marks. The letter 'X' is a character literal constant, and so are the dollar sign '$' and a space ' ' (two single quotation marks with a space between). A **string literal constant**, on the other hand, is zero or more characters enclosed in double quotation marks, such as the word "Hello", the message "Enter current weekly pay: ", and the empty string "" (two double quotation marks with no space between). Figure 4-9 shows examples of numeric, character, and string literal constants.

tip

Exponential notation, often referred to as *e notation*, provides a convenient way of writing very large and very small numbers by expressing the number as a multiple of some power of 10. The large number 3,200,000,000 written using e notation is 3.2e9, and the small number .0000000032 is 3.2e−9. The e9 says to move the decimal point nine places to the right, which is the same as multiplying the number by 10 to the ninth power. The e−9 says to move the decimal point nine places to the left, which is the same as dividing the number by 10 to the ninth power.

Figure 4-9: Examples of numeric, character, and string literal constants

Numeric literal constants	Character literal constants	String literal constants
2 3.14 3.2e6 −2300 0	'X' '$' 'b' '2' ' ' (a space enclosed in single quotation marks)	"Hello" "Enter room length: " "450" "345AB" "" (two double quotation marks with no space between)

Important note: Notice that character literal constants are enclosed in single quotation marks and string literal constants are enclosed in double quotation marks. Numeric literal constants, however, are not enclosed in any quotation marks.

When using a literal constant to initialize a memory location in a program, the data type of the literal constant should match the data type of the memory location to which it is assigned. In other words, you should use only integers to initialize memory locations having the `short` or `int` data type, and only floating-point numbers to initialize memory locations having the `float` or `double` data type. Character literal constants should be used to initialize `char` memory locations, and string literal constants to initialize `string` memory locations. Memory locations having the `bool` data type typically are initialized using either the C++ keyword `true` or the C++ keyword `false`, which stand for the Boolean values True and False, respectively.

If a memory location is a named constant, the problem description and/or IPO chart will provide the appropriate initial value to use. The problem description and IPO chart shown earlier in Figure 4-2, for example, indicate that the PI named constant should be initialized to 3.141593 (the value of pi rounded to six decimal places). The initial value for a variable, on the other hand, typically is not stated in a problem description or IPO chart, because the user supplies the value while the program is running. As a result, `short` and `int` variables generally are initialized to the integer 0. Variables of the `float` and `double` data types typically are initialized to the floating-point number 0.0. `string` variables usually are initialized to the empty string (`""`), and `char` variables to a space (`' '`). As mentioned earlier, the C++ keywords `true` and `false` are used to initialize `bool` variables.

Be aware that the Visual C++ compiler may display the warning message *'initializing' : truncation from 'double' to 'float'* when you initialize a `float` memory location to a number other than 0.0—for example, a number such as 3.1. (The warning message is displayed when you build the program.) The warning message appears because the Visual C++ compiler treats all numeric literal constants containing a decimal place as a `double` data type. When you assign a `double` number (which requires eight bytes of memory) to a `float` memory location (which can store only four bytes), the compiler warns you that it may need to truncate part of the number before it can store the number in the memory location. Some programmers simply ignore the warning message—although this practice is not recommended. Other programmers use a process called type casting to prevent the compiler from displaying the warning message; type casting is the preferred approach.

Type Casting

When a program instructs the computer to assign a value to a memory location, the computer first compares the data type of the value with the data type of the memory location to verify that the value is appropriate for the memory location. If the value's data type does not match the memory location's data type, the computer uses a process called **implicit type conversion** to convert the value to fit the memory location. For example, assume your program declares a `float` variable named `sales`. If you assign the integer 9 to the `sales` variable, the computer converts the integer to a floating-point number before storing the value in the variable; it does so by appending a decimal point and the number 0 to the end of the integer. In this case, the integer 9 is converted to the floating-point number 9.0, and it is the floating-point number 9.0 that is assigned to the `sales` variable. Similarly, if the user enters the number 100 as the sales amount, the computer assigns the number 100.0 to the `sales` variable. When a value is converted from one data type to another data type that can store larger numbers, the value is said to be **promoted**. (Figure 4-5, shown earlier, lists the values that each data type can store.) In most cases, the implicit promotion of values does not adversely affect a program's output.

Now assume that your program declares an `int` variable named `sales`. If you use a floating-point number—such as 67.45—to initialize the `sales` variable, the computer converts the floating-point number to an integer before storing the value in the variable; it does

tip

The Boolean values True and False are named in honor of the English mathematician George Boole (1815–1864), who invented Boolean algebra. You would use a `bool` variable to keep track of whether a bill has been paid—for example, either it has been paid (`true`) or it has not been paid (`false`).

tip

When you distinguish among a literal constant, a named constant, and a variable, it is helpful to remember that a literal constant is simply an item of data. Variables and named constants, on the other hand, are memory locations where literal constants are stored. Unlike the contents of a variable, the contents of a named constant cannot change while the program is running.

tip

You can learn more about initializing `bool` variables by completing Exercise 11 at the end of the Application lesson.

tip

It is not always possible to convert a value to match the memory location's data type. For example, assigning a string literal constant to a memory location that can store only integers produces an error, because the computer cannot convert a string literal constant to an integer.

so by truncating (dropping off) the decimal portion of the number. In this case, the computer converts the floating-point number 67.45 to the integer 67. As a result, the number 67, rather than the number 67.45, is assigned to the **sales** variable. Similarly, if the user enters the number 11.25 as the sales amount, the computer assigns the number 11 to the **sales** variable. When a value is converted from one data type to another data type that can store smaller numbers, the value is said to be **demoted**. The implicit demotion of values *can* adversely affect a program's output.

The computer also makes implicit type conversions when processing calculation statements that contain items having different data types. Figure 4-10 shows examples of calculation statements that result in implicit type conversions. Notice that when the computer performs an implicit type conversion in a calculation statement, you may or may not get the expected answer.

Figure 4-10: Calculation statements that result in implicit type conversions

Examples and results

Example 1
```
double price = 5.0;
double total = 0.0;
int quantity = 8;
total = price * quantity;
```

Result
assigns 40.0 to the **total** variable, which is correct

Example 2
```
int average  = 0;
double test1 = 90.0;
double test2 = 81.0;
average = (test1 + test2) / 2;
```

Result
assigns 85 to the **average** variable, which may or may not be correct

Example 3
```
double average = 0.0;
int test1      = 90;
int test2      = 81;
average = (test1 + test2) / 2;
```

Result
assigns 85.0 to the **average** variable, which is not correct

Example 4
```
double average = 0.0;
int test1      = 90;
int test2      = 81;
average = (test1 + test2) / 2.0;
```

Result
assigns 85.5 to the **average** variable, which is correct

When performing an arithmetic operation with two items having different data types, the item with the lower-ranking data type is always promoted to the higher-ranking data type. A data type ranks higher than another data type if it can store larger numbers. For example, when the computer processes the `total = price * quantity;` statement shown in Example 1 in Figure 4-10, it temporarily promotes the integer value stored in the `quantity` variable to the `double` data type to agree with the data type of the `price` variable. (Recall that the `double` data type can store larger numbers than the `int` data type.) After performing the multiplication using both `double` numbers, the computer assigns the correct result (40.0) to the `double` variable named `total`. Notice that the result of the calculation is not adversely affected by the implicit promotion of the `quantity` variable's contents.

When the computer processes the `average = (test1 + test2) / 2;` statement shown in Example 2, it first adds the contents of the `test1` variable (90.0) to the contents of the `test2` variable (81.0), giving 171.0. It then promotes the integer 2 to the `double` number 2.0 before dividing it into the 171.0; the result of the division is 85.5. The computer then demotes the `double` number 85.5 to the integer 85 before assigning it to the `int` variable, `average`; this may or may not be the intended result.

The calculation statement shown in Example 3 in Figure 4-10 is identical to the one shown in Example 2. However, in Example 3, the `test1` and `test2` variables have a data type of `int` rather than `double`, and the `average` variable has a data type of `double` rather than `int`. When the computer processes the `average = (test1 + test2) / 2;` statement shown in Example 3, it first adds the contents of the `test1` variable (90) to the contents of the `test2` variable (81), giving 171; it then divides the 171 by 2. It might be surprising to you that the result of the division is 85 rather than 85.5. When you divide an integer by another integer in C++, the result is always an integer. The computer then promotes the integer result (85) to a `double` number (85.0) before storing it in the `average` variable. It is doubtful that this is the result you were trying to obtain.

Example 4 in Figure 4-10 is identical to Example 3, with the exception of the `double` number 2.0 rather than the integer 2 in the calculation statement. When the computer processes the `average = (test1 + test2) / 2.0;` statement shown in Example 4, it first adds the contents of the `test1` variable (90) to the contents of the `test2` variable (81), giving 171. The computer then promotes the integer 171 to a `double` number (171.0) before dividing it by the `double` number 2.0. The computer assigns the correct result (85.5) to the `average` variable. Notice that the implicit promotion that occurred when the calculation statement was processed had no adverse effect on the calculation.

Many programmers consider it poor programming practice to allow the computer to make implicit type conversions in a program, because the conversions can lead to errors that are difficult to find. To prevent the computer from making an implicit type conversion when processing a program statement, all of the variables and constants that appear in the statement must be the same data type. You can accomplish this by using the same data type to declare the variables and constants; or, you can use type casting.

Type casting, also known as **explicit type conversion**, is the explicit conversion of data from one data type to another. You type cast, or explicitly convert, an item of data by enclosing the data in parentheses, and then preceding it with the C++ keyword that represents the desired data type. For example, you type cast the `double` number 3.7 to the `float` data type using `float(3.7)`. The `float` in the type cast tells the computer to treat the number within parentheses as a `float` data type rather than as a `double` data type. Figure 4-11 shows examples of type casting.

Figure 4-11: Examples of type casting

Examples and results

Example 1
```
double average = 0.0;
int test1       = 90;
int test2       = 81;
average = double(test1 + test2) / 2.0;
```

Result
assigns 85.5 to the **average** variable, which is correct

Example 2
```
double price = 5.0;
double total = 0.0;
int quantity = 8;
total = price * double(quantity);
```

Result
assigns 40.0 to the **total** variable, which is correct

When the computer processes the **average = double(test1 + test2) / 2.0;** statement shown in Example 1, it first adds the contents of the **test1** variable (90) to the contents of the **test2** variable (81), giving 171. It then promotes the integer number 171 to the **double** number 171.0 before dividing it by the **double** number 2.0. The result of the division is the **double** number 85.5, which the computer assigns to the **double** variable, **average**.

When the computer processes the **total = price * double(quantity);** statement shown in Example 2, it temporarily promotes the integer value stored in the **quantity** variable to the **double** number 8.0. It then multiplies the **double** number 8.0 by the **double** number 5.0 (which is stored in the **price** variable). The computer then assigns the result—the **double** number 40.0—to the **total** variable. Although the same answer would be achieved with implicit type conversion, the type casting makes the program's intent clear to anyone reading the program.

Figure 4-12 shows the initial values appropriate for the circle area problem's memory locations. In each case, the data type of the initial value matches the data type of the memory location, so no type casting is necessary.

Figure 4-12: Initial values assigned to memory locations for the circle area problem

Memory location	Name	Data type	Initial value
variable	radius	double	0.0
variable	radiusSquared	double	0.0
variable	area	double	0.0
named constant	PI	double	3.141593

MINI-QUIZ

Mini-Quiz 1

1) Which of the following is an invalid name for a variable?
   a. class2003
   b. gallons
   c. 88TaxAmt
   d. tuition

2) The letter 'w' is a _____.
   a. character literal constant
   b. named constant
   c. numeric literal constant
   d. string literal constant

3) "Jacob Motors" is a _____.
   a. character literal constant
   b. named constant
   c. numeric literal constant
   d. string literal constant

4) In the binary number system, the decimal number 23 is represented as
   _____.
   a. 10111
   b. 10011
   c. 11000
   d. 10001

5) The lowercase letter 'b' is stored in internal memory using the eight bits
   _____.
   a. 01100010
   b. 01100011
   c. 01100000
   d. 01010001

6) Which of the following type casts the number 75.46 to the float data type?
   a. cast(75.46)
   b. castToFloat(75.46)
   c. Float(75.46)
   d. float(75.46)

Now that you know how to select an appropriate name, data type, and initial value for a memory location, you learn how to use that information to declare a memory location in a C++ program. Begin by learning how to declare a named constant.

Declaring a Named Constant

The instruction you use to declare a named constant allows you to specify the named constant's name, data type, and initial value. Figure 4-13 shows the syntax and examples of instructions used to declare named constants in C++.

Figure 4-13: Syntax and examples of instructions that declare named constants in C++

Syntax
const *datatype constantname* **=** *value***;**
Examples
| ```
const double PI = 3.141593;
const float MAXPAY = float(15.75);
const int AGE = 65;
const bool PAID = true;
const char YES = 'Y';
const string TITLE = "IMG";
``` |

In the syntax, *datatype* is the type of data the named constant will store, *constantname* is the name of the named constant, and *value* is a literal constant that represents the value you want stored in the named constant. Words and symbols in **bold** in an instruction's syntax are required parts of the syntax. In this case, the word **const** and the **=** and **;** (semicolon) symbols are required. Items in *italics* in an instruction's syntax represent places where the programmer must supply information relative to the program. When declaring a named constant, the programmer must supply the named constant's data type, name, and value.

Notice that the instruction to declare a named constant ends with a semicolon. This is because the instruction is considered a statement in C++. As you learned in Chapter 3, a statement is an instruction that causes the computer to perform some action after it is executed, or processed, by the computer. Recall that all statements in C++ must end with a semicolon.

The **const double PI = 3.141593;** statement shown in Figure 4-13 creates a named constant whose name is **PI** and whose value is 3.141593. The statement tells the computer to set aside a small box in internal memory and to name the box **PI**. The **PI** box (memory location) will have a data type of **double** and a value of 3.141593. The keyword **const** at the beginning of the statement indicates that the **PI** memory location is a named constant, which means that its value cannot be changed later in the program. If the program contains a statement that attempts to change the value stored in the **PI** named constant, the C++ compiler will display an error message.

The second example shown in Figure 4-13, **const float MAXPAY = float(15.75);**, first converts the **double** number 15.75 to the **float** data type. It then creates the **MAXPAY** named constant and initializes it to 15.75. The third example, **const int AGE = 65;**, creates a named constant named **AGE** and initializes it to the number 65. The fourth example, **const bool PAID = true;**, creates a **bool** named constant named **PAID** and uses the C++ keyword **true** to initialize the constant. The fifth example, **const char YES = 'Y';**, creates a **char** named constant named **YES** and initializes it to the letter Y. The last example, **const string TITLE = "IMG";**, creates a **string** named constant whose name is **TITLE** and whose value is "IMG".

After you declare a named constant, you then can use its name, instead of its value, in another statement. For example, you can use the C++ statement **cout << PI;** to display the contents of the **PI** named constant on the screen; the statement will display the value 3.141593. You also can use the **PI** named constant in a C++ statement that calculates the area of a circle, like this: **area = radiusSquared * PI;**. The computer will use the value stored in the **PI** named constant (3.141593) to calculate the area.
```

Named constants make a program more self-documenting and, therefore, easier to modify because they allow you to use meaningful words in place of values that may be less clear. The named constant **PI**, for example, is much more meaningful than is the number 3.141593. Additionally, typing **PI**, rather than typing 3.141593, in a statement that calculates the area of a circle is easier and less prone to typing errors. If you do mistype **PI** in the area calculation statement—for example, if you type **Pi** rather than **PI**—the C++ compiler will display an error message. Mistyping 3.141593 in the area calculation statement, however, will not trigger an error message and will result in an incorrect answer.

Next, you learn how to declare a variable in a C++ program.

Declaring a Variable

The instruction you use to declare a variable in C++ allows you to specify the variable's name, data type, and initial value. Figure 4-14 shows the syntax and examples of instructions used to declare and initialize variables in C++. Notice that a variable declaration ends with a semicolon; this is because it is considered a C++ statement.

Figure 4-14: Syntax and examples of instructions that declare and initialize variables in C++

Syntax	
datatype variablename [= *initialvalue*];	
Examples	**Initial value**

`int age = 0;`
`float rate = 0.0;`
`float rate = float(3.5);`
`double sale = 0.0;`
`bool insured = false;`
`char grade = ' ';`
`string company = "";`
	0
	0.0
	3.5
	0.0
	false
	one space
	empty string

In the syntax, *datatype* designates the type of data the variable can store, *variablename* is the name of the variable, and *initialvalue* is usually a literal constant that represents the beginning value for the variable. Recall that items in *italics* in an instruction's syntax represent places where the programmer supplies information relative to the program. When declaring a variable, the programmer supplies the variable's data type, name, and initial value.

Notice that the = symbol and *initialvalue* appear in square brackets in the variable declaration's syntax. Items appearing in square brackets in an instruction's syntax are optional parts of the syntax. Although the = symbol and *initialvalue* are optional, recall that it is a good programming practice to initialize the variables that a program uses. A variable can be initialized to any value, as long as the value's data type matches the variable's data type. However, recall that **short** and **int** variables generally are initialized to the integer 0. Variables of the **float** and **double** data types typically are initialized to the floating-point number 0.0. **string** variables usually are initialized to the empty string (""), and **char** variables to a space (' '). The C++ keywords **true** and **false** are used to initialize **bool** variables.

tip

If you do not supply an initial value for a variable in a C++ program, the variable may contain a meaningless value, referred to by programmers as "garbage". The "garbage" is the remains of what was last stored at the memory location that the variable now occupies.

The first statement shown in Figure 4-14 creates an `int` variable named `age` and initializes it to the number 0. The second statement creates a `float` variable named `rate` and initializes it to the number 0.0. The third statement shows how you initialize a `float` variable to a number other than 0.0. Notice that you use a type cast to convert the `double` number—in this case, the number 3.5—to the `float` data type before storing it in the `rate` variable.

The fourth statement shown in Figure 4-14 creates a `double` variable named `sale` and initializes it to the number 0.0. The fifth statement creates a `bool` variable named `insured` and initializes it using the C++ keyword `false`. The sixth statement creates a `char` variable named `grade` and initializes it to a space. The last statement, `string company = "";`, creates a `string` variable named `company` and initializes it to the empty string.

Figure 4-15 shows the C++ statements you would use to declare the `radius`, `radiusSquared`, and `area` variables in the circle area problem.

Figure 4-15: C++ statements reserving the `radius`, `radiusSquared`, and `area` variables

```
double radius = 0.0;
double radiusSquared = 0.0;
double area = 0.0;
```

The C++ statements shown in Figure 4-15 tell the computer to set aside three memory locations that can store floating-point numbers. The memory locations will be named `radius`, `radiusSquared`, and `area`, and each will be initialized to the numeric literal constant 0.0.

MINI-QUIZ

Mini-Quiz 2

1) Write a C++ instruction that declares a named constant named `CITY`. Use the string literal constant "Chicago" to initialize the memory location.

2) Write a C++ instruction that declares a variable named `numberOfPeople`. Assign the data type `int` to the variable and initialize it appropriately.

3) Write a C++ instruction that declares a variable named `studentName`. Assign the data type `string` to the variable and initialize it appropriately.

4) Write a C++ instruction that declares a variable named `interestRate`. Assign the data type `double` to the variable and initialize it appropriately.

5) Write a C++ instruction that declares a `float` variable named `rate`. Initialize the variable to the number 5.6.

In the next section, you learn how to write an assignment statement, which you can use to change the contents of a variable while a program is running.

Using an Assignment Statement to Store Data in a Variable

You can use an assignment statement to change the contents of a variable while a program is running. You already are familiar with assignment statements, as you used two such statements in the program for Sarah Martin. In that program, shown earlier in Figure 4-1, you used the `raise = currentPay * raiseRate;` assignment statement to calculate Sarah's raise, and the `newPay = raise + currentPay;` statement to calculate Sarah's new weekly pay.

Figure 4-16 shows the syntax and examples of assignment statements written in the C++ language. Notice that C++ requires a semicolon at the end of an assignment statement.

Figure 4-16: Syntax and examples of assignment statements in C++

Syntax
variablename = *expression;*
Examples

Note: hoursWkd, overtime, and age are int variables, cost is a float variable, and bonus and sales are double variables. RATE is a double named constant, name is a string variable, middleInitial is a char variable, and paid is a bool variable.
 	
hoursWkd = 50;
overtime = hoursWkd - 40;
age = age + 1;
cost = float(6300.75);
bonus = sales * RATE;
name = "Jackie";
middleInitial = 'P';
paid = true;

tip
You cannot use an assignment statement to assign a value to a named constant, because the contents of a named constant cannot be changed while a program is running.

When an assignment statement is encountered in a program, the computer assigns the value of the *expression* appearing on the right side of the **assignment operator** (=) to the variable whose *variablename* appears on the left side of the assignment operator (=). The data type of the *expression*—which can include items such as literal constants, named constants, variables, and arithmetic operators—must match the data type of the variable to which it is assigned. For example, you should assign only *expressions* that represent integers to memory locations declared using the int data type, and only *expressions* that represent strings to memory locations declared using the string data type. As you learned earlier, if the data type of the *expression*'s value does not match the data type of the memory location to which the value is assigned, the computer uses a process called implicit type conversion to convert the value to fit the memory location. However, recall that implicit type conversions do not always give you the expected results. Therefore, it is considered a good programming practice to use a type cast to explicitly convert the value of the *expression* to fit the memory location.

The first assignment statement shown in Figure 4-16, hoursWkd = 50;, stores the integer 50 (a numeric literal constant) in an int variable named hoursWkd. The second assignment statement, overtime = hoursWkd - 40;, contains two int variables (hoursWkd and overtime), an arithmetic operator (−), and a numeric literal constant (40). The statement first subtracts the integer 40 from the contents of the hoursWkd variable, and then assigns the result to the overtime variable. Assuming the hoursWkd variable contains the number 50, the second assignment statement assigns the number 10 to the overtime variable.

tip
It is easy to confuse an assignment statement (hoursWkd = 50;) with a variable declaration statement (int hoursWkd = 50;) in C++. You use a variable declaration statement, which must begin with a data type, to create and initialize a new variable. You use an assignment statement to change the value stored in an existing variable. An assignment statement does not create a variable in memory.

tip

Recall that C++
treats all numbers
with a decimal
place as a double
data type.

The third assignment statement shown in Figure 4-16, `age = age + 1;`, uses an arithmetic operator (+) to add the integer 1 to the value stored in the `int` variable named `age`; it then assigns the sum to the `age` variable. If the `age` variable contains the value 16 before the computer processes the statement, it contains the value 17 after it is processed.

The fourth assignment statement, `cost = float(6300.75);`, uses a type cast to assign the number 6300.75 to the `float` variable named `cost`. The type cast tells the computer to treat the number 6300.75 as a `float` rather than as a `double`.

The fifth assignment statement, `bonus = sales * RATE;`, contains two `double` variables (`bonus` and `sales`), a `double` named constant (`RATE`), and an arithmetic operator (*). The assignment statement tells the computer to multiply the contents of the `sales` variable by the contents of the `RATE` named constant, then assign the result to the `bonus` variable.

The sixth assignment statement shown in Figure 4-16, `name = "Jackie";`, stores the string literal constant "Jackie" in a `string` variable named `name`. The seventh assignment statement, `middleInitial = 'P';`, stores the character literal constant 'P' in a `char` variable named `middleInitial`. The last assignment statement, `paid = true;`, assigns the C++ keyword `true` to a `bool` variable named `paid`.

It is important to remember that a variable can store only one value at a time. When you assign another value to the variable, the new value replaces the existing value. To illustrate this fact, assume that a C++ program contains the following statements:

```
int temp = 3;
temp = temp + 1;
temp = temp * 2;
```

When you run the program containing these statements, the three lines of code are processed as follows:

- ▶ The declaration statement `int temp = 3;` creates the `temp` variable in the computer's internal memory and initializes the variable to the integer 3.

- ▶ The assignment statement `temp = temp + 1;` adds the number 1 to the contents of the `temp` variable, giving 4. It then replaces the 3 currently stored in the `temp` variable with the number 4. Notice that the computer evaluates the *expression* appearing on the right side of the assignment operator before assigning the result to the variable whose name appears on the left side. (All programming languages process assignment statements in the same manner.)

- ▶ The assignment statement `temp = temp * 2;` first multiplies the contents of the `temp` variable (4) by 2, giving 8. It then removes the number 4 from the `temp` variable and stores the number 8 there instead.

Several of the examples shown in this lesson contain arithmetic operators, which are used to perform calculations in a program. The next section provides a more thorough discussion of arithmetic operators.

Arithmetic Operators

Most programs require the computer to perform one or more calculations. You instruct the computer to perform a calculation by writing an arithmetic expression that contains one or more arithmetic operators. Figure 4-17 lists the standard arithmetic operators in C++, along with their precedence numbers. The precedence numbers indicate the order in which the computer performs the arithmetic operations in an expression. Operations with a precedence number of 1 are performed before operations with a precedence number of 2, which are performed before operations with a precedence number of 3, and so on. However, you can use parentheses to override the order of precedence, because operations within parentheses always are performed before operations outside of parentheses.

Figure 4-17: Standard arithmetic operators and their order of precedence

Operator	Operation	Precedence number
()	override normal precedence rules	1
-	negation	2
*, /, %	multiplication, division, and modulus arithmetic	3
+, -	addition and subtraction	4

Notice that some operators shown in Figure 4-17 have the same precedence number. For example, both the addition and subtraction operator have a precedence number of 4. If an expression contains more than one operator having the same priority, those operators are evaluated from left to right. In the expression 3 + 12 / 3 − 1, for instance, the division (/) is performed first, then the addition (+), and then the subtraction (−). In other words, the computer first divides 12 by 3, then adds the result of the division (4) to 3, and then subtracts 1 from the result of the addition (7). The expression evaluates to 6.

You can use parentheses to change the order in which the operators in an expression are evaluated. The expression 3 + 12 / (3 − 1), for instance, evaluates to 9, not 6. This is because the parentheses tell the computer to subtract 1 from 3 first, then divide the difference (2) into 12, and then add the quotient (6) to 3.

One of the arithmetic operators listed in Figure 4-17, the modulus arithmetic operator (%), might be less familiar to you. The modulus arithmetic operator is used to divide two integers, and results in the remainder of the division. For example, the expression 211 % 4 (read 211 mod 4) equals 3, which is the remainder of 211 divided by 4. One use for the modulus operator is to determine whether a year is a leap year—one that has 366 days rather than 365 days. As you may know, if a year is a leap year, then its year number is evenly divisible by the number 4. In other words, if you divide the year number by 4 and the remainder is 0 (zero), then the year is a leap year. You can determine whether the year 2004 is a leap year by using the expression 2004 % 4. This expression evaluates to 0 (the remainder of 2004 divided by 4), so the year 2004 is a leap year. Similarly, you can determine whether the year 2005 is a leap year by using the expression 2005 % 4. This expression evaluates to 1 (the remainder of 2005 divided by 4), so the year 2005 is not a leap year.

Figure 4-18 shows examples of C++ statements containing arithmetic operators. For the examples, assume that the numbers 0.0 and 100.0 are stored in the **due** and **purchase** variables, respectively; both variables have the **double** data type. Also assume that the **quantity** variable is an **int** variable whose value is the number 10, and the **total** variable is an **int** variable whose value is 0.

Figure 4-18: C++ statements containing arithmetic operators

C++ statement	Result

due = purchase − (purchase * .05);
due = purchase − purchase * .05;
total = quantity + 20 / 2;
total = (quantity + 20) / 2;
total = quantity % 4 * 3;
	95.0
	95.0
	20
	15
	6

tip

The difference between the negation and subtraction operators shown in Figure 4-17 is that the negation operator is unary, whereas the subtraction operator is binary. *Unary* and *binary* refer to the number of operands required by the operator. Unary operators require one operand. For example, the negative number −3 contains the negation operator (−) and one operand (3). Unlike unary operators, binary operators require two operands. For example, the expression 4 − 3 contains the subtraction operator (−) and two operands (4 and 3).

tip

Years ending in 00 are not leap years unless they also are evenly divisible by 400.

When the computer processes the `due = purchase - (purchase * .05);` statement shown in Figure 4-18, it first performs the operation within parentheses. In this case, it multiplies the contents of the `purchase` variable by .05. The computer then subtracts the result from the contents of the `purchase` variable and assigns the difference to the `due` variable. As Figure 4-18 indicates, if the `purchase` variable contains the number 100.0, the statement tells the computer to assign the number 95.0 to the `due` variable.

The second statement shown in Figure 4-18 is identical to the first statement, except it does not contain any parentheses. Notice that the second statement produces the same result as the first statement; both statements assign the number 95.0 to the `due` variable. Because multiplication has a higher precedence than does subtraction, the computer will perform the multiplication operation before the subtraction operation even without the parentheses.

When processing the third statement, `total = quantity + 20 / 2;`, the computer first divides the number 20 by the number 2. It then adds the result to the contents of the `quantity` variable and assigns the sum to the `total` variable. As Figure 4-18 indicates, if the `quantity` variable contains the number 10, the statement tells the computer to assign the number 20 to the `total` variable.

The fourth statement shown in Figure 4-18 is identical to the third statement, except it contains parentheses. Notice that the fourth statement does not produce the same result as the third statement. The parentheses in the fourth statement, `total = (quantity + 20) / 2;`, tell the computer first to add the contents of the `quantity` variable to the number 20, and then divide the sum by the number 2 before assigning the result—in this case, 15—to the `total` variable.

When the computer processes the last statement shown in Figure 4-18, `total = quantity % 4 * 3;`, it first divides the contents of the `quantity` variable (10) by the number 4. It then multiplies the remainder (2) by the number 3 and assigns the result (6) to the `total` variable. (Recall that the modulus arithmetic operator divides two integers and results in the remainder of the division.)

MINI-QUIZ

Mini-Quiz 3

1) Write a C++ assignment statement that assigns the value 23.25 to a `float` variable named `price`.

2) Write a C++ assignment statement that assigns the letter T to a `char` variable named `insured`.

3) Write a C++ assignment statement that multiplies the number 10.75 by the contents of a `double` variable named `hours`, and then assigns the result to a `double` variable named `grossPay`.

4) Write a C++ assignment statement that multiplies the number 10.75 by the contents of an `int` variable named `hours`, and then assigns the result to a `double` variable named `grossPay`.

5) Assuming the `answer` variable is an `int` variable, the assignment statement `answer = 8 / 4 * 3 - 5 % 2;` assigns the value _____ to the `answer` variable.

6) What value will be assigned to the `answer` variable in Question 5 if the variable is a `double` variable?

Earlier, you learned how to use an assignment statement to change a variable's value while a program is running. You also can change a variable's value using data entered by the user at the keyboard.

Getting Data from the Keyboard

You already know how to use the extraction operator (>>) to get a number from the user at the keyboard, then store the number in a numeric variable. You used the extraction operator in the program created for Sarah Martin (shown earlier in Figure 4-1). As you may remember, the extraction operator appears in the `cin >> currentPay;` statement, which gets the current weekly pay amount and stores the amount in the `currentPay` variable. Likewise, it appears in the `cin >> raiseRate;` statement, which gets the raise rate and stores it in the `raiseRate` variable.

You also can use the extraction operator (>>) to get one character from the user at the keyboard and store it in a `char` variable. Additionally, you can use the extraction operator to get a string of characters from the user at the keyboard, as long as none of the characters is a space, because the extraction operator stops reading characters from the keyboard when it encounters a space in the input. To get a string of characters that contains a space, you use the C++ `getline()` function rather than the extraction operator.

The getline() Function

Figure 4-19 shows the syntax and examples of the **getline() function**, which you use to get string input from the keyboard. The `getline()` function continues getting characters from the keyboard until the user presses the Enter key.

Figure 4-19: Syntax and examples of the `getline()` **function**

Syntax
getline(cin, *stringVariablename***);**

Examples

`getline(cin, name);`
`getline(cin, city);`
`getline(cin, petName);`

As you learned in Chapter 3, a function is a block of code that performs a specific task. Functions have parentheses following their names. Some functions, such as `getline()`, require you to enter information, called **arguments**, between the parentheses. The `getline()` function requires two arguments: `cin` and *stringVariablename*. `cin` refers to the keyboard, and *stringVariablename* is the name of the `string` variable in which to store the data entered at the keyboard. In the examples shown in Figure 4-19, the data will be stored in `string` variables named `name`, `city`, and `petName`. Notice that the `getline()` function ends with a semicolon; this is because it is considered a statement in C++.

In some programs, you may need the computer to disregard, or skip, characters entered at the keyboard. You can use the `ignore()` function to accomplish this task.

The ignore() Function

In a C++ program, you can use the **ignore() function** to instruct the computer to disregard, or skip, characters entered at the keyboard. The function actually reads, then discards the characters—a process C++ programmers refer to as **consuming** the characters. Figure 4-20 shows the syntax and examples of the `ignore()` function.

tip

Recall that some functions, like `main()`, do not require any arguments.

Figure 4-20: Syntax and examples of the `ignore()` **function**

Syntax
cin.ignore([*numberOfCharacters*] [, *delimiterCharacter*]**)** ;

Examples

```
cin.ignore(3);
cin.ignore(1);
cin.ignore();
cin.ignore(100, '\n');
cin.ignore(25, '#');
```

As the syntax indicates, the `ignore()` function has two optional arguments: *numberOfCharacters* and *delimiterCharacter*. The *numberOfCharacters* argument is an integer that represents the maximum number of characters you want the function to consume. The *delimiterCharacter* argument is a character that, when consumed, stops the `ignore()` function from reading and discarding any additional characters. The `ignore()` function stops reading and discarding characters either when it consumes the number of characters specified in the *numberOfCharacters* argument or when it consumes the *delimiterCharacter*, whichever occurs first.

The first example shown in Figure 4-20 tells the computer to read and discard, or consume, three characters. The second and third examples tell the computer to consume one character; this is because if you omit the *numberOfCharacters* argument from the `ignore()` function, the default value for the argument is the number 1.

The fourth example, `cin.ignore(100, '\n');`, tells the computer to read and discard characters until either 100 characters are consumed or the newline character is consumed, whichever occurs first. The **newline character** represents the Enter key and is designated by a backslash and the letter n, enclosed in single quotation marks, like this: '\n'.

The last example shown in Figure 4-20, `cin.ignore(25, '#');`, tells the computer to read and discard characters until either 25 characters are consumed or the number symbol ('#') is consumed, whichever comes first. Figure 4-21 shows a program that requires the use of the `ignore()` function.

Figure 4-21: C++ program that requires the `ignore()` **function**

this directive
and
statement are
necessary
when using a
`string`
memory
location

ignore()
function

```cpp
#include <iostream>
#include <string>

using std::cout;
using std::cin;
using std::endl;
using std::string;

int main()
{
    //declare variables
    double sales  = 0.0;
    string stateName = "";

    //enter input items
    cout << "Enter the sales amount: ";
    cin >> sales;
    cin.ignore(100, '\n');
    cout << "Enter the state name: ";
    getline(cin, stateName);

    //display output items
    cout << "You entered sales of " << sales;
    cout << " for " << stateName << endl;

    return 0;
}   //end of main function
```

It's difficult to understand why the `ignore()` function is essential in the program shown in Figure 4-21 without first understanding how the extraction operator and the `getline()` function get keyboard input. Toward this end, you will desk-check the program using 520 as the sales amount and "New Mexico" as the state name. The program begins by declaring and initializing a **double** variable named **sales** and a **string** variable named **stateName**. The program then prompts the user to enter the sales amount. However, before allowing the user to enter the amount, the extraction operator in the `cin >> sales;` statement looks in the keyboard buffer to see if it contains any characters. The keyboard buffer is a special area in the computer's memory that stores the keystrokes entered by the user. Because the buffer is empty at this point, the extraction operator waits for the user to enter a sales amount. In this case, the user types the numbers 5, 2, and 0, then presses the Enter key to indicate that he or she is finished entering the sales amount. The computer stores the numbers 5, 2, and 0, along with the newline character ('\n'), in the keyboard buffer, and alerts the extraction operator that the buffer now contains data. The extraction operator removes the numbers 5, 2, and 0 from the buffer and stores them in the **sales** variable; however, it leaves the newline character (which represents the Enter key) in the buffer.

The next statement in the program, `cin.ignore(100, '\n');`, tells the computer to read and discard characters until either 100 characters are consumed or the newline character is consumed, whichever occurs first. In this case, the `ignore()` function needs to consume only one character—the newline character that was left in the buffer after the sales amount was entered.

The `cout << "Enter the state name: ";` statement in the program prompts the user to enter the state name, and the `getline(cin, stateName);` statement uses the `getline()` function to get the state name from the user at the keyboard. However, before allowing the user to enter the state name, the `getline()` function looks in the keyboard buffer to see if it contains any characters. Not finding any characters in the keyboard buffer at this point, the `getline()` function waits for the user to enter the state name. In this case, the user enters the string "New Mexico" and then presses the Enter key to indicate the end of the entry. The computer stores the string "New Mexico", along with the newline character ('\n'), in the keyboard buffer; it then alerts the `getline()` function that the buffer now contains data. The `getline()` function removes the string "New Mexico" from the buffer and stores it (in ASCII format) in the **stateName** variable. Unlike the extraction operator, the `getline()` function also removes the newline character from the buffer.

If you had not used the `ignore()` function prior to the `getline(cin, stateName);` statement in the program shown in Figure 4-21, the `getline()` function would have found the newline character in the buffer and would have interpreted the newline character as the end of the state name entry. [Recall that the `getline()` function continues reading characters until the user presses the Enter key, which is represented by the newline character.] As a result, the user would not be given a chance to enter the state name. Rather, the `getline()` function would have assigned the empty string to the **stateName** variable before reading and discarding the newline character from the buffer.

You may be wondering why the program shown in Figure 4-21 uses the `cin.ignore(100, '\n');` statement rather than the simpler `cin.ignore();` statement. Although both statements will consume the newline character left in the buffer after the sales amount is entered, there is an advantage to using the `cin.ignore(100, '\n');` statement in the program. To illustrate, assume that when entering the sales amount, the user types the numbers 5, 2, and 0, followed inadvertently by the letter L, and then presses the Enter key. The computer stores the numbers 5, 2, and 0, along with the letter L and the newline character, in the keyboard buffer; it then alerts the extraction operator in the `cin >> sales;` statement that the buffer now contains data. The extraction operator removes the numbers 5, 2, and 0 from the buffer and stores them in the **sales** variable; however, it leaves the letter L (which cannot be stored in a **double** variable) and the newline character in the buffer. The `cin.ignore();` statement will consume only one of the characters: the letter L. The newline character will still be in the keyboard buffer when the `getline(cin, stateName);` statement is processed. As you learned earlier, the `getline()` function will interpret the newline character as the end of the state name entry. The `cin.ignore(100, '\n');` statement, on the other hand, will consume both the letter L and the newline character. As a result, the `getline()` function will not find any characters in the buffer and will, therefore, wait for the user to enter the state name.

MINI-QUIZ

Mini-Quiz 4

1) Write a C++ statement that uses the `getline()` function to get a string of characters from the keyboard. The statement should store the characters in a variable named `streetAddress`.

2) Write a C++ statement that tells the computer to skip the very next character entered at the keyboard.

3) Which of the following tells the computer to stop reading and discarding characters either when it consumes 10 characters or when the user presses the Enter key, whichever occurs first?
   a. `cin.ignore(10, \n)`
   b. `cin.ignore(10, '\n');`
   c. `cin.ignore("\n", 10)`
   d. `cin.ignore('\n', 10);`

You now have completed Chapter 4's Concept lesson. You can either take a break or complete the end-of-lesson questions and exercises before moving on to the Application lesson.

SUMMARY

Most programs include variables, constants (named and literal), and arithmetic operators (which are used to perform calculations). Variables and named constants are computer memory locations where you can temporarily store data. The contents of a variable can change as the program is running, but the contents of a named constant cannot change. You must assign a name, data type, and initial value to each named constant you create. You also must assign a name and data type to each variable you create. Although assigning an initial value to a variable is optional in most programming languages, it is considered a good programming practice to do so to ensure that the variable does not contain garbage.

In C++, you declare and initialize a named constant using the syntax **const** *datatype constantname = value;*. You declare and initialize a variable in C++ using the syntax *datatype variablename* [*= initialvalue*];. You typically use a literal constant, which is an item of data, to initialize named constants and variables. C++ has three types of literal constants: numeric, character, and string. A numeric literal constant is a number. A character literal constant is one letter, number, or symbol enclosed in single quotation marks (' '). A string literal constant is zero or more characters enclosed in double quotation marks ("").

You can use an assignment statement, which must conform to the C++ syntax *variablename = expression;*, to store data in a variable. The data type of the *expression* must match the data type of the variable. When C++ encounters an assignment statement in a program, it assigns the value of the *expression* appearing on the right side of the assignment operator (=) to the variable whose *variablename* appears on the left side of the assignment operator. A variable can store only one item of data at any time. When you assign another item to the variable, the new data replaces the existing data.

When assigning a value to a memory location, it is important that the value fit the memory location's data type. If you assign a value that does not match the data type of the memory location, the computer uses a process called implicit type conversion to convert the value to fit the memory location. However, it is not always possible for the computer to make the conversion. You can use a type cast to explicitly convert data from one data type to another.

Most programs require the computer to perform one or more calculations. You instruct the computer to perform a calculation by writing an arithmetic expression that contains one or more arithmetic operators. Each arithmetic operator is associated with a precedence number, which controls the order in which the operation is performed in an expression. You can use parentheses to override the normal order of precedence, because operations within parentheses always are performed before operations outside of parentheses.

You can use the `getline()` function to get a string of characters entered at the keyboard. The `getline()` function stops reading characters when it encounters the Enter key in the input.

You can use the `ignore()` function to consume characters entered at the keyboard. The function stops consuming characters either when it consumes a specified number of characters or when it consumes the delimiter character, whichever occurs first.

The computer stores the characters entered at the keyboard in the keyboard buffer. Both the extraction operator and the `getline()` function remove characters from the keyboard buffer. However, unlike the extraction operator, which leaves the newline character in the keyboard buffer, the `getline()` function consumes the newline character.

ANSWERS TO MINI-QUIZZES

Mini-Quiz 1

1) c. `88TaxAmt`

2) a. character literal constant

3) d. string literal constant

4) a. `10111`

5) a. `01100010`

6) d. `float(75.46)`

Mini-Quiz 2

1) `const string CITY = "Chicago";`

2) `int numberOfPeople = 0;`

3) `string studentName = "";`

4) `double interestRate = 0.0;`

5) `float rate = float(5.6);`

Mini-Quiz 3

1) `price = float(23.25);`

2) `insured = 'T';`

3) `grossPay = 10.75 * hours;`

4) `grossPay = 10.75 * double(hours);`

5) `5`

6) `5.0`

Mini-Quiz 4

1) `getline(cin, streetAddress);`

2) `cin.ignore();` [or `cin.ignore(1);`]

3) b. `cin.ignore(10, '\n');`

QUESTIONS

1) A variable is _____.

    A. an item of data

    B. a literal constant

    C. a memory location whose value can change while the program is running

    D. a memory location whose value cannot change while the program is running

2) To create a named constant, you must assign _____ to it.

    A. a data type

    B. a name

    C. a value

    D. all of the above

3) Which of the following declares and initializes a C++ variable that can store whole numbers only?

    A. `int numItems = 0;`

    B. `int numItems = '0';`

    C. `int numItems = "0";`

    D. `numItems = 0;`

4) Which of the following is a valid name for a variable?

    A. `amt-Sold`

    B. `amt    Sold`

    C. `amt_Sold`

    D. `98SoldAmt`

5) Which of the following is not a valid name for a C++ variable?

    A. `float`

    B. `payRate`

    C. `total`

    D. `winnings`

6) Which of the following stores the letter H in a `char` variable named `initial`?

    A. `initial = 'H'`

    B. `initial = 'H';`

    C. `initial = "H"`

    D. `initial = "H";`

7) You typically initialize `int` variables in a C++ program to _____.

    A. the number 0 enclosed in double quotation marks

    B. the number 0 enclosed in single quotation marks

    C. the number 0

    D. the number 0.0

8) Which of the following C++ statements declares and initializes a **double** variable named **rate**?

A. double rate = 0.0

B. double rate = '0.0';

C. double rate = 0.0;

D. rate = 0.0;

9) Which of the following assigns the number 3.56 to a **float** variable named **payRate**?

A. payRate = 3.56(float);

B. payRate = float(3.56);

C. float(payRate) = 3.56;

D. none of the above

10) Which of the following are valid characters for a numeric literal constant?

A. a comma

B. a dollar sign ($)

C. a percent sign (%)

D. none of the above

11) Which of the following C++ statements creates a named constant called **RATE** whose value is 16.5?

A. const RATE = 16.5;

B. const double RATE = 16.5;

C. double RATE = 16.5;

D. RATE const = 16.5;

12) Assume that the following instructions are part of a valid C++ program. What is the value contained in the **number** variable after the instructions are processed?

```
int number = 0;
number = 10;
number = number + 5;
```

A. 0

B. 5

C. 10

D. 15

13) What value will be assigned to the **answer** variable as a result of the **answer = 3 + 2 * 9 % (10 - 6);** statement? (The **answer** variable is an **int** variable.)

A. 1

B. 5

C. 6

D. 11

14) In a payroll program, which one of the following items would typically be assigned to a named constant?

A. employee's name

B. FICA (Federal Insurance Contributions Act) tax rate

C. hourly pay rate

D. hours worked

15) Assume that a program needs to get the name of a city and store it in a `string` variable named `cityName`. Which of the following statements should the program use to get the information?

A. `cin >> cityName;`

B. `cin(cityName);`

C. `getline(cityName, cin);`

D. `getline(cin, cityName);`

16) Assume that a program declares an `int` variable named `hours` and two `double` variables named `payRate` and `grossPay`. The `hours` variable contains the number 40, and the `payRate` variable contains the number 5.5. Which of the following statements will assign the correct gross pay to the `grossPay` variable?

A. `grossPay = hours * payRate;`

B. `grossPay = double(hours) * payRate;`

C. `grossPay = hours * int(payRate);`

D. both A and B

17) Assume that a program declares three `int` variables named `sales1`, `sales2`, and `sales3`. The program also declares a `double` variable named `averageSales`. Which of the following statements will assign the correct average to the `averageSales` variable?

A. `averageSales = sales1 + sales2 + sales3 / double(3);`

B. `averageSales = sales1 + sales2 + sales3 / 3.0;`

C. `averageSales = double(sales1 + sales2 + sales3) / 3.0;`

D. all of the above

18) Which of the following tells the computer to consume the next 100 characters?

A. `cin.ignore(100);`

B. `cin.ignore('100');`

C. `ignore(cin, 100);`

D. none of the above

19) Assume that a program declares a `float` variable and an `int` variable. If the program contains a statement that adds the `float` variable to the `int` variable, which of the following statements is true?

A. The `float` variable's value will be temporarily converted to an `int`.

B. The `int` variable's value will be temporarily converted to a `float`.

C. The C++ compiler will display a warning message.

D. The C++ compiler will display an error message.

20) When processed, the _____ consumes the newline character.

A. `>>` operator

B. `<<` operator

C. `getline()` function

D. both A and C

Look For These
Symbols

Debugging

Discovery

EXERCISES

1) Write the statement to declare and initialize a variable that can store an item's price, which can contain decimal places. Name the variable `price` and assign the `double` data type to it. Then write an assignment statement that assigns the value 16.23 to the variable.

2) Write the statements to declare and initialize two variables: one to store an item's height and the other to store an item's width. Both dimensions can contain decimal places. Name the variables `height` and `width`, and assign the `float` data type to each. Then write an assignment statement that assigns the value 4.5 to the `height` variable. Also write an assignment statement that assigns the value 6.9 to the `width` variable.

3) Write the statement to declare and initialize a variable that can store the population of a city. Name the variable `population` and assign the `int` data type to it. Then write an assignment statement that assigns the value 60,000 to the variable.

4) Write the statement to declare and initialize a variable that can store a letter of the alphabet. Name the variable `letter` and assign the `char` data type to it. Then write an assignment statement that assigns the letter A to the variable.

5) Write a C++ statement to declare and initialize a `double` named constant called **TAXRATE** whose value is .15.

6) Write a C++ statement to declare and initialize an `int` named constant called **MAXPAY** whose value is 20.

7) Write a C++ statement to declare and initialize a `char` named constant called **INSURED** whose value is the letter Y.

8) Write a C++ statement to declare and initialize a `string` named constant called **PROMPT** whose value is the string "Press any key to continue".

9) Write a C++ statement that uses the `getline()` function to get a string of characters from the keyboard. Store the characters in a `string` variable named `company`.

10) Write a C++ statement that multiplies the contents of a `double` variable named `taxRate` by the contents of a `double` variable named `grossPay`. The statement should assign the result to a `double` variable named `tax`.

11) Assume a program needs to store the number of units in stock at the beginning of the current month, the number of units purchased during the current month, the number of units sold during the current month, and the number of units in stock at the end of the current month. (The number of units is always an integer.) Write the appropriate C++ statements to declare and initialize the necessary variables. Name the variables `beginStock`, `purchased`, `sold`, and `endStock`. Use the `int` data type to declare each variable. Then write an assignment statement that calculates the number of units in stock at the end of the current month.

12) Assume a program needs to calculate a bonus, which is always 5% of the sales. Write the appropriate C++ statements to declare and initialize the necessary memory locations. Be sure to assign a descriptive name to each memory location. Use the `double` data type for all memory locations. Then write an assignment statement that calculates the bonus.

13) Assume a program needs to calculate an employee's gross pay. The input items will be the employee's name, hours worked, and pay rate. Write the appropriate C++ statements to declare and initialize the necessary memory locations. The hours worked will always be an integer. The pay rate may contain a number with a decimal place. Then write an assignment statement that calculates the gross pay. You do not need to worry about overtime pay, because no employees work more than 40 hours.

14) In this exercise, you learn about the arithmetic assignment operators available in C++.

  A. In addition to the standard arithmetic operators, the C++ programming language also has an addition assignment operator (+=), a subtraction assignment operator (−=), a multiplication assignment operator (*=), a division assignment operator (/=), and a modulus assignment operator (%=). What is the purpose of these operators?

  B. Write a C++ statement that uses the addition assignment operator to add the number 10 to the contents of an `int` variable named `quantity`.

 15) In this exercise, you learn about the increment and decrement operators in C++.

  A. The C++ programming language has an increment operator (++) and a decrement operator (−−). What is the purpose of these operators?

  B. Write a C++ statement that uses the increment operator to increment the `quantity` variable by 1.

 16) In this exercise, you learn how the computer uses implicit type conversion to convert a value assigned within a declaration statement.

  A. If necessary, start Visual Studio .NET. Open the Ch4ConE16 Solution (Ch4ConE16 Solution.sln) file contained in the Cpp\Chap04\Ch4ConE16 Solution folder. The Ch4ConE16.cpp program initializes an `int` variable named **number** to the integer 9. It then displays the value stored in the **number** variable on the screen.

  B. Build the solution, then execute the program. The number 9 appears in the Command Prompt window. Press Enter to close the Command Prompt window.

  C. Change the number 9 in the variable declaration statement to 9.6. Save and build the solution. What warning message did you receive from the C++ compiler? Execute the program. The number 9 appears in the Command Prompt window; this indicates that the computer converted the floating-point number 9.6 to an integer before storing it in the **number** variable. Close the Command Prompt window.

  D. Change the number 9.6 in the variable declaration statement to the character '9'. Save and build the solution, then execute the program. What value appears in the Command Prompt window? What does this value represent? Close the Command Prompt window.

  E. Change the character '9' in the variable declaration statement to the string "9". Save and build the program. What happens when you assign a value whose data type cannot be converted to fit the memory location?

  F. Change the string "9" in the variable declaration statement to the number 9. Save and build the solution.

  G. Close the Output window, then use the File menu to close the solution.

17) In this exercise, you debug a C++ program.

  A. If necessary, start Visual Studio .NET. Open the Ch4ConE17 Solution (Ch4ConE17 Solution.sln) file contained in the Cpp\Chap04\Ch4ConE17 Solution folder. The Ch4ConE17.cpp program calculates a bonus amount. It then displays a message containing the salesperson's name and bonus amount.

  B. Build the solution, then execute the program. Test the program using 1000 as the sales, .03 as the bonus rate, and Harry as the name. Notice that the program is not working correctly.

  C. Make the appropriate corrections to the program, then save and build the solution.

  D. Execute the program. Test the program using 1000 as the sales, .03 as the bonus rate, and Harry as the name.

  E. When the program is working correctly, close the Output window, and then use the File menu to close the solution.

Application Lesson

Using Variables, Constants, and Arithmetic Operators in a C++ Program

Lab 4.1 - Stop and Analyze   If necessary, start Visual Studio .NET. Open the Ch4Lab1 Solution (Ch4Lab1 Solution.sln) file contained in the Cpp\Chap04\Ch4Lab1 Solution folder. Figure 4-22 shows the code entered in the Ch4Lab1.cpp file. (The line numbers are included in the figure only.) Study the code, then answer the questions.

Figure 4-22: C++ instructions entered in the C4Lab1.cpp file

```
1   //Ch4Lab1.cpp - calculates and displays the total price
2   //Created/revised by <your name> on <current date>
3
4   #include <iostream>
5
6   using std::cout;
7   using std::cin;
8   using std::endl;
9
10  int main()
11  {
12      //declare variables
13      int numCds       = 0;
14      double cdPrice    = 0.0;
15      double totalPrice = 0.0;
16
17      //get user's input
18      cout << "Number of CDs purchased: ";
19      cin >> numCds;
20      cout << "CD price: ";
21      cin >> cdPrice;
22
23      //calculate total price
24      totalPrice = double(numCds) * cdPrice;
25
26      //display total price
27      cout << "Total price: " << totalPrice << endl;
28
29      return 0;
30
31  }     //end of main function
```

Questions

1. What exactly does the Ch4Lab1.cpp program do? In other words, what does it input, process, and output?
2. Is the type cast in Line 24 necessary? Why or why not?
3. Build the solution, then execute the program. What is the total price for the purchase of three CDs at a price of 10.99 per CD? Close the Command Prompt window.
4. Execute the program again. Use the program to calculate the total price for the purchase of four CDs at a price of 5.69ab (notice the typing error) per CD; the total price should be $22.76. What does the program display? If the program's output is not correct, why didn't

the program produce the correct output, and how can you fix the program so that it does display the correct output? Close the Command Prompt window.

5. Execute the program again. Use the program to calculate the total price for the purchase of 3x (notice the typing error) CDs at a price of 3.45 per CD; the total price should be $10.35. What does the program display? If the program's output is not correct, why didn't the program produce the correct output, and how can you fix the program so that it does display the correct output? Close the Command Prompt window.

Lab 4.2 Jack Faye, the cashier at Jackson College, wants a program that the clerks can use to display a student's name and the total amount the student owes for the semester, including tuition and room and board. The tuition at Jackson College is $100 per semester hour, and room and board is $1800 per semester.

Figure 4-23 shows the IPO chart and C++ instructions for the Jackson College problem. Notice that the program uses three variables and two named constants. Variables were chosen for the student's name, hours enrolled, and total amount owed items, because the values of those items will change each time the program is executed. The semester hour and room and board fees, however, will not change and are assigned to named constants.

Figure 4-23: IPO chart and C++ instructions for the Jackson College problem

IPO chart information	C++ instructions

Input
  name
  hours enrolled
  semester hour fee ($100)
  room and board fee ($1800)
	`string name = "";`
	`int hours = 0;`
	`const int SEMHOURFEE = 100;`
	`const int ROOMBOARD = 1800;`

Processing	

Output
  name
  total amount owed
	`int total = 0;`

Algorithm
1. enter the name and
   hours enrolled
	`cout << "Enter student name: ";`
	`getline(cin, name);`
	`cout << "Enter hours enrolled: ";`
	`cin >> hours;`

2. calculate the total
   amount owed by
   multiplying the hours
   enrolled by the semester
   hour fee, then adding the
   room and board fee to
   the result
	`total = hours * SEMHOURFEE + ROOMBOARD;`

3. display the name and total amount owed	`cout << "Student name: " << name << endl;` `cout << "Total due: " << total << endl;`

Activity for Lab 4.2

In this activity, you enter the C++ instructions shown in Figure 4-23 into the computer. You then test the program to verify that it is working correctly.

To create the Jackson College program, then test the program:

1. If necessary, start Visual Studio .NET. Create a blank solution named Ch4Lab2 Solution. Save the solution in the Cpp\Chap04 folder.

2. Add an empty C++ Win32 Console Project to the solution. Name the project Ch4Lab2 Project.

3. Add a new C++ source file to the project. Name the source file Ch4Lab2.

4. Type **//Ch4Lab2.cpp - calculates and displays the total amount owed** and press **Enter**.

5. Type **//Created/revised by <your name> on <current date>**, replacing *<your name>* and *<current date>* with your name and the current date, respectively. Press **Enter** twice.

   Next, you need to include the iostream and string files in the program. Recall that the iostream file must be included in any program that uses `cin` or `cout`. The string file is necessary when using >> or `getline()` to enter data into a `string` variable or when using << to display the data contained in a `string` variable.

6. Type the following two `#include` directives, then press **Enter** twice.

   #include <iostream>

   #include <string>

   The program requires four `using` statements. The `using` statements will give the program access to the definitions of the keywords `cout`, `cin`, `endl`, and `string`.

7. Type the following four `using` statements, then press **Enter** twice.

   using std::cout;

   using std::cin;

   using std::endl;

   using std::string;

8. Complete the program by entering the `main()` function, which is shown in Figure 4-24.

Figure 4-24: Jackson College program

```cpp
//Ch4Lab2.cpp - calculates and displays the total amount owed
//Created/revised by <your name> on <current date>

#include <iostream>
#include <string>

using std::cout;
using std::cin;
using std::endl;
using std::string;

int main()
{
    //declare constants and variables
    const int SEMHOURFEE = 100;
    const int ROOMBOARD = 1800;
    string name = "";
    int hours = 0;
    int total = 0;

    //get user's input
    cout << "Enter student name: ";
    getline(cin, name);
    cout << "Enter hours enrolled: ";
    cin >> hours;

    //calculate total due
    total = hours * SEMHOURFEE + ROOMBOARD;

    //display output items
    cout << "Student name: " << name << endl;
    cout << "Total due: $" << total << endl;

    return 0;
}   //end of main function
```

enter the main() function instructions

9. Save and then build the solution. If necessary, correct any syntax errors, then save and build the solution again.

10. Execute the program by clicking **Debug** on the menu bar, then clicking **Start Without Debugging**. Rachel Woods is enrolled in 15 hours of coursework. Use the program to calculate the total amount she owes; the total amount should be $3300. Close the Command Prompt window.

11. Execute the program again. Paul Pitowski is enrolled in 20 hours of coursework. Use the program to calculate the total amount he owes; the total amount should be $3800. Close the Command Prompt window.

12. Close the Output window, then use the File menu to close the solution.

Lab 4.3 In this lab, you modify the program you created in Lab 4.2 so that it allows the user to enter the semester hour fee.

Activity for Lab 4.3

Before modifying the program created in Lab 4.2, you copy the instructions contained in the Ch4Lab2.cpp file to a new solution.

To copy the instructions contained in the Ch4Lab2.cpp file to a new solution:

1. If necessary, start Visual Studio .NET. Create a blank solution named **Ch4Lab3 Solution**. Save the solution in the Cpp\Chap04 folder.

2. Add an empty C++ Win32 Console Project to the solution. Name the project **Ch4Lab3 Project**.

3. Add a new C++ source file to the project. Name the source file **Ch4Lab3**.

4. Click **File** on the menu bar, point to **Open**, and then click **File**. The Open File dialog box opens.

5. Open the Cpp\Chap04\Ch4Lab2 Solution\Ch4Lab2 Project folder. Click **Ch4Lab2.cpp** in the list of filenames, then click the **Open** button to open the Ch4Lab2.cpp file.

6. Click **Edit** on the menu bar, then click **Select All** to select all of the instructions in the Ch4Lab2.cpp window.

7. Click **Edit**, then click **Copy** to copy the selected instructions to the clipboard.

8. Close the Ch4Lab2.cpp window by clicking the **Close** button on its title bar.

9. Click the **Ch4Lab3.cpp** tab. Click **Edit**, then click **Paste** to paste the Ch4Lab2.cpp instructions in the Ch4Lab3.cpp window.

10. Change the filename in the first program comment to **Ch4Lab3.cpp**. If necessary, change the date in the second comment.

Assume that Jack Faye, the cashier at Jackson College, now wants the clerks to be able to enter the fee for a semester hour.

To allow the user to enter the semester hour fee:

1. Make the appropriate modifications to the program.

2. Save and then build the solution. If necessary, correct any syntax errors, then save and build the solution again.

3. Execute the program. Test the program using your own sample data, then close the Command Prompt window.

4. When the program is working correctly, close the Output window, then use the File menu to close the solution.

You now have completed Chapter 4's Application lesson. You can either take a break or complete the end-of-lesson exercises.

ANSWERS TO LABS

Lab 4.1

1. The program allows the user to enter the number of CDs purchased and the price of a CD. It then calculates and displays the total purchase price of the CDs.

2. Although it is a good programming practice to include the type cast in Line 24, it is not necessary to do so. Because the `cdPrice` variable's data type is `double`, the computer will automatically promote the value stored in the `numCds` variable to `double` before calculating the total price. This is because the computer performs arithmetic operations (in this case, the multiplication operation) using the highest ranking data type.

3. The total price is $32.97.

4. The program displays the message *Total price: $22.76*, which is correct.

5. The program displays *CD price: Total price: $0*, which is not correct. When the `cin >> numCds;` statement in Line 19 is processed, the extraction operator checks the keyboard buffer for any characters. Because the keyboard buffer is empty at this point, the extraction operator waits for the user to enter some data. When you type 3x as the number of CDs purchased and then press Enter, the computer places the number 3, the letter x, and the newline character in the keyboard buffer; it then tells the extraction operator that the buffer contains data. The extraction operator in Line 19 stores the number 3 in the `numCds` variable. However, it leaves the letter x in the keyboard buffer, because a letter cannot be stored in an `int` variable. It also leaves the newline character in the buffer. When the `cin >> cdPrice;` statement in Line 21 is processed, the extraction operator checks the keyboard buffer for any characters. In this case, it finds the letter x and the newline character. Because a letter cannot be stored in an `int` variable, the extraction operator disregards the letter. The newline character then marks the end of the entry. You can fix the program by including a statement such as `cin.ignore(100, '\n');` between Lines 19 and 20. Using 100 as the *numberOfCharacters* argument in the `ignore()` function assures that the program will work correctly even when the user types several invalid characters at the end of the number of CDs entry.

Lab 4.2

No answer required.

Lab 4.3

See Figure 4-25. Modifications are shaded in the figure.

Figure 4-25

```
//Ch4Lab3.cpp - calculates and displays the total amount owed
//Created/revised by <your name> on <current date>

#include <iostream>
#include <string>

using std::cout;
using std::cin;
```

Figure 4-25 (continued)

```cpp
using std::endl;
using std::string;

int main()
{
    //declare constant and variables
    const int ROOMBOARD = 1800;
    string name     = "";
    int hours       = 0;
    int total       = 0;
    int semHourFee = 0;

    //get user's input
    cout << "Enter student name: ";
    getline(cin, name);
    cout << "Enter hours enrolled: ";
    cin >> hours;
    cin.ignore(100, '\n');
    cout << "Enter semester hour fee: ";
    cin >> semHourFee;

    //calculate total due
    total = hours * semHourFee + ROOMBOARD;

    //display output items
    cout << "Student name: " << name << endl;
    cout << "Total due: $" << total << endl;

    return 0;
}   //end of main function
```

Look For These
Symbols

Debugging

Discovery

EXERCISES

1) Acme Appliances needs a program to calculate a bonus, which is always 5% of the sales.

   A. Complete an IPO chart for this problem.

   B. Desk-check the algorithm. Use 330.50 as the sales.

   C. Use the IPO chart to code the program.

   D. Desk-check the program using the data supplied in Step B.

   E. If necessary, start Visual Studio .NET. Create a blank solution named Ch4AppE01 Solution. Save the solution in the Cpp\Chap04 folder.

   F. Add an empty C++ Win32 Console Project to the solution. Name the project Ch4AppE01 Project.

   G. Add a new C++ source file to the project. Name the source file Ch4AppE01.

   H. Enter the appropriate C++ instructions into the source file.

   I. Save and then build the solution.

   J. Execute the program. Test the program using the data supplied in Step B.

   K. When the program is working correctly, close the Output window, then use the File menu to close the solution.

2) Write a program to calculate the square of a number. The number will always be an integer.

   A. Complete an IPO chart for this problem.

   B. Desk-check the algorithm. Use 10 as the number.

   C. Use the IPO chart to code the program.

   D. Desk-check the program using the data supplied in Step B.

   E. If necessary, start Visual Studio .NET. Create a blank solution named Ch4AppE02 Solution. Save the solution in the Cpp\Chap04 folder.

   F. Add an empty C++ Win32 Console Project to the solution. Name the project Ch4AppE02 Project.

   G. Add a new C++ source file to the project. Name the source file Ch4AppE02.

   H. Enter the appropriate C++ instructions into the source file.

   I. Save and then build the solution.

   J. Execute the program. Test the program using the data supplied in Step B.

   K. When the program is working correctly, close the Output window, then use the File menu to close the solution.

3) Builders Inc. needs a program that allows the company's salesclerks to enter both the diameter of a circle (in feet) and the price of railing material per foot. The diameter and the price may contain decimal places. The program should display both the circumference of the circle and the total price of the railing material. Use 3.141593 as the value of pi.

   A. Complete an IPO chart for this problem.

   B. Desk-check the algorithm. Use 36.5 feet as the diameter and $2.35 as the price per foot of railing material.

   C. Use the IPO chart to code the program.

   D. Desk-check the program using the data supplied in Step B.

   E. If necessary, start Visual Studio .NET. Create a blank solution named Ch4AppE03 Solution. Save the solution in the Cpp\Chap04 folder.

   F. Add an empty C++ Win32 Console Project to the solution. Name the project Ch4AppE03 Project.

   G. Add a new C++ source file to the project. Name the source file Ch4AppE03.

   H. Enter the appropriate C++ instructions into the source file.

   I. Save and then build the solution.

   J. Execute the program. Test the program using the data supplied in Step B.

   K. When the program is working correctly, close the Output window, then use the File menu to close the solution.

4) A-1 Appliances needs a program that allows the store clerks to enter the number of dishwashers in stock at the beginning of the current month, the number of dishwashers purchased during the current month, and the number of dishwashers sold during the current month. The program should calculate and display the number of dishwashers in stock at the end of the current month.

   A. Complete an IPO chart for this problem.

   B. Desk-check the algorithm, using 5000 as the number of dishwashers at the beginning of the month, 1000 as the number of dishwashers purchased during the month, and 3500 as the number of dishwashers sold during the month.

   C. Use the IPO chart to code the program.

   D. Desk-check the program using the data supplied in Step B.

E. If necessary, start Visual Studio .NET. Create a blank solution named Ch4AppE04 Solution. Save the solution in the Cpp\Chap04 folder.

F. Add an empty C++ Win32 Console Project to the solution. Name the project Ch4AppE04 Project.

G. Add a new C++ source file to the project. Name the source file Ch4AppE04.

H. Enter the appropriate C++ instructions into the source file.

I. Save and then build the solution.

J. Execute the program. Test the program using the data supplied in Step B.

K. When the program is working correctly, close the Output window, then use the File menu to close the solution.

5) Tile Limited wants a program that allows the company's salesclerks to enter the length and width (in feet) of a rectangle, and the price of a square foot of tile. The length, width, and price may contain decimal places. The program should display the area of the rectangle and the total price of the tile.

A. Complete an IPO chart for this problem.

B. Desk-check the algorithm. Use 12.5 feet as the length, 14.5 feet as the width, and $3.10 as the price per square foot of tile.

C. Use the IPO chart to code the program.

D. Desk-check the program using the data supplied in Step B.

E. If necessary, start Visual Studio .NET. Create a blank solution named Ch4AppE05 Solution. Save the solution in the Cpp\Chap04 folder.

F. Add an empty C++ Win32 Console Project to the solution. Name the project Ch4AppE05 Project.

G. Add a new C++ source file to the project. Name the source file Ch4AppE05.

H. Enter the appropriate C++ instructions into the source file.

I. Save and then build the solution.

J. Execute the program. Test the program using the data supplied in Step B.

K. When the program is working correctly, close the Output window, then use the File menu to close the solution.

6) Jerome Symanski wants a program that he can use to display the number of cubic feet of water contained in a rectangular pool. (*Hint*: Find the volume of the pool.)

A. Complete an IPO chart for this problem.

B. Desk-check the algorithm, using 100 feet as the length, 30.5 feet as the width, and 4 feet as the depth.

C. Use the IPO chart to code the program. Use **double** variables for the length, width, depth, and volume.

D. Desk-check the program using the data supplied in Step B.

E. If necessary, start Visual Studio .NET. Create a blank solution named Ch4AppE06 Solution. Save the solution in the Cpp\Chap04 folder.

F. Add an empty C++ Win32 Console Project to the solution. Name the project Ch4AppE06 Project.

G. Add a new C++ source file to the project. Name the source file Ch4AppE06.

H. Enter the appropriate C++ instructions into the source file.

I. Save and then build the solution.

J. Execute the program. Test the program using the data supplied in Step B.

K. When the program is working correctly, close the Output window, then use the File menu to close the solution.

7) Temp Employers wants a program that allows the company's clerks to enter an employee's name and the number of hours the employee worked during the month. (The number of hours worked will always be an integer.) The program should display the name, number of weeks (assume a 40-hour week), days (assume an 8-hour day), and hours worked. For example, if the employee worked 70 hours during the month, the program should display 1 week, 3 days, and 6 hours.

A. Complete an IPO chart for this problem.

B. Desk-check the algorithm three times, using the following data:

Mary Claire, 88 hours worked

Jackie Smith, 111 hours worked

Sue Jones, 12 hours worked

C. Use the IPO chart to code the program.

D. Desk-check the program using the data supplied in Step B.

E. If necessary, start Visual Studio .NET. Create a blank solution named Ch4AppE07 Solution. Save the solution in the Cpp\Chap04 folder.

F. Add an empty C++ Win32 Console Project to the solution. Name the project Ch4AppE07 Project.

G. Add a new C++ source file to the project. Name the source file Ch4AppE07.

H. Enter the appropriate C++ instructions into the source file.

I. Save and then build the solution.

J. Execute the program. Test the program using the data supplied in Step B.

K. When the program is working correctly, close the Output window, then use the File menu to close the solution.

8) Colfax Industries needs a program that allows the shipping clerk to enter an item's name, the quantity of the item in inventory, and how many units of the item can be packed in a box for shipping. The program should display the item's name, the number of full boxes that can be packed from the quantity on hand, and how many of the item are left over.

A. Complete an IPO chart for this problem.

B. Desk-check the algorithm three times, using the following data:

Cleanser, 45 in inventory, six can be packed in a box

Hair Spray, 100 in inventory, three can be packed in a box

Comb, 78 in inventory, five can be packed in a box

C. Use the IPO chart to code the program.

D. Desk-check the program using the data supplied in Step B.

E. If necessary, start Visual Studio .NET. Create a blank solution named Ch4AppE08 Solution. Save the solution in the Cpp\Chap04 folder.

F. Add an empty C++ Win32 Console Project to the solution. Name the project Ch4AppE08 Project.

G. Add a new C++ source file to the project. Name the source file Ch4AppE08.

H. Enter the appropriate C++ instructions into the source file.

I. Save and then build the solution.

J. Execute the program. Test the program using the data supplied in Step B.

K. When the program is working correctly, close the Output window, then use the File menu to close the solution.

9) Your friend Joe saves pennies in a jar, which he empties every month when he goes to the bank. You are to create a program that allows him to enter the number of pennies, and then calculates and displays the number of dollars, quarters, dimes, nickels, and pennies he will receive when he trades in the pennies at the bank.

A. Complete an IPO chart for this problem.

B. Desk-check the algorithm two times, using the following data: 2311 pennies and 7333 pennies.

C. Use the IPO chart to code the program.

D. Desk-check the program using the data supplied in Step B.

E. If necessary, start Visual Studio .NET. Create a blank solution named Ch4AppE09 Solution. Save the solution in the Cpp\Chap04 folder.

F. Add an empty C++ Win32 Console Project to the solution. Name the project Ch4AppE09 Project.

G. Add a new C++ source file to the project. Name the source file Ch4AppE09.

H. Enter the appropriate C++ instructions into the source file.

I. Save and then build the solution.

J. Execute the program. Test the program using the data supplied in Step B.

K. When the program is working correctly, close the Output window, then use the File menu to close the solution.

10) A third-grade teacher at Hinsbrook Elementary School would like you to create a program that will help her students learn how to make change. The program should allow the student to enter the amount of money the customer owes and the amount of money the customer paid. The program should calculate and display the amount of change, as well as how many dollars, quarters, dimes, nickels, and pennies to return to the customer. For now, you do not have to worry about the situation where the price is greater than what the customer pays. You can always assume that the customer paid either the exact amount or more than the exact amount.

A. Complete an IPO chart for this problem.

B. Desk-check the algorithm three times, using the following data:

75.34 as the amount due and 80.00 as the amount paid

39.67 as the amount due and 50.00 as the amount paid

45.55 as the amount due and 45.55 as the amount paid

C. Use the IPO chart to code the program.

D. Desk-check the program using the data supplied in Step B.

E. If necessary, start Visual Studio .NET. Create a blank solution named Ch4AppE10 Solution. Save the solution in the Cpp\Chap04 folder.

F. Add an empty C++ Win32 Console Project to the solution. Name the project Ch4AppE10 Project.

G. Add a new C++ source file to the project. Name the source file Ch4AppE10.

H. Enter the appropriate C++ instructions into the source file.

I. Save and then build the solution.

J. Execute the program. Test the program using the data supplied in Step B.

K. When the program is working correctly, close the Output window, then use the File menu to close the solution.

11) As you learned in the Concept lesson, you can initialize a **bool** variable in C++ using either the keyword **false** or the keyword **true**. You also can use an integer—either 0 or 1—to initialize a **bool** variable. Initializing a **bool** variable to the number 0 is the same as initializing it using the keyword **false**. Initializing a **bool** variable to the number 1 is the same as initializing it using the keyword **true**. Although you can use an integer to initialize a **bool** variable, the keywords make your program more self-documenting.

A. If necessary, start Visual Studio .NET. Open the Ch4AppE11 Solution (Ch4AppE11 Solution.sln) file, which is contained in the Cpp\Chap04\Ch4AppE11 Solution folder. The program initializes a **bool** variable named **insured**, then displays its value. Build the solution, then execute the program. What does the program display in the Command Prompt window? Close the Command Prompt window.

B. Change the **bool insured = false;** statement to **bool insured = true;**. Save and then build the solution. Execute the program. What does the program display in the Command Prompt window? Close the Command Prompt window.

C. Change the **bool insured = true;** statement to **bool insured = 0;**. Save and then build the solution. Execute the program. What does the program display in the Command Prompt window? Close the Command Prompt window.

D. Change the **bool insured = 0;** statement to **bool insured = 1;**. Save and then build the solution. Execute the program. What does the program display in the Command Prompt window? Close the Command Prompt window.

E. Close the Output window, then use the File menu to close the solution.

12) In this exercise, you debug a C++ program.

A. If necessary, start Visual Studio .NET. Open the Ch4AppE12 Solution (Ch4AppE12 Solution.sln) file, which is contained in the Cpp\Chap04\Ch4AppE12 Solution folder. The program first initializes the **temp** variable. It then adds 1.5 to the variable before displaying its value.

B. Build the solution. Correct any errors, then save and build the solution again. Execute the program. When the program is working correctly, close the Output window, then use the File menu to close the solution.

13) In this exercise, you debug a C++ program.

A. If necessary, start Visual Studio .NET. Open the Ch4AppE13 Solution (Ch4AppE13 Solution.sln) file, which is contained in the Cpp\Chap04\Ch4AppE13 Solution folder. The program should calculate the average of the three sales amounts entered by the user.

B. Build the solution. Correct any errors, then save and build the solution again. Execute the program. Use the following sales amounts to test the program: 110.55, 203.45, and 100.68. Correct the program so that it produces the proper output.

C. When the program is working correctly, close the Output window, then use the File menu to close the solution.

Please visit the Testing Center at www.course.com/testingcenter for more practice on the topics covered in this chapter.

The Selection Structure

After completing this chapter, you will be able to:

▸ Use the selection structure in a program

▸ Write pseudocode for the selection structure

▸ Create a flowchart for the selection structure

▸ Code the `if` and `if/else` forms of the selection structure

▸ Write code that uses comparison operators and logical operators

▸ Convert the contents of a `char` variable to uppercase or lowercase

▸ Convert the contents of a `string` variable to uppercase or lowercase

Concept Lesson

Using the Selection Structure

The programs you created in the previous four chapters used the sequence programming structure only, where the program instructions are processed, one after another, in the order in which each appears in the program. In many programs, however, the next instruction processed depends on the result of a decision or comparison that the program must make. A payroll program, for example, typically needs to compare the number of hours the employee worked with the number 40 to determine whether the employee should receive overtime pay in addition to regular pay. Based on the result of that comparison the program then selects either an instruction that computes regular pay only or an instruction that computes regular pay plus overtime pay.

You use the **selection structure**, also called the **decision structure**, when you want a program to make a decision or comparison and then select one of two paths, depending on the result of that decision or comparison. Although the idea of using the selection structure in a program is new, the concept of the selection structure is already familiar to you, because you use it each day to make hundreds of decisions. For example, every morning you have to decide whether you are hungry and, if you are, what you are going to eat. Figure 5-1 shows other examples of selection structures you might use today.

Figure 5-1: Selection structures you might use today

	Example 1	Example 2

condition	if (it is raining)
	    wear a rain coat
	    bring an umbrella
		if (you have a test tomorrow)
		    study tonight
		else

condition		watch a movie

tip

As you may remember from Chapter 1, the selection structure is one of the three programming structures. The other two programming structures are sequence, which was covered in the previous chapters, and repetition, which is covered in Chapters 7 and 8.

In the examples shown in Figure 5-1, the portion in parentheses, called the **condition**, specifies the decision you are making and is phrased so that it results in either a true or false answer only. For example, either it's raining (true) or it's not raining (false); either you have a test tomorrow (true) or you don't have a test tomorrow (false).

If the condition is true, you perform a specific set of tasks. If the condition is false, on the other hand, you might or might not need to perform a different set of tasks. For instance, look at the first example shown in Figure 5-1. If it is raining (a true condition), then you will wear a raincoat and bring an umbrella. Notice that you do not have anything in particular to do if it is not raining (a false condition). Compare this with the second example shown in Figure 5-1. If you have a test tomorrow (a true condition), then you will study tonight. If you do not have a test tomorrow (a false condition), however, then you will watch a movie.

Like you, the computer also can evaluate a condition and then select the appropriate tasks to perform based on that evaluation. When using the selection structure in a program, the programmer must be sure to phrase the condition so that it results in either a true or a false answer only. The programmer also must specify the tasks to be performed when the condition is true and, if necessary, the tasks to be performed when the condition is false.

Most programming languages offer three forms of the selection structure: `if`, `if/else`, and `switch` (also called `case`). You learn about the `if` and `if/else` forms of the selection structure in this chapter; the `switch` form is covered in Chapter 6. Begin by learning how to show the `if` and `if/else` selection structures in pseudocode.

Including the Selection Structure in Pseudocode

Figure 5-2 shows examples of the `if` and `if/else` selection structures written in pseudocode.

Figure 5-2: Examples of the `if` and `if/else` selection structures written in pseudocode

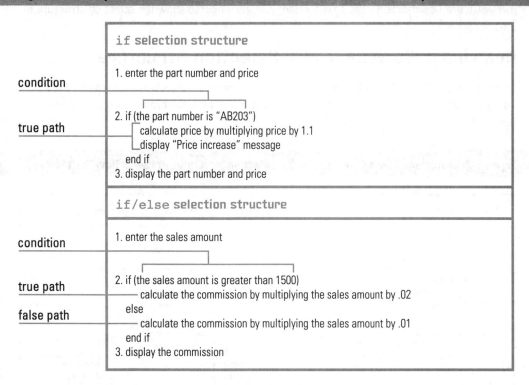

Although pseudocode is not standardized—every programmer has his or her own version— you will find some similarities among the various versions. For example, many programmers begin the selection structure with the word `if` and end the structure with the two words **end if**. They also use the word **else** to designate the instructions to be performed when the condition is false.

In the examples shown in Figure 5-2, the portion within parentheses indicates the condition to be evaluated. Notice that each condition results in either a true or a false answer only. In the first example, either the part number is "AB203" or it isn't. In the second example, either the sales amount is greater than the number 1500 or it isn't.

When the condition is true, the set of instructions following the condition is selected for processing. The instructions following the condition are referred to as the **true path**—the path you follow when the condition is true. The true path ends when you come to the **else** or, if there is no **else**, when you come to the end of the selection structure (the **end if**). After the true path instructions are processed, the instruction following the **end if** is processed. In the examples shown in Figure 5-2, the display instructions are processed after the instructions in the true path.

The instructions processed when the **if** structure's condition is false depend on whether the selection structure contains an **else**. When there is no **else**, as in the first example shown in Figure 5-2, the **if** structure ends when its condition is false, and processing continues with the instruction following the **end if**. In the first example, for instance, the "display the part number and price" instruction is processed when the part number is not "AB203". In cases where the selection structure contains an **else**, as in the second example shown in Figure 5-2, the instructions between the **else** and the **end if**—referred to as the **false path**—are processed before the instruction after the **end if** is processed. In the second example, the "calculate the commission by multiplying the sales amount by .01" instruction is processed first, followed by the "display the commission" instruction.

In addition to using pseudocode to plan algorithms, recall from Chapter 2 that programmers also use flowcharts. In the next section, you learn how to show the selection structure in a flowchart.

Drawing a Flowchart of a Selection Structure

Unlike pseudocode, which consists of short English statements, a flowchart uses standardized symbols to show the steps the computer must take to accomplish the program's goal. Figure 5-3 shows Figure 5-2's examples in flowchart form.

Figure 5-3: Examples of the if **and** if/else **selection structures drawn in flowchart form**

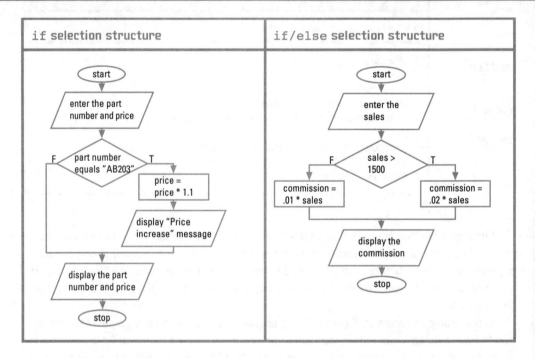

As you learned in Chapter 2, the oval in the figure is the start/stop symbol, the rectangle is the process symbol, and the parallelogram is the input/output symbol. The new symbol in the flowchart, the diamond, is called the **selection/repetition symbol**, because it is used to represent

tip

You also can mark the flowlines leading out of the diamond with a "Y" and an "N" (for yes and no).

both selection and repetition. In Figure 5-3's flowcharts, the diamonds represent the selection structure. (You learn how to use the diamond to represent repetition in Chapter 7.) Notice that inside each diamond is a comparison that evaluates to either true or false only. Each diamond also has one flowline entering the symbol and two flowlines leaving the symbol. The two flowlines leading out of the diamond should be marked so that anyone reading the flowchart can distinguish the true path from the false path. You mark the flowline leading to the true path with a "T" (for true), and you mark the flowline leading to the false path with an "F" (for false).

Next, you learn how to code the `if` and `if/else` forms of the selection structure.

tip

Recall that flowlines are the lines that connect the flowchart symbols.

Coding the Selection Structure

Figure 5-4 shows the syntax of the `if` statement, which is the statement you use to code the `if` and `if/else` forms of the selection structure in C++.

Figure 5-4: Syntax of the C++ `if` statement

if (*condition***)**
 one statement, or a block of statements enclosed in braces, to be processed
 when the condition is true
[else
 one statement, or a block of statements enclosed in braces, to be processed
 when the condition is false]
//end if

The items in square brackets ([]) in the syntax are optional. In other words, you do not always need to include the **else** portion of the syntax, referred to as the **else** clause, in an **if** statement. Items in **bold**, on the other hand, are essential components of the **if** statement. For example, the keyword **if** and the parentheses that surround the *condition* are required. The keyword **else** must be included only if the statement uses that clause.

Items in *italics* in the syntax indicate where the programmer must supply information pertaining to the current program. In an **if** statement, the programmer must supply the *condition* to be evaluated. The *condition* must be a Boolean expression, which is an expression that results in a Boolean value (true or false).

In addition to supplying the *condition*, the programmer also must supply the statements to be processed when the *condition* evaluates to true and, optionally, when the *condition* evaluates to false. If more than one statement needs to be processed, the statements must be entered as a statement block. You create a **statement block** by enclosing the statements in a set of braces ({}).

Although it is not required to do so, it is a good programming practice to use a comment, such as **//end if**, to mark the end of the **if** statement in a program. The comment will make your program easier to read and understand. It also will help you keep track of the required **if** and **else** clauses when you nest **if** statements—in other words, when you include one **if** statement inside another **if** statement. You learn how to nest **if** statements in Chapter 6.

Figure 5-5 shows the different ways of using the C++ **if** statement to code the **if** and **if/else** forms of the selection structure. Notice that, whenever multiple statements are included in a path, the statements are entered as a statement block by enclosing them in braces.

tip

Many C++ programmers include the braces even when only one statement needs to be processed. By doing so, the programmer does not need to remember to enter the braces when statements are added to the selection structure in the future. Forgetting to enter the braces is a common error made by C++ programmers.

Figure 5-5: Different ways of coding the `if` and `if/else` selection structures in C++

`if` form with one statement	`if` form with multiple statements

if (*condition*)
   one statement
//end if
	if (*condition*)
	{
	    multiple statements
	    require braces
	} //end if

`if/else` form with one statement in each path	`if/else` form with multiple statements in true path and one statement in false path	`if/else` form with multiple statements in false path and one statement in true path	`if/else` form with multiple statements in true and false paths

if (*condition*)
   one statement
else
   one statement
//end if
	if (*condition*)
	{
	    multiple statements
	    require braces
	}
	else
	   one statement
	//end if
		if (*condition*)
		   one statement
		else
		{
		    multiple statements
		    require braces
		} //end if
			if (*condition*)
			{
			    multiple statements
			    require braces
			}
			else
			{
			    multiple statements
			    require braces
			} //end if

As mentioned earlier, the *condition* specified in the `if` statement must be a Boolean expression, which is an expression that evaluates to either true or false. The expression can contain variables, constants, functions, arithmetic operators, comparison operators, and logical operators. You already know about variables, constants, functions, and arithmetic operators. You learn about comparison operators and logical operators in the following sections.

Comparison Operators

Figure 5-6 lists the **comparison operators**, also referred to as **relational operators**, that you can use to make comparisons in a C++ program. The figure also shows the order of precedence for these operators. The precedence numbers indicate the order in which the computer performs the comparisons in a C++ expression. Comparisons with a precedence number of 1 are performed before comparisons with a precedence number of 2. However, you can use parentheses to override the order of precedence.

Notice that you use two equal signs (==) to test for equality in C++. You test for inequality by using an exclamation point, which stands for *not*, followed by an equal sign (!=).

It is easy to confuse the equality operator (==), which is used to compare two values, with the assignment operator (=), which is used to assign a value to a memory location. Keep in mind that you use the C++ statement `num = 1;` to assign the number 1 to the **num** variable. However, you use the C++ *condition* `num == 1` to compare the contents of the **num** variable to the number 1.

Figure 5-6: Comparison operators in C++

Operator	Operation	Precedence number
<	less than	1
<=	less than or equal to	1
>	greater than	1
>=	greater than or equal to	1
==	equal to	2
!=	not equal to	2

Important note: Notice that four of the operators contain two symbols. When using these operators, do not include any spaces between the symbols. Also be sure you do not reverse the symbols—in other words, use >=, but don't use =>.

Figure 5-7 shows some examples of using comparison operators in the `if` statement's *condition* in C++.

Figure 5-7: Examples of comparison operators in an `if` statement's *condition*

`if` statement's *condition*	Meaning
`if (quantity < 50)`	Compares the contents of the `quantity` variable to the number 50. The *condition* will evaluate to true if the `quantity` variable contains a number that is less than 50; otherwise, it will evaluate to false.
`if (age >= 25)`	Compares the contents of the `age` variable to the number 25. The *condition* will evaluate to true if the `age` variable contains a number that is greater than or equal to 25; otherwise, it will evaluate to false.
`if (onhand == target)`	Compares the contents of the `onhand` variable to the contents of the `target` variable. The *condition* will evaluate to true if the `onhand` variable contains a number that is equal to the number in the `target` variable; otherwise, it will evaluate to false. (Both variables are `int` variables.)
`if (quantity != 7500)`	Compares the contents of the `quantity` variable to the number 7500. The *condition* will evaluate to true if the `quantity` variable contains a number that is not equal to 7500; otherwise, it will evaluate to false. (The `quantity` variable is an `int` variable.)

Notice that the expression contained in each *condition* evaluates to either true or false. All expressions containing a comparison operator result in an answer of either true or false only.

As with arithmetic operators, if an expression contains more than one comparison operator with the same precedence number, the computer evaluates the comparison operators from left to right in the expression. Keep in mind, however, that comparison operators are evaluated after any arithmetic operators in the expression. In other words, in the expression 5 − 2 > 1 + 2, the

tip

Entering a space between the symbols in a comparison operator (for example, entering > = instead of >=) is a syntax error. Reversing the symbols in a comparison operator (for example, entering => instead of >=) also is a syntax error.

tip

Be careful when comparing two floating-point numbers (numbers with a decimal place). Because some floating-point values cannot be stored, precisely, in memory, you should never compare these values for equality or inequality. Rather, test that the difference between the numbers you are comparing is less than some acceptable small value, such as .00001. You learn how to do determine whether two floating-point numbers are equal in Discovery Exercise 12 at the end of this lesson.

two arithmetic operators (− and +) are evaluated before the comparison operator (>). The result of the expression is false, as shown in Figure 5-8.

Figure 5-8: Evaluation steps for an expression containing arithmetic and comparison operators

Evaluation steps	Result
Original expression 5 − 2 is evaluated first 1 + 2 is evaluated second 3 > 3 is evaluated last	5 − 2 > 1 + 2 3 > 1 + 2 3 > 3 false

In the next two sections, you view the pseudocode, flowchart, and C++ code for two programs that contain comparison operators in an if statement.

Comparison Operator Program 1: Swapping Numeric Values

Assume you want to swap the values contained in two variables, but only if the first value is greater than the second value. Figure 5-9 shows the pseudocode, flowchart, and C++ code for a program that accomplishes this task.

Figure 5-9: Pseudocode, flowchart, and C++ code showing the if form of the selection structure

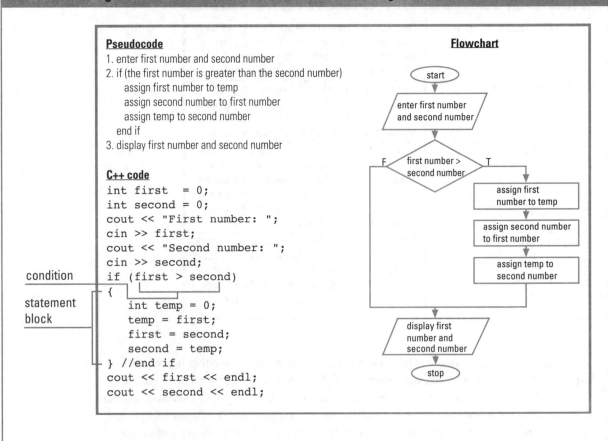

The (`first > second`) *condition* in the C++ code shown in Figure 5-9 tells the computer to compare the contents of the `first` variable to the contents of the `second` variable. If the *condition* is true, which means that the value in the `first` variable is greater than the value in the `second` variable, then the four instructions in the `if` statement's true path swap the values contained in those variables. Notice that the four instructions are enclosed in braces, forming a statement block. As you learned earlier, when more than one instruction needs to be processed when the `if` statement's *condition* is true (or false), the C++ syntax requires those instructions to be entered as a statement block.

Study closely the four instructions that swap the two values. The first instruction, `int temp = 0;`, creates and initializes a local variable named `temp`. A **local variable** can be used only within the statement block in which it is declared. In this case, because the `temp` variable is declared in the `if` statement's true path, it is local to that path and can be used only by the instructions within that path.

The second instruction, `temp = first;`, assigns the value contained in the `first` variable to the `temp` variable. In other words, it stores a copy of the `first` variable's contents in the `temp` variable. Next, the `first = second;` instruction assigns the value contained in the `second` variable to the `first` variable. Finally, the `second = temp;` instruction assigns the value contained in the `temp` variable to the `second` variable. The `temp` variable is necessary to store the contents of the `first` variable temporarily so that the swap can be made. If you did not store the `first` variable's value in the `temp` variable, the `second` variable's value would write over the value in the `first` variable, and the value in the `first` variable would be lost. Figure 5-10 illustrates the concept of swapping.

Figure 5-10: Illustration of the swapping concept

	temp	first	second
Values stored in the variables after the `cin` statements are processed	0	8	4
Result of the `temp = first;` statement	8	8	4
Result of the `first = second;` statement	8	4	4
Result of the `second = temp;` statement (completes the swapping process)	8	4	8

values were swapped

Comparison Operator Program 2: Displaying the Sum or Difference

In this program, assume you want to give the user the option of displaying either the sum of two numbers he or she enters, or the difference between the two numbers. Figure 5-11 shows the pseudocode, flowchart, and C++ code for a program that accomplishes this task.

Figure 5-11: Pseudocode, flowchart, and C++ code showing the if/else form of the selection structure

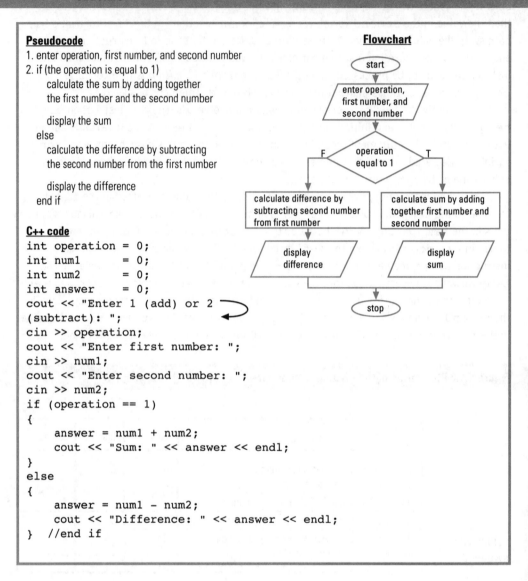

Pseudocode
1. enter operation, first number, and second number
2. if (the operation is equal to 1)
        calculate the sum by adding together
        the first number and the second number

        display the sum
    else
        calculate the difference by subtracting
        the second number from the first number

        display the difference
    end if

C++ code
```cpp
int operation = 0;
int num1      = 0;
int num2      = 0;
int answer    = 0;
cout << "Enter 1 (add) or 2
(subtract): ";
cin >> operation;
cout << "Enter first number: ";
cin >> num1;
cout << "Enter second number: ";
cin >> num2;
if (operation == 1)
{
    answer = num1 + num2;
    cout << "Sum: " << answer << endl;
}
else
{
    answer = num1 - num2;
    cout << "Difference: " << answer << endl;
}   //end if
```

The (`operation == 1`) *condition* in the C++ code shown in Figure 5-11 tells the computer to compare the contents of the `operation` variable to the number 1. If the *condition* is true, then the selection structure calculates and displays the sum of the two numbers entered by the user. If the *condition* is false, however, the selection structure calculates and displays the difference between the two numbers. Here again, because more than one instruction appears in both the true and false paths of the `if` statement, the instructions in each path are entered as a statement block.

MINI-QUIZ

Mini-Quiz 1

1) Assume that a program needs to determine whether a student's score is less than 70. If it is, the program should display the "Fail" message; otherwise, it should display the "Pass" message. Write the pseudocode for this selection structure.

2) Write a C++ `if` statement that corresponds to the pseudocode you wrote in Question 1. The student's score is stored in an `int` variable named **score**.

3) Which of the following C++ `if` clauses determines whether the **quantity** variable, which is of data type `int`, contains the number 100?
   a. `if (quantity = 100)`
   b. `if (quantity = 100);`
   c. `if (quantity == 100)`
   d. `if (quantity == 100);`

4) Which of the following C++ statements assigns the number 5 to a variable named **area**?
   a. `area = 5`
   b. `area = 5;`
   c. `area == 5`
   d. `area == 5;`

5) Write a C++ `if` clause that determines whether an `int` variable named **area** has the value 5 stored in it.

Recall that you also can use logical operators to form the `if` statement's *condition*. You learn about logical operators next.

Logical Operators

The most commonly used **logical operators**, sometimes referred to as **Boolean operators**, are And and Or. Both of these operators allow you to combine two or more *conditions* into one compound *condition*. When the **And logical operator** is used to create a compound condition, all of the conditions must be true for the compound condition to be true. However, when the **Or logical operator** is used, only one of the conditions must be true for the compound condition to be true.

C++ uses special symbols to represent the And and Or logical operators in a program. The And operator in C++ is two ampersands (`&&`), and the Or operator is two pipe symbols (`||`). The pipe symbol (|) usually is located on the same key as the backslash (\) on the computer keyboard.

The tables shown in Figure 5-12, called **truth tables**, summarize how the computer evaluates the logical operators in an expression.

tip

You learn about another logical operator, Not (!), in a later chapter.

Figure 5-12: Truth tables for the And and Or logical operators

Truth table for the && (And) operator

Value of *condition1*	Value of *condition2*	Value of *condition1 && condition2*
true	true	true
true	false	false
false	true	false
false	false	false

Truth table for the || (Or) operator

Value of *condition1*	Value of *condition2*	Value of *condition1 || condition2*
true	true	true
true	false	true
false	true	true
false	false	false

As Figure 5-12 indicates, when you use the And (`&&`) operator to combine two conditions (*condition1* `&&` *condition2*), the resulting compound condition is true only when both conditions are true. If either condition is false, or if both conditions are false, then the compound condition is false. Compare the And operator with the Or operator. When you combine conditions using the Or (`||`) operator, as in *condition1* `||` *condition2*, notice that the compound condition is false only when both conditions are false. If either condition is true, or if both conditions are true, then the compound condition is true.

If you use the `&&` (And) operator to combine two conditions in a C++ expression, the computer does not evaluate the second condition if the first condition is false. Because both conditions combined with the `&&` operator must be true for the compound condition to be true, there is no need to evaluate the second condition when the first condition is false. If, on the other hand, you use the `||` (Or) operator to combine two conditions in a C++ expression, the computer does not evaluate the second condition if the first condition is true. Because only one of the conditions combined with the `||` operator must be true for the compound condition to be true, there is no need to evaluate the second condition when the first condition is true. The concept of evaluating *condition2* based on the result of *condition1* is referred to as **short-circuit evaluation**.

In the next section, you use the truth tables to determine which logical operator is appropriate for the `if` statement's *condition*.

Using the Truth Tables

Assume that you want to pay a bonus to your A-rated salespeople—those whose monthly sales total more than $10,000. To receive a bonus, the salesperson must be rated A and he or she must sell more than $10,000 in product. Assuming the program uses a `char` variable named `rate` and an `int` variable named `sales`, you can phrase *condition1* as `rate == 'A'`, and you can phrase *condition2* as `sales > 10000`. Now the question is, should you use the And operator or the Or operator to combine both conditions into one compound condition? You can use the truth tables shown in Figure 5-12 to answer this question.

For a salesperson to receive a bonus, remember that both *condition1* (`rate == 'A'`) and *condition2* (`sales > 10000`) must be true at the same time. If either condition is false, or if both conditions are false, then the compound condition is false, and the salesperson should not receive a bonus. According to the truth tables, both the And and the Or operators evaluate the compound condition as true when both conditions are true. Only the And operator, however, evaluates the compound condition as false when either one or both of the conditions are false. The Or operator, you will notice, evaluates the compound condition as false only when *both* conditions are false. Therefore, the correct compound condition to use here is `(rate == 'A' && sales > 10000)`.

Now assume that you want to send a letter to all A-rated salespeople and all B-rated salespeople. Assuming the program uses a `char` variable named `rate`, you can phrase *condition1* as `rate == 'A'`, and you can phrase *condition2* as `rate == 'B'`. Now which operator do you use—And or Or?

At first it might appear that the And operator is the correct one to use, because the example says to send the letter to "all A-rated salespeople and all B-rated salespeople". In everyday conversations, people sometimes use the word *and* when what they really mean is *or*. Although both words do not mean the same thing, using *and* instead of *or* generally does not cause a problem because we are able to infer what another person means. Computers, however, cannot infer anything; they simply process the directions you give them, word for word. In this case, you actually want to send a letter to all salespeople with either an A or a B rating, so you need to use the Or operator to combine both conditions. As the truth tables indicate, the Or operator is the only operator that evaluates the compound condition as true if at least one of the conditions is true. The correct compound condition to use here is `(rate == 'A' || rate == 'B')`.

Like expressions containing comparison operators, expressions containing logical operators always result in an answer of either true or false. If an expression contains both an And and an Or logical operator, the And operator is evaluated first, and then the Or operator is evaluated. Figure 5-13 shows the order of precedence for the arithmetic, comparison, and logical operators you have learned so far.

Figure 5-13: Order of precedence for arithmetic, comparison, and logical operators in a C++ expression

Operator	Operation	Precedence number
()	Overrides all other normal precedence rules	1
−	Performs negation	2
*, /, %	Performs multiplication, division, and modulus arithmetic	3
+, −	Performs addition and subtraction	4
<, <=, >, >=	Less than, less than or equal to, greater than, greater than or equal to	5
==, !=	Equal to, not equal to	6
&& (And)	All conditions connected by the And operator must be true for the compound condition to be true	7
|| (Or)	Only one of the conditions connected by the Or operator needs to be true for the compound condition to be true	8

Notice that the And and Or logical operators are evaluated after any arithmetic operators or comparison operators in an expression. In other words, in the expression 12 > 0 && 12 < 10 * 2, the arithmetic operator (*) is evaluated first, followed by the two comparison operators (> and <), followed by the And logical operator (&&). The expression evaluates to true, as shown in Figure 5-14.

Figure 5-14: Evaluation steps for an expression containing arithmetic, comparison, and logical operators

Evaluation steps	Result
Original expression	12 > 0 && 12 < 10 * 2
10 * 2 is evaluated first	12 > 0 && 12 < 20
12 > 0 is evaluated second	true && 12 < 20
12 < 20 is evaluated third	true && true
true && true is evaluated last	true

MINI-QUIZ

Mini-Quiz 2

1) Using the truth tables shown in Figure 5-12, evaluate the following compound condition: (true || false).

2) Using the truth tables shown in Figure 5-12, evaluate the following compound condition: (7 > 3 && 5 < 2).

3) Using the truth tables shown in Figure 5-12, evaluate the following compound condition: (5 * 4 < 20 || false).

Next, you view the C++ code for a program that contains a logical operator in an if statement.

Logical Operator Program: Calculating Gross Pay

Assume you want to create a program that calculates and displays an employee's gross pay. To keep this example simple, assume that no one at the company works more than 40 hours per week, and everyone earns the same hourly rate, $10.65. Before making the gross pay calculation, the program should verify that the number of hours entered by the user is greater than or equal to 0, but less than or equal to 40. Programmers refer to the process of verifying that the input data is within the expected range as **data validation**. In this case, if the number of hours is valid, the program should calculate and display the gross pay; otherwise, it should display an error message alerting the user that the input data is incorrect. Figure 5-15 shows two ways of writing the C++ code for this program. Notice that the if statement in the first example uses the And (&&) logical operator, whereas the if statement in the second example uses the Or (||) logical operator.

Figure 5-15: C++ code showing the And and Or logical operators in the `if` statement's *condition*

Example 1: using the && (And) operator

```
double hours = 0.0;
double gross = 0.0;
cout << "Enter hours worked: ";
cin >> hours;
if (hours >= 0 && hours <= 40)
{
    gross = hours * 10.65;
    cout << gross << endl;
}
else
    cout << "Input error";
//end if
```

Example 2: using the || (Or) operator

```
double hours = 0.0;
double gross = 0.0;
cout << "Enter hours worked: ";
cin >> hours;
if (hours < 0 || hours > 40)
    cout << "Input error";
else
{
    gross = hours * 10.65;
    cout << gross << endl;
}   //end if
```

The (`hours >= 0 && hours <= 40`) *condition* in Example 1 shown in Figure 5-15 tells the computer to determine whether the value stored in the `hours` variable is greater than or equal to the number 0 and, at the same time, less than or equal to the number 40. If the *condition* is true, then the selection structure calculates and displays the gross pay; otherwise, it displays an error message.

The (`hours < 0 || hours > 40`) *condition* in Example 2 shown in Figure 5-15 tells the computer to determine whether the value stored in the `hours` variable is less than the number 0 or greater than the number 40. If the *condition* is true, then the selection structure displays an error message; otherwise, it calculates and displays the gross pay. Both `if` statements shown in Figure 5-15 produce the same results and simply represent two different ways of performing the same task.

In all of the programs shown so far in this lesson, the `if` statement's *condition* compared numeric values. You also can use the `if` statement's *condition* to perform character and string comparisons. First you learn how to compare characters.

Comparing Characters

Assume you want a program to display the word "Pass" if the user enters the letter P, and the word "Fail" if the user enters anything else. Figure 5-16 shows four ways of writing the C++ code for this program.

tip

As you learned in Chapter 4, character literal constants (for example, the letter 'P') are enclosed in single quotation marks, and string literal constants (for example, the word "Pass") are enclosed in double quotation marks.

Figure 5-16: C++ code showing character comparisons in the `if` statement's *condition*

Example 1: using the | | (Or) operator

```cpp
char letter = ' ';
cout << "Enter a letter: ";
cin >> letter;
if (letter == 'P' || letter == 'p')
    cout << "Pass" << endl;
else
    cout << "Fail" << endl;
//end if
```

Example 2: using the && (And) operator

```cpp
char letter = ' ';
cout << "Enter a letter: ";
cin >> letter;
if (letter != 'P' && letter != 'p')
    cout << "Fail" << endl;
else
    cout << "Pass" << endl;
//end if
```

Example 3: correct, but less efficient, solution

```cpp
char letter = ' ';
cout << "Enter a letter: ";
cin >> letter;
if (letter == 'P' || letter == 'p')
    cout << "Pass" << endl;
//end if
if (letter != 'P' && letter != 'p')
    cout << "Fail" << endl;
//end if
```

Example 4: using the `toupper()` function

```cpp
char letter = ' ';
cout << "Enter a letter: ";
cin >> letter;
letter = toupper(letter);
if (letter == 'P')
    cout << "Pass" << endl;
else
    cout << "Fail" << endl;
//end if
```

The first statement in each example shown in Figure 5-16 creates and initializes a char variable named letter. The second statement prompts the user to enter a letter, and the third statement assigns the user's response to the letter variable. The (letter == 'P' || letter == 'p') *condition* in Example 1 tells the computer to determine whether the value stored in the letter variable is either the uppercase letter P or the lower-case letter p. If the *condition* is true, which means that the variable contains one of those

tip

You learned about the ASCII codes in Chapter 3's Concept lesson. The full ASCII chart is shown in Appendix A.

two letters, then the selection structure displays the word "Pass" on the screen; otherwise, it displays the word "Fail". You may be wondering why you need to tell the computer to compare the contents of the `letter` variable to both the uppercase and lowercase version of the letter P. As is true in many programming languages, character comparisons in C++ are case sensitive. That means that the uppercase version of a letter is not the same as its lowercase counterpart. So, although a human recognizes P and p as being the same letter, a computer does not; to a computer, a P is different from a p. The reason for this differentiation is that each character on the computer keyboard is stored differently in the computer's internal memory. The uppercase letter P, for example, is stored using the eight bits 01010000 (ASCII code 80), whereas the lowercase letter p is stored using the eight bits 01110000 (ASCII code 112).

The `(letter != 'P' && letter != 'p')` *condition* in Example 2 shown in Figure 5-16 tells the computer to determine whether the value stored in the `letter` variable is *not* equal to either the uppercase letter P or the lowercase letter p. If the *condition* is true, which means that the variable does not contain either of those two letters, then the selection structure displays the word "Fail" on the screen; otherwise, it displays the word "Pass".

Rather than using one `if` statement with an `else` clause, as in Examples 1 and 2, Example 3 in Figure 5-16 uses two `if` statements with no `else` clause in either one. Although the `if` statements in Example 3 produce the same results as the `if` statement in Examples 1 and 2, they do so less efficiently. To illustrate this point, assume that the user enters the letter P in response to the "Enter a letter: " prompt. The *condition* in the first `if` statement shown in Example 3 determines whether the value stored in the `letter` variable is equal to either P or p. In this case, the *condition* evaluates to true, because the `letter` variable contains the letter P. As a result, the first `if` statement's true path displays the word "Pass" on the screen, and then the first `if` statement ends. Although the appropriate word ("Pass") already appears on the screen, the program instructs the computer to evaluate the second `if` statement's *condition* to determine whether to display the "Fail" message. The second evaluation is unnecessary and makes Example 3's code less efficient than the code shown in Examples 1 and 2.

The `if` statement shown in Example 4 in Figure 5-16 also contains a character comparison in its *condition*, but notice that the *condition* does not use a logical operator; rather, it uses the `toupper()` function.

Converting a Character to Uppercase or Lowercase

C++ provides two functions, `toupper()` and `tolower()`, that you can use to convert a character to uppercase or lowercase, respectively. The syntax of the `toupper()` function is **toupper(***charVariable***)**, and the syntax of the `tolower()` function is **tolower(***charVariable***)**. In each syntax, *charVariable* is the name of a `char` variable. Both functions copy the character stored in the *charVariable* to a temporary location in memory; they then convert the character to the appropriate case and return the result. For example, when processing the `letter = toupper(letter);` assignment statement shown in Example 4 in Figure 5-16, the `toupper()` function copies the character stored in the `letter` variable to a temporary memory location. It then converts the letter to uppercase and returns the result to the assignment statement, which assigns the result to the `letter` variable. Assuming the user enters the character p in response to the "Enter a letter:" prompt, the `letter` variable contains the character P after the assignment statement is processed. In this case, the assignment statement ensures that the letter stored in the `letter` variable is uppercase before the `if` statement's *condition* is evaluated. The `if` statement's *condition*, `(letter == 'P')`, compares the contents of the `letter` variable (which is always uppercase) to the uppercase letter P. If the `letter` variable contains the uppercase letter P, the `if` statement's true path displays the word "Pass"; otherwise, its false path displays the word "Fail".

You also can use the assignment statement `letter = tolower(letter);` in Example 4 in Figure 5-16. However, then you must change the `if` statement's *condition* to `(letter == 'p')`, because the character in the `letter` variable will always be lowercase.

tip

The toupper()
and tolower()
functions affect
only characters
that represent let-
ters of the alpha-
bet, as these are
the only characters
that have upper-
case and lowercase
forms.

tip

If the letter stored
in the *charVariable*
argument in the
toupper() and
tolower() func-
tions is already the
appropriate case,
the function simply
returns the letter.

tip

Do not include
a set of paren-
theses after the
function name in the
transform()
function's *function*
argument. Doing
so—for example,
entering toupper()
rather than
toupper—will
produce a syntax
error when the pro-
gram is compiled.

In addition to performing numeric and character comparisons in an `if` statement's *condition*, you also can perform string comparisons.

Comparing Strings

As are character comparisons, string comparisons are case-sensitive, which means that the string "Yes" is not the same as the string "YES" or the string "yes". A problem occurs when you need to include a string, entered by the user, in a comparison, because you cannot control the case in which the user enters the string. Before using a string in a comparison, you should convert it to either uppercase or lowercase, and then use the converted string in the comparison.

Converting a String to Uppercase or Lowercase

In C++ you can use the **transform() function** to convert a string to either uppercase or lowercase. Figure 5-17 shows the syntax of the `transform()` function and includes two examples of using the function in a C++ statement. The `transform()` function is defined in the algorithm file, so you must include the `#include <algorithm>` directive in any program that uses the `transform()` function.

Figure 5-17: Syntax and examples of the `transform()` **function**

Syntax
`transform(string.begin(), string.end(), string.begin(), function);`

Examples

Example 1
```
string name = "";
cout << "Enter your name: ";
getline(cin, name);
transform(name.begin(), name.end(), name.begin(), tolower);
if (name == "mary")
    cout << "Your name is Mary" << endl;
else
    cout << "Your name is not Mary" << endl;
//end if
```

Example 2
```
string item1 = "";
string item2 = "";
cout << "Enter item 1: ";
getline(cin, item1);
cout << "Enter item 2: ";
getline(cin, item2);
transform(item1.begin(), item1.end(), item1.begin(), toupper);
transform(item2.begin(), item2.end(), item2.begin(), toupper);
if (item1 == item2)
{
    instructions processed when the condition is true
}   //end if
```

In the syntax, *string* is the name of a **string** variable that contains the string you want converted, or transformed, to either uppercase or lowercase. The first two arguments in the **transform()** function specify the range of characters to transform in the *string*. To transform the entire contents of a **string** variable, you use *string*.**begin()** as the first argument, and *string*.**end()** as the second argument. *String*.**begin()** refers to the first character in the *string,* and *string*.**end()** refers to the location that is just past the end of the string in the computer's internal memory. For example, if a **string** variable named **state** contains the string "Iowa", then **state.begin()** refers to the letter *I*, and **state.end()** refers to the memory location following the letter *a*, as illustrated in Figure 5-18.

Figure 5-18: Illustration of state.begin() **and** state.end()

memory locations

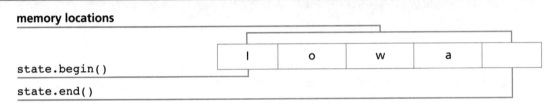

state.begin()

state.end()

The **transform()** function converts (transforms) each of the characters contained in the range specified in the function's first two arguments—beginning with the character whose location is specified in the first argument [in this case, *string*.**begin()**] and continuing up to, but not including, the character whose location is specified in the second argument [in this case, *string*.**end()**]. The function stores the results of the conversion beginning in the location specified in the function's third argument, replacing the characters currently stored at that location. For example, the third argument shown in the syntax, *string*.**begin()**, tells the function to store the transformed string in the *string* variable, beginning with the first character in the variable.

The last argument in the **transform()** function's syntax is the name of a function, and it indicates the task to be performed on the string contained in the *string* variable. To transform the string to uppercase, you use **toupper** as the *function* argument. To transform the *string* to lowercase, you use **tolower** as the *function* argument.

Study the two examples shown in Figure 5-17. The code in Example 1 prompts the user to enter a name, which the computer stores in the **name** variable. As with **char** data, there is no way to control the case in which the user enters **string** data. In this case, the user might enter the name using all uppercase letters, all lowercase letters, or a combination of uppercase and lowercase letters. To solve this problem, the **transform(name.begin(), name.end(), name.begin(), tolower);** statement converts the contents of the **name** variable to lowercase. The **if** statement's *condition*, (**name == "mary"**), then compares the contents of the **name** variable (which is lowercase) with the lowercase string "mary".

The code shown in Example 2 in Figure 5-17 prompts the user to enter two items, storing the user's responses in the **item1** and **item2** variables. The code then uses the **transform()** function to convert the contents of both variables to uppercase before using the variables in the **if** statement's *condition*. Notice that the *condition* compares the **item1** variable, whose contents are uppercase, with the **item2** variable, whose contents also are uppercase.

MINI-QUIZ

Mini-Quiz 3

1) Write a compound condition for a C++ `if` statement that determines whether the value in the `age` variable is between 30 and 40, including 30 and 40.

2) Write a compound condition for a C++ `if` statement that determines whether the `age` variable contains a value that is either less than 30 or greater than 50.

3) Write a condition for an `if` statement that determines whether the `char` variable named `key` contains the letter R (in any case).

4) Write a C++ statement that converts the contents of a `string` variable named `department` to uppercase.

5) Write a condition for an `if` statement that determines whether the `department` variable in Question 4 contains the word *Accounting*.

You now have completed Chapter 5's Concept lesson. You can either take a break or complete the end-of-lesson questions and exercises before moving on to the Application lesson.

SUMMARY

The selection structure, also called the decision structure, is one of the three programming structures; the other two programming structures are sequence and repetition. You use the selection structure when you want a program to make a decision or comparison and then select one of two paths—either the true path or the false path—based on the result of that decision or comparison. Most programming languages offer three forms of the selection structure: `if`, `if/else`, and `switch` (also referred to as `case`).

A diamond, called the selection/repetition symbol, is used in a flowchart to represent the selection structure. The diamond contains a question that has a true or false answer only. Each selection diamond has one flowline entering the symbol and two flowlines leaving the symbol. The two flowlines leading out of the diamond should be marked so it is clear to the reader which path is the true path and which is the false path.

You can use the C++ `if` statement to code both the `if` and `if/else` forms of the selection structure. If either the `if` statement's true path or false path contains more than one statement, you must enclose the statements in a set of braces (`{}`). Statements enclosed in braces are referred to as a statement block. It is a good programming practice to include an `//end if` comment to identify the end of the `if` statement in a program.

The *condition* in an `if` statement can contain variables, constants, functions, arithmetic operators, comparison operators, and logical operators. The comparison operators in C++ are `<`, `<=`, `>`, `>=`, `==`, and `!=`. If more than one comparison operator with the same precedence number appears in a C++ expression, the computer evaluates those operators from left to right in the expression. The logical operators—And and Or—are signified in C++ by the symbols `&&` and `||`, respectively. The And operator is evaluated first, then the Or operator is evaluated. All expressions containing either a relational or logical operator result in an answer of either true or false only. Arithmetic operators are evaluated before any comparison operators, which are evaluated before any logical operators.

As is true in many programming languages, character and string comparisons in C++ are case sensitive. The C++ language provides the `toupper()` and `tolower()` functions for converting characters to uppercase and lowercase, respectively. The C++ language provides the `transform()` function for converting a string to uppercase or lowercase.

ANSWERS TO MINI-QUIZZES

Mini-Quiz 1

1)
```
if (score < 70)
      display "Fail"
else
      display "Pass"
end if
```

2)
```
if (score < 70)
      cout << "Fail" << endl;
 else
      cout << "Pass" << endl;
 //end if
```

3) c. if (quantity == 100)

4) b. area = 5;

5) if (area == 5)

Mini-Quiz 2

1) true

2) false

3) false

Mini-Quiz 3

1) (age >= 30 && age <= 40)

2) (age < 30 || age > 50)

3) (toupper(key) == 'R') [or (tolower(key) == 'r')]

4) transform(department.begin(), department.end(), department.begin(), toupper);

5) (department == "ACCOUNTING")

QUESTIONS

1) Which of the following symbols is used in a flowchart to represent the selection structure?

A. diamond

B. oval

C. parallelogram

D. rectangle

2) Which of the following is the equality operator in C++?

A. !=

B. =

C. ==

D. ->

3) Which of the following is the inequality operator in C++?

A. !=

B. ==

C. ->

D. <>

4) Assume you want to determine whether the **item** variable contains either the word *Chair* or the word *Desk*. Which of the following *conditions* should you use in the **if** statement? You can assume that the **item** variable's contents are uppercase.

A. (item == "CHAIR" || item == "DESK")

B. (item = "CHAIR" || item == "DESK")

C. (item = "CHAIR" && item = "DESK")

D. (item == "CHAIR" && item == "DESK")

5) Which of the following **if** statement *conditions* compares the character stored in the **initial** variable to the letter *A* entered in either uppercase or lowercase?

A. (initial = 'a' or 'A')

B. (initial == 'a' or 'A')

C. (initial == 'A' && initial == 'a')

D. (initial == 'A' || initial == 'a')

6) The expression 3 > 6 && 7 > 4 evaluates to _____.

A. true

B. false

7) The expression 4 > 6 || 10 < 2 * 6 evaluates to _____.

A. true

B. false

8) The expression 7 >= 3 + 4 || 6 < 4 && 2 < 5 evaluates to

_____.

A. true

B. false

9) The expression 4 * 3 < (6 + 7) && 7 < 6 + 9 evaluates to
_____.

   A. true

   B. false

10) Assuming the expression does not contain parentheses, which of the following operators is performed first in the expression?

   A. arithmetic

   B. comparison

   C. logical

11) Which of the following statements converts the contents of a `string` variable named `emp` to uppercase?

   A. `transform(emp.begin(), emp.end(), emp.begin(),`
      `toupper);`

   B. `transform(emp.begin, emp.end, emp.begin, toupper);`

   C. `transform(emp.begin(), emp.end(), emp.begin(),`
      `upper);`

   D. `transform(emp.begin(), emp.end(), emp.begin(),`
      `toupper());`

12) Which of the following statements converts the contents of a `char` variable named `initial` to uppercase?

   A. `initial == toupper(initial);`

   B. `initial = toupper(initial);`

   C. `toupper(initial);`

   D. `transform(initial, toupper);`

EXERCISES

1) Write the C++ `if` statement that compares the contents of the `quantity` variable to the number 10. If the `quantity` variable contains a number that is greater than 10, display the string "Over 10"; otherwise, display the string "Not over 10".

2) Write the C++ statements that correspond to the flowchart shown in Figure 5-19.

Look For These
Symbols

Debugging

Discovery

Figure 5-19

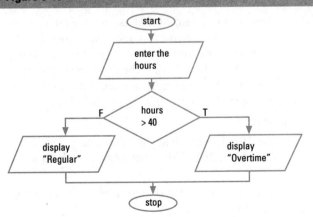

3) In this exercise, you complete a program by writing an **if** statement.

A. If necessary, start Visual Studio .NET. Open the Ch5ConE03 Solution (Ch5ConE03 Solution.sln) file, which is contained in the Cpp\Chap05\ Ch5ConE03 Solution folder.

B. Complete the program by writing an **if** statement that displays the string "Firebird" when the user enters the letter *F* (in any case).

C. Save and then build the solution.

D. Execute the program three times, using the following letters: *F*, *f*, and *x*.

E. When the program is working correctly, close the Output window, then use the File menu to close the solution.

4) In this exercise, you complete a program by writing an **if** statement.

A. If necessary, start Visual Studio .NET. Open the Ch5ConE04 Solution (Ch5ConE04 Solution.sln) file, which is contained in the Cpp\Chap05\ Ch5ConE04 Solution folder.

B. Complete the program by writing an **if** statement that displays the string "Entry error" when the user enters a number that is less than 0 otherwise, display the string "Valid number".

C. Save and then build the solution.

D. Execute the program three times, using the following numbers: 5, 0, and -3.

E. When the program is working correctly, close the Output window, then use the File menu to close the solution.

5) In this exercise, you complete a program by writing an **if** statement.

A. If necessary, start Visual Studio .NET. Open the Ch5ConE05 Solution (Ch5ConE05 Solution.sln) file, which is contained in the Cpp\Chap05\ Ch5ConE05 Solution folder.

B. Complete the program by writing an **if** statement that displays the string "Reorder" when the user enters a number that is less than 10; otherwise, display the string "OK".

C. Save and then build the solution.

D. Execute the program three times, using the following numbers: 5, 10, and 19.

E. When the program is working correctly, close the Output window, then use the File menu to close the solution.

6) In this exercise, you complete a program by writing an **if** statement.

A. If necessary, start Visual Studio .NET. Open the Ch5ConE06 Solution (Ch5ConE06 Solution.sln) file, which is contained in the Cpp\Chap05\ Ch5ConE06 Solution folder.

B. Complete the program by writing an **if** statement that assigns the number 10 to the **bonus** variable when the user enters a sales amount that is less than or equal to $250. When the user enters a sales amount that is greater than $250, prompt the user to enter the bonus rate, then multiply the user's response by the sales amount and assign the result to the **bonus** variable. After assigning the appropriate bonus amount, display the bonus amount on the screen.

C. Save and then build the solution.

D. Execute the program three times. First, use 240 as the sales amount. Second, use 250 as the sales amount. Third, use 251 as the sales amount and .05 as the bonus rate.

E. When the program is working correctly, close the Output window, then use the File menu to close the solution.

7) In this exercise, you complete a program by writing an **if** statement.

   A. If necessary, start Visual Studio .NET. Open the Ch5ConE07 Solution (Ch5ConE07 Solution.sln) file, which is contained in the Cpp\Chap05\ Ch5ConE07 Solution folder.

   B. Assume that employees working more than 40 hours receive overtime pay (time and one-half) for the hours over 40. Complete the program by writing an **if** statement that calculates the overtime pay (if any) and the gross pay. Display the overtime pay (if any) and the gross pay.

   C. Save and then build the solution.

   D. Execute the program two times. First, use 40 as the number of hours worked and 7 as the pay rate. The program should display $0 as the overtime pay and $280 as the gross pay. Second, use 42 as the number of hours worked and 10 as the pay rate. The program should display $30 as the overtime pay and $430 as the gross pay.

   E. When the program is working correctly, close the Output window, then use the File menu to close the solution.

8) In this exercise, you complete a program by writing an **if** statement.

   A. If necessary, start Visual Studio .NET. Open the Ch5ConE08 Solution (Ch5ConE08 Solution.sln) file, which is contained in the Cpp\Chap05\ Ch5ConE08 Solution folder.

   B. The program should prompt the user to enter an animal ID, then store the user's response in a **char** variable named **animal**. The program should display the string "Dog" when the **animal** variable contains the letter *D* (in any case); otherwise, it should display the string "Cat". Complete the program appropriately.

   C. Save and then build the solution.

   D. Execute the program three times, using the letters *D*, *d*, and *h*.

   E. When the program is working correctly, close the Output window, then use the File menu to close the solution.

9) In this exercise, you complete a program by writing an **if** statement.

   A. If necessary, start Visual Studio .NET. Open the Ch5ConE09 Solution (Ch5ConE09 Solution.sln) file, which is contained in the Cpp\Chap05\ Ch5ConE09 Solution folder.

   B. Complete the program by writing an **if** statement that displays the string "Valid entry" when the user enters either the integer 1, the integer 2, or the integer 3; otherwise, display the string "Entry error".

   C. Save and then build the solution.

   D. Execute the program four times, using the integers 1, 2, 3, and 4.

   E. When the program is working correctly, close the Output window, then use the File menu to close the solution.

10) In this exercise, you complete a program by writing an **if** statement.

    A. If necessary, start Visual Studio .NET. Open the Ch5ConE10 Solution (Ch5ConE10 Solution.sln) file, which is contained in the Cpp\Chap05\ Ch5ConE10 Solution folder.

    B. Complete the program by writing an **if** statement that swaps the two numbers entered by the user, but only if the first number is less than the second number.

    C. Save and then build the solution.

    D. Execute the program two times. First, use the numbers 5 and 3. The program should display "5, 3". Second, use the numbers 3 and 80. The program should display "80, 3".

    E. When the program is working correctly, close the Output window, then use the File menu to close the solution.

11) In this exercise, you complete a program by writing an **if** statement.

    A. If necessary, start Visual Studio .NET. Open the Ch5ConE11 Solution (Ch5ConE11 Solution.sln) file, which is contained in the Cpp\Chap05\ Ch5ConE11 Solution folder.

    B. Complete the program by writing an **if** statement that assigns the appropriate price. The price is based on the item number entered by the user. If the item number is AB123, then the price is $5. All other items are $10.

    C. Save and then build the solution.

    D. Execute the program three times. First, use item number AB123. The program should display $5. Second, use item number ab123. The program should display $5. Third, use item number XX345. The program should display $10.

    E. When the program is working correctly, close the Output window, then use the File menu to close the solution.

 12) Recall that you must be careful when comparing two floating-point values (values with a decimal place) for either equality or inequality. This is because some floating-point values cannot be stored, precisely, in memory. To determine whether two floating-point values are either equal or unequal, you should test that the difference between the values you are comparing is less than some acceptable small value, such as .00001.

    A. If necessary, start Visual Studio .NET. Open the Ch5ConE12 Solution (Ch5ConE12 Solution.sln) file, which is contained in the Cpp\Chap05\ Ch5ConE12 Solution folder.

    B. Study the program's code. Notice that the code divides the contents of the **num1** variable (10.0) by the contents of the **num2** variable (3.0), then stores the result (approximately 3.33333) in the **quotient** variable. An **if** statement is used to compare the contents of the **quotient** variable to the number 3.33333. The **if** statement then displays an appropriate message, indicating whether the numbers are equal.

C. Build the solution, then execute the program. Although the Command Prompt window indicates that the quotient is 3.33333, the `if` statement displays the message "No, the quotient 3.33333 is not equal to 3.33333." Close the Command Prompt window.

The proper procedure for comparing two floating-point values is first to find the difference between the values, then to compare the absolute value of that difference to a small number, such as .00001. You can use the C++ `fabs()` function to find the absolute value of a floating-point number. The absolute value of a number is a positive number that represents how far the number is from 0 on the number line. For example, the absolute value of the number 5 is 5; the absolute value of the number –5 also is 5.

To use the `fabs()` function, the program must contain the `#include <cmath>` directive.

D. Modify the program appropriately.

E. Save and then build the solution.

F. Execute the program. The `if` statement displays the message "Yes, the quotient 3.33333 is equal to 3.33333." Close the Command Prompt window.

G. When the program is working correctly, close the Output window, then use the File menu to close the solution.

13) In this exercise, you debug a C++ program.

A. If necessary, start Visual Studio .NET. Open the Ch5ConE13 Solution (Ch5ConE13 Solution.sln) file, which is contained in the Cpp\Chap05\ Ch5ConE13 Solution folder.

B. The program should display a message based on the sales amount entered by the user. Study the program's code, then build the solution.

C. Correct any errors in the program, then save and build the solution.

D. Execute the program twice. First, use 5000 as the sales amount. Second, use 20000 as the sales amount.

E. When the program is working correctly, close the Output window, then use the File menu to close the solution.

14) In this exercise, you debug a C++ program.

A. If necessary, start Visual Studio .NET. Open the Ch5ConE14 Solution (Ch5ConE14 Solution.sln) file, which is contained in the Cpp\Chap05\ Ch5ConE14 Solution folder.

B. The program should display a message based on the age entered by the user. Study the program's code, then build the solution. Correct any errors.

C. Save and then build the solution.

D. Execute the program twice. First, use John as the name and 32 as the age. Second, use Mary as the name and 16 as the age.

E. When the program is working correctly, close the Output window, then use the File menu to close the solution.

Application Lesson

Using the Selection Structure in a C++ Program

Lab 5.1 - Stop and Analyze   If necessary, start Visual Studio .NET. Open the Ch5Lab1 Solution (Ch5Lab1 Solution.sln) file contained in the Cpp\Chap05\Ch5Lab1 Solution folder. Figure 5-20 shows the code entered in the Ch5Lab1.cpp file. (The line numbers are included in the figure only.) Study the code, then answer the questions.

Figure 5-20: C++ instructions entered in the Ch5Lab1.cpp file

```
1   //Ch5Lab1.cpp - calculates and displays a commission
2   //Created/revised by <your name> on <current date>
3
4   #include <iostream>
5   #include <string>
6   #include <algorithm>
7
8   using std::cout;
9   using std::cin;
10  using std::endl;
11  using std::string;
12
13  int main()
14  {
15      //declare variables
16      string state      = "";
17      double sales      = 0.0;
18      double commission = 0.0;
19
20      //get input items
21      cout << "Enter the state name: ";
22      getline(cin, state);
23      cout << "Enter the sales amount: ";
24      cin >> sales;
25
26      //convert state to uppercase
27      transform(state.begin(), state.end(), state.begin(), toupper);
28
29      //calculate commission
30      if (state == "NEW YORK" || state == "NEW JERSEY")
31          commission = .03 * sales;
32      else
33          commission = .035 * sales;
34      //end if
35
36      //display commission
37      cout << "The commission is $" << commission << endl;
38
39      return 0;
40  }   //end of main function
```

Questions

1. What exactly does the Ch5Lab1.cpp program do? In other words, what does it input, process, and output?

2. Which salespeople receive a 3% commission? Which salespeople receive a 3.5% commission?

3. Build the solution, then execute the program. What is the commission for a New York salesperson selling $2,000 in product? Close the Command Prompt window.

4. Execute the program again. What is the commission for an Illinois salesperson selling $2,000 in product? Close the Command Prompt window.

5. Why is the instruction on Line 6 necessary?

6. What is the purpose of the statement shown on Line 27?

7. Modify the program so that it converts the state name to lowercase rather than uppercase.

8. Save and then build the solution. Execute the program. What is the commission for a New Jersey salesperson selling $800 in product? Close the Command Prompt window. Close the Output window, then use the File menu to close the solution.

Lab 5.2 Marshall Cabello is the manager of Willow Springs Health Club. Every other month, Marshall teaches a three-hour seminar titled "Healthy Living." The seminar stresses the importance of daily exercise (at least 20 minutes per day) and eating a low-fat diet (no more than 30 percent of the calories consumed should come from fat). Each time Marshall teaches the seminar, many of the participants ask him how to determine whether a specific food item is considered low-fat. Marshall has asked you to create a program that allows him to enter the number of calories and grams of fat contained in a specific food. The program then should calculate and display two values: the food's fat calories (the number of calories attributed to fat) and its fat percentage (the ratio of the food's fat calories to its total calories).

You can calculate the number of fat calories in a food by multiplying the number of fat grams contained in the food by the number 9, because each gram of fat contains 9 calories. To calculate the fat percentage, which is the percentage of a food's total calories derived from fat, you divide the food's fat calories by its total calories, then multiply the result by 100. You will use both of these calculations in the health club's algorithm.

Figure 5-21 shows the IPO chart and C++ instructions for the health club problem. Notice that the program uses four variables. Variables were chosen for the total calories, grams of fat, fat calories, and fat percentage items because the values of those items will change each time the program is executed.

Figure 5-21: IPO chart and C++ instructions for the Willow Springs Health Club problem

IPO chart information	C++ instructions

Input
total calories
grams of fat
Processing
 	
Output
fat calories
fat percentage
 	
Algorithm
1. enter the total calories
and grams of fat
	`int totalCal = 0;`
	`int fatGrams = 0;`
	
	`int fatCal = 0;`
	`double fatPercent = 0.0;`
	
	`cout << "Enter the total calories: ";`
	`cin >> totalCal;`
	`cout << "Enter the grams of fat: ";`
	`cin >> fatGrams;`

2. if (the total calories are greater
than or equal to zero and the
grams of fat are greater than or
equal to zero)
  calculate fat calories by
  multiplying grams of fat by 9
 	
  calculate fat percentage by
  dividing fat calories by
  total calories, then
  multiplying the result by 100
 	
  display fat calories and
  fat percentage
 	
else
  display error message
end if
	`if (totalCal >= 0 && fatGrams >= 0)`
	`{`
	
	  `fatCal = fatGrams * 9;`
	
	  `fatPercent = double(fatCal) /`
	  `double(totalCal) * 100.0;`
	
	  `cout << "Fat calories: " << fatCal <<`
	  `endl;`
	  `cout << "Fat percentage: " <<`
	  `fatPercent << endl;`
	
	`}`
	`else`
	  `cout << "Input error" << endl;`
	`//end if`

As Figure 5-21 indicates, the program's output is the fat calories and fat percentage, and its input is the total calories and grams of fat. First, the program gets the two input values from the user; it then validates both values. If both input values are greater than or equal to zero, the program calculates the fat calories and fat percentage, then displays both calculated values on the screen. However, if both input values are not greater than or equal to zero, the program displays an error message on the screen.

Activity for Lab 5.2

In this activity, you enter the C++ instructions shown in Figure 5-21 into the computer. You then test the program to verify that it is working correctly.

To create the Willow Springs Health Club program, then test the program:

1. If necessary, start Visual Studio .NET. Create a blank solution named Ch5Lab2 Solution. Save the solution in the Cpp\Chap05 folder.

2. Add an empty C++ Win32 Console Project to the solution. Name the project Ch5Lab2 Project.

3. Add a new C++ source file to the project. Name the source file Ch5Lab2.

4. Type **//Ch5Lab2.cpp - calculates and displays a food's fat calories and fat percentage** and press **Enter**.

5. Type **//Created/revised by *<your name>* on *<current date>*,** replacing *<your name>* and *<current date>* with your name and the current date, respectively. Press **Enter** twice.

6. Type **#include <iostream>** and press **Enter** twice.

7. Type the following three `using` statements, then press **Enter** twice.

    using std::cout;

    using std::cin;

    using std::endl;

8. Complete the program by entering the `main()` function, which is shown in Figure 5-22.

Figure 5-22: Willow Springs Health Club program

enter the
main()
function
instructions

```cpp
//Ch5Lab2.cpp - calculates and displays a food's fat
calories and fat percentage
//Created/revised by <your name> on <current date>

#include <iostream>

using std::cout;
using std::cin;
using std::endl;

int main()
{
    int totalCal      = 0;
    int fatGrams      = 0;
    int fatCal        = 0;
    double fatPercent = 0.0;

    //enter input data
    cout << "Enter the total calories: ";
    cin >> totalCal;
    cout << "Enter the grams of fat: ";
    cin >> fatGrams;

    //validate input data
    if (totalCal >= 0 && fatGrams >= 0)
    {
        //valid data - calculate fat calories and fat
        percentage
        fatCal = fatGrams * 9;
        fatPercent = double(fatCal) / double(totalCal)
        * 100.0;
        cout << "Fat calories: " << fatCal << endl;
        cout << "Fat percentage: " << fatPercent << endl;
    }
    else
        //invalid data - display error message
        cout << "Input error" << endl;
    //end if

    return 0;
}   //end of main function
```

9. Save and then build the solution. If necessary, correct any syntax errors, then save and build the solution again.

10. Execute the program by clicking **Debug** on the menu bar, then clicking **Start Without Debugging**. Use the program to calculate the fat calories and fat percentage for a food that contains 150 total calories and 6 grams of fat. The fat calories should be 54, and the fat percentage should be 36. Close the Command Prompt window.

11. Execute the program again. What are the fat calories and fat percentage for a food that contains 105 total calories and 2 grams of fat? Close the Command Prompt window.

12. Execute the program again. Use 100 for the total calories and –3 for the grams of fat. The program should display the message "Input Error". Close the Command Prompt window.

13. Execute the program again. Use −7 for the total calories and 20 for the grams of fat. What does the program display? Close the Command Prompt window.

14. Execute the program again. Use −6 for the total calories and −6 for the grams of fat. What does the program display? Close the Command Prompt window.

15. Close the Output window, then use the File menu to close the solution.

Lab 5.3 In this lab, you modify the `if` statement in the program you created in Lab 5.2. In the modified statement, the true path handles the invalid data, and the false path handles the valid data.

Activity for Lab 5.3

Before modifying the program created in Lab 5.2, you copy the instructions contained in the Ch5Lab2.cpp file to a new solution.

To copy the instructions contained in the Ch5Lab2.cpp file to a new solution:

1. If necessary, start Visual Studio .NET. Create a blank solution named **Ch5Lab3 Solution**. Save the solution in the Cpp\Chap05 folder.

2. Add an empty C++ Win32 Console Project to the solution. Name the project **Ch5Lab3 Project**.

3. Add a new C++ source file to the project. Name the source file **Ch5Lab3**.

4. Click **File** on the menu bar, point to **Open**, and then click **File**. The Open File dialog box opens.

5. Open the Cpp\Chap05\Ch5Lab2 Solution\Ch5Lab2 Project folder. Click **Ch5Lab2.cpp** in the list of filenames, then click the **Open** button to open the Ch5Lab2.cpp file.

6. Click **Edit** on the menu bar, then click **Select All** to select all of the instructions in the Ch5Lab2.cpp window.

7. Click **Edit**, then click **Copy** to copy the selected instructions to the clipboard.

8. Close the Ch5Lab2.cpp window by clicking the **Close** button on its title bar.

9. Click the **Ch5Lab3.cpp** tab. Click **Edit**, then click **Paste** to paste the Ch5Lab2.cpp instructions in the Ch5Lab3.cpp window.

10. Change the filename in the first program comment to **Ch5Lab3.cpp**. If necessary, change the date in the second comment.

Currently, the instructions in the `if` statement's true path are processed when the data is valid, and the instructions in the false path are processed when the data is not valid. Your task is to modify the program so that the true path instructions are processed when the data is invalid, and the false path instructions are processed when the data is valid.

To modify the program, then test the program:

1. Make the appropriate modifications to the program.

2. Save and then build the solution. If necessary, correct any syntax errors, then save and build the solution again.

3. Execute the program. Test the program using your own sample data, then close the Command Prompt window.

4. When the program is working correctly, close the Output window, then use the File menu to close the solution.

You now have completed Chapter 5's Application lesson. You can either take a break or complete the end-of-lesson exercises.

ANSWERS TO LABS

Lab 5.1

1. The program allows the user to enter a state name and a sales amount. It then calculates and displays a commission amount.

2. Salespeople in both New York and New Jersey receive a 3% commission. Salespeople in all other states receive a 3.5% commission.

3. A New York salesperson selling $2,000 in product earns a $60 commission.

4. An Illinois salesperson selling $2,000 in product earns a $70 commission.

5. The `#include <algorithm>` instruction on Line 6 is necessary because the program uses the `transform()` function.

6. The statement on Line 27 uses the `transform()` function to convert the contents of the `state` variable to uppercase before using the variable in the `if` statement's *condition* on Line 30.

7. See Figure 5-23. Modifications are shaded in the figure.

Figure 5-23

```cpp
1   //Ch5Lab1.cpp - calculates and displays a commission
2   //Created/revised by <your name> on <current date>
3
4   #include <iostream>
5   #include <string>
6   #include <algorithm>
7
8   using std::cout;
9   using std::cin;
10  using std::endl;
11  using std::string;
12
13  int main()
14  {
15      //declare variables
16      string state      = "";
17      double sales      = 0.0;
18      double commission = 0.0;
19
20      //get input items
21      cout << "Enter the state name: ";
22      getline(cin, state);
23      cout << "Enter the sales amount: ";
24      cin >> sales;
25
26      //convert state to lowercase
27      transform(state.begin(), state.end(), state.begin(), tolower);
28
29      //calculate commission
30      if (state == "new york" || state == "new jersey")
31          commission = .03 * sales;
32      else
33          commission = .035 * sales;
34      //end if
35
36      //display commission
37      cout << "The commission is $" << commission << endl;
38
39      return 0;
40  }   //end of main function
```

8. A New Jersey salesperson selling $800 in product earns a $24 commission.

Lab 5.2

Step 11: The program displays 18 as the fat calories and 17.1429 as the fat percentage.

Steps 12, 13, and 14: The program displays the "Input error" message.

Lab 5.3

See Figure 5-24. Modifications are shaded in the figure.

Figure 5-24

```cpp
//Ch5Lab3.cpp - calculates and displays a food's fat
calories and fat percentage
//Created/revised by <your name> on <current date>

#include <iostream>

using std::cout;
using std::cin;
using std::endl;

int main()
{
    int totalCal     = 0;
    int fatGrams     = 0;
    int fatCal       = 0;
    double fatPercent = 0.0;

     //enter input data
     cout << "Enter the total calories: ";
     cin >> totalCal;
     cout << "Enter the grams of fat: ";
     cin >> fatGrams;

     //validate input data
     if (totalCal < 0 || fatGrams < 0)
         //invalid data - display error message
         cout << "Input error" << endl;
     else
     {
         //valid data - calculate fat calories and fat
         percentage
         fatCal = fatGrams * 9;
         fatPercent = double(fatCal) / double(totalCal)
         * 100.0;
         cout << "Fat calories: " << fatCal << endl;
         cout << "Fat percentage: " << fatPercent << endl;
     }   //end if

    return 0;
}   //end of main function
```

EXERCISES

1) In this exercise, you create a program that displays an employee's name and gross pay.

A. Figure 5-25 shows the partially completed IPO chart for the payroll program. Employees working more than 40 hours should be paid time and one-half for the hours worked over 40. Complete the IPO chart.

Figure 5-25

Input	Processing	Output
name hours worked pay rate	Processing items: none Algorithm:	name gross pay

B. If necessary, start Visual Studio .NET. Open the Ch5AppE01 Solution (Ch5AppE01 Solution.sln) file, which is contained in the Cpp\Chap05\ Ch5AppE01 Solution folder.

C. Use the IPO chart you completed in Step A to complete the program.

D. Complete a desk-check table for the program. First, use Jack Henderson as the name, 35 as the hours worked, and 10 as the hourly pay rate. Then, use Mary Matiez as the name, 45 as the hours worked, and 7.50 as the hourly pay rate.

E. Save and then build the solution.

F. Execute the program. Use the data from Step D to test the program.

G. When the program is working correctly, close the Output window, then use the File menu to close the solution.

2) In this exercise, you create a program that displays a bonus amount.

A. Figure 5-26 shows the partially completed IPO chart for the bonus program. The program should calculate and display a bonus amount. The bonus rate is 10% on the first $12,000 of sales, and 15% on sales more than $12,000. (For example, a salesperson selling $15,000 in product should receive a bonus in the amount of $1,650.) Complete the IPO chart.

Figure 5-26

Input	Processing	Output
sales	Processing items: none Algorithm:	bonus

B. If necessary, start Visual Studio .NET. Open the Ch5AppE02 Solution (Ch5AppE02 Solution.sln) file, which is contained in the Cpp\Chap05\ Ch5AppE02 Solution folder.

C. Use the IPO chart you completed in Step A to complete the program.

D. Complete a desk-check table for the program, using the following sale amounts: 5000 and 96000.

E. Save and then build the solution.

F. Execute the program. Use the data from Step D to test the program.

G. When the program is working correctly, close the Output window, then use the File menu to close the solution.

3) In this exercise, you modify the program shown in Figure 4-22 in Chapter 4's Application lesson. The modified program will verify that both the number of CDs purchased and the purchase price are greater than 0.

A. If necessary, start Visual Studio .NET. Open the Ch5AppE03 Solution (Ch5AppE03 Solution.sln) file, which is contained in the Cpp\Chap05\ Ch5AppE03 Solution folder.

B. Modify the program appropriately.

C. Save and then build the solution.

D. Execute the program. Test the program using your own sample data.

E. When the program is working correctly, close the Output window, then use the File menu to close the solution.

4) In this exercise, you create a program that displays the average of three test scores entered by the user.

A. Complete an IPO chart for the average program. Be sure to validate the input data. To be valid, each test score must be greater than or equal to 0. If one or more test scores are not valid, the program should display an appropriate message.

B. Complete a desk-check table for the algorithm, using the following two groups of test scores:

95.5, 76, and 59

45, −78, and 30 (notice the minus sign before the number 78)

C. If necessary, start Visual Studio .NET. Create a blank solution named Ch5AppE04 Solution. Save the solution in the Cpp\Chap05 folder.

D. Add an empty C++ Win32 Console Project to the solution. Name the project Ch5AppE04 Project.

E. Add a new C++ source file to the project. Name the source file Ch5AppE04.

F. Enter the appropriate C++ instructions into the source file.

G. Save and then build the solution.

H. Execute the program. Test the program using the data supplied in Step B.

I. When the program is working correctly, close the Output window, then use the File menu to close the solution.

5) In this exercise, you create a program that displays the total amount a company owes for a seminar. The seminar charge is $80 per person.

A. Complete an IPO chart for the seminar program. The input is the number of seminar registrants, which should be greater than 0, but less than 50. Display an appropriate error message when the number of registrants is invalid.

B. Complete a desk-check table for the algorithm, using the following data: 5 and −20.

C. If necessary, start Visual Studio .NET. Create a blank solution named Ch5AppE05 Solution. Save the solution in the Cpp\Chap05 folder.

D. Add an empty C++ Win32 Console Project to the solution. Name the project Ch5AppE05 Project.

E. Add a new C++ source file to the project. Name the source file Ch5AppE05.

F. Enter the appropriate C++ instructions into the source file.

G. Save and then build the solution.

H. Execute the program. Test the program using the data supplied in Step B.

I. When the program is working correctly, close the Output window, then use the File menu to close the solution.

6) In this exercise, you create a program that displays a shipping charge.

A. Complete an IPO chart for the shipping charge program. The shipping charge is based on the state name entered by the user, as shown in the following table:

State	Shipping charge ($)
Hawaii	30
Oregon	30

If the user enters any other state name, the program should display the message "Incorrect state".

B. Complete a desk-check table for the algorithm, using the following data: Hawaii, Kentucky, and Oregon.

C. If necessary, start Visual Studio .NET. Create a blank solution named Ch5AppE06 Solution. Save the solution in the Cpp\Chap05 folder.

D. Add an empty C++ Win32 Console Project to the solution. Name the project Ch5AppE06 Project.

E. Add a new C++ source file to the project. Name the source file Ch5AppE06.

F. Enter the appropriate C++ instructions into the source file.

G. Save and then build the solution.

H. Execute the program. Test the program using the data supplied in Step B.

I. When the program is working correctly, close the Output window, then use the File menu to close the solution.

7) In this exercise, you complete a program that displays the result of dividing two numbers.

A. If necessary, start Visual Studio .NET. Open the Ch5AppE07 Solution (Ch5AppE07 Solution.sln) file, which is contained in the Cpp\Chap05\ Ch5AppE07 Solution folder. The program should display a quotient.

B. Study the existing code. Notice that the code to calculate the quotient is missing from the program. Complete the program by entering the appropriate code. Be sure to always divide the larger number by the smaller number.

C. Save and then build the solution.

D. Execute the program twice. First, use the numbers 40 and 10. Second, use the numbers 9 and 81.

E. When the program is working correctly, close the Output window, then use the File menu to close the solution.

8) In this exercise, you create a program that displays a shipping charge.

A. Complete an IPO chart for the shipping charge program. The shipping charge is based on the state name entered by the user, as shown in the following table:

State	Shipping charge ($)
Alabama	25
Alaska	50

If the user enters any other state name, the shipping charge should be 0 (zero).

(*Hint*: You can nest an `if` statement, which means you can place one `if` statement inside another `if` statement.)

B. If necessary, start Visual Studio .NET. Open the Ch5AppE08 Solution (Ch5AppE08 Solution.sln) file, which is contained in the Cpp\Chap05\ Ch5AppE08 Solution folder.

C. Use the IPO chart you completed in Step A to complete the program.

D. Complete a desk-check table for the program, using the following state names: Alabama, Alaska, and Illinois.

E. Save and then build the solution.

F. Execute the program. Use the data from Step D to test the program.

G. When the program is working correctly, close the Output window, then use the File menu to close the solution.

9) In this exercise, you debug a C++ program.

A. If necessary, start Visual Studio .NET. Open the Ch5AppE09 Solution (Ch5AppE09 Solution.sln) file, which is contained in the Cpp\Chap05\ Ch5AppE09 Solution folder.

B. The program should display a message when the sales amount is greater than or equal to zero, but it is not working correctly. Study the program's code, then build the solution.

C. Execute the program. Test the program by entering 21500 as the sales amount. Close the Command Prompt window.

D. Correct any errors in the program, then save and build the solution.

E. Execute the program. Test the program by entering 21500 as the sales amount. Close the Command Prompt window.

F. When the program is working correctly, close the Output window, then use the File menu to close the solution.

Please visit the Testing Center at www.course.com/testingcenter for more practice on the topics covered in this chapter.

More on the Selection Structure

After completing this chapter, you will be able to:

- Include a nested selection structure in pseudocode and in a flowchart

- Code a nested selection structure in C++

- Recognize common logic errors in selection structures

- Include the `switch` form of the selection structure in pseudocode and in a flowchart

- Code the `switch` form of the selection structure in C++

- Format numeric output in C++

Concept Lesson

Nested Selection Structures

As you learned in Chapter 5, you use the selection structure when you want a program to make a decision and then select one of two paths—either the true path or the false path—based on the result of that decision. Both paths in a selection structure can include instructions that declare and initialize variables, perform calculations, and so on; both also can include other selection structures. When either a selection structure's true path or its false path contains another selection structure, the inner selection structure is referred to as a **nested selection structure**, because it is contained (nested) within the outer selection structure.

You use a nested selection structure when more than one decision must be made before the appropriate action can be taken. For example, assume you want to create a voter eligibility program that displays one of three messages. The messages and the criteria for displaying each message are shown here:

Message	Criteria
"You are too young to vote."	person is younger than 18 years old
"You can vote."	person is at least 18 years old and is registered to vote
"You need to register before you can vote."	person is at least 18 years old but is not registered to vote

As the chart indicates, the person's age and voter registration status determine the appropriate message to display. If the person is younger than 18 years old, the program should display the message "You are too young to vote." However, if the person is at least 18 years old, the program should display one of two different messages. The correct message to display is determined by the person's voter registration status. If the person is registered, then the appropriate message is "You can vote."; otherwise, it is "You need to register before you can vote." Notice that determining the person's voter registration status is important only *after* his or her age is determined. You can think of the decision regarding the age as being the **primary decision**, and the decision regarding the registration status as being the **secondary decision**, because whether the registration decision needs to be made depends on the result of the age decision. The primary decision is always made by the outer selection structure, while the secondary decision is always made by the inner (nested) selection structure.

Figure 6-1 shows the pseudocode and C++ code for the voter eligibility program, and Figure 6-2 shows the corresponding flowchart. In both figures, the outer selection structure determines the age (the primary decision), and the nested selection structure determines the voter registration status (the secondary decision). Notice that the nested selection structure appears in the outer selection structure's true path in both figures.

Figure 6-1: Pseudocode and C++ code showing the nested selection structure in the true path

<u>**Pseudocode**</u>
1. enter the age
2. if (the age is greater than or equal to 18)
           enter the registration status
           if (the registration status is Y)
                 display "You can vote."
           else
                 display "You need to register before you can vote."
           end if
    else
           display "You are too young to vote."
    end if

<u>**C++ code**</u>
```cpp
cout << "Enter your age: ";
cin >> age;
if (age >= 18)
{
    cout << "Are you registered to vote? (Y/N): ";
    cin >> status;
    status = toupper(status);
    if (status == 'Y')
        cout << "You can vote." << endl;
    else
        cout << "You need to register before you can vote." << endl;
    //end if
}
else
    cout << "You are too young to vote." << endl;
//end if
```

Note: The lines connecting the `if`, `else`, and `end if` in the pseudocode and code are included in the figure to help you see which clauses are related to each other.

Figure 6-2: Flowchart showing the nested selection structure in the true path

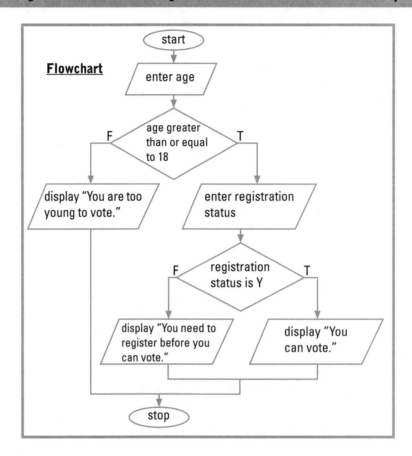

As both figures indicate, the program first gets the age from the user. The condition in the outer selection structure then checks whether the age is greater than or equal to 18. If the condition is false, it means that the person is not old enough to vote. In that case, only one message—the "You are too young to vote." message—is appropriate. After the message is displayed, both the outer selection structure and the program end.

If the outer selection structure's condition is true, on the other hand, it means that the person *is* old enough to vote. Before displaying the appropriate message, the instructions in the outer selection structure's true path first get the registration status from the user. A nested selection structure then is used to determine whether the person is registered. If he or she is registered, the instruction in the nested selection structure's true path displays the "You can vote." message. Otherwise, the instruction in the nested selection structure's false path displays the "You need to register before you can vote." message. After the appropriate message is displayed, both selection structures and the program end. Notice that the nested selection structure in this program is processed only when the outer selection structure's condition is true.

Figures 6-3 and 6-4 show the pseudocode, C++ code, and flowchart for a different version of the voter eligibility program. As in the previous version, the outer selection structure in this version determines the age (the primary decision), and the nested selection structure determines the voter registration status (the secondary decision). In this version of the program, however, the nested selection structure appears in the false path of the outer selection structure.

Figure 6-3: Pseudocode and C++ code showing the nested selection structure in the false path

<u>**Pseudocode**</u>

1. enter the age
2. if (the age is less than 18)
       display "You are too young to vote."
   else
       enter the registration status
       if (the registration status is Y)
           display "You can vote."
       else
           display "You need to register before you can vote."
       end if
   end if

<u>**C++ code**</u>

```cpp
cout << "Enter your age: ";
cin >> age;
if (age < 18)
    cout << "You are too young to vote." << endl;
else
{
    cout << "Are you registered to vote? (Y/N): ";
    cin >> status;
    if (status == 'Y')
        cout << "You can vote." << endl;
    else
        cout << "You need to register before you can vote." << endl;
    //end if
} //end if
```

Note: The lines connecting the `if`, `else`, and `end if` in the pseudocode and code are included in the figure to help you see which clauses are related to each other.

Figure 6-4: Flowchart showing the nested selection structure in the false path

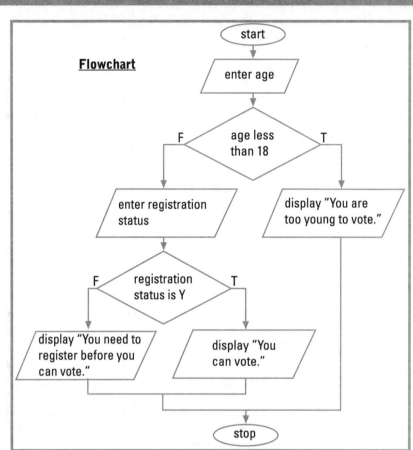

Like the version shown earlier, this version of the voter eligibility program first gets the age from the user. However, rather than checking whether the age is greater than or equal to 18, the outer selection structure in this version checks whether the age is less than 18. If the condition is true, the instruction in the outer selection structure's true path displays the "You are too young to vote." message. If the condition is false, the instructions in the outer selection structure's false path first get the registration status from the user, then use a nested selection structure to determine whether the person is registered. If the person is registered, the instruction in the nested selection structure's true path displays the "You can vote." message. Otherwise, the instruction in the nested selection structure's false path displays the "You need to register before you can vote." message. Unlike in the previous version, the nested selection structure in this version of the program is processed only when the outer selection structure's condition is false.

Notice that both versions of the voter eligibility program produce the same results. Neither version is better than the other; each simply represents a different way of solving the same problem.

Next, view another example of a nested selection structure.

Another Example of a Nested Selection Structure

In Lab 5.2 in Chapter 5's Application lesson, you created a program for Marshall Cabello, the manager of Willow Springs Health Club. As you may remember, the program allows Marshall to enter the number of calories and grams of fat contained in a specific food. The program then calculates and displays two values: the food's fat calories and its fat percentage.

Now suppose that Marshall wants you to modify the program so that it displays the message "This food is high in fat." when a food's fat percentage is greater than 30%; otherwise, the program should display the message "This food is not high in fat." The modified health club program, which uses a nested selection structure, is shown in Figure 6-5.

Figure 6-5: Modified health club program containing a nested selection structure

```cpp
//Modified Ch6Lab2.cpp
//Calculates and displays a food's fat calories and fat percentage
//Created/revised by <your name> on <current date>

#include <iostream>

using std::cout;
using std::cin;
using std::endl;

int main()
{
    int totalCal      = 0;
    int fatGrams      = 0;
    int fatCal        = 0;
    double fatPercent = 0.0;

    //enter input data
    cout << "Enter the total calories: ";
    cin >> totalCal;
    cout << "Enter the grams of fat: ";
    cin >> fatGrams;

    //validate input data
    if (totalCal >= 0 && fatGrams >= 0)
    {
        //valid data - calculate fat calories and fat percentage
        fatCal = fatGrams * 9;
        fatPercent = double(fatCal) / double(totalCal) * 100.0;
        cout << "Fat calories: " << fatCal << endl;
        cout << "Fat percentage: " << fatPercent << endl;
        if (fatPercent > 30.0)
            cout << "This food is high in fat." << endl;
        else
            cout << "This food is not high in fat." << endl;
        //end if
    }
    else
        //invalid data - display error message
        cout << "Input error" << endl;
    //end if

    return 0;
}   //end of main function
```

nested
selection
structure

outer
selection
structure

In this case, the outer selection structure's condition, which represents the primary decision, determines whether the user's input (total calories and grams of fat) is valid. If the condition is false, the instruction in the outer selection structure's false path displays an error message on the screen. However, if the condition is true, the instructions in the outer selection structure's true path both calculate and display the fat calories and fat percentage, then use a nested selection structure to determine whether the secondary decision—which checks whether the fat percentage is greater than 30.0—is true or false. If the fat percentage is greater than 30.0, the nested selection structure's true path displays the message "This food is high in fat." Otherwise, the nested selection structure's false path displays the message "This food is not high in fat." As in the voter eligibility program, the result of the primary decision in the health club program determines whether the secondary decision needs to be made.

MINI-QUIZ

Mini-Quiz 1

1) Assume you want to create a program that displays the message "Highest honors" when a student's test score is 90 or above. When the test score is 70 through 89, the program should display the message "Good job". For all other test scores, the program should display the message "Retake the test". Write the pseudocode for this program's selection structure.

2) Write the C++ code that corresponds to the pseudocode you wrote in Question 1. The student's score is stored in an `int` variable named `score`.

3) Assume that the manager of a golf course has asked you to create a program that displays the appropriate fee to charge a golfer. The club uses the following fee schedule:

Fee	Criteria
0	Club members
15	Non-members golfing on Monday through Thursday
25	Non-members golfing on Friday through Sunday

In this program, which is the primary decision and which is the secondary decision? Why?

In the next section, you learn some of the common logic errors made when writing selection structures. Being aware of these errors will help to prevent you from making them.

Logic Errors in Selection Structures

Typically, logic errors commonly made when writing selection structures are a result of one of the following mistakes:

1. Using a logical operator rather than a nested selection structure
2. Reversing the primary and secondary decisions
3. Using an unnecessary nested selection structure

The XYZ Company's vacation program can be used to demonstrate each of these logic errors. Assume that the company employs both full-time and part-time employees. Only full-time employees receive a paid vacation, as shown here:

Vacation weeks	Criteria
0	Part-time employees
2	Full-time employees working at the company for 5 years or fewer
3	Full-time employees working at the company for more than 5 years

Your task is to create a program that allows the user to enter the employee's status—either F for full-time or P for part-time—and the number of years the employee has worked for the company. If the employee is full-time, the program should display the number of vacation weeks the employee has earned, then the program should end. If the employee is not full-time, the program should simply end without displaying anything.

As the vacation chart indicates, the employee's status—either full-time or part-time—is a factor in determining whether the employee receives any paid vacation. If the employee is entitled to a paid vacation, then the number of years he or she has worked for the company determines the appropriate number of vacation weeks. In this case, the decision regarding the employee's status is the primary decision, and the decision regarding the years employed is the secondary decision, because whether the years employed decision needs to be made depends on the result of the status decision.

Figure 6-6 shows a correct algorithm for the vacation program.

Figure 6-6: A correct algorithm for the vacation program

Correct algorithm for the vacation program

```
1. enter the status and years
2. if (the status is F)
      if (the years are greater than 5)
            display "3-week vacation"
      else
            display "2-week vacation"
      end if
end if
```

tip
You also can write the condition in the nested selection structure shown in Figure 6-6 as follows: *if (the years are less than or equal to 5)*. The nested structure's true path then would contain the instruction *display "2-week vacation"*, and its false path would contain the instruction *display "3-week vacation"*.

To observe why the algorithm shown in Figure 6-6 is correct, you will desk-check it using the following test data:

Data for first desk-check
Status: F
Years: 4

Data for second desk-check
Status: F
Years: 15

Data for third desk-check
Status: P
Years: 11

The algorithm should display "2-week vacation" for the first set of test data, "3-week vacation" for the second set, and nothing for the third set.

Using the first set of test data, the user enters F as the status and 4 as the years. The outer selection structure's condition determines whether the status is F; it is, so the nested selection structure's condition checks whether the years are greater than 5. The years are not greater than 5, so the nested selection structure's false path displays the message "2-week vacation," which is correct. After doing so, both selection structures and the program end.

Using the second set of test data, the user enters F as the status and 15 as the years. The outer selection structure's condition determines whether the status is F; it is, so the nested selection structure's condition checks whether the years are greater than 5. The years are greater than 5, so the nested selection structure's true path displays the message "3-week vacation", which is correct. After doing so, both selection structures and the program end.

Using the third set of test data, the user enters P as the status and 11 as the years. The outer selection structure's condition determines whether the status is F. The status is not F, so the outer selection structure and the program end. Notice that the nested selection structure is not processed when the outer selection structure's condition is false. Figure 6-7 shows the results of desk-checking the correct algorithm shown in Figure 6-6.

Figure 6-7: Results of desk-checking the correct algorithm shown in Figure 6-6

Desk-check	Result
First: using F as the status and 4 as the years Second: using F as the status and 15 as the years Third: using P as the status and 11 as the years	"2-week vacation" displayed "3-week vacation" displayed Nothing is displayed

In the next section, you view and desk-check another algorithm for the vacation program. You will find that the algorithm does not produce the desired results because it contains a logical operator instead of a nested selection structure.

Using a Logical Operator Rather Than a Nested Selection Structure

One common error made when writing selection structures is to use a logical operator in the outer selection structure's condition when a nested selection structure is needed. Figure 6-8 shows an example of this error in the vacation algorithm. The correct algorithm is included in the figure for comparison.

Figure 6-8: Correct algorithm and an incorrect algorithm containing the first logic error

logical operator used rather than a nested selection structure

Correct algorithm	Incorrect algorithm

1. enter the status and years
2. if (the status is F)
    if (the years are greater than 5)
        display "3-week vacation"
    else
        display "2-week vacation"
    end if
end if
	1. enter the status and years
	2. if (the status is F and the years are greater than 5)
	    display "3-week vacation"
	else
	    display "2-week vacation"
	end if

Notice that the incorrect algorithm uses one selection structure, rather than two selection structures, and the selection structure's condition contains the logical operator *and*. Consider why the selection structure in the incorrect algorithm cannot be used in place of the selection structures in the correct algorithm. In the correct algorithm, the outer and nested selection structures indicate that a hierarchy exists between the status and years employed decisions: The status decision is always made first, followed by the years employed decision (if necessary). In the incorrect algorithm, on the other hand, the logical operator in the selection structure's condition indicates that no hierarchy exists between the status and years employed decisions; each has equal weight and neither is dependent on the other, which is incorrect. To better understand why this algorithm is incorrect, you will desk-check it using the same test data you used to desk-check the correct algorithm.

After the user enters the first set of test data—F as the status and 4 as the years—the selection structure's condition in the incorrect algorithm determines whether the status is F and, at the same time, the years are greater than 5. Only one of these conditions is true, so the compound condition evaluates to false and the selection structure's false path displays the message "2-week vacation" before both the selection structure and the program end. Even though the algorithm's selection structure is phrased incorrectly, notice that the incorrect algorithm produces the same result as the correct algorithm.

After the user enters the second set of test data—F as the status and 15 as the years—the selection structure's condition in the incorrect algorithm determines whether the status is F and, at the same time, the years are greater than 5. Both conditions are true, so the compound condition is true and the selection structure's true path displays the message "3-week vacation" before both the selection structure and the program end. Here again, using the second set of test data, the incorrect algorithm produces the same result as the correct algorithm.

After the user enters the third set of test data—P as the status and 11 as the years—the selection structure's condition in the incorrect algorithm determines whether the status is F and, at the same time, the years are greater than 5. Only one of these conditions is true, so the compound condition is false and the selection structure's false path displays the message "2-week vacation" before both the selection structure and the program end. Notice that the incorrect algorithm produces erroneous results for the third set of test data; according to Figure 6-7, the algorithm should not have displayed anything using this data. As you learned in Chapter 2, it is important to desk-check an algorithm several times, using different test data. In this case, if you had used only the first two sets of data to desk-check the incorrect algorithm, you would not have discovered the error.

Figure 6-9 shows the results of desk-checking the incorrect algorithm shown in Figure 6-8. As indicated in the figure, the results of the first and second desk-checks are correct, but the result of the third desk-check is not correct.

Figure 6-9: Results of desk-checking the incorrect algorithm shown in Figure 6-8

correct results	**Desk-check**	**Result**
incorrect result	First: using F as the status and 4 as the years Second: using F as the status and 15 as the years Third: using P as the status and 11 as the years	"2-week vacation" displayed "3-week vacation" displayed "2-week vacation" displayed

Next, you view and desk-check another algorithm for the vacation program. You will find that this algorithm also does not produce the desired results; this is because the primary and secondary decisions are reversed in the selection structures.

tip

As you learned in Chapter 5, when you use the logical operator *and* to combine two conditions in a selection structure, both conditions must be true for the compound condition to be true. If at least one of the conditions is false, then the compound condition is false and the instructions in the selection structure's false path (assuming there is a false path) are processed.

Reversing the Primary and Secondary Decisions

Another common error made when writing a selection structure that contains a nested selection structure is to reverse the primary and secondary decisions — in other words, put the secondary decision in the outer selection structure, and put the primary decision in the nested selection structure. Figure 6-10 shows an example of this error in the vacation algorithm. The correct algorithm is included in the figure for comparison.

Figure 6-10: Correct algorithm and an incorrect algorithm containing the second logic error

	Correct algorithm	Incorrect algorithm

primary and secondary decisions reversed	1. enter the status and years
	2. if (the status is F)
	  if (the years are greater than 5)
	    display "3-week vacation"
	
	  else
	    display "2-week vacation"
	  end if
	end if
		1. enter the status and years
		2. if (the years are greater than 5)
		  if (the status is F)
		    display "3-week vacation"
		
		  else
		    display "2-week vacation"
		  end if
		end if

Unlike the selection structures in the correct algorithm, which determine the employment status before determining the number of years employed, the selection structures in the incorrect algorithm determine the number of years employed before determining the employment status. Consider how this difference changes the algorithm. In the correct algorithm, the selection structures indicate that only employees whose status is full-time receive a paid vacation, which is correct. The selection structures in the incorrect algorithm, on the other hand, indicate that all employees who have been with the company for more than 5 years receive a paid vacation, which is not correct. Desk-check the incorrect algorithm to see the results.

After the user enters the first set of test data — F as the status and 4 as the years — the condition in the outer selection structure determines whether the years are greater than 5. The years are not greater than 5, so both the outer selection structure and the program end. Notice that the incorrect algorithm does not display the expected message, "2-week vacation".

After the user enters the second set of test data — F as the status and 15 as the years — the condition in the outer selection structure determines whether the years are greater than 5; they are, so the condition in the nested selection structure determines whether the status is F. The status is F, so the nested selection structure's true path displays the message "3-week vacation", which is correct.

After the user enters the third set of test data — P as the status and 11 as the years — the condition in the outer selection structure determines whether the years are greater than 5; they are, so the condition in the nested selection structure determines whether the status is F. The status is not F, so the nested selection structure's false path displays the message "2-week vacation", which is not correct.

Figure 6-11 shows the results of desk-checking the incorrect algorithm shown in Figure 6-10. As indicated in the figure, only the results of the second desk-check are correct.

Figure 6-11: Results of desk-checking the incorrect algorithm shown in Figure 6-10

	Desk-check	Result
only this result is correct	First: using F as the status and 4 as the years Second: using F as the status and 15 as the years Third: using P as the status and 11 as the years	Nothing is displayed "3-week vacation" displayed "2-week vacation" displayed

Next, you view and desk-check another algorithm for the vacation program. This algorithm contains the third logic error—using an unnecessary nested selection structure. Like the correct algorithm, this algorithm produces the desired results; however, it does so in a less efficient manner than the correct algorithm.

Using an Unnecessary Nested Selection Structure

Another common error made when writing selection structures is to include an unnecessary nested selection structure. In most cases, a selection structure containing this error still produces the correct results. The only problem is that it does so less efficiently than selection structures that are properly structured. Figure 6-12 shows an example of this error in the vacation algorithm. The correct algorithm is included in the figure for comparison.

Figure 6-12: Correct algorithm and an inefficient algorithm containing the third logic error

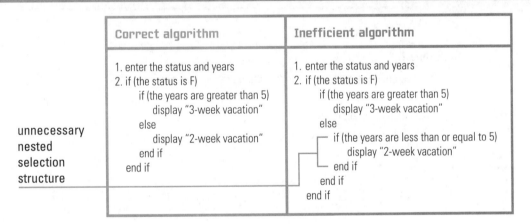

	Correct algorithm	Inefficient algorithm

unnecessary nested selection structure	1. enter the status and years
	2. if (the status is F)
	    if (the years are greater than 5)
	        display "3-week vacation"
	    else
	        display "2-week vacation"
	    end if
	end if
		1. enter the status and years
		2. if (the status is F)
		    if (the years are greater than 5)
		        display "3-week vacation"
		    else
		        if (the years are less than or equal to 5)
		            display "2-week vacation"
		        end if
		    end if
		end if

Unlike the correct algorithm, which contains two selection structures, the inefficient algorithm contains three selection structures. Notice that the condition in the third selection structure determines whether the years are less than or equal to 5, and is processed only when the condition in the second selection structure is false; in other words, it is processed only when the years are not greater than 5. However, if the years are not greater than 5, then they would have to be either less than or equal to 5, so the third selection structure is unnecessary. To better understand the error in the inefficient algorithm, you will desk-check the algorithm.

After the user enters the first set of test data—F as the status and 4 as the years—the first selection structure's condition determines whether the status is F; it is, so the second selection structure's condition determines whether the years are greater than 5. The years are not greater than 5, so the third selection structure's condition checks whether the years are less than or equal to 5—an unnecessary decision. In this case, 4 is less than 5, so the third selection structure's true path displays the message "2-week vacation", which is correct. After doing so, the three selection structures and the program end.

After the user enters the second set of test data—F as the status and 15 as the years—the first selection structure's condition determines whether the status is F; it is, so the second selection structure's condition determines whether the years are greater than 5. The years are greater than 5, so the second selection structure's true path displays the message "3-week vacation", which is correct. After doing so, the first and second selection structures and the program end.

After the user enters the third set of test data—P as the status and 11 as the years—the condition in the first selection structure determines whether the status is F; it isn't, so the first selection structure and the program end.

Figure 6-13 shows the results of desk-checking the inefficient algorithm shown in Figure 6-12. As indicated in the figure, although the results of the three desk-checks are correct, the result of the first desk-check is obtained in a less efficient manner.

Figure 6-13: Results of desk-checking the inefficient algorithm shown in Figure 6-12

correct result is obtained in a less efficient manner

Desk-check	Result
First:　　using F as the status and 4 as the years Second: using F as the status and 15 as the years Third:　　using P as the status and 11 as the years	"2-week vacation" displayed "3-week vacation" displayed Nothing is displayed

MINI-QUIZ

Mini-Quiz 2

1) List the three errors commonly made when writing selection structures.

2) Which of the errors from Question 1 makes the selection structure inefficient, but still produces the correct results?

Some algorithms require selection structures that are capable of choosing from several alternatives. You can create such selection structures, commonly referred to as multiple-path or extended selection structures, using either the if/else or switch form of the selection structure. First learn how to use the if/else form.

Using the if/else Form to Create Multiple-Path Selection Structures

At times, you may need to create a selection structure that can choose from several alternatives. For example, assume you are asked to create a program that displays a message based on a letter grade that the user enters. Figure 6-14 shows the valid letter grades and their corresponding messages.

Figure 6-14: Letter grades and messages

Letter grade	Message
A	Excellent
B	Above Average
C	Average
D	Below Average
F	Below Average

As Figure 6-14 indicates, if the letter grade is an A, then the program should display the message "Excellent". If the letter grade is a B, then the program should display the message "Above Average", and so on. Figure 6-15 shows two versions of the C++ code for the grade problem. Both versions use the if/else form of the selection structure to display the appropriate message.

Figure 6-15: Two versions of the C++ code for the grade problem

Version 1

```cpp
cout << "Grade: ";
cin >> grade;
grade = toupper(grade);

if (grade == 'A')
    cout << "Excellent" << endl;
else
    if (grade == 'B')
        cout << "Above Average" << endl;
    else
        if (grade == 'C')
            cout << "Average" << endl;
        else
            if (grade == 'D' || grade == 'F')
                cout << "Below Average" << endl;
            else
                cout << "Error" << endl;
            //end if
        //end if
    //end if
//end if
```

Figure 6-15: Two versions of the C++ code for the grade problem (continued)

you can use one comment to mark the end of the entire structure

you can include another statement on the same line as the else

Version 2

```cpp
cout << "Grade: ";
cin >> grade;
grade = toupper(grade);

if (grade == 'A')
    cout << "Excellent" << endl;
else if (grade == 'B')
    cout << "Above Average" << endl;
else if (grade == 'C')
    cout << "Average" << endl;
else if (grade == 'D' || grade == 'F')
    cout << "Below Average" << endl;
else cout << "Error" << endl;
//end ifs
```

Although you can write the `if/else` form of the selection structure using either of the two methods shown in Figure 6-15, the second method provides a much more convenient way of writing this logic.

In addition to using the `if/else` form to create multiple-path selection structures, you also can use the `switch` form.

Using the `switch` Form to Create Multiple-Path Selection Structures

It is often simpler and clearer to use the `switch` form of the selection structure, rather than the `if/else` form, in situations where the selection structure has many paths from which to choose. Figure 6-16 shows the flowchart and pseudocode for the grade problem, using the `switch` form of the selection structure.

Figure 6-16: Flowchart and pseudocode showing the switch form of the selection structure

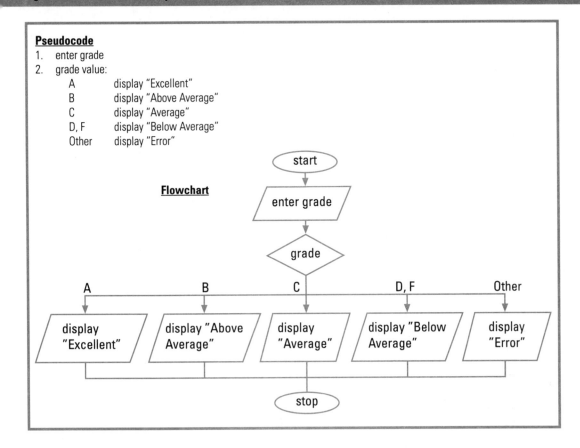

Pseudocode
1. enter grade
2. grade value:

A	display "Excellent"
B	display "Above Average"
C	display "Average"
D, F	display "Below Average"
Other	display "Error"

Notice that the flowchart symbol for the **switch** form of the selection structure is the same as the flowchart symbol for the **if** and **if/else** forms—a diamond. However, unlike the **if** and **if/else** diamond, the **switch** diamond does not contain a condition requiring a true or false answer. Instead, the **switch** diamond contains an expression—in this case, grade—whose value determines which path is chosen.

Like the **if** and **if/else** diamond, the **switch** diamond has one flowline leading into the symbol. Unlike the **if** and **if/else** diamond, however, the **switch** diamond has many flowlines leading out of the symbol. Each flowline represents a possible path for the selection structure. The flowlines must be marked appropriately, indicating which value(s) are necessary for each path to be chosen.

Figure 6-17 shows the syntax of the **switch** statement, which is used to code the **switch** form of the selection structure in C++. It also shows how to use the **switch** statement to code the grade problem.

tip

In some programming languages—for example, Visual Basic—the switch form of the selection structure is called the case form.

Figure 6-17: Syntax and an example of the C++ switch statement

Syntax

```
switch (selectorExpression)
{
case value1:    one or more statements
[case value2:    one or more statements]
[case valueN:    one or more statements]
[default:        one or more statements processed when the selectorExpression does
                 not match any of the values]
} //end switch
```

Example

```
cout << "Enter grade: ";
cin >> grade;
grade = toupper(grade);

switch (grade)
{
case 'A':        cout << "Excellent" << endl;
                 break;
case 'B':        cout << "Above Average" << endl;
                 break;
case 'C':        cout << "Average" << endl;
                 break;
case 'D':
case 'F':        cout << "Below Average" << endl;
                 break;
default:         cout << "Error" << endl;
}   //end switch
```

case clause

selector-Expression

a break statement tells the computer to exit the switch statement

default clause

tip

The default clause can appear anywhere within the switch statement. However, for clarity, it is recommended that you place the default clause at the end of the switch statement.

The **switch** statement begins with the **switch** clause, followed by an opening brace; the statement ends with a closing brace. It is a good programming practice to document the end of the **switch** statement with the **//end switch** comment, as shown in Figure 6-17.

The **switch** clause is composed of the keyword **switch** followed by a *selectorExpression* enclosed in parentheses. The *selectorExpression* can contain any combination of variables, constants, functions, and operators, as long as the combination results in a value whose data type is either **bool**, **char**, **short**, **int**, or **long**. In the **switch** statement shown in the example in Figure 6-17, the *selectorExpression* contains a **char** variable named **grade**.

Between the **switch** statement's opening and closing braces are the individual **case** clauses, each representing a different path that the selection structure can follow. You can have as many **case** clauses as necessary in a **switch** statement. If a **default** clause is included in the **switch** statement, it usually is the last clause in the statement.

Each of the individual clauses within the switch statement (except for the default clause) contains a *value*, followed by a colon. The data type of the *value* should be compatible with the data type of the *selectorExpression*. In other words, if the *selectorExpression* is a numeric variable, the *values* in the case clauses should be numeric. Likewise, if the *selectorExpression* is a char variable, the *values* should be characters. The *values* in the case clauses can be literal constants, named constants, or expressions composed of literal and named constants. In the switch statement shown in the example in Figure 6-17, the data type of the *values* in the case clauses ('A', 'B', 'C', 'D', and 'F') is char to match the data type of the *selectorExpression* (grade).

Following the colon in each case clause are one or more statements that are processed when the *selectorExpression* matches that case's *value*. Notice that the statements within a case clause are not entered as a statement block—in other words, the statements are not enclosed in braces.

After the computer processes the instructions in the case clause whose *value* matches the *selectorExpression*, you typically want the computer to leave the switch statement without processing the remaining instructions in the statement. You do so by including the break statement as the last statement in the case clause. The break statement tells the computer to leave ("break out of") the switch statement at that point. If you do not use the break statement to leave the switch statement, the computer continues processing the remaining instructions in the statement, which may or may not be what you want to happen. After processing the break statement, the computer then processes the instruction that follows the switch statement's closing brace. To better understand the switch statement, you will desk-check the code shown in the example in Figure 6-17 using the grades *b*, *D*, and *X*.

Desk-Checking the Grade Program

Assume the user enters the letter *b* in response to the "Enter grade: " prompt shown in the example in Figure 6-17. The code stores the uppercase equivalent of the user's input (B) in the grade variable, which then is used as the *selectorExpression* in the program's switch statement. When processing the switch statement, the computer compares the value of the *selectorExpression* with the *value* listed in each of the case clauses, one case clause at a time beginning with the first. If a match is found, the computer processes the instructions contained in that case clause until it encounters either a break statement or the switch statement's closing brace (which marks the end of the selection structure). The computer then skips to the instruction following the switch statement's closing brace. In this case, the value of the *selectorExpression*—the letter *B*—does not match the letter contained in the first case clause (which is 'A'); however, it does match the letter contained in the second case clause. The first statement in the second case clause is cout << "Above Average" << endl;, which displays the message "Above Average" on the screen. The next statement in the second case clause is break;, which tells the computer to skip the remaining instructions in the switch statement, and continue processing with the instruction that follows the switch statement's closing brace.

Now assume the user enters the letter *D* in response to the "Enter grade: " prompt shown in the example in Figure 6-17. As before, the code stores the uppercase equivalent of the user's input in the grade variable, which then is used as the *selectorExpression* in the program's switch statement. The computer compares the value of the *selectorExpression* (*D*) with the *value* listed in each of the case clauses, one case clause at a time beginning with the first. In this case, the letter *D* matches the letter listed in the fourth case clause. However, notice that there is no statement to the immediate right of the case 'D': clause. So, what (if anything) will appear when the grade is *D*?

tip

Recall from Chapter 3 that character literal constants are enclosed in single quotation marks in C++ code.

tip

In Exercises 10 and 11 at the end of this lesson, you learn what happens when you do not use the break statement to break out of the switch statement.

tip

If the default
clause is not the
last clause in the
switch state-
ment, you will need
to include a break
statement at the
end of the clause.

Recall that, when the *value* of the *selectorExpression* matches the *value* in a `case` clause, the computer processes the instructions contained in that clause until it encounters either a `break` statement or the `switch` statement's closing brace. In this case, not finding any instructions in the `case 'D':` clause, the computer continues processing with the instructions in the next clause—the `case 'F':` clause. The first instruction in the `case 'F':` clause displays the message "Below Average", which is the correct message to display, and the second instruction tells the computer to break out of the `switch` statement. In other words, the `cout << "Below Average" << endl;` and `break;` statements are processed when the grade is the letter *D*. The computer then skips to the instruction following the `switch` statement's closing brace. As this example shows, you can process the same instructions for more than one *value* by listing each *value* in a separate `case` clause, as long as the clauses appear together in the `switch` statement. The last `case` clause in the group of related clauses should contain the instructions you want the computer to process when one of the *values* in the group matches the *selectorExpression*. Only the last `case` clause in the group of related clauses should contain the `break` statement.

Finally, assume the user enters the letter *X* as the grade. Notice that the letter *X* does not appear as a *value* in any of the `case` clauses. If the *selectorExpression* does not match any of the *values* listed in the `case` clauses, the computer processes the instructions contained in the `default` clause (if there is one). The instruction in the `default` clause shown in the example in Figure 6-17 displays the message "Error" on the screen. If the `default` clause is the last clause in the `switch` statement, as it is in Figure 6-17, the computer then skips to the instruction following the `switch` statement's closing brace. Figure 6-18 shows the results of desk-checking the code shown in the example in Figure 6-17.

Figure 6-18: Results of desk-checking the grade program example shown in Figure 6-17

Desk-check	Result
First: using b	"Above Average" displayed
Second: using D	"Below Average" displayed
Third: using X	"Error" displayed

MINI-QUIZ

Mini-Quiz 3

1) Assume you want to create a program that displays the message "Highest honors" when a student's test score is 90 or above. When the test score is 70 through 89, the program should display the message "Good job". For all other test scores, the program should display the message "Retake the test". Write the appropriate C++ code, using the shorter version of the `if/else` form of the selection structure.

2) If the *selectorExpression* used in the `switch` statement is a numeric variable, then the values listed in each `case` clause should be _____.

3) The _____ statement tells the computer to leave the `switch` statement at that point.

4) If the *selectorExpression* in the `switch` statement is the `int` variable `code`, which of the following `case` clauses is valid?
   a. `case "2":`
   b. `case 2:`
   c. `case 2;`
   d. `case == 2`

Next, you learn how to format a program's numeric output.

Formatting Numeric Output

In a C++ program, numbers containing a decimal point are displayed in either fixed-point or e (exponential) notation, depending on the size of the number. Smaller numbers—those containing six or fewer digits to the left of the decimal point—usually are displayed in fixed-point notation. For example, the number 1,234.56 would be displayed in fixed-point notation as 1234.56. Larger numbers—those containing more than six digits to the left of the decimal point—typically are displayed in e notation. The number 1,225,000.00, for example, would be displayed in e notation as 1.225e+006. Unless you are a scientist, engineer, or mathematician, you are used to viewing numbers in fixed-point notation rather than in e notation.

You can use the **setiosflags stream manipulator** to display a program's numeric output in fixed-point notation only. To use the manipulator, the program must contain the `#include <iomanip>` directive, as well as the `using std::ios;` and `using std::setiosflags;` statements. Figure 6-19 shows the syntax of the `setiosflags` stream manipulator and includes two examples of using the manipulator in a C++ statement.

Figure 6-19: Syntax and examples of the `setiosflags` **stream manipulator**

Syntax
setiosflags(*flag* **)**
Examples

`cout << setiosflags(ios::fixed);`
`cout << sales << endl;`
 	
`cout << setiosflags(ios::fixed) << sales << endl;`

When displaying numbers using the `setiosflags` stream manipulator, you typically use `ios::fixed` as the *flag* argument. The `ios::fixed` *flag* tells the computer to display floating-point numbers in fixed notation only. Keep in mind that the `setiosflags` manipulator must appear before the first number you want formatted. The manipulator remains in effect until the computer encounters another program statement that changes the *flag*.

In the first example shown in Figure 6-19, the `cout << setiosflags(ios::fixed);` statement tells the computer to use fixed-point notation when displaying the program's numeric output on the screen. In this case, the numeric output is stored in the `sales` variable. You also can include the `setiosflags` stream manipulator in the same `cout` statement as the output, as long as it appears before the output; this is shown in the second example in the figure.

To control the number of decimal places displayed in a number, you use the C++ **setprecision stream manipulator**. To use the `setprecision` manipulator, the program must contain the `#include <iomanip>` directive and the `using std::setprecision;` statement. Figure 6-20 shows the syntax of the `setprecision` stream manipulator and includes three examples of using the manipulator in a C++ statement.

Figure 6-20: Syntax and examples of the `setprecision` **stream manipulator**

Syntax
setprecision(_numberOfDecimalPlaces)_
Examples

```
cout << setprecision(2);
cout << sales << endl;

cout << setprecision(2) << sales << endl;

cout << setiosflags(ios::fixed) << setprecision
(0) << sales << endl;
```

The _numberOfDecimalPlaces_ argument in the syntax is an integer that specifies the number of decimal places to display in each number. In the first example shown in Figure 6-20, the `cout << setprecision(2);` statement tells the computer to display the program's numeric output with two digits to the right of the decimal point. You also can include the `setprecision` stream manipulator in the same `cout` statement as the output, as long as it appears before the output; this is shown in the second example in the figure. The last example shows how you can use both the `setiosflags` and `setprecision` manipulators in the same `cout` statement. In this case, the statement tells the computer to display the output as a fixed-point number with zero decimal places. Like the `setiosflags` manipulator, the `setprecision` manipulator remains in effect until the computer encounters another program statement that changes the _numberOfDecimalPlaces_.

You now have completed Chapter 6's Concept lesson. You can either take a break or complete the end-of-lesson questions and exercises before moving on to the Application lesson.

SUMMARY

You can nest a selection structure within either the true path or false path of another selection structure. You use a nested selection structure when more than one decision must be made before the appropriate action can be taken. The outer selection structure always represents the primary decision, while the nested (or inner) selection structure represents the secondary decision.

Typically, logic errors commonly made when writing selection structures are a result of one of the following mistakes: using a logical operator when a nested selection structure is needed, or reversing the primary and secondary decisions, or using an unnecessary nested selection structure.

Some algorithms require selection structures that are capable of choosing from several alternatives. You can code such selection structures using either the `if/else` or `switch` form of the selection structure.

The flowchart symbol for the `switch` form of the selection structure is a diamond. The diamond should contain an expression; the expression's value controls which alternative is chosen. The `switch` diamond has one flowline leading into the symbol, and many flowlines leading out of the symbol. Each flowline represents a possible path for the selection structure and should be marked to indicate which value(s) are necessary for each path to be chosen. In C++, you use the **switch** statement, along with the **break** statement, to code the **switch** form of the selection structure.

You can use the **setiosflags** stream manipulator to display a program's numeric output in fixed-point notation only. To control the number of decimal places displayed in a number, you use the **setprecision** stream manipulator.

ANSWERS TO MINI-QUIZZES

Mini-Quiz 1

1) if (score >= 90)
   display "Highest honors"
else
  if (score >= 70)
    display "Good job"
  else
    display "Retake the test"
  end if
end if

2)
```
if (score >= 90)
        cout << "Highest honors" << endl;
else
        if (score >= 70)
                cout << "Good job" << endl;
        else
                cout << "Retake the test" << endl;
        //end if
//end if
```

3) The decision regarding the member status is the primary decision. The decision regarding the day of the week is the secondary decision, because whether it needs to be made depends on the result of the member status decision.

Mini-Quiz 2

1) Using a logical operator when a nested selection structure is needed
Reversing the primary and secondary decisions
Using an unnecessary nested selection structure

2) Using an unnecessary nested selection structure

Mini-Quiz 3

1)
```
if (score >= 90)
        cout << "Highest honors" << endl;
else if (score >= 70)
        cout << "Good job" << endl;
else cout << "Retake the test" << endl;
//end ifs
```

2) numeric

3) break

4) b. case 2:

QUESTIONS

Use the code shown in Figure 6-21 to answer Questions 1 through 3.

Figure 6-21

```
if (number <= 100)
    number = number * 2;
else
    if (number > 500)
        number = number * 3;
    //end if
//end if
```

1) Assume the **number** variable contains the number 90. What value will be in the **number** variable after the code shown in Figure 6-21 is processed?

A. 0

B. 90

C. 180

D. 270

2) Assume the **number** variable contains the number 1000. What value will be in the **number** variable after the code shown in Figure 6-21 is processed?

A. 0

B. 1000

C. 2000

D. 3000

3) Assume the **number** variable contains the number 200. What value will be in the **number** variable after the code shown in Figure 6-21 is processed?

A. 0

B. 200

C. 400

D. 600

Use the code shown in Figure 6-22 to answer Questions 4 through 7.

Figure 6-22

```
if (id == 1)
    cout << "Janet" << endl;
else if (id == 2 || id == 3)
    cout << "Paul" << endl;
else if (id == 4)
    cout << "Jerry" << endl;
else cout << "Sue" << endl;
//end ifs
```

4) What, if anything, will the code shown in Figure 6-22 display when the `id` variable contains the number 2?

A. Jerry

B. Paul

C. Sue

D. nothing

5) What, if anything, will the code shown in Figure 6-22 display when the `id` variable contains the number 4?

A. Jerry

B. Paul

C. Sue

D. nothing

6) What, if anything, will the code shown in Figure 6-22 display when the `id` variable contains the number 3?

A. Jerry

B. Paul

C. Sue

D. nothing

7) What, if anything, will the code shown in Figure 6-22 display when the `id` variable contains the number 8?

A. Jerry

B. Paul

C. Sue

D. nothing

8) You can use the C++ _____ statement to code the `switch` form of the selection structure.

A. `case`

B. `case of`

C. `struc`

D. `switch`

9) Which of the following flowchart symbols represents the `switch` form of the selection structure?

A. diamond

B. hexagon

C. parallelogram

D. rectangle

10) If the *selectorExpression* used in the `switch` statement is a `char` variable named `code`, which of the following `case` clauses is valid?

A. `case "3":`

B. `case '3':`

C. `case 3;`

D. `case = 3`

Use the code shown in Figure 6-23 to answer Questions 11 through 13.

Figure 6-23

```
switch (id)
{
case 1:   cout << "Janet" << endl;
          break;
case 2:   cout << "Paul" << endl;
          break;
case 3:
case 5:   cout << "Jerry" << endl;
          break;
default:  cout << "Sue" << endl;
} //end switch
```

11) What, if anything, will the code shown in Figure 6-23 display when the id variable contains the number 2?

    A. Jerry

    B. Paul

    C. Sue

    D. nothing

12) What, if anything, will the code shown in Figure 6-23 display when the id variable contains the number 4?

    A. Jerry

    B. Paul

    C. Sue

    D. nothing

13) What, if anything, will the code shown in Figure 6-23 display when the id variable contains the number 3?

    A. Jerry

    B. Paul

    C. Sue

    D. nothing

14) Which of the following statements will display the contents of the `sales` variable in fixed-point notation with zero decimal places?

    A. `cout << setiosflags(ios::fixed) <<`
       `setprecision(0) << sales << endl;`

    B. `cout << setprecision(0)`
       `<< setiosflags(ios::fixed) << sales << endl;`

    C. `cout << setprecision(0);`
       `cout << setiosflags(ios::fixed);`
       `cout << sales << endl;`

    D. all of the above

Look For These Symbols

Debugging

Discovery

EXERCISES

1) Write the C++ `if` statement that compares the contents of the `quantity` variable to the number 10. If the `quantity` variable contains a number that is equal to 10, display the string "Equal". If the `quantity` variable contains a number that is greater than 10, display the string "Over 10". If the `quantity` variable contains a number that is less than 10, display the string "Not over 10".

2) Write the C++ code that corresponds to the flowchart shown in Figure 6-24.

Figure 6-24

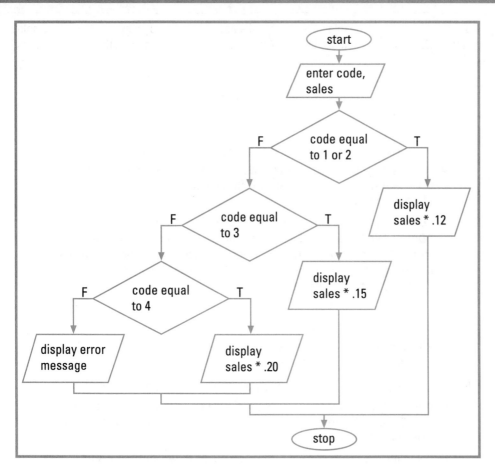

3) Write the C++ code that corresponds to the flowchart shown in Figure 6-25.

Figure 6-25

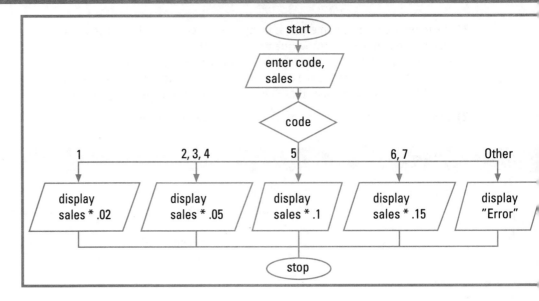

4) In this exercise, you complete a program by writing a selection structure.

   A. If necessary, start Visual Studio .NET. Open the Ch6ConE04 Solution (Ch6ConE04 Solution.sln) file, which is contained in the Cpp\Chap06\ Ch6ConE04 Solution folder.

   B. Complete the program by writing an **if** statement that displays the string "Dog" when the **animal** variable contains the number 1. Display the string "Cat" when the **animal** variable contains the number 2. Display the string "Bird" when the **animal** variable contains anything other than the number 1 or the number 2.

   C. Save and then build the solution.

   D. Execute the program three times, using the following numbers: 1, 2, and 5.

   E. When the program is working correctly, close the Output window, then use the File menu to close the solution.

5) In this exercise, you complete a program by writing a selection structure.

   A. If necessary, start Visual Studio .NET. Open the Ch6ConE05 Solution (Ch6ConE05 Solution.sln) file, which is contained in the Cpp\Chap06\ Ch6ConE05 Solution folder.

   B. Complete the program by writing a **switch** statement that displays the month corresponding to the number entered by the user. For example, when the user enters the number 1, the program should display the string "January". When the user enters an invalid number (one that is not in the range 1 through 12), the program should display an appropriate error message.

   C. Save and then build the solution.

   D. Execute the program three times, using the following numbers: 3, 7, and 20.

   E. When the program is working correctly, close the Output window, then use the File menu to close the solution.

6) In this exercise, you complete a program by writing a selection structure.

   A. If necessary, start Visual Studio .NET. Open the Ch6ConE06 Solution (Ch6ConE06 Solution.sln) file, which is contained in the Cpp\Chap06\ Ch6ConE06 Solution folder.

B. Complete the program by writing an `if` statement that assigns the number 25 to the **bonus** variable when the user enters a sales amount that is greater than or equal to $100, but less than or equal to $250. When the user enters a sales amount that is greater then $250, assign the number 50 to the **bonus** variable. When the user enters a sales amount that is less than $100, assign the number 0 to the **bonus** variable.

C. Save and then build the solution.

D. Execute the program three times, using the following sales amounts: 100, 300, and 40.

E. When the program is working correctly, close the Output window, then use the File menu to close the solution.

7) In this exercise, you complete a program by writing a selection structure.

A. If necessary, start Visual Studio .NET. Open the Ch6ConE07 Solution (Ch6ConE07 Solution.sln) file, which is contained in the Cpp\Chap06\ Ch6ConE07 Solution folder.

B. The program should display the appropriate seminar fee, which is based on the membership status and age entered by the user. Use the following information to complete the program:

Seminar fee	Criteria
10	Club member less than 65 years old
5	Club member at least 65 years old
20	Non-member

C. Save and then build the solution.

D. Execute the program three times. For the first test, use M as the status and 65 as the age. For the second test, use m as the status and 40 as the age. For the third test, use N as the status.

E. When the program is working correctly, close the Output window, then use the File menu to close the solution.

8) In this exercise, you complete a program by writing a selection structure.

A. If necessary, start Visual Studio .NET. Open the Ch6ConE08 Solution (Ch6ConE08 Solution.sln) file, which is contained in the Cpp\Chap06\ Ch6ConE08 Solution folder.

B. The program should display the appropriate grade based on the average of three test scores entered by the user. (Each test is worth 100 points.) Use the following information to complete the program:

Test average	Grade
90–100	A
80–89	B
70–79	C
60–69	D
below 60	F

C. Save and then build the solution.

D. Execute the program three times. For the first test, use scores of 90, 95, and 100. For the second test, use scores of 83, 72, and 65. For the third test, use scores of 40, 30, and 20.

E. When the program is working correctly, close the Output window, then use the File menu to close the solution.

9) In this exercise, you complete a program by writing a selection structure.

A. If necessary, start Visual Studio .NET. Open the Ch6ConE09 Solution (Ch6ConE09 Solution.sln) file, which is contained in the Cpp\Chap06\ Ch6ConE09 Solution folder.

B. The program should display the class rank, which is based on the code entered by the user. Use the information below to complete the program. Be sure to use the **switch** statement.

Code	Rank
1	Freshman
2	Sophomore
3	Junior
4	Senior
other	Error

C. Save and then build the solution.

D. Execute the program three times, using the following codes: 1, 3, and 5.

E. When the program is working correctly, close the Output window, then use the File menu to close the solution.

10) In this exercise, you experiment with the **switch** statement.

A. If necessary, start Visual Studio .NET. Open the Ch6ConE10 Solution (Ch6ConE10 Solution.sln) file, which is contained in the Cpp\Chap06\ Ch6ConE10 Solution folder.

B. Build the solution, then execute the program. When you are prompted to enter a grade, type d and press Enter. What, if anything, did the **switch** statement display on the screen? Close the Command Prompt window.

C. Enter a **break;** statement in the **case 'd':** clause. Save and then build the solution. Execute the program. When you are prompted to enter a grade, type d and press Enter. What, if anything, did the **switch** statement display on the screen? Close the Command Prompt window.

D. Remove the **break;** statement from the **case 'd':** clause. Also remove the **break;** statement from the **case 'f':** clause. Save and then build the solution. Execute the program. When you are prompted to enter a grade, type d and press Enter. What, if anything, did the **switch** statement display on the screen? Close the Command Prompt window.

E. Put the **break;** statement back in the **case 'f':** clause, then save and build the solution. Execute the program. When you are prompted to enter a grade, type d and press Enter. Close the Command Prompt window.

F. Close the Output window, then use the File menu to close the solution.

11) In this exercise, you experiment with the **switch** statement.

A. If necessary, start Visual Studio .NET. Open the Ch6ConE11 Solution (Ch6ConE11 Solution.sln) file, which is contained in the Cpp\Chap06\Ch6ConE11 Solution folder. The program uses the **switch** statement to display the names of the gifts mentioned in the song "The Twelve Days of Christmas."

B. Build the solution, then execute the program. When you are prompted to enter the day, type the number 1 and press Enter. You will notice that the names of the gifts for the first through the twelfth day appear in the Command Prompt window. Close the Command Prompt window.

C. Execute the program again. When you are prompted to enter the day, type the number 9 and press Enter. The names of the gifts for the ninth through the twelfth day appear in the Command Prompt window. Close the Command Prompt window.

D. Modify the program so that it displays only the name of the gift corresponding to the day entered by the user. For example, when the user enters the number 4, the program should display the "4 calling birds" message only.

E. Save and then build the solution. Execute the program. When you are prompted to enter the day, type the number 4 and press Enter. The "4 calling birds" message should appear on the screen. Close the Command Prompt window.

F. Close the Output window, then use the File menu to close the solution.

12) In this exercise, you use both the `if` and `switch` statements.

A. If necessary, start Visual Studio .NET. Open the Ch6ConE12 Solution (Ch6ConE12 Solution.sln) file, which is contained in the Cpp\Chap06\ Ch6ConE12 Solution folder. The program should calculate and display the price of an order, based on the number of units ordered and the customer's status (either 1 for wholesaler or 2 for retailer). The price per unit is shown in Figure 6-26.

Figure 6-26

Wholesaler		Retailer	
Number of units	Price per unit ($)	Number of units	Price per unit ($)
1 through 4	10	1 through 3	15
5 and over	9	4 through 8	14
		9 and over	12

B. Complete the program appropriately. Use a `switch` statement to determine the customer's status. If the user enters a status other than 1 or 2, display an appropriate error message. Use an `if` statement to determine the price per unit. If the user enters an invalid number of units (in other words, a negative number or 0), display an appropriate error message.

C. Save and then build the solution. Execute the program. Test the program using the number 1 as the status and 5 as the number of units ordered. The Command Prompt window should show that the price of the order is $45. Close the Command Prompt window.

D. Execute the program again. Test the program using 2 as the status and 2 as the number of units ordered. The Command Prompt window should show that the price of the order is $30. Close the Command Prompt window.

E. Execute the program again. Test the program using 4 as the status and 3 as the number of units ordered. An appropriate error message should appear in the Command Prompt window. Close the Command Prompt window.

F. Execute the program again. Test the program using 2 as the status and −5 as the number of units ordered. An appropriate error message should appear in the Command Prompt window. Close the Command Prompt window.

G. When the program is working correctly, close the Output window, then use the File menu to close the solution.

13) In this exercise, you debug a C++ program.

A. If necessary, start Visual Studio .NET. Open the Ch6ConE13 Solution (Ch6ConE13 Solution.sln) file, which is contained in the Cpp\Chap06\ Ch6ConE13 Solution folder. The program should display "Illinois" when the user enters a state code of 1, "Kentucky" when the user enters a state code of 2, "New Hampshire" when the user enters a state code of 3, "Vermont" when the user enters a state code of 4, and "Massachusetts" when the user enters a state code of 5.

B. Study the program's code, then build the solution.

C. Correct any errors in the program, then save and build the solution.

D. Execute the program. Test the program six times, using state codes of 1, 2, 3, 4, 5, and 6.

E. When the program is working correctly, close the Output window, then use the File menu to close the solution.

Application Lesson

Using the Selection Structure in a C++ Program

Lab 6.1 - Stop and Analyze   If necessary, start Visual Studio .NET. Open the Ch6Lab1 Solution (Ch6Lab1 Solution.sln) file contained in the Cpp\Chap06\Ch6Lab1 Solution folder. Figure 6-27 shows the code entered in the Ch6Lab1.cpp file. (The line numbers are included in the figure only.) Study the code, then answer the questions.

Figure 6-27: C++ instructions entered in the Ch6Lab1.cpp file

```
1  //Ch6Lab1.cpp - converts American dollars to British pounds, or
2  //Mexican pesos, or Japanese yen
3  //Created/revised by <your name> on <current date>
4
5  #include <iostream>
6  #include <iomanip>
7
8  using std::cout;
9  using std::cin;
10 using std::endl;
11 using std::setprecision;
12 using std::ios;
13 using std::setiosflags;
14
15 int main()
16 {
17     //declare variables
18     int choice              = 0;
19     double originalDollars  = 0.0;
20     double convertedDollars = 0.0;
21
22     //get input items
23     cout << "1 British pounds" << endl;
24     cout << "2 Mexican pesos" << endl;
25     cout << "3 Japanese yen" << endl;
26     cout << "Enter 1, 2, or 3: ";
27     cin >> choice;
28     cout << "Enter number of American dollars: ";
29     cin >> originalDollars;
30
31     //display output in fixed-point notation
32     //with two decimal places
33     cout << setiosflags(ios::fixed) << setprecision(2);
34
35     //convert American dollars
36     if (choice == 1)
37     {
38         convertedDollars = originalDollars * .626881;
39         cout << "British pounds: " << convertedDollars << endl;
```

Figure 6-27: C++ instructions entered in the Ch6Lab1.cpp file (continued)

```
40      }
41      else if (choice == 2)
42      {
43          convertedDollars = originalDollars * 10.392;
44          cout << "Mexican pesos: " << convertedDollars << endl;
45      }
46      else
47      {
48          convertedDollars = originalDollars * 118.24;
49          cout << "Japanese yen: " << convertedDollars << endl;
50      }   //end ifs
51
52      return 0;
53 }    //end of main function
```

Questions

1. What exactly does the Ch6Lab1.cpp program do? In other words, what does it input, process, and output?
2. Are the braces in lines 37 and 40 necessary? Why or why not?
3. Build the solution, then execute the program. Use the program to convert 100 American dollars to Japanese yen. What is the answer? Close the Command Prompt window.
4. Execute the program again. Use the program to convert 50 American dollars to British pounds. What is the answer? Close the Command Prompt window.
5. Execute the program again. Use the program to convert 10 American dollars to Mexican pesos. What is the answer? Close the Command Prompt window.
6. Execute the program again. What happens when the user enters the number 4 in response to the first prompt, and the number 500 in response to the second prompt? Is this correct? If not, what *should* the program display? Close the Command Prompt window.
7. Modify the program so that it displays an error message when the user enters an invalid number in response to the first prompt. If the number is invalid, the program should not ask the user to enter the number of American dollars.
8. Save and then build the solution. Execute the program. What happens when the user enters an invalid number in response to the first prompt? Close the Command Prompt window. Close the Output window, then use the File menu to close the solution.

Lab 6.2 Jennifer Yardley is the owner of Golf Pro, a U.S. company that sells golf equipment both domestically and abroad. Each of Golf Pro's salespeople receives a commission based on the total of his or her domestic and foreign sales. Jennifer has asked you to create a program that she can use to calculate and display a salesperson's commission.

Many companies pay their sales force a commission rather than, or in addition to, a salary or hourly wage. A commission is a percentage of the sales made by the salesperson. Some companies use a fixed rate to calculate the commission, while others—like Golf Pro—use a rate that varies with the amount of sales. Figure 6-28 shows Golf Pro's commission schedule, along with examples of using the schedule to calculate the commission on three different sales amounts.

Figure 6-28: Commission schedule and examples

Sales	Commission
1 – 100,000 100,001 – 400,000 400,001 and over	2% * sales 2,000 + 5% * sales over 100,000 17,000 + 10% * sales over 400,000

Example 1:   Sales: 15,000
                Commission: 2% * 15,000 = $300

Example 2:   Sales: 250,000
                Commission: 2000 + 5% * (250,000 – 100,000) = $9,500

Example 3:   Sales: 500,000
                Commission: 17,000 + 10% * (500,000 – 400,000) = $27,000

Notice that the commission for each range in the schedule is calculated differently. For instance, the commission for sales in the first range—1 through 100,000—is calculated by multiplying the sales amount by 2%. As Example 1 shows, sales of $15,000 would earn a $300 commission. The commission for sales in the second range—100,001 through 400,000—is calculated by multiplying the amount of sales more than 100,000 by 5%, and then adding $2,000 to the result. As Example 2 shows, sales of $250,000 would earn a $9,500 commission. The commission for sales starting at 400,001 is calculated by multiplying the amount of sales more than 400,000 by 10%, then adding $17,000 to the result. Example 3 indicates that sales of $500,000 would earn a $27,000 commission.

Figure 6-29 shows the IPO chart and C++ instructions for the Golf Pro problem. Notice that the program uses two variables and three named constants. Variables were chosen for the sales and commission amounts, because the values of those items will change each time the program is executed. The commission rates, however, will not change and are assigned to named constants.

Figure 6-29: IPO chart and C++ instructions for the Golf Pro problem

IPO chart information	C++ instructions

Input
   sales
   range 1 commission rate (2%)
   range 2 commission rate (5%)
   range 3 commission rate (10%)
Processing
 	
Output
 commission
 	
Algorithm
1. enter the sales
 	
2. if (the sales are less
   than or equal to zero)
     display "The sales amount
     must be greater than 0."
 	
  else
 	
   if (the sales are less than or
   equal to 100,000)
     calculate commission by
     multiplying the sales by
     COMM_RATE1
   else if (the sales are less than
     or equal to 400,000)
     calculate commission using
     the following expression:
     2000 + COMM_RATE2 * (sales −
     100,000)
   else calculate commission using
     the following expression:
     17,000 + COMM_RATE3 * (sales
     − 400,000)
   end ifs
 	
   display the commission
 	
  end if
	`double sales = 0.0;`
	`const double COMM_RATE1 = .02;`
	`const double COMM_RATE2 = .05;`
	`const double COMM_RATE3 = .1;`
	
	`double commission = 0.0;`
	
	`cout << "Enter the sales amount: ";`
	`cin >> sales;`
	
	`if (sales <= 0)`
	
	`    cout << "The sales amount must be `⤶
	`    greater than 0." << endl;`
	
	`else`
	`{`
	`    if (sales <= 100000)`
	
	`        commission = sales * COMM_RATE1;`
	
	`    else if (sales <= 400000)`
	
	`        commission = 2000 + COMM_RATE2 *`
	`        (sales - 100000);`
	
	`    else commission = 17000 + COMM_RATE3 *`
	`        (sales - 400000);`
	
	`    //end ifs`
	
	`    cout << setiosflags(ios::fixed)`
	`        << setprecision(2);`
	`    cout << "Commission: $" << commission `⤶
	`    << endl;`
	`}   //end if`

As Figure 6-29 indicates, the program's output is the commission, and its input is the sales amount and commission rates. First, the program gets the sales amount from the user. If the sales amount is less than or equal to 0, the program displays the "The sales must be greater than 0." message and the program ends. However, if the sales are not less than or equal to 0, the program determines the appropriate sales range and then calculates and displays the commission.

Activity for Lab 6.2

In this activity, you enter the C++ instructions shown in Figure 6-29 into the computer. You then test the program to verify that it is working correctly.

To create the Golf Pro program, then test the program:

1. If necessary, start Visual Studio .NET. Create a blank solution named Ch6Lab2 Solution. Save the solution in the Cpp\Chap06 folder.

2. Add an empty C++ Win32 Console Project to the solution. Name the project Ch6Lab2 Project.

3. Add a new C++ source file to the project. Name the source file Ch6Lab2.

4. Type **//Ch6Lab2.cpp - calculates and displays a commission** and press **Enter**.

5. Type **//Created/revised by *<your name>* on *<current date>***, replacing *<your name>* and *<current date>* with your name and the current date, respectively. Press **Enter** twice.

6. Type **#include <iostream>** and press **Enter**, then type **#include <iomanip>** and press **Enter** twice.

7. Type the following six `using` statements, then press **Enter** twice.

   using std::cout;
   using std::cin;
   using std::endl;
   using std::setprecision;
   using std::ios;
   using std::setiosflags;

8. Complete the program by entering the `main()` function, which is shown in Figure 6-30.

Figure 6-30: Golf Pro program

```
//Ch6Lab2.cpp - calculates and displays a commission
//Created/revised by <your name> on <current date>

#include <iostream>
#include <iomanip>

using std::cout;
using std::cin;
using std::endl;
using std::setprecision;
using std::ios;
using std::setiosflags;
```

Figure 6-30: Golf Pro program (continued)

enter the
main()
function
instructions

```cpp
int main()
{
    //declare constants and variables
    const double COMM_RATE1 = .02;
    const double COMM_RATE2 = .05;
    const double COMM_RATE3 = .1;
    double sales       = 0.0;
    double commission = 0.0;

    //get input item
    cout << "Enter the sales amount: ";
    cin >> sales;

    //validate sales amount
    if (sales <= 0)
        //if the sales amount is invalid, display an
        error message
        cout << "The sales amount must be greater than
        0." << endl;
    else
    {
        //calculate commission
        if (sales <= 100000)
            commission = sales * COMM_RATE1;
        else if (sales <= 400000)
            commission = 2000 + COMM_RATE2 * (sales -
            100000);
         else commission = 17000 + COMM_RATE3 * (sales
         - 400000);
        //end ifs

        //display commission
        cout << setiosflags(ios::fixed) << setprecision(2);
        cout << "Commission: $" << commission << endl;
    }   //end if

    return 0;
}   //end of main function
```

9. Save and then build the solution. If necessary, correct any syntax errors, then save and build the solution again.

10. Execute the program by clicking **Debug** on the menu bar, then clicking **Start Without Debugging**. Use the program to calculate the commission for a salesperson selling $15,000 in product. The commission should be $300.00. Close the Command Prompt window.

11. Execute the program again. What is the commission on $250,000 in sales? Close the Command Prompt window.

12. Execute the program again. What is the commission on $500,000 in sales? Close the Command Prompt window.

13. Execute the program again. Enter −89 as the sales amount. The program should display the "The sales amount must be greater than 0." message. Close the Command Prompt window.

14. Close the Output window, then use the File menu to close the solution.

Lab 6.3 In this lab, you modify the program from Lab 6.1 by replacing the `if` statements with a `switch` statement.

Activity for Lab 6.3

Before modifying the program from Lab 6.1, you copy the instructions contained in the Ch6Lab1.cpp file to a new solution.

To copy the instructions contained in the Ch6Lab1.cpp file to a new solution:

1. If necessary, start Visual Studio .NET. Create a blank solution named **Ch6Lab3 Solution**. Save the solution in the Cpp\Chap06 folder.

2. Add an empty C++ Win32 Console Project to the solution. Name the project **Ch6Lab3 Project**.

3. Add a new C++ source file to the project. Name the source file **Ch6Lab3**.

4. Click **File** on the menu bar, point to **Open**, then click **File**. The Open File dialog box opens.

5. Open the Cpp\Chap06\Ch6Lab1 Solution\Ch6Lab1 Project folder. Click **Ch6Lab1.cpp** in the list of filenames, then click the **Open** button to open the Ch6Lab1.cpp file.

6. Click **Edit** on the menu bar, then click **Select All** to select all of the instructions in the Ch6Lab1.cpp window.

7. Click **Edit**, then click **Copy** to copy the selected instructions to the clipboard.

8. Close the Ch6Lab1.cpp window by clicking the **Close** button on its title bar.

9. Click the **Ch6Lab3.cpp** tab to make the Ch6Lab3.cpp window the active window. Click **Edit**, then click **Paste** to paste the Ch6Lab1.cpp instructions in the Ch6Lab3.cpp window.

10. Change the filename in the first program comment to **Ch6Lab3.cpp**. If necessary, change the date in the second comment.

Currently, the program uses `if` statements to convert the American dollars to British pounds, Mexican pesos, or Japanese yen. Your task is to replace the `if` statements with a `switch` statement.

To modify the program, then test the program:

1. Make the appropriate modifications to the program.

2. Save and then build the solution. If necessary, correct any syntax errors, then save and build the solution again.

3. Execute the program. Test the program using your own sample data, then close the Command Prompt window.

4. When the program is working correctly, close the Output window, then use the File menu to close the solution.

You now have completed Chapter 6's Application lesson. You can either take a break or complete the end-of-lesson exercises.

ANSWERS TO LABS

Lab 6.1

1. The program allows the user to enter a number. The number indicates whether the user wants to convert the American dollars, which are input by the user, to British pounds, Mexican pesos, or Japanese yen. The program then converts the American dollars to the user's choice and displays the answer on the screen.

2. The braces on Lines 37 and 40 are necessary. The braces mark the beginning and end of a statement block, which is necessary when a path in the selection structure requires more than one instruction.

3. 11824.00

4. 31.34

5. 103.92

6. The program displays 59120.00 as the number of Japanese yen. This is because the last **else** clause is processed when the **choice** variable contains anything other than 1 or 2. Rather than displaying the number of Japanese yen, the program should display an error message.

7. See Figure 6-31. Modifications are shaded in the figure.

Figure 6-31

```
1  //Ch6Lab1.cpp - converts American dollars to British pounds, or
2  //Mexican pesos, or Japanese yen
3  //Created/revised by <your name> on <current date>
4
5  #include <iostream>
6  #include <iomanip>
7
8  using std::cout;
9  using std::cin;
10 using std::endl;
11 using std::setprecision;
12 using std::ios;
13 using std::setiosflags;
14
15 int main()
16 {
```

Figure 6-31 (continued)

```
17      //declare variables
18      int choice             = 0;
19      double originalDollars  = 0.0;
20      double convertedDollars = 0.0;
21
22      //get input items
23      cout << "1 British pounds" << endl;
24      cout << "2 Mexican pesos" << endl;
25      cout << "3 Japanese yen" << endl;
26      cout << "Enter 1, 2, or 3: ";
27      cin >> choice;
28
29      if (choice < 1 || choice > 3)
30          cout << "Invalid choice";
31      else
32      {
33          cout << "Enter number of American dollars: ";
34          cin >> originalDollars;
35
36          //display output in fixed-point notation
37          //with two decimal places
38          cout << setiosflags(ios::fixed) << setprecision(2);
39
40          //convert American dollars
41          if (choice == 1)
42          {
43              convertedDollars = originalDollars * .626881;
44              cout << "British pounds: " << convertedDollars
                     << endl;
45          }
46          else if (choice == 2)
47          {
48              convertedDollars = originalDollars * 10.392;
49              cout << "Mexican pesos: " << convertedDollars
                     << endl;
50          }
51          else
52          {
53              convertedDollars = originalDollars * 118.24;
54              cout << "Japanese yen: " << convertedDollars
                     << endl;
55          }   //end ifs
56      } //end if
57
58      return 0;
59 }    //end of main function
```

8. The program displays the "Invalid choice" message.

Lab 6.2

Step 11: $9500.00

Step 12: $27000.00

Lab 6.3

See Figure 6-32. Modifications are shaded in the figure.

Figure 6-32

```cpp
//Ch6Lab3.cpp - converts American dollars to British pounds, or
//Mexican pesos, or Japanese yen
//Created/revised by <your name> on <current date>

#include <iostream>
#include <iomanip>

using std::cout;
using std::cin;
using std::endl;
using std::setprecision;
using std::ios;
using std::setiosflags;

int main()
{
    //declare variables
    int choice               = 0;
    double originalDollars  = 0.0;
    double convertedDollars = 0.0;

    //get input items
    cout << "1 British pounds" << endl;
    cout << "2 Mexican pesos" << endl;
    cout << "3 Japanese yen" << endl;
    cout << "Enter 1, 2, or 3: ";
    cin >> choice;

    if (choice < 1 || choice > 3)
        cout << "Invalid choice" << endl;
    else
    {
        cout << "Enter number of American dollars: ";
        cin >> originalDollars;

        //display output in fixed-point notation
        //with two decimal places
        cout << setiosflags(ios::fixed) << setprecision(2);

        //convert American dollars
        switch (choice)
        {
        case 1:     convertedDollars = originalDollars * .626881;
                    cout << "British pounds: "
                    << convertedDollars << endl;
                    break;
        case 2:     convertedDollars = originalDollars * 10.392;
                    cout << "Mexican pesos: " << convertedDollars
                    << endl;
```

```
              break;
    default:  convertedDollars = originalDollars * 118.24;
              cout << "Japanese yen: " << convertedDollars
              << endl;
    }    //end switch
}    //end if

    return 0;
}    //end of main function
```

EXERCISES

Look For These Symbols

Debugging

Discovery

1) In this exercise, you modify the program you created in Lab 6.2 so that it calculates the commission for five sales ranges, rather than three sales ranges.

A. If necessary, start Visual Studio .NET. Create a new solution named Ch6AppE01 Solution. Add an empty C++ Win32 Console Project to the solution. Name the project Ch6AppE01 Project. Add a new C++ source file to the project. Name the source file Ch6AppE01. Open the Ch6Lab2.cpp file. Copy the instructions contained in the Ch6Lab2.cpp file to the Ch6AppE01.cpp file, then close the Ch6Lab2.cpp file.

B. Change the filename in the first comment to Ch6AppE01.cpp. Change the date in the second comment, if necessary. Figure 6-33 shows Golf Pro's new commission rate schedule.

Figure 6-33

Sales	Commission
1–100,000	2% * sales
100,001–200,000	4% * sales
200,001–300,000	6% * sales
300,001–400,000	8% * sales
400,001 and over	10% * sales

C. Modify the program to accommodate the new commission rate schedule. Use the shorter version of the `if/else` form of the selection structure.

D. Save and then build the solution.

E. Execute the program four times, using the following sales amounts: 15000, 250000, 500000, and −1. (The Command Prompt window should display the following commission amounts: $300.00, $15000.00, $50000.00, and "The sales amount must be greater than 0.", respectively.)

F. When the program is working correctly, close the Output window, then use the File menu to close the solution.

2) In this exercise, you create a program that displays the total amount of money a company owes for a seminar.

A. Complete an IPO chart for the problem. The seminar fee per person is based on the number of people the company registers, as shown in the following table. (For example, if the company registers seven people, then the total amount owed by the company is $560.)

Number of registrants	Fee per person
1–4	$100
5–10	$ 80
11 or more	$ 60

If the user enters the number 0 or a negative number, the program should display an appropriate error message.

B. If necessary, start Visual Studio .NET. Create a blank solution named Ch6AppE02 Solution. Save the solution in the Cpp\Chap06 folder.

C. Add an empty C++ Win32 Console Project to the solution. Name the project Ch6AppE02 Project.

D. Add a new C++ source file to the project. Name the source file Ch6AppE02.

E. Enter the appropriate C++ instructions into the source file. Use the IPO chart you created in Step A to code the program. Display the total amount owed with a dollar sign and no decimal places.

F. Complete a desk-check table for the program, using the following data: 4, 8, 12, 0, and –2.

G. Save and then build the solution.

H. Execute the program. Use the data from Step F to test the program.

I. When the program is working correctly, close the Output window, then use the File menu to close the solution.

3) In this exercise, you create a program that displays a shipping charge.

A. Complete an IPO chart for the problem. The shipping charge is based on the state code, as shown in the following table. Use the **switch** form of the selection structure to display the appropriate shipping charge.

State code	Shipping charge ($)
1	25
2	30
3	40
4	40
5	30
6	30

If the user enters any other state code, the program should display the message "Incorrect state code".

B. If necessary, start Visual Studio .NET. Open the Ch6AppE03 Solution (Ch6AppE03 Solution.sln) file, which is contained in the Cpp\Chap06\ Ch6AppE03 Solution folder.

C. Use the IPO chart you created in Step A to code the program.

D. Complete a desk-check table for the program, using the following data: 1, 2, 3, 4, 5, 6, 7, and –2.

E. Save and then build the solution.

F. Execute the program. Use the data from Step D to test the program.

G. When the program is working correctly, close the Output window, then use the File menu to close the solution.

4) In this exercise, you create a program that displays the price of a concert ticket.

A. Complete an IPO chart for the problem. The concert ticket's price is based on the seat location, as shown in the following table. (The user should be able to enter the seat location using either an uppercase or lowercase letter.)

Seat location	Concert ticket price ($)
B (box)	75
P (Pavilion)	30
L (Lawn)	21

If the user enters any other seat location, the program should display the message "Invalid location".

B. If necessary, start Visual Studio .NET. Open the Ch6AppE04 Solution (Ch6AppE04 Solution.sln) file, which is contained in the Cpp\Chap06\ Ch6AppE04 Solution folder.

C. Use the IPO chart you created in Step A to code the program.

D. Complete a desk-check table for the program, using the following data: B, p, L, and g.

E. Save and then build the solution.

F. Execute the program. Use the data from Step D to test the program.

G. When the program is working correctly, close the Output window, then use the File menu to close the solution.

5) In this exercise, you create a program that displays the number of vacation weeks due an employee.

A. Complete an IPO chart for the problem. The number of vacation weeks is based on the number of years the employee has been with the company, as shown in the following table.

Years with the company	Weeks of vacation
0	0
1–5	1
6–10	2
11 and over	3

If the user enters a negative number of years, the program should display the message "Invalid years".

B. If necessary, start Visual Studio .NET. Open the Ch6AppE05 Solution (Ch6AppE05 Solution.sln) file, which is contained in the Cpp\Chap06\ Ch6AppE05 Solution folder.

C. Use the IPO chart you created in Step A to code the program.

D. Complete a desk-check table for the program, using the following data: 0, 2, 10, 11, and −2.

E. Save and then build the solution.

F. Execute the program. Use the data from Step D to test the program.

G. When the program is working correctly, close the Output window, then use the File menu to close the solution.

6) In this exercise, you create a program that displays the number of daily calories needed to maintain your current weight.

A. Complete an IPO chart for the problem, using the information shown in Figure 6-34.

Figure 6-34

Female:

*To maintain your current weight:
Moderately active: total calories per day = weight multiplied by 12 calories per pound
Relatively inactive: total calories per day = weight multiplied by 10 calories per pound

Male:

*To maintain your current weight:
Moderately active: total calories per day = weight multiplied by 15 calories per pound
Relatively inactive: total calories per day = weight multiplied by 13 calories per pound

*Formulas from ViaHealth

B. If necessary, start Visual Studio .NET. Open the Ch6AppE06 Solution (Ch6AppE06 Solution.sln) file, which is contained in the Cpp\Chap06\ Ch6AppE06 Solution folder.

C. Use the IPO chart you created in Step A to code the program.

D. Complete a desk-check table for the program, using the following data: (F stands for female, M for male, A for active, and I for inactive.)

- F, I, 150
- F, A, 120
- M, I, 180
- M, A, 200

Also desk-check the program two additional times: first, using an invalid gender status of G, then using a valid gender status of F, but an invalid activity status of B.

E. Save and then build the solution.

F. Execute the program. Use the data from Step D to test the program.

G. When the program is working correctly, close the Output window, then use the File menu to close the solution.

7) In this exercise, you create a program that displays a message indicating whether a student passed or failed a course.

A. Create an IPO chart for the problem. The program will need to get two test scores from the user. Both scores should be positive numbers and can include 0. Both numbers also can contain a decimal place. If the first number is negative, the program should not ask the user to enter the second number; rather, it should display an appropriate error message before the program ends. If both numbers are positive, on the other hand, the program should calculate the average of the two numbers. If the average is at least 70, the program should display the message "Pass"; otherwise, it should display the message "Fail".

B. If necessary, start Visual Studio .NET. Open the Ch6AppE07 Solution (Ch6AppE07 Solution.sln) file, which is contained in the Cpp\Chap06\ Ch6AppE07 Solution folder.

C. Use the IPO chart you created in Step A to code the program.

D. Complete a desk-check table for the program, using the following data: 95 and 73, 65 and 50, 0 and 100, 80 and −3, and −1.

E. Save and then build the solution.

F. Execute the program. Use the data from Step D to test the program.

G. When the program is working correctly, close the Output window, then use the File menu to close the solution.

8) In this exercise, you create a program that adds, subtracts, multiplies, or divides two integers entered by the user.

A. Complete an IPO chart for the problem. The program will need to get a letter (A for addition, S for subtraction, M for multiplication, or D for division) and two integers from the user. If the user enters an invalid letter, the program should not ask the user for the two integers; rather, it should display an appropriate error message before the program ends. If the letter is A (or a), the program should calculate and display the sum of both numbers entered by the user. If the letter is S (or s), the program should calculate and display the difference between both numbers (subtracting the second number from the first number), but only if the first number is larger than, or equal to, the second number. If the first number is smaller than the second number, the program should swap both numbers before calculating and displaying the difference. If the letter is M (or m), the program should calculate and display the product of both integers. If the letter is D (or d), the program should divide both integers, always dividing the larger number by the smaller number.

B. If necessary, start Visual Studio .NET. Open the Ch6AppE08 Solution (Ch6AppE08 Solution.sln) file, which is contained in the Cpp\Chap06\ Ch6AppE08 Solution folder.

C. Use the IPO chart you created in Step A to code the program.

D. Complete a desk-check table for the program, using the following eight sets of data:

- A, 10, 20
- a, 45, 15
- S, 65, 50
- s, 7, 13
- G
- M, 10, 20
- d, 45, 15
- d, 50, 100

E. Save and then build the solution.

F. Execute the program. Use the data from Step D to test the program.

G. When the program is working correctly, close the Output window, then use the File menu to close the solution.

9) In this exercise, you learn how to include a Boolean value in a **switch** statement.

A. If necessary, start Visual Studio .NET. Open the Ch6AppE09 Solution (Ch6AppE09 Solution.sln) file, which is contained in the Cpp\Chap06\ Ch6AppE09 Solution folder.

B. Replace the **if** statement with a **switch** statement.

C. Save and then build the solution.

D. Execute the program. Test the program appropriately.

E. When the program is working correctly, close the Command Prompt window and the Output window, then use the File menu to close the solution.

 10) In this exercise, you debug a C++ program.

A. If necessary, start Visual Studio .NET. Open the Ch6AppE10 Solution (Ch6AppE10 Solution.sln) file, which is contained in the Cpp\Chap06\ Ch6AppE10 Solution folder. The program should display the salary amount corresponding to the code entered by the user. A code of 1 corresponds to a salary amount of $45,000. Codes of 2 and 5 correspond to a salary amount of $33,000. Codes of 3 and 4 correspond to a salary amount of $25,000.

B. Study the program's code, then build the solution.

C. Correct any errors in the program, then save and build the solution. Execute the program. Test the program using a code of 2. $33,000 should appear in the Command Prompt window.

D. When the program is working correctly, close the Output window, then use the File menu to close the solution.

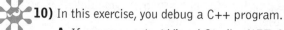 Please visit the Testing Center at www.course.com/testingcenter for more practice on the topics covered in this chapter.

The Repetition Structure

After completing this chapter, you will be able to:

- Include a repetition structure in pseudocode and in a flowchart

- Code a pretest loop using the C++ `while` statement

- Initialize and update counters and accumulators

- Code a pretest loop using the C++ `for` statement

Concept Lesson

Using the Repetition Structure

As you learned in Chapter 1, the three control structures used in programs are sequence, selection, and repetition. Every program contains the sequence structure, in which the program instructions are processed, one after another, in the order in which each appears in the program. Most programs also contain the selection structure, which you learned about in Chapters 5 and 6. Recall that programmers use the selection structure when they need the computer to make a decision and then take the appropriate action based on the result of that decision.

In addition to including the sequence and selection structures, most programs also include the repetition structure. Programmers use the **repetition structure**, referred to more simply as a **loop**, when they need the computer to repeatedly process one or more program instructions until some condition is met, at which time the repetition structure ends. For example, you may want to process a set of instructions—such as the instructions to calculate net pay—for each employee in a company. Or, you may want to process a set of instructions until the user enters a negative sales amount, which indicates that he or she has no more sales amounts to enter.

A repetition structure can be either a pretest loop or a posttest loop. In both types of loops, the condition is evaluated with each repetition, or iteration, of the loop. In a **pretest loop**, the evaluation occurs before the instructions within the loop are processed, while in a **posttest loop**, the evaluation occurs after the instructions within the loop are processed. Depending on the result of the evaluation, the instructions in a pretest loop may never be processed. The instructions in a posttest loop, however, always will be processed at least once. Of the two types of loops, the pretest loop is the most commonly used. You learn about the pretest loop in this chapter. The posttest loop is covered in Chapter 8.

Pretest Loops

As you already know, not all problems require a loop in their solutions. Consider, for example, Acme Hardware's problem description and IPO chart shown in Figure 7-1.

Figure 7-1: Problem description and IPO chart for Acme Hardware

Problem description		
At the beginning of each year, the president of Acme Hardware is paid a 10% bonus. The bonus is based on the amount of sales made by the company during the previous year. The payroll clerk wants a program that can be used to calculate and display the amount of the president's bonus.		
Input	**Processing**	**Output**
bonus rate (10%) sales	Processing items: none Algorithm: 1. enter the sales 2. calculate the bonus by multiplying the sales by the bonus rate 3. display the bonus	bonus

tip

As with the sequence and selection structures, you already are familiar with the repetition structure. For example, shampoo bottles typically include a direction that tells you to repeat the "apply shampoo to hair," "lather," and "rinse" steps until your hair is clean.

tip

Pretest and posttest loops are also called top-driven and bottom-driven loops, respectively.

tip

As you can with selection structures, you also can nest repetition structures, which means that you can place one repetition structure within another repetition structure. Nested repetition structures are covered in Chapter 8.

The problem description for Acme Hardware indicates that the bonus for only one employee needs to be displayed. Therefore, the enter, calculate, and display steps contained in the algorithm will be processed only once. Because no steps in the algorithm need to be repeated, the algorithm does not require a loop.

Now, however, consider the O'Donnell Incorporated problem description and IPO chart shown in Figure 7-2.

Figure 7-2: Problem description and IPO chart for O'Donnell Incorporated

Problem description
In January of each year, O'Donnell Incorporated pays a 10% bonus to each of its salespeople. The bonus is based on the amount of sales made by the salesperson during the previous year. The payroll clerk wants a program that can be used to calculate and display each salesperson's bonus amount.

Input	Processing	Output

bonus rate (10%)
sales
	Processing items: none
	
	Algorithm 1:
	1. enter the sales
	2. calculate the bonus by multiplying the sales by the bonus rate
	3. display the bonus
	
	Algorithm 2:
	1. enter the sales
	2. repeat while (the sales are not equal to -1)
	    calculate the bonus by multiplying the sales by the bonus rate
	
	    display the bonus
	    enter the sales
	  end repeat while
		bonus

displays the bonus for one salesperson only

displays the bonus for as many salespeople as desired

The problem description for O'Donnell Incorporated is similar to the problem description for Acme Hardware, except it indicates that the bonus for more than one employee needs to be calculated and displayed. You could use either of the algorithms shown in Figure 7-2's IPO chart to solve the O'Donnell Incorporated problem. However, as you will learn shortly, the second algorithm is a much better choice.

The first algorithm shown in Figure 7-2 is identical to the Acme Hardware algorithm shown in Figure 7-1; neither algorithm contains a loop. Although the first algorithm shown in Figure 7-2 can be used to solve the O'Donnell Incorporated problem, the algorithm is inefficient for that purpose, because it displays only one bonus amount. A program based on this algorithm would need to be executed once for each salesperson receiving a bonus. In other words, if O'Donnell Incorporated has 100 salespeople, the payroll clerk would need to execute the program 100 times to calculate and display each salesperson's bonus amount.

The second algorithm shown in Figure 7-2 contains a loop and represents a more efficient solution to the O'Donnell Incorporated problem. After executing a program based on the second algorithm, the payroll clerk can calculate and display the bonus amount for as many salespeople as desired. The payroll clerk indicates when he or she is finished calculating and displaying bonus amounts by entering −1 (a negative number one) as the sales amount. Figure 7-3 identifies the important components of the loop shown in the second algorithm.

Figure 7-3: Components of a loop

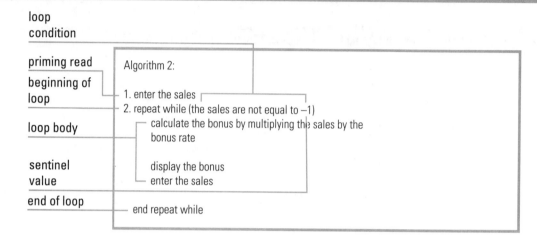

With very rare exceptions, every loop has a loop condition and a loop body. In a pretest loop, the **loop condition** appears at the beginning of the loop and determines the number of times the instructions within the loop are processed. The instructions within the loop are referred to as the **loop body**. Similar to a selection structure condition, a loop condition must result in either a true or false answer only. In the loop shown in Figure 7-3, for example, if the sales amount entered by the user is not equal to −1, then the loop condition evaluates to true. Otherwise, in which case the user entered −1 as the sales amount, the loop condition evaluates to false.

Some loops, such as the one shown in Figure 7-3, require the user to enter a special value to end the loop. Values that are used to end loops are referred to as **sentinel values**. In the loop shown in Figure 7-3, the sentinel value is −1. The sentinel value should be one that is easily distinguishable from the valid data recognized by the program. The number 1000, for example, would not be a good sentinel value for the loop in Figure 7-3, because it is possible that a salesperson could have made that amount of sales. The number −1, on the other hand, is a good sentinel value for the loop, because a sales amount cannot be negative.

When the loop condition evaluates to true, the one or more instructions listed in the loop body are processed; otherwise, these instructions are skipped over. Because the loop condition in a pretest loop is evaluated before any of the instructions within the loop body are processed, it is possible that the loop body instructions may not be processed at all; this would occur when the loop condition initially evaluates to false. For example, if the payroll clerk at O'Donnell Incorporated enters the number −1 as the first sales amount, the loop condition shown in Figure 7-3 will evaluate to false, and the instructions in the loop body will be skipped over.

After each processing of the loop body instructions, the loop condition is reevaluated to determine whether the instructions should be processed again. The loop's instructions are processed and its condition evaluated until the condition evaluates to false, at which time the loop ends and processing continues with the instruction immediately following the end of the loop.

tip

Values used to end loops are also called trip values or trailer values.

Notice that the pseudocode shown in Figure 7-3 contains two "enter the sales" instructions: One of the instructions appears in Step 1, which is above the loop, and the other appears as the last instruction in the loop body. The "enter the sales" instruction that appears above the loop is referred to as the **priming read**, because it is used to prime (prepare or set up) the loop. In this case, the priming read gets only the first sales amount from the user. This first value is compared to the sentinel value (−1) and determines whether the loop body instructions are processed at all. If the loop body instructions are processed, the "enter the sales" instruction that appears within the loop body gets the remaining sales amounts (if any) from the user.

It may be easier to visualize a pretest loop by viewing it in a flowchart.

Flowcharting a Pretest Loop

Figure 7-4 shows the O'Donnell Incorporated algorithm in flowchart form.

Figure 7-4: O'Donnell Incorporated algorithm shown in flowchart form

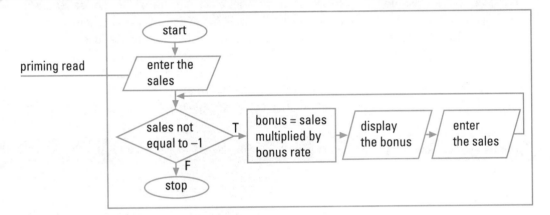

priming read

tip

The flowchart shown in Figure 7-4 illustrates why the loop is referred to as a pretest loop. Notice that the repetition diamond, which contains the loop condition, appears *before* the symbols in both the true and false paths.

tip

The symbol located immediately above the repetition diamond represents the instruction processed immediately before the loop condition is evaluated the first time.

Recall that the oval in a flowchart is the start/stop symbol, the rectangle is the process symbol, the parallelogram is the input/output symbol, and the diamond is the selection/repetition symbol. In Figure 7-4's flowchart, the diamond indicates the beginning of a repetition structure (loop). As with the selection structure diamond, which you learned about in Chapter 5, the repetition structure diamond contains a comparison that has a true or false answer only. The comparison represents the loop condition, which determines whether the instructions within the loop body are processed.

Like the selection diamond, the repetition diamond has two flowlines leaving the symbol. The flowline marked with a "T" (for true) leads to the loop body—the instructions processed when the loop condition evaluates to true. The flowline marked with an "F" (for false) leads to the instructions that are processed when the loop condition evaluates to false.

Unlike the selection diamond, the repetition diamond has two flowlines leading into the diamond, rather than one. One of the flowlines comes from the symbol located immediately above the diamond. In the flowchart shown in Figure 7-4, this symbol is the parallelogram that represents the priming read, which gets only the first sales amount from the user. Notice that the parallelogram has a flowline that flows into the repetition diamond.

The second flowline leading into the repetition diamond flows from the repetition structure's true path, which contains the loop body instructions. In the flowchart shown in Figure 7-4, for example, the flowline leading out of the "enter the sales" parallelogram in the true path flows back up to the repetition diamond. Notice that the two flowlines leading into the repetition diamond, as well as the symbols and flowlines within the true path, form a circle or loop. It is this loop that distinguishes the repetition structure from the selection structure in a flowchart.

To help you understand how a loop operates in a program, you will desk-check the algorithm shown in Figure 7-4 using the following sales data: 10000, 25000, and −1. The first input parallelogram shown in Figure 7-4's flowchart gets the first sales amount from the user. Figure 7-5 shows the first sales amount—10000—recorded in the desk-check table.

Figure 7-5: First sales amount recorded in the desk-check table

bonus rate	sales	bonus
.10	10000	

The next symbol in the flowchart is the repetition diamond. This diamond represents the beginning of a pretest loop that repeats its instructions as long as (or while) the user enters a sales amount that is not −1. Before processing the loop instructions, the loop condition compares the sales amount entered by the user to the number −1. In this case, the loop condition evaluates to true, because 10000 is not equal to −1. Recall that when the loop condition evaluates to true, the instructions in the loop body are processed. The first two instructions in the loop body shown in Figure 7-4 calculate and then display the bonus amount. Figure 7-6 shows the first salesperson's bonus information recorded in the desk-check table.

Figure 7-6: First salesperson's bonus information recorded in the desk-check table

bonus rate	sales	bonus
.10	10000	1000

The last instruction in the loop body shown in Figure 7-4 is contained in an input parallelogram, and it gets the next salesperson's sales—in this case, 25000—from the user. After getting the sales, the loop condition, which appears in the repetition diamond located at the top of the loop, is reevaluated to determine whether the loop should be processed again (a true condition) or end (a false condition). In this case, the condition evaluates to true, because 25000 is not equal to −1. Because of this, the bonus amount is calculated and then displayed on the screen. Figure 7-7 shows the second salesperson's information recorded in the desk-check table.

Figure 7-7: Second salesperson's information recorded in the desk-check table

bonus rate	sales	bonus
.10	~~10000~~ 25000	~~1000~~ 2500

The input parallelogram that appears as the last flowchart symbol in the loop body then gets the next salesperson's sales from the user. In this case, the user enters the sentinel value (−1) as the sales, as shown in Figure 7-8.

Figure 7-8: Sentinel value recorded in the desk-check table

	bonus rate	sales	bonus
sentinel value	.10	~~10000~~ ~~25000~~ -1	~~1000~~ 2500

Next, the loop condition is reevaluated to determine whether the loop should be processed again (a true condition) or end (a false condition). In this case, the loop condition evaluates to false, because the sales amount entered by the user is equal to −1. Recall that when the loop condition evaluates to false, the loop instructions are skipped over and processing continues with the instruction immediately following the end of the loop. In Figure 7-4's flowchart, the stop oval, which marks the end of the algorithm, follows the loop.

You can code the pretest loop in C++ using either the while statement or the for statement. First, you learn how to use the while statement.

Using the while Statement to Code a Pretest Loop

Figure 7-9 shows the syntax of the while statement, which you can use to code a pretest loop in a C++ program.

Figure 7-9: Syntax of the C++ while **statement**

```
while (loop condition)
    one statement, or a block of statements enclosed in braces, to be processed as long as the loop
    condition evaluates to true
//end while
```

Items in **bold** in the syntax—in this case, the keyword while and the parentheses that surround the loop condition—are essential components of the while statement. Items in italics indicate where the programmer must supply information pertaining to the current program. In the while statement, the programmer must supply the loop condition to be evaluated. The loop condition must be a Boolean expression, which is an expression that evaluates to either true or false. The loop condition can contain variables, constants, functions, arithmetic operators, comparison operators, and logical operators.

In addition to supplying the loop condition, the programmer also must supply the statements to be processed when the loop condition evaluates to true. If more than one statement needs to be processed, the statements must be entered as a statement block. Recall that you create a statement block by enclosing the statements in a set of braces ({}).

Although it is not required to do so, it is a good programming practice to use a comment, such as //end while, to mark the end of the while statement. The comment will make your program easier to read and understand.

Figure 7-10 shows the C++ code for the O'Donnell Incorporated algorithm, which contains a pretest loop.

tip

Some C++ programmers enclose the loop body in braces even when it contains only one statement, but this is not required by the C++ syntax. However, including the braces in a loop that contains only one statement is convenient, because you will not need to remember to enter the braces if additional statements are added to the loop in the future. Forgetting to enter the braces around a statement block is a common error made by programmers.

Figure 7-10: C++ statements for the O'Donnell Incorporated algorithm

IPO chart information	C++ instructions

Input
  bonus rate (10%)
  sales
Processing
  none
Output
  bonus
	`const double RATE = .1;`
	`double sales = 0.0;`
	
	`double bonus = 0.0;`

Algorithm 1. enter the sales	`cout << "Enter the first sales amount: ";` `cin >> sales;`
2. repeat while (the sales are not equal to –1)	`while (sales != -1)` `{`
calculate the bonus by multiplying the sales by the bonus rate	`    bonus = sales * RATE;`
display the bonus	`    cout << bonus << endl;`
enter the sales	`    cout << "Enter the next sales amount: ";` `    cin >> sales;`
end repeat while	`} //end while`

Take a closer look at the statements shown in Figure 7-10. The first three statements declare and initialize the **RATE** named constant and the **sales** and **bonus** variables. The `cout << "Enter the first sales amount: ";` statement prompts the user to enter the first sales amount, and the `cin >> sales;` statement stores the user's response in the **sales** variable. The `while (sales != -1)` clause compares the value stored in the **sales** variable to the sentinel value (–1). If the **sales** variable does not contain the sentinel value, the instructions within the loop body are processed. Those instructions calculate and display the bonus, then prompt the user to enter the next sales amount, and store the user's response in the **sales** variable. Each time the user enters a sales amount the **while** clause compares the sales amount to the sentinel value. When the user enters the sentinel value—in this case, –1—as the sales amount, the loop instructions are skipped over and processing continues with the line immediately below the end of the loop.

Keep in mind that if you forget to enter the `cin >> sales;` statement within the program's loop, the loop will process its instructions indefinitely, because there will be no way to change the value stored in the **sales** variable. A loop that processes its instructions indefinitely is referred to as either an **endless loop** or an **infinite loop**. Usually, you can stop a program that contains an endless loop by pressing Ctrl+c (press and hold down the Ctrl key as you press the letter c); you also can use the Command Prompt window's Close button.

tip

You can practice stopping a program that contains an endless loop by completing Exercise 17 at the end of this lesson.

MINI-QUIZ

Mini-Quiz 1

1) Write a C++ `while` clause that processes the loop instructions as long as the value in the `quantity` variable is greater than the number 0.

2) Write a C++ `while` clause that stops the loop when the value in the `quantity` variable is less than the number 0.

3) Write a C++ `while` clause that processes the loop instructions as long as the value in the `inStock` variable is greater than the value in the `reorder` variable.

4) Write a C++ `while` clause that processes the loop instructions as long as the value in the `letter` variable is either Y or y. (The `letter` variable is a `char` variable.)

5) Which of the following is a good sentinel value for a program that inputs the number of hours each employee worked this week?
    a. −9
    b. 32
    c. 45.5
    d. 7

6) The input instruction that appears above a pretest loop is called the _____.

Many times a program will need to display a subtotal, a total, or an average. You calculate this information using a repetition structure that includes a counter, or an accumulator, or both.

Using Counters and Accumulators

Counters and accumulators are used within a repetition structure to calculate subtotals, totals, and averages. A **counter** is a numeric variable used for counting something—such as the number of employees paid in a week. An **accumulator** is a numeric variable used for accumulating (adding together) something—such as the total dollar amount of a week's payroll.

Two tasks are associated with counters and accumulators: initializing and updating. **Initializing** means to assign a beginning value to the counter or accumulator. Typically, counters and accumulators are initialized to 0; however, they can be initialized to any number, depending on the value required by the algorithm. The initialization task is done before the loop is processed, because it needs to be done only once.

Updating, also called **incrementing**, means adding a number to the value stored in the counter or the accumulator. The number can be either positive or negative, integer or non-integer. A counter is always incremented by a constant value—typically the number 1—whereas an accumulator is incremented by a value that varies. The assignment statement that updates a counter or an accumulator is placed within the loop in a program, because the update task must be performed each time the loop instructions are processed. You use both a counter and an accumulator in the Sales Express program, which you view next.

The Sales Express Program

Assume that Sales Express wants a program that the sales manager can use to display the average amount the company sold during the prior year. The sales manager will enter the amount of each salesperson's sales. The program will use a counter to keep track of the number of sales amounts entered by the sales manager, and an accumulator to total those sales amounts. After all of the sales amounts are entered, the program will calculate the average sales amount by dividing the value stored in the accumulator by the value stored in the

tip

Counters are used to answer the question, "How many?"—for example, "How many salespeople live in Virginia?" Accumulators are used to answer the question, "How much?"—for example, "How much did the salespeople sell this quarter?"

counter. It then will display the average sales amount on the screen. Figure 7-11 shows the IPO chart information and C++ code for the Sales Express problem.

Figure 7-11: IPO chart information and C++ code for the Sales Express problem

	IPO chart information	C++ instructions
initialization		

Input
  sales

```cpp
double sales = 0.0;
```

Processing
  number of salespeople (counter)
  total sales (accumulator)

```cpp
int totalPeople = 0;
double totalSales = 0.0;
```

Output
  average sales

```cpp
double average = 0.0;
```

Algorithm
1. enter the sales

```cpp
cout << "Enter the first sales amount: ";
cin >> sales;
```

2. repeat while (the sales are
   greater than or equal to 0)
       add 1 to the number of
       salespeople

```cpp
while (sales >= 0)
{
    totalPeople = totalPeople + 1;
```

update

       add the sales to the total
       sales

```cpp
    totalSales = totalSales + sales;
```

verify that the counter is not 0 before using it as the divisor in an expression

       enter the sales

```cpp
    cout << "Enter the next sales
    amount: ";
    cin >> sales;
```

   end repeat while

```cpp
}   //end while
```

3. if (the number of salespeople is
   not equal to 0)
       calculate the average sales
       by dividing the total sales by
       the number of salespeople

```cpp
if (totalPeople != 0)
{
    average = totalSales /
    double(totalPeople);
```

       display the average sales

```cpp
    cout << setiosflags(ios::fixed);
    cout << setprecision(2);
    cout << average << endl;
}
```

   else
       display an error message

```cpp
else
    cout << "You didn't enter any
    sales." << endl;
```

   end if

```cpp
//end if
```

tip

The "enter the sales" step located above the loop in the algorithm shown in Figure 7-11 is the priming read.

As Figure 7-11 indicates, the input for the Sales Express problem is each salesperson's sales amount, and the output is the average sales amount. The algorithm uses two processing items: a counter that keeps track of the number of salespeople and an accumulator that keeps track of the total sales. Notice in the C++ code that the counter (an `int` variable) is initialized to 0, and the accumulator (a `double` variable) is initialized to 0.0. To better understand counters and accumulators, you will desk-check the Sales Express code using the following sales data: 30000, 40000, and −3.

After declaring and initializing the appropriate variables, the program prompts the user to enter the first sales amount, then stores the user's response in the **sales** variable, as shown in Figure 7-12.

Figure 7-12: First sales amount recorded in the desk-check table

sales	totalPeople	totalSales	average
~~0.0~~ 30000.0	0	0.0	0.0

The **while (sales >= 0)** clause begins a pretest loop that repeats the loop body instructions as long as (or while) the user enters a sales amount that is greater than or equal to 0. The loop stops when the user enters the sentinel value, which, in this program, is any sales amount that is less than 0. Notice that, unlike the loop in the O'Donnell Incorporated algorithm, the loop in the Sales Express algorithm has more than one sentinel value. In the Sales Express algorithm, any number that is less than 0 can be used to stop the loop.

If the sales amount entered by the user is greater than or equal to 0, as it is in this case, the instructions in the loop body are processed. The first two instructions update the **totalPeople** counter variable by adding 1 to it, and update the **totalSales** accumulator variable by adding the sales amount to it. The updates are shown in Figure 7-13's desk-check table.

Figure 7-13: Desk-check table showing the first update to the counter and accumulator

sales	totalPeople	totalSales	average
~~0.0~~ 30000.0	~~0~~ 1	~~0.0~~ 30000.0	0.0

The last two instructions in the loop body prompt the user to enter the next sales amount, then store the user's response—in this case, 40000—in the **sales** variable. The loop condition **while (sales >= 0)** then is reevaluated to determine whether the loop should be processed again (a true condition) or simply end (a false condition). Here again, the loop condition evaluates to true, because 40000 is greater than 0. Because of this, the loop instructions increment the **totalPeople** variable by 1, and increment the **totalSales** variable by the sales amount, as shown in Figure 7-14.

Figure 7-14: Desk-check table showing the second update to the counter and accumulator

sales	totalPeople	totalSales	average
~~0.0~~ ~~30000.0~~ 40000.0	~~0~~ ~~1~~ 2	~~0.0~~ ~~30000.0~~ 70000.0	0.0

The last two instructions in the loop body prompt the user to enter the next sales amount, and then store the user's response—in this case, −3, which is a sentinel value—in the **sales** variable. The loop condition **while (sales >= 0)** then is reevaluated to determine whether the loop should be processed again or simply end. In this case, the loop condition evaluates to false, because −3 is not greater than or equal to 0. When the loop condition evaluates to false, the loop ends, and processing continues with the statement immediately following the loop.

In the Sales Express program, the statement following the loop is an **if** statement. The **if** statement's condition verifies that the **totalPeople** variable does not contain the number 0. This verification is necessary because the first instruction in the **if** statement's true path uses the **totalPeople** variable as the divisor when calculating the average, and the computer cannot divide by 0. If the **totalPeople** variable contains the number 0, the **if** statement's false path displays an appropriate message. However, if the **totalPeople** variable contains a value other than 0, as it does in this case, the **if** statement's true path calculates and displays the average sales amount (35000) on the screen before the program ends. Figure 7-15 shows the completed desk-check table for the Sales Express program.

Figure 7-15: Completed desk-check table for the Sales Express program

	sales	totalPeople	totalSales	average
	~~0.0~~ ~~30000.0~~ ~~40000.0~~	~~0~~ ~~1~~ 2	~~0.0~~ ~~30000.0~~ 70000.0	~~0.0~~ 35000.0
sentinel value	−3			

MINI-QUIZ

Mini-Quiz 2

1) A(n) _____ is updated by an amount that varies.

2) Write a C++ assignment statement that updates the **quantity** counter variable by 2.

3) Write a C++ assignment statement that updates the **total** counter variable by −3.

4) Write a C++ assignment statement that updates the **totalPurchases** accumulator variable by the value stored in the **purchases** variable.

In both the O'Donnell Incorporated and Sales Express programs, the termination of the loop is controlled by the user entering a sentinel value. The termination of a loop also can be controlled by the program itself; typically, this is done using a counter.

Counter-Controlled Pretest Loops

Assume that Jasper Music Company wants a program that allows the sales manager to enter the quarterly sales amount made in each of three regions: Region 1, Region 2, and Region 3. The program should calculate the total quarterly sales and then display the total amount on the screen. Figure 7-16 shows the IPO chart information and C++ code for the Jasper Music Company problem.

Figure 7-16: IPO chart information and C++ code for the Jasper Music Company problem

IPO chart information	C++ instructions
Input region's quarterly sales	`int regionSales = 0;`
Processing counter (1 through 3)	`int numRegion = 1;`
Output total quarterly sales (accumulator)	`int totalSales = 0;`

Algorithm
1. repeat while (the counter is less than or equal to 3)
　　enter the region's quarterly sales
 	
　　add the region's quarterly sales to the total quarterly sales
 	
　　add 1 to the counter
end repeat while
2. display the total quarterly sales
	`while (numRegion <= 3)`
	`{`
	`   cout << "Enter Region " << numRegion`
	`   << "'s quarterly sales: ";`
	`   cin >> regionSales;`
	
	`   totalSales = totalSales + regionSales;`
	
	`   numRegion = numRegion + 1;`
	`}   //end while`
	`cout << setiosflags(ios::fixed);`
	`cout << setprecision(2);`
	`cout << totalSales << endl;`

As Figure 7-16 indicates, the input is each region's quarterly sales amount, and the output is the total quarterly sales amount. The solution uses one processing item: a counter that will keep track of the number of times the loop instructions are repeated. In this case, the loop instructions need to be repeated three times, once for each sales region. Notice in the C++ code that the counter variable, named **numRegion**, is initialized to the number 1, which corresponds to the first sales region. To understand how a counter is used to stop a program, you will desk-check the code shown in Figure 7-16.

The first three statements in the code create and initialize three variables named **regionSales**, **numRegion**, and **totalSales**. Figure 7-17 shows the desk-check table after these statements are processed.

Figure 7-17: Desk-check table showing initialization of variables

regionSales	numRegion	totalSales
0	1	0

The while (numRegion <= 3) clause in the code begins a pretest loop that repeats its instructions as long as (or while) the value in the numRegion counter variable is less than or equal to 3. The loop stops when the value in the numRegion variable is greater than 3. At this point in the program, the value stored in the numRegion variable is less than 3, so the loop condition evaluates to true and the loop instructions are processed. The first statement in the loop body prompts the user to enter Region 1's quarterly sales, and the second statement stores the user's response in the regionSales variable. Assume that the user enters the number 2500. The third statement adds Region 1's quarterly sales (2500) to the value stored in the totalSales accumulator variable (0), giving 2500. The last statement in the loop body increments the numRegion counter variable by 1, giving 2. Figure 7-18 shows the desk-check table after the loop instructions are processed the first time.

Figure 7-18: Results of processing the loop instructions the first time

regionSales	numRegion	totalSales
~~0~~ 2500	~~1~~ 2	~~0~~ 2500

The loop condition while (numRegion <= 3) then is reevaluated to determine whether the loop should be processed again (a true condition) or simply end (a false condition). Here again, the loop condition evaluates to true, because the contents of the numRegion counter variable (2) is less than 3. Because of this, the loop instructions prompt the user to enter Region 2's quarterly sales, then store the user's response in the regionSales variable. Assume that the user enters the number 6000. The loop instructions add Region 2's quarterly sales (6000) to the value stored in the totalSales accumulator (2500), giving 8500. The instructions then increment the numRegion counter variable by 1, giving 3. Figure 7-19 shows the desk-check table after the loop body instructions are processed the second time.

Figure 7-19: Results of processing the loop instructions the second time

regionSales	numRegion	totalSales
~~0~~ ~~2500~~ 6000	~~1~~ ~~2~~ 3	~~0~~ ~~2500~~ 8500

The loop condition `while (numRegion <= 3)` then is reevaluated to determine whether the loop should be processed again or end. Here again, the loop condition evaluates to true, because the contents of the `numRegion` counter variable (3) is equal to 3. Because of this, the loop instructions prompt the user to enter Region 3's quarterly sales, and then store the user's response in the `regionSales` variable. Assume that the user enters the number 2000. The loop instructions add Region 3's quarterly sales (2000) to the value stored in the `totalSales` accumulator (8500), giving 10500. The instructions then increment the `numRegion` counter variable by 1, giving 4. Figure 7-20 shows the desk-check table after the loop body instructions are processed the third (and last) time.

Figure 7-20: Results of processing the loop instructions the third time

regionSales	numRegion	totalSales
0̶	1̶	0̶
2̶5̶0̶0̶	2̶	2̶5̶0̶0̶
6̶0̶0̶0̶	3̶	8̶5̶0̶0̶
2000	4	10500

The loop condition `while (numRegion <= 3)` then is reevaluated to determine whether the loop should be processed again or end. At this point, the loop condition evaluates to false, because the contents of the `numRegion` counter variable (4) is not less than or equal to 3. Because of this, the loop ends and processing continues with the instruction located immediately below the loop; that instruction displays the contents of the `totalSales` variable on the screen. Notice that the quarterly sales program itself, rather than the user, controls the termination of the loop.

Recall that, in addition to using the `while` statement, you also can use the `for` statement to code a pretest loop in C++.

Using the `for` Statement to Code a Pretest Loop

As you can with the `while` statement, you also can use the `for` statement to code any pretest loop. However, the most common use for the `for` statement is to code pretest loops whose processing is controlled by a counter. This is because the `for` statement provides a more compact way of writing that type of loop. Figure 7-21 shows the syntax of the `for` statement in C++.

Figure 7-21: Syntax of the C++ `for` statement

semicolon

semicolon

```
for ([initialization]; loop condition; [update])
     one statement, or a block of statements enclosed in braces, to be processed
     as long as the loop condition evaluates to true
//end for
```

Note: Items in **bold** are required. Items in square brackets ([]) are optional. Items in *italics* indicate places where the programmer must supply information pertaining to the current program.

tip

A common error made by C++ programmers is to separate the three items of information in the `for` clause with two commas rather than with two semicolons.

The `for` statement begins with the `for` clause, followed by the body of the loop, which contains the one or more statements that you want the loop to repeat. If the loop body contains more than one statement, the statements must be entered as a statement block, which means they must be enclosed in a set of braces ({}). Although it is not required by the C++ syntax, it is helpful to use a comment, such as `//end for`, to document the end of the `for` statement.

As the syntax shown in Figure 7-21 indicates, the `for` clause contains three arguments separated by two semicolons. In most `for` clauses, the first argument, *initialization*, creates and initializes a counter variable. The `for` statement uses the counter variable to keep track of the number of times the loop instructions are processed. The second argument in the `for` clause, *loop condition*, specifies the condition that must be true for the loop to continue processing the loop body instructions. The loop condition must be a Boolean expression; in other words, it must be an expression that evaluates to either true or false. The loop condition can contain variables, constants, functions, arithmetic operators, comparison operators, and logical operators. The loop stops when the loop condition evaluates to false. The third argument in the `for` clause, *update*, usually contains an expression that updates the counter variable specified in the *initialization* argument.

In the remaining sections in this lesson, you view three examples of the `for` statement.

Example 1 – Displaying the Numbers 1 Through 3

Figure 7-22 shows a `for` statement that displays the numbers 1 through 3 on the screen.

Figure 7-22: `for` statement displays the numbers 1 through 3

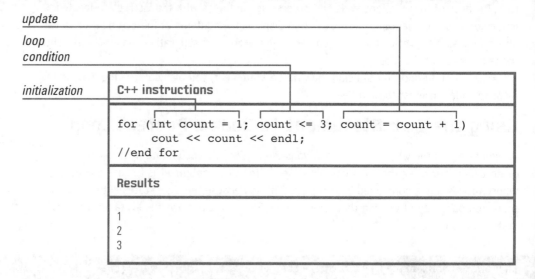

update

loop condition

initialization

```
C++ instructions

for (int count = 1; count <= 3; count = count + 1)
    cout << count << endl;
//end for
```

```
Results

1
2
3
```

Desk-checking the C++ instructions shown in Figure 7-22 will help you to understand how the `for` statement works. When the computer encounters a `for` statement in a program, it first processes the code shown in the `for` clause's *initialization* argument. The code shown in the *initialization* argument is processed only once, at the beginning of the loop. In the case of the `for` statement shown in Figure 7-22, the computer creates an `int` variable named `count` and initializes the variable to the number 1, as shown in Figure 7-23.

Figure 7-23: Desk-check table showing the result of processing the *initialization* argument

Next, the computer processes the code shown in the **for** clause's *loop condition* argument to determine whether to process the loop body instructions. In the case of the *loop condition* argument shown in Figure 7-22, the computer processes the instruction contained in the loop body only when the value stored in the **count** variable is less than or equal to the number 3. Currently, the value stored in the **count** variable is the number 1, so the loop body instruction is processed and displays the **count** variable's value (1) on the screen. Unlike the *initialization* argument, which is processed only once, the *loop condition* argument is processed with each repetition, or iteration, of the loop.

Next, the computer processes the code shown in the **for** clause's *update* argument. The *update* argument shown in Figure 7-22 instructs the computer to add the number 1 to the value stored in the **count** variable, giving 2. Like the *loop condition* argument, the *update* argument is processed with each repetition of the loop. Figure 7-24 shows the result of processing the *update* argument for the first time.

Figure 7-24: Desk-check table showing the result of processing the *update* argument for the first time

After processing the *update* code for the first time, the computer processes the *loop condition* code again to determine whether to process the loop body instructions once more. In the case of the program shown in Figure 7-22, the **count** variable's value still is less than or equal to 3, so the computer displays the **count** variable's value (2) on the screen.

After processing the loop body instructions, the computer processes the *update* argument again. The *update* argument shown in Figure 7-22 increments the **count** variable by 1, giving 3, as shown in Figure 7-25.

Figure 7-25: Desk-check table showing the result of processing the *update* argument for the second time

count
~~1~~
~~2~~
3

tip

Like the while statement, the for statement evaluates the loop condition *before* the loop body instructions are processed.

Next, the computer processes the *loop condition* code again to determine whether to process the loop body instructions another time. In this case, the `count` variable's value still is less than or equal to 3, so the computer displays the `count` variable's value (3) on the screen.

After processing the loop body instructions, the computer processes the *update* argument again. The *update* argument shown in Figure 7-22 increments the `count` variable by 1, giving 4, as shown in Figure 7-26.

Figure 7-26: Desk-check table showing the result of processing the *update* argument for the third time

count
~~1~~
~~2~~
~~3~~
4

Next, the computer processes the *loop condition* code again to determine whether to process the loop body instructions another time. In this case, the `count` variable's value is not less than or equal to three, so the computer does not process the loop body instruction. Rather, the loop ends (the *update* argument is not processed this time) and the computer processes the instruction following the end of the `for` statement. Notice that the value in the `count` variable is the number four when the loop stops.

Now view an example of a `for` statement that contains more than one instruction in the loop body.

Example 2 – Calculating and Displaying a Commission

Figure 7-27 shows a `for` statement that calculates and displays a commission using commission rates of .1, .15, .2, and .25. Notice that the loop body contains more than one instruction, and the instructions are entered as a statement block by enclosing them in a set of braces ({}).

Figure 7-27: for statement calculates and displays a commission

```
C++ instructions

double sales = 0.0;
double comm  = 0.0;
cout << setiosflags(ios::fixed) << setprecision(0);
cout << "Enter the sales: ";
cin >> sales;
for (double rate = .1; rate <= .25; rate = rate + .05)
{
    comm = sales * rate;
    cout << "Commission: $" << comm << endl;
}  //end for
```

Results (assuming the user enters 25000 as the sales amount)

Commission: $2500
Commission: $3750
Commission: $5000
Commission: $6250

Figure 7-28 shows the steps the computer follows when processing the code shown in Figure 7-27. Notice that the **for** statement stops when the value stored in the **rate** variable is .3.

Figure 7-28: Processing steps for the code shown in Figure 7-27

Processing steps

1. Computer creates and initializes the **sales** variable to 0.0.
2. Computer creates and initializes the **comm** variable to 0.0.
3. Computer sets the appropriate format for floating-point numbers.
4. Computer prompts user for sales amount.
5. Computer stores user's response in the **sales** variable.
6. Computer creates the **rate** variable and initializes it to .1 (*initialization* code).
7. Computer determines whether value in **rate** variable is less than or equal to .25 (*loop condition* code). It is.
8. Computer calculates the commission and displays "Commission: $2500" on the screen (loop body instructions).
9. Computer adds .05 to value stored in **rate** variable, giving .15 (*update* code).
10. Computer determines whether value in **rate** variable is less than or equal to .25 (*loop condition* code). It is.
11. Computer calculates the commission and displays "Commission: $3750" on the screen (loop body instructions).
12. Computer adds .05 to value stored in **rate** variable, giving .2 (*update* code).
13. Computer determines whether value in **rate** variable is less than or equal to .25 (*loop condition* code). It is.
14. Computer calculates the commission and displays "Commission: $5000" on the screen (loop body instructions).
15. Computer adds .05 to value stored in **rate** variable, giving .25 (*update* code).

Figure 7-28: Processing steps for the code shown in Figure 7-27 (continued)

Processing steps
16. Computer determines whether value in **rate** variable is less than or equal to .25 (*loop condition* code). It is.
17. Computer calculates the commission and displays "Commission: $6250" on the screen (loop body instructions).
18. Computer adds .05 to value stored in **rate** variable, giving .3 (*update* code).
19. Computer determines whether value in **rate** variable is less than or equal to .25 (*loop condition* code). It is not.
20. Loop ends and the computer processes the instruction following the end of the **for** statement.

Finally, view an example of a **for** statement that does not use the *initialization* and *update* arguments.

Example 3 – Calculating and Displaying a Bonus

Although the most common use for the **for** statement is to code loops whose processing is controlled by a counter, you actually can use the **for** statement to code any pretest loop. For example, the **for** statement shown in Figure 7-29's code, which calculates and displays a bonus, is controlled by the user rather than by a counter.

Figure 7-29: for statement calculates and displays a bonus

tip

You also can omit the *loop condition* argument in the for clause. When doing so, however, you need to include the break statement in the loop body to stop the loop. You learned about the break statement in Chapter 6.

C++ instructions

semicolon after the *initialization*

loop condition

semicolon after the *loop condition*

```
const double RATE = .1;
double sales = 0.0;
double bonus = 0.0;
cout << setiosflags(ios::fixed) << setprecision(0);
cout << "Enter the first sales amount: ";
cin >> sales;
for (; sales > 0;)
{
    bonus = sales * RATE;
    cout << "Bonus: $" << bonus << endl;
    cout << "Enter the next sales amount: ";
    cin >> sales;
}   //end for
```

Results (assuming the user enters sales amounts of 4000, 3000, and –1)

Bonus: $400
Bonus: $300

Notice that the **for** clause shown in Figure 7-29 contains only the *loop condition* argument. Although the *initialization* and *update* arguments are omitted from the **for** clause, the semicolons after the *initialization* and *loop condition* arguments must be included. Figure 7-30 shows the steps the computer follows when processing the code shown in Figure 7-29.

Figure 7-30: Processing steps for the code shown in Figure 7-29

Processing steps

1. Computer creates and initializes the **RATE** constant to .1.
2. Computer creates and initializes the **sales** variable to 0.0.
3. Computer creates and initializes the **bonus** variable to 0.0.
4. Computer sets the appropriate format for floating-point numbers.
5. Computer prompts user for sales amount. Assume the user enters the number 4000.
6. Computer stores the user's response (4000) in the **sales** variable.
7. Computer determines whether the value in the **sales** variable is greater than 0 (*loop condition* code). It is.
8. Computer calculates the bonus and displays "Bonus: $400" on the screen. It then prompts the user for another sales amount and stores the user's response in the **sales** variable (loop body instructions). Assume the user enters the number 3000.
9. Computer determines whether the value in the **sales** variable is greater than 0 (*loop condition* code). It is.
10. Computer calculates the bonus and displays "Bonus: $300" on the screen. It then prompts the user for another sales amount and stores the user's response in the **sales** variable (loop body instructions). Assume the user enters the number −1.
11. Computer determines whether the value in the **sales** variable is greater than 0 (*loop condition* code). It is not.
12. Loop ends and the computer processes the instruction following the end of the **for** statement.

As Figure 7-30 indicates, the **for** statement stops when the user enters a sales amount that is less than or equal to 0.

tip
Whether you use the `for` statement or the `while` statement to code the loop shown in Figure 7-29 is a matter of personal preference.

MINI-QUIZ

Mini-Quiz 3

1) Assume a program declares an `int` variable named **evenNum** and initializes it to 2. Write a C++ `while` loop that uses the **evenNum** variable to display the even integers between 1 and 9.

2) Which of the following `for` clauses processes the loop instructions as long as the value stored in the **x** variable is less than or equal to the number 100?
   a. `for (int x = 10; x <= 100; x = x + 10)`
   b. `for (int x = 10, x <= 100, x = x + 10)`
   c. `for (int x == 10; x <= 100; x = x + 10)`
   d. `for (int x = x + 10; x <= 100; x = 10)`

3) What is the value stored in the **x** variable when the loop corresponding to the `for` clause in Question 2 ends?
   a. 100
   b. 111
   c. 101
   d. 110

4) Write a `for` clause that processes the loop instructions as long as the value stored in the **x** variable is greater than 0. The **x** variable should be an `int` variable. Initialize the variable to the number 25 and increment it by −5 with each repetition of the loop.

5) What is the value stored in the **x** variable when the loop corresponding to the `for` clause in Question 4 ends?

6) Write a `for` statement that displays the even integers between 1 and 9 on the screen. Use **num** as the name of the counter variable.

You now have completed Chapter 7's Concept lesson. You can either take a break or complete the end-of-lesson questions and exercises before moving on to the Application lesson.

SUMMARY

Programmers use the repetition structure, also called a loop, when they need the computer to repeatedly process one or more program instructions until some condition is met, at which time the repetition structure ends. A repetition structure can be either a pretest loop or a posttest loop. In a pretest loop, the loop condition is evaluated before the instructions within the loop are processed. In a posttest loop, the evaluation occurs after the instructions within the loop are processed. Of the two types of loops, the pretest loop is the most commonly used.

Almost every loop has a loop condition and a loop body. The loop condition appears at the beginning of a pretest loop and determines the number of times the instructions within the loop, referred to as the loop body, are processed. The loop condition must result in either a true or false answer only. When the loop condition evaluates to true, the one or more instructions listed in the loop body are processed; otherwise, these instructions are skipped over.

Some loops require the user to enter a special value, called a sentinel value, to end the loop. You should use a sentinel value that is easily distinguishable from the valid data recognized by the program. Other loops are terminated by the program itself, through the use of a counter.

The input instruction that appears above the pretest loop is referred to as the priming read, because it is used to prime (prepare or set up) the loop. The priming read gets only the first value from the user. The input instruction that appears within the loop gets the remaining values.

The flowchart symbol for the repetition structure (loop) is the repetition/selection diamond. You can use either the `while` statement or the `for` statement to code a pretest loop in C++.

Counters and accumulators are used within a repetition structure to calculate subtotals, totals, and averages. All counters and accumulators must be initialized and updated. Counters are updated by a constant value, whereas accumulators are updated by an amount that varies.

ANSWERS TO MINI-QUIZZES

Mini-Quiz 1

1) `while (quantity > 0)`

2) `while (quantity >= 0)`

3) `while (inStock > reorder)`

4) `while (toupper(letter) == 'Y') [or while (letter == 'Y' || letter == 'y')]`

5) a. −9

6) priming read

Mini-Quiz 2

1) accumulator

2) `quantity = quantity + 2;`

3) `total = total + -3;` (or `total = total - 3;`)

4) `totalPurchases = totalPurchases + purchases;`

Mini-Quiz 3

1) `while (evenNum < 9)` [or while (evenNum <= 8)]

```
{
    cout << evenNum << endl;
    evenNum = evenNum + 2;
}//end while
```

2) a. `for (int x = 10; x <= 100; x = x + 10)`

3) d. 110

4) `for (int x = 25; x > 0; x = x -5)` [or
`for (int x = 25; x > 0; x = x + -5)`]

5) 0 (zero)

6) `for(int num = 2; num <= 8; num = num + 2)`
`        cout << num << endl;`

QUESTIONS

1) The `while` loop is referred to as _____ loop, because the loop `condition` is tested at the beginning of the loop.

   A. a beginning

   B. an initial

   C. a pretest

   D. a priming

2) The loop condition in a flowchart is represented by _____.

   A. a diamond

   B. an oval

   C. a parallelogram

   D. a rectangle

3) A numeric variable used for counting something is called _____.

   A. an accumulator

   B. an adder

   C. a constant

   D. a counter

4) Counters and accumulators must be initialized and _____.

    A. added

    B. displayed

    C. updated

    D. none of the above

5) _____ are always incremented by a constant amount, whereas _____ are incremented by an amount that varies.

    A. Accumulators, counters

    B. Counters, accumulators

6) Which of the following statements correctly updates the counter variable named `numEmployees`?

    A. `numEmployees = 0;`

    B. `numEmployees = numEmployees + numEmployees;`

    C. `numEmployees = numEmployees + sumSalary;`

    D. `numEmployees = numEmployees + 1;`

7) Which of the following statements correctly updates the accumulator variable named `total`?

    A. `total = 0;`

    B. `total = total + total;`

    C. `total = total + sales;`

    D. `total = total + 1;`

8) Which of the following is a good sentinel value for a program that allows the user to enter a person's age?

    A. −4

    B. 350

    C. 999

    D. all of the above

9) Which of the following `while` clauses stops the loop when the value in the `age` variable is less than the number 0?

    A. `while (age < 0)`

    B. `while age >= 0;`

    C. `while (age >= 0);`

    D. `while (age >= 0)`

Refer to Figure 7-31 to answer Questions 10 through 13.

Figure 7-31

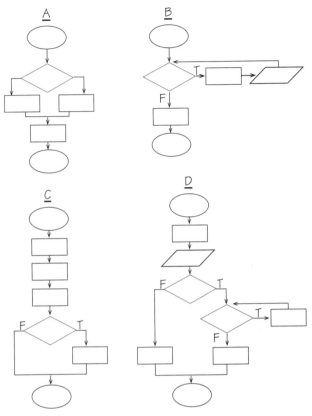

10) Which of the following control structures are used in Figure 7-31's flowchart A? (Select all that apply.)

   A. sequence

   B. selection

   C. repetition

11) Which of the following control structures are used in Figure 7-31's flowchart B? (Select all that apply.)

   A. sequence

   B. selection

   C. repetition

12) Which of the following control structures are used in Figure 7-31's flowchart C? (Select all that apply.)

   A. sequence

   B. selection

   C. repetition

13) Which of the following control structures are used in Figure 7-31's flowchart D? (Select all that apply.)

   A. sequence

   B. selection

   C. repetition

14) Values that are used to end loops are referred to as _____ values.

A. end

B. finish

C. sentinel

D. stop

15) Assume a program allows the user to enter one or more numbers. The first input instruction will get the first number only and is referred to as the _____ read.

A. entering

B. initializer

C. priming

D. starter

16) How many times will the `cout << count << endl;` statement in the following loop be processed?

```
for (int count = 1; count < 6; count = count + 1)
    cout << count << endl;
//end for
```

A. 0

B. 1

C. 5

D. 6

17) What is the value stored in the `count` variable when the loop in Question 16 ends?

A. 1

B. 5

C. 6

D. 7

18) How many times will the `cout << count << endl;` statement in the following loop be processed?

```
for (int count = 4; count <= 10; count = count + 2)
    cout << count << endl;
//end for
```

A. 0

B. 3

C. 4

D. 12

19) What is the value stored in the `count` variable when the loop in Question 18 ends?

A. 4

B. 6

C. 10

D. 12

Look For These
Symbols

Debugging

Discovery

EXERCISES

1) In this exercise, you complete a program by writing a repetition structure.

   A. If necessary, start Visual Studio .NET. Open the Ch7ConE01 Solution (Ch7ConE01 Solution.sln) file, which is contained in the Cpp\Chap07\ Ch7ConE01 Solution folder.

   B. Complete the program by entering a `while` clause that stops the loop when the user enters a number that is less than 0.

   C. Save and then build the solution.

   D. Execute the program. Test the program using the following data: 4, 10, 0, and –3.

   E. When the program is working correctly, close the Output window, and then use the File menu to close the solution.

2) In this exercise, you complete a program by writing a repetition structure.

   A. If necessary, start Visual Studio .NET. Open the Ch7ConE02 Solution (Ch7ConE02 Solution.sln) file, which is contained in the Cpp\Chap07\ Ch7ConE02 Solution folder.

   B. Complete the program by entering a `while` clause that stops the loop when the user enters the letter "N" (in any case).

   C. Save and then build the solution.

   D. Execute the program. Test the program using the following data: a, 4, $, and n.

   E. When the program is working correctly, close the Output window, then use the File menu to close the solution.

3) In this exercise, you complete a program by writing a repetition structure.

   A. If necessary, start Visual Studio .NET. Open the Ch7ConE03 Solution (Ch7ConE03 Solution.sln) file, which is contained in the Cpp\Chap07\ Ch7ConE03 Solution folder.

   B. Complete the program by entering a `while` clause that processes the loop instructions as long as the user enters a number that is greater than 0.

   C. Save and then build the solution.

   D. Execute the program. Test the program using the following data: 8, 100, and 0.

   E. When the program is working correctly, close the Output window, then use the File menu to close the solution.

4) In this exercise, you complete a program by writing a repetition structure.

   A. If necessary, start Visual Studio .NET. Open the Ch7ConE04 Solution (Ch7ConE04 Solution.sln) file, which is contained in the Cpp\Chap07\ Ch7ConE04 Solution folder.

   B. Complete the program by entering a `while` clause that processes the loop instructions as long as the user enters the letter "Y" (in any case).

   C. Save and then build the solution.

   D. Execute the program. Test the program using the following three sets of data: y and 100, Y and 200, and n. (The total sales should be 300.)

   E. Execute the program again. When you are asked if you want to enter a sales amount, type N and press Enter. Notice that you were not asked to enter the sales amount. Explain why.

   F. When the program is working correctly, close the Output window, then use the File menu to close the solution.

5) In this exercise, you complete a program by writing a repetition structure.

A. If necessary, start Visual Studio .NET. Open the Ch7ConE05 Solution (Ch7ConE05 Solution.sln) file, which is contained in the Cpp\Chap07\ Ch7ConE05 Solution folder.

B. Complete the program by entering a **while** statement that displays the word "Hello" on the screen 10 times.

C. Save and then build the solution.

D. Execute the program. The word "Hello" (without the quotation marks) should appear on the screen 10 times.

E. When the program is working correctly, close the Output window, then use the File menu to close the solution.

6) In this exercise, you complete a program by writing a repetition structure.

A. If necessary, start Visual Studio .NET. Open the Ch7ConE06 Solution (Ch7ConE06 Solution.sln) file, which is contained in the Cpp\Chap07\ Ch7ConE06 Solution folder.

B. Complete the program by entering a **while** statement that displays the numbers 20, 40, 60, 80, 100, 120, 140, 160, and 180 on the screen. Use the flowchart shown in Figure 7-32 to enter the appropriate code.

Figure 7-32

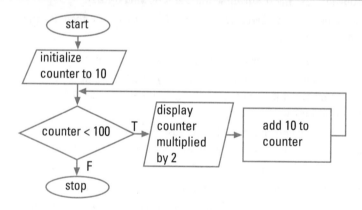

C. Save and then build the solution.

D. Execute the program. The numbers 20, 40, 60, 80, 100, 120, 140, 160, and 180 should appear on the screen.

E. When the program is working correctly, close the Output window, then use the File menu to close the solution.

7) What will appear on the screen when the code shown in Figure 7-33 is processed, assuming the code is included in a valid C++ program? What is the value in the **temp** variable when the loop stops? Complete a desk-check table for this code.

Figure 7-33

```
int temp = 0;
while (temp < 5)
{
    cout << temp << endl;
    temp = temp + 1;
} //end while
```

8) What will appear on the screen when the code shown in Figure 7-34 is processed, assuming the code is included in a valid C++ program? What is the value in the `totEmp` variable when the loop stops? Complete a desk-check table for this code.

Figure 7-34

```
int totEmp = 0;
while (totEmp <= 5)
{
    cout << totEmp << endl;
    totEmp = totEmp + 2;
}//end while
```

9) Write an assignment statement that updates a counter variable named `numStudents` by 1.

10) Write an assignment statement that updates a counter variable named `quantity` by −5.

11) Write an assignment statement that updates an accumulator variable named `total` by the value in the `sales` variable.

12) Write an assignment statement that updates an accumulator variable named `total` by the value in the `gross` variable.

13) In this exercise, you complete a program by writing a repetition structure.

   A. If necessary, start Visual Studio .NET. Open the Ch7ConE13 Solution (Ch7ConE13 Solution.sln) file, which is contained in the Cpp\Chap07\ Ch7ConE13 Solution folder.

   B. Complete the program by entering a **for** statement that displays the word "Hello" on the screen 10 times.

   C. Save and then build the solution.

   D. Execute the program. The word "Hello" (without the quotation marks) should appear on the screen 10 times.

   E. When the program is working correctly, close the Output window, then use the File menu to close the solution.

14) In this exercise, you complete a program by writing a repetition structure.

   A. If necessary, start Visual Studio .NET. Open the Ch7ConE14 Solution (Ch7ConE14 Solution.sln) file, which is contained in the Cpp\Chap07\ Ch7ConE14 Solution folder.

   B. Complete the program by entering a **for** statement that displays the numbers 10, 20, 30, 40, 50, 60, 70, 80, 90, and 100 on the screen.

   C. Save and then build the solution.

   D. Execute the program. The numbers 10, 20, 30, 40, 50, 60, 70, 80, 90, and 100 should appear on the screen.

   E. When the program is working correctly, close the Output window, then use the File menu to close the solution.

15) What will appear on the screen when the code shown in Figure 7-35 is processed, assuming the code is included in a valid C++ program? What is the value in the `temp` variable when the loop stops? Complete a desk-check table for this code.

Figure 7-35

```cpp
for (int temp = 0; temp < 5; temp = temp + 1)
    cout << temp << endl;
//end for
```

16) What will appear on the screen when the code shown in Figure 7-36 is processed, assuming the code is included in a valid C++ program? What is the value in the `totEmp` variable when the loop stops? Complete a desk-check table for this code.

Figure 7-36

```cpp
for (int totEmp = 0; totEmp <= 5; totEmp = totEmp + 2)
    cout << totEmp << endl;
//end for
```

17) In this exercise, you learn two ways to stop a program that is in an endless (infinite) loop.

  A. If necessary, start Visual Studio .NET. Open the Ch7ConE17 Solution (Ch7ConE17 Solution.sln) file, which is contained in the Cpp\Chap07\ Ch7ConE17 Solution folder.

  B. Build the solution, then execute the program. Notice that the program results in an endless (infinite) loop. You can tell that the program is in an endless loop because it displays the number 0 over and over again in the Command Prompt window.

  C. On most systems, you can stop a program that is in an endless loop by pressing Ctrl+c (press and hold down the Ctrl key as you press the letter c). Use the Ctrl+c key combination to stop the program. The Command Prompt window closes.

  D. Execute the program again. You also can use the Command Prompt window's Close button to stop a program that is in an endless loop. Click the Command Prompt window's Close button. The Command Prompt window closes.

  E. Close the Output window, then use the File menu to close the solution.

 18) In this exercise, you learn about the increment and decrement operators in C++.

  A. The C++ programming language has an increment operator (++) and a decrement operator (−−). What is the purpose of these operators?

  B. If necessary, start Visual Studio .NET. Open the Ch7ConE18 Solution (Ch7ConE18 Solution.sln) file, which is contained in the Cpp\Chap07\ Ch7ConE18 Solution folder.

  C. Complete the program by writing a `for` statement that displays the numbers 10 through 1 on the screen.

  D. Save and then build the solution.

  E. Execute the program. The numbers 10, 9, 8, 7, 6, 5, 4, 3, 2, and 1 should appear on the screen.

  F. When the program is working correctly, close the Output window, then use the File menu to close the solution.

 19) When included in a valid C++ program, the code shown in Figure 7-37 should display the numbers 1, 2, 3, and 4 on the screen. The code is not working properly. Correct the code.

Figure 7-37

```
int num = 1;
while (num < 5)
    cout << num << endl;
//end while
```

 20) When included in a valid C++ program, the code shown in Figure 7-38 should print the commission amount for each salesperson. The commission amount is calculated by multiplying the sales amount by .1. The code is not working properly. Correct the code.

Figure 7-38

```
double sales = 0.0;
cout << "Enter a sales amount: ";
cin >> sales;
while (sales > 0)
{
    cout << sales * .1 << endl;
} //end while
```

Application Lesson

Using the Repetition Structure in a C++ Program

Lab 7.1 - Stop and Analyze   If necessary, start Visual Studio .NET. Open the Ch7Lab1 Solution (Ch7Lab1 Solution.sln) file contained in the Cpp\Chap07\Ch7Lab1 Solution folder. Figure 7-39 shows the code entered in the Ch7Lab1.cpp file. (The line numbers are included in the figure only.) Study the code, then answer the questions.

Figure 7-39: C++ instructions entered in the Ch7Lab1.cpp file

```cpp
1  //Ch7Lab1.cpp - calculates the average temperature
2  //Created/revised by <your name> on <current date>
3
4  #include <iostream>
5  #include <iomanip>
6
7  using std::cout;
8  using std::cin;
9  using std::endl;
10 using std::setprecision;
11 using std::ios;
12 using std::setiosflags;
13
14 int main()
15 {
16     //declare variables
17     int numberOfTemps = 0;   //counter
18     int totalTemp     = 0;   //accumulator
19     int temp          = 0;
20     double average    = 0.0;
21
22     //get first temperature
23     cout << "Enter first temperature (999 to stop): ";
24     cin >> temp;
25
26     while (temp != 999)
27     {
28         //update counter and accumulator
29         numberOfTemps = numberOfTemps + 1;
30         totalTemp = totalTemp + temp;
31
32         //get remaining temperatures
33         cout << "Enter next temperature (999 to stop): ";
34         cin >> temp;
35     }   //end while
36
37     //verify that the counter is greater than zero
38     if (numberOfTemps > 0)
39     {
40         //calculate and display average temperature
41         average = double(totalTemp) / double(numberOfTemps);
```

Figure 7-39: C++ instructions entered in the Ch7Lab1.cpp file (continued)

```
42              cout << setiosflags(ios::fixed) << setprecision(1);
43              cout << "Average temperature: " << average << endl;
44      }
45      else
46              //display message
47              cout << "No temperatures were entered." << endl;
48      //end if
49
50      return 0;
51 }   //end of main function
```

Questions

1. What exactly does the Ch7Lab1.cpp program do? In other words, what does it input, process, and output?
2. Why do you think the number 999 was chosen as the sentinel value for this program? Would a negative number be a good sentinel value for this program? Why or why not?
3. Why is the selection structure in Lines 38 through 48 necessary?
4. Is the type cast in Line 41 necessary? Why or why not?
5. What is the purpose of the statement shown on Line 42?
6. Why was the counter initialized to 0 rather than 1?
7. Build the solution, then execute the program. Enter the following three temperatures followed by the sentinel value: 78, 85, and 67. What is the average temperature? Close the Command Prompt window.
8. Execute the program again. Enter the sentinel value. What appears in the Command Prompt window? Close the Command Prompt window. Close the Output window, then use the File menu to close the solution.
9. Create a blank solution named Ch7Lab1 For Solution. Save the solution in the Cpp\Chap07 folder.
10. Add an empty C++ Win32 Console Project to the solution. Name the project Ch7Lab1 For Project.
11. Add a new C++ source file to the project. Name the source file Ch7Lab1 For.
12. Open the Ch7Lab1.cpp file contained in the Cpp\Ch7Lab1 Solution\Ch7Lab1 Project folder. Copy the file's contents to the clipboard. Close the Ch7Lab1.cpp window, then paste the instructions into the Ch7Lab1 For.cpp window. Change the filename in the first comment to Ch7Lab1 For.cpp.
13. Modify the program so that it uses a **for** statement rather than a **while** statement.
14. Save and then build the solution. Execute the program. Enter the sentinel value. What appears in the Command Prompt window? Close the Command Prompt window.
15. Execute the program again. Enter the following four temperatures followed by the sentinel value: −3, 32, −10, and 40. What is the average temperature? Close the Command Prompt window. Close the Output window, then use the File menu to close the solution.

Lab 7.2 Next Monday is career day at your alma mater. Professor Krelina, one of your computer programming instructors, has asked you to be a guest speaker in her Introduction to Programming class. You gladly accept this speaking engagement and begin planning your presentation. You decide to show the students how to create a program that will calculate their grade in Professor Krelina's class.

Professor Krelina assigns four projects and two tests to the students in her Introduction to Programming class. Each project is worth 50 points, and each test is worth 100 points. Figure 7-40 shows the grading scale that Professor Krelina uses to assign a grade to each student in her class.

Figure 7-40: Professor Krelina's grading scale

Total points earned	Grade
360–400	A
320–359	B
280–319	C
240–279	D
below 240	F

Figure 7-41 shows the IPO chart and C++ instructions for the Professor Krelina problem.

Figure 7-41: IPO chart and C++ instructions for the Professor Krelina problem

IPO chart information	C++ instructions
Input score	`double score = 0.0;`
Processing	
Output total points earned grade	`double totalPoints = 0.0;` `char grade = ' ';`
Algorithm 1. enter the first score	`cout << "First score (negative number to stop): ";` `cin >> score;`

2. repeat while (score is greater than or equal to zero)
 	
add the score to the total points earned
 	
enter the next score
 	
end repeat while
	`while (score >= 0)`
	
	`{`
	`    totalPoints = totalPoints + score;`
	
	`    cout << "Next score (negative number to stop): ";`
	`    cin >> score;`
	`}    //end while`

3. if (total points earned >= 360)
        assign A as grade
    else if (total points earned >= 320)
        assign B as grade
    else if (total points earned >= 280)
        assign C as grade
    else if (total points earned >= 240)
        assign D as grade
    else assign F as grade
    end ifs
	`if (totalPoints >= 360)`
	`    grade = 'A';`
	`else if (totalPoints >= 320)`
	`    grade = 'B';`
	`else if (totalPoints >= 280)`
	`    grade = 'C';`
	`else if (totalPoints >= 240)`
	`    grade = 'D';`
	`else grade = 'F';`
	`//end ifs`

4. display the total points earned 5. display the grade	`cout << "Total points: " << totalPoints << endl;` `cout << "Grade: " << grade << endl;`

As the IPO chart indicates, the program requires three memory locations to store the values of its input and output items. You will store the values in variables, because the values will be different each time the program is executed. You will use the **double** data type for the variables that store the score and total points earned, and the **char** data type for the variable that stores the grade. The total points earned variable will be an accumulator, because it will need to accumulate, or add together, the project and test scores entered by the user.

The first step in the algorithm is the priming read, which gets the first score from the user. The next step is a pretest loop that repeats its instructions as long as (or while) the user enters a score that is greater than or equal to 0. Notice that the instructions within the loop add the score to the total points earned accumulator and then get another score from the user. The loop stops when the user enters the sentinel value. In this case, any number that is less than 0 can be used as the sentinel value.

The third step in the algorithm is a selection structure that assigns the appropriate grade based on the total number of points earned. The last steps in the algorithm are to display the total number of points earned and the grade.

Activity for Lab 7.2

In this activity, you enter the C++ instructions shown in Figure 7-41 into the computer. You then test the program to verify that it is working correctly.

To create the Professor Krelina program, then test the program:

1. If necessary, start Visual Studio .NET. Create a blank solution named Ch7Lab2 Solution. Save the solution in the Cpp\Chap07 folder.

2. Add an empty C++ Win32 Console Project to the solution. Name the project Ch7Lab2 Project.

3. Add a new C++ source file to the project. Name the source file Ch7Lab2.

4. Type **//Ch7Lab2.cpp - calculates the total points earned on projects** and press **Enter**.

5. Type **//and tests, then assigns a grade, and then displays the** and press **Enter**.

6. Type **//total points earned and grade** and press **Enter**.

7. Type **//Created/revised by <your name> on <current date>**, replacing <your name> and <current date> with your name and the current date, respectively. Press **Enter** twice.

8. Type **#include <iostream>** and press **Enter** twice.

9. Type the following three using statements, and then press **Enter** twice.

   using std::cout;
   using std::cin;
   using std::endl;

10. Complete the program by entering the main ( ) function, which is shown in Figure 7-42.

Figure 7-42: Professor Krelina program

```cpp
//Ch7Lab2.cpp - calculates the total points earned on projects
//and tests, then assigns a grade, and then displays the
//total points earned and grade
//Created/revised by <your name> on <current date>

#include <iostream>

using std::cout;
using std::cin;
using std::endl;

int main()
{
    //declare variables
    double score       = 0.0;
    double totalPoints = 0.0;   //accumulator
    char grade         = ' ';

    //get first score
    cout << "First score (negative number to stop): ";
    cin >> score;

    while (score >= 0)
    {
        //add score to accumulator
        totalPoints = totalPoints + score;
        //get next score
        cout << "Next score (negative number to stop): ";
        cin >> score;
    }   //end while

    //assign grade
    if (totalPoints >= 360)
        grade = 'A';
    else if (totalPoints >= 320)
        grade = 'B';
    else if (totalPoints >= 280)
        grade = 'C';
    else if (totalPoints >= 240)
        grade = 'D';
    else grade = 'F';
    //end ifs

    //display total points and grade
    cout << "Total points: " << totalPoints << endl;
    cout << "Grade: " << grade << endl;

    return 0;
}   //end of main function
```

enter the main() function instructions

11. Save and then build the solution. If necessary, correct any syntax errors, then save and build the solution again.

12. Execute the program. Enter the following six scores followed by the sentinel value, which can be any negative number: 45, 40, 45, 41, 96, and 89. The total points earned should be 356, and the grade should be B. Close the Command Prompt window.

13. Execute the program again. What are the total points earned and grade for the following six scores: 35, 35, 40, 43, 75, and 69? Close the Command Prompt window.

14. Execute the program again. What does the program display when you enter a negative number for the first score? Close the Command Prompt window.

15.. Close the Output window, then use the File menu to close the solution.

Lab 7.3 In this lab, you modify the program you created in Lab 7.2. The modified program will allow the user to enter four project scores and two test scores only.

Activity for Lab 7.3

Before modifying the program created in Lab 7.2, you copy the instructions contained in the Ch7Lab2.cpp file to a new solution.

To copy the instructions contained in the Ch7Lab2.cpp file to a new solution:

1. If necessary, start Visual Studio .NET. Create a blank solution named **Ch7Lab3 Solution**. Save the solution in the Cpp\Chap07 folder.

2. Add an empty C++ Win32 Console Project to the solution. Name the project **Ch7Lab3 Project**.

3. Add a new C++ source file to the project. Name the source file **Ch7Lab3**.

4. Use the File menu to open the Ch7Lab2.cpp file contained in the Cpp\Chap07\Ch7Lab2 Solution\Ch7Lab2 Project folder. Select the contents of the file, then copy the contents to the clipboard.

5. Close the Ch7Lab2.cpp window.

6. Click the **Ch7Lab3.cpp** tab, then paste the instructions from the clipboard into the Ch7Lab3.cpp window.

7. Change the filename in the first program comment to **Ch7Lab3.cpp**. If necessary, change the date in the second comment.

Currently, the program uses a `while` statement to get any number of scores from the user. Your task is to modify the program so that it uses two `for` statements rather than a `while` statement. The first `for` statement should allow the user to enter four project scores. The second `for` statement should allow the user to enter two test scores.

To modify the program, then test the program:

1. Make the appropriate modifications to the program.

2. Save and then build the solution. If necessary, correct any syntax errors, then save and build the solution again.

3. Execute the program. Test the program using your own sample data, then close the Command Prompt window.

4. When the program is working correctly, close the Output window, then use the File menu to close the solution.

You now have completed Chapter 7's Application lesson. You can either take a break or complete the end-of-lesson exercises.

ANSWERS TO LABS

Lab 7.1

1. The program allows the user to enter temperatures until he or she enters the number 999. It calculates the number of temperatures entered, the total of the temperatures, and the average temperature. It displays the average temperature.

2. The number 999 was chosen as a sentinel value because it is not a valid temperature. A negative number was not chosen as a sentinel value because a temperature can be a negative number.

3. The selection structure is necessary because it prevents the program from calculating the average when the counter variable (`numberOfTemps`) contains the number 0. Without the selection structure, the program would attempt to calculate the average even when the counter variable contained 0. When this happened, the program would result in an error, because the computer cannot divide by 0.

4. The type cast in Line 41 is necessary. Without the type cast, the quotient obtained when the computer divided the `totalTemp` variable (an `int`) by the `numberOfTemps` variable (also an `int`) would be an integer. Recall that in C++, when two `int` variables are used in a division operation, the result is always an integer.

5. The statement on Line 42 tells the computer to display the program's numeric output in fixed-point notation with one decimal place.

6. The counter reflects the number of temperatures entered. Therefore, it should be initialized to 0 at the beginning of the program and updated only when a temperature is entered.

7. The average temperature is 76.7.

8. The message "No temperatures were entered." appears in the Command Prompt window.

13. See Figure 7-43. Modifications are shaded in the figure.

Figure 7-43

```
1 //Ch7Lab1 For.cpp - calculates the average temperature
2 //Created/revised by <your name> on <current date>
3
4 #include <iostream>
5 #include <iomanip>
6
7 using std::cout;
8 using std::cin;
9 using std::endl;
```

Figure 7-43 (continued)

```
10  using std::setprecision;
11  using std::ios;
12  using std::setiosflags;
13
14  int main()
15  {
16      //declare variables
17      int numberOfTemps = 0;   //counter
18      int totalTemp    = 0;   //accumulator
19      int temp         = 0;
20      double average   = 0.0;
21
22      //get first temperature
23      cout << "Enter first temperature (999 to stop): ";
24      cin >> temp;
25
26      for (; temp != 999;)
27      {
28          //update counter and accumulator
29          numberOfTemps = numberOfTemps + 1;
30          totalTemp = totalTemp + temp;
31
32          //get remaining temperatures
33          cout << "Enter next temperature (999 to stop): ";
34          cin >> temp;
35      }   //end for
36
37      //verify that the counter is greater than zero
38      if (numberOfTemps > 0)
39      {
40          //calculate and display average temperature
41          average = double(totalTemp) / double(numberOfTemps);
42          cout << setiosflags(ios::fixed) << setprecision(1);
43          cout << "Average temperature: " << average << endl;
44      }
45      else
46          //display message
47          cout << "No temperatures were entered." << endl;
48      //end if
49
50      return 0;
51  }   //end of main function
```

14. The message "No temperatures were entered." appears in the Command Prompt window.

15. The average temperature is 14.8.

Lab 7.2

Step 13: The total points earned are 297, and the grade is C.

Step 14: The program displays the following:

Total points: 0

Grade: F

Lab 7.3

See Figure 7-44. Modifications are shaded in the figure.

Figure 7-44

```cpp
//Ch7Lab3.cpp - calculates the total points earned on projects
//and tests, then assigns a grade, and then displays the
//total points earned and grade
//Created/revised by <your name> on <current date>

#include <iostream>

using std::cout;
using std::cin;
using std::endl;

int main()
{
    //declare variables
    double score        = 0.0;
    double totalPoints = 0.0;   //accumulator
    char grade          = ' ';

    //get four project scores
    for (int numProjects = 1; numProjects < 5; numProjects =
    numProjects + 1)
    {
        cout << "Enter project " << numProjects << " score: ";
        cin >> score;
        //add project score to accumulator
        totalPoints = totalPoints + score;
    }    //end for

    //get two test scores
    for (int numTests = 1; numTests < 3; numTests =
    numTests + 1)
    {
        cout << "Enter test " << numTests << " score: ";
        cin >> score;
        //add test score to accumulator
        totalPoints = totalPoints + score;
    }    //end for
```

Figure 7-44 (continued)

```
    //assign grade
    if (totalPoints >= 360)
        grade = 'A';
    else if (totalPoints >= 320)
        grade = 'B';
    else if (totalPoints >= 280)
        grade = 'C';
    else if (totalPoints >= 240)
        grade = 'D';
    else grade = 'F';
    //end ifs

    //display total points and grade
    cout << "Total points: " << totalPoints << endl;
    cout << "Grade: " << grade << endl;

    return 0;
}    //end of main function
```

EXERCISES

1) In this exercise, you modify the program you created in Lab 7.2 in this lesson. The modified program should verify that a score more than 100 points is correct.

   A. If necessary, start Visual Studio .NET. Create a blank solution named Ch7AppE01 Solution. Save the solution in the Cpp\Chap07 folder.

   B. Add an empty C++ Win32 Console Project to the solution. Name the project Ch7AppE01 Project.

   C. Add a new C++ source file to the project. Name the source file Ch7AppE01.

   D. Use the File menu to open the Ch7Lab2.cpp file contained in the Cpp\Chap07\Ch7Lab2 Solution\Ch7Lab2 Project folder. Select the contents of the file, then copy the contents to the clipboard.

   E. Close the Ch7Lab2.cpp window.

   F. Click the Ch7AppE01.cpp tab, then paste the instructions from the clipboard into the Ch7AppE01.cpp window.

   G. Change the filename in the first program comment to Ch7AppE01.cpp. If necessary, change the date in the second comment.

   H. Make the following modifications to the program. If the user enters a score that is over 100 points, the program should ask the user if the score is correct. The program should not add a score that is more than 100 to the accumulator unless the user responds that the score is correct.

   I. Save and then build the solution.

   J. Execute the program. Enter 70 for the first score and 105 for the next score. When you are prompted to verify the score, respond that the score is not correct. Then enter 100 and −2 for the next score and sentinel value. The program should display 170 as the total points and F as the grade.

   K. Execute the program. Enter 70 for the first score and 105 for the next score. When you are prompted to verify the score, respond that the score is correct. Then enter 100 and −2 for the next score and sentinel value. The program should display 275 as the total points and D as the grade.

Look For These Symbols

Debugging

Discovery

L. Now test the program using the following two sets of data.

45, 40, 45, 41, 96, 89, −1

35, 35, 40, 43, 75, 69, −3

M. When the program is working correctly, close the Output window, then use the File menu to close the solution.

2) In this exercise, you create a program that displays the sum of the monthly sales amounts made in four regions: North, South, East, and West.

A. Create an IPO chart for the problem. Use a `while` loop to allow the user to enter each of the four sales amounts, one at a time.

B. If necessary, start Visual Studio .NET. Open the Ch7AppE02 Solution (Ch7AppE02 Solution.sln) file, which is contained in the Cpp\Chap07\Ch7AppE02 Solution folder.

C. Use the IPO chart you created in Step A to code the program.

D. Complete a desk-check table for the program, using 2000, 3000, 2500, and 1500 as the first set of sales amounts, and 39000, 45000, 25000, and 56000 as the second set of sales amounts.

E. Save and then build the solution.

F. Execute the program. Use the first set of sales amounts from Step D to test the program.

G. Execute the program again. Use the second set of sales amounts from Step D to test the program.

H. When the program is working correctly, close the Output window, then use the File menu to close the solution.

3) In this exercise, you create a program that displays an employee's name when the employee's ID is entered at the keyboard. The IDs and their corresponding names are as follows:

ID	Name
1234	Sue Nguyen
1345	Janice Blackfeather
3456	Allen Kraus
4567	Margie O'Donnell

If the user enters an ID other than the ones listed above, the program should display the message "Incorrect ID – Please try again".

A. Create an IPO chart for the problem. Use a `while` loop to allow the user to enter each ID, one at a time. (Be sure to use an appropriate sentinel value.)

B. If necessary, start Visual Studio .NET. Open the Ch7AppE03 Solution (Ch7AppE03 Solution.sln) file, which is contained in the Cpp\Chap07\ Ch7AppE03 Solution folder.

C. Use the IPO chart you created in Step A to code the program.

D. Complete a desk-check table for the program, using 1345 as the first ID, 4567 as the second ID, and your sentinel value as the third ID.

E. Save and then build the solution.

F. Execute the program. Use the data from Step D to test the program.

G. When the program is working correctly, close the Output window, then use the File menu to close the solution.

4) In this exercise, you create a program that displays the registration information for programming seminars. The price per person depends on the number of people a company registers. (For example, if a company registers four people, then the amount owed by that company is $400.) The following table shows the charges per registrant.

Number of registrants	Charge per person ($)
1–3	150
4–9	100
10 or more	90

A. Create an IPO chart for the problem. Use a `while` loop to allow the user to enter the number of people a company registers. The program should allow the user to enter the number registered for as many companies as desired. Be sure to use an appropriate sentinel value. The program should display the total number of people registered, the total charge, and the average charge per registrant. (For example, if one company registers 4 people and a second company registers 2 people, then the total number of people registered is 6, the total charge is $700, and the average charge per registrant is $116.67.)

B. If necessary, start Visual Studio .NET. Open the Ch7AppE04 Solution (Ch7AppE04 Solution.sln) file, which is contained in the Cpp\Chap07\Ch7AppE04 Solution folder.

C. Use the IPO chart you created in Step A to code the program.

D. Complete a desk-check table for the program, using 3 as the number of people registered by the first company, 12 as the number registered by the second company, and 9 as the number registered by the third company; then enter your sentinel value.

E. Save and then build the solution.

F. Execute the program. Use the data from Step D to test the program.

G. When the program is working correctly, close the Output window, then use the File menu to close the solution.

5) In this exercise, you add a loop to an existing program. The program displays a ticket price based on a seat location entered by the user.

A. If necessary, start Visual Studio .NET. Open the Ch7AppE05 Solution (Ch7AppE05 Solution.sln) file, which is contained in the Cpp\Chap07\ Ch7AppE05 Solution folder. The program prompts the user to enter a seat location, then displays the ticket price.

B. Modify the program so that it allows the user to enter as many seat locations as desired.

C. Save and then build the solution.

D. Execute the program. Test the program using the following data: L, b, p, a, and your sentinel value.

E. When the program is working correctly, close the Output window, then use the File menu to close the solution.

6) In this exercise, you add a loop and a counter to an existing program. The program displays the number of vacation weeks based on the number of years an employee has been with the company.

A. If necessary, start Visual Studio .NET. Open the Ch7AppE06 Solution (Ch7AppE06 Solution.sln) file, which is contained in the Cpp\Chap07\ Ch7AppE06 Solution folder. The program prompts the user to enter the number of years an employee has been with the company, then displays the appropriate number of vacation weeks.

B. Modify the program so that it allows the user to enter the number of years for as many employees as desired. Also add the appropriate code to calculate and display the total number of employees entered.

C. Save and then build the solution.

D. Execute the program. Test the program using the following data: 0, 4, 7, 20, and your sentinel value.

E. When the program is working correctly, close the Output window, then use the File menu to close the solution.

7) In this exercise, you complete a program that displays the product of the odd integers from 1 through 13 (in other words, the result of multiplying 1 * 3 * 5 and so on).

A. If necessary, start Visual Studio .NET. Open the Ch7AppE07 Solution (Ch7AppE07 Solution.sln) file, which is contained in the Cpp\Chap07\ Ch7AppE07 Solution folder.

B. Complete the program by entering the appropriate **for** statement.

C. Save and then build the solution.

D. Execute the program.

E. When the program is working correctly, close the Output window, then use the File menu to close the solution.

8) In this exercise, you complete a program that displays the numbers 0 through 117, in increments of 9.

A. If necessary, start Visual Studio .NET. Open the Ch7AppE08 Solution (Ch7AppE08 Solution.sln) file, which is contained in the Cpp\Chap07\ Ch7AppE08 Solution folder.

B. Complete the program by entering the appropriate **for** statement.

C. Save and then build the solution.

D. Execute the program.

E. When the program is working correctly, close the Output window, then use the File menu to close the solution.

9) In this exercise, you complete a program that displays the squares of the even numbers from 10 through 25.

A. If necessary, start Visual Studio .NET. Open the Ch7AppE09 Solution (Ch7AppE09 Solution.sln) file, which is contained in the Cpp\Chap07\ Ch7AppE09 Solution folder.

B. Complete the program by entering the appropriate **for** and **while** statements.

C. Save and then build the solution.

D. Execute the program.

E. When the program is working correctly, close the Output window, then use the File menu to close the solution.

10) In this exercise, you complete a program that displays the first 10 Fibonacci numbers (1, 1, 2, 3, 5, 8, 13, 21, 34, and 55). Notice that, beginning with the third number in the series, each Fibonacci number is the sum of the prior two numbers. In other words, 2 is the sum of 1 plus 1, 3 is the sum of 1 plus 2, 5 is the sum of 2 plus 3, and so on.

    A. If necessary, start Visual Studio .NET. Open the Ch7AppE10 Solution (Ch7AppE10 Solution.sln) file, which is contained in the Cpp\Chap07\ Ch7AppE10 Solution folder.

    B. Complete the program by entering the appropriate **for** statement and code.

    C. Save and then build the solution.

    D. Execute the program.

    E. When the program is working correctly, close the Output window, then use the File menu to close the solution.

11) In this exercise, you create a program that displays a pattern of asterisks. (*Hint:* You can nest repetition structures.)

    A. If necessary, start Visual Studio .NET. Open the Ch7AppE11 Solution (Ch7AppE11 Solution.sln) file, which is contained in the Cpp\Chap07\ Ch7AppE11 Solution folder.

    B. Enter the C++ instructions to display the following pattern of asterisks (2 asterisks, 4 asterisks, 6 asterisks, 8 asterisks, 10 asterisks, and 12 asterisks).

```
**
****
******
********
**********
************
```

    C. Save and then build the solution.

    D. Execute the program. When the program is working correctly, close the Output window, then use the File menu to close the solution.

12) In this exercise, you debug a C++ program.

    A. If necessary, start Visual Studio .NET. Open the Ch7AppE12 Solution (Ch7AppE12 Solution.sln) file, which is contained in the Cpp\Chap07\ Ch7AppE12 Solution folder. This program should display the squares of the numbers from 1 through 5; in other words, it should display the numbers 1, 4, 9, 16, and 25.

    B. Build the solution, then execute the program. Notice that the program results in an endless loop. Stop the program either by pressing Ctrl+c or by clicking the Command Prompt window's Close button.

    C. Correct the program's code, then save and build the solution.

    D. Execute the program. When the program is working correctly, close the Output window, then use the File menu to close the solution.

13) In this exercise, you debug a C++ program.

A. If necessary, start Visual Studio .NET. Open the Ch7AppE13 Solution (Ch7AppE13 Solution.sln) file, which is contained in the Cpp\Chap07\ Ch7AppE13 Solution folder. This program should display the number of positive integers entered by the user, and the number of negative integers entered by the user. The program should stop when the user enters the number 0.

B. Build the solution, then execute the program. Test the program by entering the following integers: 4, 6, –4, 23, –9, and 0. Notice that the program is not working correctly.

C. Correct the program's code, then save and build the solution.

D. Execute the program. Use the data from Step B to test the program.

E. When the program is working correctly, close the Output window, then use the File menu to close the solution.

 Please visit the Testing Center at www.course.com/testingcenter for more practice on the topics covered in this chapter.

More on the Repetition Structure

After completing this chapter, you will be able to:

- Show the posttest repetition structure in pseudocode and in a flowchart

- Code a posttest loop using the C++ `do while` statement

- Nest repetition structures

Concept Lesson

Posttest Loops

As you learned in Chapter 7, programmers use the repetition structure, referred to more simply as a loop, when they need the computer to repeatedly process one or more program instructions until some condition is met, at which time the repetition structure ends. Recall that a repetition structure can be either a pretest loop or a posttest loop. You learned about the pretest loop in Chapter 7; you learn about the posttest loop in this chapter.

As is true of the condition in a pretest loop, the condition in a posttest loop is evaluated with each repetition, or iteration, of the loop. However, unlike the evaluation in a pretest loop, the evaluation in a posttest loop occurs *after* the instructions within the loop are processed, rather than *before* the instructions are processed.

Figure 8-1 shows the problem description and IPO chart for O'Donnell Incorporated. The IPO chart contains two algorithms (written in pseudocode) that could be used to calculate and display a bonus for each of the company's salespeople. Algorithm 1, which you viewed in Chapter 7's Concept lesson, uses a pretest loop to repeat the appropriate instructions; Algorithm 2 uses a posttest loop to accomplish the same task.

tip

Posttest loops also are called bottom-driven loops.

Figure 8-1: Problem description and IPO chart for O'Donnell Incorporated

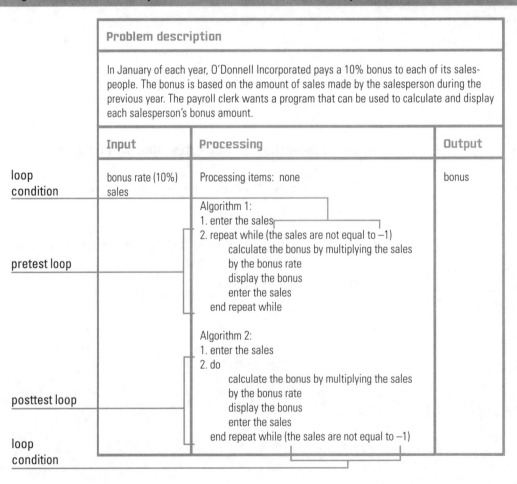

	Problem description		
	In January of each year, O'Donnell Incorporated pays a 10% bonus to each of its salespeople. The bonus is based on the amount of sales made by the salesperson during the previous year. The payroll clerk wants a program that can be used to calculate and display each salesperson's bonus amount.		
	Input	Processing	Output
loop condition	bonus rate (10%) sales	Processing items: none	bonus

pretest loop		Algorithm 1:
		1. enter the sales
		2. repeat while (the sales are not equal to −1)
		  calculate the bonus by multiplying the sales
		  by the bonus rate
		  display the bonus
		  enter the sales
		end repeat while	

posttest loop		Algorithm 2:
		1. enter the sales
		2. do
		  calculate the bonus by multiplying the sales
		  by the bonus rate
		  display the bonus
		  enter the sales	

loop condition		end repeat while (the sales are not equal to −1)	

tip

As you learned in Chapter 7, the loop body instructions are not processed if the loop condition in a pretest loop initially evaluates to false.

As Figure 8-1 shows, the first step in Algorithm 1 is to enter a sales amount. The second step is a pretest loop whose loop condition compares the sales amount entered by the user with the sentinel value, −1. If the sales amount is not the sentinel value, the loop body instructions calculate and display the bonus amount, and then get another sales amount from the user. The loop condition then compares the sales amount with the sentinel value to determine whether the loop body instructions should be processed again. The loop repeats the loop body instructions as long as (or while) the user does not enter the sentinel value, −1, as the sales amount.

Compare the steps in Algorithm 2 to the steps in Algorithm 1. Like the first step in Algorithm 1, the first step in Algorithm 2 is to enter a sales amount. The second step in Algorithm 2, however, is a posttest loop rather than a pretest loop. You can tell that Algorithm 2's second step is a posttest loop because it begins with the word **do**, rather than with the words **repeat while** followed by the loop condition. In a posttest loop, the words **repeat while** and the loop condition appear at the *end* of the loop, which indicates that the loop condition is evaluated only *after* the instructions in the loop body are processed.

Like the loop body instructions in Algorithm 1, the loop body instructions in Algorithm 2 calculate and display the salesperson's bonus, then get another sales amount from the user. The loop condition, which appears at the bottom of the posttest loop, then compares the sales amount with the sentinel value (−1) to determine whether the instructions in the loop body should be processed again. In a posttest loop, only the second and subsequent sales amounts are compared to the sentinel value; the first sales amount is not compared to the sentinel value, as it is in a pretest loop. Although it is possible that the instructions contained in a pretest loop might never be processed, the instructions contained in a posttest loop always are processed at least once. You should use a posttest loop only when you are sure that the loop body instructions can and should be processed at least once. You often find a posttest loop in programs that allow the user to select from a menu, such as a game program. This type of program uses the posttest loop to control the display of the menu, which must appear on the screen at least once.

It may be easier to understand the difference between a pretest loop and a posttest loop by viewing both loops in flowchart form.

Flowcharting a Posttest Loop

Figure 8-2 shows the O'Donnell Incorporated algorithms in flowchart form. The flowcharts illustrate why the loops are referred to as pretest and posttest loops. Notice that the repetition diamond, which contains the loop condition, appears at the top of a pretest loop, but it appears at the bottom of a posttest loop.

Figure 8-2: O'Donnell Incorporated algorithms shown in flowchart form

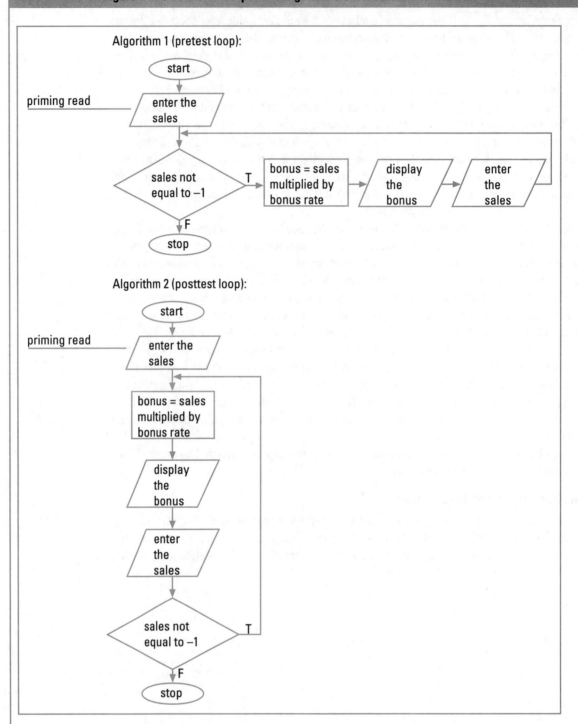

To help you understand how a posttest loop operates in a program, you will desk-check Algorithm 2 shown in Figure 8-2 using the following sales data: 10000, 25000, and −1. The first instruction in the flowchart gets the first sales amount (10000) from the user; recall that this instruction is referred to as the priming read. The next instruction calculates the bonus and is the first instruction in the loop body. Notice that the first sales amount is not compared to the sentinel value in a posttest loop. Figure 8-3 shows the first salesperson's sales and bonus amounts recorded in the desk-check table.

Figure 8-3: First salesperson's sales and bonus amounts recorded in the desk-check table

bonus rate	sales	bonus
.10	10000	1000

The second instruction in the loop body displays the bonus on the screen, and the third instruction gets the next salesperson's sales (25000) from the user. Figure 8-4 shows the second salesperson's sales amount recorded in the desk-check table.

Figure 8-4: Second salesperson's sales amount recorded in the desk-check table

bonus rate	sales	bonus
.10	~~10000~~ 25000	1000

The next symbol in the flowchart is the repetition diamond, which contains the loop condition and marks the end of the posttest loop. The loop condition compares the sales amount entered by the user with the sentinel value, −1, to determine whether the loop should be processed again (a true condition) or end (a false condition). Notice that this is the first time the loop condition is evaluated. In this case, the loop condition evaluates to true, because 25000 is not equal to −1. As is true in a pretest loop, when the loop condition in a posttest loop evaluates to true, the instructions in the loop body are processed. Those instructions calculate and display the bonus for the second salesperson, and then get another sales amount (in this case, the sentinel value) from the user. Figure 8-5 shows the sentinel value recorded in the desk-check table.

Figure 8-5: Sentinel value recorded in the desk-check table

	bonus rate	sales	bonus
sentinel value	.10	~~10000~~ ~~25000~~ −1	~~1000~~ 2500

The loop condition then is reevaluated to determine whether the loop should be processed again or end. In this case, the loop condition evaluates to false, because the sales amount entered by the user is equal to the sentinel value, −1. As is true in a pretest loop, when the loop condition in a posttest loop evaluates to false, the loop instructions are skipped over and processing continues with the instruction immediately following the end of the loop. In Algorithm 2's flowchart, the stop oval, which marks the end of the algorithm, follows the loop.

MINI-QUIZ

Mini-Quiz 1

1) In a _____ loop, the loop condition is evaluated *after* the loop instructions are processed, while in a _____ loop, the evaluation occurs *before* the loop instructions are processed.
   a. pretest, posttest
   b. posttest, pretest

2) The instructions in a _____ loop always are processed at least once, while the instructions in a _____ loop might never be processed.
   a. pretest, posttest
   b. posttest, pretest

3) Assume that a program contains a posttest loop that repeats the loop body instructions until the user enters a negative number. How many times will the loop condition be evaluated if the user enters the numbers 5, 8, 9, and −1, respectively?

Next, you learn how to code the posttest loop.

Coding the Posttest Loop

Figure 8-6 shows the syntax of the **do while** statement, which you use to code a posttest loop in a C++ program.

tip

As you learned in Chapter 7, you can use the C++ while statement to code a pretest loop.

Figure 8-6: Syntax of the C++ do while statement

notice that the do while statement ends with a semicolon

```
do
    one statement, or a block of statements enclosed in braces, to be processed
    one time, and thereafter as long as the loop condition evaluates to true
while (loop condition);
```

Items in **bold** in the syntax—in this case, the keywords **do** and **while**, the parentheses that surround the loop condition, and the semicolon—are essential components of the **do while** statement. Items in italics indicate where the programmer must supply information pertaining to the current program. In the **do while** statement, the programmer must supply the loop condition to be evaluated. As is true in the C++ **while** statement, the loop condition must be a Boolean expression, which is an expression that evaluates to either true or false. The loop condition can contain variables, constants, functions, arithmetic operators, comparison operators, and logical operators.

In addition to supplying the loop condition, the programmer also must supply the statements to be processed when the loop condition evaluates to true. If more than one statement needs to be processed, the statements must be entered as a statement block. Recall that you create a statement block by enclosing the statements in a set of braces ({}).

Figure 8-7 shows how you can use the C++ **do while** statement to code the O'Donnell Incorporated algorithm.

tip

Recall that some C++ programmers enclose the loop body in braces even when it contains only one statement, but this is not required by the C++ syntax.

Figure 8-7: C++ do while statement included in the code for the O'Donnell Incorporated algorithm

IPO chart information	C++ instructions

Input
bonus rate (10%)
sales
Processing
none
Output
bonus
 	
Algorithm
1. enter the sales
 	
2. do
 	
   calculate the bonus
   by multiplying the
   sales by the bonus
   rate
 	
   display the bonus
 	
   enter the sales
 	
end repeat while (the
sales are not equal to
−1)
	`const double RATE = .1;`
	`double sales = 0.0;`
	
	`double bonus = 0.0;`
	
	`cout << "Enter the first sales amount: ";`
	`cin >> sales;`
	
	`do`
	`{`
	
	`    bonus = sales * RATE;`
	
	`    cout << bonus << endl;`
	
	`    cout << "Enter the next sales amount: ";`
	`    cin >> sales;`
	`} while (sales != -1);`

braces
mark the
start and
end of the
statement
block

do while
statement
ends with a
semicolon

Take a closer look at the instructions shown in Figure 8-7. The first three instructions declare and initialize the **RATE** named constant and the **sales** and **bonus** variables. The `cout << "Enter the first sales amount: ";` statement prompts the user to enter the first sales amount, and the `cin >> sales;` statement stores the user's response in the **sales** variable. The do clause, which appears next in the program, simply marks the beginning of the posttest loop.

The first instruction in the posttest loop calculates the bonus amount, and the second instruction displays the bonus amount on the screen. The third instruction in the loop prompts the user to enter the next sales amount, and the fourth instruction stores the user's response in the **sales** variable. Notice that the four instructions in the loop body are processed *before* the `while (sales != -1);` clause is evaluated. The `while (sales != -1);` clause compares the value stored in the **sales** variable to the sentinel value (−1). If the **sales** variable does not contain the sentinel value, the instructions within the loop body are processed again. Otherwise, the instructions are skipped over and processing continues with the line immediately below the end of the loop.

tip

As you learned in Chapter 7, if you forget to enter the `cin >> sales;` statement within the program's loop, the loop will process its instructions indefinitely. Usually, you can stop a program that contains an infinite (or endless) loop by pressing Ctrl+c; you also can use the Command Prompt window's Close button.

MINI-QUIZ

Mini-Quiz 2

1) The `do while` clause marks the beginning of the C++ `do while` statement.
   a. True
   b. False

2) The `while` clause in the C++ `do while` statement ends with a semicolon.
   a. True
   b. False

3) Write a C++ `while` clause that processes a posttest loop's instructions as long as the value in the `quantity` variable is greater than the number 0.

In Chapter 6, you learned how to nest selection structures. You also can nest repetition structures, which means you can place one repetition structure inside another repetition structure.

Nested Repetition Structures

In a nested repetition structure, one loop, referred to as the **inner loop**, is placed entirely within another loop, called the **outer loop**. Although the idea of nested loops may sound confusing, you already are familiar with the concept. A clock, for instance, uses nested loops to keep track of the time. For simplicity, consider a clock's second and minute hands only. You can think of the second hand as being the inner loop and the minute hand as being the outer loop. As you know, the second hand on a clock moves one position, clockwise, for every second that has elapsed. Only after the second hand completes its processing—in this case, only after it moves 60 positions—does the minute hand move one position, clockwise. The second hand then begins its journey around the clock again. Figure 8-8 illustrates the logic used by a clock's second and minute hands.

Figure 8-8: Nested loops used by a clock

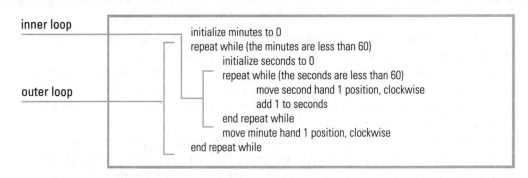

inner loop

outer loop

```
initialize minutes to 0
repeat while (the minutes are less than 60)
        initialize seconds to 0
        repeat while (the seconds are less than 60)
                move second hand 1 position, clockwise
                add 1 to seconds
        end repeat while
        move minute hand 1 position, clockwise
end repeat while
```

As indicated in Figure 8-8, the outer loop corresponds to a clock's minute hand, and the inner loop corresponds to a clock's second hand. Notice that the entire inner loop is contained within the outer loop, which must be true for the loops to be nested and to work correctly.

You will use a nested repetition structure in the Max Beauty Supply program, which you view next.

The Max Beauty Supply Program

Assume that Max Beauty Supply divides its sales territory into two regions: Region 1 and Region 2. The company's sales manager wants a program that allows him to enter each

tip

Although both loops in Figure 8-8 are pretest loops, you also could write the logic using two posttest loops or a combination of a pretest and a posttest loop.

region's sales amounts. The program then should calculate and display the total amount sold in each region. Figure 8-9 shows the IPO chart information and C++ code for the Max Beauty Supply program. Notice that the program contains an outer loop and an inner loop, and that the entire inner loop is contained within the outer loop.

Figure 8-9: IPO chart information and C++ code for the Max Beauty Supply problem

IPO chart information	C++ instructions
Input sales	`double sales = 0.0;`
Processing region counter (1 and 2)	`int region = 1;`
Output region counter total region sales (accumulator)	`double totRegSales = 0.0;`
Algorithm 1. repeat while (the region counter is less than 3)	`while (region < 3)` `{`

enter the sales	`    cout << "First sales amount for`
	`    Region " << region << ":";`
	`    cin >> sales;`

repeat while (the sales are greater than 0)	`    while (sales > 0)` `    {`
add the sales to the total region sales	`        totRegSales = totRegSales + sales;`

enter the sales	`        cout << "Next sales amount for`
	`        Region " << region << ":";`
	`        cin >> sales;`

end repeat while	`    }   //end while`
display the region counter and total region sales	`    cout << "Region " << region << " sales: "` `    << totRegSales << endl;`
add 1 to the region counter	`    region = region + 1;`
assign 0 to the total region sales	`    totRegSales = 0.0;`
end repeat while 2. display "End of program"	`}   //end while` `cout << "End of program" << endl;`

As Figure 8-9 indicates, the input for the Max Beauty Supply problem is the sales amounts made in each region; the output is each region's total sales amount. The problem requires an accumulator to total the sales amounts made in each region. It also requires a counter to keep track of the region numbers (1 and 2). Notice in the C++ code that the `region` counter variable is initialized to the first region number, 1.

After declaring and initializing the appropriate variables, the outer loop's `while (region < 3)` clause begins a pretest loop that repeats its instructions while the value in the `region` variable is less than 3. At this point in the program, the value stored in the `region` variable is 1, so the outer loop condition evaluates to true and the outer loop instructions are processed.

The first two instructions in the outer loop prompt the user to enter the first sales amount, and then store the user's response in the `sales` variable. The third instruction in the outer loop is the inner loop's `while (sales > 0)` clause, which begins a pretest loop that repeats its instructions while the sales amount entered by the user is greater than 0.

The first instruction in the inner loop adds the amount stored in the `sales` variable to the contents of the `totRegSales` accumulator variable. The last two instructions in the inner loop prompt the user to enter the next sales amount, then store the user's response in the `sales` variable. The inner loop condition then is reevaluated to determine whether the inner loop instructions should be processed again. The inner loop continues to process its instructions until the user enters either the number 0 or a negative number, at which time the inner loop ends. Figure 8-10 shows the status of the desk-check table, assuming the user enters the following sales amounts for Region 1: 25000, 30000, 10000, −1.

Figure 8-10: Desk-check table after processing Region 1's data

sales	region	totRegSales
~~0.0~~	1	~~0.0~~
~~25000.0~~		~~25000.0~~
~~30000.0~~		~~55000.0~~
~~10000.0~~		65000.0
−1.0		

When the inner loop ends, the next statement processed is the one that appears immediately below the inner loop in the program—in this case, the `cout << "Region " << region << " sales: " << totRegSales << endl;` statement. This statement displays the region number (1) along with the total sales made in Region 1 (65000).

Next, the computer processes the `region = region + 1;` statement, which adds 1 to the value stored in the `region` counter variable, giving 2. The `totRegSales = 0.0;` statement then reinitializes the `totRegSales` accumulator variable to 0, as shown in Figure 8-11.

tip

When loops are nested, the outer loop typically reinitializes the counters and accumulators updated within the inner loop. In the Max Beauty Supply program, only the `totRegSales` accumulator is updated within the inner loop, so that is the only variable reinitialized by the outer loop.

Figure 8-11: Desk-check table after updating the counter and reinitializing the accumulator

sales	region	totRegSales
~~0.0~~	~~1~~	~~0.0~~
~~25000.0~~	2	~~25000.0~~
~~30000.0~~		~~55000.0~~
~~10000.0~~		~~65000.0~~
−1.0		0.0

The outer loop condition, `while (region < 3)`, then is reevaluated to determine whether the outer loop should be processed again. Here again, the outer loop condition evaluates to true, because the value stored in the **region** variable (2) is less than 3. Because of this, the outer loop instructions are processed again.

The first two instructions in the outer loop prompt the user to enter the first sales amount, and then store the user's response in the **sales** variable. The third instruction in the outer loop is the inner loop's **while (sales > 0)** clause, which begins a pretest loop that repeats its instructions while the sales amount entered by the user is greater than 0.

The first instruction in the inner loop adds the sales amount stored in the **sales** variable to the **totRegSales** accumulator variable. The last two instructions in the inner loop prompt the user to enter the next sales amount, then store the user's response in the **sales** variable. The inner loop condition then is reevaluated to determine whether the inner loop instructions should be processed again. The inner loop continues to process its instructions until the user enters either the number 0 or a negative number, at which time the inner loop ends. Figure 8-12 shows the status of the desk-check table, assuming the user enters the following sales amounts for Region 2: 13000, 10000, −1.

Figure 8-12: Desk-check table after processing Region 2's data

sales	region	totRegSales
~~0.0~~	~~1~~	~~0.0~~
~~25000.0~~	2	~~25000.0~~
~~30000.0~~		~~55000.0~~
~~10000.0~~		~~65000.0~~
~~-1.0~~		~~0.0~~
~~13000.0~~		~~13000.0~~
~~10000.0~~		23000.0
−1.0		

When the inner loop ends, the next statement processed is the one that appears immediately below the inner loop in the program—in this case, the **cout << "Region " << region << " sales: " << totRegSales << endl;** statement. This statement displays the region number (2) along with the total sales made in Region 2 (23000).

Next, the computer processes the **region = region + 1;** statement, which adds 1 to the value stored in the **region** counter variable, giving 3. The **totRegSales = 0.0;** statement then reinitializes the **totRegSales** accumulator variable to 0, as shown in Figure 8-13.

Figure 8-13: Desk-check table after updating the counter and reinitializing the accumulator

sales	region	totRegSales
~~0.0~~	~~1~~	~~0.0~~
~~25000.0~~	~~2~~	~~25000.0~~
~~30000.0~~	3	~~55000.0~~
~~10000.0~~		~~65000.0~~
~~-1.0~~		~~0.0~~
~~13000.0~~		~~13000.0~~
~~10000.0~~		~~23000.0~~
−1.0		0.0

The outer loop condition, `while (region < 3)`, then is reevaluated to determine whether the outer loop should be processed again. At this point, the outer loop condition evaluates to false, because the value stored in the `region` variable (3) is not less than 3. Because of this, the outer loop ends and processing continues with the instruction located immediately below the outer loop. In this case, processing continues with the `cout << "End of program" << endl;` statement.

Figure 8-14 shows another way of writing the code for the Max Beauty Supply program. This version of the program uses a `for` statement and a `do while` statement, rather than two `while` statements.

Figure 8-14: Another version of the Max Beauty Supply program

IPO chart information	C++ instructions
Input sales	`double sales = 0.0;`
Processing region counter (1 and 2)	(the `region` counter variable is initialized in the `for` statement)
Output region counter total region sales (accumulator)	`double totRegSales = 0.0;`
Algorithm 1. repeat while (the region counter is less than 3)	`for (int region = 1; region < 3; region = region + 1)` `{`
enter the sales	`cout << "First sales amount for Region " << region << ":";` `cin >> sales;`
do	`do` `{`
add the sales to the total region sales	`totRegSales = totRegSales + sales;`
enter the sales	`cout << "Next sales amount for Region " << region << ":";` `cin >> sales;`
end repeat while (the sales are greater than 0)	`} while (sales > 0);`
display the region counter and total region sales	`cout << "Region " << region << " sales: " << totRegSales << endl;`
add 1 to the region counter	(the `region` counter is updated in the `for` statement)
assign 0 to the total region sales	`totRegSales = 0.0;`
end repeat while 2. display "End of program"	`}   //end for` `cout << "End of program" << endl;`

Mini-Quiz 3

1) For nested loops to work correctly, the entire _____ loop must be contained within the _____ loop.
   a. inner, outer
   b. outer, inner

2) Assume a program declares two `int` variables named `firstLoop` and `secondLoop`. Both variables are initialized to the number 1. Write the C++ code that uses these variables to display the numbers 1 through 3 on four lines, as follows.

1	2	3
1	2	3
1	2	3
1	2	3

You now have completed Chapter 8's Concept lesson. You can either take a break or complete the end-of-lesson questions and exercises before moving on to the Application lesson.

SUMMARY

A repetition structure can be either a pretest loop or a posttest loop. In a pretest loop, the loop condition is evaluated *before* the instructions in the loop body are processed. In a posttest loop, on the other hand, the loop condition is evaluated *after* the instructions in the loop body are processed. Depending on the result of the evaluation, the instructions in a pretest loop may never be processed. The instructions in a posttest loop, however, always are processed at least once. As you learned in Chapter 7, you can use either the `while` statement or the `for` statement to code a pretest loop in C++. You use the `do while` statement to code a posttest loop in C++.

You can nest repetition structures, which means that you can place one repetition structure inside another repetition structure. For repetition structures to be nested and work correctly, the entire inner loop must be contained within the outer loop.

ANSWERS TO MINI-QUIZZES

Mini-Quiz 1

1) b. posttest, pretest

2) b. posttest, pretest

3) three

Mini-Quiz 2

1) b. False

2) a. True

3) `while (quantity > 0);`

Mini-Quiz 3

1) a. inner, outer

2)
```
while (firstLoop <= 4)
{
    while (secondLoop <= 3)
    {
        cout << secondLoop;
        cout << " ";
        secondLoop = secondLoop + 1;
    }  //end while
    cout << endl;
    firstLoop = firstLoop + 1;
    secondLoop = 1;
}  //end while
```

QUESTIONS

1) The condition in the **do while** statement is evaluated _____ the instructions in the loop body are processed.

A. after

B. before

2) The loop body instructions in the _____ statement always are processed at least once.

A. do while

B. for

C. while

D. both A and B

3) What numbers appear on the screen when the computer processes the following code?

```
int x = 1;
do
{
    cout << x << endl;
    x = x + 1;
} while (x < 5);
```

A. 0, 1, 2, 3, 4

B. 0, 1, 2, 3, 4, 5

C. 1, 2, 3, 4

D. 1, 2, 3, 4, 5

4) What numbers appear on the screen when the computer processes the following code?

```
int x = 20;
do
{
        cout << x << endl;
        x = x - 4;
} while (x > 10);
```

A. 16, 12, 8

B. 16, 12

C. 20, 16, 12, 8

D. 20, 16, 12

5) What is the value stored in the **x** variable when the loop in Question 4 stops?

A. 0

B. 8

C. 10

D. 12

6) What numbers appear on the screen when the computer processes the following code?

```
int total = 1;
do
{
        cout << total << endl;
        total = total + 2;
} while (total >= 3);
```

A. 1

B. 1, 3

C. 1, 3, 5

D. 0, 1, 3

7) What appears on the screen when the computer processes the following code?

```
for (int x = 1; x < 3; x = x + 1)
{
    for (int y = 1; y < 4; y = y + 1)
            cout << "*";
        //end for
      cout << endl;
} //end for
```

A. ***
   ***

B. ***
   ***
   ***

C. **
   **
   **

D. ***
   ***
   ***
   ***

8) What number appears on the screen when the computer processes the following code?

```cpp
int sum = 0;
int y = 0;
do
{
        for (int x = 1; x < 5; x = x + 1)
              sum = sum + x;
        //end for
        y = y + 1;
} while (y < 3);
cout << sum << endl;
```

A. 5

B. 8

C. 15

D. 30

Look For These
Symbols

Debugging

Discovery

EXERCISES

1) Write a C++ `while` clause that stops a posttest loop when the value in the `quantity` variable is less than the number 0.

2) Write a C++ `while` clause that processes a posttest loop's instructions as long as the value in the `inStock` variable is greater than the value in the `reorder` variable.

3) Write a C++ `while` clause that processes a posttest loop's instructions as long as the value in the `letter` variable is the letter Y in either uppercase or lowercase. (The `letter` variable is a `char` variable.)

4) Assume a program declares an `int` variable named `evenNum` and initializes it to 2. Write the C++ code, using the `do while` statement and the `evenNum` variable, to display the even integers between 1 and 9 on the screen.

5) In this exercise, you use a nested loop to display a pattern of asterisks.

A. If necessary, start Visual Studio .NET. Open the Ch8ConE05 Solution (Ch8ConE05 Solution.sln) file, which is contained in the Cpp\Chap08\ Ch8ConE05 Solution folder.

B. Complete the program by entering the instructions to display the following pattern of asterisks (2 asterisks, 4 asterisks, 6 asterisks, 8 asterisks, and 10 asterisks).

```
**

****

******

********

**********
```

C. Save and then build the solution.

D. Execute the program.

E. When the program is working correctly, close the Output window, then use the File menu to close the solution.

6) In this exercise, you use a nested loop to display a pattern of asterisks.

A. If necessary, start Visual Studio .NET. Open the Ch8ConE06 Solution (Ch8ConE06 Solution.sln) file, which is contained in the Cpp\Chap08\ Ch8ConE06 Solution folder.

B. Complete the program by entering the instructions to display the following pattern of asterisks (9 asterisks, 8 asterisks, 7 asterisks, 6 asterisks, 5 asterisks, 4 asterisks, 3 asterisks, 2 asterisks, and 1 asterisk).

```
* * * * * * * * *
* * * * * * * *
* * * * * * *
* * * * * *
* * * * *
* * * *
* * *
* *
*
```

C. Save and then build the solution.

D. Execute the program.

E. When the program is working correctly, close the Output window, then use the File menu to close the solution.

7) In this exercise, you modify the program you created in Exercise 5 so that it allows the user to specify the outer loop's ending value (which determines the largest number of asterisks to display) and its increment value (the number of asterisks to repeat).

A. If necessary, start Visual Studio .NET. Open the Ch8ConE07 Solution (Ch8ConE07 Solution.sln) file, which is contained in the Cpp\Chap08\ Ch8ConE07 Solution folder.

B. Click File on the menu bar, point to Open, and then click File. Open the Ch8ConE05.cpp file, which is contained in the Cpp\Chap08\Ch8ConE05 Solution\Ch8ConE05 Project folder. Select all of the **main( )** function's code, then copy the code to the clipboard. Close the Ch8ConE05.cpp window, then paste the code in the Ch8ConE07.cpp window.

C. Modify the program so that it allows the user to specify the outer loop's ending and increment values.

D. Save and then build the solution.

E. Execute the program. Test the program by entering the number 4 as the maximum number of asterisks and the number 1 as the increment value. The program should display the following pattern of asterisks (1 asterisk, 2 asterisks, 3 asterisks and 4 asterisks).

```
*
* *
* * *
* * * *
```

F. Execute the program again. This time, enter the number 9 as the maximum number of asterisks and the number 3 as the increment value. The program should display the following pattern of asterisks (3 asterisks, 6 asterisks, and 9 asterisks).

```
* * *

* * * * * *

* * * * * * * * *
```

G. When the program is working correctly, close the Output window, then use the File menu to close the solution.

8) In this exercise, you modify the program you created in Exercise 6 so that it allows the user to display the asterisks using either of the following two patterns:

<u>Pattern 1</u> (9 asterisks, 8 asterisks, 7 asterisks, 6 asterisks, 5 asterisks, 4 asterisks, 3 asterisks, 2 asterisks, and 1 asterisk)

```
* * * * * * * * *

* * * * * * * *

* * * * * * *

* * * * * *

* * * * *

* * * *

* * *

* *

*
```

<u>Pattern 2</u> (1 asterisk, 2 asterisks, 3 asterisks, 4 asterisks, 5 asterisks, 6 asterisks, 7 asterisks, 8 asterisks, and 9 asterisks)

```
*

* *

* * *

* * * *

* * * * *

* * * * * *

* * * * * * *

* * * * * * * *

* * * * * * * * *
```

A. If necessary, start Visual Studio .NET. Open the Ch8ConE08 Solution (Ch8ConE08 Solution.sln) file, which is contained in the Cpp\Chap08\ Ch8ConE08 Solution folder.

B. Click File on the menu bar, point to Open, and then click File. Open the Ch8ConE06.cpp file, which is contained in the Cpp\Chap08\Ch8ConE06 Solution\Ch8ConE06 Project folder. Select all of the **main( )** function's code, then copy the code to the clipboard. Close the Ch8ConE06.cpp window, then paste the code in the Ch8ConE08.cpp window.

C. Modify the program appropriately.

D. Save and then build the solution.

E. Execute the program. Display the asterisks using pattern 1.

F. Execute the program again. Display the asterisks using pattern 2.

G. When the program is working correctly, close the Output window, then use the File menu to close the solution.

9) In this exercise, you modify the program you created in Exercise 5 so that it allows the user to process the program's code as many times as desired.

A. If necessary, start Visual Studio .NET. Open the Ch8ConE09 Solution (Ch8ConE09 Solution.sln) file, which is contained in the Cpp\Chap08\ Ch8ConE09 Solution folder.

B. Click File on the menu bar, point to Open, and then click File. Open the Ch8ConE05.cpp file, which is contained in the Cpp\Chap08\Ch8ConE05 Solution\Ch8ConE05 Project folder. Select all of the **main( )** function's code, then copy the code to the clipboard. Close the Ch8ConE05.cpp window, then paste the code in the Ch8ConE09.cpp window.

C. Modify the program so that it allows the user to process the code as many times as desired.

D. Save and then build the solution.

E. Execute the program. Test the program by processing its code three times.

F. When the program is working correctly, close the Output window, then use the File menu to close the solution.

10) In this exercise, you debug a C++ program.

A. If necessary, start Visual Studio .NET. Open the Ch8ConE10 Solution (Ch8ConE10 Solution.sln) file, which is contained in the Cpp\Chap08\ Ch8ConE10 Solution folder.

B. Build the solution, then execute the program. The program should display the total sales amount ($11000) for two departments, but it is not working correctly.

C. Correct the program's code, then save and build the solution.

D. Execute the program. When the program is working correctly, close the Output window, then use the File menu to close the solution.

Application Lesson

Using a Nested Repetition Structure in a C++ Program

Lab 8.1 - Stop and Analyze   If necessary, start Visual Studio .NET. Open the Ch8Lab1 Solution (Ch8Lab1 Solution.sln) file contained in the Cpp\Chap08\Ch8Lab1 Solution folder. Figure 8-15 shows the code entered in the Ch8Lab1.cpp file. (The line numbers are included in the figure only.) Study the code, then answer the questions.

Figure 8-15: C++ instructions entered in the Ch8Lab1.cpp file

```
1   //Ch8Lab1.cpp - simulates a clock's hour and minute hands
2   //Created/revised by <your name> on <current date>
3
4   #include <iostream>
5
6   using std::cout;
7   using std::endl;
8
9   int main()
10  {
11    for (int hour = 0; hour < 3; hour = hour + 1)
12    {
13        //display hour
14        cout << "Hour: " << hour << endl;
15        for (int minute = 0; minute < 60; minute = minute + 1)
16            //display minute
17            cout << "          Minute: " << minute << endl;
18        //end for
19    }  //end for
20
21    return 0;
22  } //end of main function
```

Questions

1. What is the Ch8Lab1.cpp program's output?
2. What value is stored in the `hour` variable when the outer loop ends?
3. What value is stored in the `minute` variable when the inner loop ends?
4. How else could you have written the outer loop's condition?
5. How else could you have written the inner loop's condition?
6. How many times will the instructions in the outer loop be processed?
7. Build the solution, then execute the program. Scroll up the Command Prompt window to view its contents, then close the Command Prompt window.
8. Create a blank solution named Ch8Lab1 Do Solution. Save the solution in the Cpp\Chap08 folder.
9. Add an empty C++ Win32 Console Project to the solution. Name the project Ch8Lab1 Do Project.
10. Add a new C++ source file to the project. Name the source file Ch8Lab1 Do.
11. Open the Ch8Lab1.cpp file contained in the Cpp\Ch8Lab1 Solution\Ch8Lab1 Project folder. Copy the file's contents to the clipboard. Close the Ch8Lab1.cpp window, then paste the instructions into the Ch8Lab1 Do.cpp window. Change the filename in the first comment to Ch8Lab1 Do.cpp.

12. Modify the program so that it uses two **do while** statements rather than two **for** statements.
13. Save and then build the solution. Execute the program. Scroll up the Command Prompt window to view its contents, which should be identical to what you observed in Step 7. Close the Command Prompt window.
14. Close the Output window, then use the File menu to close the solution.

Lab 8.2 Mrs. Johnson teaches second grade at Allen Primary Center. Last month, Mrs. Johnson began teaching multiplication to the students. She has asked you to create a program that she can use to display multiplication tables for her students. Figure 8-16 shows a sample of a multiplication table. In this case, the multiplication table is for the number 6.

Figure 8-16: Sample multiplication table for the number 6

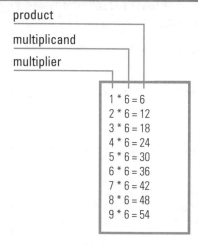

```
product
multiplicand
multiplier

        1 * 6 = 6
        2 * 6 = 12
        3 * 6 = 18
        4 * 6 = 24
        5 * 6 = 30
        6 * 6 = 36
        7 * 6 = 42
        8 * 6 = 48
        9 * 6 = 54
```

The first column of the multiplication table should always contain the numbers 1 through 9; these numbers represent the multiplier. The number to display in the third column depends on the value entered by the user. For example, if the user enters the number 6, then the number 6 should appear in the third column, as shown in Figure 8-16. However, if the user enters the number 12, then the number 12 should appear in the third column. The number in the third column is called the multiplicand. The last column in the multiplication table is the result of multiplying the multiplier by the multiplicand and is called the product of the two numbers. Figure 8-17 shows the IPO chart and C++ instructions for the multiplication table problem.

Figure 8-17: IPO chart and C++ instructions for the multiplication table problem

IPO chart information	C++ instructions

Input
  multiplicand
  answer to "another table?" question
Processing
  none
Output
  multiplicand
  multiplier
  product
	`int multiplicand = 0;`
	`char anotherTable = ' ';`
	
	(the `multiplier` variable is initialized in the **for** statement)
	`int product = 0;`

Figure 8-17: IPO chart and C++ instructions for the multiplication table problem (continued)

IPO chart information	C++ instructions
Algorithm 1. do	`do` `{`
enter the multiplicand	`    cout << "Enter the multiplicand: ";` `    cin >> multiplicand;`
assign 1 to the multiplier	`(the ` `multiplier` ` variable is initialized in the ` `for` ` statement)`

repeat while (multiplier < 10)	`    for (int multiplier = 1; multiplier < 10;`
	`    multiplier = multiplier + 1)`
	`    {`

calculate product = multiplier * multiplicand	`        product = multiplier * multiplicand;`

display multiplier, multiplicand,
     and product
	`        cout << multiplier << " * " <<`
	`        multiplicand << " = " <<`
	`        product << endl;`

add 1 to the multiplier end repeat while	`    (the ` `multiplier` ` variable is updated in the ` `for` ` statement)` `    }   //end for`

enter answer to "another table?"
   question
	`    cout << "Do you want to display`
	`    another multiplication table? (Y/N) ";`
	`    cin >> anotherTable;`

end repeat while (answer to "another table?" question is Y)	`} while (toupper(anotherTable) == 'Y');`

As the IPO chart indicates, the multiplication table program requires four memory locations to store the values of its input and output items. You will store the values in variables, because the values will be different each time the program is executed. You will use the `int` data type for the variables that store the multiplicand, multiplier, and product, and the `char` data type for the variable that stores the answer to the "another table?" question.

Notice that the program uses two repetition structures: a posttest loop and a pretest loop. Also notice that the pretest loop is contained entirely within the posttest loop. The posttest loop keeps track of whether the user wants to display more than one multiplication table. The pretest loop is responsible for displaying the multiplication table(s).

Activity for Lab 8.2

In this activity, you enter the C++ instructions shown in Figure 8-17 into the computer. You then test the program to verify that it is working correctly.

To create the multiplication table program, then test the program:

1. If necessary, start Visual Studio .NET. Create a blank solution named Ch8Lab2 Solution. Save the solution in the Cpp\Chap08 folder.

2. Add an empty C++ Win32 Console Project to the solution. Name the project Ch8Lab2 Project.

3. Add a new C++ source file to the project. Name the source file Ch8Lab2.

4. Type **//Ch8Lab2.cpp – displays one or more multiplication tables** and press **Enter**.

5. Type **//Created/revised by *<your name>* on *<current date>***, replacing *<your name>* and *<current date>* with your name and the current date, respectively. Press **Enter** twice.

6. Type **#include <iostream>** and press **Enter** twice.

7. Type the following three `using` statements, then press **Enter** twice.

   using std::cout;

   using std::cin;

   using std::endl;

8. Complete the program by entering the `main()` function, which is shown in Figure 8-18.

Figure 8-18: Multiplication table program

```cpp
//Ch8Lab2.cpp - displays one or more multiplication tables
//Created/revised by <your name> on <current date>

#include <iostream>

using std::cout;
using std::cin;
using std::endl;

int main()
{
    //declare variables
    char anotherTable = ' ';
    int multiplicand  = 0;
    int product       = 0;

    do
    {
        //get the multiplicand
        cout << "Enter the multiplicand: ";
        cin >> multiplicand;

        //display the multiplication table
        for (int multiplier = 1; multiplier < 10;
        multiplier = multiplier + 1)
        {
            product = multiplier * multiplicand;
            cout << multiplier << " * " << multiplicand
                 << " = " << product << endl;
        }   //end for

        cout << "Do you want to display another
        multiplication table? (Y/N) ";
        cin >> anotherTable;
    } while (toupper(anotherTable) == 'Y');

    return 0;
}   //end of main function
```

enter the `main()` function instructions

9.   Save and then build the solution. Verify that the program generated no warnings.

10. Execute the program. When you are prompted to enter the multiplicand, type **6** and press **Enter**. The program displays the multiplication table for the number 6.

11. Type **y** and press **Enter** in response to the "Do you want to display another multiplication table? (Y/N)" prompt.

12. When you are prompted to enter the multiplicand, type **2** and press **Enter**. The program displays the multiplication table for the number 2.

13. Type **n** and press **Enter** in response to the "Do you want to display another multiplication table? (Y/N)" prompt. The multiplication program ends. Close the Command Prompt window.

14. Close the Output window, then use the File menu to close the solution.

Lab 8.3   In this lab, you modify the program you created in Lab 8.2. The modified program will use a posttest loop (rather than a pretest loop) to display the multiplication table(s).

Activity for Lab 8.3

Before modifying the program created in Lab 8.2, you copy the instructions contained in the Ch8Lab2.cpp file to a new solution.

To copy the instructions contained in the Ch8Lab2.cpp file to a new solution:

1.   If necessary, start Visual Studio .NET. Create a blank solution named **Ch8Lab3 Solution**. Save the solution in the Cpp\Chap08 folder.

2.   Add an empty C++ Win32 Console Project to the solution. Name the project **Ch8Lab3 Project**.

3.   Add a new C++ source file to the project. Name the source file **Ch8Lab3**.

4.   Use the File menu to open the Ch8Lab2.cpp file contained in the Cpp\Chap08\ Ch8Lab2 Solution\Ch8Lab2 Project folder. Select the contents of the file, then copy the contents to the clipboard.

5.   Close the Ch8Lab2.cpp window.

6.   Click the **Ch8Lab3.cpp** tab, then paste the instructions from the clipboard into the Ch8Lab3.cpp window.

7.   Change the filename in the first program comment to **Ch8Lab3.cpp**. If necessary, change the date in the second comment.

Currently, the program uses a `for` statement to display the multiplication table(s). Your task is to modify the program so that it uses a `do while` statement rather than a `for` statement.

To modify the program, then test the program:

1.   Make the appropriate modifications to the program.

2.   Save and then build the solution. If necessary, correct any syntax errors, then save and build the solution again.

3. Execute the program. Test the program using your own sample data, then close the Command Prompt window.

4. When the program is working correctly, close the Output window, then use the File menu to close the solution.

You now have completed Chapter 8's Application lesson. You can either take a break or complete the end-of-lesson exercises.

ANSWERS TO LABS

Lab 8.1

1. The program displays the hours and minutes.

2. The hour variable contains the number 3 when the outer loop ends.

3. The minute variable contains the number 60 when the inner loop ends.

4. You also can write the outer loop's condition as hour <= 2.

5. You also can write the inner loop's condition as minute <= 59.

6. The instructions in the outer loop will be processed three times.

12. See Figure 8-19.

Figure 8-19

```
1  //Ch8Lab1 Do.cpp - simulates a clock's hour and minute hands
2  //Created/revised by <your name> on <current date>
3
4  #include <iostream>
5
6  using std::cout;
7  using std::cin;
8  using std::endl;
9
10 int main()
11 {
12   //declare variables
13   int hour   = 0;
14   int minute = 0;
15
16   do
17   {
18       //display hour
19       cout << "Hour: " << hour << endl;
20       minute = 0;
21       do
22       {
23           //display minute
```

Figure 8-19 (continued)

```
24              cout << "          Minute: " << minute << endl;
25              minute = minute + 1;   //update minute
26          }   while (minute < 60);
27          hour = hour + 1;     //update hour
28      } while (hour < 3);
29
30      return 0;
31 }   //end of main function
```

Lab 8.2

No answer required.

Lab 8.3

See Figure 8-20. Modifications are shaded in the figure.

Figure 8-20

```
//Ch8Lab3.cpp - displays one or more multiplication tables
//Created/revised by <your name> on <current date>

#include <iostream>

using std::cout;
using std::cin;
using std::endl;

int main()
{
    //declare variables
    char anotherTable = ' ';
    int multiplicand  = 0;
    int product       = 0;

    do
    {
        //get the multiplicand
        cout << "Enter the multiplicand: ";
        cin >> multiplicand;

        //display the multiplication table
        int multiplier = 1;
        do
        {
            product = multiplier * multiplicand;
```

Figure 8-20 (continued)

```
            cout << multiplier << " * " << multiplicand
                 << " = " << product << endl;
            multiplier = multiplier + 1;
      }  while (multiplier < 10);

         cout << "Do you want to display another
         multiplication table? (Y/N) ";
         cin >> anotherTable;
    }  while (toupper(anotherTable) == 'Y');

    return 0;
}    //end of main function
```

EXERCISES

Look For These
Symbols

Debugging

Discovery

1) In this exercise, you modify the program you created in Lab 8.2 so that it uses two `while` statements, rather than a `do while` statement and a `for` statement.

   A. If necessary, start Visual Studio .NET. Create a blank solution named Ch8AppE01 Solution. Save the solution in the Cpp\Chap08 folder.

   B. Add an empty C++ Win32 Console Project to the solution. Name the project Ch8AppE01 Project.

   C. Add a new C++ source file to the project. Name the source file Ch8AppE01.

   D. Use the File menu to open the Ch8Lab2.cpp file contained in the Cpp\Chap08\ Ch8Lab2 Solution\Ch8Lab2 Project folder. Select the contents of the file, then copy the contents to the clipboard.

   E. Close the Ch8Lab2.cpp window.

   F. Click the Ch8AppE01.cpp tab, then paste the instructions from the clipboard into the Ch8AppE01.cpp window.

   G. Change the filename in the first program comment to Ch8AppE01.cpp. If necessary, change the date in the second comment.

   H. Replace the `do while` and `for` statements with `while` statements.

   I. Save and then build the solution.

   J. Execute the program. Display the multiplication tables for the numbers 5 and 3.

   K. When the program is working correctly, close the Output window, then use the File menu to close the solution.

2) In this exercise, you modify the Max Beauty Supply program shown in Figure 8-14 so that it uses a `for` statement instead of a `do while` statement.

   A. If necessary, start Visual Studio .NET. Open the Ch8AppE02 Solution (Ch8AppE02 Solution.sln) file, which is contained in the Cpp\Chap08\ Ch8AppE02 Solution folder.

   B. Replace the `do while` statement with a `for` statement. Assume that each region has four sales amounts.

   C. Save and then build the solution.

D. Execute the program. Test the program using the following sales amounts:

Region 1 sales: 400, 200, 500, 600

Region 2 sales: 100, 900, 400, 700

E. When the program is working correctly, close the Output window, then use the File menu to close the solution.

3) In this exercise, you modify the program you created in Lab 7.2 in Chapter 7. The modified program will allow the user to display the grade for as many students as needed.

A. If necessary, start Visual Studio .NET. Create a blank solution named Ch8AppE03 Solution. Save the solution in the Cpp\Chap08 folder.

B. Add an empty C++ Win32 Console Project to the solution. Name the project Ch8AppE03 Project.

C. Add a new C++ source file to the project. Name the source file Ch8AppE03.

D. Use the File menu to open the Ch7Lab2.cpp file contained in the Cpp\Chap07\ Ch7Lab2 Solution\Ch7Lab2 Project folder. Select the contents of the file, then copy the contents to the clipboard.

E. Close the Ch7Lab2.cpp window.

F. Click the Ch8AppE03.cpp tab, then paste the instructions from the clipboard into the Ch8AppE03.cpp window.

G. Change the filename in the first program comment to Ch8AppE03.cpp. If necessary, change the date in the second comment.

H. Modify the program appropriately.

I. Save and then build the solution.

J. Execute the program. Test the program using your own sample data for three students.

K. When the program is working correctly, close the Output window, then use the File menu to close the solution.

4) In this exercise, you create a program that displays the sum of the sales amounts made in each of four regions (North, South, East, and West) during a three-month period. The program also should display the total sales made during the three months.

A. If necessary, start Visual Studio .NET. Open the Ch8AppE04 Solution (Ch8AppE04 Solution.sln) file, which is contained in the Cpp\Chap08\ Ch8AppE04 Solution folder.

B. Complete the program by entering the C++ code that allows the user to enter four sets (one set for each region) of three sales amounts (one sales amount for each month). The program should display each region's total sales for the three-month period, and the company's total sales for the three-month period.

C. Save and then build the solution.

D. Execute the program. Use the following four sets of data to test the program:

2000, 4000, 3000
2000, 5000, 5000
3000, 2000, 1000
4000, 1000, 6000

E. When the program is working correctly, close the Output window, then use the File menu to close the solution.

5) In this exercise, you modify the program you created in Lab 5.2 in Chapter 5. The modified program will allow the user to display the fat calories and fat percentage as many times as desired.

A. If necessary, start Visual Studio .NET. Create a blank solution named Ch8AppE05 Solution. Save the solution in the Cpp\Chap08 folder.

B. Add an empty C++ Win32 Console Project to the solution. Name the project Ch8AppE05 Project.

C. Add a new C++ source file to the project. Name the source file Ch8AppE05.

D. Use the File menu to open the Ch5Lab2.cpp file contained in the Cpp\Chap05\Ch5Lab2 Solution\Ch5Lab2 Project folder. Select the contents of the file, then copy the contents to the clipboard.

E. Close the Ch5Lab2.cpp window.

F. Click the Ch8AppE05.cpp tab, then paste the instructions from the clipboard into the Ch8AppE05.cpp window.

G. Change the filename in the first program comment to Ch8AppE05.cpp. If necessary, change the date in the second comment.

H. Modify the program appropriately.

I. Save and then build the solution.

J. Execute the program. Test the program using your own sample data.

K. When the program is working correctly, close the Output window, then use the File menu to close the solution.

6) In this exercise, you modify the O'Donnell Incorporated program shown in Figure 8-7 so that it uses a **for** statement instead of a **do while** statement.

A. If necessary, start Visual Studio .NET. Open the Ch8AppE06 Solution (Ch8AppE06 Solution.sln) file, which is contained in the Cpp\Chap08\Ch8AppE06 Solution folder.

B. Replace the **do while** statement with a **for** statement. Assume the program needs to calculate the bonus amounts for five salespeople.

C. Save and then build the solution.

D. Execute the program. Test the program using your own sample data.

E. When the program is working correctly, close the Output window, then use the File menu to close the solution.

7) In this exercise, you modify the program you created in Lab 8.2. The modified program will use two **for** statements rather than a **do while** statement and a **for** statement.

A. If necessary, start Visual Studio .NET. Create a blank solution named Ch8AppE07 Solution. Save the solution in the Cpp\Chap08 folder.

B. Add an empty C++ Win32 Console Project to the solution. Name the project Ch8AppE07 Project.

C. Add a new C++ source file to the project. Name the source file Ch8AppE07.

D. Use the File menu to open the Ch8Lab2.cpp file contained in the Cpp\Chap08\Ch8Lab2 Solution\Ch8Lab2 Project folder. Select the contents of the file, then copy the contents to the clipboard.

E. Close the Ch8Lab2.cpp window.

F. Click the Ch8AppE07.cpp tab, then paste the instructions from the clipboard into the Ch8AppE07.cpp window.

G. Change the filename in the first program comment to Ch8AppE07.cpp. If necessary, change the date in the second comment.

H. Replace the `do while` statement with a `for` statement.

I. Save and then build the solution.

J. Execute the program. Display the multiplication tables for the numbers 9 and 12.

K. When the program is working correctly, close the Output window, then use the File menu to close the solution.

 8) In this exercise, you debug a C++ program.

A. If necessary, start Visual Studio .NET. Open the Ch8AppE08 Solution (Ch8AppE08 Solution.sln) file, which is contained in the Cpp\Chap08\ Ch8AppE08 Solution folder.

B. Build the solution, then execute the program.

C. Correct the program's code, then save and build the solution.

D. Execute the program. When the program is working correctly, close the Output window, then use the File menu to close the solution.

 Please visit the Testing Center at www.course.com/testingcenter for more practice on the topics covered in this chapter.

Value-Returning Functions

After completing this chapter, you will be able to:

- Raise a number to a power

- Generate random numbers

- Create and invoke a function that returns a value

- Pass information, *by value*, to a function

- Write a function prototype

- Understand a variable's scope and lifetime

Concept Lesson

Functions

As you learned in Chapter 3, a function is a block of code that performs a task. Every C++ program contains at least one function—`main()`—and most contain many more. Programmers use functions for two reasons. First, functions allow the programmer to avoid duplicating code in different parts of a program. If a program needs to perform the same task several times, it is more efficient to enter the appropriate code once, in a function, then simply call the function to perform its task when needed. Second, functions allow large and complex programs, which typically are written by a team of programmers, to be broken into small and manageable tasks; each member of the team can be assigned one of the tasks to code as a function. When each programmer has completed his or her function, all of the functions then are gathered together into one program. Typically, the `main()` function in the program is responsible for calling (or invoking) each of the other functions when needed.

All functions are categorized as either value-returning functions or void functions. Value-returning functions return a value, whereas void functions do not return a value. You learn about value-returning functions in this chapter, and about void functions in Chapter 10.

Value-Returning Functions

A **value-returning function** is a function that, after completing its assigned task, returns precisely one value. In most cases, the value is returned to the statement that called the function. Typically, such statements display the function's return value, use the return value in a calculation, or assign the return value to a variable.

Some value-returning functions are built into the C++ language. Examples of built-in value-returning functions with which you are already familiar are the `getline()` and `toupper()` functions. Recall that the `getline()` function returns the string of characters entered by the user at the keyboard, and the `toupper()` function returns the uppercase equivalent of a string.

In the next two sections, you learn how to use value-returning functions that are built into the C++ language for the purpose of raising a number to a power and also generating random numbers.

Raising a Number to a Power

Some mathematical expressions—for example, the πr^2 expression for calculating the area of a circle—require you to raise a number to a power; you use the `pow()` function for this purpose. The **pow() function** raises a number to a power and then returns the result as a `double` number. To use the `pow()` function in a program, the program must contain the `#include <cmath>` directive and the `using std::pow;` statement. Figure 9-1 shows the syntax of the `pow()` function and includes three examples of using the function in a C++ statement.

tip

Any function, not just `main()`, can call another function.

tip

The ability to create functions within a program allows more than one programmer to work on a program at the same time, decreasing the time it takes to write the program.

tip

The `main()` function is also a value-returning function. However, it returns its one value to the operating system.

Figure 9-1: Syntax and examples of the pow() **function**

Syntax
pow(x, y)

Examples and results

```
cube = pow(4, 3);
```
assigns the number 64 to the **cube** variable

```
cout << pow(100.0, .5);
```
displays the number 10 on the screen

```
area = 3.141593 * pow(radius, 2);
```
assuming the **radius** variable contains the number 5, assigns the number 78.5398 to the **area** variable

tip

Recall that the items appearing within the parentheses following a function's name are called arguments.

In the syntax, x is the number you want raised to power y. For example, the **cube = pow(4, 3);** statement shown in Figure 9-1 raises the number 4 to the third power. In other words, it multiplies the number 4 by itself three times (4 * 4 * 4). The statement then assigns the result (64) to the **cube** variable.

The **cout << pow(100.0, .5);** statement raises the number 100 to the .5 power, which is the same as finding the square root of the number. The statement displays the number 10 on the screen.

The **area = 3.141593 * pow(radius, 2);** statement raises the number contained in the **radius** variable to the second power. It then multiplies the result by 3.141593 and assigns the product to the **area** variable. If the **radius** variable contains the number 5, the statement assigns the number 78.5398 to the **area** variable.

Next, you learn how to generate random numbers in a program.

Generating Random Numbers

Many programs require the use of random numbers. Examples of such programs include lottery programs and programs used to practice elementary math skills. Most programming languages have a built-in function for generating random numbers; the function is commonly referred to as the random number generator. In C++, the random number generator is the **rand() function**.

The **rand()** function returns a positive integer that is greater than or equal to 0, but less than or equal to RAND_MAX, a constant that is built into the C++ language. Although the value of RAND_MAX varies with different systems, its value is always at least 32,767.

In C++, you must initialize the random number generator in each program in which it is used. Typically, the initialization task is performed at the beginning of the program. If you do not initialize the random number generator, it generates the same series of numbers each time the program is executed. This repetition occurs because the random number generator in C++ does not generate true random numbers. Rather, it generates pseudo-random numbers based on a mathematical formula included in the random number generator's code.

You initialize the random number generator using the **srand()** function. Like the **rand()** function, the **srand()** function is built into the C++ language. However, unlike the **rand()** function, the **srand()** function is a void function, which means it does not return a value.

The syntax of the **srand()** function is **srand(**seed**)**, where seed is a number that represents the starting point for the **rand()** function (the random number generator). Most C++ programmers use the built-in **time()** function as the seed. The **time()** function is a

tip

If you want to view the value of RAND_MAX for your computer system, complete Discovery Exercise 12 at the end of this lesson.

value-returning function that returns the current time (according to your computer system's clock) in seconds. The **time()** function ensures that the random number generator is initialized with a unique number each time the program is executed. To use the **time()** function in a program, the program must contain the **#include <ctime>** directive. Figure 9-2 shows the syntax of the **rand()**, **srand()**, and **time()** functions. It also includes examples of using each function.

Figure 9-2: Syntax of the rand(), srand(), and time() functions

Syntax
rand( ) **srand(**_seed_**)** **time(0)**
Examples and results

`srand(int(time(0)));`
initializes the random number generator [the **rand( )** function], using the **time( )** function as the _seed_
 	
`randomNum = rand();`
assigns to the **randomNum** variable a random positive integer that is greater than or equal to 0, but less than or equal to RAND_MAX

The **srand(int(time(0)));** statement shown in Figure 9-2 initializes the random number generator using the **time()** function as the _seed_. The **randomNum = rand();** statement shown in the figure first generates a random positive integer that is greater than or equal to 0, but less than or equal to RAND_MAX, then assigns the integer to the **randomNum** variable.

In most programs that use random numbers, you will need to generate numbers within a more specific range—for example, numbers from 1 through 10 only, or numbers from 10 through 100. Figure 9-3 shows the syntax of the expression you use to specify the range of numbers you want the program to generate. The figure also includes examples of using the expression in a C++ statement.

Figure 9-3: Syntax and examples of the expression used to generate specific random numbers

Syntax
lowerbound + **rand()** % (_upperbound_ – _lowerbound_ + **1**)
Examples and results

`cout << 1 + rand() % (10 - 1 + 1);`
displays a random integer from 1 through 10 on the screen
 	
`randomNum = 10 + rand() % (100 - 10 + 1);`
assigns to the **randomNum** variable a random integer from 10 through 100

tip
Recall from Chapter 4 that % is the modulus arithmetic operator, which divides two integers and results in the remainder of the division.

In the expression's syntax, *lowerbound* is the lowest number in the range, and *upperbound* is the highest number in the range. The `cout << 1 + rand() % (10 - 1 + 1);` statement shown in Figure 9-3 displays a random integer from 1 through 10 on the screen. Before displaying the random integer, the computer first evaluates the expression within parentheses. In this case, the `10 - 1 + 1` expression evaluates to 10. The computer then finds the remainder after dividing the random number, which is generated by the `rand()` function, by 10. If the `rand()` function generated the number 7, for instance, the remainder after performing the division is 7. Finally, the computer adds the number 1 to the remainder (7), displays the result (8) on the screen. Figure 9-4 shows the results of the `cout << 1 + rand() % (10 - 1 + 1);` statement using sample values produced by the `rand()` function.

Figure 9-4: Results of the `cout << 1 + rand() % (10 - 1 + 1);` statement using sample `rand()` values

rand() **value**	**Statement containing** rand() **value**	**Result**
7	`cout << 1 + 7 % (10 - 1 + 1);` Evaluation of random number expression: Step 1: 1 + 7 % 10 Step 2: 1 + 7 Step 3: 8	displays 8 on the screen
323	`cout << 1 + 323 % (10 - 1 + 1);` Evaluation of random number expression: Step 1: 1 + 323 % 10 Step 2: 1 + 3 Step 3: 4	displays 4 on the screen
30000	`cout << 1 + 30000 % (10 - 1 + 1);` Evaluation of random number expression: Step 1: 1 + 30000 % 10 Step 2: 1 + 0 Step 3: 1	displays 1 on the screen

You can use the second statement shown earlier in Figure 9-3, `randomNum = 10 + rand() % (100 - 10 + 1);`, to assign a random integer from 10 through 100 to the `randomNum` variable. Before assigning the random integer, the computer first evaluates the expression within parentheses. In this case, the `100 - 10 + 1` expression evaluates to 91. The computer then finds the remainder after dividing the random number, which is generated by the `rand()` function, by 91. If the `rand()` function generated the number 352, for instance, the remainder after performing the division would be 79. Finally, the computer adds the number 10 to the remainder (79) and assigns the result (89) to the `randomNum` variable. Figure 9-5 shows the result of the `randomNum = 10 + rand() % (100 - 10 + 1);` statement using sample values produced by the `rand()` function.

Figure 9-5: Results of the `randomNum = 10 + rand() % (100 - 10 + 1);`
statement using sample `rand()` **values**

rand() value	Statement containing rand() value	Result
352	`randomNum = 10 + 352 % (100 - 10 + 1);` Evaluation of random number expression: Step 1: 10 + 352 % 91 Step 2: 10 + 79 Step 3: 89	assigns 89 to the **randomNum** variable
4	`randomNum = 10 + 4 % (100 - 10 + 1);` Evaluation of random number expression: Step 1: 10 + 4 % 91 Step 2: 10 + 4 Step 3: 14	assigns 14 to the **randomNum** variable
2500	`randomNum = 10 + 2500 % (100 - 10 + 1);` Evaluation of random number expression: Step 1: 10 + 2500 % 91 Step 2: 10 + 43 Step 3: 53	assigns 53 to the **randomNum** variable

In addition to using the value-returning functions built into the C++ language, you also can create your own value-returning functions. In this book, functions you create are referred to as **program-defined functions**, because the function definitions are contained in the program itself rather than in a different file.

Creating Program-Defined Value-Returning Functions

Figure 9-6 shows the syntax used to create (or define) a value-returning function in a C++ program. The figure also shows an example of a value-returning function whose task is to calculate the area of a rectangle and then return the result.

Figure 9-6: Syntax and an example of a program-defined value-returning function in C++

Syntax	function header

returnDataType functionName(\[*parameterList*\]) ———
{
    one or more statements
    return *expression*;
}
 	
Note: Items within square brackets (\[\]) in the syntax are optional. Items in **bold**, however, are essential components of the syntax. Items in *italics* indicate where the programmer must supply information pertaining to the current program.
	function body

Example	

`int calcRectangleArea(int len, int wid)`
`{`
    `return len * wid;`
`}    //end of calcRectangleArea function`
	function definition

As Figure 9-6 indicates, a function is composed of a function header and a function body.

Function Header

The **function header** is the first line in a function definition and is so named because it appears at the top (head) of the function. The function header specifies the type of data the function returns (if any), as well as the function's name and an optional *parameterList*. The *parameterList* lists the data type and name of memory locations used by the function to store information passed to it. Notice that a function header does not end with a semicolon. This is because a function header is not considered a statement in C++.

The function header for a value-returning function begins with *returnDataType*, where *returnDataType* indicates the data type of the value returned by the function. If the function returns an integer, as does the `calcRectangleArea()` function shown in Figure 9-6, *returnDataType* will be `int`; however, it will be `char` if the function returns a character.

The function header also specifies the name of the function. The rules for naming functions are the same as for naming variables. To make your programs more self-documenting and easier to understand, you should use meaningful names that describe the task the function performs. In the example shown in Figure 9-6, the name `calcRectangleArea()` indicates that the function calculates the area of a rectangle.

In Chapter 4, you learned that the items of information you send (pass) to a function are called arguments; more specifically, they are called **actual arguments**. An actual argument can be a variable, named constant, literal constant, or keyword. When an actual argument is a variable, the variable can be passed either *by value* or *by reference*. When a variable is passed **by value**, only the value stored in the variable is passed to the function. When a variable is passed **by reference**, on the other hand, the address of the variable in the computer's internal memory is passed. Unless you specify otherwise, variables in C++ are automatically passed *by value*. For now, you do not need to concern yourself with passing *by reference*, because all variables passed to functions in this chapter are passed *by value*. You learn how to pass variables *by reference* in Chapter 10.

tip

As you will learn in Chapter 10, you use the keyword `void` as the *returnDataType* for functions that do not return a value.

tip

You can use any of the C++ data types listed in Chapter 4's Figure 4-5 as the *returnDataType* for a value-returning function.

tip

The rules for naming variables in C++, which also should be followed for naming C++ functions, are shown in Chapter 4's Figure 4-3.

You pass information to a function when you want the function to process the information in some way. In the case of the `calcRectangleArea()` function shown in Figure 9-6, you pass the length and width of the rectangle. To calculate the area of a rectangle having a length of 2 feet and a width of 3 feet, for example, you use the expression `calcRectangleArea(2, 3)` in a C++ statement. The `calcRectangleArea(2, 3)` expression calls (invokes) the `calcRectangleArea()` function, passing it the literal constants 2 and 3. Similarly, to calculate the area of a rectangle whose length and width measurements are stored in the `length` and `width` variables, respectively, you use the expression `calcRectangleArea(length, width)` in a C++ statement. The `calcRectangleArea(length, width)` expression calls the `calcRectangleArea()` function, passing it the values stored in the `length` and `width` variables.

When you pass a literal constant, a keyword, a named constant, or a variable's value to a function, the function stores the value it receives in a memory location. The name and data type of the memory locations that a function uses to store the values passed to it are listed in the function's *parameterList*, which appears within parentheses in the function header. The `calcRectangleArea()` function's *parameterList* in Figure 9-6, for example, indicates that the function uses two `int` variables named `len` and `wid` to store the values passed to it.

Each memory location listed in the *parameterList* is referred to as a **formal parameter**. The number of formal parameters included in the *parameterList* should agree with the number of actual arguments passed to the function. If you pass one actual argument, then the function needs only one formal parameter to store the value of that argument. Similarly, a function that is passed three actual arguments when called requires three formal parameters in its *parameterList*. Each formal parameter must be assigned a data type and name. If a *parameterList* contains more than one formal parameter, you use a comma to separate one parameter from another.

In addition to having the same number of formal parameters as actual arguments, the data type and position of each formal parameter in the *parameterList* must agree with the data type and position of its corresponding actual argument in the *argumentList*. For instance, if the actual argument is a variable whose data type is `int`, then the formal parameter that will store the variable's value should have a data type of `int`. Likewise, if two actual arguments are passed to a function—the first one being a character and the second one being a number with a decimal place—the first formal parameter should have a data type of `char`, and the second formal parameter should have a data type of either `float` or `double`.

Not every function requires information to be passed to it, so not every function has formal parameters listed in its function header. Functions that do not require a *parameterList* have an empty set of parentheses after the function's name.

In addition to a function header, a function definition also includes a function body.

Function Body

The **function body** contains the instructions the function must follow to perform its assigned task. The function body begins with the opening brace ({) and ends with the closing brace (}). Although only one statement appears in the function body shown in Figure 9-6, a function body typically contains many statements.

In most cases, the last statement in the function body of a value-returning function is **return** *expression*;, where *expression* represents the value the function returns to the statement that called it. The **return** statement alerts the computer that the function has completed its task, and it ends the function. The data type of the *expression* in the **return** statement must agree with the *returnDataType* specified in the function header.

tip

You also can define a default value for one or more of the formal parameters listed in the function header. If a formal parameter has a default value, then you do not need to provide an actual argument for it when you call the function. Defining default values for formal parameters is beyond the scope of this book.

tip

Rather than using an empty set of parentheses to indicate that a function does not receive any information, some C++ programmers enter the C++ keyword void within the parentheses.

MINI-QUIZ

Mini-Quiz 1

1) Assume a program uses the statement `discount = calcDisc(300.45);` to call the `calcDisc()` function. The function returns a number having a decimal place. Which of the following is a valid function header for the `calcDisc()` function?
   a. `calcDisc(double sales)`
   b. `double calcDisc(sales);`
   c. `double calcDisc(double sales)`
   d. `double calcDisc(double sales);`

2) Write a function header for a function named `calcTotal()`. The function will be passed two integers when it is called. Use the variable names `sale1` and `sale2` as the formal parameters. The function will return an integer.

3) Assume a program uses the statement `cout << calcGross (hours, rate) << endl;` to call the `calcGross()` function. Also assume that `hours` is an `int` variable, and `rate` is a `double` variable. The function header used in the program is `double calcGross(double hoursWkd, payRate)`, which is incorrect. Correct the function header.

4) Write the C++ statement that instructs the `calcGross()` function to return the contents of the `grossPay` variable.

Most C++ programmers enter the function definitions below the `main()` function in a program. When a function definition appears below the `main()` function, you must enter a function prototype above the `main()` function. You learn about function prototypes in the next section.

Using a Function Prototype

A **function prototype** is a statement that specifies the function's name, the data type of its return value (if any), and the data type of each of its formal parameters. A program will have one function prototype for each function defined below the `main()` function. You usually place the function prototypes at the beginning of the program, after the `#include` directives and `using` statements.

A function prototype alerts the compiler that the function will be defined later in the program. It may help to think of the function prototypes in a program as being similar to the table of contents in a book. Each prototype, like each entry in a table of contents, is simply a preview of what will be expanded on later in the program (or in the book). In the programs you create in this book, you will place the function definitions after the `main()` function, then use function prototypes to declare the functions above the `main()` function.

Figure 9-7 shows the syntax of a function prototype. It also shows the function prototype for the `calcRectangleArea()` function shown in Figure 9-6.

tip

If the function definition appears above the `main()` function in a program, then you do not need to include a function prototype for the function. The function prototype is necessary only when the function is defined after the `main()` function.

tip

Some programmers also include the name of each formal parameter in the function prototype, but this is optional.

only the data types of the formal parameters are necessary

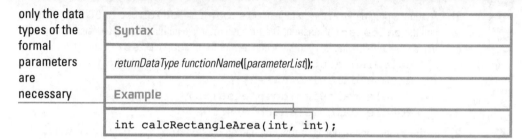

Figure 9-7: Syntax and an example of a function prototype

Syntax
returnDataType functionName([*parameterList*]);
Example
`int calcRectangleArea(int, int);`

If you compare the function prototype shown in Figure 9-7 to the function header shown in Figure 9-6, you will notice two differences: First, the function prototype ends with a semicolon, whereas the function header does not. Second, the function header contains both the data type and name of each formal parameter, but the function prototype contains only the data type.

In the next section, you learn how the computer processes a function when a statement within the program calls the function.

Processing a Function

You call a program-defined function in exactly the same way as you call a built-in function—by including its name and actual arguments (if any) in a statement. When the computer processes a statement containing a program-defined function, the computer first locates the function's code. In a C++ program, this code typically is located after the `main()` function. If the function call contains an *argumentList*, the computer passes the values of the actual arguments (assuming the variables included in the *argumentList* are passed *by value*) to the called function. The function receives these values and stores them in the memory locations listed in the function's *parameterList*. Then the computer processes the function's code and, in the case of a value-returning function, the computer returns the appropriate value to the statement that called the function. This is the same process the computer uses when processing a statement containing a built-in function, such as the `cube = pow(4, 3);` statement. The only difference is that the computer locates a program-defined function's code in the current program rather than in a different file. (Recall that the `pow()` function's code is contained in the cmath file.)

Most C++ programmers enter the function definitions below the `main()` function in a C++ program. Many programmers also use a comment (such as `//***** function definitions*****`) to separate the `main()` function's code from the code for the function definitions.

Figure 9-8 shows an example of calling and defining a value-returning function in a C++ program. The function call appears in the `main()` function and is shaded in the figure.

Figure 9-8: Example of calling and defining a value-returning function in a C++ program

```
main() and calcRectangleArea() functions
```

```
//function prototype
int calcRectangleArea(int, int);

int main()
{
   int length = 2;
   int width  = 3;
   int area   = 0;
   area = calcRectangleArea(length, width);
   cout << area << endl;
   return 0;
}   //end of main function

//*****function definitions*****
int calcRectangleArea(int len, int wid)
{
      return len * wid;
}   //end of calcRectangleArea function
```

two actual arguments

two formal parameters

Notice that the quantity and data type of the actual arguments match the quantity and data type of the corresponding formal parameters. Also notice that the names of the formal parameters do not need to be identical to the names of their corresponding actual arguments. In this case, the function call contains two actual arguments named `length` and `width`, and the corresponding function header contains two formal parameters named `len` and `wid`. Both the actual arguments and the formal parameters are of data type `int`.

Desk-checking the program shown in Figure 9-8 will help you understand how the computer processes a program-defined function when it appears in a statement.

Desk-Checking the Program Shown in Figure 9-8

The first three statements in the `main()` function create and initialize three `int` variables named `length`, `width`, and `area`. Figure 9-9 shows the contents of memory after the variable declaration statements are processed.

Figure 9-9: Contents of memory after the variable declaration statements are processed

main() function's variables

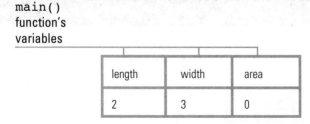

length	width	area
2	3	0

The fourth statement, `area = calcRectangleArea(length, width);`, calls the `calcRectangleArea()` function, passing it two actual arguments: an `int` variable named `length` and an `int` variable named `width`. Recall that unless specified otherwise, variables in C++ are passed *by value*, which means that only the contents of the variables are passed to the function. In this case, the computer passes the numbers 2 and 3 to the `calcRectangleArea()` function.

At this point, the computer temporarily leaves the `main()` function to process the code contained in the `calcRectangleArea()` function, beginning with the function header. In this case, the *parameterList* in the `calcRectangleArea()` function header tells the computer to reserve two memory locations—an `int` variable named `len` and an `int` variable named `wid`. After reserving the `len` and `wid` variables, the computer stores the values passed to the function—in this case, the numbers 2 and 3—in the variables, as shown in Figure 9-10.

Figure 9-10: Contents of memory after the `calcRectangleArea()` function header is processed

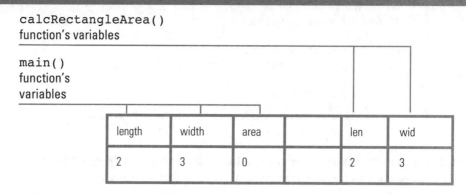

Next, the computer processes the `return len * wid;` statement contained in the `calcRectangleArea()` function body. The statement first multiplies the value stored in the `len` variable (2) by the value stored in the `wid` variable (3), then returns the result (6) to the statement that called the function. In this case the `calcRectangleArea()` function was called by the `area = calcRectangleArea(length, width);` statement in the `main()` function. After processing the `calcRectangleArea()` function's `return` statement, the computer removes the `len` and `wid` variables from memory, then the `calcRectangleArea()` function ends. Figure 9-11 shows the contents of memory after the `calcRectangleArea()` function has completed its task and returned its value. Notice that only the `main()` function's variables are still in the computer's memory.

Figure 9-11: Contents of memory after the `calcRectangleArea()` function completes its task and returns its value

main()
function's
variables

length	width	area
2	3	~~0~~ 6

The `area = calcRectangleArea(length, width);` statement in the `main()` function assigns the value returned to it (6) to the `area` variable. Next, the computer processes the `cout << area << endl;` statement, which displays the contents of the `area` variable on the screen. Finally, the computer processes the `main()` function's `return 0;` statement, which returns the number 0 to the operating system to indicate that the program ended normally. After processing the `return 0;` statement, the computer removes the `length`, `width`, and `area` variables from memory, then the program ends.

At this point, you may be wondering why the program needs to pass the contents of the `length` and `width` variables to the `calcRectangleArea()` function. Why can't the function just use both variables in its `return` statement, like this: `return length * width;`? You also may be wondering why the computer removes the `len` and `wid` variables from memory after it processes the `calcRectangleArea()` function's `return` statement, but waits until after it processes the `main()` function's `return` statement before it removes the `length`, `width`, and `area` variables. Why are the variables removed from memory at different times? To answer these questions, you need to learn about the scope and lifetime of a variable.

The Scope and Lifetime of a Variable

A variable's **scope**, which can be either local or global, indicates which portions of a program can use the variable. A variable's **lifetime**, on the other hand, indicates how long the variable remains in the computer's memory. The scope and lifetime typically are determined by where you declare the variable in the program. Variables declared within a function, and those that appear in a function's *parameterList*, have a local scope and are referred to as **local variables**. Local variables can be used only by the function in which they are declared or in whose *parameterList* they appear. Local variables remain in memory until the function ends. In the case of a value-returning function, the function ends after the computer processes the function's `return` statement.

Unlike local variables, **global variables** are declared outside of any function in the program, and they remain in memory until the program ends. Also unlike a local variable, a global variable can be used by any statement in the program. Declaring a variable as global rather than local allows unintentional errors to occur when a function that should not have access to the variable inadvertently changes the variable's contents. Because of this, you should avoid using global variables in your programs. If more than one function needs access to the same variable, it is better to create a local variable in one of the functions and then pass that variable only to the other functions that need it.

In the program shown earlier in Figure 9-8, the `length`, `width`, and `area` variables are local to the `main()` function, because that is the function in which they are declared. Therefore, only the `main()` function can use the `length`, `width`, and `area` variables; the `calcRectangleArea()` function is not even aware of the existence of these variables in memory. If you want the `calcRectangleArea()` function to use the values stored in the `length` and `width` variables, you must pass each variable's value to the function.

The `len` and `wid` variables, which appear in the `calcRectangleArea()` function's *parameterList*, are local to the `calcRectangleArea()` function. Therefore, only the `calcRectangleArea()` function can use the `len` and `wid` variables.

As mentioned earlier, local variables remain in memory until the function in which they are created ends. This explains why the `len` and `wid` variables are removed from memory after the computer processes the `calcRectangleArea()` function's `return` statement, and why the computer waits until after it processes the `main()` function's `return` statement before it removes the `length`, `width`, and `area` variables from memory.

Now that you understand the concepts of scope and lifetime, you will view and desk-check another program that calls and defines a value-returning function.

tip

You can experiment with the concepts of scope and lifetime by completing Discovery Exercise 11 at the end of this lesson.

Another Example of Calling and Defining Value-Returning Functions

The program shown in Figure 9-12 calls and defines two value-returning functions. The function calls appear in the main() function and are shaded in the figure.

Figure 9-12: A program that calls and defines two value-returning functions

two actual
arguments,
two formal
parameters

no actual
arguments,
no formal
parameters

```
main(), getSales(), and calcBonus() functions

//function prototypes
int getSales();
double calcBonus(int, double);

int main()
{
    int salesAmt    = 0;
    double bonusAmt = 0.0;

    salesAmt = getSales();

    bonusAmt = calcBonus(salesAmt, .05);

    cout << bonusAmt << endl;
    return 0;
}   //end of main function


//*****function definitions*****
int getSales()
{
    int sales = 0;
    cout << "Enter sales: ";
    cin >> sales;
    return sales;
}   //end of getSales function

double calcBonus(int dollars, double rate)
{
    double bonusAmt = 0.0;
    bonusAmt = double(dollars) * rate;
    return bonusAmt;
}   //end of calcBonus function
```

The first two statements in the main() function create and initialize two local variables: an int variable named salesAmt and a double variable named bonusAmt. Both variables can be used only by the main() function, and both remain in memory until the main() function's return statement is processed. Figure 9-13 shows the contents of memory after the variable declaration statements in the main() function are processed.

Figure 9-13: Contents of memory after the variable declaration statements in the `main()` function are processed

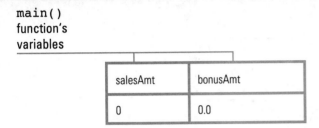

main()
function's
variables

salesAmt	bonusAmt
0	0.0

When the computer encounters the `salesAmt = getSales();` statement in the program, it temporarily leaves the `main()` function to process the instructions in the `getSales()` function, beginning with the function header. The `getSales()` function header does not contain any formal parameters, which indicates that the function will not receive any information when it is called.

The first statement in the `getSales()` function body creates and initializes a local `int` variable named `sales`. The `sales` variable can be used only by the `getSales()` function, and it remains in memory until the `getSales()` function's `return` statement is processed.

The next two statements in the `getSales()` function body prompt the user to enter a sales amount, then store the user's response in the `sales` variable. Figure 9-14 shows the contents of memory at this point, assuming the user enters the number 1575 as the sales amount.

Figure 9-14: Contents of memory after the user enters the sales amount

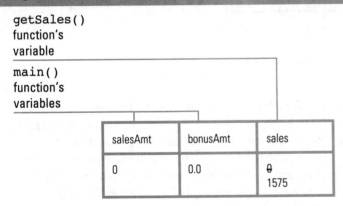

getSales()
function's
variable

main()
function's
variables

salesAmt	bonusAmt	sales
0	0.0	~~0~~ 1575

Next, the computer processes the `return sales;` statement contained in the `getSales()` function body. The statement returns the contents of the `sales` variable (1575) to the statement that called the function. In this case, the `getSales()` function was called by the `salesAmt = getSales();` statement in the `main()` function. The statement assigns the return value (1575) to the `salesAmt` variable, as shown in Figure 9-15.

Figure 9-15: Contents of memory after the `return sales;` **statement is processed**

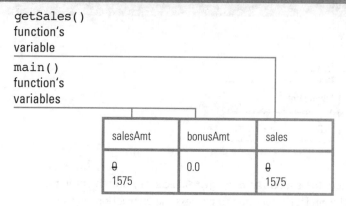

getSales()
function's
variable

main()
function's
variables

salesAmt	bonusAmt	sales
~~0~~ 1575	0.0	~~0~~ 1575

After processing the `getSales()` function's `return` statement, the computer removes the `sales` variable from memory, then the `getSales()` function ends. Figure 9-16 shows the contents of memory after the `getSales()` function has completed its task and returned its value. Notice that only the `main()` function's variables are still in memory.

Figure 9-16: Contents of memory after the `getSales()` **function completes its task and returns its value**

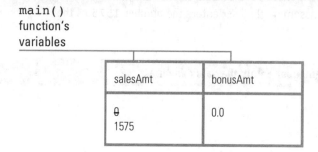

main()
function's
variables

salesAmt	bonusAmt
~~0~~ 1575	0.0

Next, the computer processes the `bonusAmt = calcBonus(salesAmt, .05);` statement in the `main()` function. Here again, the computer temporarily leaves the `main()` function; in this case, it does so to process the code in the `calcBonus()` function. The *parameterList* in the `calcBonus()` function header tells the computer to create two local variables—an `int` variable named `dollars` and a `double` variable named `rate`. After creating both variables, the computer stores the first value passed to the function (the contents of the `salesAmt` variable) in the first formal parameter (the `dollars` variable). It then stores the second value passed to the function (the number .05) in the second formal parameter (the `rate` variable), as shown in Figure 9-17.

Figure 9-17: Contents of memory after the `calcBonus()` function header is processed

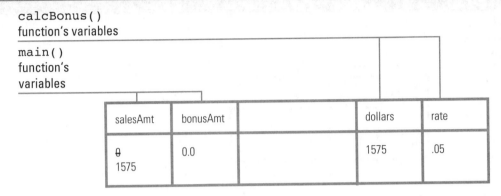

calcBonus()
function's variables

main()
function's
variables

salesAmt	bonusAmt		dollars	rate
~~0~~ 1575	0.0		1575	.05

The first statement in the `calcBonus()` function body reserves an additional local variable. The variable, named **bonusAmt**, has a data type of **double**. The second statement in the function body multiplies the contents of the **dollars** variable (1575) by the contents of the **rate** variable (.05), and assigns the result (78.75) to the **bonusAmt** variable, as shown in Figure 9-18.

Figure 9-18: Contents of memory after the bonus is calculated

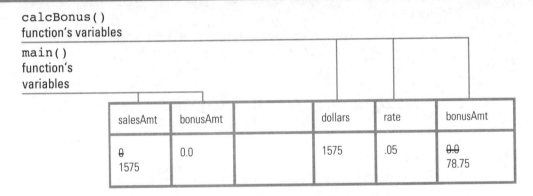

calcBonus()
function's variables

main()
function's
variables

salesAmt	bonusAmt		dollars	rate	bonusAmt
~~0~~ 1575	0.0		1575	.05	~~0.0~~ 78.75

Notice that the computer's memory contains two locations having the same name, **bonusAmt**. When the variable's name appears in a statement, the computer uses the position of the statement in the program to determine which of the two locations to use. If the program statement appears in the **main()** function, the computer uses the **bonusAmt** variable located in the **main()** function's section in memory. However, if the program statement appears in the **calcBonus()** function, the computer uses the **bonusAmt** variable located in the **calcBonus()** function's section of memory.

Next, the computer processes the **return bonusAmt;** statement, which returns the contents of the **calcBonus()** function's **bonusAmt** variable (78.75) to the statement that called the function. In this case, the **calcBonus()** function was called by the **bonusAmt = calcBonus(salesAmt, .05);** statement in the **main()** function. The statement assigns the value returned to it to the **main()** function's **bonusAmt** variable. At this point, the computer removes the **calcBonus()** function's local variables (**dollars**, **rate**, and **bonusAmt**) from memory. Figure 9-19 shows the contents of memory after the **calcBonus()** function completes its task and returns its value. Notice that only the variables local to the **main()** function are still in memory.

tip

For clarity, it is recommended that you use unique variable names throughout the program.

Figure 9-19: Contents of memory after the `calcBonus()` function completes its task and returns its value

main()
function's
variables

salesAmt	bonusAmt
~~0~~ 1575	~~0.0~~ 78.75

After processing the `bonusAmt = calcBonus(salesAmt, .05);` statement, the computer processes the `cout << bonusAmt << endl;` statement, which displays the contents of the `main()` function's `bonusAmt` variable (78.75) on the screen. The `return 0;` statement then returns the number 0 to the operating system, indicating that the program ended normally. After processing the `return 0;` statement, the computer removes the `main()` function's local variables (`salesAmt` and `bonusAmt`) from memory, then the program ends.

MINI-QUIZ

Mini-Quiz 2

1) The data type and name of each formal parameter must match the data type and name of its corresponding actual argument.
   a. True
   b. False

2) Unless specified otherwise, variables in a C++ program are passed _____, which means that only the contents of the variables are passed.

3) A variable's _____ indicates which portions of a program can use the variable.

4) Assume two functions declare a variable having the same name. How does the computer know which variable to use?

You now have completed Chapter 9's Concept lesson. You can either take a break or complete the end-of-lesson questions and exercises before moving on to the Application lesson.

SUMMARY

Programmers use functions for two reasons: Functions allow the programmer to avoid duplicating code in different parts of a program, and they allow large and complex programs to be broken into small and manageable tasks. You call a function by including its name and actual arguments (if any) in a statement.

All functions are classified as either value-returning functions or void functions. A value-returning function returns a value after completing its assigned task; a void function does not return a value.

The C++ language contains the `pow()` function for raising a number to a power. It also contains the `rand()` function for generating random numbers. The `rand()`

function returns a positive integer that is greater than or equal to 0, but less than or equal to RAND_MAX. You initialize the `rand()` function using the `srand()` and `time()` functions.

A function is composed of a function header and a function body. The function header is the first line in the function definition. The function header specifies the type of data the function returns, as well as the name of the function and an optional *parameterList* enclosed in parentheses. The *parameterList* contains the data type and name of each formal parameter the function uses to store the data passed to it. The number and sequence of formal parameters included in the *parameterList* should agree with the number and sequence of actual arguments passed to the function. Additionally, the data type of each formal parameter must agree with the data type of its corresponding actual argument. The name of each formal parameter typically is different than the name of the actual argument to which it corresponds. Functions that do not require a *parameterList* will have an empty set of parentheses after the function's name. Unless specified otherwise, variables in C++ are passed to a function *by value*, which means that only the contents of the variables are passed.

The function body in a function definition contains the instructions the function must follow to perform its assigned task. The function body begins with an opening brace and ends with a closing brace. The last statement in the function body of a value-returning function typically is one that instructs the function to return its value.

A program will have one function prototype for each function defined below the `main()` function.

A variable's scope, which can be either local or global, indicates which portions of a program can use the variable. A variable's lifetime, on the other hand, indicates how long the variable remains in the computer's memory. Local variables can be used only by the function in which they are created, and they remain in memory until the function ends. Global variables, which you should avoid using, can be used anywhere in the program, and they remain in memory until the program ends.

If more than one memory location has the same name, and the name appears in a statement, the computer uses the position of the statement within the program to determine which memory location to use. For clarity, you should use unique variable names within a program.

ANSWERS TO MINI-QUIZZES

Mini-Quiz 1

1) c. `double calcDisc(double sales)`

2) `int calcTotal(int sale1, int sale2)`

3) `double calcGross(int hoursWkd, double payRate)`

4) `return grossPay;`

Mini-Quiz 2

1) b. False

2) *by value*

3) scope

4) By the position of the statement that refers to the variable in the program

QUESTIONS

1) A function whose function header is `double calcShipping()` is an example of a _____ function.

   A. value-returning

   B. void

2) Value-returning functions can return _____.

   A. one value only

   B. one or more values

   C. the number 0 only

   D. none of the above

3) The function header specifies _____.

   A. the data type of the function's return value

   B. the name of the function

   C. the function's formal parameters

   D. all of the above

4) Which of the following is false?

   A. The number of actual arguments should agree with the number of formal parameters.

   B. The data type of each actual argument should match the data type of its corresponding formal parameter.

   C. The name of each actual argument should be identical to the name of its corresponding formal parameter.

   D. When you pass information to a function *by value*, the function stores the value of each item it receives in a separate memory location.

5) Each memory location listed in the *parameterList* in the function header is referred to as _____.

   A. an actual argument

   B. an actual parameter

   C. a formal argument

   D. a formal parameter

6) In a C++ function, the function body ends with the _____.

   A. { (opening brace)

   B. } (closing brace)

   C. ; (semicolon)

   D. `return` statement

7) Assume a program uses the statement `tax = calcTax(sales);` to call the `calcTax()` function. (`sales` is a `float` variable.) The function returns a number having a decimal place. Which of the following is a valid function header for the `calcTax()` function?

   A. `calcTax(float sales);`

   B. `float calcTax(salesAmount)`

   C. `float calcTax(float salesAmount)`

   D. `float calcTax(int sales);`

8) Which of the following is a valid function header for a function (named `fee`) that receives an integer first and a number with a decimal place second, then returns a number with a decimal place?

A. `fee(int base, double rate);`

B. `int fee(int base, double rate)`

C. `double fee(double base, int rate)`

D. `double fee(int base, double rate)`

9) Which of the following is a valid function prototype for the function described in Question 8?

A. `fee(int base, double rate);`

B. `int fee(int, double)`

C. `double fee(int base, double rate)`

D. `double fee(int, double);`

10) Which of the following instructs a function to return the contents of the `stateTax` variable to the `main()` function?

A. `restore stateTax;`

B. `return stateTax`

C. `return to main(stateTax);`

D. none of the above

11) If the statement `netPay = calcNet(gross, taxes);` passes the contents of the `gross` and `taxes` variables to the `calcNet()` function, the variables are said to be passed _____.

A. *by address*

B. *by content*

C. *by reference*

D. *by value*

12) Assume a program contains a function named `displayGross()`. When the computer processes the `displayGross()` function's `return` statement, _____.

A. it removes the function's local variables (if any) from memory, then continues program execution with the statement immediately following the one that called the function

B. it removes the function's local variables (if any) from memory, then continues program execution with the statement that called the function

C. it removes the function's global variables (if any) from memory, then continues program execution with the statement immediately following the one that called the function

D. it removes the function's global variables (if any) from memory, then continues program execution with the statement that called the function

13) A variable's _____ indicates which portions of a program can use the variable.

A. lifetime

B. range

C. scope

D. span

14) Assume a variable named `beginBalance` appears in a function's *parameterList*. Which of the following statements is true?

A. The `beginBalance` variable remains in memory until the computer processes the function's `return` statement.

B. The `beginBalance` variable is called a functional variable.

C. The `beginBalance` variable can be used anywhere in the program.

D. both A and B

15) Assume a program contains three functions named `main()`, `calcGross()`, and `displayGross()`. Both the `main()` and `calcGross()` functions declare a variable named `pay`. The `pay` variable name also appears in the `displayGross()` function header. When the computer processes the statement `pay = hours * rate;` in the `calcGross()` function, it multiplies the contents of the `hours` variable by the contents of the `rate` variable, then _____.

A. stores the result in the `calcGross()` function's `pay` variable

B. stores the result in the `displayGross()` function's `pay` variable

C. stores the result in the `main()` function's `pay` variable

D. displays an error message because you can't have three memory locations with the same name

16) Which of the following is equivalent to the mathematical expression 5^3?

A. `cube(5)`

B. `pow(3, 5)`

C. `pow(5, 3)`

D. none of the above

17) Which of the following displays a random number in the range 3 through 9?

A. `1 + rand() % (9 - 3 + 1)`

B. `3 + rand() % (9 - 3 + 1)`

C. `3 + rand() % (9 + 3 - 1)`

D. `9 + rand() % (9 + 1 - 3)`

18) You use the _____ statement to initialize the random number generator in C++.

A. `init(int(time(0)));`

B. `rand(int(time(0)));`

C. `srand(int(time(0)));`

D. none of the above

Look For These
Symbols

Debugging

Discovery

EXERCISES

1) Write the C++ code for a function that receives an integer passed to it. The function, named `halveNumber()`, should divide the integer by 2, then return the result (which may contain a decimal place).

2) Write the C++ code for a function that prompts the user to enter a character, then stores the user's response in a `char` variable. The function should return the character entered by the user. (The function will not have any actual arguments passed to it.) Name the function `getChar()`.

3) Write the C++ code for a function that receives four integers. The function should calculate the average of the four integers, then return the result (which may contain a decimal place). Name the function `calcAverage()`.

4) Write the function prototype for the function described in Exercise 3.

5) Write the C++ code for a function that receives two numbers that both have a decimal place. The function should divide the first number by the second number, then return the result. Name the function `quotient()`.

6) Write the C++ statement that adds the cube of the number stored in the `num1` variable to the square of the number stored in the `num2` variable and assigns the result to the `total` variable.

7) Write the C++ statement that assigns to the `answer` variable the result of the following expression: $x^2 * y^3$.

8) Write the C++ statement that assigns to the `rate` variable the result of the following expression: $(future / present)^{1 - term} - 1$.

9) Write the C++ statement that displays (on the screen) a random number in the range 50 through 100.

10) Desk-check the program shown in Figure 9-20. Show the desk-check table after the first four statements in the `main()` function are processed, after the `calcEnd()` function's `return` statement is processed (but before local variables are removed from memory), and after the `calcEnd()` function's local variables are removed from memory.

Figure 9-20

`main()` **and** `calcEnd()` **functions**

```cpp
//function prototype
int calcEnd(int, int, int);

int main()
{
    int begVal     = 1000;
    int purchase   = 500;
    int sale       = 200;
    int endVal     = 0;

    endVal = calcEnd(begVal, purchase, sale);
    cout << endVal << endl;
    return 0;
}       //end of main function

//*****function definitions*****
int calcEnd(int b, int p, int sale)
{
    int endValue = 0;
    endValue = b + p - sale;
    return endValue;
}       //end of calcEnd function
```

11) In this exercise, you experiment with the concepts of scope and lifetime.

A. If necessary, start Visual Studio .NET. Open the Ch9ConE11 Solution (Ch9ConE11 Solution.sln) file, which is contained in the Cpp\Chap09\Ch9ConE11 Solution folder.

B. Build the solution. The C++ compiler displays an error message indicating that the `calcDoubleNumber()` function does not recognize the `number` variable. This error occurs because the `number` variable is local to the `main()` function. To fix this error, you can either pass the `number` variable's value to the `calcDoubleNumber()` function or create a global variable named `number`. Passing the variable's value is the preferred way for the `main()` function to communicate with the `calcDoubleNumber()` function. However, to give you an opportunity to see how global variables work in a program, you will fix the program's error by creating a global variable named `number`.

C. Close the Output and Task List windows.

D. Change the `int number = 0;` statement in the `main()` function to a comment by preceding the statement with `//`.

E. Recall that global variables are declared outside of any functions in the program. In the blank line below the `//declare global variable` comment, type `int number = 0;` and press Enter. Because the `number` variable is now a global variable, both the `main()` and `calcDoubleNumber()` functions have access to it. You can verify that by running the program.

F. Save and then build the solution. Execute the program. When prompted for a number, type 5 and press Enter. The Command Prompt window shows that doubling the number 5 results in the number 10.

G. Close the Command Prompt and Output windows, then use the File menu to close the solution.

12) In this exercise, you learn more about the RAND_MAX constant.

A. If necessary, start Visual Studio .NET. Open the Ch9ConE12 Solution (Ch9ConE12 Solution.sln) file, which is contained in the Cpp\Chap09\ Ch9ConE12 Solution folder.

B. The program should display the value of the RAND_MAX constant. Complete the program appropriately.

C. Save and then build the solution. Execute the program. The value of RAND_MAX appears in the Command Prompt window.

D. Close the Command Prompt and Output windows, then use the File menu to close the solution.

13) Assume a C++ function named `calcCommission()` is passed three items of information when it is called by the `main()` function: a `string` variable followed by two `double` variables. (The variables are passed *by value*.) The `calcCommission()` function returns a number with a decimal place. Rewrite the following function header correctly.

```
calcCommission(name, double sales, double rate);
```

Application Lesson

Using Value-Returning Functions in a C++ Program

Lab 9.1 - Stop and Analyze   If necessary, start Visual Studio .NET. Open the Ch9Lab1 Solution (Ch9Lab1 Solution.sln) file contained in the Cpp\Chap09\Ch9Lab1 Solution folder. Figure 9-21 shows the code entered in the Ch9Lab1.cpp file. (The line numbers are included in the figure only.) Study the code, then answer the questions.

Figure 9-21: C++ instructions entered in the Ch9Lab1.cpp file

```
1   //Ch9Lab1.cpp - simulates a number guessing game
2   //Created/revised by <your name> on <current date>
3
4   #include <iostream>
5   #include <ctime>
6
7   using std::cout;
8   using std::cin;
9   using std::endl;
10
11  int main()
12  {
13      //declare variables
14      int randomNumber = 0;
15      int numberGuess  = 0;
16
17      //generate random number from 1 through 10
18      srand(int(time(0)));
19      randomNumber = 1 + rand() % (10 - 1 + 1);
20
21      //get first number guess from user
22      cout << "Guess a number from 1 through 10: ";
23      cin >> numberGuess;
24
25      while (numberGuess != randomNumber)
26      {
27          cout << "Sorry, guess again: ";
28          cin >> numberGuess;
29      }   //end while
30
31      cout << "Yes, the number was " << randomNumber << endl;
32
33      return 0;
34  }   //end of main function
```

Questions

1. What is the purpose of Line 18?
2. If the **rand()** function in Line 19 returns the number 453, what number will be assigned to the **randomNumber** variable?
3. Build the solution, then execute the program. Enter as many guesses as necessary until you guess the number.
4. Close the Command Prompt window.

5. Create a blank solution named Ch9Lab1 Step 5 Solution. Save the solution in the Cpp\Chap09 folder.

6. Add an empty C++ Win32 Console Project to the solution. Name the project Ch9Lab1 Step 5 Project.

7. Add a new C++ source file to the project. Name the source file Ch9Lab1 Step 5.

8. Open the Ch9Lab1.cpp file contained in the Cpp\Ch9Lab1 Solution\Ch9Lab1 Project folder. Copy the file's contents to the clipboard. Close the Ch9Lab1.cpp window, then paste the instructions into the Ch9Lab1 Step 5.cpp window. Change the filename in the first comment to Ch9Lab1 Step 5.cpp.

9. Modify the program so that it allows the user to make only three incorrect guesses. When the user has made the third incorrect guess, display the random number on the screen.

10. Save and then build the solution. Execute the program. Test the program appropriately. Close the Command Prompt window.

11. Close the Output window, then use the File menu to close the solution.

Lab 9.2 After weeks of car shopping, David Liu still hasn't decided what car to purchase. Recently, David has noticed that many car dealers, in an effort to boost sales, are offering buyers a choice of either a large cash rebate or an extremely low financing rate, much lower than the rate David would pay by financing the car through his local credit union. David is not sure whether to take the lower financing rate from the dealer or take the rebate and then finance the car through the credit union. He has asked you to create a program that he can use to calculate and display the monthly payments using both options.

In this program, you need to calculate a periodic payment on a loan for David. The formula to calculate the payment is $principal * rate / (1 - (rate + 1)^{-term})$, where *principal* is the amount of the loan, *rate* is the periodic interest rate, and *term* is the number of periodic payments. Figure 9-22 shows two examples of using the periodic payment formula to calculate the periodic payment on a loan.

Figure 9-22: Periodic payment formula and examples

Periodic payment formula: $principal * rate / (1 - (rate + 1)^{-term})$

Note: When you apply for a loan, the lender typically quotes you an annual interest rate, and the term is expressed in years.

Example 1 – calculate the annual payment for a loan of $9000 for 3 years at 5% interest

Principal:	9000
Annual rate:	.05
Term (years):	3
Formula:	$9000 * .05 / (1 - (.05 + 1)^{-3})$
Annual payment:	$3304.88 (rounded to two decimal places)

Example 2 – calculate the monthly payment for a loan of $12,000 for 5 years at 6% interest

Principal:	12,000
Monthly rate:	.005 (annual rate of .06 divided by 12)
Term (months):	60 (5 years multiplied by 12)
Formula:	$12,000 * .005 / (1 - (.005 + 1)^{-60})$
Monthly payment:	$231.99 (rounded to two decimal places)

Example 1 uses the periodic payment formula to calculate the annual payment for a $9000 loan for three years at 5% interest; the annual payment is $3304.88 (rounded to two decimal places). In other words, if you borrow $9000 for three years at 5% interest, you would need to make three annual payments of $3304.88 to pay off the loan.

Example 2 uses the periodic payment formula to calculate the monthly payment for a $12,000 loan for five years at 6% interest. To pay off this loan, you would need to make 60 payments of $231.99. Notice that, before you can calculate the monthly payment, you need to convert the annual interest rate to a monthly interest rate by dividing the annual rate by 12. You also need to convert the term, which is expressed in years, to months by multiplying the number of years by 12. You will use the periodic payment formula to calculate David Liu's monthly car payment if he accepts the dealer's rebate and finances the car through his credit union. You also will use the formula to calculate David's monthly payment if he chooses the car dealer's lower financing rate instead of the rebate.

In this program, you will use a program-defined value-returning function named `calcPayment()`, which will be responsible for calculating the monthly payments. Figure 9-23 shows the IPO chart and C++ instructions for the `main()` function in the program.

Figure 9-23: IPO chart and C++ instructions for the `main()` function

IPO chart information	C++ instructions

Input
  car price
  rebate
  credit union rate (annual)
  dealer rate (annual)
  term (years)
	`double carPrice = 0.0;`
	`double rebate = 0.0;`
	`double creditRate = 0.0;`
	`double dealerRate = 0.0;`
	`int term = 0;`

Processing
  monthly credit union rate
  monthly dealer rate
  number of months
	`double mthCreditRate = 0.0;`
	`double mthDealerRate = 0.0;`
	`int numMonths = 0;`

Output
  credit union payment
  dealer payment
	`double creditPay = 0.0;`
	`double dealerPay = 0.0;`

Algorithm
1. enter the car price, rebate, credit union rate, dealer rate, and term
 	
2. calculate the monthly credit union rate by dividing the credit union rate by 12
	`cout << "Car price: ";`
	`cin >> carPrice;`
	`cout << "Rebate: ";`
	`cin >> rebate;`
	`cout << "Credit union rate: ";`
	`cin >> creditRate;`
	`cout << "Dealer rate: ";`
	`cin >> dealerRate;`
	`cout << "Term in years: ";`
	`cin >> term;`
	`mthCreditRate = creditRate / 12;`

tip

The variables shown in Figure 9-23 are local to the `main()` function and remain in memory until the `main()` function's return statement is processed.

Figure 9-23: IPO chart and C++ instructions for the `main()` **function (continued)**

IPO chart information	C++ instructions
3. calculate the monthly dealer rate by dividing the dealer rate by 12	`mthDealerRate = dealerRate / 12;`
4. calculate the number of months by multiplying the term by 12	`numMonths = term * 12;`
5. call the calcPayment() function to calculate the credit union payment; pass the function the car price – rebate, monthly credit union rate, and number of months	`creditPay = calcPayment(carPrice - rebate, mthCreditRate, numMonths);`
6. call the calcPayment() function to calculate the dealer payment; pass the function the car price, monthly dealer rate, and number of months	`dealerPay = calcPayment(carPrice, mthDealerRate, numMonths);`

7. display the credit union payment and the dealer payment	`cout << "Credit union payment: $"`
	`    << creditPay << endl;`
	`cout << "Dealer payment: $"`
	`    << dealerPay << endl;`

As the IPO chart indicates, the output is the monthly payment to the credit union and the monthly payment to the car dealer. To display the output, the program must know the car price, rebate, credit union rate, dealer rate, and term.

According to the algorithm, the `main()` function first will have the user enter the five input items. It then will convert the two annual rates to monthly rates, and the term, which is stated in years, to months. The `main()` function then will call the `calcPayment()` function to calculate the credit union and dealer payments. Lastly, the `main()` function will display both payments on the screen.

Figure 9-24 shows the IPO chart and C++ instructions for the `calcPayment()` function.

tip
The variables shown in Figure 9-24 are local to the `calcPayment()` function and remain in memory until the function's return statement is processed.

Figure 9-24: IPO chart and C++ instructions for the `calcPayment()` function

IPO chart information	C++ instructions
Input principal monthly rate number of months	`double calcPayment(double prin, double monthRate, int months)`
Processing none	
Output monthly payment	`double monthPay = 0.0;`
Algorithm 1. calculate the monthly payment using the formula: principal * monthly rate / 1 – (monthly rate + 1)$^{-months}$	`monthPay = prin * monthRate /` `  (1 - pow(monthRate + 1, -months));`
2. return the monthly payment	`return monthPay;`

Notice that the `calcPayment()` function's output is the monthly payment. Also notice that the function needs to know three items of information to calculate the monthly payment: the principal, monthly rate, and number of months. The values of these items will be passed to the `calcPayment()` function by the `main()` function. For example, when calling the `calcPayment()` function to calculate the credit union payment, the `main()` function will pass the difference between the car price and the rebate as the principal; it also will pass the monthly credit union rate and the number of months. Likewise, when calling the `calcPayment()` function to calculate the dealer payment, the `main()` function will pass the car price as the principal, and also the monthly dealer rate and the number of months.

Activity for Lab 9.2

In this activity, you enter the C++ instructions shown in Figures 9-23 and 9-24 into the computer. You then test the program to verify that it is working correctly.

To create the David Liu program, then test the program:

1. If necessary, start Visual Studio .NET. Create a blank solution named Ch9Lab2 Solution. Save the solution in the Cpp\Chap09 folder.

2. Add an empty C++ Win32 Console Project to the solution. Name the project Ch9Lab2 Project.

3. Add a new C++ source file to the project. Name the source file Ch9Lab2.

4. Type **//Ch9Lab2.cpp – displays monthly payments** and press **Enter**.

5. Type **//Created/revised by <your name> on <current date>**, replacing <your name> and <current date> with your name and the current date, respectively. Press **Enter** twice.

6. Type the following three #include directives, then press **Enter** twice.

```
#include <iostream>
#include <iomanip>
#include <cmath>
```

7. Type the following six using statements, then press **Enter** twice.

```
using std::cout;
using std::cin;
using std::endl;
using std::setprecision;
using std::ios;
using std::setiosflags;
```

8. Type **//function prototype** and press **Enter**, then type **double calcPayment(double, double, int);** and press **Enter** twice.

9. Complete the program by entering the main() and calcPayment() functions, which are shown in Figure 9-25.

Figure 9-25: David Liu program

tip

Recall that the data type and sequence of the formal parameters in a function's *parameterList* must match the data type and sequence of the actual arguments passed to the function and listed in the *argumentList*.

enter the code for the main() and calc-Payment() functions

```
//Ch9Lab2.cpp - displays monthly payments
//Created/revised by <your name> on <current date>

#include <iostream>
#include <iomanip>
#include <cmath>

using std::cout;
using std::cin;
using std::endl;
using std::setprecision;
using std::ios;
using std::setiosflags;

//function prototype
double calcPayment(double, double, int);

int main()
{
    //declare variables
    double carPrice       = 0.0;
    double rebate         = 0.0;
    double creditRate     = 0.0;
    double dealerRate     = 0.0;
    int term              = 0;
    double mthCreditRate  = 0.0;
    double mthDealerRate  = 0.0;
    int numMonths         = 0;
    double creditPay      = 0.0;
    double dealerPay      = 0.0;

    //get input items
    cout << "Car price: ";
    cin >> carPrice;
```

Figure 9-25: David Liu program (continued)

```cpp
        cout << "Rebate: ";
        cin >> rebate;
        cout << "Credit union rate: ";
        cin >> creditRate;
        cout << "Dealer rate: ";
        cin >> dealerRate;
        cout << "Term in years: ";
        cin >> term;

        //convert annual items to monthly items
        mthCreditRate = creditRate / 12;
        mthDealerRate = dealerRate / 12;
        numMonths = term * 12;

        //call function to calculate payments
        creditPay = calcPayment(carPrice - rebate,
            mthCreditRate, numMonths);
        dealerPay = calcPayment(carPrice,
            mthDealerRate, numMonths);

        //display payments
        cout << setiosflags(ios::fixed) << setprecision(2);
        cout << "Credit union payment: $"
            << creditPay << endl;
        cout << "Dealer payment: $"
            << dealerPay << endl;

        return 0;
}   //end of main function

//*****function definitions*****
double calcPayment(double prin, double monthRate, int
months)
{
    double monthPay = 0.0;

    //calculate and return payment
    monthPay = prin * monthRate /
        (1 - pow(monthRate + 1, -months));
    return monthPay;
}   //end of calcPayment function
```

enter the code for the main() and calcPayment() functions

10. Save and then build the solution. Verify that the program generated no warnings.

11. Execute the program. When you are prompted to enter the car price, type **16000** and press **Enter**. When you are prompted to enter the rebate, type **3000** and press **Enter**.

12. When prompted for the credit union rate, type **.08** and press **Enter**. When prompted for the dealer rate, type **.03** and press **Enter**.

13. When prompted for the term, type **4** and press **Enter**. The program calculates and displays the two monthly payments ($317.37 and $354.15), as shown in Figure 9-26.

Figure 9-26: Monthly payments displayed in the Command Prompt window

14. Close the Command Prompt window.

15. Close the Output window, then use the File menu to close the solution.

Lab 9.3 In this lab, you modify the program you created in Lab 9.2. The modified program will not use any processing items.

Activity for Lab 9.3

Before modifying the program created in Lab 9.2, you copy the instructions contained in the Ch9Lab2.cpp file to a new solution.

To copy the instructions contained in the Ch9Lab2.cpp file to a new solution:

1. If necessary, start Visual Studio .NET. Create a blank solution named **Ch9Lab3 Solution**. Save the solution in the Cpp\Chap09 folder.

2. Add an empty C++ Win32 Console Project to the solution. Name the project **Ch9Lab3 Project**.

3. Add a new C++ source file to the project. Name the source file **Ch9Lab3**.

4. Use the File menu to open the Ch9Lab2.cpp file contained in the Cpp\Chap09\Ch9Lab2 Solution\Ch9Lab2 Project folder. Select the contents of the file, then copy the contents to the clipboard.

5. Close the Ch9Lab2.cpp window.

6. Click the **Ch9Lab3.cpp** tab, then paste the instructions from the clipboard into the Ch9Lab3.cpp window.

7. Change the filename in the first program comment to **Ch9Lab3.cpp**. If necessary, change the date in the second comment.

Currently, the program uses three processing items. Your task is to modify the program so that it does not use any processing items.

To modify the program, then test the program:

1. Make the appropriate modifications to the program.

2. Save and then build the solution. If necessary, correct any syntax errors, then save and build the solution again.

3. Execute the program. Test the program using your own sample data, then close the Command Prompt window.

4. When the program is working correctly, close the Output window, then use the File menu to close the solution.

You now have completed Chapter 9's Application lesson. You can either take a break or complete the end-of-lesson exercises.

ANSWERS TO LABS

Lab 9.1

1. Line 18 initializes the **rand()** function, which is the random number generator in C++.

2. 4

5. See Figure 9-27.

Figure 9-27

```
//Ch9Lab1 Step 5.cpp – simulates a number guessing game
//Created/revised by <your name> on <current date>

#include <iostream>
#include <ctime>

using std::cout;
using std::cin;
using std::endl;

int main()
{
    //declare variables
    int randomNumber = 0;
    int numberGuess  = 0;
    int counter      = 0;

    //generate random number from 1 through 10
    srand(int(time(0)));
    randomNumber = 1 + rand() % (10 - 1 + 1);
```

Figure 9-27 (continued)

```
    //get first number guess from user
    cout << "Guess a number from 1 through 10: ";
    cin >> numberGuess;

    while (numberGuess != randomNumber && counter < 2)
    {
        counter = counter + 1;
        cout << "Sorry, guess again: ";
        cin >> numberGuess;
    }    //end while

    if (numberGuess != randomNumber)
        cout << "Sorry, the number was " << randomNumber << endl;
    else
        cout << "Yes, the number was " << randomNumber << endl;
    //end if

    return 0;
}    //end of main function
```

Lab 9.2

No answer required.

Lab 9.3

See Figure 9-28.

Figure 9-28

```
//Ch9Lab3.cpp - displays monthly payments
//Created/revised by <your name> on <current date>

#include <iostream>
#include <iomanip>
#include <cmath>

using std::cout;
using std::cin;
using std::endl;
using std::setprecision;
using std::ios;
using std::setiosflags;

//function prototype
double calcPayment(double, double, int);
```

Figure 9-28 (continued)

```cpp
int main()
{
    //declare variables
    double carPrice      = 0.0;
    double rebate        = 0.0;
    double creditRate    = 0.0;
    double dealerRate    = 0.0;
    int term             = 0;
    double creditPay     = 0.0;
    double dealerPay     = 0.0;

    //get input items
    cout << "Car price: ";
    cin >> carPrice;
    cout << "Rebate: ";
    cin >> rebate;
    cout << "Credit union rate: ";
    cin >> creditRate;
    cout << "Dealer rate: ";
    cin >> dealerRate;
    cout << "Term in years: ";
    cin >> term;

    //call function to calculate payments
    creditPay = calcPayment(carPrice - rebate,
        creditRate / 12, term * 12);
    dealerPay = calcPayment(carPrice,
        dealerRate / 12, term * 12);

    //display payments
    cout << setiosflags(ios::fixed) << setprecision(2);
    cout << "Credit union payment: $"
        << creditPay << endl;
    cout << "Dealer payment: $"
        << dealerPay << endl;

    return 0;
}   //end of main function

//*****function definitions*****
double calcPayment(double prin, double monthRate, int months)
{
    double monthPay = 0.0;

    //calculate and return payment
    monthPay = prin * monthRate /
        (1 - pow(monthRate + 1, -months));
    return monthPay;
}   //end of calcPayment function
```

Look For These
Symbols

Debugging

Discovery

EXERCISES

1) In this exercise, you create a program that converts a Fahrenheit temperature to a Celsius temperature.

   A. If necessary, start Visual Studio .NET. Open the Ch9AppE01 Solution (Ch9AppE01 Solution.sln) file, which is contained in the Cpp\Chap09\ Ch9AppE01 Solution folder.

   B. Use the IPO charts shown in Figure 9-29 to complete the program. Notice that the program contains three functions: `main()`, `getFahrenheit()`, and `calcCelsius()`. Display the Celsius temperature as an integer.

Figure 9-29

`main()` function

Input	Processing	Output
Fahrenheit temperature	Processing items: none Algorithm: 1. Fahrenheit temperature = getFahrenheit() 2. Celsius temperature = calcCelsius(Fahrenheit temperature) 3. display the Celsius temperature	Celsius temperature

`getFahrenheit()` function

Input	Processing	Output
	Processing items: none Algorithm: 1. enter the Fahrenheit temperature 2. return the Fahrenheit temperature	Fahrenheit temperature

`calcCelsius()` function

Input	Processing	Output
Fahrenheit temperature	Processing items: none Algorithm: 1. Celsius temperature = 5.0 / 9.0 * (Fahrenheit temperature −32) 2. return the Celsius temperature	Celsius temperature

C. Complete a desk-check table for the program, using the following Fahrenheit temperatures: 32 degrees F and 212 degrees F.

D. Save and then build the solution.

E. Execute the program. Use the data from Step C to test the program.

F. When the program is working correctly, close the Output window, then use the File menu to close the solution.

2) In this exercise, you create a program that displays a bonus.

A. If necessary, start Visual Studio .NET. Open the Ch9AppE02 Solution (Ch9AppE02 Solution.sln) file, which is contained in the Cpp\Chap09\ Ch9AppE02 Solution folder.

B. Use the IPO charts shown in Figure 9-30 to complete the program. Notice that the program contains three functions: `main()`, `getSales()`, and `calcBonus()`. Display the bonus amount with two decimal places and a dollar sign.

Figure 9-30

`main()` function

Input	Processing	Output
sales	Processing items: none Algorithm: 1. sales = getSales() 2. bonus = calcBonus(sales) 3. display the bonus	bonus

`getSales()` function

Input	Processing	Output
	Processing items: none Algorithm: 1. enter the sales 2. return the sales	sales

`calcBonus()` function

Input	Processing	Output
sales	Processing items: none Algorithm: 1. bonus = sales * .1 2. return the bonus	bonus

C. Complete a desk-check table for the program, using the following sales amounts: 24,500 and 134,780.

D. Save and then build the solution.

E. Execute the program. Use the data from Step C to test the program.

F. When the program is working correctly, close the Output window, then use the File menu to close the solution.

3) In this exercise, you modify the program you created in Lab 7.2 in Chapter 7. The modified program will use a value-returning function.

A. If necessary, start Visual Studio .NET. Open the Ch9AppE03 Solution (Ch9AppE03 Solution.sln) file, which is contained in the Cpp\Chap09\ Ch9AppE03 Solution folder.

B. Modify the program so that it uses a function to assign and return the grade.

C. Save and then build the solution.

D. Execute the program. Test the program appropriately.

E. When the program is working correctly, close the Output window, then use the File menu to close the solution.

4) In this exercise, you create a program that calculates the average of three test scores.

A. Write the IPO charts for a program that contains three value-returning functions: `main()`, `getTestScore()`, and `calcAverage()`. The `main()` function should call the `getTestScore()` function to get and return each of three test scores. The test scores may contain a decimal place. (Hint: The `main()` function will need to call the `getTestScore()` function three times.) The `main()` function then should call the `calcAverage()` function to calculate the average of the three test scores. When the `calcAverage()` function has completed its task, the `main()` function should display the average on the screen.

B. If necessary, start Visual Studio .NET. Create a blank solution named Ch9AppE04 Solution. Save the solution in the Cpp\Chap09 folder.

C. Add an empty C++ Win32 Console Project to the solution. Name the project Ch9AppE04 Project.

D. Add a new C++ source file to the project. Name the source file Ch9AppE04.

E. Enter the appropriate C++ instructions into the source file. Use the IPO charts you created in Step A to code the program. Display the average with one decimal place.

F. Complete a desk-check table for the program, using the following two groups of test scores:

95, 83, 76

54, 89, 77

G. Save and then build the solution.

H. Execute the program. Use the data from Step F to test the program.

I. When the program is working correctly, close the Output window, then use the File menu to close the solution.

5) In this exercise, you create a program that displays an employee's gross pay.

A. Write the IPO charts for a program that contains four value-returning functions: `main()`, `getHoursWorked()`, `getPayRate()`, and `calcGross()`. The `main()` function should call each function, then display the gross pay on the computer screen. When coding the `calcGross()` function, you do not have to worry about overtime pay. You can assume that everyone works 40 or fewer hours per week. The hours worked and rate of pay may contain a decimal place.

B. If necessary, start Visual Studio .NET. Create a blank solution named Ch9AppE05 Solution. Save the solution in the Cpp\Chap09 folder.

C. Add an empty C++ Win32 Console Project to the solution. Name the project Ch9AppE05 Project.

D. Add a new C++ source file to the project. Name the source file Ch9AppE05.

E. Enter the appropriate C++ instructions into the source file. Use the IPO charts you created in Step A to code the program. Display the gross pay with a dollar sign and two decimal places.

F. Complete a desk-check table for the program, using the following two sets of data:

25.5 hours, $12 per hour

40 hours, $11.55 per hour

G. Save and then build the solution.

H. Execute the program. Use the data from Step F to test the program.

I. When the program is working correctly, close the Output window, then use the File menu to close the solution.

6) In this exercise, you modify the program you created in Lab 9.2 so that it uses a function that does not return a value.

A. If necessary, start Visual Studio .NET. Open the Ch9AppE06 Solution (Ch9AppE06 Solution.sln) file, which is contained in the Cpp\Chap09\ Ch9AppE06 Solution folder.

B. Create a function named `displayPayment()`. The function should accept a monthly payment, then display the monthly payment on the screen. Unlike the functions you learned about in this chapter, the `displayPayment()` function will not return a value. Functions that do not return a value have a *returnDataType* of `void`.

C. Enter the appropriate function prototype for the `displayPayment()` function.

D. Modify the `main()` function so that it calls the `displayPayment()` function to display each monthly payment.

E. Save and then build the solution.

F. Execute the program. Enter 9000 as the car price, 500 as the rebate, .09 as the credit union rate, .03 as the dealer rate, and 2 as the term. Is it better to finance the car through the credit union or through the car dealer?

G. When the program is working correctly, close the Output window, then use the File menu to close the solution.

7) In this exercise, you debug a C++ program.

A. Open the Ch9AppE07 Solution (Ch9AppE07 Solution.sln) file, which is contained in the Cpp\Chap09\Ch9AppE07 Solution folder. The program should calculate and display the miles per gallon, but it is not working correctly. Study the program's code, then build the solution.

B. Correct any errors in the program, then save and build the solution again.

C. Execute the program. Enter 200 as the number of miles and 15 as the number of gallons. The miles per gallon should be 13.3.

D. When the program is working correctly, close the Output window, then use the File menu to close the solution.

Please visit the Testing Center at www.course.com/testingcenter for more practice on the topics covered in this chapter.

Void Functions

Objectives

After completing this chapter, you will be able to:

- Create and invoke a function that does not return a value

- Pass information, *by reference*, to a function

Concept Lesson

tip

You can use program-defined functions to streamline the main() function. By removing the detail from main() and leaving only the function names, which should be descriptive, the main() function provides an overview of the program.

tip

Another advantage of using a function to perform a repetitive task is that, if the task needs to be modified in the future, you need to make the modification in only one place—the function.

tip

As you learned in Chapter 9, value-returning functions typically are called from statements that display the function's return value, use the return value in a calculation, or assign the return value to a variable.

More About Functions

As you learned in Chapter 9, programmers use functions for two reasons. First, functions allow the programmer to avoid duplicating code in different parts of a program. If a program needs to perform the same task several times, it is more efficient to enter the appropriate code once, in a function, then simply call the function to perform its task when needed. Second, functions allow large and complex programs, which typically are written by a team of programmers, to be broken into small and manageable tasks. Each member of the team is assigned one of the tasks to code as a function. When writing a payroll program, for example, one team member might code the function that calculates the federal withholding tax, while another might code the function that calculates the state income tax. When each programmer has completed his or her function, all of the functions then are gathered together into one program. Typically, the `main()` function in the program is responsible for calling each of the other functions when needed. However, any function can call another function.

Recall that all functions fall into one of two categories: value-returning or void. Value-returning functions return precisely one value to the statement that called the function. You learned how to create and invoke value-returning functions in Chapter 9. Unlike value-returning functions, void functions do not return a value. You learn how to create void functions in this chapter.

Creating Void Functions

A **void function** is a function that does not return a value after completing its assigned task. You might want to use a void function in a program simply to display information (such as a title and column headings) at the top of each page in a report. Rather than repeat the necessary code several times in the program, you can enter the code once, in a void function, then call the function whenever the program needs to display the information. A void function is appropriate in this situation because the function does not need to return a value after completing its task.

Figure 10-1 shows the syntax used to create (or define) a void function in a C++ program. It also shows an example of a void function whose task is to display a straight line.

Figure 10-1: Syntax and an example of creating and invoking a void function in C++

Syntax

function header →

```
void functionName([parameterList])
{
    one or more statements
}
```

function body

Example

function prototype →

```
void displayLine();

int main()
{
    displayLine();

    cout << "ABC Company" << endl;

    displayLine();

    return 0;
}   //end of main function

//*****function definitions*****
void displayLine()
{
    cout << "-----------" << endl;
}   //end of displayLine function
```

function call →

function call →

function definition →

tip

Recall that a function header in a C++ program does not end with a semicolon because it is not considered a statement.

There are two differences between the syntax of a value-returning function (shown in Figure 9-6 in Chapter 9) and the syntax of a void function. First, the function header in a void function begins with the keyword **void**, rather than with a data type. The keyword **void** indicates that the function does not return a value. Second, the function body in a void function does not contain a **return** *expression*; statement, which is required in the function body of a value-returning function. The **return** statement is not necessary in a void function body because a void function does not return a value.

As you do with a value-returning function, you call a void function by including its name and actual arguments (if any) in a statement. However, unlike a call to a value-returning function, a call to a void function appears as a statement by itself, rather than as part of another statement. For example, notice that each call to the **displayLine()** function in Figure 10-1 is a self-contained statement.

When the computer processes a statement that calls a program-defined void function, the computer first locates the function's code in the program. If the function call contains an *argumentList*, the computer passes the values of the actual arguments (assuming the variables included in the *argumentList* are passed *by value*) to the called function. The function receives these values and stores them in the formal parameters listed in its *parameterList*. Then the computer processes the void function's code. When processing has finished, the computer continues program execution with the statement immediately below the one that called the function. In Figure 10-1's example, for instance, the computer continues program execution with the **cout << "ABC Company" << endl;** statement after processing the **displayLine()** function's code the first time. It continues with the statement **return 0;** after processing the function's code the second time.

MINI-QUIZ

Mini-Quiz 1

1) A void function header in C++ begins with the keyword _____.

2) Which of the following C++ statements correctly calls a void function named `displayTaxes()`, passing it two `double` variables named `federal` and `state`?
   a. `cout << displayTaxes(federal, state) << endl;`
   b. `taxes = displayTaxes(federal, state);`
   c. `displayTaxes(federal, state);`
   d. all of the above

3) Write the function header for the `displayTaxes()` function in Question 2. Use the names `fedTax` and `stateTax` for the formal parameters.

4) The `return` statement typically is the last statement in a C++ void function.
   a. True
   b. False

In Chapter 9, you learned that a variable can be passed to a function either *by value* or *by reference*. In the remainder of this lesson, you learn more about passing variables to functions.

Passing Variables

Each variable you create in a program has both a value and a unique address that represents the location of the variable in the computer's internal memory. Most programming languages allow you to pass either the variable's value (referred to as passing *by value*) or its address (referred to as passing *by reference*) to the receiving function. The method you choose—*by value* or *by reference*—depends on whether you want the receiving function to have access to the variable in memory—in other words, whether you want to allow the receiving function to change the contents of the variable.

Although the idea of passing information *by value* and *by reference* may sound confusing at first, it is a concept with which you already are familiar. To illustrate, assume that you have a savings account at a local bank. During a conversation with a friend, you mention the amount of money you have in the account. Telling someone the amount of money in your account is similar to passing a variable *by value*. Knowing the balance in your account doesn't give your friend access to your bank account. It merely gives your friend some information that he or she can use—perhaps to compare to the amount of money he or she has saved.

The savings account example also provides an illustration of passing information *by reference*. To deposit money to or withdraw money from your account, you must provide the bank teller with your account number. The account number represents the location of your account at the bank and allows the teller to change the account balance. Giving the teller your bank account number is similar to passing a variable *by reference*. The account number allows the teller to change the contents of your bank account, just as the variable's address allows the receiving function to change the contents of the variable passed to the function.

Before learning how to pass a variable *by reference*, review passing *by value*.

Passing Variables *by Value*

As you learned in Chapter 9, when you pass a variable *by value*, the computer passes only the contents of the variable to the receiving function. When only the contents are passed, the receiving function is not given access to the variable in memory, so it cannot change the value stored inside the variable. You pass a variable *by value* when the receiving function needs to *know* the variable's contents, but the receiving function does not need to *change* the contents. Recall that, unless specified otherwise, variables are automatically passed *by value* in C++.

tip

Recall from the Overview that the internal memory of a computer is like a large post office, where each memory cell, like each post office box, has a unique address.

tip

In the programs you created in Chapter 9, all of the variables passed to functions were passed *by value* because none of the programs required the receiving function to change the contents of the variables passed to it.

Figure 10-2 shows a C++ program that calculates and displays a salesperson's total sales and his or her bonus. Notice that the program's `main()` function calls a void function named `calcAndDisplay()`, passing it three variables *by value*.

Figure 10-2: Example of passing variables *by value*

```
function
prototype   ──┌──void calcAndDisplay(double, double, double);

                int main()
                {
                    double sale1     = 0.0;
                    double sale2     = 0.0;
                    double bonusRate = 0.0;

                    //enter input items
                    cout << "Enter first sale: ";
                    cin >> sale1;
                    cout << "Enter second sale: ";
                    cin >> sale2;
                    cout << "Enter bonus rate: ";
                    cin >> bonusRate;

function call              //calculate and display total sales and bonus
            ──────────────calcAndDisplay(sale1, sale2, bonusRate);
                    return 0;
                }   //end of main function

                //*****function definitions*****
              ──void calcAndDisplay(double s1, double s2, double rate)
                {
                    double total = 0.0;
function            double bonus = 0.0;
definition
                    //calculate and display the total sales and bonus
                    total = s1 + s2;
                    bonus = total * rate;
                    cout << "Total: $" << total << endl;
                    cout << "Bonus: $" << bonus << endl;
              ──}   //end of calcAndDisplay function
```

Because the `calcAndDisplay()` function shown in Figure 10-2 is a void function, its function call (which is shaded in the figure) appears as a statement by itself. Notice that the number, data type, and sequence of the actual arguments in the function call match the number, data type, and sequence of the corresponding formal parameters in both the function header and function prototype. Also notice that the names of the formal parameters do not need to be identical to the names of their corresponding actual arguments. In fact, for clarity, it is better to use different names for the actual arguments and formal parameters. To review the concept of passing *by value*, you will desk-check the program shown in Figure 10-2.

Desk-checking Figure 10-2's Program

The first three statements in the `main()` function shown in Figure 10-2 create and initialize three `double` variables named `sale1`, `sale2`, and `bonusRate`. These variables are local to the `main()` function, and they remain in memory until the `main()` function's `return 0;` statement is processed.

The next six statements prompt the user to enter two sale amounts and the bonus rate, and store the user's responses in the three **double** variables. Assume that the user enters the numbers 2350.25, 3000.75, and .1. Figure 10-3 shows the contents of memory after the first nine statements in the **main()** function are processed.

Figure 10-3: Contents of memory after the first nine statements in the main() function are processed

main()
function's
variables

sale1	sale2	bonusRate
0.0 2350.25	0.0 3000.75	0.0 .1

tip

As you learned in Chapter 9, variables in a C++ program are passed, automatically, *by value*.

tip

Recall that the variables listed in a function header are local to the function, which means they can be used only by the function.

The **calcAndDisplay(sale1, sale2, bonusRate);** statement in the **main()** function calls the **calcAndDisplay()** function, passing it three variables *by value*, which means that only the contents of the variables are passed to the function. In this case, the computer passes the numbers 2350.25, 3000.75, and .1 to the **calcAndDisplay()** function.

At this point, the computer leaves the **main()** function, temporarily, to process the code contained in the **calcAndDisplay()** function. The **calcAndDisplay()** function header indicates that the computer should create three local **double** variables named **s1**, **s2**, and **rate**. The computer stores the values passed to the function in these local variables, as shown in Figure 10-4.

Figure 10-4: Contents of memory after the calcAndDisplay() function header is processed

calcAnd-
Display()
function's
variables

main()
function's
variables

sale1	sale2	bonusRate		s1	s2	rate
0.0 2350.25	0.0 3000.75	0.0 .1		2350.25	3000.75	.1

Next, the computer processes the statements contained in the **calcAndDisplay()** function body. The first two statements create and initialize two local **double** variables named **total** and **bonus**. The third statement adds together the contents of the **s1** and **s2** variables, then assigns the sum (5351.00) to the **total** variable. The fourth statement multiplies the contents of the **total** variable by the contents of the **rate** variable, then assigns the product (535.10) to the **bonus** variable, as shown in Figure 10-5.

Figure 10-5: Contents of memory after the first four statements in the calcAndDisplay() function are processed

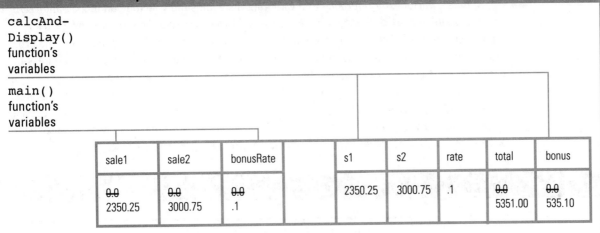

The last two statements in the **calcAndDisplay()** function display the contents of the **total** and **bonus** variables on the screen. When the computer encounters the **calcAndDisplay()** function's closing brace, which marks the end of the function, it removes the function's local variables (**s1**, **s2**, **rate**, **total**, and **bonus**) from memory. It then continues program execution with the statement immediately following the one that called the **calcAndDisplay()** function. In this case, program execution continues with the **return 0;** statement in the **main()** function. Figure 10-6 shows the contents of memory after the **calcAndDisplay()** function has completed its task. Notice that only the **main()** function's local variables (**sale1**, **sale2**, and **bonusRate**) remain in the computer's memory.

Figure 10-6: Contents of memory after the calcAndDisplay() function ends

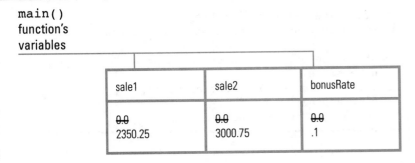

The **return 0;** statement in the **main()** function is the next statement processed. The statement returns the number 0 to the operating system to indicate that the program ended normally. The computer then removes the **main()** function's local variables (**sale1**, **sale2**, and **bonusRate**) from memory before ending the program.

Next, you learn how to pass variables *by reference*.

Passing Variables *by Reference*

In addition to passing a variable's value to a function, most programming languages also allow you to pass a variable's address—in other words, its location in the computer's internal memory. Passing a variable's address is referred to as passing *by reference*, and it gives the

tip

A void function's local variables are removed from memory when the computer encounters the function's closing brace. A value-returning function's local variables, on the other hand, are removed from memory after the function's return statement is processed.

receiving function access to the variable being passed. You pass a variable *by reference* when you want the receiving function to change the contents of the variable.

To pass a variable *by reference* to a C++ function, you simply include an ampersand (&), called the **address-of operator**, before the name of the corresponding formal parameter in the function header. If the function definition appears below the `main()` function in the program, you also must include the address-of operator in the function prototype. The address-of operator tells the computer to pass the variable's address rather than its contents.

Figure 10-7 shows a C++ program that calculates and displays the average of two test scores. Notice that the program's `main()` function calls a void function named `getScores()`, passing it two variables *by reference*. You can tell that the variables are passed *by reference* because the address-of operator appears in both the function prototype and function header.

Figure 10-7: Example of passing variables *by reference*

```
                        //function prototype
                        void getScores(double &, double &);
address-of
operator
                        int main()
                        {
                            double test1 = 0.0;
                            double test2 = 0.0;
                            double avg   = 0.0;

                            //enter input items
function call            getScores(test1, test2);

                            //calculate and display average
                            avg = (test1 + test2) / 2.0;
                            cout << "Average: " << avg << endl;
                            return 0;
                        }   //end of main function

                        //*****function definitions*****
                        void getScores(double &score1, double &score2)
address-of              {
operator                    cout << "Enter first test score: ";
                            cin >> score1;
                            cout << "Enter second test score: ";
                            cin >> score2;
                        }   //end of getScores function
```

tip

The statement that calls a function does not indicate whether an item is passed *by value* or *by reference*. To determine how an item is passed, you need to examine the *parameterList* in either the function header or function prototype.

Because the `getScores()` function is a void function, its function call, which is shaded in the figure, appears as a statement by itself. Notice that the number, data type, and sequence of the actual arguments in the function call match the number, data type, and sequence of the corresponding formal parameters in both the function header and function prototype. Also notice that the names of the formal parameters do not need to be identical to the names of their corresponding actual arguments. Additionally, notice that the address-of operator appears before the name of the formal parameter in the function header, and it appears after the data type and a space in the function prototype. Desk-checking the program shown in Figure 10-7 will help you understand the concept of passing *by reference*.

Desk-checking Figure 10-7's Program

The first three statements in the `main()` function shown in Figure 10-7 create and initialize three `double` variables named `test1`, `test2`, and `avg`. Figure 10-8 shows the contents of memory after these statements are processed.

Figure 10-8: Contents of memory after the first three statements in the `main()` function are processed

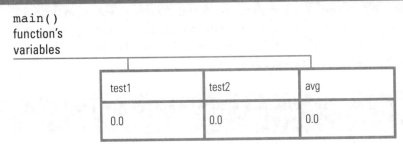

The `getScores(test1, test2);` statement in the `main()` function calls the `getScores()` function, passing it two variables. Both variables are passed *by reference*, which means that each variable's address in memory, rather than its contents, are passed. At this point, the computer temporarily leaves the `main()` function to process the code contained in the `getScores()` function.

The `getScores()` function header indicates that the function receives the addresses of two `double` variables. When you pass a variable's address to a function, the computer uses the address to locate the variable in memory; it then assigns the name appearing in the function header to the memory location. In this case, for example, the computer locates the `test1` and `test2` variables in memory, and assigns the names `score1` and `score2`, respectively, to these locations. At this point, each of the two memory locations has two names: one assigned by the `main()` function, and the other assigned by the `getScores()` function, as shown in Figure 10-9.

Figure 10-9: Contents of memory after the `getScores()` function header is processed

variable
belonging
only to
`main()`

variables
belonging
to both
`main()` and
get-
`Scores()`

test1 [main()] score1 [getScores()]	test2 [main()] score2 [getScores()]	avg
0.0	0.0	0.0

As Figure 10-9 indicates, only one of the memory locations shown in the figure—the one named **avg**—belongs strictly to the **main()** function. The other two memory locations shown in the figure belong to both the **main()** and **getScores()** functions. Although both functions can access these two memory locations, each function uses a different name to do so. The **main()** function, for example, uses the names **test1** and **test2** to refer to these memory locations. The **getScores()** function, on the other hand, uses the names **score1** and **score2**.

After processing the **getScores()** function header, the computer processes the statements contained in the function body. Those statements prompt the user to enter two test scores and store the user's responses in the **score1** and **score2** variables. Assume the user enters the numbers 93 and 84. Figure 10-10 shows the contents of memory after the four statements in the **getScores()** function are processed.

Figure 10-10: Contents of memory after the four statements in the getScores() function are processed

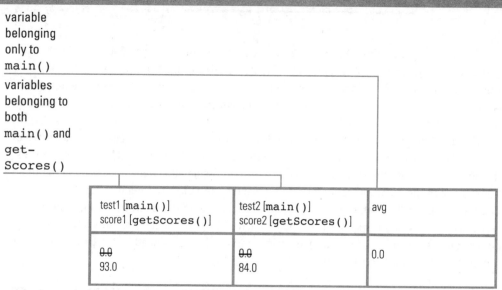

Changing the contents of the **score1** and **score2** variables also changes the contents of the **test1** and **test2** variables, respectively. This is because the names refer to the same locations in memory.

When the computer encounters the **getScores()** function's closing brace, it removes the **score1** and **score2** names assigned to the **main()** function's **test1** and **test2** variables. Program execution then continues with the statement immediately following the one that called the **getScores()** function. In this case, program execution continues with the **avg = (test1 + test2) / 2.0;** statement in the **main()** function. Figure 10-11 shows the contents of memory after the **getScores()** function ends. Notice that only the **main()** function's local variables (**test1, test2,** and **avg**) remain in the computer's memory.

tip

A void function uses variables that are passed *by reference* to send information back to the function that called it. A value-returning function, on the other hand, uses its return value to send information back to the function that called it.

Figure 10-11: Contents of memory after the `getScores()` **function ends**

main()
function's
variables

test1	test2	avg
~~0.0~~ 93.0	~~0.0~~ 84.0	0.0

The `avg = (test1 + test2) / 2.0;` statement in the `main()` function adds the contents of the `test1` variable to the contents of the `test2` variable. It then divides the sum (177) by two and assigns the result (88.5) to the `avg` variable, as shown in Figure 10-12.

Figure 10-12: Contents of memory after the average is calculated

main()
function's
variables

test1	test2	avg
~~0.0~~ 93.0	~~0.0~~ 84.0	~~0.0~~ 88.5

Next, the computer processes the `cout << "Average: " << avg << endl;` statement, which displays the average test score on the screen. When the computer encounters the `return 0;` statement, it removes the `main()` function's local variables (`test1`, `test2`, and `avg`) from memory before ending the program.

Mini-Quiz 2

1) Write the function header for a C++ void function named `getInput()`. The function is passed the addresses of the `main()` function's `hours` and `rate` variables. The variables are of the `double` data type. Use the names `hoursWkd` and `payRate` for the formal parameters.

2) Write the statement to call the `getInput()` function in Question 1.

3) Write the function prototype for the `getInput()` function in Question 1.

4) A void function's local variables are removed from memory when the computer encounters the function's _____.

MINI-QUIZ

Next, view a program that passes variables both *by value* and *by reference*.

Passing Variables *by Value* and *by Reference*

In the program shown earlier in Figure 10-2, the variables passed to the
`calcAndDisplay()` function are passed *by value*. In Figure 10-7's program, on the other
hand, the variables are passed to the `getScores()` function *by reference*. You also can mix
the way variables are passed when a function is called, passing some *by reference* and others
by value, as shown in Figure 10-13's program.

Figure 10-13: Example of passing variables *by value* and *by reference*

passed
by value

passed *by
reference*

function call

```
//function prototype
void calc(double, double, double &, double &);

int main()
{
    double salary    = 0.0;
    double raiseRate = 0.0;
    double raise     = 0.0;
    double newSalary = 0.0;

    //enter input items
    cout << "Enter current salary: ";
    cin >> salary;
    cout << "Enter raise rate: ";
    cin >> raiseRate;

    //calculate raise and new salary
    calc(salary, raiseRate, raise, newSalary);

    //display raise and new salary
    cout << "Raise: " << raise << endl;
    cout << "New salary: " << newSalary << endl;
    return 0;
}   //end of main function

//*****function definitions*****
void calc(double current, double rate, double &increase, double &pay)
{
    increase = current * rate;
    pay = current + increase;
}   //end of calc function
```

tip

Recall that when
you pass a variable
by value, the vari-
able's contents are
passed. When you
pass a variable *by
reference*, on the
other hand, the
variable's address
in memory is
passed.

The program shown in Figure 10-13 calculates and displays an employee's raise and new
salary amounts, given the employee's current salary amount and the raise rate. The first four
statements in the `main()` function create and initialize four `double` variables named
`salary`, `raiseRate`, `raise`, and `newSalary`. The next four statements prompt the user
to enter the current salary amount and the raise rate, and store the user's responses in the
`salary` and `raiseRate` variables. Assume that the user enters the numbers 34500 and
.06 for the salary and rate, respectively. Figure 10-14 shows the contents of memory after the
first eight statements in the `main()` function are processed.

Figure 10-14: Contents of memory after the first eight statements in the `main()` function are processed

```
main()
function's
variables
```

salary	raiseRate	raise	newSalary
~~0.0~~ 34500.0	~~0.0~~ .06	0.0	0.0

Next, the computer processes the `calc(salary, raiseRate, raise, newSalary);` statement, which calls the `calc()` function, passing it four variables. The `salary` and `raiseRate` variables are passed *by value*, because the receiving function needs to *know* the values stored in these variables, but it does not need to change those values. The `raise` and `newSalary` variables are passed *by reference*, because it is the receiving function's responsibility to calculate the raise and new salary amounts and then store the results in these memory locations.

At this point, the computer temporarily leaves the `main()` function to process the code contained in the `calc()` function. The `double current, double rate` portion of the `calc()` function header tells the computer to create two `double` memory locations named `current` and `rate`. These memory locations will store the values of the `salary` and `raiseRate` variables passed to the function. The `double &increase, double &pay` portion of the `calc()` function header tells the computer to assign the name `increase` to the `main()` function's `raise` variable, and assign the name `pay` to the `main()` function's `newSalary` variable. Figure 10-15 shows the contents of memory after the `calc()` function header is processed.

Figure 10-15: Contents of memory after the `calc()` function header is processed

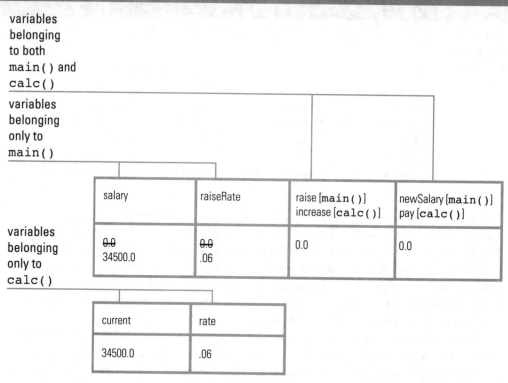

The statements contained in the `calc()` function body are processed next. The first statement multiplies the contents of the `current` variable by the contents of the `rate` variable, then assigns the result (2070) to the `increase` variable. The second statement adds together the contents of the `current` and `increase` variables, then assigns the sum (36570) to the `pay` variable, as shown in Figure 10-16.

Figure 10-16: Contents of memory after the two statements in the `calc()` **function body are processed**

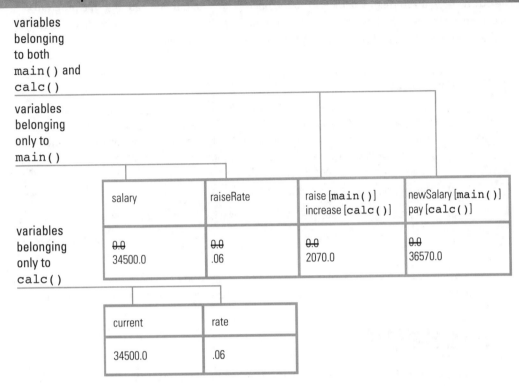

variables
belonging
to both
`main()` and
`calc()`

variables
belonging
only to
`main()`

variables
belonging
only to
`calc()`

salary	raiseRate	raise [`main()`] increase [`calc()`]	newSalary [`main()`] pay [`calc()`]
~~0.0~~ 34500.0	~~0.0~~ .06	~~0.0~~ 2070.0	~~0.0~~ 36570.0

current	rate
34500.0	.06

When the computer encounters the `calc()` function's closing brace, it removes the
`increase` and `pay` names assigned to the `main()` function's `raise` and `newSalary`
variables. It also removes the `calc()` function's `current` and `rate` variables from memory. Program execution then continues with the statement immediately following the one that
called the `calc()` function. In this case, program execution continues with the `cout <<`
`"Raise: " << raise << endl;` statement in the `main()` function. Figure 10-17
shows the contents of memory after the `calc()` function ends. Notice that only the `main()`
function's local variables (`salary`, `raiseRate`, `raise`, and `newSalary`) remain in the
computer's memory.

Figure 10-17: Contents of memory after the `calc()` **function ends**

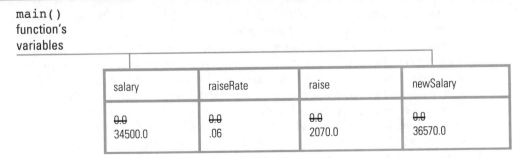

`main()`
function's
variables

salary	raiseRate	raise	newSalary
~~0.0~~ 34500.0	~~0.0~~ .06	~~0.0~~ 2070.0	~~0.0~~ 36570.0

The `cout << "Raise: " << raise << endl;` statement in the `main()` function is the next statement processed and displays the raise amount on the screen. The

cout << "New salary: " << newSalary << endl; statement then displays the new salary amount. When the computer processes the last statement in the main() function— return 0; —it returns the number 0 to the operating system to indicate that the program ended normally. The computer then removes the main() function's local variables (salary, raiseRate, raise, and newSalary) from memory before ending the program.

MINI-QUIZ

Mini-Quiz 3

1) Write the function header for a C++ void function named calcTaxes(). The function is passed the value of the main() function's gross variable and the addresses of the main() function's federal and state variables. The variables are of the double data type. Use the names pay, fedTax, and stateTax for the formal parameters.

2) Write the statement to call the calcTaxes() function in Question 1.

3) Write the function prototype for the calcTaxes() function in Question 1.

You now have completed Chapter 10's Concept lesson. You can either take a break or complete the end-of-lesson questions and exercises before moving on to the Application lesson.

SUMMARY

All functions fall into one of two categories: value-returning or void. A value-returning function returns precisely one value to the statement that called the function. A void function, on the other hand, does not return a value after completing its assigned task.

Like a value-returning function, a void function is composed of a function header and a function body. However, unlike a value-returning function, the function header for a void function begins with the keyword void, rather than with a data type. Also unlike a value-returning function, the function body for a void function does not contain a return statement.

As you do with a value-returning function, you call a void function by including its name and actual arguments (if any) in a statement. However, unlike a call to a value-returning function, a call to a void function appears as a statement by itself, rather than as part of another statement. When the computer finishes processing a void function's code, it continues program execution with the statement immediately below the one that called the function.

Variables can be passed to functions either *by value* or *by reference*. When you pass a variable *by value*, only the value stored inside the variable is passed to the receiving function. The receiving function is not given access to a variable passed *by value*, so it cannot change the variable's contents. When you pass a variable *by reference*, on the other hand, its address in memory is passed to the receiving function, allowing the receiving function to change the variable's contents. Unless specified otherwise, variables in C++ are passed automatically *by value*. To pass a variable *by reference* in a C++ program, you include the address-of operator (&) before the corresponding formal parameter's name in the function header. If the function definition appears below the main() function in the program, you also must include the address-of operator in the function prototype. The address-of operator tells the computer to pass the variable's address rather than its contents.

ANSWERS TO MINI-QUIZZES

Mini-Quiz 1

1) `void`

2) c. `displayTaxes(federal, state);`

3) `void displayTaxes(double fedTax, double stateTax)`

4) b. False

Mini-Quiz 2

1) `void getInput(double &hoursWkd, double &payRate)`

2) `getInput(hours, rate);`

3) `void getInput(double &, double &);`

4) `closing brace (})`

Mini-Quiz 3

1) `void calcTaxes(double pay, double &fedTax, double &stateTax)`

2) `calcTaxes(gross, federal, state);`

3) `void calcTaxes(double, double &, double &);`

QUESTIONS

1) Which of the following is false?

A. A void function does not return a value after completing its assigned task.

B. A void function call typically appears as its own statement in a C++ program.

C. A void function cannot receive any items of information when it is called.

D. A void function header begins with the keyword **void**.

2) Which of the following C++ statements correctly calls a void function named `displayHeading()`, passing it one `string` variable named `companyName`?

A. `cout << displayHeading(string companyName);`

B. `cout << displayHeading(companyName);`

C. `displayHeading(string companyName);`

D. `displayHeading(companyName);`

3) Which of the following function prototypes is correct for a void function named `calcEndingBalance()`? The function is passed the value of two `int` variables.

A. `void calcEndingBalance(int, int);`

B. `void calcEndingBalance(int, int)`

C. `void calcEndingBalance(int &, int &);`

D. `int calcEndingBalance(void);`

4) Assume that a void function named `calcEndingInventory()` receives four `int` variables from the `main()` function: `beginInventory`, `sales`, `purchases`, and `endingInventory`. The function's task is to calculate the ending inventory, based on the beginning inventory, sales, and purchase amounts passed to the function. The function should store the result in the `endingInventory` memory location. Which of the following function headers is correct?

A. `void calcEndingInventory(&int b, &int s, &int p, &int e)`

B. `void calcEndingInventory(int b, int s, int p, int e)`

C. `void calcEndingInventory(int &b, int &s, int &p, int e)`

D. `void calcEndingInventory(int b, int s, int p, int &e)`

5) Which of the following statements calls the `calcEndingInventory()` function described in Question 4?

A. `calcEndingInventory(int, int, int, int);`

B. `calcEndingInventory(beginInventory, sales, purchases, &endingInventory);`

C. `calcEndingInventory(beginInventory, sales, purchases, endingInventory);`

D. `calcEndingInventory(int beginInventory, int sales, int purchases, int &endingInventory);`

6) In C++, variables are passed automatically _____.

A. *by address*

B. *by number*

C. *by reference*

D. *by value*

7) If you want the receiving function to change the contents of a variable, you must pass the variable _____.

A. *by address*

B. *by number*

C. *by reference*

D. *by value*

8) To determine whether an item is being passed *by value* or *by reference*, you must examine either the _____ or the _____.

A. function call, function header

B. function call, function prototype

C. function header, function prototype

D. function header, function body

9) Which of the following is false?

A. You enclose a function's statements in a set of braces.

B. The function header is considered a C++ statement, so it must end with a semicolon.

C. The keyword `void` tells the computer that the function does not return a value.

D. An empty set of parentheses after the function's name in the function header tells you that the function does not receive any information.

10) Which of the following calls a function named `displayName()`, passing it no actual arguments?

A. `call displayName();`

B. `displayName;`

C. `displayName()`

D. `displayName();`

11) Assume a program contains a void function named `displayName()`. Which of the following is a correct function prototype for this function, assuming that the function requires no formal parameters?

A. `displayName();`

B. `void displayName;`

C. `void displayName();`

D. `void displayName(none);`

12) When the computer encounters a void function's closing brace, it continues program execution with _____.

A. the statement immediately above the one that called the function

B. the statement that called the function

C. the statement immediately below the one that called the function

13) A program will have one function prototype for each function defined in the function definitions section of the program. (Assume that the function definitions section is located below the `main()` function.)

A. True

B. False

14) Variables that can be used only by the function in which they are declared are called _____ variables.

A. global

B. local

C. separate

D. void

15) Which of the following is false?

A. When you pass a variable *by reference*, the receiving function can change the variable's contents.

B. When you pass a variable *by value*, the receiving function creates a local variable that it uses to store the passed value.

C. Unless specified otherwise, all variables in C++ are passed *by value*.

D. To pass a variable *by reference* in C++, you place an ampersand (&) before the variable's name in the statement that calls the function.

16) Assume a program contains a void function named `calcNewPrice()`. The function receives two `double` variables named `oldPrice` and `newPrice`. The function multiplies the contents of the `oldPrice` variable by 1.1, then stores the result in the `newPrice` variable. Which of the following is the best function prototype for this function?

A. `void calcNewPrice(double, double);`

B. `void calcNewPrice(double &, double);`

C. `void calcNewPrice(double, double &);`

D. `void calcNewPrice(double &, double &);`

17) Which of the following can be used to call the `calcNewPrice()` function in Question 16?

A. `calcNewPrice(double oldPrice, double newPrice);`

B. `calcNewPrice(&oldPrice, newPrice);`

C. `calcNewPrice(oldPrice, &newPrice);`

D. `calcNewPrice(oldPrice, newPrice);`

18) Which of the following is false?

A. The names of the formal parameters in the function header must be identical to the names of the actual arguments in the function call.

B. When listing the formal parameters in a function header, you include each parameter's data type and name.

C. The formal parameters should be the same data type as the actual arguments.

D. If a function call passes an `int` variable first and a `char` variable second, the receiving function should receive an `int` variable first and a `char` variable second.

Look For These
Symbols

Debugging

Discovery

EXERCISES

1) Write the C++ code for a void function named `halveNumber()`. The function receives an integer passed to it. It then divides the integer by 2 and displays the result on the computer screen.

2) Write the C++ code for a void function that prompts the user to enter the name of an item, then stores the user's response in the `string` variable whose address is passed to the function. Name the function `getItemName()`.

3) Write the C++ code for a void function that receives four `int` variables: the first two *by value* and the last two *by reference*. The function should calculate the sum of and the difference between the two variables passed *by value*, then store the results in the variables passed *by reference*. When calculating the difference, subtract the contents of the second variable from the contents of the first variable. Name the function `calcSumAndDiff()`.

4) Write the C++ code for a void function that receives three `double` variables: the first two *by value* and the last one *by reference*. The function should divide the first variable by the second variable, then store the result in the third variable. Name the function `quotient()`.

5) Write the C++ code for a void function that receives a `string` variable *by value*. The function should display the string on the computer screen. Name the function `displayName()`.

6) Desk-check the program shown in Figure 10-18. Show the desk-check table after the first four statements in the `main()` function are processed, after the `calcEnd()` function's statement is processed, and after the `calcEnd()` function ends.

Figure 10-18

```
//function prototype
void calcEnd(int, int, int, int &);

int main()
{
    int begVal    = 1000;
    int purchase = 500;
    int sale      = 200;
    int endVal    = 0;

    calcEnd(begVal, purchase, sale, endVal);

    cout << endVal << endl;
    return 0;
}   //end of main function

//*****function definitions*****
void calcEnd(int beg, int pur, int sale, int &ending)
{
    ending = beg + pur - sale;
}   //end of calcEnd function
```

7) In this exercise, you experiment with passing *by value* and *by reference*.

   A. If necessary, start Visual Studio .NET. Open the Ch10ConE07 Solution
   (Ch10ConE07 Solution.sln) file, which is contained in the Cpp\Chap10\
   Ch10ConE07 Solution folder. Notice that the **main()** function passes the
   age variable *by value* to the **getAge()** function.

   B. Build the solution, then execute the program. When prompted to enter your
   age, type your age and press Enter. Notice that the program displays the number 0, rather than your age, in the message. This is because the **age** variable is
   passed *by value* to the **getAge()** function.

   C. Close the Command Prompt and Output windows.

   D. Modify the program so that it passes the **age** variable *by reference* to the
   getAge() function.

   E. Save and then build the solution.

   F. Execute the program. When prompted to enter your age, type your age and
   press Enter. Notice that, this time, the program displays your age in the message. This is because the **age** variable is passed *by reference* to the
   getAge() function. Close the Command Prompt window.

   G. When the program is working correctly, close the Output window, then use the
   File menu to close the solution.

8) In this exercise, you learn about a common error made when using arithmetic
expressions in a program.

   A. If necessary, start Visual Studio .NET. Open the Ch10ConE08 Solution
   (Ch10ConE08 Solution.sln) file, which is contained in the Cpp\Chap10\
   Ch10ConE08 Solution folder.

   B. Study the existing code. Although the **calcTax1()** and **calcTax2()** functions use slightly different formulas for calculating the sales tax, both formulas
   should produce the same result.

C. Build the solution, then execute the program. Notice that the `calcTax1()` function displays $2.63 as the sales tax, which is correct. The `calcTax2()` function, however, displays $1.75 as the sales tax, which is incorrect.

D. Close the Command Prompt and Output windows.

In C++, dividing an integer by an integer results in an integer. In the `calcTax2()` function, for example, dividing the `saleAmt` variable (which is an `int` variable) by the integer 1000 results in the integer 1. Multiplying the integer 1 by the contents of the `taxRate` variable (1.75) results in an incorrect sales tax amount.

E. Modify the formula in the `calcTax2()` function so that it tells the computer to divide the `saleAmt` variable by the `double` value 1000.0.

F. Save and then build the solution.

G. Execute the program. This time, both functions produce the same sales tax amount. Close the Command Prompt window.

H. Change the 1000.0 in the `calcTax2()` function's formula to 1000. Now modify the formula in the `calcTax2()` function so that it tells the computer to divide the `saleAmt` variable, treated as a `double`, by the integer 1000.

I. Save and then build the solution.

J. Execute the program. Here again, both functions produce the same sales tax amount. Close the Command Prompt window.

K. When the program is working correctly, close the Output window, then use the File menu to close the solution.

9) In this exercise, you debug a C++ program.

A. If necessary, start Visual Studio .NET. Open the Ch10ConE09 Solution (Ch10ConE09 Solution.sln) file, which is contained in the Cpp\Chap10\ Ch10ConE09 Solution folder.

B. Build the solution. Correct any errors.

C. Save and then build the solution.

D. Execute the program. When prompted to enter your name, type your name and press Enter. Close the Command Prompt window.

E. When the program is working correctly, close the Output window, then use the File menu to close the solution.

10) In this exercise, you debug a C++ program.

A. If necessary, start Visual Studio .NET. Open the Ch10ConE10 Solution (Ch10ConE10 Solution.sln) file, which is contained in the Cpp\Chap10\ Ch10ConE10 Solution folder.

B. Build the solution. Correct any errors.

C. Save and then build the solution.

D. Execute the program. Test the program using the numbers 10 and 20. The program should display the number 30 as the sum of both numbers. Close the Command Prompt window.

E. When the program is working correctly, close the Output window, then use the File menu to close the solution.

Application Lesson

Using Void Functions in a C++ Program

Lab 10.1 - Stop and Analyze   If necessary, start Visual Studio .NET. Open the Ch10Lab1 Solution (Ch10Lab1 Solution.sln) file contained in the Cpp\Chap10\Ch10Lab1 Solution folder. Figure 10-19 shows the code entered in the Ch10Lab1.cpp file. (The line numbers are included in the figure only.) Study the code, then answer the questions.

Figure 10-19: C++ instructions entered in the Ch10Lab1.cpp file

```cpp
1   //Ch10Lab1.cpp - converts American dollars to British pounds, or
2   //Mexican pesos, or Japanese yen
3   //Created/revised by <your name> on <current date>
4
5   #include <iostream>
6   #include <iomanip>
7
8   using std::cout;
9   using std::cin;
10  using std::endl;
11  using std::setprecision;
12  using std::ios;
13  using std::setiosflags;
14
15  //function prototypes
16  void displayMenu();
17  void convertDols(double, double, double &);
18
19  int main()
20  {
21      //declare variables
22      int choice            = 0;
23      double origDollars      = 0.0;
24      double convertedDollars = 0.0;
25      double rate            = 0.0;
26
27      //display output in fixed-point notation
28      //with two decimal places
29      cout << setiosflags(ios::fixed) << setprecision(2);
30
31      //get menu choice
32      displayMenu();
33      cout << "Enter 1, 2, 3, or 4: ";
34      cin >> choice;
35
36      while (choice > 0 && choice < 4)
37      {
38          //get dollars to convert
39          cout << "Enter number of American dollars: ";
40          cin >> origDollars;
41
42          //assign rate
43          if (choice == 1)          //British
44              rate = .626881;
```

Figure 10-19: C++ instructions entered in the Ch10Lab1.cpp file (continued)

```
45              else if (choice == 2)     //Mexican
46                  rate = 10.392;
47              else
48                  rate = 118.24;        //Japanese
49              //end ifs
50
51              convertDols(origDollars, rate, convertedDollars);
52              cout << convertedDollars << endl << endl;
53
54              //get menu choice
55              displayMenu();
56              cout << "Enter 1, 2, 3, or 4: ";
57              cin >> choice;
58      }   //end while
59
60      return 0;
61      }   //end of main function
62
63   //*****function definitions*****
64   void displayMenu()
65   {
66      cout << "1 British pounds" << endl;
67      cout << "2 Mexican pesos" << endl;
68      cout << "3 Japanese yen" << endl;
69      cout << "4 Stop program" << endl;
70   }   //end of displayMenu function
71
72   void convertDols(double orig, double r, double &newDols)
73   {
74      newDols = orig * r;
75   }   //end of convertDols function
```

Questions

1. Which lines in the program indicate how a variable is being passed to the `convertDols()` function?

2. Why are the `origDollars` and `rate` variables passed *by value*, while the `convertedDollars` variable is passed *by reference*?

3. Build the solution, then execute the program. Use the program to convert 100 American dollars to Japanese yen. What is the answer?

4. Use the program to convert 50 American dollars to British pounds. What is the answer?

5. Use the program to convert 10 American dollars to Mexican pesos. What is the answer?

6. Stop the program, then close the Command Prompt window.

7. Create a blank solution named Ch10Lab1 Step 7 Solution. Save the solution in the Cpp\Chap10 folder.

8. Add an empty C++ Win32 Console Project to the solution. Name the project Ch10Lab1 Step 7 Project.

9. Add a new C++ source file to the project. Name the source file Ch10Lab1 Step 7.

10. Open the Ch10Lab1.cpp file contained in the Cpp\Ch10Lab1 Solution\Ch10Lab1 Project folder. Copy the file's contents to the clipboard. Close the Ch10Lab1.cpp window, then paste the instructions into the Ch10Lab1 Step 7.cpp window. Change the filename in the first comment to Ch10Lab1 Step 7.cpp.

11. Modify the program so that it uses a void function to assign the conversion rate. Name the function `assignRate()`.

12. Save and then build the solution. Execute the program. Test the program appropriately, then close the Command Prompt window.

13. Close the Output window, then use the File menu to close the solution.

Lab 10.2 Jane Hernandez is employed by the public works office in Allenton, a small rural town with a population of 500. Each month, Jane uses a calculator to calculate each customer's water bill—a time-consuming task and one that is prone to errors. She has asked you to create a program that she can use to make the appropriate calculations, then display the customer's name, gallons of water used, and water charge. The charge for water is $1.75 per 1000 gallons, or .00175 per gallon.

In this program, you will use three program-defined void functions named `getInput()`, `calcBill()`, and `displayBill()`. The `getInput()` function will be assigned the task of getting the user input (customer name, current meter reading, and previous meter reading). A void function is appropriate in this case because the `getInput()` function needs to get three values for the `main()` function, and a value-returning function can return only one value. The `calcBill()` function will be responsible for calculating both the gallons used and the water charge. Here again, a void function is appropriate because the `calcBill()` function needs to calculate more than one value for the `main()` function. The `displayBill()` function will be responsible for displaying the output (customer name, gallons used, and water charge) on the screen. The `displayBill()` function also should be a void function, because it will not need to return a value to the `main()` function after completing its task. Figure 10-20 shows the IPO chart and C++ instructions for the `main()`, `getInput()`, `calcBill()`, and `displayBill()` functions in the program.

Figure 10-20: IPO chart and C++ instructions for the water department program

`main()` function

IPO chart information	C++ instructions

Input
  customer name
  current reading (gallons)
  previous reading (gallons)
  rate per gallon (.00175)
	`string name = "";`
	`int current = 0;`
	`int previous = 0;`
	`const double RATE = .00175;`

Processing none	

Output
  customer name
  gallons used
  water charge
	
	`int gallons = 0;`
	`double charge = 0.0;`

Algorithm
1. getInput(customer name,
   current reading,
   previous reading)
2. calcBill(current reading,
   previous reading, rate
   per gallon, gallons used,
   water charge)
3. displayBill(customer name,
   gallons used, water charge)
	
	`getInput(name, current, previous);`
	
	`calcBill(current, previous, RATE, gallons,`
	`charge);`
	
	`displayBill(name, gallons, charge);`

Figure 10-20: IPO chart and C++ instructions for the water department program (continued)

`getInput()` function

IPO chart information	C++ instructions

Input
   address of customer name
   address of current reading
   address of previous reading
 Processing
   none
 Output
   customer name
   current reading
   previous reading
	`void getInput(string &cust, int &cur,`
	 `int &prev)`

Algorithm
 1. enter the customer name,
    current reading, and
    previous reading
	`cout << "Customer name: ";`
	 `getline(cin, cust);`
	 `cout << "Current reading: ";`
	 `cin >> cur;`
	 `cout << "Previous reading: ";`
	 `cin >> prev;`

`calcBill()` function

IPO chart information	C++ instructions

Input
   current reading
   previous reading
   rate per gallon
   address of gallons used
   address of water charge
 Processing
   none
 Output
   gallons used
   water charge
	`void calcBill(int c, int p, double r,`
	 `int &gal, double &due)`

Algorithm
 1. calculate gallons
    used by subtracting
    previous reading
    from current reading
 2. calculate water charge by
    multiplying gallons used
    by rate per gallon
	`gal = c - p;`
	
	 `due = gal * r;`

Figure 10-20: IPO chart and C++ instructions for the water department program (continued)

`displayBill()` function

IPO chart information	C++ instructions
Input customer name gallons used water charge **Processing** none **Output** customer name gallons used water charge	`void displayBill(string cust, int used,` `double amtDue)`

Algorithm
1. display the customer
   name, gallons used,
   and water charge
	`cout << "Customer name: " << cust << endl;`
	`cout << "Gallons used: " << used << endl;`
	`cout << "Water charge: $" << amtDue << endl;`

According to the information shown in Figure 10-20, the `main()` function first will call the `getInput()` function, whose task is to get the required information from the user. Notice that the `getInput()` function's output is the customer name, current reading, and previous reading. For the function to perform its task, the `main()` function must pass it the addresses of the variables where the customer name, current reading, and previous reading should be stored.

After the `getInput()` function performs its task, the `main()` function will call the `calcBill()` function to make the appropriate calculations. Notice that the `calcBill()` function's output is the gallons used and the water charge. For the function to perform the necessary calculations, the `main()` function must pass it the current reading, the previous reading, the rate per gallon, and the memory addresses of the variables where the gallons used and water charge should be stored.

Finally, the `main()` function will call the `displayBill()` function, whose task is to display the appropriate information on the screen. Notice that the `displayBill()` function's output is the customer name, gallons used, and water charge. For the function to perform its task, it must receive the name, usage, and charge information from the `main()` function.

Activity for Lab 10.2

In this activity, you enter the C++ instructions shown in Figure 10-20 into the computer. You then test the program to verify that it is working correctly.

To create the water department program, then test the program:

1. If necessary, start Visual Studio .NET. Create a blank solution named Ch10Lab2 Solution. Save the solution in the Cpp\Chap10 folder.

2. Add an empty C++ Win32 Console Project to the solution. Name the project Ch10Lab2 Project.

3. Add a new C++ source file to the project. Name the source file Ch10Lab2.

4. Type **//Ch10Lab2.cpp – calculates and displays a water bill** and press **Enter**.

5. Type **//Created/revised by <*your name*> on <*current date*>**, replacing <*your name*> and <*current date*> with your name and the current date, respectively. Press **Enter** twice.

6. Type the following three #include directives, then press **Enter** twice:

   #include <iostream>
   #include <string>
   #include <iomanip>

7. Type the following seven using statements, then press **Enter** twice.
   using std::cout;
   using std::cin;
   using std::endl;
   using std::string;
   using std::setprecision;
   using std::ios;
   using std::setiosflags;

8. Type **//function prototypes** and press **Enter**, then type the following three
   function prototypes and press **Enter** twice.

   void getInput(string &, int &, int &);
   void calcBill(int, int, double, int &, double &);
   void displayBill(string, int, double);

9. Complete the program by entering the main(), getInput(), calcBill(),
   and displayBill() functions, which are shown in Figure 10-21.

Figure 10-21: Water department program

```
//Ch10Lab2.cpp - calculates and displays a water bill
//Created/revised by <your name> on <current date>

#include <iostream>
#include <string>
#include <iomanip>

using std::cout;
using std::cin;
using std::endl;
using std::string;
using std::setprecision;
using std::ios;
using std::setiosflags;

//function prototypes
void getInput(string &, int &, int &);
void calcBill(int, int, double, int &, double &);
void displayBill(string, int, double);

int main()
{
    //declare variables
    string name = "";
    int current = 0;
    int previous = 0;
    const double RATE = .00175;
    int gallons = 0;
    double charge = 0.0;
```

enter
this code

Figure 10-21: Water department program (continued)

```cpp
    //display output in fixed-point notation
    //with two decimal places
    cout << setiosflags(ios::fixed) << setprecision(2);

    //call functions to get input and
    //calculate and display water bill
    getInput(name, current, previous);
    calcBill(current, previous, RATE, gallons, charge);
    displayBill(name, gallons, charge);

    return 0;
}   //end of main function

//*****function definitions*****
void getInput(string &cust, int &cur, int &prev)
{
    //get customer information
    cout << "Customer name: ";
    getline(cin, cust);
    cout << "Current reading: ";
    cin >> cur;
    cout << "Previous reading: ";
    cin >> prev;
}   //end of getInput function

void calcBill(int c, int p, double r, int &gal, double &due)
{
    //calculate gallons used and amount due
    gal = c - p;
    due = gal * r;
}   //end of calcBill function

void displayBill(string cust, int used, double amtDue)
{
    cout << "Customer name: " << cust << endl;
    cout << "Gallons used: " << used << endl;
    cout << "Water charge: $" << amtDue << endl;
}   //end of displayBill function
```

enter
this code

10. Save and then build the solution. Verify that the program generated no warnings.

11. Execute the program. When you are prompted to enter the customer's name, type **Joe Brown** and press **Enter**.

12. When prompted for the current reading, type **9000** and press **Enter**. When prompted for the previous reading, type **8000** and press **Enter**. The program calculates and displays the water bill, as shown in Figure 10-22.

Figure 10-22: Water bill displayed in the Command Prompt window

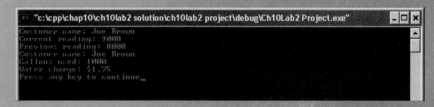

13. Close the Command Prompt window.

14. Close the Output window, then use the File menu to close the solution.

Lab 10.3 In this lab, you modify the program you created in Lab 10.2. The modified program will use two void functions, rather than one void function, to calculate the number of gallons used and the water charge.

Activity for Lab 10.3

Before modifying the program created in Lab 10.2, copy the instructions contained in the Ch10Lab2.cpp file to a new solution.

To copy the instructions contained in the Ch10Lab2.cpp file to a new solution:

1. If necessary, start Visual Studio .NET. Create a blank solution named Ch10Lab3 Solution. Save the solution in the Cpp\Chap10 folder.

2. Add an empty C++ Win32 Console Project to the solution. Name the project Ch10Lab3 Project.

3. Add a new C++ source file to the project. Name the source file Ch10Lab3.

4. Use the File menu to open the Ch10Lab2.cpp file contained in the Cpp\Chap10\Ch10Lab2 Solution\Ch10Lab2 Project folder. Select the contents of the file, then copy the contents to the clipboard.

5. Close the Ch10Lab2.cpp window.

6. Click the **Ch10Lab3.cpp** tab, then paste the instructions from the clipboard into the Ch10Lab3.cpp window.

7. Change the filename in the first program comment to Ch10Lab3.cpp. If necessary, change the date in the second comment.

Currently, the program uses one void function to calculate both the number of gallons used and the water charge. Your task is to modify the program so that it uses one void function to calculate the number of gallons used and another void function to calculate the water charge.

To modify the program, then test the program:

1. Make the appropriate modifications to the program.

2. Save and then build the solution. If necessary, correct any syntax errors, then save and build the solution again.

3. Execute the program. Test the program using your own sample data, then close the Command Prompt window.

4. When the program is working correctly, close the Output window, then use the File menu to close the solution.

You now have completed Chapter 10's Application lesson. You can either take a break or complete the end-of-lesson exercises.

ANSWERS TO LABS

Lab 10.1

1. Lines 17 and 72.

2. The `origDollars` and `rate` variables are passed *by value* because the `convertDols()` function needs to know only the value stored in those variables. The `convertedDollars` variable is passed *by reference* because the `convertDols()` function needs to store a value in the variable.

3. 11824.00

4. 31.34

5. 103.92

7. See Figure 10-23.

Figure 10-23

```
1   //Ch10Lab1 Step 7.cpp – converts American dollars to British pounds, or
2   //Mexican pesos, or Japanese yen
3   //Created/revised by <your name> on <current date>
4
5   #include <iostream>
6   #include <iomanip>
7
8   using std::cout;
9   using std::cin;
10  using std::endl;
11  using std::setprecision;
12  using std::ios;
13  using std::setiosflags;
14
15  //function prototypes
16  void displayMenu();
17  void assignRate(int, double &);
18  void convertDols(double, double, double &);
19
20  int main()
21  {
22      //declare variables
23      int choice             = 0;
24      double origDollars     = 0.0;
25      double convertedDollars = 0.0;
26      double rate            = 0.0;
27
28      //display output in fixed-point notation
29      //with two decimal places
30      cout << setiosflags(ios::fixed) << setprecision(2);
31
32      //get menu choice
33      displayMenu();
34      cout << "Enter 1, 2, 3, or 4: ";
```

Figure 10-23 (continued)

```
35      cin >> choice;
36
37      while (choice > 0 && choice < 4)
38      {
39            //get dollars to convert
40            cout << "Enter number of American dollars: ";
41            cin >> origDollars;
42
43            //assign rate
44            assignRate(choice, rate);
45
46            convertDols(origDollars, rate, convertedDollars);
47            cout << convertedDollars << endl << endl;
48
49            //get menu choice
50            displayMenu();
51            cout << "Enter 1, 2, 3, or 4: ";
52            cin >> choice;
53      }    //end while
54
55      return 0;
56 }    //end of main function
57
58  //*****function definitions*****
59 void displayMenu()
60 {
61      cout << "1 British pounds" << endl;
62      cout << "2 Mexican pesos" << endl;
63      cout << "3 Japanese yen" << endl;
64      cout << "4 Stop program" << endl;
65 }    //end of displayMenu function
66
67  void assignRate(int selection, double &convertRate)
68 {
69      if (selection == 1)         //British
70          convertRate = .626881;
71      else if (selection == 2)    //Mexican
72          convertRate = 10.392;
73      else
74          convertRate = 118.24;   //Japanese
75      //end ifs
76 }    //end of assignRate function
77
78  void convertDols(double orig, double r, double &newDols)
79 {
80      newDols = orig * r;
81 }    //end of convertDols function
```

Lab 10.2

No answer required.

Lab 10.3

See Figure 10-24. Modifications are shaded in the figure.

Figure 10-24

```cpp
//Ch10Lab3.cpp - calculates and displays a water bill
//Created/revised by <your name> on <current date>

#include <iostream>
#include <string>
#include <iomanip>

using std::cout;
using std::cin;
using std::endl;
using std::string;
using std::setprecision;
using std::ios;
using std::setiosflags;

//function prototypes
void getInput(string &, int &, int &);
void calcGallons(int, int, int &);
void calcCharge(double, int, double &);
void displayBill(string, int, double);

int main()
{
    //declare variables
    string name = "";
    int current = 0;
    int previous = 0;
    const double RATE = .00175;
    int gallons = 0;
    double charge = 0.0;

    //display output in fixed-point notation
    //with two decimal places
    cout << setiosflags(ios::fixed) << setprecision(2);

    //call functions to get input and
    //calculate and display water bill
    getInput(name, current, previous);
    calcGallons(current, previous, gallons);
    calcCharge(RATE, gallons, charge);
    displayBill(name, gallons, charge);

    return 0;
}   //end of main function

//*****function definitions*****
void getInput(string &cust, int &cur, int &prev)
{
    //get customer information
    cout << "Customer name: ";
    getline(cin, cust);
    cout << "Current reading: ";
    cin >> cur;
    cout << "Previous reading: ";
    cin >> prev;
}   //end of getInput function
```

Figure 10-24 (continued)

```cpp
void calcGallons(int c, int p, int &gal)
{
    //calculate gallons used
    gal = c - p;
}   //end of calcGallons function

void calcCharge(double r, int gal, double &due)
{
    //calculate amount due
    due = gal * r;
}   //end of calcCharge function

void displayBill(string cust, int used, double amtDue)
{
    cout << "Customer name: " << cust << endl;
    cout << "Gallons used: " << used << endl;
    cout << "Water charge: $" << amtDue << endl;
}   //end of displayBill function
```

Look For These
Symbols

Debugging

Discovery

EXERCISES

1) In this exercise, you create a simple payroll program using a **main()** function and four void functions.

   A. Figure 10-25 shows the partially completed IPO charts for the payroll program. Complete the Input and Output columns of the IPO charts for the four void functions named **getInput()**, **calcFedTaxes()**, **calcNetPay()**, and **displayInfo()**. The FWT (Federal Withholding Tax) rate is 20% of the weekly salary, and the FICA (Federal Insurance Contributions Act) rate is 8% of the weekly salary.

Figure 10-25

main() function

Input	Processing	Output
name weekly salary FWT rate (.2) FICA rate (.08)	Processing items: none Algorithm: 1. getInput(name, weekly salary) 2. calcFedTaxes(weekly salary, FWT rate, FICA rate, FWT, FICA) 3. calcNetPay(weekly salary, FWT, FICA, weekly net pay) 4. displayInfo(name, FWT, FICA, weekly net pay)	name FWT FICA weekly net pay

Figure 10-25 (continued)

`getInput()` **function**

Input	Processing	Output
	Processing items: none Algorithm: 1. enter the name and weekly salary	

`calcFedTaxes()` **function**

Input	Processing	Output
	Processing items: none Algorithm: 1. calculate the FWT by multiplying the weekly salary by the FWT rate 2. calculate the FICA by multiplying the weekly salary by the FICA rate	

`calcNetPay()` **function**

Input	Processing	Output
	Processing items: none Algorithm: 1. calculate the weekly net pay by subtracting the FWT and FICA from the weekly salary	

`displayInfo()` **function**

Input	Processing	Output
	Processing items: none Algorithm: 1. display the name, FWT, FICA, and weekly net pay	

B. If necessary, start Visual Studio .NET. Open the Ch10AppE01 Solution (Ch10AppE01 Solution.sln) file, which is contained in the Cpp\Chap10\ Ch10AppE01 Solution folder.

C. Use the IPO charts you completed in Step A to complete the program. Display the taxes and net pay with two decimal places.

D. Complete a desk-check table for the program, using Samuel Montez as the employee's name and 500 as the weekly salary, then using Barbara Jacks as the employee's name and 650 as the weekly salary.

E. Save and then build the solution.

F. Execute the program. Use the data from Step D to test the program.

G. When the program is working correctly, close the Output window, then use the File menu to close the solution.

2) In this exercise, you create a program that converts a Fahrenheit temperature to a Celsius temperature. The program uses a `main()` function and three void functions.

A. Figure 10-26 shows the partially completed IPO charts for the temperature program. Complete the IPO charts for the `main()` function and the three void functions named `getFahrenheit()`, `calcCelsius()`, and `displayCelsius()`.

Figure 10-26

`main()` function

Input	Processing	Output
Fahrenheit temperature	Processing items: none Algorithm: 1. getFahrenheit( ) 2. calcCelsius( ) 3. displayCelsius( )	Celsius temperature

`getFahrenheit()` function

Input	Processing	Output
	Processing items: none Algorithm: 1. enter the Fahrenheit temperature	

`calcCelsius()` function

Input	Processing	Output
	Processing items: none Algorithm: 1. calculate the Celsius temperature as follows: 5.0/9.0 * (Fahrenheit temperature − 32)	

`displayCelsius()` function

Input	Processing	Output
	Processing items: none Algorithm: 1. display the Celsius temperature	

B. If necessary, start Visual Studio .NET. Open the Ch10AppE02 Solution (Ch10AppE02 Solution.sln) file, which is contained in the Cpp\Chap10\ Ch10AppE02 Solution folder.

C. Use the IPO charts you completed in Step A to complete the program. Display the Celsius temperature with zero decimal places.

D. Complete a desk-check table for the program, using the following Fahrenheit temperatures: 32 degrees F and 212 degrees F.

E. Save and then build the solution.

F. Execute the program. Use the data from Step D to test the program.

G. When the program is working correctly, close the Output window, then use the File menu to close the solution.

3) In this exercise, you create a program that displays a 10% bonus. The program uses a **main()** function and three void functions.

A. Figure 10-27 shows the partially completed IPO charts for the bonus program. Complete the IPO charts for the **main()** function and the three void functions named **getSales()**, **calcBonus()**, and **displayBonus()**.

Figure 10-27

main() function

Input	Processing	Output
sales bonus rate (.1)	Processing items: none Algorithm: 1. getSales( ) 2. calcBonus( ) 3. displayBonus( )	bonus

getSales() function

Input	Processing	Output
	Processing items: Algorithm:	

calcBonus() function

Input	Processing	Output
	Processing items: Algorithm:	

Figure 10-27 (continued)

`displayBonus()` function

Input	Processing	Output
	Processing items:	
	Algorithm:	

B. If necessary, start Visual Studio .NET. Open the Ch10AppE03 Solution (Ch10AppE03 Solution.sln) file, which is contained in the Cpp\Chap10\ Ch10AppE03 Solution folder.

C. Use the IPO charts you completed in Step A to complete the program. Display the bonus amount with a dollar sign and two decimal places.

D. Complete a desk-check table for the program, using the following sale amounts: 24,500 and 134,780.

E. Save and then build the solution.

F. Execute the program. Use the data from Step D to test the program.

G. When the program is working correctly, close the Output window, then use the File menu to close the solution.

4) In this exercise, you modify the program you created in Lab 9.2 in Chapter 9. The modified program uses a void function to calculate the monthly car payments.

A. If necessary, start Visual Studio .NET. Open the Ch10AppE04 Solution (Ch10AppE04 Solution.sln) file, which is contained in the Cpp\Chap10\ Ch10AppE04 Solution folder.

B. Copy the instructions from the Ch9Lab2.cpp file into the Ch10AppE04.cpp window. The Ch9Lab2.cpp file is contained in the Cpp\Chap09\Ch9Lab2 Solution\Ch9Lab2 Project folder.

C. Change the filename in the first program comment to Ch10AppE04.cpp. If necessary, change the date in the second comment.

D. Modify the program so that it uses a void function, rather than a value-returning function, to calculate the monthly payments.

E. Save and then build the solution.

F. Execute the program. Enter 16000 as the car price, 3000 as the rebate, .08 as the credit union rate, .03 as the dealer rate, and 4 as the term. The program should display $317.37 as the credit union payment and $354.15 as the dealer payment.

G. When the program is working correctly, close the Output window, then use the File menu to close the solution.

5) In this exercise, you create a program that calculates the average of three test scores. The program uses two value-returning functions and two void functions.

A. Write the IPO charts for a program that contains four functions: `main()`, `getTestScores()`, `calcAverage()`, and `displayAverage()`. The `main()` function should call the void `getTestScores()` function, whose task is to get three test scores. (The test scores might contain a decimal place.) The `main()` function then should call the value-returning `calcAverage()` function to calculate and return the average of the three test scores. When the `calcAverage()` function has completed its task, the main() function should call the void **displayAverage()** function to display the average of the three scores on the screen.

B. If necessary, start Visual Studio .NET. Create a blank solution named Ch10AppE05 Solution. Save the solution in the Cpp\Chap10 folder.

C. Add an empty C++ Win32 Console Project to the solution. Name the project Ch10AppE05 Project.

D. Add a new C++ source file to the project. Name the source file Ch10AppE05.

E. Enter the appropriate C++ instructions into the source file. Use the IPO charts you created in Step A to code the program. Display the average with one decimal place.

F. Complete a desk-check table for the program, using the following two groups of test scores:

95.5, 83, 76

54, 89, 77

G. Save and then build the solution.

H. Execute the program. Use the data from Step F to test the program.

I. When the program is working correctly, close the Output window, then use the File menu to close the solution.

6) In this exercise, you modify the program you created in Lab 10.2 so that it uses two value-returning functions, rather than one void function, to calculate the gallons used and the water charge.

A. If necessary, start Visual Studio .NET. Create a blank solution named Ch10AppE06 Solution. Save the solution in the Cpp\Chap10 folder.

B. Add an empty C++ Win32 Console Project to the solution. Name the project Ch10AppE06 Project.

C. Add a new C++ source file to the project. Name the source file Ch10AppE06.

D. Copy the instructions from the Ch10Lab2.cpp file into the Ch10AppE06.cpp window. The Ch10Lab2.cpp file is contained in the Cpp\Chap10\Ch10Lab2 Solution\Ch10Lab2 Project folder. Change the filename in the first comment to Ch10AppE06.cpp.

E. Replace the **calcBill()** function with two value-returning functions named **calcGallons()** and **calcCharge()**. The **calcGallons()** function should calculate and return the number of gallons used. The **calcCharge()** function should calculate and return the water charge.

F. Save and then build the solution.

G. Execute the program. Enter Sue Jones as the name, 6000 as the current reading, and 3000 as the previous reading.

H. When the program is working correctly, close the Output window, then use the File menu to close the solution.

7) In this exercise, you create a simple payroll program that uses four value-returning functions named **main()**, **calcFwt()**, **calcFica()**, and **calcNetPay()**. The program also uses two void functions named **getInput()** and **displayInfo()**.

A. Figure 10-28 shows the partially completed IPO charts for the payroll program. Complete the IPO charts appropriately. The FWT (Federal Withholding Tax) rate is 20% of the weekly salary, and the FICA (Federal Insurance Contributions Act) rate is 8% of the weekly salary. Remember that only the **getInput()** and **displayInfo()** functions are void functions.

Figure 10-28

main() function

Input	Processing	Output
name weekly salary FWT rate (.2) FICA rate (.08)	Processing items: none Algorithm: 1. getInput( ) 2. FWT = calcFwt( ) 3. FICA = calcFica( ) 4. weekly net pay = calcNetPay( ) 5. displayInfo( )	name FWT FICA weekly net pay

getInput() function

Input	Processing	Output
	Processing items: none Algorithm:	

calcFwt() function

Input	Processing	Output
	Processing items: none Algorithm:	

calcFica() function

Input	Processing	Output
	Processing items: none Algorithm:	

calcNetPay() function

Input	Processing	Output
	Processing items: none Algorithm:	

Figure 10-28 (continued)

`displayInfo()` **function**

Input	Processing	Output
	Processing items: none Algorithm:	

    B. If necessary, start Visual Studio .NET. Open the Ch10AppE07 Solution (Ch10AppE07 Solution.sln) file, which is contained in the Cpp\Chap10\ Ch10AppE07 Solution folder.

    C. Use the IPO charts you completed in Step A to complete the program. Display the taxes and net pay with a dollar sign and two decimal places.

    D. Complete a desk-check table for the program, using Bonnie James as the employee's name and 350 as the weekly salary, then using Drew Carlisle as the employee's name and 700 as the weekly salary.

    E. Save and then build the solution.

    F. Execute the program. Use the data from Step D to test the program.

    G. When the program is working correctly, close the Output window, then use the File menu to close the solution.

8) In this exercise, you learn how to pass a named constant so that the receiving function cannot change the value passed to it.

    A. If necessary, start Visual Studio .NET. Open the Ch10AppE08 Solution (Ch10AppE08 Solution.sln) file, which is contained in the Cpp\Chap10\ Ch10AppE08 Solution folder.

The water bill program that you created in Lab 10.2 passed the value of the **RATE** named constant to the `calcBill()` function. The `calcBill()` function stored the value it received (.00175) in the `r` variable. Because the passed value was stored in a variable, the value could be changed by the `calcBill()` function. First verify that the `calcBill()` function can change the value stored in the `r` variable.

    B. Insert a blank line above the `gal = c - p;` statement in the `calcBill()` function. In the blank line, type `r = 1.5;`.

    C. Save and then build the solution. Execute the program. Enter your name as the customer name, 3000 as the current reading, and 2000 as the previous reading. Rather than displaying $1.75 as the water charge, the program displays $1500.00.

    D. Close the Command Prompt and Output windows.

    E. To prevent the `calcBill()` function from changing the water rate, you must indicate that the value being passed is a constant. Make the appropriate modifications to the `calcBill()` function's prototype and header.

    F. Save and then build the solution. The compiler displays an error message indicating that the contents of the `r` variable in the `r = 1.5;` statement is a constant.

    G. Delete the `r = 1.5;` statement from the `calcBill()` function.

H. Save and then build the solution. Execute the program. Enter your name as the customer name, 3000 as the current reading, and 2000 as the previous reading. The program correctly displays 1000 and $1.75 as the gallons used and water charge, respectively.

I. When the program is working correctly, close the Output window, then use the File menu to close the solution.

9) In this exercise, you debug a C++ program.

A. If necessary, start Visual Studio .NET. Open the Ch10AppE09 Solution (Ch10AppE09 Solution.sln) file, which is contained in the Cpp\Chap10\ Ch10AppE09 Solution folder.

B. The program should display an employee's gross pay, but it is not working correctly. Study the program's code, then build the solution.

C. Correct any errors in the program, then save and build the solution.

D. Execute the program. Test the program by entering 35 as the hours worked, and 10 as the pay rate. Close the Command Prompt window.

E. When the program is working correctly, close the Output window, then use the File menu to close the solution.

10) In this exercise, you debug a C++ program.

A. If necessary, start Visual Studio .NET. Open the Ch10AppE10 Solution (Ch10AppE10 Solution.sln) file, which is contained in the Cpp\Chap10\ Ch10AppE10 Solution folder.

B. The program should display a bonus amount, but it is not working correctly. Study the program's code, then build the solution.

C. Execute the program. Test the program by entering 10500 as the sales and .05 as the bonus rate. Notice that the program does not display the correct bonus amount. Close the Command Prompt window.

D. Correct the errors in the program, then save and build the solution. Execute the program again, using the data from Step C to test the program. Close the Command Prompt window.

E. When the program is working correctly, close the Output window, then use the File menu to close the solution.

Please visit the Testing Center at www.course.com/testingcenter for more practice on the topics covered in this chapter.

Arrays

Objectives

After completing this chapter, you will be able to:

- Declare and initialize a one-dimensional array

- Manipulate a one-dimensional array

- Pass a one-dimensional array to a function

- Use parallel one-dimensional arrays

- Declare and initialize a two-dimensional array

- Enter data into a two-dimensional array

Concept Lesson

Using Arrays

All of the variables you have used so far have been simple variables. A **simple variable**, also called a **scalar variable**, is one that is unrelated to any other variable in memory. In many programs, however, you may need to reserve a block of variables, referred to as an array.

An **array** is a group of variables that have the same name and data type and are related in some way. For example, each variable in the array might contain an inventory quantity, or each might contain a state name, or each might contain an employee record (name, Social Security number, pay rate, and so on). It may be helpful to picture an array as a group of small, adjacent boxes inside the computer's memory. You can write information to the boxes and you can read information from the boxes; you just cannot *see* the boxes.

Programmers use arrays to temporarily store related data in the internal memory of the computer. Examples of data stored in an array would be the federal withholding tax tables in a payroll program and a price list in an order entry program. Storing data in an array increases the efficiency of a program, because data can be both written to and read from internal memory much faster than it can be written to and read from a file on a disk. Additionally, after the data is entered into an array, which typically is done at the beginning of the program, the program can use the data as many times as desired. A payroll program, for example, can use the federal withholding tax tables stored in an array to calculate the amount of each employee's federal withholding tax.

The most commonly used arrays are one-dimensional and two-dimensional. You learn about one-dimensional arrays first, and then you learn about two-dimensional arrays. Arrays having more than two dimensions, which are used in scientific and engineering programs, are beyond the scope of this book.

One-Dimensional Arrays

You can visualize a **one-dimensional array** as a column of variables. Each variable in a one-dimensional array is identified by a unique number, called a **subscript**, which the computer assigns to the variable when the array is created. The subscript indicates the variable's position in the array. The first variable in a one-dimensional array is assigned a subscript of 0, the second a subscript of 1, and so on. You refer to each variable in an array by the array's name and the variable's subscript, which is specified in a set of square brackets immediately following the array name. For example, to refer to the first variable in a one-dimensional array named `prices`, you use `prices[0]`—read "`prices` sub zero." Similarly, to refer to the third variable in the `prices` array, you use `prices[2]`. Figure 11-1 illustrates this naming convention.

Figure 11-1: Names of the variables in a one-dimensional array named `prices`

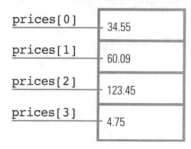

```
prices[0]     34.55
prices[1]     60.09
prices[2]     123.45
prices[3]     4.75
```

tip

The variables in an array are stored in consecutive memory locations in the computer's internal memory.

tip

It takes longer for the computer to access the information stored in a disk file because the computer must wait for the disk drive to locate the needed information and then read the information into internal memory.

tip

You also can visualize a one-dimensional array as a row of variables, rather than as a column of variables.

Before you can use an array, you first must declare (create) it. It also is a good programming practice to initialize the array. Figure 11-2 shows the syntax for declaring and initializing a one-dimensional array in C++. The figure also includes several examples of using the syntax to declare and initialize one-dimensional arrays.

Figure 11-2: Syntax and examples of declaring and initializing a one-dimensional array

Syntax
datatype arrayname[*numberOfElements*] =**{***initialValues***}**;

Examples and results

```
char letters[3] = {'A', 'B', 'C'};
```

declares and initializes a three-element `char` array named `letters`

```
string names[4] = {"Barb",
                    "Nancy",
                    "Bill",
                    "Samuel"};
```

declares and initializes a four-element `string` array named `names`

```
string states[4] = {"", "", "", ""};
            or
string states[4] = {""};
```

declares and initializes a four-element `string` array named `states`; each element is initialized to the empty string

```
int nums[3] = {0, 0, 0};
            or
int nums[3] = {0};
```

declares and initializes a three-element `int` array named `nums`; each element is initialized to 0

```
double prices[5] = {6.5};
```

declares and initializes a five-element `double` array named `prices`; the first element is initialized to 6.5, while the others are initialized to 0.0

tip

The = {*initialValues*} section of the syntax shown in Figure 11-2 is optional. Typically, optional items are enclosed in square brackets ([]) in the syntax. In this case, the square brackets were omitted so as not to confuse them with the square brackets that are required by the syntax.

In the syntax for declaring a one-dimensional array, *datatype* is the type of data the array variables, referred to as **elements**, will store. Recall that each of the elements (variables) in an array has the same data type. *Arrayname* is the name of the array; the name must follow the same rules as for variables. In the syntax, *numberOfElements* is an integer that specifies the size of the array—in other words, the number of elements you want in the array. To declare an array that contains 10 elements, for example, you enter the number 10 as the *numberOfElements*. Notice that you enclose the *numberOfElements* in square brackets ([]).

tip

As you learned in Chapter 4, the garbage found in uninitialized variables is the remains of what was last stored at the memory location that the variable now occupies.

As mentioned earlier, it is a good programming practice to initialize the elements (variables) in an array to ensure that they will not contain garbage. You can initialize the array elements at the same time you declare the array simply by entering one or more values, separated by commas, in the *initialValues* section of the syntax, as shown in Figure 11-2. Notice that you enclose the *initialValues* section in braces ({}).

Carefully study the examples shown in Figure 11-2. In the first example, the statement `char letters[3] = {'A', 'B', 'C'};` declares a `char` array named `letters` that contains three elements. It initializes the first element in the array to the letter A, the second element to B, and the third element to C, as shown in Figure 11-3.

Figure 11-3: Illustration of the `letters` array in memory

```
letters[0]                              A

letters[1]                              B

letters[2]                              C
```

Similar to the way each house on a street is identified by a unique address, each element in an array is identified by a unique number, called a **subscript**. The computer assigns the subscript to each of the array elements when it creates the array in memory. The first element in a one-dimensional array is assigned a subscript of 0, the next element is assigned a subscript of 1, and so on, as indicated in Figure 11-3.

You refer to each element in the array by the array's name and the element's subscript, which is specified in square brackets ([]) immediately following the name. For example, `letters[0]`—read "`letters` sub zero"—refers to the first element in the `letters` array, and `letters[2]` refers to the third element in the array.

As Figure 11-3 indicates, the three-element array will have subscripts of 0, 1, and 2. Notice that the last subscript is one number less than the number of elements in the array. This is because the first subscript is 0 rather than 1.

tip

Although Microsoft Visual C++ .NET initializes the uninitialized elements in an array (assuming you have provided at least one initial value), not all C++ compilers do.

The statement shown in the second example in Figure 11-2, `string names[4] = {"Barb", "Nancy", "Bill", "Samuel"};` declares a `string` array that contains four elements. The elements are named `names[0]`, `names[1]`, `names[2]`, and `names[3]`. The statement initializes the first element to the string "Barb", the second to "Nancy", and so on.

You can use either of the two statements shown in the third example in Figure 11-2 to declare a `string` array and initialize its elements to the empty string. The `string states[4] = {"", "", "", ""};` statement provides an initial value for each of the four array elements, whereas the `string states[4] = {""};` statement provides only one value. When you do not specify an initial value for each of the elements in a `string` array, the Microsoft Visual C++ .NET compiler stores the empty string in the uninitialized elements.

tip

If you inadvertently provide more values in the *initialValues* section than the number of array elements, the Microsoft Visual C++ .NET compiler displays a syntax error message when you compile the program. However, not all C++ compilers display a message when this error occurs. Rather, some compilers store the extra values in memory locations adjacent to, but not reserved for, the array.

The fourth example in Figure 11-2 shows two statements that you can use to declare an `int` array and initialize its elements to the number 0. The `int nums[3] = {0, 0, 0};` statement provides an initial value for each of the three array elements, whereas the `int nums[3] = {0};` statement provides only one value. When you do not provide an initial value for each of the elements in a numeric array, the Microsoft Visual C++ .NET compiler initializes the uninitialized array elements only if you provide at least one value in the *initialValues* section of the statement that declares the array. If you omit the *initialValues* section from the declaration statement—for example, if you use the `int nums[3];` statement to declare an array—the Microsoft Visual C++ .NET compiler does not automatically initialize the elements, so the array elements will contain garbage.

The last example in Figure 11-2, `double prices[5] = {6.5};`, declares a five-element **double** array named **prices**, and it initializes the first element to the number 6.5. Because the statement does not provide an initial value for the remaining elements in the array, the Microsoft Visual C++ .NET compiler initializes the remaining elements to 0.0.

After declaring and initializing an array, you can use various methods to store other data in the array.

Storing Data in a One-Dimensional Array

You can use a variety of ways to enter data into an array. The examples shown in Figure 11-4, for instance, can be used to enter data into the arrays declared in Figure 11-2.

Figure 11-4: Examples of entering data into a one-dimensional array

Examples and results

`letters[0] = 'X';`
`letters[1] = 'Y';`
`letters[2] = 'Z';`
 	
assigns the letters X, Y, and Z to the **letters** array, replacing the letters A, B, and C

`names[1] = "Helen";` assigns the name Helen to the second element in the **names** array, replacing the name Nancy

`int sub = 0;`
`while (sub < 4)`
`{`
`    states[sub] = "";`
`    sub = sub + 1;`
`}   //end while`
 	
assigns the empty string to each element in the **states** array; provides another means of initializing the array

`for (int x = 1; x <= 3; x = x + 1)`
`    nums[x - 1] = x * x;`
`//end for`
 	
assigns the squares of the numbers from 1 through 3 to the **nums** array, replacing the data stored in the array

`for (int x = 0; x < 5; x = x + 1)`
`{`
`    cout << "Enter price: ";`
`    cin >> prices[x];`
`}   //end for`
 	
stores the values entered by the user in the **prices** array, replacing the data stored in the array

The three assignment statements shown in the first example in Figure 11-4 assign the letters X, Y, and Z to the `letters` array, replacing the array's initial values (A, B, and C). In the second example, the `names[1] = "Helen";` statement assigns the name "Helen" to the second element in the `names` array, replacing the name "Nancy" that was stored in the element when the array was initialized.

You can use the code shown in the third example in Figure 11-4 to initialize each element in the `states` array to the empty string. The code shown in the fourth example assigns the squares of the numbers from one through three to the `nums` array, writing over the array's initial values. Notice that the number one must be subtracted from the value stored in the `x` variable when assigning the squares to the array; this is because the first array element has a subscript of zero rather than one. The code shown in the last example replaces the data stored in the `prices` array with the values entered by the user.

MINI-QUIZ

Mini-Quiz 1

1) Write a C++ statement that declares and initializes a 20-element `int` array named `quantities`. Initialize the array elements to the number zero.

2) Write a C++ statement that declares and initializes a 10-element `string` array named `items`. Initialize the array elements to the empty string.

3) The first subscript in a 25-element array is the number _____.

4) The last subscript in a 25-element array is the number _____.

5) Write a C++ statement that assigns the number seven to the fourth element in the `ages` array.

Now that you know how to declare, initialize, and enter data into a one-dimensional array, you learn how to manipulate an array in a program.

Manipulating One-Dimensional Arrays

The variables (elements) in an array can be used just like any other variables. For example, you can assign values to them, use them in calculations, display their contents, and so on. In the next several sections, you view sample functions that demonstrate how one-dimensional arrays are used in a program. More specifically, the functions will show you how to perform the following tasks using a one-dimensional array:

1. Display the contents of an array
2. Access an array element using its subscript
3. Search an array
4. Calculate the average of the data stored in a numeric array
5. Find the highest value stored in an array
6. Update the array elements
7. Sort the array elements

Begin by viewing a function that displays the contents of a one-dimensional array.

Displaying the Contents of a One-Dimensional Array

Many times, a function needs simply to display the contents of an array used by the program. The `displayMonths()` function shown in Figure 11-5 demonstrates how you can display the contents of an array named `months`.

tip

In most applications, the values stored in an array come from a file on the computer's disk and are assigned to the array using a loop. However, so that you can follow the code and its results more easily, most of the functions you view in this lesson initialize the array to the appropriate data when the array is created.

Figure 11-5: `displayMonths()` **function**

C++ instructions

```cpp
void displayMonths()
{
    //declare array
    string months[12] = {"JAN", "FEB", "MAR",
                         "APR", "MAY", "JUNE",
                         "JULY", "AUG", "SEPT",
                         "OCT", "NOV", "DEC"};

    //display contents of array
    for (int x = 0; x < 12; x = x + 1)
        cout << months[x] << endl;
    //end for
}   //end of displayMonths function
```

Results (displayed on the screen)

```
JAN
FEB
MAR
APR
MAY
JUNE
JULY
AUG
SEPT
OCT
NOV
DEC
```

tip
The loop in the function shown in Figure 11-5 stops when the x variable contains the number 12, which is one number more than the highest subscript in the array.

The `displayMonths()` function declares a 12-element, one-dimensional `string` array named `months`, and uses the names of the 12 months to initialize the array. The function then uses a loop to display the contents of each array element on the screen. The first time the loop is processed, the `x` variable in the `for` statement contains the number 0, and the statement `cout << months[x] << endl;` displays the contents of the `months[0]` element— JAN—on the screen. When the loop is processed the second time, the `x` variable contains the number 1, and the `cout << months[x] << endl;` statement displays the contents of the `months[1]` element—FEB—on the screen, and so on. The computer repeats the loop instructions for each element in the `months` array, beginning with the element whose subscript is 0 and ending with the element whose subscript is 11. The computer stops processing the loop when the value contained in the `x` variable is the number 12. As Figure 11-5 indicates, the function displays the names of the 12 months on the computer screen.

Next, you view a function that uses the array subscript to access the appropriate element in an array.

Using the Subscript to Access an Element in a One-Dimensional Array

Assume that XYZ Corporation pays its managers based on six different salary codes, 1 through 6. Each code corresponds to a different salary amount. You can use the function shown in Figure 11-6 to display the salary amount corresponding to the code entered by the user.

Figure 11-6: `displaySalary()` **function**

```
C++ instructions

void displaySalary()
{
    //declare variable and array
    int code = 0;
    int salaries[6] = {25000, 35000, 55000,
                        70000, 80200, 90500};

    //get code, then display corresponding salary
    cout << "Enter the salary code (1-6): ";
    cin >> code;
    if (code < 1 || code > 6)
        cout << "Invalid code" << endl;
    else
        cout << salaries[code - 1] << endl;
    //end if
}   //end of displaySalary function
```

Results (displayed on the screen)

55000   (assuming the user enters the number 3)
Invalid code (assuming the user enters the number 8)

tip

Before accessing an array element, a function always should verify that the subscript is valid—in other words, that it is in range. If the function uses a subscript that is not in range, the computer displays an error message and the function ends abruptly.

The `displaySalary()` function declares an `int` variable named `code` and a six-element, one-dimensional `int` array named `salaries`. The function uses six salary amounts to initialize the array. The salary amount for code 1 is stored in the `salaries[0]` element. Code 2's salary amount is stored in the `salaries[1]` element, and so on. Notice that the salary code is one number more than its corresponding array subscript.

Next, the `displaySalary()` function prompts the user to enter the salary code, and then stores the user's response in the `code` variable. The selection structure in the function determines whether the code entered by the user is invalid. In this case, invalid codes are numbers that are less than 1 or greater than 6. If the code is not valid, the function displays an appropriate message; otherwise, it displays the corresponding salary from the `salaries` array. Notice that, to access the correct element in the `salaries` array, the number 1 must be subtracted from the contents of the `code` variable. This is because the salary code entered by the user is one number more than its associated array subscript. As Figure 11-6 indicates, the function displays the number 55000 when the user enters a code of 3. When the user enters a code of 8, the program displays the message "Invalid code".

In the next section, you learn how to search a one-dimensional array.

Searching a One-Dimensional Array

Assume that the sales manager at Jacobsen Motors wants a function that allows him to determine the number of salespeople selling above a certain amount, which he will enter. To accomplish this task, the function will need to search the array, looking for values that are greater than the amount entered by the sales manager. The function shown in Figure 11-7 shows you how to search an array.

Figure 11-7: `searchArray()` **function**

```
C++ instructions

void searchArray()
{
    //declare variables and array
    int count = 0;        //counter variable
    int searchFor = 0;    //number to search for
    int sales[5] = {45000, 35000, 25000, 60000, 23000};

    //get number to search for
    cout << "Enter sales amount: ";
    cin >> searchFor;

    //search for numbers greater than searchFor value
    for (int x = 0; x < 5; x = x + 1)
        if (sales[x] > searchFor)
            count = count + 1;
        //end if
    //end for

    //display count
    cout << "Count: " << count << endl;
}   //end of searchArray function

Results (displayed on the screen)

Count: 2   (assuming the user enters the number 40000)
Count: 0   (assuming the user enters the number 60000)
```

The `searchArray()` function declares two `int` variables named `count` and `searchFor`. It also declares a five-element, one-dimensional `int` array named `sales` and uses five sales amounts to initialize the array. Next, the function prompts the user to enter a sales amount, and it stores the user's response in the `searchFor` variable. The loop in the function repeats its instructions for each element in the array, beginning with the element whose subscript is 0 and ending with the element whose subscript is 4.

The selection structure in the loop compares the contents of the current array element with the contents of the `searchFor` variable. If the array element contains a number that is greater than the number stored in the `searchFor` variable, the selection structure's true path adds the number 1 to the value stored in the `count` variable. In the `searchArray()` function, the `count` variable is used as a counter to keep track of the number of salespeople selling over the amount entered by the sales manager.

When the loop ends, which is when the `x` variable contains the number 5, the `cout << "Count: " << count << endl;` statement displays the contents of the `count` variable on the screen. As Figure 11-7 indicates, the function displays "Count: 2" if the sales manager enters 40000 as the sales amount, and it displays "Count: 0" if he enters 60000 as the sales amount.

Next, you learn how to calculate the average of the data stored in a numeric array.

Calculating the Average Amount Stored in a One-Dimensional Numeric Array

Professor Jeremiah wants a function that calculates and displays the average test score earned by his students on the final exam. The `displayAverage()` function shown in Figure 11-8 can be used to accomplish this task.

Figure 11-8: `displayAverage()` **function**

C++ instructions

```cpp
void displayAverage()
{
    //declare variables and array
    double total = 0.0;    //accumulator variable
    double avg = 0.0;      //average score
    double scores[5] = {98, 100, 56, 74, 35};


    //accumulate scores
    for (int x = 0; x < 5; x = x + 1)
        total = total + scores[x];
    //end for

    //calculate and display average
    avg = total / 5.0;
    cout << "Average: " << avg << endl;
}   //end of displayAverage function
```

Results (displayed on the screen)

Average: 72.6

The `displayAverage()` function declares two **double** variables named **total** and **avg**. It also declares a five-element, one-dimensional **double** array named **scores** and uses five test scores to initialize the array. The loop in the function adds the score contained in each array element to the **total** variable. In the `displayAverage()` function, the **total** variable is used as an accumulator to add up the test scores. When the loop ends, which is when the **x** variable contains the number 5, the `avg = total / 5.0;` statement calculates the average test score, and the `cout << "Average: " << avg << endl;` statement displays the average test score on the screen. As Figure 11-8 indicates, the program displays "Average: 72.6".

Mini-Quiz 2

1) Which of the following C++ statements displays the contents of the first element in the `items` array?
   a. `cout << items[0] << endl;`
   b. `cout << items[1] << endl;`
   c. `cout << items(0) << endl;`
   d. `cout << items(1) << endl;`

2) Which of the following C++ statements assigns the string "BX45" to the third element in a `string` array named `items`?
   a. `items[2] = "BX45";`
   b. `items[3] = "BX45";`
   c. `items[2] == "BX45";`
   d. `items(3) = "BX45";`

3) Assume that the `inventory` array is declared using the statement `int inventory[20] = {0};`. Also assume that the `x` variable, which keeps track of the array subscripts, is initialized to 0. Which of the following C++ `while` clauses tells the computer to process the loop instructions for each element in the array?
   a. `while (x > 20)`
   b. `while (x < 20)`
   c. `while (x >= 20)`
   d. `while (x <= 20)`

4) Assume that the `bonus` array is declared using the statement `double bonus[10] = {0.0};`. Also assume that the `x` variable, which keeps track of the array subscripts, is initialized to 0. Write the C++ code to display the contents of the `bonus` array.

In the next section, you learn how to determine the highest value stored in a one-dimensional array.

Determining the Highest Value Stored in a One-Dimensional Array

Sharon Johnson keeps track of the amount of money she spends each week on groceries. She would like a function that displays the highest amount spent in a week. Similar to the `searchArray()` function shown earlier in Figure 11-7, the `displayHighest()` function will need to search the array. However, rather than looking in the array for values that are greater than a specific amount, the function will look for the highest amount in the array, as shown in Figure 11-9.

Figure 11-9: `displayHighest()` **function**

C++ instructions

```cpp
void displayHighest()
{
    //declare array
    double dollars[5] = {25.6, 30.25, 50.0, 20.0, 25.45};
    //declare variables
    double high = dollars[0];   //store first array value
                                //in the high variable
    int x = 1;                  //begin search with the
                                //second element

    //search for highest value
    while (x < 5)
    {
        if (dollars[x] > high)
            high = dollars[x];
        //end if
        x = x + 1;
    }   //end while

    //display highest value
    cout << "Highest: " << high << endl;
}   //end of displayHighest function
```

Results (displayed on the screen)

Highest: 50

---

tip

Notice that the loop shown in Figure 11-9 searches the second through the last element in the `dollars` array. The first element is not included in the search because it is already stored in the `high` variable.

The `displayHighest()` function declares a five-element, one-dimensional `double` array named `dollars`, and it initializes the array to the amounts that Sharon spent on groceries during the last five weeks. The function also declares a `double` variable named `high` and an `int` variable named `x`. The `high` variable is used to keep track of the highest value stored in the `dollars` array and is initialized using the value stored in the first array element. The `x` variable is used to keep track of the array subscripts. Notice that the function initializes the `x` variable to the number 1, which is the subscript corresponding to the second element in the `dollars` array.

The first time the loop in the `displayHighest()` function is processed, the selection structure within the loop compares the value stored in the second array element—`dollars [1]`—with the value stored in the `high` variable. (Recall that the `high` variable contains the same value as the first array element at this point.) If the value stored in the second array element is greater than the value stored in the `high` variable, then the statement `high = dollars[x];` assigns the array element value to the `high` variable. The statement `x = x + 1;` then adds the number 1 to the `x` variable, giving 2. The next time the loop is processed, the selection structure compares the value stored in the third array element—`dollars[2]`—with the value stored in the `high` variable, and so on.

When the loop ends, which is when the `x` variable contains the number 5, the `displayHighest()` function displays the contents of the `high` variable on the screen. As Figure 11-9 indicates, the function displays "Highest: 50".

Next, you learn how to update the values stored in a one-dimensional array.

Updating the Values Stored in a One-Dimensional Array

The sales manager at Jillian Company wants a function that allows her to increase the price of each item the company sells. She also wants the function to display each item's new price on the screen. The **updateArray()** function shown in Figure 11-10 will perform these tasks.

Figure 11-10: updateArray() **function**

C++ instructions

```
void updateArray()
{
     //declare variable and array
     double increase = 0.0;   //stores increase amount
     double prices[4] = {150.35, 35.6, 75.75, 25.3};

     //get increase amount
     cout << "Enter increase: ";
     cin >> increase;

     cout << setiosflags(ios::fixed)
          << setprecision(2);

     //update each array element
     for (int x = 0; x < 4; x = x + 1)
     {
         prices[x] = prices[x] + increase;
         cout << "New price: $" << prices[x] << endl;
     }    //end for
}   //end of updateArray function
```

Results (displayed on the screen)

New price: $155.35   (assuming the user enters the number 5)
New price: $40.60
New price: $80.75
New price: $30.30

The **updateArray()** function declares a **double** variable named **increase**. It also declares a four-element, one-dimensional **double** array named **prices** and uses four **double** numbers to initialize the array. Next, the function prompts the user to enter the amount of the increase and stores the user's response in the **increase** variable. The loop in the function then repeats its instructions for each element in the **prices** array.

The first instruction in the loop, **prices[x] = prices[x] + increase;**, updates the contents of the current array element by adding the increase amount to it. The **cout << "New price: $" << prices[x] << endl;** statement then displays the updated contents on the screen. The loop ends when the **x** variable contains the number 4. Figure 11-10 shows the values displayed by the function when the user enters the number 5 as the increase amount. Notice that each new price is $5 more than the corresponding original price.

Next, you learn how to sort the data stored in a one-dimensional array.

Sorting the Data Stored in a One-Dimensional Array

At times, a function might need to arrange the contents of an array in either ascending or descending order. Arranging data in a specific order is called **sorting**. When an array is sorted in ascending order, the first element in the array contains the smallest value, and the last element contains the largest value. When an array is sorted in descending order, on the other hand, the first element contains the largest value, and the last element contains the smallest value. Over the years, many different sorting algorithms have been developed. In this lesson, you learn how to use the bubble sort algorithm.

The bubble sort provides a quick and easy way to sort the items stored in an array, as long as the number of items is relatively small—for example, fewer than 50. The bubble sort algorithm works by comparing adjacent array elements and interchanging (swapping) the ones that are out of order. The algorithm continues comparing and swapping until the data in the array is sorted. To illustrate the logic of a bubble sort, manually sort the numbers 9, 8, and 7 in ascending order. Assume that the three numbers are stored in an array named `num`. Figure 11-11 shows the `num` array values before, during, and after the bubble sort.

Figure 11-11: Array values before, during, and after the bubble sort

	Comparison	Swap	Result/Comparison	Swap	Result
Pass 1:					
num[0]	9⌐	Yes	8		8
num[1]	8⌐		9⌐	Yes	7
num[2]	7		7⌐		9
Pass 2:					
num[0]	8⌐	Yes	7		7
num[1]	7⌐		8⌐	No	8
num[2]	9		9⌐		9

The bubble sort algorithm begins by comparing the first value in the array with the second value. If the first value is less than or equal to the second value, then no swap is made. However, if the first value is greater than the second value, then both values are interchanged. In this case, the first value (9) is greater than the second value (8), so the values are swapped as shown in the Result/Comparison column in Figure 11-11.

After comparing the first value in the array with the second, the algorithm then compares the second value with the third. In this case, 9 is greater than 7, so the two values are swapped as shown in the Result column in Figure 11-11.

At this point, the algorithm has completed its first time through the entire array— referred to as a pass. Notice that, at the end of the first pass, the largest value (9) is stored in the last position of the array. The bubble sort gets its name from the fact that as the larger values drop to the bottom of the array, the smaller values rise, like bubbles, to the top.

Now observe what the algorithm does on its second pass through the array. The bubble sort algorithm begins the second pass by comparing the first value in the array to the second value. In this case, 8 is greater than 7, so the two values are interchanged as shown in Figure 11-11. Then the second value is compared to the third. In this case, 8 is not greater than 9, so no swap is made. Notice that at the end of the second pass, the data in the array is sorted.

Figure 11-12 shows the `sortAndDisplay()` function, which uses the bubble sort to sort the contents of an array in ascending order. The function then displays the contents of the sorted array on the screen.

Figure 11-12: `sortAndDisplay()` **function**

C++ instructions

```cpp
void sortAndDisplay()
{
   //declare array
   int num[4] = {3, 6, 2, 5};

   //declare variables used in bubble sort code
   int x        = 0;    //keeps track of subscripts
   int temp     = 0;    //variable used for swapping
   int maxSub   = 3;    //maximum subscript
   int lastSwap = 0;    //indicates position of last swap
   char swap    = 'Y';  //indicates whether a swap was made

   //repeat loop instructions as long as a swap was made
   while (swap == 'Y')
   {
      swap = 'N';   //assume that no swaps are necessary
      x = 0;        //begin comparing with first array
                    //element

      //compare adjacent array elements to determine
      //whether a swap is necessary
      while (x < maxSub)
      {
         if (num[x] > num[x + 1])
         {
            //a swap is necessary
            temp = num[x];
            num[x] = num[x + 1];
            num[x + 1] = temp;
            swap = 'Y';
            lastSwap = x;
         } //end if
         x = x + 1;   //increment subscript
      } //end while

      maxSub = lastSwap;  //reset maximum subscript
   } //end while

   //display sorted array
   x = 0;
   while (x < 4)
   {
      cout << num[x] << endl;
      x = x + 1;
   } //end while
}  //end of sortAndDisplay function
```

code for the bubble sort algorithm

Results (displayed on the screen)

```
2
3
5
6
```

You can better understand the bubble sort algorithm by desk-checking the code shown in Figure 11-12. Figure 11-13 shows the completed desk-check tables.

Figure 11-13: Completed desk-check tables for the code shown in Figure 11-12

num[0]	num[1]	num[2]	num[3]
~~3~~ 2	~~6~~ ~~2~~ 3	~~2~~ ~~6~~ 5	~~5~~ 6

x	temp	maxSub	lastSwap	swap
~~0~~ ~~0~~ ~~1~~ 2 ~~3~~ ~~0~~ ~~1~~ 2 ~~0~~	~~0~~ ~~6~~ ~~6~~ 3	~~3~~ ~~2~~ 0	~~0~~ ~~1~~ ~~2~~ 0	~~Y~~ ~~N~~ ~~Y~~ ~~Y~~ ~~N~~ ~~Y~~ N
~~0~~ ~~1~~ 2 ~~3~~ 4				

result of bubble sort code

result of display code

Mini-Quiz 3

1) Write an `if` clause that determines whether the value stored in the current array element is less than the value stored in the `low` variable. The name of the array is `prices`. Use `x` as the name of the variable that keeps track of the array subscripts.

2) Write a `while` loop that subtracts the number 3 from each of the elements in an array named `numbers`. The `numbers` array has 50 elements. Use `x` as the name of the variable that keeps track of the array subscripts. You can assume that the `x` variable is initialized to 0.

3) The process of arranging data in alphabetical or numerical order is called _____.

Next, you learn how to pass a one-dimensional array to a function.

Passing a One-Dimensional Array to a Function

Figure 11-14 shows a program that passes a one-dimensional array named `prices` to a function named `displayArray()`. The `displayArray()` function displays the contents of the array on the screen.

Figure 11-14: Program showing a one-dimensional array passed to a function

C++ instructions

```cpp
#include <iostream>

using std::cout;
using std::cin;
using std::endl;

//function prototype
void displayArray(double []);

int main()
{
    //declare array
    double prices[4] = {56.76, 78.34, 23.12, 5.34};

    //display the contents of the array
    displayArray(prices);

    return 0;
}   //end of main function

//*****function definitions*****
void displayArray(double dollars[])
{
    for (int x = 0; x < 4; x = x + 1)
        cout << dollars[x] << endl;
    //end for
}   //end of displayArray function
```

Results (displayed on the screen)

```
56.76
78.34
23.12
5.34
```

The **main()** function in the program shown in Figure 11-14 declares and initializes a one-dimensional **double** array named **prices**. It then calls the **displayArray()** function to display the contents of the array on the screen.

Study closely the **displayArray()** function prototype, function call, and function header, which are shaded in Figure 11-14. As you know, data can be passed to a function either *by value* or *by reference*. Recall that scalar variables in C++ are passed automatically *by value*. To pass a scalar variable *by reference* in C++, you need to include the address-of (&) operator before the formal parameter's name in the receiving function's header. You also need to include the & operator in the receiving function's prototype.

Unlike scalar variables, arrays in C++ are automatically passed *by reference* rather than *by value*. When you pass an array, the computer passes the address of only the first array element to the receiving function. Because array elements are stored in contiguous locations in memory, the receiving function needs to know only where the first element is located in memory. From there, the function can easily locate the other elements.

tip

Passing an array *by reference* is more efficient than passing it *by value*. Because many arrays are large, passing *by value* would consume a great deal of memory and time since the computer would need to duplicate the array in the receiving function's formal parameter.

Because arrays are passed automatically *by reference*, you do not include the address-of (&) operator before the formal parameter's name in the function header, as you do when passing scalar variables *by reference*. You also do not include the & operator in the function prototype. To pass an array to a function, you need simply to enter the data type and name of the formal parameter, followed by an empty set of square brackets, in the receiving function's header. You also enter the data type and an empty set of square brackets in the receiving function's prototype. As Figure 11-14 shows, you can pass the `prices` array to the `displayArray()` function by entering `double dollars[]` in the `displayArray()` function header and entering `double []` in the `displayArray()` function prototype.

Next, you learn about parallel one-dimensional arrays.

Using Parallel One-Dimensional Arrays

Takoda Tapahe owns a small gift shop named Takoda Treasures. She has asked you to create a program that displays the price of the item whose product ID she enters. Figure 11-15 shows a portion of the gift shop's price list.

Figure 11-15: A portion of the gift shop's price list

Product ID	Price
BX35	13
CR20	10
FE15	12
KW10	24
MM67	4

Recall that all of the variables in an array have the same data type. So how can you store a price list, which includes a string (the product ID) and a number (the price), in an array? One way of doing so is to use two one-dimensional arrays: a `string` array to store the product IDs and an `int` array to store the prices. Both arrays are illustrated in Figure 11-16.

Figure 11-16: Illustration of a price list stored in two one-dimensional arrays

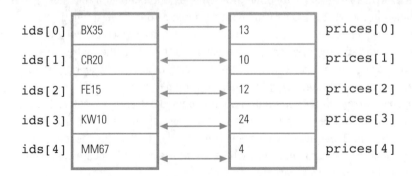

The arrays shown in Figure 11-16 are referred to as parallel arrays. **Parallel arrays** are two or more arrays whose elements are related by their position—in other words, by their subscript—in the arrays. The `ids` and `prices` arrays shown in Figure 11-16 are parallel arrays because each element in the `ids` array corresponds to the element located in the same position in the `prices` array. For example, the first element in the `ids` array corresponds to the first element in the `prices` array. In other words, the item whose product ID is BX35 (`ids[0]`) has a price of $13 (`prices[0]`). Likewise, the second elements in both arrays—the elements with a subscript of 1—also are related; the item whose product ID is CR20 (`ids[1]`) has a price of $10 (`prices[1]`). The same relationship is true for the remaining elements in both arrays. If you want to know an item's price, you simply locate the item's ID in the `ids` array and then view its corresponding element in the `prices` array. Figure 11-17 shows a program that Takoda can use to display the price of an item based on the product ID she enters.

Figure 11-17: Takoda Treasures program using parallel arrays

```
#include <iostream>
#include <string>
#include <algorithm>

using std::cout;
using std::cin;
using std::endl;
using std::string;

int main()
{
    //declare variable and arrays
    string searchForId = "";
    string ids[5] = {"BX35", "CR20", "FE15", "KW10", "MM67"};
    int prices[5] = {13, 10, 12, 24, 4};

    //get ID to search for, then convert to uppercase
    cout << "Enter ID (X to exit): ";
    getline(cin, searchForId);
    transform(searchForId.begin(), searchForId.end(),
        searchForId.begin(), toupper);

    while (searchForId != "X")
    {
        //locate position of product ID in the ids array
        int y = 0;     //keeps track of array subscripts
        while (y < 5 && ids[y] != searchForId)
            y = y + 1;
        //end while

        //if ID was found, display price from prices array
        //otherwise, display error message
        if (y < 5)
            cout << "Price: $" << prices[y] << endl;
        else
            cout << "Product ID is not valid." << endl;
        //end if

        //get ID to search for, then convert to uppercase
        cout << "Enter ID (X to exit): ";
```

parallel arrays

Figure 11-17: Takoda Treasures program using parallel arrays (continued)

C++ instructions

```cpp
        getline(cin, searchForId);
        transform(searchForId.begin(), searchForId.end(),
           searchForId.begin(), toupper);
    }   //end while

    return 0;
}   //end of main function
```

Results (displayed on the screen)

Price: $12 (assuming the user enters FE15 as the product ID)
Product ID is not valid. (assuming the user enters XX89 as the product ID)

The program shown in Figure 11-17 declares a `string` variable named `searchForId` and two parallel one-dimensional arrays: a five-element `string` array named `ids` and a five-element `int` array named `prices`. The program stores each item's ID in the `ids` array and stores each item's price in the corresponding location in the `prices` array. The program then prompts the user to enter a product ID, and it stores the user's response in the `searchForId` variable. The `transform()` function is used to convert the contents of the `searchForId` variable to uppercase, to match the case of the product IDs stored in the `ids` array.

The computer processes the instructions contained in the program's outer loop as long as the user does not enter the letter X (in any case) as the product ID. The first instruction in the body of the outer loop declares and initializes an `int` variable named `y` to keep track of the array subscripts. The second instruction is the beginning of a nested loop.

The nested loop continues to add the number 1 to the `y` variable as long as the `y` variable contains a value that is less than 5 and, at the same time, the product ID has not been located in the `ids` array. The nested loop stops when either of the following conditions is true: the `y` variable contains the number 5 (which indicates that the loop reached the end of the array without finding the product ID) or the product ID is located in the array.

After the nested loop completes its processing, the `if` statement in the program compares the number stored in the `y` variable with the number 5. If the `y` variable contains a number that is less than 5, it indicates that the loop stopped processing because the product ID was located in the `ids` array. In that case, the statement `cout << "Price: $" << prices[y] << endl;` displays the corresponding price from the `prices` array. However, if the `y` variable contains a number that is not less than 5, it indicates that the loop stopped processing because it reached the end of the `ids` array without finding the product ID. In that case, the message "Product ID is not valid." is displayed.

The program then prompts the user to enter another product ID, and it stores the user's response in the `searchForId` variable. The `transform()` function is used to convert the contents of the `searchForId` variable to uppercase, to match the case of the product IDs stored in the `ids` array. Processing then continues with the `while (searchForId != "X")` clause. This clause compares the contents of the `searchForId` variable with the letter X to determine whether the instructions in the outer loop should be processed again.

As Figure 11-17 indicates, the Takoda Treasures program displays the message "Price: $12" when the user enters FE15 as the product ID. The program displays the message "Product ID is not valid." when the user enters XX89 as the product ID.

MINI-QUIZ

Mini-Quiz 4

1) Parallel arrays are arrays whose elements are related by their _____ in the arrays.

2) Assume that the `employNumber` and `employName` arrays are parallel arrays. If an employee's number is located in `employNumber[3]`, then his or her name is located in _____.

3) Parallel arrays must have the same data type.
    a. True
    b. False

Recall that, in addition to using one-dimensional arrays, some programs also utilize two-dimensional arrays. You learn how to create and manipulate two-dimensional arrays in the remainder of this lesson.

Two-Dimensional Arrays

As you learned earlier, you can visualize a one-dimensional array as a column of variables. A **two-dimensional array**, however, resembles a table in that the variables are in rows and columns.

Recall that, before you can use an array, you first must declare (create) it. Also recall that it is a good programming practice to initialize an array when it is created. Figure 11-18 shows the syntax for declaring and initializing a two-dimensional array in C++. The figure also includes several examples of using the syntax to declare and initialize two-dimensional arrays.

Figure 11-18: Syntax and examples of declaring and initializing a two-dimensional array

Syntax
datatype arrayname[*numberOfRows*][*numberOfColumns*] = {{*initialValues*}, {*initialValues*},...{*initialValues*}};

Examples and results

```
char grades[3][2] =
    {{'A', 'A'}, {'B', 'C'}, {'D', 'B'}};
```

declares and initializes a three-row, two-column `char` array named `grades`

```
string names[2][2] =
    {{"Bob", "Sue"}, {"Bill", "Tom"}};
```

declares and initializes a two-row, two-column `string` array named `names`

```
int nums[2][4] = {0};
    or
int nums[2][4] = {{0}, {0}};
    or
int nums[2][4] = {{0,0,0,0}, {0,0,0,0}};
```

declares and initializes a two-row, four-column `int` array named `nums`; each element is initialized to 0

Figure 11-18: Syntax and examples of declaring and initializing a two-dimensional array (continued)

Examples and results
```double prices[5][6] = {2.0};```   declares a five-row, six-column **double** array named **prices**; the first element is initialized to 2.0, while the others are initialized to 0.0

In the syntax for declaring a two-dimensional array, *arrayname* is the name of the array, and *datatype* is the type of data the array variables will store. Recall that each of the variables (elements) in an array has the same data type. The *numberOfRows* and *numberOfColumns* sections in the syntax are integers that specify the number of rows and columns, respectively, in the array. To declare an array that contains three rows and two columns, for example, you enter the number 3 as the *numberOfRows* and enter the number 2 as the *numberOfColumns*, as shown in the first example in Figure 11-18. Notice that the *numberOfRows* is enclosed in square brackets ([]) in the syntax, and so is the *numberOfColumns*.

As mentioned earlier, it is a good programming practice to initialize the elements (variables) in an array to ensure that they will not contain garbage. You can initialize the array elements in a two-dimensional array by entering a separate *initialValues* section, enclosed in braces, for each row in the array. If the array has two rows, for example, then the statement that declares and initializes the array can have a maximum of two *initialValues* sections. If the array has five rows, then the declaration statement can have a maximum of five *initialValues* sections.

Within the individual *initialValues* sections, you enter one or more values separated by commas. The maximum number of values you enter corresponds to the maximum number of columns in the array. If the array contains 10 columns, for example, then you can include up to 10 values in each *initialValues* section.

In addition to the set of braces that surrounds each individual *initialValues* section, notice in the syntax that a set of braces also surrounds all of the *initialValues* sections.

Carefully study the examples shown in Figure 11-18. In the first example, the **char grades[3][2] = {{'A', 'A'}, {'B', 'C'}, {'D', 'B'}};** statement declares a **char** array named **grades** that contains three rows and two columns. The statement initializes the first row in the array to the grades A and A, the second row to the grades B and C, and the third row to the grades D an B, as shown in Figure 11-19.

Figure 11-19: Illustration of the two-dimensional **grades** array in memory

grades[0][0]	A	A	grades[0][1]
grades[1][0]	B	C	grades[1][1]
grades[2][0]	D	B	grades[2][1]

As Figure 11-19 shows, the first row in a two-dimensional array is row 0, and the first column is column 0. You refer to each element in a two-dimensional array by the array's name followed by the row subscript (in square brackets) and the column subscript (also in square brackets). For example, `grades[0][0]`—read "`grades` sub zero zero"—refers to the element located in row 0, column 0 in the `grades` array. Similarly, `grades[2][1]` refers to the element located in row 2, column 1 in the array.

The `string names[2][2] = {{"Bob", "Sue"}, {"Bill", "Tom"}};` statement shown in Figure 11-18 creates a `string` array having two rows and two columns. The statement uses the names "Bob" and "Sue" to initialize the first row in the array, and the names "Bill" and "Tom" to initialize the second row.

You can use any of the statements shown in Example 3 in Figure 11-18 to declare and initialize (to 0) a two-dimensional `int` array named **nums**. Recall that when you don't provide an initial value for each of the elements in a numeric array, Microsoft Visual C++ .NET stores the number 0 in the uninitialized elements.

The last example shown in Figure 11-18 declares and initializes a two-dimensional `double` array named **prices**. The element located in the first row, first column of the array will be initialized to 2.0; the remaining elements will be initialized to 0.0.

After declaring a two-dimensional array, you can use various methods to store data in the array.

Storing Data in a Two-Dimensional Array

You can use a variety of ways to enter data into a two-dimensional array. The examples shown in Figure 11-20, for instance, can be used to enter data into a two-dimensional array. Notice that you use two loops to access every element in a two-dimensional array. One of the loops keeps track of the row subscript, while the other keeps track of the column subscript.

Figure 11-20: Examples of entering data into a two-dimensional array

Examples and results

```
int scores[4][2] = {0};

for (int rows = 0; rows < 4; rows = rows + 1)
   for (int cols = 0; cols < 2; cols = cols + 1)
   {
      cout << "Enter the score: ";
      cin >> scores[rows][cols];
   } //end for
//end for
```

assigns to the **scores** array the values entered by the user at the keyboard

Figure 11-20: Examples of entering data into a two-dimensional array (continued)

Examples and results

```cpp
int average[10][2] = {0};

int rows = 0;
int cols = 0;
double num1 = 0.0;
double num2 = 0.0;
while (rows < 10)
{
    while (cols < 2)
    {
        cout << "First number: ";
        cin >> num1;
        cout << "Second number: ";
        cin >> num2;
        averages[rows][cols] = (num1 + num2) / 2.0;
        cols = cols + 1;
    }   //end while
    rows = rows + 1;
    cols = 0;
}   //end while
```

assigns to the **averages** array the averages of the numbers entered by the user at the keyboard

The code shown in the first example in Figure 11-20 uses two **for** statements to assign values to the two-dimensional **scores** array, which has four rows and two columns. The code shown in the second example uses two **while** statements to assign values to the two-dimensional **averages** array, which has 10 rows and two columns.

MINI-QUIZ

Mini-Quiz 5

1) Write a C++ statement that declares a four-row, two-column **int** array named **quantities**.

2) A five-row, four-column array has a total of _____ elements.

3) A six-row, three-column array has row subscripts of _____ through _____, and column subscripts of _____ through _____.

4) Write a C++ assignment statement that stores the number 5 in the second row, third column of a two-dimensional array named **quantities**.

You now have completed Chapter 11's Concept lesson. You can either take a break or complete the end-of-lesson questions and exercises before moving on to the Application lesson.

SUMMARY

An array is a group of variables that have the same name and data type and are related in some way. The most commonly used arrays in programs are one-dimensional and two-dimensional. You can visualize a one-dimensional array as a column of variables. A two-dimensional array, on the other hand, resembles a table in that it has rows and columns. Programmers use arrays to temporarily store related data in the internal memory of the computer. By doing so, a programmer can increase the efficiency of a program, because data can be both written to and read from internal memory much faster than it can be written to and read from a file on a disk. Additionally, after the data is entered into an array, which typically is done at the beginning of the program, the program can use the data as many times as desired.

You must declare an array before you can use it. After declaring an array, you can use a variety of ways to enter data into the array.

Each of the array elements in a one-dimensional array is assigned a unique number, called a subscript. The first element is assigned a subscript of 0, the next element is assigned a subscript of 1, and so on. Because the first array subscript is 0, the last subscript in an array is always one number less than the number of elements. You refer to each element in a one-dimensional array by the array's name and the element's subscript, which is specified in square brackets immediately following the name.

Parallel arrays are two or more arrays whose elements are related by their subscript (or position) in the arrays.

The syntax for creating and initializing a two-dimensional array is similar to the syntax for creating and initializing a one-dimensional array. The two-dimensional array syntax, however, requires the programmer to provide both the number of rows and the number of columns in the array, rather than just the number of array elements.

Just as each element in a one-dimensional array is identified by a unique subscript, each element in a two-dimensional array is identified by a unique combination of two subscripts. The first subscript represents the element's row location in the array, and the second represents its column location. The computer assigns the subscripts to the elements when the array is created in memory. The first row subscript in a two-dimensional array is 0. The first column subscript also is 0.

You need to use two loops to access every element in a two-dimensional array. One of the loops keeps track of the row subscript, while the other keeps track of the column subscript.

ANSWERS TO MINI-QUIZZES

Mini-Quiz 1

1) `int quantities[20] = {0};`
2) `string items[10] = {""};`
3) 0
4) 24
5) `ages[3] = 7;`

Mini-Quiz 2

1) a. `cout << items[0] << endl;`

2) a. `items[2] = "BX45";`

3) b. `while (x < 20)`

4)
```
while (x < 10)
{
    cout << bonus[x] << endl;
    x = x + 1;
} //end while
```

Mini-Quiz 3

1) `if (prices[x] < low)`

2)
```
while (x < 50)
{
    numbers[x] = numbers[x] - 3;
    x = x + 1;
} //end while
```

3) `sorting`

Mini-Quiz 4

1) subscripts (or position)

2) `employName[3]`

3) b. False

Mini-Quiz 5

1) `int quantities[4][2] = {0};`

2) 20

3) 0, 5, 0, 2

4) `quantities[1][2] = 5;`

QUESTIONS

1) Which of the following is false?

    A. The elements in an array are related in some way.

    B. All of the elements in an array have the same data type.

    C. All of the elements in a one-dimensional array have the same subscript.

    D. The first element in a one-dimensional array has a subscript of 0.

2) Elements in a one-dimensional array are identified by a unique _____.

    A. combination of two subscripts

    B. data type

    C. subscript

    D. symbol

3) Which of the following statements declares a five-element array named `population`?

A. `int population[4] = {0};`

B. `int population[5] = {0};`

C. `int population[5] = 0`

D. `int population[5] = {0}`

Use the `sales` array shown in Figure 11-21 to answer Questions 4 through 8.

Figure 11-21

10000	12000	900	500	20000

4) The `sales[3] = sales[3] + 10;` statement will _____.

A. replace the 500 amount with 10

B. replace the 500 amount with 510

C. replace the 900 amount with 910

D. result in an error

5) The `sales[4] = sales[4 - 2];` statement will _____.

A. replace the 20000 amount with 900

B. replace the 20000 amount with 19998

C. replace the 500 amount with 12000

D. result in an error

6) The `cout << sales[0] + sales[1] << endl;` statement will _____.

A. display 22000

B. display 10000 + 12000

C. display `sales[0] + sales[1]`

D. result in an error

7) Which of the following `if` clauses can be used to verify that the array subscript, named `x`, is valid for the `sales` array?

A. `if (sales[x] >= 0 && sales[x] < 4)`

B. `if (sales[x] >= 0 && sales[x] <= 4)`

C. `if (x >= 0 && x < 4)`

D. `if (x >= 0 && x <= 4)`

8) Which of the following will correctly add 100 to each variable in the `sales` array? (You can assume that the `x` variable is initialized to 0.)

A.
```
while (x <= 4)
     x = x + 100;
//end while
```

B. while (x <= 4)
```
    {
        sales = sales + 100;
        x = x + 1;
    } //end while
```
C. while (sales < 5)
```
    {
        sales[x] = sales[x] + 100;
    } //end while
```
D. while (x <= 4)
```
    {
        sales[x] = sales[x] + 100;
        x = x + 1;
    } //end while
```

Use the **nums** array shown in Figure 11-22 to answer Questions 9 through 13. The **x** and **total** variables are **int** variables and are initialized to 0. The **avg** variable is a **double** variable and is initialized to 0.0.

Figure 11-22

10	5	7	2

9) Which of the following correctly calculates and displays the average of the **nums** array elements?

A. while (x < 4)
```
    {
        nums[x] = total + total;
        x = x + 1;
    }    //end while
    avg = double(total) / double(x);
    cout << avg << endl;
```
B. while (x < 4)
```
    {
        total = total + nums[x];
        x = x + 1;
    }    //end while
    avg = double(total) / double(x);
    cout << avg << endl;
```

```
C. while (x < 4)
   {
        total = total + nums[x];
        x = x + 1;
   }    //end while
   avg = double(total) / double(x) - 1.0;
   cout << avg << endl;
D. while (x < 4)
   {
        total = total + nums[x];
        x = x + 1;
   }    //end while
   avg = double(total) / double(x - 1);
   cout << avg << endl;
```

10) The code in Question 9's answer A displays _____.

    A. 0

    B. 5

    C. 6

    D. 8

11) The code in Question 9's answer B displays _____.

    A. 0

    B. 5

    C. 6

    D. 8

12) The code in Question 9's answer C displays _____.

    A. 0

    B. 5

    C. 6

    D. 8

13) The code in Question 9's answer D displays _____.

    A. 0

    B. 5

    C. 6

    D. 8

14) The first element in a two-dimensional array has a row subscript of _____ and a column subscript of _____.

    A. 0, 0

    B. 0, 1

    C. 1, 0

    D. 1, 1

15) The individual elements in a two-dimensional array are identified by a unique
_____.

A. combination of two subscripts

B. data type

C. order

D. subscript

16) Which of the following statements creates a two-dimensional `int` array named
`sales` that contains three rows and four columns?

A. `int sales[3, 4] = {0};`

B. `int sales[4, 3] = {0};`

C. `int sales[3][4] = {0};`

D. `int sales[4][3] = {0};`

Use the **sales** array shown in Figure 11-23 to answer Questions 17 through 20.

Figure 11-23

10000	12000	900	500	20000
350	600	700	800	100

17) The statement `sales[1][3] = sales[1][3] + 10;` will
_____.

A. replace the 900 amount with 910

B. replace the 500 amount with 510

C. replace the 700 amount with 710

D. replace the 800 amount with 810

18) The statement `sales[0][4] = sales[0][4 - 2];` will _____.

A. replace the 20000 amount with 900

B. replace the 20000 amount with 19998

C. replace the 20000 amount with 19100

D. result in an error

19) The statement `cout << sales[0][3] + sales[1][3] << endl;`
will _____.

A. display 1300

B. display 1600

C. display `sales[0][3] + sales[1][3]`

D. result in an error

20) Which of the following `if` clauses can be used to verify that the array subscripts
named `row` and `column` are valid for the `sales` array?

A. `if (sales[row][column] >= 0 && sales[row][column] < 5)`

B. `if (sales[row][column] >= 0 && sales[row][column] <= 5)`

C. `if (row >= 0 && row < 3 && column >= 0 && column < 6)`

D. `if (row >= 0 && row <= 1 && column >= 0 && column <= 4)`

21) Assume that the `city` and `zip` arrays are parallel arrays. Which of the following statements displays the city name associated with the zip code stored in `zip[8]`?

A. `cout << city[zip[8]] << endl;`

B. `cout << city(zip[8]) << endl;`

C. `cout << city[8] << endl;`

D. `cout << city(8) << endl;`

EXERCISES

1) Write the C++ statement to declare and initialize a one-dimensional `int` array named `numbers`. The array should have 20 elements.

2) Write the C++ statement to store the value 7 in the second element contained in a one-dimensional `int` array named `numbers`.

3) Write the C++ statement to declare and initialize a one-dimensional `double` array named `rates` that has five elements. Use the following numbers to initialize the array: 6.5, 8.3, 4.0, 2.0, and 10.5.

4) Write the C++ code to display (on the screen) the contents of a one-dimensional `double` array named `rates`. The array has five elements. Use the `for` statement.

5) Rewrite the code from Exercise 4 using the `while` statement.

6) Write the C++ code to calculate the average of the elements included in a one-dimensional `double` array named `rates`. The array has five elements. Display the average on the screen. Use the `for` statement.

7) Rewrite the code from Exercise 6 using the `while` statement.

8) Write the C++ code to display (on the screen) the largest number stored in a one-dimensional `double` array named `rates`. The array has five elements. Use the `while` statement.

9) Rewrite the code from Exercise 8 using the `for` statement.

10) Write the C++ code to subtract the number 1 from each element in a one-dimensional `double` array named `rates`. The array has five elements. Use the `while` statement.

11) Rewrite the code from Exercise 10 using the `for` statement.

12) Write the C++ code to multiply by 2 the number stored in the first element included in a one-dimensional `int` array named `nums`. Store the result in the `numDoubled` variable.

13) Write the C++ code to add together the numbers stored in the first and second elements included in a one-dimensional `int` array named `nums`. Display the sum on the screen.

14) Write the C++ code to declare and initialize a two-dimensional `double` array named `balances`. The array should have four rows and six columns.

15) Write the C++ code to store the number 100 in each element in the `balances` array declared in Exercise 14. Use the `for` statement.

Look For These Symbols

Debugging

Discovery

16) Rewrite the code from Exercise 15 using the `while` statement.

17) Write the statement to assign the C++ keyword **true** to the variable located in the third row, first column of a **boolean** array named **answers**.

18) Write the C++ code to add together the number stored in the first row, first column of the **nums** array, and the number stored in the second row, second column of the **nums** array. Display the sum on the screen.

19) In this exercise, you debug a C++ program.

A. If necessary, start Visual Studio .NET. Open the Ch11ConE19 Solution (Ch11ConE19 Solution.sln) file, which is contained in the Cpp\Chap11\ Ch11ConE19 Solution folder.

B. Study the existing code, then build the solution. Correct any errors in the program, then save and build the solution.

C. Execute the program.

D. When the program is working correctly, close the Output window, then use the File menu to close the solution.

Application Lesson

Using an Array in a C++ Program

Lab 11.1 - Stop and Analyze   If necessary, start Visual Studio .NET. Open the Ch11Lab1 Solution (Ch11Lab1 Solution.sln) file contained in the Cpp\Chap11\Ch11Lab1 Solution folder. Figure 11-24 shows the code entered in the Ch11Lab1.cpp file. (The line numbers are included in the figure only.) The **domestic** array contains the company's domestic sales amounts for the period January through June. The **international** array contains the company's international sales amounts for the same period. Study the code, then answer the questions.

Figure 11-24: C++ instructions entered in the Ch11Lab1.cpp file

```
1   //Ch11Lab1.cpp - calculates the total company sales
2   //Created/revised by <your name> on <current date>
3
4   #include <iostream>
5
6   using std::cout;
7   using std::cin;
8   using std::endl;
9
10  int main()
11  {
12   //declare variable and arrays
13   int total = 0;
14   int domestic[6] = {12000, 45000, 32000, 67000, 24000, 55000};
15   int international[6] = {10000, 56000, 42000, 23000, 12000, 34000};
16
17   //accumulate sales
18   for (int x = 0; x < 6; x = x + 1)
19      total = total + domestic[x] + international[x];
20   //end for
21
22   //display total sales
23   cout << "Total sales: $" << total << endl;
24
25   return 0;
26  }    //end of main function
```

Questions

1. What relationship exists between the **domestic** and **international** arrays?

2. What value is stored in the **domestic[1]** variable?

3. What is the highest subscript in the **international** array?

4. If the **for** clause was changed to **for (int x = 1; x <= 6; x = x + 1)**, how would this affect the assignment statement included in the **for** loop?

5. Build the solution, then execute the program. What are the total company sales?

6. Close the Command Prompt window.

7. Create a blank solution named Ch11Lab1 Step 7 Solution. Save the solution in the Cpp\Chap11 folder.

8. Add an empty C++ Win32 Console Project to the solution. Name the project Ch11Lab1 Step 7 Project.

9. Add a new C++ source file to the project. Name the source file Ch11Lab1 Step 7.

10. Open the Ch11Lab1.cpp file contained in the Cpp\Ch11Lab1 Solution\Ch11Lab1 Project folder. Copy the file's contents to the clipboard. Close the Ch11Lab1.cpp window, then paste the instructions into the Ch11Lab1 Step 7.cpp window. Change the filename in the first comment to Ch11Lab1 Step 7.cpp.

11. Modify the program so that it uses a two-dimensional array named **company**, rather than two one-dimensional arrays.

12. Save and then build the solution. Execute the program. Test the program appropriately, then close the Command Prompt window.

13. Close the Output window, then use the File menu to close the solution.

Lab 11.2　Martha Stenwaldt has asked you to create a program that allows her to enter the monthly rainfall amounts for the previous year. The program should then allow her to either display the monthly rainfall amounts on the screen or calculate and display the total rainfall amount.

In this program, you will use two program-defined void functions named `displayMonthly()` and `displayTotal()`. Both functions will be passed the contents of a one-dimensional array named `rainfall`. The `rainfall` array will contain the 12 monthly rainfall amounts entered by the user. The `displayMonthly()` function will display the contents of the array on the screen, and the `displayTotal()` function will sum the rainfall amounts and display the total on the screen. Void functions are appropriate in this case because neither function needs to return a value to the `main()` function. Figure 11-25 shows the IPO chart and C++ instructions for the `main()`, `displayMonthly()`, and `displayTotal()` functions in the program.

Figure 11-25: IPO chart and C++ instructions for the rainfall program

`main()` function

IPO chart information	C++ instructions
Input menu choice 12 monthly rainfall amounts **Processing** none **Output** none	`int choice = 0;` `double rainfall[12] = {0.0};`

Algorithm
1. get 12 monthly rainfall amounts
 	
2. display output in fixed-point
   notation with two decimal places
3. do
      display menu
 	
   get menu choice
 	
   if (choice is 1)
     displayMonthly(rainfall)
   else if (choice is 2)
     displayTotal(rainfall)
   end ifs
end repeat while (choice is 1 or
choice is 2)
	`for (int x = 0; x < 12; x = x + 1)`
	`{`
	    `cout << "Enter rainfall for month "`
	    `<< x + 1 << ": ";`
	    `cin >> rainfall[x];`
	`}    //end for`
	`cout << setiosflags(ios::fixed)`
	`<< setprecision(2);`
	`do`
	`{`
	    `cout << endl;`
	    `cout << "1    Display monthly`
	    `rainfall amounts" << endl;`
	    `cout << "2    Display total`
	    `rainfall" << endl;`
	    `cout << "3    End program"`
	    `<< endl;`
	    `cout << "Enter your choice: ";`
	    `cin >> choice;`
	    `if (choice == 1)`
	        `displayMonthly(rainfall);`
	    `else if (choice == 2)`
	        `displayTotal(rainfall);`
	    `//end ifs`
	`} while (choice == 1 or choice == 2);`

`displayMonthly()` function

IPO chart information	C++ instructions
Input rainfall array **Processing** none **Output** 12 monthly rainfall amounts	`void displayMonthly(double rain[])`

Algorithm
1. display heading
2. display contents of array
	`cout << "Monthly rainfall amounts:";`
	`for (int x = 0; x < 12; x = x + 1)`
	    `cout << rain[x] << endl;`
	`//end for`

Figure 11-25: IPO chart and C++ instructions for the rainfall program (continued)

displayTotal() function

IPO chart information	C++ instructions

Input
  rainfall array
Processing
  none
Output
  total rainfall
 	
Algorithm
1. calculate total rainfall
 	
2. display total rainfall
	`void displayTotal(double rain[])`
	
	`double total = 0.0;`
	
	`for (int x = 0; x < 12; x = x + 1)`
	`    total = total + rain[x];`
	`//end for`
	`cout << "Total rainfall: " <<`
	`total << endl;`

According to the information shown in Figure 11-25, the `main()` function first will get the 12 rainfall amounts from the user. It then will display a menu that allows the user to select from three different options. If the user chooses to display the monthly rainfall amounts, the `main()` function calls the `displayMonthly()` function, passing it the `rainfall` array. The `displayMonthly()` function uses a `for` loop to display the 12 monthly rainfall amounts on the screen. However, if the user chooses to display the total rainfall amount, the `main()` function calls the `displayTotal()` function, passing it the `rainfall` array. The `displayTotal()` function uses a `for` loop to accumulate the 12 monthly rainfall amounts. It then displays the total rainfall amount on the screen. The program ends when the user chooses the third option on the menu.

Activity for Lab 11.2

In this activity, you enter the C++ instructions shown in Figure 11-25 into the computer. You then test the program to verify that it is working correctly.

To create the rainfall program, then test the program:

1. If necessary, start Visual Studio .NET. Create a blank solution named **Ch11Lab2 Solution**. Save the solution in the Cpp\Chap11 folder.

2. Add an empty C++ Win32 Console Project to the solution. Name the project **Ch11Lab2 Project**.

3. Add a new C++ source file to the project. Name the source file **Ch11Lab2**.

4. Type **//Ch11Lab2.cpp –displays the monthly rainfall amounts** and press **Enter**.

5. Type **//or the total annual rainfall** and press **Enter**.

6. Type **//Created/revised by <*your name*> on <*current date*>**, replacing <*your name*> and <*current date*> with your name and the current date, respectively. Press **Enter** twice.

7. Type the following two `#include` directives, then press **Enter** twice.

   ```
   #include <iostream>
   #include <iomanip>
   ```

8. Type the following six `using` statements, then press **Enter** twice.

```
using std::cout;
using std::cin;
using std::endl;
using std::setprecision;
using std::ios;
using std::setiosflags;
```

9. Type **//function prototypes** and press **Enter**, then type the following two function prototypes, then press **Enter** twice.

```
void displayMonthly(double [ ]);
void displayTotal(double [ ]);
```

10. Complete the program by entering the `main()`, `displayMonthly()`, and `displayTotal()` functions, which are shown in Figure 11-26.

Figure 11-26: Rainfall program

```
//Ch11Lab2.cpp - displays the monthly rainfall amounts
//or the total annual rainfall
//Created/revised by <your name> on <current date>

#include <iostream>
#include <iomanip>

using std::cout;
using std::cin;
using std::endl;
using std::setprecision;
using std::ios;
using std::setiosflags;

//function prototypes
void displayMonthly(double [ ]);
void displayTotal(double [ ]);

int main()
{
    //declare variable and array
    int choice = 0;
    double rainFall[12] = {0.0};

    //get rainfall amounts
    for (int x = 0; x < 12; x = x + 1)
    {
        cout << "Enter rainfall for month " << x + 1 << ": ";
        cin >> rainFall[x];
    }   //end for

    //display output in fixed-point notation
    //with two decimal places
    cout << setiosflags(ios::fixed) << setprecision(2);
```

enter
this code

Figure 11-26: Rainfall program (continued)

enter
this code

```cpp
        do
        {
            cout << endl;
            cout << "1      Display monthly rainfall amounts" << endl;
            cout << "2      Display total rainfall" << endl;
            cout << "3      End program" << endl;
            cout << "Enter your choice: ";
            cin >> choice;

            if (choice == 1)
                displayMonthly(rainFall);
            else if (choice == 2)
                displayTotal(rainFall);
            //end ifs
        } while (choice == 1 || choice == 2);

        return 0;
}       //end of main function

//*****function definitions*****
void displayMonthly(double rain[])
{
    cout << "Monthly rainfall amounts:" << endl;
    for (int x = 0; x < 12; x = x + 1)
        cout << rain[x] << endl;
    //end for
}       //end of displayMonthly function

void displayTotal(double rain[])
{
    double total = 0.0;    //accumulator
    for (int x = 0; x < 12; x = x + 1)
        total = total + rain[x];
    //end for
    cout << "Total rainfall: " << total << endl;
}       //end of displayTotal function
```

11. Save and then build the solution. Verify that the program generated no warnings.

12. Execute the program. Enter the following 12 rainfall amounts: 2.44, 2.36, 2.76, 1.2, .4, .07, .04, .23, .54, .63, 1.54, 2.16

13. When you are prompted to enter your choice from the menu, type **2** and press **Enter**. The program calculates and displays the total rainfall amount, as shown in Figure 11-27.

Figure 11-27: Total rainfall amount displayed in the Command Prompt window

```
"c:\cpp\chap11\ch11lab2 solution\ch11lab2 project\debug\Ch11Lab2 Project.exe"
Enter rainfall for month 1: 2.44
Enter rainfall for month 2: 2.36
Enter rainfall for month 3: 2.76
Enter rainfall for month 4: 1.2
Enter rainfall for month 5: .4
Enter rainfall for month 6: .07
Enter rainfall for month 7: .04
Enter rainfall for month 8: .23
Enter rainfall for month 9: .54
Enter rainfall for month 10: .63
Enter rainfall for month 11: 1.54
Enter rainfall for month 12: 2.16

1      Display monthly rainfall amounts
2      Display total rainfall
3      End program
Enter your choice: 2
Total rainfall: 14.37

1      Display monthly rainfall amounts
2      Display total rainfall
3      End program
Enter your choice: _
```

total rainfall amount

14. Type **1** in response to the "Enter your choice:" prompt, then press **Enter**. The program displays the 12 monthly rainfall amounts on the screen.

15. Type **3** in response to the "Enter your choice:" prompt, then press **Enter** to end the program.

16. Close the Command Prompt window.

17. Close the Output window, then use the File menu to close the solution.

Lab 11.3   In this lab, you modify the program you created in Lab 11.2. The modified program will use one void function and one value-returning function, rather than two void functions. The void function will display the 12 monthly rainfall amounts on the screen. The value-returning function will calculate the total rainfall amount and then return the total to the `main()` function, which will display the total on the screen.

Activity for Lab 11.3

Before modifying the program created in Lab 11.2, you copy the instructions contained in the Ch11Lab2.cpp file to a new solution.

To copy the instructions contained in the Ch11Lab2.cpp file to a new solution:

1. If necessary, start Visual Studio .NET. Create a blank solution named Ch11Lab3 Solution. Save the solution in the Cpp\Chap11 folder.

2. Add an empty C++ Win32 Console Project to the solution. Name the project Ch11Lab3 Project.

3. Add a new C++ source file to the project. Name the source file Ch11Lab3.

4. Use the File menu to open the Ch11Lab2.cpp file contained in the Cpp\Chap11\Ch11Lab2 Solution\Ch11Lab2 Project folder. Select the contents of the file, then copy the contents to the clipboard.

5. Close the Ch11Lab2.cpp window.

6. Click the **Ch11Lab3.cpp** tab, then paste the instructions from the clipboard into the Ch11Lab3.cpp window.

7. Change the filename in the first program comment to **Ch11Lab3.cpp**. If necessary, change the date in the second comment.

Currently, the `displayTotal()` function is a void function that calculates and displays the total rainfall amount. Your task is to change the function's name to `calcTotal()` and also make the function a value-returning function. The `calcTotal()` function should calculate the total rainfall amount and then return the result to the `main()` function, which should display the result on the screen.

> **To modify the program, then test the program:**
> 1. Make the appropriate modifications to the program.
> 2. Save and then build the solution. If necessary, correct any syntax errors, then save and build the solution again.
> 3. Execute the program. Test the program using your own sample data, then close the Command Prompt window.
> 4. When the program is working correctly, close the Output window, then use the File menu to close the solution.

You now have completed Chapter 11's Application lesson. You can either take a break or complete the end-of-lesson exercises.

ANSWERS TO LABS

Lab 11.1

1. The **domestic** and **international** arrays are parallel arrays.
2. 45000
3. 5
4. You would need to change the assignment statement to `total = total + domestic[x - 1] + international[x - 1];`.
5. $412000
7. See Figure 11-28.

Figure 11-28

```
1   //Ch11Lab1 Step 7.cpp - calculates the total company sales
2   //Created/revised by <your name> on <current date>
3
4   #include <iostream>
5
6   using std::cout;
7   using std::cin;
8   using std::endl;
9
10  int main()
11  {
12    //declare variable and arrays
13    int total = 0;
```

Figure 11-28 (continued)

```
14   int company[2][6] = {{12000, 45000, 32000, 67000, 24000, 55000},
15   {10000, 56000, 42000, 23000, 12000, 34000}};
16
17   //accumulate sales
18   for (int row = 0; row < 2; row = row + 1)
19     for (int col = 0; col < 6; col = col + 1)
20         total = total + company[row][col];
21     //end for
22   //end for
23
24   //display total sales
25   cout << "Total sales: $" << total << endl;
26
27   return 0;
28 }    //end of main function
```

Lab 11.2

No answer required.

Lab 11.3

See Figure 11-29. Modifications are shaded in the figure.

Figure 11-29

```
//Ch11Lab3.cpp - displays the monthly rainfall amounts
//or the total annual rainfall
//Created/revised by <your name> on <current date>

#include <iostream>
#include <iomanip>

using std::cout;
using std::cin;
using std::endl;
using std::setprecision;
using std::ios;
using std::setiosflags;

//function prototypes
void displayMonthly(double []);
double calcTotal(double []);

int main()
{
    //declare variable and array
    int choice = 0;
    double totalRainfall = 0.0;
```

Figure 11-29 (continued)

```cpp
    double rainFall[12] = {0.0};

    //get rainfall amounts
    for (int x = 0; x < 12; x = x + 1)
    {
        cout << "Enter rainfall for month " << x + 1 << ": ";
        cin >> rainFall[x];
    }   //end for

    //display output in fixed-point notation
    //with two decimal places
    cout << setiosflags(ios::fixed) << setprecision(2);

    do
    {
        cout << endl;
        cout << "1     Display monthly rainfall amounts" << endl;
        cout << "2     Display total rainfall" << endl;
        cout << "3     End program" << endl;
        cout << "Enter your choice: ";
        cin >> choice;

        if (choice == 1)
            displayMonthly(rainFall);
        else if (choice == 2)
        {
            totalRainfall = calcTotal(rainFall);
            cout << "Total rainfall: " << totalRainfall << endl;
        } //end ifs
    }   while (choice == 1 || choice == 2);

    return 0;
}   //end of main function

//*****function definitions*****
void displayMonthly(double rain[])
{
    cout << "Monthly rainfall amounts:" << endl;
    for (int x = 0; x < 12; x = x + 1)
        cout << rain[x] << endl;
    //end for
}   //end of displayMonthly function

double calcTotal(double rain[])
{
    double total = 0.0;    //accumulator
    for (int x = 0; x < 12; x = x + 1)
        total = total + rain[x];
    //end for
    return total;
}   //end of calcTotal function
```

Look For These
Symbols

Debugging

Discovery

EXERCISES

1) In this exercise, you modify the program you created in Lab 11.2 so that it includes functions that calculate the following: the average rainfall amount, the highest rainfall amount, and the lowest rainfall amount.

   A. If necessary, start Visual Studio .NET. Open the Ch11AppE01 Solution (Ch11AppE01 Solution.sln) file, which is contained in the Cpp\Chap11\ Ch11AppE01 Solution folder. Notice that the array is initialized in the `main()` function.

   B. Add three additional functions to the program: `displayAvg()`, `displayHigh()`, and `displayLow()`. The `displayAvg()`, `displayHigh()`, and `displayLow()` functions should display the average rainfall amount, the highest rainfall amount, and the lowest rainfall amount, respectively. Modify the program appropriately.

   C. Save and then build the solution.

   D. Execute the program. Display the monthly rainfall amounts, the average rainfall amount, the total rainfall amount, the highest rainfall amount, and the lowest rainfall amount.

   E. When the program is working correctly, close the Output window, then use the File menu to close the solution.

2) In this exercise, you complete a program that displays the number of days in a month.

   A. If necessary, start Visual Studio .NET. Open the Ch11AppE02 Solution (Ch11AppE02 Solution.sln) file, which is contained in the Cpp\Chap11\ Ch11AppE02 Solution folder.

   B. Declare a 12-element, one-dimensional `int` array named **days**. Assign the number of days in each month to the array. (Use 28 for February.)

   C. Code the program so that it displays (on the screen) the number of days in the month corresponding to the number entered by the user. For example, if the user enters the number 1, the program should display 31 on the screen. The program should display an appropriate message if the user enters an invalid number.

   D. Save and then build the solution.

   E. Execute the program. Use the following numbers to test the program: 20, 1, 2, 3, 4, 5, 6, 7, 8, 9, 10, 11, 12, and –1 (sentinel value).

   F. When the program is working correctly, close the Output window, then use the File menu to close the solution.

3) In this exercise, you complete a program that displays the lowest value stored in an array.

   A. If necessary, start Visual Studio .NET. Open the Ch11AppE03 Solution (Ch11AppE03 Solution.sln) file, which is contained in the Cpp\Chap11\ Ch11AppE03 Solution folder.

   B. Code the program so that it displays (on the screen) the lowest score stored in the **scores** array.

   C. Save and then build the solution.

   D. Execute the program. A message containing the lowest score should appear on the screen.

   E. When the program is working correctly, close the Output window, then use the File menu to close the solution.

4) In this exercise, you complete a program that updates the prices stored in a one-dimensional array.

A. If necessary, start Visual Studio .NET. Open the Ch11AppE04 Solution (Ch11AppE04 Solution.sln) file, which is contained in the Cpp\Chap11\ Ch11AppE04 Solution folder.

B. Code the program so that it asks the user for a percentage amount by which each price should be increased. The program then should increase each price in the `prices` array by that amount. (For example, if the user enters the number 15, then each element in the array should be increased by 15%.) After increasing each price, the program should display the contents of the `prices` array on the screen.

C. Save and then build the solution.

D. Execute the program. Increase each price by 5%. Each price displayed on the screen should be 5% more than the prices originally stored in the `prices` array. Close the Command Prompt window.

E. When the program is working correctly, close the Output window, then use the File menu to close the solution.

5) In this exercise, you modify the program you completed in Exercise 4. The modified program will allow the user to update a specific price.

A. If necessary, start Visual Studio .NET. Open the Ch11AppE05 Solution (Ch11AppE05 Solution.sln) file, which is contained in the Cpp\Chap11\ Ch11AppE05 Solution folder.

B. Click File on the menu bar, point to Open, and then click File. Open the Ch11AppE04.cpp file, which is contained in the Cpp\Chap11\Ch11AppE04 Solution\Ch11AppE04 Project folder. Select the `main()` function. Copy the code to the clipboard. Close the Ch11AppE04.cpp window, then paste the code in the Ch11AppE05.cpp window.

C. Modify the program so that it also asks the user to enter a number from 1 through 10. If the user enters the number 1, the program should update the first price in the array. If the user enters the number 2, the program should update the second price in the array, and so on. Use a loop that stops asking the user for a number when the user enters a number that is less than or equal to 0, or greater than 10.

D. Save and then build the solution.

E. Execute the program. Increase the second price by 10%. Then increase the tenth price by 2%. Finally, decrease the first price by 10%. (*Hint*: To decrease a price, enter a negative number.)

F. Stop the loop. The first price displayed on the screen should be 10% less than the original first price. The second price should be 10% more than the original second price, and the tenth price should be 2% more than the original tenth price. Close the Command Prompt window.

G. When the program is working correctly, close the Output window, then use the File menu to close the solution.

6) In this exercise, you code a program that displays the number of students earning a specific score.

A. If necessary, start Visual Studio .NET. Open the Ch11AppE06 Solution (Ch11AppE06 Solution.sln) file, which is contained in the Cpp\Chap11\ Ch11AppE06 Solution folder.

B. Enter the code that prompts the user to enter a score from 0 through 100. The program should display (on the computer screen) the number of students earning that score.

C. Save and then build the solution.

D. Execute the program. Use the program to answer the following questions:

How many students earned a score of 72?

How many students earned a score of 88?

How many students earned a score of 20?

How many students earned a score of 99?

E. Close the Command Prompt window.

F. When the program is working correctly, close the Output window, then use the File menu to close the solution.

7) In this exercise, you modify the program you completed in Exercise 6. The modified program will allow the user to display the number of students earning a score in a specific range.

A. If necessary, start Visual Studio .NET. Open the Ch11AppE07 Solution (Ch11AppE07 Solution.sln) file, which is contained in the Cpp\Chap11\ Ch11AppE07 Solution folder.

B. Click File on the menu bar, point to Open, and then click File. Open the Ch11AppE06.cpp file, which is contained in the Cpp\Chap11\Ch11AppE06 Solution\Ch11AppE06 Project folder. Select the `main()` function. Copy the code to the clipboard. Close the Ch11AppE06.cpp window, then paste the code in the Ch11AppE07.cpp window.

C. Modify the program so that it prompts the user to enter a minimum score and a maximum score. The program then should display (on the screen) the number of students who earned a score within that range.

D. Save and then build the solution.

E. Execute the program. Use the program to answer the following questions:

How many students earned a score between 70 and 79, including 70 and 79?

How many students earned a score between 65 and 85, including 65 and 85?

How many students earned a score between 0 and 50, including 0 and 50?

F. Stop the program, then close the Command Prompt window.

G. When the program is working correctly, close the Output window, then use the File menu to close the solution.

8) In this exercise, you complete a program that displays the sum of the numbers stored in a two-dimensional array.

A. If necessary, start Visual Studio .NET. Open the Ch11AppE08 Solution (Ch11AppE089 Solution.sln) file, which is contained in the Cpp\Chap11\ Ch11AppE08 Solution folder.

B. Complete the program by entering the code to sum the values stored in the `quantities` array. Also enter the code to display the sum on the screen.

C. Save and then build the solution.

D. Execute the program. The sum of the numbers stored in the array should appear in the Command Prompt window. Close the Command Prompt window.

E. When the program is working correctly, close the Output window, then use the File menu to close the solution.

9) In this exercise, you create a program that uses a two-dimensional array. The program displays the highest score earned on the midterm and the highest score earned on the final.

   A. If necessary, start Visual Studio .NET. Open the Ch11AppE09 Solution (Ch11AppE09 Solution.sln) file, which is contained in the Cpp\Chap11\ Ch11AppE09 Solution folder.

   B. Complete the program by entering the code to display the highest score on the midterm and the highest score on the final.

   C. Save and then build the solution.

   D. Execute the program. The program should display the highest score earned on the midterm and the highest score earned on the final. Close the Command Prompt window.

   E. When the program is working correctly, close the Output window, then use the File menu to close the solution.

10) In this exercise, you determine the number of times a value appears in a two-dimensional array.

   A. If necessary, start Visual Studio .NET. Open the Ch11AppE10 Solution (Ch11AppE10 Solution.sln) file, which is contained in the Cpp\Chap11\ Ch11AppE10 Solution folder.

   B. Complete the program by entering the code to display the number of times each of the numbers 1 through 9 appears in the two-dimensional **numbers** array. Also enter the code to display the nine counts on the screen. For example, the number 1 appears two times in the array, the number 2 appears four times, and so on.

   C. Save and then build the solution.

   D. Execute the program. The nine counts should appear in the Command Prompt window. Close the Command Prompt window.

   E. When the program is working correctly, close the Output window, then use the File menu to close the solution.

11) In this exercise, you use two parallel arrays. Ms. Jenkins uses the grade table shown in Figure 11-30 for her Introduction to Computers course. She wants a program that displays the grade after she enters the total points earned.

Figure 11-30

Minimum points	Maximum points	Grade
0	299	F
300	349	D
350	399	C
400	449	B
450	500	A

A. If necessary, start Visual Studio .NET. Open the Ch11AppE11 Solution (Ch11AppE11 Solution.sln) file, which is contained in the Cpp\Chap11\Ch11AppE11 Solution folder.

B. Store the minimum points in a one-dimensional `int` array named `minPoints`. Store the grade in a parallel, one-dimensional `string` array named `grade`. The program should display the appropriate grade after Ms. Jenkins enters the number of points earned by a student. Include a loop that allows Ms. Jenkins to enter as many values as desired.

C. Save and then build the solution.

D. Execute the program. Test the program four times, using the following amounts: 455, 210, 400, and 349. The program should display grades of A, F, B, and D.

E. When the program is working correctly, close the Output window, then use the File menu to close the solution.

12) In this exercise, you use three parallel numeric arrays. You search one of the arrays and then display its corresponding values from the other two arrays.

A. If necessary, start Visual Studio .NET. Open the Ch11AppE12 Solution (Ch11AppE12 Solution.sln) file, which is contained in the Cpp\Chap11\Ch11AppE12 Solution folder.

B. The program should prompt the user to enter a product ID. It then should search for the product ID in the `id` array, and then display the corresponding price and quantity from the `prices` and `quantities` array. Allow the user to display the price and quantity for as many product IDs as desired without having to execute the program again.

C. Save and then build the solution.

D. Execute the program. Test the program appropriately.

E. When the program is working correctly, close the Output window, then use the File menu to close the solution.

13) In this exercise, you learn how to pass a two-dimensional array to a function.

A. If necessary, start Visual Studio .NET. Open the Ch11AppE13 Solution (Ch11AppE13 Solution.sln) file, which is contained in the Cpp\Chap11\Ch11AppE13 Solution folder.

B. Complete the program by entering the code to pass the two-dimensional `sales` array to the `calcTotal()` function.

C. Save and then build the solution.

D. Execute the program. The program should display total sales of $412000 in the Command Prompt window. Close the Command Prompt window.

E. When the program is working correctly, close the Output window, then use the File menu to close the solution.

14) In this exercise, you debug a C++ program.

    A. If necessary, start Visual Studio .NET. Open the Ch11AppE14 Solution (Ch11AppE14 Solution.sln) file, which is contained in the Cpp\Chap11\Ch11AppE14 Solution folder. The program prompts the user to enter the amount by which each quantity is to be increased or decreased. It then displays the old and new quantities on the screen.

    B. Build the solution. Correct any errors in the program, then save and build the solution.

    C. Execute the program. When you are prompted to enter a number, type 5 and press Enter. The Command Prompt window should show the old and new quantities. Notice that the program is not working correctly. Close the Command Prompt window.

    D. Correct any errors in the program, then save and build the solution.

    E. Execute the program. When the program is working correctly, close the Output window, then use the File menu to close the solution.

Please visit the Testing Center at www.course.com/testingcenter for more practice on the topics covered in this chapter.

String Manipulation

Objectives

After completing this chapter, you will be able to:

- Determine the number of characters contained in a string

- Remove characters from a string

- Access characters contained in a string

- Replace characters in a string

- Insert characters within a string

- Search a string for another string

- Compare a portion of a `string` variable's contents to another string

- Duplicate a character within a `string` variable

- Concatenate strings

Concept Lesson

Manipulating Strings

Many times, a program will need to manipulate (process) string data. For example, a program may need to verify that an inventory part number begins with a specific letter. Or, it may need to determine whether the last three characters in an employee number are valid. In this chapter, you learn several ways of manipulating strings in C++. You begin by learning how to determine the number of characters contained in a string.

Determining the Number of Characters Contained in a String

In many programs, it is necessary to determine the number of characters contained in a string. For example, a program that expects the user to enter a 10-digit phone number needs to verify that the user entered the required number of characters. You can use a `string` variable's **length() function** to determine the number of characters contained in the variable. The syntax of the `length()` function is shown in Figure 12-1 along with several examples of using the function.

Figure 12-1: Syntax and examples of the `length()` function

Syntax
string.**length()**

Examples and results

```
string name = "Paul Blackfeather";
cout << name.length() << endl;
```

displays the number 17 on the screen

```
string phone = "";
cout << "10-digit phone number: ";
getline(cin, phone);
while (phone.length() == 10)
{
        instructions to process when the loop condition is true
        cout << "10-digit phone number: ";
        getline(cin, phone);
}  //end while
```

gets a phone number from the user, then repeats the loop body instructions while the number of characters contained in the **phone** variable is equal to the number 10

Figure 12-1: Syntax and examples of the `length()` **function (continued)**

Examples and results

```
string part = "";
cout << "Part number: ";
getline(cin, part);
if (part.length() >= 4)
{
            instructions to process when the condition is true
}
else
{
            instructions to process when the condition is false
} //end if
```

gets a part number from the user, and then determines whether the **part** variable contains
at least four characters

tip

The `length()`
function returns an
unsigned integer.
Therefore, you will
need to use the
`int` type cast when
assigning the return
value to an `int`
variable; otherwise,
the C++ compiler
will display a warn-
ing message indi-
cating that a loss of
data can occur. You
learn more about
this type of error in
Lab 12.1 in the
Application lesson.

In the `length()` function's syntax, *string* is the name of a `string` variable whose
length you want to determine. The `length()` function returns the number of characters contained in the `string` variable.

The code shown in the first example in Figure 12-1 assigns the string "Paul Blackfeather" to
a `string` variable named **name**. It then uses the `length()` function to display the number
of characters contained in the **name** variable; the number 17 will appear on the screen.

The code shown in the second example prompts the user to enter a 10-digit phone number
and stores the user's response in a `string` variable named **phone**. The `while`
`(phone.length() == 10)` clause uses the `length()` function to return the number of
characters contained in the **phone** variable, comparing the function's return value to the
number 10.

The code shown in the third example in Figure 12-1 prompts the user to enter a part
number, and stores the user's response in a `string` variable named **part**. The `if`
`(part.length() >= 4)` clause then determines whether the **part** variable contains at
least four characters.

Next, you learn how to remove characters from a string.

Removing Characters from a String

At times, an application may need to remove one or more characters from an item of data
entered by the user. For example, an application may need to remove a dollar sign from the
beginning of a sales amount. Or, it may need to remove a percent sign from the end of a tax rate.

In C++, you can use the **erase() function** to remove one or more characters located anywhere in a `string` variable. Figure 12-2 shows the syntax of the `erase()` function and
includes several examples of using the function.

tip

The *subscript* and *count* arguments can be numeric literal constants or the names of numeric variables.

Figure 12-2: Syntax and examples of the `erase()` **function**

Syntax
string.**erase**(*subscript*[, *count*])

Examples and results

```
string name = "John Cober";
name.erase(0, 5);
```

changes the contents of the **name** variable to "Cober"

```
string name = "John";
name.erase(2, 1);
```

changes the contents of the **name** variable to "Jon"

```
string name = "Janis";
name.erase(3, 2);
```

changes the contents of the **name** variable to "Jan"

```
string name = "Paul Blackfeather";
name.erase(5);
```

changes the contents of the **name** variable to "Paul"

Each character in a string is assigned a unique number, called a **subscript**, that indicates the character's position in the string. The first character in a string has a subscript of 0, the second character has a subscript of 1, and so on. In the **erase()** function's syntax, *subscript* is the subscript of the first character you want removed from the *string*, and *count* is the number of characters you want removed. For example, to remove only the first character from a string, you use the number 0 as the *subscript*, and the number 1 as the *count*. To remove the fourth through eighth characters, you use the number 3 as the *subscript*, and the number 5 as the *count*. Notice that the *count* argument is optional, as indicated by the square brackets in the syntax. If you omit the *count* argument, the **erase()** function removes all characters from the *subscript* position through the end of the string.

Study closely the four examples shown in Figure 12-2. The **name.erase(0, 5);** statement shown in the first example tells the computer to remove the first five characters from the string stored in the **name** variable. In this case, the computer removes the letters J, o, h, and n, and the space character from the string "John Cober". After the statement is processed, the **name** variable contains the string "Cober".

The **name.erase(2, 1);** statement shown in the second example tells the computer to remove one character, beginning with the character whose subscript is 2, from the string stored in the **name** variable. The character with an index of 2 is the third character in the string "John"—in this case, the letter "h". After the statement is processed, the **name** variable contains the string "Jon".

You can use the **name.erase(3, 2);** statement shown in the third example to remove two characters, beginning with the character whose subscript is 3, from the string stored in the `name` variable. In this case, the letters "i" and "s" are removed, changing the contents of the `name` variable from "Janis" to "Jan".

The `name.erase(5);` statement shown in the last example in Figure 12-2 removes all of the characters from the `name` variable beginning with the character in position five, which is the space character. In this case, the statement removes the space character along with the string "Blackfeather". After the statement is processed, the `name` variable contains the string "Paul".

Next, you learn how to access characters contained in a string.

Accessing Characters Contained in a String

At times, an application may need to access one or more characters contained in a string. For example, an application may need to determine whether the letter "K" appears as the third character in a string. Or, it may need to display only the string's first five characters. In C++, you can use the **substr() function** to access any number of characters contained in a `string` variable. (The "substr" stands for "substring".) Figure 12-3 shows the syntax of the `substr()` function and includes several examples of using the function.

Figure 12-3: Syntax and examples of the `substr()` function

Syntax
string.**substr**(*subscript*[, *count*])

Examples and results

```
string name = "Peggy Ryan";
string first = "";
string last = "";
first = name.substr(0, 5);
last = name.substr(6);
```

assigns "Peggy" to the `first` variable, and assigns "Ryan" to the `last` variable

```
string sales = "";
cout << "Enter the sales amount: ";
getline(cin, sales);
if (sales.substr(0, 1) == "$")
    sales = sales.substr(1);
//end if
```

determines whether the string stored in the `sales` variable begins with the dollar sign; if it does, assigns the contents of the variable, excluding the dollar sign, to the `sales` variable

```
string rate = "";
cout << "Enter the rate: ";
getline(cin, rate);
if (rate.substr(rate.length() - 1, 1) == "%")
    rate = rate.substr(0, rate.length() - 1);
//end if
```

determines whether the string stored in the `rate` variable ends with the percent sign; if it does, assigns the contents of the variable, excluding the percent sign, to the `rate` variable

The `substr()` function contains two arguments: *subscript* and *count*. *Subscript* is the subscript of the first character you want to access in the *string*. As you learned earlier, the first character in a string has a subscript of 0, the second character has a subscript of 1, and so on. The *count* argument, which is optional, specifies the number of characters you want to access. The `substr()` function returns a string that contains *count* number of characters, beginning with the character whose subscript is specified in the *subscript* argument. If you omit the *count* argument, the `substr()` function returns all characters from the *subscript* position through the end of the string.

Study closely the three examples shown in Figure 12-3. In the first example, the `first = name.substr(0, 5);` statement assigns the first five characters contained in the `name` variable ("Peggy") to the `first` variable. The `last = name.substr(6);` statement assigns all of the characters contained in the `name` variable, beginning with the character whose subscript is 6, to the `last` variable. In this case, the statement assigns "Ryan" to the `last` variable.

The `sales.substr(0, 1) == "$"` condition shown in the second example uses the `substr()` function to determine whether the string stored in the `sales` variable begins with the dollar sign. If it does, the `sales = sales.substr(1);` statement assigns all of the characters from the `sales` variable, beginning with the character whose subscript is 1, to the `sales` variable. The `sales = sales.substr(1);` statement is equivalent to the `sales.erase(0, 1);` statement.

The `rate.substr(rate.length() - 1, 1) == "%"` condition shown in the last example in Figure 12-3 uses the `substr()` and `length()` functions to determine whether the string stored in the `rate` variable ends with the percent sign. If it does, the `rate = rate.substr(0, rate.length() - 1);` statement assigns all of the characters contained in the `rate` variable, excluding the last character (which is the percent sign), to the `rate` variable. The `rate = rate.substr(0, rate.length() - 1);` statement is equivalent to the statement `rate.erase(rate.length() - 1, 1);`.

MINI-QUIZ

Mini-Quiz 1

1) Which of the following C++ `while` clauses processes the loop instructions as long as the number of characters contained in a `string` variable named `employee` is greater than 20?
   a. `while (employee.length > 20)`
   b. `while (employee.length() > 20)`
   c. `while (length(employee) > 20)`
   d. `while (length.employee > 20)`

2) Write a C++ `if` clause that determines whether a `string` variable named `code` contains five characters.

3) Assume the `name` variable contains the string "Carol P. Smith". Write a C++ statement to change the contents of the `name` variable to "Carol Smith". Use the `erase()` function.

4) Assume the `cityState` variable contains the string "Los Angeles, CA". Write the C++ statement to assign the state ID ("CA") to a `string` variable named `city`. Use the `substr()` function.

Next, you learn how to replace a sequence of characters in a string with another sequence of characters.

Replacing Characters in a String

In C++, you can use the **replace() function** to replace a sequence of characters in a `string` variable with another sequence of characters. For example, you can use the `replace()` function to replace area code "800" with area code "877" in a phone number. Figure 12-4 shows the syntax of the `replace()` function and includes several examples of using the function.

Figure 12-4: Syntax and examples of the `replace()` **function**

tip
The *replacementString* argument can be a string literal constant or the name of a `string` variable.

Syntax
string.**replace**(*subscript, count, replacementString*)
Examples and results

`string phone = "1-800-111-0000";`
`phone.replace(2, 3, "877");`
 	
changes the contents of the **phone** variable to 1-877-111-0000

`string item = "ABCX34";`
`item.replace(3, 1, "D");`
 	
changes the contents of the **item** variable to ABD234

`string name = "Jamie Leonard";`
`name.replace(6, 7, "Kent");`
 	
changes the contents of the **name** variable to Jamie Kent

In the `replace()` function's syntax, *string* is the name of a `string` variable that contains the one or more characters you want to replace. The *subscript* argument specifies where—in other words, in what character position—to begin replacing characters in the *string*. The *count* argument indicates the number of characters to replace, and the *replacementString* argument contains the string that will replace the characters in the *string*.

In the first example shown in Figure 12-4, the `phone.replace(2, 3, "877");` statement replaces the "800" in the **phone** variable with "877". After the statement is processed, the **phone** variable contains 1-877-111-0000.

In the second example, the `item.replace(3, 1, "D");` statement replaces the letter X, which is located in position three in the **item** variable, with the letter "D". In other words, the statement changes the value stored in the **item** variable from "ABCX34" to "ABCD34".

The `name.replace(6, 7, "Kent");` statement shown in the last example in Figure 12-4 replaces the string "Leonard"—which is the seven characters, beginning in position six, in the **name** variable—with the string "Kent". The statement changes the value stored in the **name** variable from "Jamie Leonard" to "Jamie Kent".

Next, you learn how to insert characters anywhere within a string.

Inserting Characters within a String

In C++, you can use the **insert() function** to insert characters within a `string` variable. For example, you can use the `insert()` function to insert an employee's middle initial within his or her name. Or, you can use it to insert parentheses around the area code in a phone number. Figure 12-5 shows the syntax of the `insert()` function and includes two examples of using the function.

Figure 12-5: Syntax and examples of the `insert()` function

Syntax
string.**insert**(*subscript*, *insertString*)

Examples and results
``
string name = "Rob Smith";
name.insert(4, "T. ");
```
changes the contents of the **name** variable to Rob T. Smith |
| ```
string phone = "3120501111";
phone.insert(0, "(");
phone.insert(4, ")");
phone.insert(8, "-");
```
changes the contents of the **phone** variable to (312)050-1111 |

In the `insert()` function's syntax, *subscript* specifies where in the *string* you want the *insertString* inserted. To insert the *insertString* at the beginning of the *string*, you use the number 0 as the *subscript*. To insert the *insertString* beginning with the second character in the *string*, you use the number 1 as the *subscript*, and so on. The `insert()` function returns a string with the appropriate characters inserted.

The `name.Insert(4, "T. ");` statement shown in the first example in Figure 12-5 tells the computer to insert the *insertString*—in this case, "T. " (the letter T, a period, and a space)—in the **name** variable. The letter T is inserted in position four, which makes it the fifth character in the *string*. The period and space are inserted in positions five and six, making them the sixth and seventh characters in the *string*. After the statement is processed, the **name** variable contains the string "Rob T. Smith".

In the second example shown in Figure 12-5, the `phone.insert(0, "(");` statement changes the contents of the **phone** variable from "3120501111" to "(3120501111". The `phone.insert(4, ")");` statement then changes the contents of the variable from "(3120501111" to "(312)0501111", and the `phone.insert(8, "-");` statement changes the contents of the variable from "(312)0501111" to "(312)050-1111".

Next, you learn how to search a string to determine whether it contains a specific sequence of characters.

Searching a String

In C++, you can use the **find() function** to search a `string` variable to determine whether it contains a specific sequence of characters. For example, you can use the `find()` function to determine whether the area code "312" appears in a phone number, or whether the street name "Elm Street" appears in an address. Figure 12-6 shows the syntax of the `find()` function and includes several examples of using the function.

Figure 12-6: Syntax and examples of the `find()` function

Syntax
string.**find**(*searchString*, *subscript*)

Examples and results

```
string zip = "60611";
cout << zip.find("61", 0) << endl;
```

searches the `zip` variable, beginning with the first character (which is in position zero), to determine whether the variable contains the *searchString* "61", then displays the result (2) on the screen

```
string address = "";
int location = 0;
cout << "Enter the address: ";
getline(cin, address);
transform(address.begin(), address.end(), address.begin(), toupper);
location = int(address.find("MAIN", 0));
if (location >= 0)
        instructions to process when the condition is true
//end if
```

gets an address from the user and assigns it to the `address` variable, then converts the `address` variable to uppercase, then searches the `address` variable, beginning with the first character (which is in position zero), to determine whether the variable contains the *searchString* "MAIN", then assigns the result to the `location` variable, and then determines whether the `location` variable contains a value that is greater than or equal to 0

```
string part = "";
int location = 0;
cout << "Part number: ";
getline(cin, part);
transform(part.begin(), part.end(), part.begin(), tolower);
location = int(part.find("x", 3));
if (location >= 0)
        instructions to process when the condition is true
//end if
```

gets a part number from the user and assigns it to the `part` variable, then converts the `part` variable to lowercase, then searches the `part` variable, beginning with the fourth character (which is in position three), to determine whether the variable contains the *searchString* "x", then assigns the result to the `location` variable, and then determines whether the `location` variable contains a value that is greater than or equal to 0

tip

The `find()` function is case-sensitive.

tip

The *searchString* argument can be a string literal constant or it can be the name of a `string` variable that contains the string you want to find.

tip

The `find()` function returns an unsigned integer. Therefore, you need to use the `int` type cast when assigning the return value to an `int` variable, as shown in the second and third examples in Figure 12-6. Otherwise, the C++ compiler will display a warning message indicating that a loss of data can occur. You learn more about this type of error in Lab 12.1 in the Application lesson.

In the `find()` function's syntax, *string* is the name of a `string` variable whose contents you want to search, and *searchString* is the string for which you are searching. The *subscript* argument specifies the starting position for the search—in other words, the character at which the search should begin.

The `find()` function searches for the *searchString* in the *string*, starting with the character in position *subscript* in the *string*. If the *searchString* is contained within the *string*, then the `find()` function returns a number that indicates the beginning position of the *searchString* within the *string*. The function returns the number −1 if the *searchString* is not contained within the *string*.

Study the examples shown in Figure 12-6. The `cout << zip.find("61", 0) << endl;` statement shown in the first example searches for the *searchString* "61" in the `zip` variable, beginning with the first character (which is in position zero) in the variable. It then displays the result—in this case, the number 2—on the screen. The number 2 is displayed because the *searchString* "61" begins in character position two in the `zip` variable.

The code shown in the second example prompts the user to enter an address and stores the user's response in a `string` variable named `address`. The `transform()` function converts the contents of the `address` variable to uppercase. The `location = int(address.find ("MAIN", 0));` statement searches for the *searchString* "MAIN" in the `address` variable, beginning with the first character in the variable. The statement assigns the number returned by the `find()` function to an `int` variable named `location`. If the `address` variable contains the address "123 MAIN STREET", the `find()` function stores the number 4 in the `location` variable, because the *searchString* "MAIN" begins in character position four in the `address` variable. However, if the `address` variable contains the address "12 HAMPTON AVENUE", the `find()` function stores the number –1 in the `location` variable, because the *searchString* "MAIN" is not contained within the `address` variable. The `if (location >= 0)` clause uses the value stored in the `location` variable to determine whether the *searchString* was located within the *string*. If the *searchString* was found, the `location` variable's value will be greater than or equal to 0; otherwise, the value will be –1.

The code shown in the last example in Figure 12-6 prompts the user to enter a part number, storing the user's response in a `string` variable named `part`. The `transform()` function converts the contents of the `part` variable to lowercase. The statement `location = int(part.find("x", 3));` searches for the *searchString* "x" in the `part` variable, beginning with the character in position three (the fourth character) in the variable. The statement assigns the number returned by the `find()` function to an `int` variable named `location`. If the `part` variable contains the part number "678x34", the `find()` function stores the number 3 in the `location` variable, because the *searchString* "x" begins in character position three in the `part` variable. Similarly, if the `part` variable contains the part number "34561x", the `find()` function stores the number 5 in the `location` variable, because the *searchString* "x" begins in character position five in the `part` variable. However, if the `part` variable contains the part number "12x533", the `find()` function stores the number –1 in the `location` variable, because the *searchString* "x" does not appear in character positions three through five in the `part` variable. The `if (location >= 0)` clause uses the number stored in the `location` variable to determine whether the *searchString* is contained within the *string*.

MINI-QUIZ

Mini-Quiz 2

1) Which of the following changes the contents of a `string` variable named `city` from "Los Angeles, CA" to "Los Angeles" ?
   a. `city.replace(11, "");`
   b. `city.replace(", CA", "");`
   c. `city.replace(4, 11, "");`
   d. `city.replace(11, 4, "");`

2) Write a C++ statement that changes the contents of a `string` variable named `cityState` from "Los Angeles CA" to "Los Angeles, CA". Use the `insert()` function.

3) Write a C++ statement that searches for a comma in a `string` variable named `cityState`, then displays the result on the computer screen. Use the `find()` function.

4) Assuming the `cityState` variable contains the string "Los Angeles, CA", what will the statement from Question 3 display on the computer screen?

Next, you learn how to compare a portion of a `string` variable's contents to another string.

Comparing a Portion of a `string` Variable's Contents to Another String

As you already know, you can use the comparison operators (>, >=, <, <=, ==, and !=) to compare two strings. For example, the condition in the `while (name != "done")` clause uses the inequality comparison operator to compare the contents of the `name` variable to the string "done". In some programs, rather than comparing two entire strings, you may need to compare a portion of one string to another string. For instance, you may need to compare the last two characters in the `employNum` variable to the string "12" to determine whether the employee works in the Accounting department, which has a department code of 12. In C++, you use the **compare() function** to compare a portion of a `string` variable's contents to another string. Figure 12-7 shows the syntax of the `compare()` function and includes several examples of using the function.

Figure 12-7: Syntax and examples of the `compare()` function

Syntax
string1.**compare**(*subscript, count, string2*)

Examples and results

```
string employNum = "24012";
int x = 0;
x = employNum.compare(0, 2, "24");
```

the `compare()` function assigns the number 0 to **x**, because the first two characters in the `employNum` variable are equal to the string "24"

```
string employNum = "24012";
int x = 0;
x = employNum.compare(3, 2, "12");
```

the `compare()` function assigns the number 0 to **x**, because the two characters in the `employNum` variable, beginning with the character in position three (the number 1), are equal to the string "12"

```
string name = "Smith, Janet";
int x = 0;
x = name.compare(0, 5, "Jones");
```

the `compare()` function assigns the number 1 to **x**, because the first character in the `name` variable (S) comes after the first character in the string "Jones" (J) in the ASCII coding scheme

tip

The `compare()` function is case-sensitive.

Figure 12-7: Syntax and examples of the `compare()` **function (continued)**

Examples and results

```
string name = "Smith, Janet";
int x = 0;
x = name.compare(0, 5, "Smyth");
```

the `compare()` function assigns the number –1 to `x`, because the character in position
two in the `name` variable (i) comes before the character in position two in the string
"Smyth" (y) in the ASCII coding scheme

```
string item1 = "33442AB";
string item2 = "2AB";
int x = 0;
x = item1.compare(4, 3, item2);
```

the `compare()` function assigns the number 0 to `x`, because the three characters in the
`item1` variable, beginning with the character in position four (the number 2), are equal to
the string stored in the `item2` variable

The ASCII codes
are shown in
Appendix A.

In the `compare()` function's syntax, *string1* and *string2* are the two strings you want to
compare. *String1* is the name of a `string` variable, and *string2* can be a string literal constant or the name of a `string` variable. The *subscript* argument specifies where in *string1* — in
other words, with which character in *string1* — the comparison should begin. The *count* argument indicates the number of characters in *string1* to compare to the characters in *string2*.

The `compare()` function compares *string2* to the number of characters specified in the
count argument in *string1*, starting in position *subscript* in *string1*. The function returns the
number 0 if *string2*'s characters are equal to the specified characters in *string1*. If *string2*'s
characters are not equal to the specified characters in *string1*, the function returns either the
number –1 or the number 1, depending on the ASCII values of the first characters that are different in each string. For example, assume *string1* is "bill" and *string2* is "belt". The first characters in both strings are the same — "b". The second characters, however, are different:
string1's second character is the letter "i" (which has an ASCII value of 105) and *string2*'s
second character is the letter "e" (which has an ASCII value of 101). Because *string1*'s character comes after (is greater than) *string2*'s character in the ASCII coding scheme, the
`compare()` function returns the number 1. However, if the situation is reversed — in other
words, if *string1* is "belt" and *string2* is "bill" — the `compare()` function returns –1 to indicate that *string1*'s character ("e") comes before (is less than) *string2*'s character ("i").

Study each of the examples shown in Figure 12-7. The `compare()` function shown in the
first example compares the string "24" (*string2*) to two characters in the `employNum` variable
(*string1*), beginning with the first character in the `employNum` variable. The function returns
the number 0, because the first two characters contained in the `employNum` variable (24) are
equal to the string "24". The code assigns the function's return value to an `int` variable
named `x`.

The `compare()` function shown in the second example compares the string "12"
(*string2*) to two characters in the `employNum` variable (*string1*), beginning with the character located in position three in the `employNum` variable. The character located in position
three in the `employNum` variable is the number 1, which is actually the fourth character in
the variable. (Recall that the first character in a string is in position zero.) Therefore, the two
characters that will be compared in the `employNum` variable are the characters one and

two. The `compare()` function returns the number 0, because the two characters contained in the `employNum` variable, beginning with the character in position three, are equal to the two characters in the string "12". The code assigns the function's return value to an `int` variable named `x`.

The `compare()` function shown in the third example compares the string "Jones" (*string2*) to the first five characters in the `name` variable (*string1*). Notice that the first character in each string is different: it is "S" in *string1* and "J" in *string2*. In this case, the `compare()` function returns the number 1, because the first character in *string1* (S) comes after the first character in *string2* (J) in the ASCII coding scheme. The code assigns the function's return value to an `int` variable named `x`.

The `compare()` function shown in the fourth example compares the string "Smyth" (*string2*) to the first five characters in the `name` variable (*string1*). Notice that both strings are equal up to the third character: the third character in *string1* is "i", and the third character in *string2* is "y". In this case, the `compare()` function returns the number −1, because the third character in *string1* (i) comes before the third character in *string2* (y) in the ASCII coding scheme. The code assigns the function's return value to an `int` variable named `x`.

The `compare()` function shown in the last example in Figure 12-7 compares the contents of the `item2` variable (*string2*) to three characters in the `item1` variable (*string1*), beginning with the character in position four in the `item1` variable. The three characters that will be compared in the `item1` variable are 2AB. In this example, the `compare()` function returns the number 0, because the three characters contained in the `item1` variable, beginning with the character in position four, are equal to the contents of the `item2` variable (2AB). The code assigns the function's return value to an `int` variable named `x`.

In the next section, you learn how to duplicate a character within a `string` variable.

Duplicating a Character within a string Variable

In C++, you can use the **assign() function** to duplicate one character a specified number of times, then assign the resulting string to a `string` variable. Figure 12-8 shows the syntax of the `assign()` function and includes two examples of using the function.

Figure 12-8: Syntax and examples of the `assign()` function

Syntax
string.**assign**(*count, character*)
Examples and results

<pre>string hyphens = "";
hyphens.assign(10, '-');</pre>

assigns 10 hyphens to the `hyphens` variable

<pre>char letter = ' ';
string letters = "";
cout << "Enter a letter: ";
cin >> letter;
letters.assign(4, letter);</pre>

prompts the user to enter a letter, then assigns the user's input to the `letter` variable, and then duplicates the letter four times and assigns the result to the `letters` variable

tip

If the *character* argument in the `assign()` function is a character literal constant, it must be enclosed in single quotation marks.

In the syntax, *string* is the name of a `string` variable that will store the duplicated characters. The *count* argument is either a numeric literal constant or the name of a numeric variable, and it indicates the number of times you want to duplicate the character specified in the function's *character* argument. The *character* argument can be either a character literal constant or the name of a `char` variable.

In the first example shown in Figure 12-8, the `hyphens.assign(10, '-');` statement duplicates the hyphen character 10 times, then stores the resulting string in the `hyphens` variable. In the second example, the `letters.assign(4, letter);` statement duplicates the contents of the `letter` variable four times, then assigns the resulting string to the `letters` variable. If the `letter` variable contains the asterisk (*) character, the statement assigns four asterisks(****) to the `letters` variable.

Finally, you learn how to concatenate strings (link them together).

Concatenating Strings

Connecting (or linking) strings together is called **concatenating**. In C++, you use the concatenation operator, which is the + sign, to concatenate strings. Figure 12-9 shows examples of using the concatenation operator in a C++ statement.

Figure 12-9: Examples of using the concatenation operator

Examples and results
```string first = "Jerome";string last = "Jacobs";string full = "";full = first + " " + last;```concatenates the contents of the `first` variable, a space, and the contents of the `last` variable, and then assigns the result (Jerome Jacobs) to the `full` variable
```string sentence = "How are you";sentence = sentence + "?";```concatenates the contents of the **sentence** variable and a question mark, then assigns the result (How are you?) to the **sentence** variable
```string hyphens = "";for (int count = 1; count <= 5; count = count + 1)   hyphens = hyphens + "-";//end forcout << hyphens << endl;```concatenates five hyphens within the **hyphens** variable, then displays the contents of the **hyphens** variable (-----) on the computer screen

In the first example shown in Figure 12-9, the `full = first + " " + last;` statement concatenates the contents of the `first` variable (Jerome), a space, and the contents of the `last` variable (Jacobs). It assigns the concatenated string (Jerome Jacobs) to the `full` variable.

In the second example, the `sentence = sentence + "?";` statement concatenates the contents of the `sentence` variable (How are you) and a question mark (?). It then assigns the concatenated string (How are you?) to the `sentence` variable.

In the last example shown in Figure 12-9, the `hyphens = hyphens + "-";` statement concatenates a hyphen (-) to the current contents of the `hyphens` variable. In this case, five hyphens will be assigned to the `hyphens` variable, because the `hyphens = hyphens + "-";` statement appears within a loop whose instructions will be processed five times. After the loop completes its processing, the contents of the `hyphens` variable (-----) are displayed on the screen. Although you could use the code shown in the last example to assign five hyphens to the `hyphens` variable, it is much easier to use the `hyphens.assign(5, '-');` statement.

MINI-QUIZ

Mini-Quiz 3

1) Assume a `string` variable named `state` contains two uppercase letters. Which of the following C++ statements compares the first character stored in the `state` variable to the string "K" and assigns the return value to an `int` variable named `returnValue`?
   a. `returnValue = compare(state, 0, 1, "K");`
   b. `returnValue = compare(state, 1, 0, "K");`
   c. `returnValue = state.compare("K", 0, 1);`
   d. `returnValue = state.compare(0, 1, "K");`

2) Which of the following C++ statements assigns four exclamation points to a `string` variable named `temp`, then concatenates the contents of the `temp` variable to a `string` variable named `sentence`?
   a. `sentence = sentence + temp.assign(4, '!');`
   b. `sentence = temp + temp.assign('!', 4);`
   c. `sentence = sentence.assign(temp, 4, '!');`
   d. `sentence = sentence & temp.assign(4, '!');`

3) Which of the following C++ statements concatenates the opening parentheses, the contents of the `areaCode` variable, and the closing parentheses, then assigns the result to the `displayAreaCode` variable?
   a. `displayAreaCode = "(" & areaCode & ")";`
   b. `displayAreaCode = "(" + areaCode + ")";`
   c. `displayAreaCode = "(" + "areaCode" + ")";`
   d. `displayAreaCode = "( + areaCode + )";`

You now have completed Chapter 12's Concept lesson. You can either take a break or complete the end-of-lesson questions and exercises before moving on to the Application lesson.

SUMMARY

String manipulation is a common task performed by many programs. Figure 12-10 summarizes the string manipulation techniques you learned about in this lesson.

Figure 12-10: String manipulation techniques

Technique	Syntax	Purpose
+ concatenation operator		concatenate strings
`assign()` function	*string*.**assign(***count*, *character***)**	duplicate a character within a `string` variable
`compare()` function	*string1*.**compare(***subscript*, *count*, *string2***)**	compare a portion of a `string` variable's contents to another string
`erase()` function	*string*.**erase(***subscript*[, *count*]**)**	remove one or more characters located anywhere in a `string` variable
`find()` function	*string*.**find(***searchString*, *subscript***)**	search a `string` variable to determine whether it contains a specific sequence of characters
`insert()` function	*string*.**insert(***subscript*, *insertString***)**	insert characters within a `string` variable
`length()` function	*string*.**length()**	determine the number of characters contained in a `string` variable
`replace()` function	*string*.**replace(***subscript*, *count*, *replacementString***)**	replace a sequence of characters in a `string` variable with another sequence of characters
`substr()` function	*string*.**substr(***subscript*[, *count*]**)**	access any number of characters contained in a `string` variable

ANSWERS TO MINI-QUIZZES

Mini-Quiz 1

1) b. `while (employee.length() > 20)`

2) `if (code.length() == 5)`

3) `name.erase(6, 3);`

4) `city = cityState.substr(13);` [or `city = cityState.substr(13, 2);`]

Mini-Quiz 2

1) d. `city.replace(11, 4, "");`

2) `cityState.insert(11, ",");`

3) `cout << cityState.find(",", 0) << endl;`

4) `11`

Mini-Quiz 3

1) d. `returnValue = state.compare(0, 1, "K");`

2) a. `sentence = sentence + temp.assign(4, '!');`

3) b. `displayAreaCode = "(" + areaCode + ")";`

QUESTIONS

1) Which of the following C++ statements displays the number of characters contained in a **string** variable named **address**?

A. cout << address.length() << endl;

B. cout << numChars(address) << endl;

C. cout << length(address) << endl;

D. cout << size.address << endl;

2) Assume that the **amount** variable contains the string "$56.55". Which of the following C++ statements removes the dollar sign from the variable's contents?

A. amount.erase("$");

B. amount.erase(0, 1);

C. amount = amount.substr(1);

D. both B and C

3) Assume that the **state** variable contains the string "MI   " (the letters M and I followed by three spaces). Which of the following C++ statements removes the three spaces from the variable's contents?

A. state.erase("   ");

B. state.erase(3, "");

C. state.remove(2, 3);

D. none of the above

4) The subscript of the first character in a string is _____.

A. 0 (zero)

B. 1 (one)

5) Which of the following **if** clauses can be used to determine whether the string stored in the **part** variable begins with the letter A?

A. if (part.begins("A"))

B. if (part.beginswith("A"))

C. if (part.substr(0, 1) == "A")

D. if (part.substr(1) == "A")

6) Which of the following **if** clauses can be used to determine whether the string stored in the **part** variable ends with the letter B?

A. if (part.ends("B"))

B. if (part.endswith("B")

C. if (part.substr(part.length() - 1, 1) == "B")

D. none of the above

7) Which of the following C++ statements assigns the first three characters in the **part** variable to the **code** variable?

A. code = part.assign(0, 3);

B. code = part.substr(0, 3);

C. code = part.substr(1, 3);

D. code = part.substring(0, 3);

8) Assume that the `word` variable contains the string "Bells". Which of the following C++ statements changes the contents of the `word` variable to "Bell"?

A. `word.erase(word.length() - 1, 1);`

B. `word.replace(word.length() - 1, 1, "");`

C. `word = word.substr(0, word.length() - 1);`

D. all of the above

9) Which of the following C++ statements changes the contents of the `word` variable from "men" to "mean"?

A. `word.addTo(2, "a");`

B. `word.insert(2, "a");`

C. `word.insert(3, "a");`

D. none of the above

10) Assuming that the `msg` variable contains the string "Happy holidays", the `cout << msg.find("day", 0) << endl;` statement displays _____ on the screen.

A. −1

B. 0

C. 10

D. 11

11) Assuming that the `msg` variable contains the string "Happy holidays", the `cout << msg.find("Day", 0) << endl;` statement displays _____ on the screen.

A. −1

B. 0

C. 10

D. 11

12) Which of the following `if` clauses can be used to determine whether the `amount` variable contains a comma?

A. `if (amount.contains(","))`

B. `if (amount.substr(",") > 0)`

C. `if (int(amount.find(",", 0)) >= 0)`

D. none of the above

13) Which of the following C++ statements compares the first four characters in a `string` variable named `address` to the string "1123", then assigns the result to an `int` variable named `result`?

A. `result = address.compare(0, 4, "1123");`

B. `result = address.compare(1, 4, "1123");`

C. `result = address.compare(4, 0, "1123");`

D. `result = compare(address, 0, 4, "1123");`

14) If the `address` variable contains the string "1125", what will the correct statement in Question 13 assign to the `result` variable?

A. −1

B. 0

C. 1

D. 4

15) Which of the following C++ statements searches for the string "CA" in a `string` variable named `state`, then assigns the result to an `int` variable named `result`? The search should begin with the character located in position five in the `state` variable. (You can assume that the `state` variable's contents are uppercase.)

A. `result = int(find(state, 5, "CA"));`

B. `result = int(state.find(5, "CA"));`

C. `result = int(state.find("CA", 5));`

D. `result = int(state.find("CA", 5, 2));`

16) If the `state` variable contains the string "San Francisco, CA", what will the correct statement in Question 15 assign to the `result` variable?

A. −1

B. 0

C. 11

D. 15

17) Which of the following C++ statements replaces the two characters located in positions four and five in a `string` variable named `code` with the string "AB"?

A. `code.replace(2, 4, "AB");`

B. `code.replace(4, 2, "AB");`

C. `code.replace(4, 5, "AB");`

D. `replace(code, 4, "AB");`

18) Which of the following C++ statements assigns five asterisks (*) to a `string` variable named `divider`?

A. `divider.assign(5, '*');`

B. `divider.assign(5, "*");`

C. `divider.assign('*', 5);`

D. `assign(divider, '*', 5);`

19) Which of the following C++ statements concatenates the contents of a `string` variable named `city`, a comma, a space, and the contents of a `string` variable named `state`, then assigns the result to a `string` variable named `cityState`?

A. `cityState = "city" + ", "  + "state";`

B. `cityState = city + ", " + state;`

C. `cityState = city & ", " & state;`

D. `cityState = "city,  + state";`

20) Which of the following can be used to assign the fifth character in the `word` variable to the `letter` variable?

A. `letter = word.substr(4);`

B. `letter = word.substr(4, 1);`

C. `letter = word(5).substring;`

D. `letter = substring(word, 5);`

Look For These
Symbols

Debugging

Discovery

EXERCISES

1) Write the C++ statement that displays on the screen the number of characters contained in the **msg** variable.

2) Write the C++ statement that removes the first two characters from the **name** variable. Use the **erase()** function.

3) Write the code that uses the **find()** function to determine whether the string stored in the **rate** variable ends with the percent sign. If it does, the code should use the **replace()** function to remove the percent sign from the variable's contents.

4) Assume that the **part** variable contains the string "ABCD34G". Write the C++ statement that assigns the 34 in the **part** variable to the **code** variable.

5) Assume that the **amount** variable contains the string "3,123,560". Write the code to remove the commas from the contents of the variable.

6) Write the C++ statement to change the contents of the **word** variable from "mouse" to "mouth".

7) Write the C++ statement to change the contents of the **word** variable from "mend" to "amend".

8) Write the code to determine whether the **address** variable contains the street name "Elm Street" (entered in uppercase, lowercase, or a combination of uppercase and lowercase). Begin the search with the first character in the **address** variable and assign the result to the **subNum** variable.

9) Assume a **string** variable named **name** contains a string in uppercase letters. Write a C++ statement that compares the first two characters in the **name** variable to the string "SM". The statement should assign the return value to an **int** variable named **returnValue**.

10) Write a C++ statement that searches for the name "SMITH" in a **string** variable named **name**, then assigns the beginning location of the name to an **int** variable named **startLocation**. The search should begin with the first character in the **name** variable. (You can assume that the **name** variable's contents are uppercase.)

11) Write a C++ statement that searches for the percent sign (%) in a **string** variable named **rate**, then assigns the location of the percent sign to an **int** variable named **location**. Begin the search with the second character in the variable.

12) Write a C++ statement that replaces with the letter "B" the first character in a **string** variable named **code**.

13) Write a C++ statement that assigns the first four characters in a **string** variable named **street** to a **string** variable named **number**.

14) Write the code that uses the **assign()** function to assign 10 asterisks to a **string** variable named **total**. The code should then concatenate the contents of the **total** variable to the contents of the **dollars** variable and assign the resulting string to the **total** variable.

15) In this exercise, you complete a program that displays a row of hyphens.

A. If necessary, start Visual Studio .NET. Open the Ch12ConE15 Solution (Ch12ConE15 Solution.sln) file, which is contained in the Cpp\Chap12\ Ch12ConE15 Solution folder.

B. The program prompts the user to enter one or more words. Complete the program by entering a statement that uses the C++ length() and assign() functions to display a row of hyphens below the word(s) on the screen. Display the same number of hyphens as there are characters in the word(s).

C. Save and then build the solution.

D. Execute the program. Test the program two times, using the words "Las Vegas" and "computer".

E. When the program is working correctly, close the Output window, then use the File menu to close the solution.

16) In this exercise, you complete a program that compares two strings.

A. If necessary, start Visual Studio .NET. Open the Ch12ConE16 Solution (Ch12ConE16 Solution.sln) file, which is contained in the Cpp\Chap12\ Ch12ConE16 Solution folder.

B. The program prompts the user to enter two one-character strings. Complete the program by entering a statement that uses the C++ compare() function to compare the two strings. Do not change the case of either string. The statement should assign the function's return value to the **compareValue** variable. Also enter an **if** statement that displays the message "Equal" if the two strings are equal. However, if the two strings are not equal, the **if** statement should display the string that comes first in the ASCII coding scheme, followed by a space and the remaining string. Display the information on the same line.

C. Save and then build the solution.

D. Execute the program. Test the program by entering the following three sets of data: a and a, b and d, f and C. (The ASCII coding scheme is shown in Appendix A.)

E. When the program is working correctly, close the Output window, then use the File menu to close the solution.

17) In this exercise, you complete a program that searches a **string** variable.

A. If necessary, start Visual Studio .NET. Open the Ch12ConE17 Solution (Ch12ConE17 Solution.sln) file, which is contained in the Cpp\Chap12\Ch12ConE17 Solution folder.

B. The program prompts the user to enter one or more letters. Complete the program by entering a statement that converts the user's response to lowercase. Also enter a statement that assigns to the **location** variable the beginning location of the letters in the **alphabet** variable.

C. Save and then build the solution.

D. Execute the program. Test the program four times, using the following strings: A, z, mnop, and $.

E. When the program is working correctly, close the Output window, then use the File menu to close the solution.

18) In this exercise, you complete a program that removes characters from a string.

    A. If necessary, start Visual Studio .NET. Open the Ch12ConE18 Solution (Ch12ConE18 Solution.sln) file, which is contained in the Cpp\Chap12\ Ch12ConE18 Solution folder.

    B. The program prompts the user to enter a phone number that includes a hyphen. Complete the program by entering a statement that replaces the hyphen with the empty string.

    C. Save and then build the solution.

    D. Execute the program. Test the program two times, using the following phone numbers: 555-5555 and 999-9999.

    E. When the program is working correctly, close the Output window, then use the File menu to close the solution.

19) In this exercise, you complete a program that accesses the characters in a string.

    A. If necessary, start Visual Studio .NET. Open the Ch12ConE19 Solution (Ch12ConE19 Solution.sln) file, which is contained in the Cpp\Chap12\ Ch12ConE19 Solution folder.

    B. The program prompts the user to enter a five-character part number. Complete the program by entering an **if** statement that verifies that the user entered exactly five characters. If the user did not enter exactly five characters, display an appropriate error message. However, if the user entered five characters, assign the first three characters to the **item** variable and assign the last two characters to the **color** variable. After making the appropriate assignments, display the contents of the **item** and **color** variables.

    C. Save and then build the solution.

    D. Execute the program. Test the program two times, using the following part numbers: 123ab and 456.

    E. When the program is working correctly, close the Output window, then use the File menu to close the solution.

20) In this exercise, you complete a program that concatenates strings.

    A. If necessary, start Visual Studio .NET. Open the Ch12ConE20 Solution (Ch12ConE20 Solution.sln) file, which is contained in the Cpp\Chap12\ Ch12ConE20 Solution folder.

    B. The program prompts the user to enter a city name, state name, and ZIP code. Complete the program by entering a statement that concatenates the city name, a comma, a space, the state name, two spaces, and the ZIP code. Assign the concatenated string to the **cityStateZip** variable.

    C. Save and then build the solution.

    D. Execute the program. Test the program by entering your city, state, and ZIP code.

    E. When the program is working correctly, close the Output window, then use the File menu to close the solution.

Application Lesson

Using String Manipulation in a C++ Program

Lab 12.1 - Stop and Analyze   If necessary, start Visual Studio .NET. Open the Ch12Lab1 Solution (Ch12Lab1 Solution.sln) file contained in the Cpp\Chap12\Ch12Lab1 Solution folder. Figure 12-11 shows the code entered in the Ch12Lab1.cpp file. (The line numbers are included in the figure only.) Study the code, then answer the questions.

Figure 12-11: C++ instructions entered in the Ch12Lab1.cpp file

```cpp
1 //Ch12Lab1.cpp - remove any parentheses and
2 //hyphens from a phone number
3 //Created/revised by <your name> on <current date>
4
5 #include <iostream>
6 #include <string>
7
8 using std::cout;
9 using std::cin;
10 using std::endl;
11 using std::string;
12
13 int main()
14 {
15     //declare variables
16     string phone       = "";
17     string currentChar = "";
18     int numChars       = 0;
19     int subscript      = 0;
20
21     //get phone number
22     cout << "Enter a phone number: ";
23     cin >> phone;
24
25     //assign number of characters to variable
26     numChars = int(phone.length());
27
28     //remove any parentheses or hyphens
29     while (subscript < numChars)
30     {
31         currentChar = phone.substr(subscript, 1);
32         if (currentChar == "("
33             || currentChar == ")"
34             || currentChar == "-")
35         {
36             phone.erase(subscript, 1);
37             numChars = numChars - 1;
38         }
```

Figure 12-11: C++ instructions entered in the Ch12Lab1.cpp file (continued)

```
39            else
40                subscript = subscript + 1;
41            //end if
42    }   //end while
43
44    //display phone number
45    cout << phone << endl;
46
47    return 0;
48 }   //end of main function
```

Questions

1. What is the purpose of the loop in Lines 29 through 42?

2. What is the purpose of the statement in Line 31?

3. What is the purpose of the selection structure in Lines 32 through 41?

4. Why is the statement in Line 37 necessary?

5. Why is the statement in Line 40 processed only when the current character is not the opening parentheses, closing parentheses, or hyphen? In other words, why isn't it necessary to update the `subscript` variable when the character is the opening parentheses, closing parentheses, or hyphen?

6. Change Line 26 to `numChars = phone.length();`. Save and then build the solution. What warning message appears in the Output window?

7. Change Line 26 to `numChars = int(phone.length());`. Save and then build the solution. Execute the program. Enter (500)123-4567 as the phone number. What phone number appears in the Command Prompt window?

8. Close the Command Prompt window.

9. Close the Output window, then use the File menu to close the solution.

Lab 12.2 On days when the weather is bad and the students cannot go outside to play, Mr. Mitchell, who teaches second grade at Hinsbrook School, spends recess time playing a simplified version of the Hangman game with his class. Mr. Mitchell feels that the game is both fun (the students love playing the game) and educational (the game allows the students to observe how letters are used to form words). Mr. Mitchell has asked you to create a program that two students can use to play the game on the computer. Figure 12-12 shows the IPO chart and C++ instructions for the program.

Figure 12-12: IPO chart and C++ instructions for the Hangman game program

IPO chart information	C++ instructions

Input

original word (from player 1)
```
string origWord = "";
```
letter (from player 2)
```
string letter = "";
```

Processing

dash replaced
```
char dashReplaced = 'F';
```
game over
```
char gameOver = 'F';
```
number of incorrect guesses
```
int numIncorrect = 0;
```

Output

guessed word (five dashes when program begins
```
string guessWord = "";
```

Algorithm

1. do
   get original word

   end repeat while(original word does not contain five characters)
2. convert original word to uppercase

3. clear the contents of the Command Prompt window
4. display the five dashes in the guessed word
5. repeat while(the game is not over)
   get a letter

   convert letter to uppercase

   repeat for each letter in the original word
     if (the current character in the word matches the letter)
       replace the dash with the letter
       indicate that a dash was replaced
     end if
   end repeat for

   if (a dash was replaced)

     display the status of the guessed word

   if (the guessed word does not contain any dashes)
     the game is over
     display "Great guessing!"

   else
     set dashReplaced to false
   end if

```
do
{
      cout << "Enter the original word: ";
      getline(cin, origWord);
} while (origWord.length() != 5);
transform(origWord.begin(), origWord.end(),
origWord.begin(), toupper);
system("cls");

cout << "Guess this word: " << guessWord << endl;

while (gameOver == 'F')
{
    cout << "Enter a letter: ";
    cin >> letter;
    transform(letter.begin(), letter.end(),
    letter.begin(), toupper);

    for(int x = 0; x < 5; x = x + 1)
    {
        if (origWord.substr(x, 1) == letter)
        {
            guessWord.replace(x, 1, letter);

            dashReplaced = 'T';

        } //end if
    } //end for

    if (dashReplaced == 'T')
    {
        cout << "Guess this word: " <<
        guessWord << endl;

        if (guessWord.find("-", 0) == -1)
        {
            gameOver = 'T';
            cout << "Great guessing!" << endl;
        }
        else
            dashReplaced = 'F';
    //end if
}
```

Figure 12-12: IPO chart and C++ instructions for the Hangman game program (continued)

IPO chart information	C++ instructions

else
  add 1 to the number of
  incorrect guesses
  if(the number of incorrect
  guesses is 10)
    the game is over
    display "Sorry, the word
    was " and the word
  end if
  end if
} //end while
	``cpp
	else
	{
	    numIncorrect = numIncorrect + 1;
	    if (numIncorrect == 10)
	    {
	        gameOver = 'T';
	        cout << "Sorry, the word was "
	            << origWord << endl;
	    } //end if
	} //end if
	} //end while```

Activity for Lab 12.2

In this activity, you enter the C++ instructions shown in Figure 12-12 into the computer. You then test the program to verify that it is working correctly.

To create the Hangman game program, then test the program:

1. If necessary, start Visual Studio .NET. Create a blank solution named Ch12Lab2 Solution. Save the solution in the Cpp\Chap12 folder.

2. Add an empty C++ Win32 Console Project to the solution. Name the project Ch12Lab2 Project.

3. Add a new C++ source file to the project. Name the source file Ch12Lab2.

4. Type **//Ch12Lab2.cpp – simulates a Hangman game** and press **Enter**.

5. Type **//Created/revised by <*your name*> on <*current date*>**, replacing <*your name*> and <*current date*> with your name and the current date, respectively. Press **Enter** twice.

6. Type the following three #include directives, then press **Enter** twice:

   #include <iostream>
   #include <algorithm>
   #include <string>

7. Type the following four using statements, then press **Enter** twice.

   using std::cout;
   using std::cin;
   using std::endl;
   using std::string;

8. Complete the program by entering the main() function, which is shaded in Figure 12-13.

Figure 12-13: Hangman game program

```cpp
//Ch12Lab2.cpp - simulates a Hangman game
//Created/revised by <your name> on <current date>

#include <iostream>
#include <algorithm>
#include <string>

using std::cout;
using std::cin;
using std::endl;
using std::string;

int main()
{
    //declare variables
    string origWord      = "";
    string letter        = "";
    char dashReplaced = 'F';
    char gameOver        = 'F';
    int numIncorrect  = 0;
    string guessWord   = "-----";

    //get the original word from player 1
    do
    {
        cout << "Enter the original word: ";
        getline(cin, origWord);
    } while(origWord.length() != 5);

    //convert the original word to uppercase
    transform(origWord.begin(), origWord.end(), origWord.
    begin(), toupper);

    //clear the contents of the Command Prompt window, then
    //display the five dashes in the guessed word
    system("cls");
    cout << "Guess this word: " << guessWord << endl;

    //allow player 2 to guess a letter
    //the game is over when either the word is guessed or
    //player 2 makes 10 incorrect guesses
    while (gameOver == 'F')
    {
        //get a letter from player 2, then convert the
        //letter to uppercase
        cout << "Enter a letter: ";
        cin >> letter;
        transform(letter.begin(), letter.end(), letter.begin(),
        toupper);

        //search for the letter in the original word
        for (int x = 0; x < 5; x = x + 1)
        {
            if (origWord.substr(x, 1) == letter)
```

Figure 12-13: Hangman game program (continued)

```cpp
            {
                //replace the appropriate dash with the letter
                guessWord.replace(x, 1, letter);
                //indicate that a replacement was made
                dashReplaced = 'T';
            }   //end if
        }   //end for

        //determine whether a replacement was made
        if (dashReplaced == 'T')
        {
            //display the status of the guessed word
            cout << "Guess this word: " << guessWord << endl;

            //if the word does not contain any dashes, then
            //the user guessed the word, so the game is over
            if (guessWord.find("-", 0) == -1)
            {
                gameOver = 'T';
                cout << "Great guessing!" << endl;
            }
            else
                dashReplaced = 'F';
            //end if

        }
        else  //processed when no dash was replaced
        {
            //update the counter variable
            numIncorrect = numIncorrect + 1;
            //determine whether player 2 made 10 incorrect guesses
            if (numIncorrect == 10)
            {
                //the game is over
                gameOver = 'T";
                cout << "Sorry, the word was " << origWord << endl;
            } //end if
        }   //end if
    }   //end while
    return 0;
}   //end of main function
```

9. Save and then build the solution. Verify that the program generated no warnings.

10. Execute the program. When you are prompted to enter the original word, type **apple** and press **Enter**. See Figure 12-14.

Figure 12-14: Dashes and prompt displayed in the Command Prompt window

11. When you are prompted to enter a letter, type **e** and press **Enter**. The program replaces, with the letter e, the last dash in the word, as shown in Figure 12-15.

Figure 12-15: Status of the guessed word

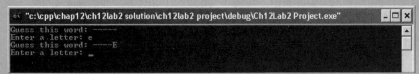

12. Type **k** in response to the "Enter a letter: " prompt, then press **Enter**. Because the letter k does not appear in the word, the program prompts you to enter another letter.

13. Type **p** in response to the "Enter a letter: " prompt, then press **Enter**. The program replaces, with the letter p, the second and third dash in the word.

14. Type **a** in response to the "Enter a letter: " prompt, then press **Enter**. The program replaces, with the letter a, the first dash in the word.

15. Type **l** in response to the "Enter a letter: " prompt, then press **Enter**. The program replaces, with the letter l, the fourth dash in the word. The program also displays the "Great guessing!" message, because you have guessed all of the letters in the word. See Figure 12-16.

Figure 12-16: Result of guessing the word

16. Close the Command Prompt window.

17. Execute the program. On your own, test the program to verify that it accepts exactly five characters in the word.

18. On your own, test the program to verify that it allows you to enter only 10 incorrect guesses, then close the Command Prompt window.

19. Close the Output window, then use the File menu to close the solution.

Lab 12.3 In this lab, you modify the program you created in Lab 12.2. The modified program will allow player 1 to enter a word of any length.

Activity for Lab 12.3

Before modifying the program created in Lab 12.2, you copy the instructions contained in the Ch12Lab2.cpp file to a new solution.

To copy the instructions contained in the Ch12Lab2.cpp file to a new solution:

1. If necessary, start Visual Studio .NET. Create a blank solution named Ch12Lab3 Solution. Save the solution in the Cpp\Chap12 folder.

2. Add an empty C++ Win32 Console Project to the solution. Name the project Ch12Lab3 Project.

3. Add a new C++ source file to the project. Name the source file Ch12Lab3.

4. Use the File menu to open the Ch12Lab2.cpp file contained in the Cpp\Chap12\Ch12Lab2 Solution\Ch12Lab2 Project folder. Select the contents of the file, then copy the contents to the clipboard.

5. Close the Ch12Lab2.cpp window.

6. Click the **Ch12Lab3.cpp** tab, then paste the instructions from the clipboard into the Ch12Lab3.cpp window.

7. Change the filename in the first program comment to **Ch12Lab3.cpp**. If necessary, change the date in the second comment.

Currently, the Hangman program allows player 1 to enter only a five-character word. Your task is to modify the program so that player 1 can enter a word of any length.

To modify the program, then test the program:

1. Make the appropriate modifications to the program.

2. Save and then build the solution. If necessary, correct any syntax errors, then save and build the solution again.

3. Execute the program. Test the program using your own sample data, then close the Command Prompt window.

4. When the program is working correctly, close the Output window, then use the File menu to close the solution.

You now have completed Chapter 12's Application lesson. You can either take a break or complete the end-of-lesson exercises.

ANSWERS TO LABS

Lab 12.1

1. The purpose of the loop is to access each character in the **phone** variable, one character at a time.

2. The statement in Line 31 assigns the current character from the **phone** variable to the **currentChar** variable.

3. The selection structure compares the current character with the opening and closing parentheses and the hyphen. If the current character is the opening parentheses, closing parentheses, or the hyphen, the statement in Line 36 removes the current character from the **phone** variable. The statement in Line 37 then subtracts the number 1 from the **numChars** variable, which keeps track of the number of characters in the **phone** variable. If the current character is not the opening parentheses, closing parentheses, or the hyphen, the statement in Line 40 adds the number 1 to the **subscript** variable, which allows the loop to access the next character in the **phone** variable.

4. Originally, the **numChars** variable contains the number of characters stored in the **phone** variable. For example, if the **phone** variable contains 111-2222, the **numChars** variable will initially contain the number 8. When the statement in Line 36 removes a character from the **phone** variable, there is one less character in the variable. For example, when the statement in Line 36 removes the hyphen from 111-2222, the **phone** variable contains seven characters rather than eight. If you did not subtract 1 from the **numChars** variable, the loop condition would attempt to access the eighth character in the **phone** variable, even though the variable now contains only seven characters.

5. Assume that the **phone** variable contains (500)333-4444. The statement in Line 31 assigns the opening parentheses, whose subscript is 0, to the **currentChar** variable. When the statement in Line 36 removes the opening parentheses from the **phone** variable, the number 5 becomes the first character in the variable and, therefore, it has a subscript of 0. In other words, when you remove a character from a variable, the next character in the variable assumes the same subscript. However, when a character is not removed from the variable, you need to update the subscript to access the next character in the variable.

6. This warning message appears: warning C4267: '=' : conversion from 'size_t' to 'int', possible loss of data.

7. The phone number 5001234567 appears in the Command Prompt window.

Lab 12.2
No answer required.

Lab 12.3
See Figure 12-17. Modifications are shaded in the figure.

Figure 12-17

```
//Ch12Lab3.cpp - simulates a Hangman game
//Created/revised by <your name> on <current date>

#include <iostream>
#include <algorithm>
#include <string>

using std::cout;
using std::cin;
using std::endl;
using std::string;

int main()
```

Figure 12-17 (continued)

```cpp
{
    //declare variables
    string origWord    = "";
    string letter      = "";
    char dashReplaced = 'F';
    char gameOver      = 'F';
    int numIncorrect  = 0;
    string guessWord   = "";
    int numChars      = 0;

    //get the original word from player 1
    cout << "Enter the original word: ";
    getline(cin, origWord);
    numChars = int(origWord.length());

    //convert the original word to uppercase
    transform(origWord.begin(), origWord.end(), origWord.begin(), toupper);

    //clear the contents of the Command Prompt window, then
    //display the dashes in the guessed word
    system("cls");
    cout << "Guess this word: " << guessWord.assign(numChars, '-') << endl;

    //allow player 2 to guess a letter
    //the game is over when either the word is guessed or
    //player 2 makes 10 incorrect guesses
    while (gameOver == 'F')
    {
        //get a letter from player 2, then convert the
        //letter to uppercase
        cout << "Enter a letter: ";
        cin >> letter;
        transform(letter.begin(), letter.end(), letter.begin(), toupper);

        //search for the letter in the original word
        for (int x = 0; x < numChars; x = x + 1)
        {
            if (origWord.substr(x, 1) == letter)
            {
                //replace the appropriate dash with the letter
                guessWord.replace(x, 1, letter);
                //indicate that a replacement was made
                dashReplaced = 'T';
            }  //end if
        }   //end for

        //determine whether a replacement was made
        if (dashReplaced == 'T')
        {
            //display the status of the guessed word
            cout << "Guess this word: " << guessWord << endl;

            //if the word does not contain any dashes, then
```

Figure 12-17 (continued)

```
                //the user guessed the word, so the game is over
                if (guessWord.find("-", 0) == -1)
                {
                    gameOver = 'T';
                    cout << "Great guessing!" << endl;
                }
                else
                    dashReplaced = 'F';
                    //end if
                }
                else  //processed when no dash was replaced
                {
                    //update the counter variable
                    numIncorrect = numIncorrect + 1;
                    //determine whether player 2 made 10 incorrect guesses
                    if (numIncorrect == 10)
                {
                    //the game is over
                    gameOver = 'T';
                    cout << "Sorry, the word was " << origWord << endl;
                } //end if
            }  //end if
        }  //end while
    return 0;
}  //end of main function
```

EXERCISES

Look For These
Symbols

1) In this exercise, you modify the program you created in Lab 12.3 so that it allows
   the user to make four more incorrect guesses than there are letters in the word.

   A. If necessary, start Visual Studio .NET. Create a blank solution named
   Ch12AppE01 Solution. Save the solution in the Cpp\Chap12 folder.

Debugging

   B. Add an empty C++ Win32 Console Project to the solution. Name the project
   Ch12AppE01 Project.

   C. Add a new C++ source file to the project. Name the source file Ch12AppE01.

   D. Use the File menu to open the Ch12Lab3.cpp file contained in the
   Cpp\Chap12\Ch12Lab3 Solution\Ch12Lab3 Project folder. Select the contents
   of the file, then copy the contents to the clipboard.

Discovery

   E. Close the Ch12Lab3.cpp window.

   F. Click the Ch12AppE01.cpp tab, then paste the instructions from the clipboard
   into the Ch12AppE01.cpp window.

   G. Change the filename in the first program comment to Ch12AppE01.cpp. If
   necessary, change the date in the second comment.

   H. Modify the program appropriately.

   I. Save and then build the solution.

   J. Execute the program. Test the program using your own sample data.

   K. When the program is working correctly, close the Output window, then use the
   File menu to close the solution.

2) In this exercise, you complete a program that displays a shipping charge based on the ZIP code entered by the user.

A. If necessary, start Visual Studio .NET. Open the Ch12AppE02 Solution (Ch12AppE02 Solution.sln) file, which is contained in the Cpp\Chap12\Ch12AppE02 Solution folder.

B. The program should display the appropriate shipping charge based on the ZIP code entered by the user. To be valid, the ZIP code must contain exactly five digits, and the first three digits must be either "605" or "606". All ZIP codes beginning with "605" have a $25 shipping charge. All ZIP codes beginning with "606" have a $30 shipping charge. All other ZIP codes are invalid and the program should display an appropriate message. Code the program appropriately.

C. Save and then build the solution.

D. Execute the program. Use the following ZIP codes to test the program: 60677, 60511, and 60344.

E. When the program is working correctly, close the Output window, then use the File menu to close the solution.

3) In this exercise, you complete a program that displays the color of an item.

A. If necessary, start Visual Studio .NET. Open the Ch12AppE03 Solution (Ch12AppE03 Solution.sln) file, which is contained in the Cpp\Chap12\ Ch12AppE03 Solution folder.

B. Code the program so that it displays the color of the item whose item number is entered by the user. All item numbers contain exactly five characters. All items are available in four colors: blue, green, red, and white. The third character in the item number indicates the item's color, as follows:

Character	Color
B or b	Blue
G or g	Green
R or r	Red
W or w	White

For example, if the user enters 12b45, the program should display the word "Blue" on the screen. If the item number does not contain exactly five characters, or if the third character is not one of the characters listed above, the program should display an appropriate message on the screen.

C. Save and then build the solution.

D. Execute the program. Test the program using the following item numbers: 12x, 12b45, 99G44, abr55, 78w99, and 23abc.

E. When the program is working correctly, close the Output window, then use the File menu to close the solution.

4) In this exercise, you complete a program that allows the user to guess a letter chosen randomly by the computer.

A. If necessary, start Visual Studio .NET. Open the Ch12AppE04 Solution (Ch12AppE04 Solution.sln) file, which is contained in the Cpp\Chap12\ Ch12AppE04 Solution folder.

B. The program assigns the letters of the alphabet to a `string` variable named `letters`. It also prompts the user to enter a letter. Complete the program by entering instructions to do the following:

- generate a random number that can be used to select one of the letters from the `letters` variable and assign the selected letter to the `randomLetter` variable

- verify that the user entered exactly one letter

- if the user did not enter exactly one letter, display an appropriate error message

- if the user entered exactly one letter, compare the lowercase version of the letter to the random letter

- allow the user to enter a letter until he or she guesses the random letter

- if the letter entered by the user is the same as the random letter, display the message "You guessed the correct letter.", then end the program

- if the random letter appears after the user's letter in the alphabet, display the message "The correct letter comes after the letter", followed by a space, the user's letter, and a period

- if the random letter appears before the user's letter in the alphabet, display the message "The correct letter comes before the letter", followed by a space, the user's letter, and a period

C. Save and then build the solution.

D. Execute the program. Test the program by entering one or more letters. The program should stop when you have guessed the correct letter.

E. When the program is working correctly, close the Output window, then use the File menu to close the solution.

5) In this exercise, you learn about the `size()` function. Like the `length()` function, the `size()` function returns the number of characters contained in a `string` variable.

A. If necessary, start Visual Studio .NET. Open the Ch12AppE05 Solution (Ch12AppE05 Solution.sln) file, which is contained in the Cpp\Chap12\Ch12AppE05 Solution folder.

B. Complete the program by entering the code to display the number of characters contained in the `name` variable. Use the `size()` function.

C. Save and then build the solution.

D. Execute the program. The program should display the number 10 in the Command Prompt window. Close the Command Prompt window.

E. When the program is working correctly, close the Output window, then use the File menu to close the solution.

6) In this exercise, you debug a C++ program.

A. If necessary, start Visual Studio .NET. Open the Ch12AppE06 Solution (Ch12AppE06 Solution.sln) file, which is contained in the Cpp\Chap12\Ch12AppE06 Solution folder. The program should display the price based on the last character in the customer number.

B. Build the solution. Correct any errors in the program, then save and build the solution.

C. Execute the program. Test the program four times, using the following customer numbers: 12x, 34W, 56a, and 23. If necessary, correct any logic errors in the program.

D. Close the Command Prompt window.

E. When the program is working correctly, close the Output window, then use the File menu to close the solution.

Please visit the Testing Center at www.course.com/testingcenter for more practice on the topics covered in this chapter.

Sequential Access Files

Objectives

After completing this chapter, you will be able to:

- Open a sequential access file

- Determine whether a file was opened successfully

- Write data to a sequential access file

- Read data from a sequential access file

- Include a delimiter character in the `getline()` function

- Test for the end of a sequential access file

- Close a sequential access file

Concept Lesson

File Types

In addition to getting information from the keyboard and sending information to the screen, a program also can get information from and send information to a file on a disk. Getting information from a file is referred to as "reading the file," and sending information to a file is referred to as "writing to the file." Files to which information is written are called **output files**, because the files store the output produced by a program. Files that are read by the computer are called **input files**, because a program uses the information in these files as input.

You can create three different types of files in C++: sequential, random, and binary. The file type refers to how the information in the file is accessed. The information in a sequential access file is always accessed sequentially—in other words, in consecutive order from the beginning of the file through the end of the file. The information stored in a random access file can be accessed either in consecutive order or in random order. The information in a binary access file can be accessed by its byte location in the file. You learn about sequential access files in this chapter. Random and binary access files are not covered in this book.

Using Sequential Access Files

A **sequential access file** is often referred to as a **text file**, because it is composed of lines of text. The text might represent a memo or a report, as shown in Examples 1 and 2 in Figure 13-1. Or, it might be a list of employee names, as shown in Example 3 in Figure 13-1.

Figure 13-1: Examples of sequential access files

```
Examples

Example 1 – memo
To all employees:

Effective January 1, 2004, the cost of dependent
coverage will increase from $35 to $38.50 per month.

Jefferson Williams
Insurance Manager


Example 2 – report
ABC Industries Sales Report

State          Sales
California      15000
Montana         10000
Wyoming          7000
                -----
Total sales:   $32000


Example 3 – list of employee names
Bonnel#Jacob
Carlisle#Donald
Eberg#Jack
Hou#Chang
```

Sequential access files are similar to cassette tapes in that each line in the file, like each song on a cassette tape, is both stored and retrieved in consecutive order (sequentially). In other words, before you can record (store) the fourth song on a cassette tape, you first must record songs one through three. Likewise, before you can write (store) the fourth line in a sequential access file, you first must write lines one through three. The same holds true for retrieving a song from a cassette tape and a line of text from a sequential access file. To listen to the fourth song on a cassette tape, you must play (or fast-forward through) the first three songs. Likewise, to read the fourth line in a sequential access file, you first must read the three lines that precede it.

Before a sequential access file can be written to or read from, it must be created and opened.

Creating and Opening a Sequential Access File

In previous chapters, you used stream objects to perform standard input and output operations in a program. The standard input stream object, `cin`, refers to the computer keyboard. The standard output stream object, `cout`, refers to the computer screen. For a program to use the `cin` and `cout` objects, it must include the iostream file; recall that you do so using the `#include <iostream>` directive. The iostream file contains the definitions of the `istream` and `ostream` classes from which the `cin` and `cout` objects, respectively, are created. You do not have to create the `cin` and `cout` objects in a program, as C++ creates the objects in the iostream file for you.

Just as you do to perform standard input and output operations in a program, you use objects to perform file input and output operations. However, unlike the standard `cin` and `cout` objects, which C++ creates, the programmer must create the input and output file objects used in a program. For a program to create a file object, it must include the fstream file; you do so using the `#include <fstream>` directive. The fstream file contains the definitions of the `ifstream` (*input file stream*) and `ofstream` (*output file stream*) classes, which allow you to create input and output file objects, respectively. In addition to the `#include <fstream>` directive, a program that creates an input file also should include the `using std::ifstream;` statement and the `using ios;` statement. Similarly, a program that creates an output file should include the `using std::ofstream;` and `using ios;` statements. Figure 13-2 shows the syntax and examples of creating input and output file objects.

tip

All objects in C++ are created from a class and are referred to as instances of the class. For example, a `cin` object is an instance of the `istream` class, and an input file object is an instance of the `ifstream` class.

Figure 13-2: Syntax and examples of creating file objects

Syntax
To create an input file object: **ifstream** *object*; To create an output file object: **ofstream** *object*;
Examples and results
`ifstream inFile;` creates an input file object named `inFile`
`ifstream inEmploy;` creates an input file object named `inEmploy`
`ofstream outFile;` creates an output file object named `outFile`
`ofstream outSales;` creates an output file object named `outSales`

In each syntax shown in Figure 13-2, *object* is the name of the file object you want to create. Notice that the names of the input file objects in the figure begin with the two letters `in`, and the names of the output file objects begin with the three letters `out`. Although the C++ syntax does not require you to begin file object names with either `in` or `out`, using this naming convention helps to distinguish a program's input file objects from its output file objects.

You use the input and output file objects, along with the C++ **open() function**, to open actual files on your computer's disk. Figure 13-3 shows the syntax of the `open()` function and describes the *modes* that are used to open a sequential access file. The figure also includes several examples of using the syntax.

Figure 13-3: Syntax and examples of the open() **function**

Syntax
object.**open**(*filename*[, *mode*]);

mode	Description
`ios::in`	Used with an `ifstream` object. Opens the file for input, which allows the computer to read the file's contents. This is the default *mode* for input files.
`ios::app`	Used with an `ofstream` object. Opens the file for append, which allows the computer to write new data to the end of the existing data in the file. If the file does not exist, the file is created before data is written to it.
`ios::out`	Used with an `ofstream` object. Opens the file for output, which creates a new, empty file to which data can be written. If the file already exists, its contents are erased before the new data is written. This is the default *mode* for output files.

Examples and results
`inFile.open("sales.txt", ios::in);` opens the sales.txt file for input
`inFile("sales.txt");` opens the sales.txt file for input
`outFile.open("payroll.txt", ios::out);` opens the payroll.txt file for output
`outFile.open("payroll.txt");` opens the payroll.txt file for output
`outEmploy.open("employ.txt", ios::app);` opens the employ.txt file for append
`outEmploy.open("a:\employ.txt", ios::app);` opens the employ.txt file (contained on the A drive) for append

In the syntax of the **open()** function, *object* is the name of either an **ifstream** or an **ofstream** file object, and *filename* is the name of the file you want to open on the computer's disk. The *filename* argument must be either a string or a **string** variable that contains the file's name. If the file you want to open is not in the same location as the program file, you must enter the file's full path in the *filename* argument. The **open()** function opens the file whose name is specified in the *filename* argument and associates it with the file object whose name is specified in the syntax as *object*.

The *mode* argument, which is optional in the **open()** function's syntax, indicates how the file is to be opened. As shown in Figure 13-3, you use the **ios::in** *mode* to open an input file. When you open a file for input, it allows the computer to read the data stored in the file. The **ios::out** and **ios::app** *modes*, on the other hand, are used to open output files. Both of these *modes* allow the computer to write data to the file. You use the **ios::app** (**app** stands for *append*) *mode* when you want to add data to the end of an existing file. If the file does not exist, the computer creates the file for you. You use the **ios::out** *mode* to open a new, empty file for output. If the file already exists, the computer erases the contents of the file before writing any data to it. The two colons (**::**) in each mode are called the **scope resolution operator** and indicate that the **in**, **out**, and **app** keywords are defined in the **ios** class.

As Figure 13-3 indicates, you can use either the **inFile.open("sales.txt", ios::in);** statement or the **inFile.open("sales.txt");** statement to open the sales.txt file for input. In C++, all files associated with an **ifstream** file object are opened automatically for input. Therefore, if you do not specify a *mode* when opening an input file, C++ uses the default *mode* **ios::in**.

Unlike files associated with an **ifstream** object, files associated with an **ofstream** object are opened automatically for output. In other words, **ios::out** is the default *mode* when opening output files, which explains why you can use either the **outFile.open("payroll.txt", ios::out);** statement or the **outFile.open("payroll.txt");** statement to open the payroll.txt file for output. In cases where the program needs to add data to the end of the existing data stored in an output file, you need to specify the **ios::app** *mode* in the **open()** function. The **outEmploy.open("employ.txt", ios::app);** statement, for example, tells the computer to open for append the employ.txt file, which is contained in the same location as the program file. However, you would need to use the **outFile.open("a:\employ.txt", ios:app);** statement to open for append the employ.txt file located on the A drive.

The computer uses a file pointer to keep track of the next character either to read from or write to a file. When you open a file for input, the computer positions the file pointer at the beginning of the file, immediately before the first character. When you open a file for output, the computer also positions the file pointer at the beginning of the file, but recall that the file is empty. (As you learned earlier, opening a file for output tells the computer to create a new, empty file or erase the contents of an existing file.) However, when you open a file for append, the computer positions the file pointer immediately after the last character in the file. Figure 13-4 illustrates the position of the file pointer when files are opened for input, output, and append.

tip

If you do not supply the file's full path in the *filename* argument, the **open()** function assumes that the file is located in the same folder as the program file.

Figure 13-4: Position of the file pointer when files are opened for input, output, and append

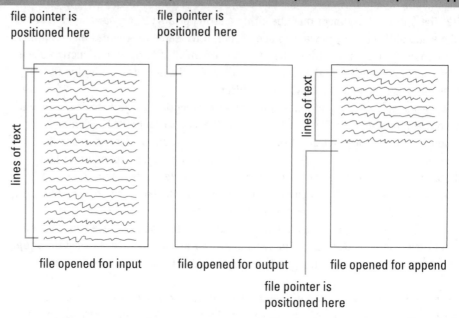

file pointer is positioned here

file pointer is positioned here

lines of text

lines of text

file opened for input

file opened for output

file opened for append

file pointer is positioned here

MINI-QUIZ

Mini-Quiz 1

1) To use either an input or output file, the program must include the _____ file.
   a.   filestream
   b.   fstream
   c.   instream
   d.   iofilestream

2) The _____ mode tells the computer to open a file for input.
   a.   `add::ios`
   b.   `in::file`
   c.   `ios::app`
   d.   `ios::in`

3) Write the C++ statement to create an output file object named `outName`.

4) Which of the following statements uses the `outName` file object created in Question 3 to open an output file named items.txt? New information should be written following the current information in the file.
   a.   `outName.open("items.txt", ios::in);`
   b.   `outName.open("items.txt", ios::out);`
   c.   `outName.open("items.txt", ios::app);`
   d.   `outName.open("items.txt", ios::add);`

Before attempting to either read data from or write data to a file, you always should verify that the file was opened successfully.

Determining Whether a File Was Opened Successfully

It is possible for the `open()` function to fail when attempting to open a file. For example, the `open()` function will not be able to create an output file on a disk that is either full or write-protected. It also will not be able to open an input file that does not exist. Before attempting to either read from or write to a file, you should use the C++ **is_open() function** to determine whether the file was opened successfully. Figure 13-5 shows the syntax of the `is_open()` function and includes examples of using the function.

Figure 13-5: Syntax and examples of the `is_open()` **function**

Syntax
object.**is_open();**

Examples and results

``
if (outFile.is_open() == true)
    instructions to process if the file was opened
else
    instructions to process if the file could not be opened
//end if
``
verifies whether the file was opened successfully, then takes the appropriate action based on the results

``
if (outFile.is_open())
    instructions to process if the file was opened
else
    instructions to process if the file could not be opened
//end if
``
verifies whether the file was opened successfully, then takes the appropriate action based on the results

``
if (outFile.is_open() == false)
    instructions to process if the file could not be opened
else
    instructions to process if the file was opened
//end if
``
verifies whether the file could not be opened, then takes the appropriate action based on the results

``
if (!outFile.is_open())
    instructions to process if the file could not be opened
else
    instructions to process if the file was opened
//end if
``
verifies whether the file could not be opened, then takes the appropriate action based on the results

not logical operator

In the `is_open()` function's syntax, *object* is the name of a file object in the program. If the file was opened successfully, the `is_open()` function returns the Boolean value `true`; otherwise it returns the Boolean value `false`. Most times, you will use the `is_open()` function in an `if` statement's *condition*, as shown in the examples in Figure 13-5.

As Figure 13-5 shows, you can use either of the *conditions* shown in the first two examples to determine whether the file was opened successfully. The `outFile.is_open() == true` *condition* compares the `is_open()` function's return value to the Boolean value `true`. Recall that a return value of `true` indicates that the file was opened successfully. As the second example indicates, you can omit the `== true` text from the *condition* and simply use `outFile.is_open()`.

Unlike the *conditions* in the first two examples, the *conditions* in the third and fourth examples determine whether the file could not be opened. In the third example, the `outFile.is_open() == false` condition compares the `is_open()` function's return value to the Boolean value `false`. Recall that a return value of `false` indicates that the file could not be opened. As the fourth example indicates, you can omit the `== false` text from the *condition*, but to do so you must begin the *condition* with an exclamation point(!). The **!** is the Not logical operator in C++, and its purpose is to reverse the truth-value of the *condition*. In other words, if the value of the *condition* is true, then the value of !*condition* is false. Likewise, if the value of the *condition* is false, then the value of !*condition* is true.

Next, you learn how to write information to a sequential access file.

Writing Information to a Sequential Access File

Figure 13-6 shows the syntax you use to write information to a sequential access file. The figure also includes examples of using the syntax.

Figure 13-6: Syntax and examples of writing information to a sequential access file

Syntax
object **<<** *data*;
Examples and results
`outFile << "ABC Company" << endl;` writes the string "ABC Company" to the file, then advances the file pointer to the next line in the file

`outFile << "Gross pay: ";`
`outFile << gross << endl;`
writes the string "Gross pay: " and the contents of the **gross** variable to the file, then advances the file pointer to the next line in the file

`outFile << name << endl;` writes the contents of the **name** variable to the file, then advances the file pointer to the next line in the file
`outFile << name << '#' << salary << endl;` writes the contents of the **name** variable, followed by the number sign (#) and the contents of the **salary** variable to the file, then advances the file pointer to the next line in the file

In the syntax shown in Figure 13-6, *object* is the name of an `ofstream` object in the program, and *data* is the information you want written to the file. The first example shown in the figure writes the string "ABC Company" to the file associated with the `outFile` object, and then advances the file pointer to the next line in the file. The `outFile << "Gross pay: ";` statement in the second example writes the string "Gross pay: " to the file, but leaves the file pointer after the last character written—in this case, after the space character. The `outFile << gross << endl;` statement then writes the contents of the **gross** variable to the file, and then advances the file pointer to the next line in the file. Assuming the **gross** variable contains the number 450, the second example writes "Gross pay: 450" (without the quotes) to the file before advancing the file pointer.

In many programs, a sequential access file is used to store fields and records. A **field** is a single item of information about a person, place, or thing—for example, a name, a salary, a Social Security number, or a price. A **record** is one or more related fields that contain all of the necessary data about a specific person, place, or thing. The college you are attending keeps a student record on you. Your student record might contain the following fields: your Social Security number, name, address, phone number, credits earned, grades earned, grade point average, and so on. The place where you are employed also keeps a record on you. Your employee record might contain your Social Security number, name, address, phone number, starting date, salary or hourly wage, and so on.

To distinguish one record from another in the file, programmers typically write each record on a separate line in the file. You do so by including the `endl` stream manipulator at the end of the statement that writes the record. The `outFile << name << endl;` statement shown in the third example in Figure 13-6, for instance, writes a record that contains one field—in this case, the name stored in the `name` variable—to the file associated with the `outFile` object. The `endl` stream manipulator writes an invisible character—referred to as the newline character—at the end of the record. As you learned in Chapter 4, the newline character represents the Enter key. The newline character advances the file pointer to the next line in the file immediately after the record is written.

When writing to a file a record that contains more than one field, programmers typically separate each field with a character literal constant; '#' is most commonly used. In the last example shown in Figure 13-6, the `outFile << name << '#' << salary << endl;` statement writes a record that contains two fields: the name stored in the `name` variable and the salary amount stored in the `salary` variable. The statement writes the record on a separate line in the file, with the # character separating the data in the name field from the data in the salary field.

Next, you learn how to read information from a sequential access file.

Reading Information from a Sequential Access File

Figure 13-7 shows the syntax you use to read information from a sequential access file. The figure also includes examples of using the syntax.

tip
You will not see the newline character when you open a sequential access file, because the character is invisible.

tip
You can verify that the information was written correctly to a sequential access file by opening the file in the Visual C++ .NET editor. To do so, click File on the menu bar, point to Open, and then click File. When the Open File dialog box opens, click the Files of type list arrow, then click All Files (*.*).

Figure 13-7: Syntax and examples of reading information from a sequential access file

Syntax
To read numeric and `char` information: *object* **>>** *variable*;   To read `string` information: **getline**(*object, variable*[, *delimCharacter*]);
Examples and results

`double salary = 0.0;`
 `inFile >> salary;`
 reads a number from the file and stores the number in the `salary` variable

`char letter = ' ';`
 `inFile >> letter;`
 reads a character from the file and stores the character in the `letter` variable

Figure 13-7: Syntax and examples of reading information from a sequential access file (continued)

Examples and results

```
string name = "";
getline(inFile, name);
```
reads a string from the file and stores the string in the **name** variable

```
string name = "";
double salary = 0.0;
getline(inFile, name, '#');
inFile >> salary;
```
reads a string from the file and stores the string in the **name** variable, then consumes the #
character, and then reads a number from the file and stores the number in the **salary**
variable

In each syntax shown in Figure 13-7, *object* is the name of an **ifstream** object in the
program, and *variable* is the name of the variable that will store the information read from
the file. Notice that you use the extraction operator (>>) to read **char** and numeric data
from a file. In the first example shown in the figure, the **inFile >> salary;** statement
reads a number from the file associated with the **inFile** object and stores the number in
the **salary** variable. In the second example, the **inFile >> letter;** statement reads a
character from the file and stores the character in the **letter** variable.

To read string data from a sequential access file, you use the **getline()** function. The
delimCharacter argument in the **getline()** function's syntax indicates where the string
ends by specifying the character that follows the last character in the string. Notice that the
delimCharacter is optional in the syntax; if you omit the *delimCharacter* argument, the
default *delimCharacter* is the newline character. When the **getline()** function encounters
the *delimCharacter*, it consumes the *delimCharacter*. As you learned in Chapter 4, when a
function consumes a character, it means that the function reads and discards the character.

In the third example shown in Figure 13-7, the **getline(inFile, name);** statement
reads a string from the file. Because the **getline()** function does not specify a
delimCharacter, the function stops reading when it encounters the newline character. The
function stores the string in the **name** variable and then consumes the newline character.

In the last example shown in Figure 13-7, the **getline(inFile, name, '#');**
statement reads a string from the file. In this case, the **getline()** function's
delimCharacter argument indicates that the string ends with the character immediately preceding the # character. After storing the string in the **name** variable, the **getline()** function consumes the # character. The next statement in the example, **inFile >> salary;**,
reads a number from the file and stores the number in the **salary** variable.

tip

In the getline()
function's
syntax shown in
Figure 13-7,
delimCharacter is
short for "delimiter
character".

tip

As you learned in
Chapter 4, the new-
line character is
designated by '\n'.

MINI-QUIZ

Mini-Quiz 2

1) The `is_open()` function returns _____ if the `open()` function could not open the file.

2) Which of the following statements writes the contents of the `quantity` variable to the inventory.txt file, which is associated with a file object named `outInv`?
   a. `inventory.txt << quantity << endl;`
   b. `ofstream << quantity << endl;`
   c. `outInv << quantity << endl;`
   d. `outInv >> quantity >> endl;`

3) Which of the following statements writes a record to the test.txt file, which is associated with a file object named `outFile`? The record contains two scores; the scores are stored in the `score1` and `score2` variables.
   a. `test.txt << score1 << score2 << endl;`
   b. `ofstream << score1 << '#' <<  score2 << endl;`
   c. `outFile << score1 << score2 << endl;`
   d. `outFile << score1 << '#' << score2 << endl;`

4) Which of the following statements reads a record written by the statement from Question 2 and stores the record in the `number` variable? The inventory.txt file is associated with a file object named `inInv`.
   a. `ifstream >> number;`
   b. `inventory.txt >> number;`
   c. `inInv << number;`
   d. `inInv >> number;`

In most cases, a program will need to read a sequential access file from its beginning to its end. In the next section, you learn how to test for the end of a file.

Testing for the End of a Sequential Access File

Recall that the computer uses a file pointer to keep track of the current line in the file. When a program first opens a sequential access file for input, the computer positions the file pointer before the first line. Each time the program reads a line from the file, the computer moves the file pointer to the beginning of the next line. The only exception to this positioning occurs when the last line is read. At that time, the computer positions the file pointer after the last line in the file.

Most times, a program will need to read each line contained in a sequential access file, one line at a time. You can do so using a repetition structure along with the `eof()` (*end of file*) function. The **eof() function** determines whether the last line has been read. In other words, it determines whether the file pointer is located after the last line in the file. Figure 13-8 shows the syntax of the `eof()` function and includes examples of using the function.

tip

Recall that sequential access files are read sequentially, one line after another, beginning with the first line and ending with the last line.

Figure 13-8: Syntax and examples of the `eof()` **function**

Syntax
object.**eof()**

Examples and results
| ```
inFile >> salary;
while (inFile.eof() == false)
{
        instructions to process when it is not the end of the file
        inFile >> salary;
}   //end while
``` <br> reads each record from the file, stopping when the end of the file is reached |
| ```
inFile >> salary;
while (!inFile.eof())
{
        instructions to process when it is not the end of the file
        inFile >> salary;
}   //end while
``` <br> reads each record from the file, stopping when the end of the file is reached |

not logical operator *(points to `!inFile.eof()`)*

In the syntax, *object* is the name of an `ifstream` object in the program. If the file pointer is located after the last line in the file, the `eof()` function returns the Boolean value `true` when the program attempts to read the next record; otherwise, it returns the Boolean value `false`.

In the first example shown in Figure 13-8, the `inFile.eof() == false` *condition* stops the loop when the end of the file has been reached. As the second example indicates, you can omit the `== false` text from the *condition*, but to do so you must begin the *condition* with the Not logical operator (`!`).

Finally, you learn how to close a sequential access file.

Closing a Sequential Access File

To prevent the loss of data, you should close a sequential access file as soon as you are finished using it. You close a file using the **close() function**. Figure 13-9 shows the syntax of the `close()` function and includes examples of using the function.

Figure 13-9: Syntax and examples of the `close()` **function**

Syntax
object.**close()**

Examples and results
`inFile.close();`   closes the file associated with the `inFile` object
`outFile.close();`   closes the file associated with the `outFile` object

In the syntax, *object* is the name of either an `ifstream` or an `ofstream` object in the program. The `close()` function does not require the name of the file to close, because the computer automatically closes the file whose name is associated with the file object specified as *object*. Recall that the `open()` function associates the filename with the file object when the file is opened.

As Figure 13-9 indicates, you use the `inFile.close();` statement to close the input file associated with the `inFile` object. You use the `outFile.close();` statement to close the output file associated with the `outFile` object.

tip

Because it is so easy to forget to close the files used in a program, you should enter the statement to close the file as soon as possible after entering the one that opens it.

MINI-QUIZ

Mini-Quiz 3

1) Which of the following `while` clauses tells the computer to read each record in the inventory.txt file while the file pointer is not at the end of the file? The file object is named `inInv`.
   a. `while (inventory.txt.end())`
   b. `while (inInv.end())`
   c. `while (!inInv.eof())`
   d. `while (!inventory.txt.eof())`

2) If the file pointer is not at the end of the file, the `eof()` function returns the value _____

3) Write the statement to close the inventory.txt file, which is associated with a file object named `outInv`.

You now have completed Chapter 13's Concept lesson. You can either take a break or complete the end-of-lesson questions and exercises before moving on to the Application lesson.

SUMMARY

Sequential access files can be either input files or output files. Input files are those whose contents are read by a program, and output files are those to which a program writes data.

For a program to use a sequential access file, it must contain the `#include <fstream>` directive. You use the `ifstream` and `ofstream` classes, which are defined in the fstream file, to create input or output file objects, respectively. The file objects are used to represent the actual files stored on your computer's disk. After creating the file object, you then use the `open()` function to open the file for input, output, or append.

Before attempting to either read data from or write data to a file, you should verify that the file was opened successfully. You can use the `is_open()` function to determine whether the file was opened successfully. The `is_open()` function returns the Boolean value `true` if the `open()` function was able to open the file. It returns the Boolean value `false` if the `open()` function could not open the file.

To distinguish one record from another in a sequential access file, programmers usually write each record on a separate line in the file. You do so by including the `endl` stream manipulator at the end of the statement that writes the record to the file. If the record contains more than one field, programmers use a character to separate the data in one field from the data in another field; the '#' character is the most commonly used.

When reading data from a file, you use the `eof()` function to determine whether the file pointer is at the end of the file. If a program attempts to read past the end of the file, the `eof()` function returns the Boolean value `true`; otherwise, it returns the Boolean value `false`.

When a program is finished with a file, you should use the `close()` function to close it. Failing to close an open file can result in the loss of data.

ANSWERS TO MINI-QUIZZES

Mini-Quiz 1

1) b. fstream

2) d. ios::in

3) ofstream outName;

4) c. outName.open("items.txt", ios::app);

Mini-Quiz 2

1) false

2) c. outInv << quantity << endl;

3) d. outFile << score1 << '#' << score2 << endl;

4) d. inInv >> number;

Mini-Quiz 3

1) c. while (!inInv.eof())

2) false

3) outInv.close();

QUESTIONS

1) A _____ is a single item of information about a person, place, or thing.
   A. field
   B. file
   C. record
   D. none of the above

2) A group of related fields that contains all of the data about a specific person, place, or thing is called a _____.
   A. field
   B. file
   C. record
   D. none of the above

3) For a program to create a file object, it must include the _____ file.
   A. fileStream
   B. fstream
   C. outFile
   D. sequential

4) You use the _____ class to instantiate an output file object.

   A. `cout`

   B. `fstream`

   C. `ofstream`

   D. `outstream`

5) Which of the following statements creates an object named `outPayroll` that represents an output file in the program?

   A. `fstream outPayroll;`

   B. `ofstream outPayroll;`

   C. `outPayroll as ofstream;`

   D. `outPayroll as outstream;`

6) Which of the following statements opens the payroll.txt file for output? The file is associated with the `outPayroll` object.

   A. `outPayroll.open("payroll.txt");`

   B. `outPayroll.open("payroll.txt", ios::out);`

   C. `outPayroll.open("payroll.txt", ios::output);`

   D. both A and B

7) To add records to the end of an existing output file, you use the _____ *mode* in the `open()` function.

   A. `add`

   B. `ios::add`

   C. `ios::app`

   D. `ios::out`

8) You use the _____ function to close a sequential access file.

   A. `close()`

   B. `end()`

   C. `exit()`

   D. `finish()`

9) To determine whether the `open()` function was successful, you use the

   _____.

   A. `is_open()`

   B. `isopen()`

   C. `isFileOpen()`

   D. `is_FileOpen()`

10) Which of the following writes the contents of the `city` variable to an output file named address.txt? The file is associated with the `outFile` object.

   A. `address.txt << city << endl;`

   B. `ofstream << city << endl;`

   C. `outFile << city << endl;`

   D. `outFile >> city >> endl;`

11) Which of the following reads a number from an input file named managers.txt and stores the number in the `salary` variable? The file is associated with the `inFile` object.

A. `managers.dat << salary;`

B. `ifstream << salary;`

C. `inFile << salary;`

D. none of the above

12) Which of the following writes the contents of the `city` and `state` variables to an output file named address.txt? The file is associated with the `outFile` object.

A. `address.txt << city << state << endl;`

B. `ofstream << city << state << endl;`

C. `outFile >> city << state << endl;`

D. `outFile << city << '#' << state << endl;`

13) Which of the following `while` clauses tells the computer to repeat the loop instructions until the end of the file is reached? The file is associated with the `inFile` object.

A. `while (inFile.eof())`

B. `while (!ifstream.eof())`

C. `while (!inFile.eof())`

D. `while (!ifstream.fail())`

14) Which of the following statements creates an object named `inPayroll` that represents an input file in the program?

A. `instream inPayroll;`

B. `ifstream inPayroll;`

C. `inPayroll as ifstream;`

D. `inPayroll as ifstream;`

15) Which of the following statements opens the payroll.txt file for input? The file is associated with the `inFile` object.

A. `inFile.open("payroll.txt", ios::app);`

B. `inFile.open("payroll.txt");`

C. `inFile.open("payroll.txt", ios::in);`

D. both B and C

EXERCISES

Look For These
Symbols

Debugging

Discovery

1) Write the statement to declare an input file object named `inSales`.

2) Write the statement to open a sequential access file named jansales.txt for input. The file is associated with the `inSales` object.

3) Write the statement to open a sequential access file named firstQtr.txt for append. The file is associated with the `outSales` object.

4) Write the statement to open a sequential access file named febsales.txt for output. The file is associated with the `outSales` object.

5) Write an `if` clause that determines whether an output file was opened successfully. The file is associated with the `outSales` object.

6) Assume you want to write the string "Employee" and the string "Name" to the sequential access file associated with the `outFile` variable. Each string should appear on a separate line in the file. Write the code to accomplish this task.

7) Assume you want to write the contents of a `string` variable named `capital` and the newline character to the sequential access file associated with the `outFile` variable. Write the code to accomplish this task.

8) Write the statement to read a string from the sequential access file associated with the `inFile` variable. Assign the string to the `textLine` variable.

9) Write the statement to read a number from the sequential access file associated with the `inFile` variable. Assign the number to the `number` variable.

10) Assume you want to read a sequential access file, line by line, and display each line on the computer screen. The file is associated with the `inFile` object. Assign each line to a `string` variable named `textLine`. Write the code to accomplish this task.

11) Write a `while` clause that tells the computer to stop processing the loop instructions when the end of the file has been reached. The file is associated with the `inFile` object.

12) Write the statement to close the jansales.txt file, which is associated with the `outFile` variable.

13) Mary Conrad wants a program that allows her to save each letter of the alphabet in a sequential access file. She will enter the letters from the keyboard.

A. If necessary, start Visual Studio .NET. Open the Ch13ConE13 Solution (Ch13ConE13 Solution.sln) file, which is contained in the Cpp\Chap13\ Ch13ConE13 Solution folder.

B. Code the program. Name the sequential access file letters.txt. Open the file for output.

C. Save and then build the solution.

D. Execute the program. Enter the 26 letters of the alphabet, one at a time. Close the Command Prompt window.

E. Click File on the menu bar, point to Open, and then click File. Click the Files of type list arrow, then click All Files (*.*) in the list. Open the letters.txt file. The file should contain 26 letters. Each letter should appear on a separate line in the file. Close the letters.txt window.

F. When the program is working correctly, close the Output window, then use the File menu to close the solution.

14) Cheryl Perry wants a program that saves the squares of the numbers from 1 through 25 in a sequential access file.

A. If necessary, start Visual Studio .NET. Open the Ch13ConE14 Solution (Ch13ConE14 Solution.sln) file, which is contained in the Cpp\Chap13\ Ch13ConE14 Solution folder.

B. Code the program. Name the sequential access file squares.txt. Open the file for output.

C. Save and then build the solution.

D. Execute the program. Close the Command Prompt window.

E. Click File on the menu bar, point to Open, and then click File. Click the Files of type list arrow, then click All Files (*.*) in the list. Open the squares.txt file. The file should contain 25 numbers. Each number should appear on a separate line in the file. Close the squares.txt window.

F. When the program is working correctly, close the Output window, then use the File menu to close the solution.

15) The manager of Checks Inc. wants a program that saves each week's total payroll amount in a sequential access file.

  A. If necessary, start Visual Studio .NET. Open the Ch13ConE15 Solution (Ch13ConE15 Solution.sln) file, which is contained in the Cpp\Chap13\ Ch13ConE15 Solution folder.

  B. Code the program. Name the sequential access file payroll.txt. Open the file for append. Use a negative number as the sentinel value.

  C. Save and then build the solution.

  D. Execute the program. Enter the following two payroll amounts: 45678.99 and 67000.56. Stop the program by entering a negative number, then close the Command Prompt window.

  E. Execute the program again. Enter the following two payroll amounts: 25000.89 and 35600.55. Stop the program by entering a negative number, then close the Command Prompt window.

  F. Click File on the menu bar, point to Open, and then click File. Click the Files of type list arrow, then click All Files (*.*) in the list. Open the payroll.txt file. The file should contain the four amounts listed in Steps D and E. Each amount should appear on a separate line in the file. Close the payroll.txt window.

  G. When the program is working correctly, close the Output window, then use the File menu to close the solution.

16) The manager of Boggs Inc. wants a program that saves the price of each inventory item in a sequential access file.

  A. If necessary, start Visual Studio .NET. Open the Ch13ConE16 Solution (Ch13ConE16 Solution.sln) file, which is contained in the Cpp\Chap13\ Ch13ConE16 Solution folder.

  B. Code the program. Use a negative number as the sentinel value. Name the sequential access file prices.txt. Open the file for append.

  C. Save and then build the solution.

  D. Execute the program. Enter the following two prices: 10.50 and 15.99. Stop the program by entering a negative number, then close the Command Prompt window.

  E. Execute the program again. Enter the following three prices: 20, 76.54, and 17.34. Stop the program by entering a negative number, then close the Command Prompt window.

  F. Click File on the menu bar, point to Open, and then click File. Click the Files of type list arrow, then click All Files (*.*) in the list. Open the prices.txt file. The file should contain the five amounts listed in Steps D and E. Each amount should appear on a separate line in the file. Close the prices.txt window.

  G. When the program is working correctly, close the Output window, then use the File menu to close the solution.

17) Mary Conrad wants a program that counts the number of letters stored in the file that you created in Exercise 13.

  A. Use Windows to copy the letters.txt file from the Cpp\Chap13\Ch13ConE13 Solution\Ch13ConE13 Project folder to the Cpp\Chap13\Ch13ConE17 Solution\ Ch13ConE17 Project folder.

  B. If necessary, start Visual Studio .NET. Open the Ch13ConE17 Solution (Ch13ConE17 Solution.sln) file, which is contained in the Cpp\Chap13\ Ch13ConE17 Solution folder.

  C. Code the program. Display the count on the computer screen.

D. Save and then build the solution. Execute the program. The program should display the number 26 in the Command Prompt window. Close the Command Prompt window.

E. When the program is working correctly, close the Output window, then use the File menu to close the solution.

18) Cheryl Perry wants a program that displays the sum of the numbers stored in the file that you created in Exercise 14.

A. Use Windows to copy the squares.txt file from the Cpp\Chap13\Ch13ConE14 Solution\Ch13ConE14 Project folder to the Cpp\Chap13\Ch13ConE18 Solution\Ch13ConE18 Project folder.

B. If necessary, start Visual Studio .NET. Open the Ch13ConE18 Solution (Ch13ConE18 Solution.sln) file, which is contained in the Cpp\Chap13\Ch13ConE18 Solution folder.

C. Code the program. Display the sum on the computer screen.

D. Save and then build the solution. Execute the program. The program should display the number 5525 in the Command Prompt window. Close the Command Prompt window.

E. When the program is working correctly, close the Output window, then use the File menu to close the solution.

19) The manager of Checks Inc. wants a program that calculates and displays the total of the weekly payroll amounts stored in the file that you created in Exercise 15.

A. Use Windows to copy the payroll.txt file from the Cpp\Chap13\Ch13ConE15 Solution\Ch13ConE15 Project folder to the Cpp\Chap13\Ch13ConE19 Solution\Ch13ConE19 Project folder.

B. If necessary, start Visual Studio .NET. Open the Ch13ConE19 Solution (Ch13ConE19 Solution.sln) file, which is contained in the Cpp\Chap13\Ch13ConE19 Solution folder.

C. Code the program. Display the total amount with a dollar sign and two decimal places on the computer screen.

D. Save and then build the solution. Execute the program. The program should display the number $173280.99 in the Command Prompt window. Close the Command Prompt window.

E. When the program is working correctly, close the Output window, then use the File menu to close the solution.

20) The manager of Boggs Inc. wants a program that calculates and displays the average price of the company's inventory items. The price of each inventory item is stored in the file that you created in Exercise 16.

A. Use Windows to copy the prices.txt file from the Cpp\Chap13\Ch13ConE16 Solution\Ch13ConE16 Project folder to the Cpp\Chap13\Ch13ConE20 Solution\Ch13ConE20 Project folder.

B. If necessary, start Visual Studio .NET. Open the Ch13ConE20 Solution (Ch13ConE20 Solution.sln) file, which is contained in the Cpp\Chap13\Ch13ConE20 Solution folder.

C. Code the program. Display the average price with a dollar sign and two decimal places on the computer screen.

D. Save and then build the solution. Execute the program. The program should display the number $28.07 in the Command Prompt window. Close the Command Prompt window.

E. When the program is working correctly, close the Output window, then use the File menu to close the solution.

21) The manager of Stellar Company wants a program that saves the company's payroll codes and corresponding salaries in a sequential access file.

A. If necessary, start Visual Studio .NET. Open the Ch13ConE21 Solution (Ch13ConE21 Solution.sln) file, which is contained in the Cpp\Chap13\ Ch13ConE21 Solution folder.

B. Code the program. Name the sequential access file codes.txt. Open the file for output. When writing the records to the file, use the # character to separate one field from another.

C. Save and then build the solution.

D. Execute the program. Enter the following codes and salaries:

Code	Salary
A	27200
B	15000
C	23000
D	12000
E	25500

E. Close the Command Prompt window.

F. Click File on the menu bar, point to Open, and then click File. Click the Files of type list arrow, then click All Files (*.*) in the list. Open the codes.txt file. The file should contain five records, each having two fields separated by the # character. Close the codes.txt window.

G. When the program is working correctly, close the Output window, then use the File menu to close the solution.

22) The manager of Boggs Inc. wants a program that records, in a sequential access file, the inventory number, quantity, and price of the items in inventory.

A. If necessary, start Visual Studio .NET. Open the Ch13ConE22 Solution (Ch13ConE22 Solution.sln) file, which is contained in the Cpp\Chap13\ Ch13ConE22 Solution folder.

B. Code the program. Name the sequential access file inventory.txt. Open the file for output. When writing the records to the file, use the # character to separate one field from another.

C. Save and then build the solution.

D. Execute the program. Enter the following inventory numbers, quantities, and prices:

Inventory number	Quantity	Price ($)
20AB	400	5
30CD	550	9
45XX	600	20

E. Close the Command Prompt window.

F. Click File on the menu bar, point to Open, and then click File. Click the Files of type list arrow, then click All Files (*.*) in the list. Open the inventory.txt file. The file should contain three records, each having three fields separated by the # character. Close the inventory.txt window.

G. When the program is working correctly, close the Output window, then use the File menu to close the solution.

23) The manager of Stellar Company wants a program that displays the codes and salaries stored in the file that you created in Exercise 21.

A. Use Windows to copy the codes.txt file from the Cpp\Chap13\Ch13ConE21 Solution\Ch13ConE21 Project folder to the Cpp\Chap13\Ch13ConE23 Solution\Ch13ConE23 Project folder.

B. If necessary, start Visual Studio .NET. Open the Ch13ConE23 Solution (Ch13ConE23 Solution.sln) file, which is contained in the Cpp\Chap13\ Ch13ConE23 Solution folder.

C. Code the program. Display the information in two columns on the computer screen. Display the column headings "Code" and "Salary".

D. Save and then build the solution. Execute the program. The program should display the fives codes and salaries stored in the codes.txt file. Close the Command Prompt window.

E. When the program is working correctly, close the Output window, then use the File menu to close the solution.

24) The manager of Boggs Inc. wants a program that calculates and displays the total dollar value of the items in inventory. The inventory numbers, quantities, and prices are stored in the file that you created in Exercise 22.

A. Use Windows to copy the inventory.txt file from the Cpp\Chap13\Ch13ConE22 Solution\Ch13ConE22 Project folder to the Cpp\Chap13\Ch13ConE24 Solution\ Ch13ConE24 Project folder.

B. If necessary, start Visual Studio .NET. Open the Ch13ConE24 Solution (Ch13ConE24 Solution.sln) file, which is contained in the Cpp\Chap13\ Ch13ConE24 Solution folder.

C. Code the program. Display the information in three columns on the computer screen. Use the column headings "Number", "Quantity", and "Price". Display the prices and total dollar value with a dollar sign and two decimal places.

D. Save and then build the solution. Execute the program. The program should display the three inventory numbers, quantities, and prices stored in the inventory.txt file. It should also display the total dollar value. Close the Command Prompt window.

E. When the program is working correctly, close the Output window, then use the File menu to close the solution.

25) In this exercise, you debug a C++ program.

A. If necessary, start Visual Studio .NET. Open the Ch13ConE25 Solution (Ch13ConE25 Solution.sln) file, which is contained in the Cpp\Chap13\ Ch13ConE25 Solution folder.

B. Study the existing code, then build the solution.

C. Execute the program. Enter Chair as the item name and 10 as the quantity, then enter Table as the item name and 20 as the quantity. Enter x as the item name. Close the Command Prompt window.

D. Click File on the menu bar, point to Open, and then click File. Click the Files of type list arrow, then click All Files (*.*) in the list. Open the items.txt file, which is contained in the Cpp\Chap13\Ch13ConE25 Solution\Ch13ConE25 Project folder. Notice that the file is empty. Close the items.txt window.

E. Correct any errors in the program, then save and build the program again. Enter Chair as the item name and 10 as the quantity, then enter Table as the item name and 20 as the quantity. Enter x as the item name. Close the Command Prompt window.

F. Open the items.txt file. This time, the file should contain the two records. Close the items.txt window.

G. When the program is working correctly, close the Output window, then use the File menu to close the solution.

Application Lesson

Using a Sequential Access File in a C++ Program

Lab 13.1 - Stop and Analyze If necessary, start Visual Studio .NET. Open the Ch13Lab1 Solution (Ch13Lab1 Solution.sln) file contained in the Cpp\Chap13\Ch13Lab1 Solution folder. Figure 13-10 shows the code entered in the Ch13Lab1.cpp file. (The line numbers are included in the figure only.) Study the code, then answer the questions.

Figure 13-10: C++ instructions entered in the Ch13Lab1.cpp file

```cpp
1 //Ch13Lab1.cpp - records state names and capitals
2 //in a sequential access file
3 //Created/revised by <your name> on <current date>
4
5 #include <iostream>
6 #include <string>
7 #include <algorithm>
8 #include <fstream>
9
10 using std::cout;
11 using std::cin;
12 using std::endl;
13 using std::string;
14 using std::ofstream;
15 using std::ios;
16
17 int main()
18 {
19     //declare variables
20     string state   = "";
21     string capital = "";
22
23     //create file object and open the file
24     ofstream outFile;
25     outFile.open("statecapitals.txt", ios::out);
26
27     //determine whether the file was opened successfully
28     if (outFile.is_open())
29     {
30         //get state name
31         cout << "Enter a state name (X to stop): ";
32         getline(cin, state);
33         transform(state.begin(), state.end(),
34             state.begin(), toupper);
35
36         while (state != "X")
37         {
38             //get the capital
39             cout << "Enter the capital: ";
40             getline(cin, capital);
41             transform(capital.begin(),
```

Figure 13-10: C++ instructions entered in the Ch13Lab1.cpp file (continued)

```
42                          capital.end(), capital.begin(), toupper);
43
44              //write the record to the file
45              outFile << state << '#' << capital << endl;
46
47              //get another state name
48              cout << "Enter a state name (X to stop): ";
49              getline(cin, state);
50              transform(state.begin(), state.end(),
51                  state.begin(), toupper);
52          }   //end while
53
54          //close the file
55          outFile.close();
56      }
57      else
58          cout << "The file could not be opened." << endl;
59      //end if
60
61      return 0;
62 } //end of main function
```

Questions

1. Why is the instruction in Line 8 necessary?

2. The program writes records to a sequential access file. How many fields are in each record and what are the fields?

3. Assume that you run the program, enter three records, and then stop the program. Also assume that you then run the program again, enter two records, and then stop the program. If you open the statecapitals.txt file, how many records will the file contain? Why?

4. How can you modify the program so that it saves the previous records no matter how many times the program is run?

5. What is another way of writing the `if` clause in Line 28?

6. What is the purpose of the # character in Line 45?

7. Why is the statement in Line 55 necessary?

8. Save and then build the solution.

9. Execute the program. Enter the following three state and capital names and the sentinel value: Oregon, Salem, New Jersey, Trenton, Ohio, Columbus, X. Close the Command Prompt window, then close the Output window.

10. Open the statecapitals.txt file, which is contained in the Cpp\Chap13\Ch13Lab1 Solution\ Ch13Lab1 Project folder. What does the file contain? Close the statecapitals.txt window.

11. Use the File menu to close the solution.

Lab 13.2 Jane Jacobs, the owner of a flower shop named Flowers Express, has asked you to create a program that she can use to record (in a sequential access file) each salesperson's name and sales amount. The program also should allow her to display the total of the sales amounts stored in the file.

The Flowers Express program will contain four functions: `main()`, `displayMenu()`, `addRecords()`, and `displayTotal()`. Figure 13-11 shows the IPO chart and C++ instructions for the `main()` function, and Figure 13-12 shows the IPO chart and C++ instructions for the `displayMenu()` function.

Figure 13-11: IPO chart and C++ instructions for the `main()` **function**

IPO chart information	C++ instructions

Input
 menu choice
Processing
 	
Output
 	
Algorithm
1. call function to display menu
2. repeat while (menu choice is not 3)
 	
  if (menu choice is 1)
    call function to add records
  else if (menu choice is 2)
    call function to display total
  else
    display "Invalid menu choice"
  end ifs
  call function to display menu
end repeat while
	`int menuChoice = 0;`
	
	`menuChoice = displayMenu();`
	`while (menuChoice != 3)`
	`{`
	  `if (menuChoice == 1)`
	    `addRecords();`
	  `else if (menuChoice == 2)`
	    `displayTotal();`
	  `else`
	    `cout << "Invalid menu choice" << endl;`
	  `//end ifs`
	  `menuChoice = displayMenu();`
	`} //end while`

Figure 13-12: IPO chart and C++ instructions for the `displayMenu()` **function**

IPO chart information	C++ instructions

Input
 	
Processing
 	
Output
 choice
 	
Algorithm
1. display menu options
 	
2. get the menu choice
 	
3. return choice
	
	`int choice = 0;`
	
	`cout << "Options" << endl;`
	`cout << "1  Add Records" << endl;`
	`cout << "2  Display Total Sales" << endl;`
	`cout << "3  Exit Program" << endl;`
	`cout << "Enter menu option: ";`
	`cin >> choice;`
	`cin.ignore(1);`
	`return choice;`

The `main()` function begins by declaring and initializing an `int` variable named `menuChoice`. It then calls the `displayMenu()` function to display a menu that contains three options: Add Records, Display Total Sales, and Exit Program. After displaying the menu, the `displayMenu()` function prompts the user to enter his or her menu choice: 1 to add records, 2 to display the total sales, and 3 to exit the program. The `displayMenu()` function returns the user's response to the `main()` function, which assigns the value to the `menuChoice` variable.

The `while (menuChoice != 3)` clause in the `main()` function repeats the loop body instructions as long as the `menuChoice` variable does not contain the number 3. (Recall that menu choice 3 indicates that the user wants to exit the program.) The first instruction in the loop body is a selection structure that compares the contents of the `menuChoice` variable to the number 1. If the `menuChoice` variable contains the number 1, the `main()` function calls the `addRecords()` function to add one or more records to the sequential access file. When the `addRecords()` function completes its processing, the `main()` function calls the `displayMenu()` function to display the menu.

If the `menuChoice` variable does not contain the number 1, the nested selection structure in the loop body compares the contents of the `menuChoice` variable to the number 2. If the `menuChoice` variable contains the number 2, the `main()` function calls the `displayTotal()` function to total the sales amounts in the sequential access file and then display the total on the screen. When the `displayTotal()` function completes its processing, the `main()` function calls the `displayMenu()` function to display the menu.

If the menuChoice variable contains a value other than 1, 2, or 3, the `main()` function displays an appropriate error message before calling the `displayMenu()` function to display the menu.

Figure 13-13 shows the IPO chart and C++ instructions for the `addRecords()` function.

Figure 13-13: IPO chart and C++ instructions for the `addRecords()` function

IPO chart information	C++ instructions
Input name sales amount **Processing**	`string name = "";` `int sales = 0;`
Output record written to a sequential access file	`ofstream outFile;`

Algorithm
1. open the file for append
2. if (the file was opened)
 	
  get name
 	
  repeat while (name is not X)
 	
    get sales amount
 	
    write record to the file
    get name
 	
  end repeat while
  close the file
 	
  else
    display the "File could
    not be opened." message
  end if
	``` outFile.open("sales.txt", ios::app);```
	``` if (outFile.is_open())```
	``` {```
	``` cout << "Enter name (X to stop): ";```
	``` getline(cin, name);```
	``` while (name != "X" && name != "x")```
	``` {```
	``` cout << "Enter sales: ";```
	``` cin >> sales;```
	``` cin.ignore();```
	``` outFile << name << '#' << sales << endl;```
	``` cout << "Enter name (X to stop): ";```
	``` getline(cin, name);```
	``` } //end while```
	``` outFile.close();```
	``` }```
	``` else```
	``` cout << "File could not be opened." << endl;```
	``` //end if```

The addRecords() function creates an output file object named outFile. It also uses the open() function to open a file named sales.txt for append, and uses the is_open() function to determine whether the file was opened successfully. If the is_open() function returns the Boolean value false, the addRecords() function displays an appropriate error message; otherwise, the instructions in the if statement's true path are processed.

The instructions in the if statement's true path prompt the user to enter a name, storing the user's response in the name variable. Next, the while clause indicates that the loop body instructions should be repeated as long as the name variable contains a value other than X or x.

The first two statements in the loop body prompt the user to enter a sales amount and store the user's response in the sales variable. The cin.ignore(); statement instructs the computer to consume the newline character that remains in the cin stream after the sales amount is entered. The outFile << name << '#' << sales << endl; statement then writes a record to the file; the record contains the contents of the name variable, the # character, and the contents of the sales variable. After writing the record, the program prompts the user to enter another name. When the loop completes its processing, which occurs when the user enters either the letter X or the letter x, the outFile.close(); statement closes the output file before the addRecords() function ends.

Figure 13-14 shows the IPO chart and C++ instructions for the displayTotal() function.

Figure 13-14: IPO chart and C++ instructions for the displayTotal() function

IPO chart information	C++ instructions

Input
record read from a
sequential access file
name
sales amount
Processing
 	
Output
total sales amount
 	
Algorithm
1. open the file for input
2. if (the file was opened)
 	
  read a record from the file
 	
  repeat while (not eof)
 	
   add the sales amount to the
   total sales amount
   read a record from the file
 	
  end repeat while
  close the file
  display the total sales amount
 	
 else
  display the "File could
  not be opened." message
end if
	`ifstream inFile;`
	
	`string name = "";`
	`int sales = 0;`
	
	`int total = 0;`
	
	`inFile.open("sales.txt", ios::in);`
	`if (inFile.is_open())`
	`{`
	   `getline(inFile, name, '#');`
	   `inFile >> sales;`
	   `inFile.ignore();`
	   `while (!inFile.eof())`
	   `{`
	     `total = total + sales;`
	
	     `getline(inFile, name, '#');`
	     `inFile >> sales;`
	     `inFile.ignore();`
	   `} //end while`
	   `inFile.close();`
	   `cout << endl << "Total sales $"`
	     `<< total << endl << endl;`
	`}`
	`else`
	  `cout << "File could not be opened." << endl;`
	
	`//end if`

The `displayTotal()` function creates an input file object named `inFile`. It also uses the `open()` function to open the sales.txt file for input, and uses the `is_open()` function to determine whether the file was opened successfully. If the `is_open()` function returns the Boolean value `false`, the `displayTotal()` function displays an appropriate error message; otherwise, the instructions in the `if` statement's true path are processed.

The instructions in the `if` statement's true path read a record from the file, assigning the name to the `name` variable and assigning the sales to the `sales` variable. The `while` clause tells the computer to repeat the loop body instructions as long as the file pointer is not at the end of the file.

The first statement in the loop body adds the sales amount to the accumulator variable `total`. The remaining instructions in the loop body read another record from the file. When the loop completes its processing, which occurs when the file pointer is at the end of the sequential access file, the last two statements in the `if` statement's true path close the input file and then display the total sales amount on the screen.

Activity for Lab 13.2

In this activity, you enter the C++ instructions shown in Figures 13-11 through 13-14 into the computer. You then test the program to verify that it is working correctly.

To create the Flowers Express program, then test the program:

1. If necessary, start Visual Studio .NET. Create a blank solution named Ch13Lab2 Solution. Save the solution in the Cpp\Chap13 folder.

2. Add an empty C++ Win32 Console Project to the solution. Name the project Ch13Lab2 Project.

3. Add a new C++ source file to the project. Name the source file Ch13Lab2.

4. Type **//Ch13Lab2.cpp – saves records to a sequential access file** and press **Enter**.

5. Type **//and also displays the total sales amount** and press **Enter**.

6. Type **//Created/revised by <*your name*> on <*current date*>**, replacing <*your name*> and <*current date*> with your name and the current date, respectively. Press **Enter** twice.

7. Type the following three `#include` directives, then press **Enter** twice:

   #include <iostream>
   #include <string>
   #include <fstream>

8. Type the following seven `using` statements, then press **Enter** twice:

   using std::cout;
   using std::cin;
   using std::endl;
   using std::string;
   using std::ifstream;
   using std::ofstream;
   using std::ios;

9. Type **//function prototypes** and press **Enter**, then type the following three function prototypes and press **Enter** twice:

   int displayMenu();
   void addRecords();
   void displayTotal();

10. Complete the program by entering the main(), displayMenu(), addRecords(), and displayTotal() functions, which are shaded in Figure 13-15.

Figure 13-15: Flowers Express program

```cpp
//Ch13Lab2.cpp - saves records to a sequential access file
//and also displays the total sales amount
//Created/revised by <your name> on <current date>

#include <iostream>
#include <string>
#include <fstream>

using std::cout;
using std::cin;
using std::endl;
using std::string;
using std::ifstream;
using std::ofstream;
using std::ios;

//function prototypes
int displayMenu();
void addRecords();
void displayTotal();

int main()
{
    //declare variable
    int menuChoice = 0;

    //display menu and get choice
    menuChoice = displayMenu();

    //call appropriate function
    //or display error message
    while (menuChoice != 3)
    {
        if (menuChoice == 1)
            addRecords();
        else if (menuChoice == 2)
            displayTotal();
        else
            cout << "Invalid menu choice" << endl;
        //end ifs

        //display menu and get choice
        menuChoice = displayMenu();
    } //end while
```

Figure 13-15: Flowers Express program (continued)

```cpp
    return 0;
}   //end of main function

//*****function definitions*****
int displayMenu()
{
    //declare variable
    int choice = 0;

    //display menu
    cout << "Options" << endl;
    cout << "1  Add Records" << endl;
    cout << "2  Display Total Sales" << endl;
    cout << "3  Exit Program" << endl;

    //get user's choice, then return the choice
    cout << "Enter menu option: ";
    cin >> choice;
    cin.ignore(1);
    return choice;
}   //end of displayMenu function

void addRecords()
{
    //declare variables
    string name = "";
    int sales = 0;

    //create file object and open the file
    ofstream outFile;
    outFile.open("sales.txt", ios::app);

    //determine whether the file was opened
    if (outFile.is_open())
    {
        //get the name
        cout << "Enter name (X to stop): ";
        getline(cin, name);
        while (name != "X" && name != "x")
        {
            //get the sales amount
            cout << "Enter sales: ";
            cin >> sales;
            cin.ignore();
            //write the record
            outFile << name << '#' << sales << endl;
            //get another name
            cout << "Enter name (X to stop): ";
            getline(cin, name);
        } //end while
```

Figure 13-15: Flowers Express program (continued)

```cpp
            //close the file
            outFile.close();
    }
    else
            cout << "File could not be opened." << endl;
    //end if
}   //end of addRecords function

void displayTotal()
{
    //declare variables
    string name = "";
    int sales = 0;
    int total = 0;

    //create file object and open the file
    ifstream inFile;
    inFile.open("sales.txt", ios::in);

    //determine whether the file was opened
    if (inFile.is_open())
    {
        //read a record
        getline(inFile, name, '#');
        inFile >> sales;
        inFile.ignore();
        while (!inFile.eof())
        {
                //accumulate the sales amount
                total = total + sales;
                //read another record
                getline(inFile, name, '#');
                inFile >> sales;
                inFile.ignore();
        } //end while

        //close the file
        inFile.close();

        //display the total sales amount
        cout << endl << "Total sales $"
            << total << endl << endl;
    }
    else
            cout << "File could not be opened." << endl;
    //end if
}   //end of displayTotal function
```

11. Save and then build the solution. Verify that the program generated no warnings.

12. Execute the program. The menu appears in the Command Prompt window, as shown in Figure 13-16.

Figure 13-16: Menu shown in the Command Prompt window

13. Type the number **1** and press **Enter** to add records to the sales.txt file. When you are prompted to enter the name, type **John Hammil** and press **Enter**. When prompted to enter the sales amount, type **3000** and press **Enter**.

14. Use the program to enter the following names and sales amounts:

Name	Sales amount
Carol Wroberg	**2000**
Sean Nunez	**1000**
Drew Merriweather	**4500**
Jake Treadle	**4650**
x	

15. When the menu appears in the Command Prompt window, type **2** and press **Enter** to display the total sales amount. The Command Prompt window indicates that the total sales amount is $15150, as shown in Figure 13-17.

Figure 13-17: Command Prompt window showing the total sales amount

```
c:\cpp\chap13\ch13lab2 solution\ch13lab2 project\debug\Ch13Lab2 Project.exe
Enter menu option: 1
Enter name (X to stop): John Hammil
Enter sales: 3000
Enter name (X to stop): Carol Wroberg
Enter sales: 2000
Enter name (X to stop): Sean Nunez
Enter sales: 1000
Enter name (X to stop): Drew Merriweather
Enter sales: 4500
Enter name (X to stop): Jake Treadle
Enter sales: 4650
Enter name (X to stop): x
Options
1  Add Records
2  Display Total Sales
3  Exit Program
Enter menu option: 2

Total sales $15150

Options
1  Add Records
2  Display Total Sales
3  Exit Program
Enter menu option:
```

16. When the menu appears in the Command Prompt window, type **3** and press **Enter** to end the program.

17. Close the Command Prompt window.

18. Close the Output window, then use the File menu to close the solution.

Lab 13.3 In this lab, you modify the program you created in Lab 13.2. The modified program will allow the user to display the contents of the sales.txt file.

Activity for Lab 13.3

Before modifying the program created in Lab 13.2, you copy the instructions contained in the Ch13Lab2.cpp file to a new solution.

To copy the instructions contained in the Ch13Lab2.cpp file to a new solution:

1. If necessary, start Visual Studio .NET. Create a blank solution named **Ch13Lab3 Solution**. Save the solution in the Cpp\Chap13 folder.

2. Add an empty C++ Win32 Console Project to the solution. Name the project **Ch13Lab3 Project**.

3. Add a new C++ source file to the project. Name the source file **Ch13Lab3**.

4. Use the File menu to open the Ch13Lab2.cpp file contained in the Cpp\Chap13\Ch13Lab2 Solution\Ch13Lab2 Project folder. Select the contents of the file, then copy the contents to the clipboard.

5. Close the Ch13Lab2.cpp window.

6. Click the **Ch13Lab3.cpp** tab, then paste the instructions from the clipboard into the Ch13Lab3.cpp window.

7. Change the filename in the first program comment to **Ch13Lab3.cpp**. If necessary, change the date in the second comment.

Currently, the Flowers Express program allows the user to add records to the sales.txt file and also display the total of the sales amounts stored in the file. Your task is to modify the program so that it also allows the user to display the contents of the sales.txt file.

To modify the program, then test the program:

1. Make the appropriate modifications to the program.

2. Save and then build the solution. If necessary, correct any syntax errors, then save and build the solution again.

3. Execute the program. Use the program to enter the following records:

Name	Sales amount
Carol Jean	3000
Jeffrey Hober	5560
Mary Leatter	2500
x	

4. Use the program to display the total sales amount.

5. Use the program to display the contents of the sales.txt file.

6. When the program is working correctly, close the Output window, then use the File menu to close the solution.

You now have completed Chapter 13's Application lesson. You can either take a break or complete the end-of-lesson exercises.

ANSWERS TO LABS

Lab 13.1

1. The #include <fstream> directive in Line 8 tells the computer to include the fstream file in the program. The fstream file is necessary because it contains the definitions of the **ifstream** and **ofstream** classes, which allow you to create input and output file objects, respectively.

2. Each record contains two fields—a state field and a capital field.

3. The statecapitals.txt file will contain only the two records written when the program was run the second time. Because the file is opened for output, the file will be erased each time the program is run.

4. To save the previous records, open the file for append by changing the *mode* in the **open()** function to **ios::app**.

5. You also can write the if clause as if (outFile.is_open() == true).

6. The # character separates the state name from the capital name.

7. The statement in Line 55 closes the output file. Neglecting to close a file can result in a loss of data.

10. The statecapitals.txt file contains the following three records:

OREGON#SALEM
NEW JERSEY#TRENTON
OHIO#COLUMBUS

Lab 13.2

No answer required.

Lab 13.3

See Figure 13-18. Modifications are shaded in the figure.

Figure 13-18

```
//Ch13Lab3.cpp - saves records to a sequential access file
//and also displays the total sales amount
//Created/revised by <your name> on <current date>

#include <iostream>
#include <string>
#include <fstream>

using std::cout;
using std::cin;
using std::endl;
using std::string;
using std::ifstream;
using std::ofstream;
using std::ios;
```

Figure 13-18 (continued)

```cpp
//function prototypes
int displayMenu();
void addRecords();
void displayTotal();
void displayFile();

int main()
{
    //declare variable
     int menuChoice = 0;
     //display menu and get choice
    menuChoice = displayMenu();

    //call appropriate function
    //or display error message
    while (menuChoice != 4)
    {
        if (menuChoice == 1)
            addRecords();
        else if (menuChoice == 2)
            displayTotal();
        else if (menuChoice == 3)
            displayFile();
        else
            cout << "Invalid menu choice" << endl;
        //end ifs

      //display menu and get choice
     menuChoice = displayMenu();
    } //end while

    return 0;
}   //end of main function

//*****function definitions*****
int displayMenu()
{
    //declare variable
    int choice = 0;

    //display menu
    cout << "Options" << endl;
    cout << "1  Add Records" << endl;
    cout << "2  Display Total Sales" << endl;
    cout << "3 Display File" << endl;
    cout << "4  Exit Program" << endl;

    //get user's choice, then return the choice
    cout << "Enter menu option: ";
    cin >> choice;
    cin.ignore(1);
    return choice;
}   //end of displayMenu function
```

Figure 13-18 (continued)

```cpp
void addRecords()
{
    //declare variables
    string name = "";
    int sales = 0;

    //create file object and open the file
    ofstream outFile;
    outFile.open("sales.txt", ios::app);

    //determine whether the file was opened
    if (outFile.is_open())
    {
        //get the name
        cout << "Enter name (X to stop): ";
        getline(cin, name);
        while (name != "X" && name != "x")
        {
            //get the sales amount
            cout << "Enter sales: ";
            cin >> sales;
            cin.ignore();
            //write the record
            outFile << name << '#' << sales << endl;
            //get another name
            cout << "Enter name (X to stop): ";
            getline(cin, name);
        } //end while

        //close the file
        outFile.close();
    }
    else
        cout << "File could not be opened." << endl;
    //end if
}   //end of addRecords function

void displayTotal()
{
    //declare variables
    string name = "";
    int sales = 0;
    int total = 0;

    //create file object and open the file
    ifstream inFile;
    inFile.open("sales.txt", ios::in);
```

Figure 13-18 (continued)

```cpp
        //determine whether the file was opened
        if (inFile.is_open())
        {
            //read a record
            getline(inFile, name, '#');
            inFile >> sales;
            inFile.ignore();
            while (!inFile.eof())
            {
                //accumulate the sales amount
                total = total + sales;
                //read another record
                getline(inFile, name, '#');
                inFile >> sales;
                inFile.ignore();
            } //end while

            //close the file
            inFile.close();

            //display the total sales amount
            cout << endl << "Total sales $"
                << total << endl << endl;
        }
        else
            cout << "File could not be opened." << endl;
        //end if
}   //end of displayTotal function

void displayFile()
{
    //declare variables
    string line = "";

    //create file object and open the file
    ifstream inFile;
    inFile.open("sales.txt", ios::in);

    //determine whether the file was opened
    if (inFile.is_open())
    {
        //read a line from the file
        getline(inFile, line);
        while (!inFile.eof())
        {
            //display the line
            cout << line << endl;
            //read another line from the file
            getline(inFile, line);
        } //end while

        //close the file
        inFile.close();
    }
    else
        cout << "File could not be opened." << endl;
    //end if
}   //end of displayFile function
```

EXERCISES

1) Consolidated Advertising wants a program that its managers can use to record various cities and their corresponding ZIP codes in a sequential access file. The program also should allow managers to look up a ZIP code in the file and display its corresponding city.

A. If necessary, start Visual Studio .NET. Open the Ch13AppE01 Solution (Ch13AppE01 Solution.sln) file, which is contained in the Cpp\Chap13\ Ch13AppE01 Solution folder.

B. Code the program.

C. Save and then build the solution. Execute the program. First, enter the following ZIP codes and cities:

ZIP code	City
60561	Darien
60544	Hinsdale
60137	Glen Ellyn
60135	Downers Grove
60136	Burr Ridge

D. Next, display the city corresponding to the following ZIP codes: 60135, 60544, and 55555. The program should display Downers Grove, Hinsdale, and an error message.

E. When the program is working correctly, close the Output window, then use the File menu to close the solution.

2) Each salesperson at BobCat Motors is assigned a code that consists of two characters. The first character is either the letter F for full-time employee or the letter P for part-time employee. The second character is either a 1 (indicating the salesperson sells new cars) or a 2 (indicating the salesperson sells used cars). The names of BobCat's salespeople, along with their codes, are contained in a sequential access file named namecode.txt.

A. If necessary, start Visual Studio .NET. Open the Ch13AppE02 Solution (Ch13AppE02 Solution.sln) file, which is contained in the Cpp\Chap13\ Ch13AppE02 Solution folder.

B. Code the program so that it prompts the user to enter the code (F1, F2, P1, or P2). The program should search the namecode.txt file for that code, then display only the names of the salespeople assigned that code.

C. Save and then build the solution.

D. Execute the program. Test the program by entering the code F2. The program should display three records: Mary Jones, Joel Adkari, and Janice Paulo.

E. When the program is working correctly, close the Output window, then use the File menu to close the solution.

3) In this exercise, you update a sequential access file.

A. If necessary, start Visual Studio .NET. Click File on the menu bar, point to Open, and then click File. Open the numbers.txt file, which is contained in the Cpp\Chap13\Ch13AppE03 Solution\Ch13AppE03 Project folder. The sequential access file contains one numeric field. Close the numbers.txt window.

B. Open the Ch13AppE03 Solution (Ch13AppE03 Solution.sln) file, which is contained in the Cpp\Chap13\Ch13AppE03 Solution folder.

C. Code the program so that it reads the numbers from the numbers.txt file. The program should add the number 1 to each number, then write the new value to another sequential file. Name the updated sequential file updatednumbers.txt.

D. Save and then build the solution.

E. Execute the program. Close the Command Prompt window, then open the updatednumbers.txt file. Each number in the file should be one greater than its corresponding number in the numbers.txt file. Close the updatednumbers.txt window.

F. When the program is working correctly, close the Output window, then use the File menu to close the solution.

4) In this exercise, you read the numbers contained in a sequential access file, then write only the even numbers to a new sequential access file.

A. If necessary, start Visual Studio .NET. Click File on the menu bar, point to Open, and then click File. Open the numbers.txt file, which is contained in the Cpp\Chap13\Ch13AppE04 Solution\Ch13AppE04 Project folder. The sequential access file contains one numeric field. Close the numbers.txt window.

B. Open the Ch13AppE04 Solution (Ch13AppE04 Solution.sln) file, which is contained in the Cpp\Chap13\Ch13AppE04 Solution folder.

C. Code the program so that it reads the numbers from the numbers.txt file. The program should write only the even numbers to a new sequential file named evennumbers.txt. *Hint:* Use the % (modulus arithmetic) operator, which you learned about in Chapter 4.

D. Save and then build the solution.

E. Execute the program. Close the Command Prompt window, then open the evennumbers.txt file. Only even numbers should appear in the file. Close the evennumbers.txt window.

F. When the program is working correctly, close the Output window, then use the File menu to close the solution.

5) In this exercise, you create a program that reads and displays the records contained in the statecapitals.txt file, which you created in Lab 13.1.

A. If necessary, start Visual Studio .NET. Open the Ch13AppE05 Solution (Ch13AppE05 Solution.sln) file, which is contained in the Cpp\Chap13\ Ch13AppE05 Solution folder.

B. Code the program so that it reads and displays the contents of the statecapitals .txt file, which is contained in the Cpp\Chap13\Ch13AppE05 Solution\ Ch13AppE05 Project folder. Display the city name, a comma, and the state name.

C. Save and then build the solution.

D. Execute the program. The content of the statecapitals.txt file appears in the Command Prompt window. Close the Command Prompt window.

E. When the program is working correctly, close the Output window, then use the File menu to close the solution.

6) In this exercise, you debug a C++ program.

A. If necessary, start Visual Studio .NET. Click File on the menu bar, point to Open, and then click File. Open the records.txt file, which is contained in the Cpp\Chap13\Ch13AppE06 Solution\Ch13AppE06 Project folder. The sequential access file contains a **string** field and two numeric fields. Close the records.txt window.

B. Open the Ch13AppE06 Solution (Ch13AppE06 Solution.sln) file, which is contained in the Cpp\Chap13\Ch13AppE06 Solution folder. The Ch13AppE06.cpp program should display the records contained in the records.txt file. A comma should separate one field from the next.

C. Study the existing code, then build the solution.

D. Execute the program. Correct any errors in the program, then save and build the solution.

E. When the program is working correctly, close the Output window, then use the File menu to close the solution.

 Please visit the Testing Center at www.course.com/testingcenter for more practice on the topics covered in this chapter.

Classes and Objects

After completing this chapter, you will be able to:

- Differentiate between procedure-oriented and object-oriented programming

- Define the terms used in object-oriented programming

- Create a class

- Create a default constructor

- Create an object from a class

Concept Lesson

Programming Methods

Currently, the two most popular methods used to create computer programs are the procedure-oriented method and the object-oriented method. When using the procedure-oriented method to create a program, the programmer concentrates on the major tasks that the program needs to perform. A payroll program, for example, typically performs several major tasks, such as calculating the gross pay, calculating the taxes, and calculating the net pay. A programmer using the procedure-oriented method usually assigns each major task to a function, which is the primary component in a procedure-oriented program. You used the procedure-oriented method to develop the programs that you created in the previous chapters.

Different from the procedure-oriented method, which focuses on the individual tasks the program must perform, the object-oriented method requires the programmer to focus on the objects that a program can use to accomplish its goal. A payroll program, for example, might utilize a time card object, an employee object, and a paycheck object. The primary component in an object-oriented program is an object. In this chapter, you learn more about object-oriented programming. You also learn how to create simple object-oriented programs.

Object-Oriented Programming

Unlike the procedure-oriented method of programming, the object-oriented method allows the programmer to use familiar objects to solve problems. The ability to use objects that model things found in the real world makes problem solving much easier. For example, assume that the manager of a flower shop asks you to create a program that keeps track of the shop's daily sales revenue. Thinking in terms of the objects used to represent revenue—cash, checks, credit card receipts, and so on—will make the sales revenue problem easier to solve. Additionally, because each object is viewed as an independent unit, an object can be used in more than one program, usually with little or no modification. A check object used in the sales revenue program, for example, also can be used in a payroll program (which issues checks to employees) and an accounts payable program (which issues checks to creditors). The ability to use an object for more than one purpose saves programming time and money—a fact that contributes to the popularity of object-oriented programming.

Although you may have either heard or read that object-oriented programming is difficult to learn, do not be intimidated. Admittedly, creating object-oriented programs does take some practice. However, you already are familiar with many of the concepts upon which object-oriented programming is based. Much of the anxiety of object-oriented programming stems from the terminology used when discussing it. Many of the terms are unfamiliar, because they typically are not used in everyday conversations. The next section will help to familiarize you with the terms used in discussions about object-oriented programming.

Object-Oriented Programming Terminology

When discussing object-oriented programs, you will hear programmers use the term *OOP* (pronounced like *loop*). **OOP** is an acronym for object-oriented programming, which, as you know, is a programming methodology based on objects. An **object** is anything that can be seen, touched, or used; in other words, an object is nearly any *thing*. The objects used in an object-oriented program can take on many different forms. The menus, buttons, and list boxes included in most Windows programs are objects. An object also can represent something encountered in real life—such as a wristwatch, a car, a credit card receipt, or an employee.

Every object has attributes and behaviors. The **attributes** are the characteristics that describe the object. When you tell someone that your wristwatch is a Farentino Model 35A, you are describing the watch (an object) in terms of some of its attributes—in this case, its maker and model number. A watch also has many other attributes, such as a crown, dial, hour hand, minute hand, movement, and so on.

An object's **behaviors**, on the other hand, are the operations (actions) that the object is capable of performing. A watch, for example, can keep track of the time. Some watches also can keep track of the date. Still others can illuminate their dials when a button on the watch is pushed.

You also will hear the term *class* in OOP discussions. Similar to a pattern or blueprint, a **class** is a set of instructions used to create an object. Every object used in an object-oriented program comes from a class. A class contains—or, in OOP terms, it **encapsulates**—all of the attributes and behaviors that describe the object the class creates. The blueprint for the Farentino Model 35A watch, for example, encapsulates all of the watch's attributes and behaviors. Objects created from a class are referred to as **instances** of the class, and are said to be "instantiated" from the class. All Farentino Model 35A watches are instances of the Farentino Model 35A class.

Abstraction is another term used in OOP discussions. **Abstraction** refers to the hiding of the internal details of an object from the user. Hiding the internal details helps prevent the user from making inadvertent changes to the object. The internal mechanism of a watch, for example, is enclosed (hidden) in a case to protect the mechanism from damage. Attributes and behaviors that are not **hidden** are said to be **exposed** to the user. Exposed on a Farentino Model 35A watch are the crown used to set the hour and minute hands, and the button used to illuminate the dial. The idea behind abstraction is to expose to the user only those attributes and behaviors that are necessary to use the object, and to hide everything else.

Another OOP term, **inheritance**, refers to the fact that you can create one class from another class. The new class, called the **derived class**, inherits the attributes and behaviors of the original class, called the **base class**. For example, the Farentino company might create a blueprint of the Model 35B watch from the blueprint of the Model 35A watch. The Model 35B blueprint (the derived class) will inherit all of the attributes and behaviors of the Model 35A blueprint (the base class), but it then can be modified to include an additional feature, such as an alarm.

Finally, you also will hear the term *polymorphism* in OOP discussions. **Polymorphism** is the object-oriented feature that allows the same instruction to be carried out differently depending on the object. For example, you open a door, but you also open an envelope, a jar, and your eyes. You can set the time, date, and alarm on a Farentino watch. Although the meaning of the verbs *open* and *set* are different in each case, you can understand each instruction because the combination of the verb and the object makes the instruction clear. Figure 14-1 uses the wristwatch example to illustrate most of the OOP terms discussed in this section.

tip

The class itself is not an object; only an instance of the class is an object.

tip

The term *encapsulate* means "to enclose in a capsule." In the context of OOP, the "capsule" is a class.

tip

Keep the OOP terms and definitions in mind as you proceed through the remaining sections in this lesson.

tip

Although you can define and code a C++ class in just a matter of minutes, the objects produced by such a class probably will not be of much use. The creation of a good class—one whose objects can be used in a variety of ways by many different programs—requires a lot of time, patience, and planning.

Figure 14-1: Illustration of OOP terms

A watch's attributes and behaviors are encapsulated into the blueprint. Some attributes and behaviors are hidden; some are exposed.

base class

Blueprint of a Farentino Model 35A

Attributes (Data)	Behaviors
Maker	Track time
Model number	Track date
Crown	Illuminate dial
Dial	
Hour hand	
Minute hand	
Movement	

derived class inherits properties of base class

Blueprint of a Farentino Model 35B

Attributes (Data)	Behaviors
Farentino Model 35A attributes	Farentino Model 35A behaviors
Alarm	Ring alarm

objects— instances of a class

MINI-QUIZ

Mini-Quiz 1

1) OOP is an acronym for _____.

2) A class is an object.
   a. True
   b. False

3) An object created from a class is called _____.
   a. an attribute
   b. an instance of the class
   c. the base class
   d. the derived class

4) The operations (actions) that an object can perform are called its _____.

Next, you learn how to define a class in C++.

Defining a Class in C++

Every object used in a program is created from a class. A `string` variable, for example, is an object created from the `string` class. A class defines the attributes and behaviors of the object it creates. The `string` class, for instance, defines the attributes and behaviors of a `string` object.

In addition to using the classes provided by the C++ language, you also can create your own classes. Like the C++ classes, your classes also must specify the attributes and behaviors of the objects they create.

In C++, you create a class using a **class definition**. All class definitions contain two sections: a declaration section and an implementation section. First, you learn about the declaration section.

The Declaration Section of the Class Definition

The **declaration section** of the class definition contains the C++ **class** statement, which specifies the name of the class, as well as the attributes and behaviors included in the class. Figure 14-2 shows the syntax of the **class** statement and includes an example of using the statement to define a simple `Date` class. You can use the `Date` class to create a `Date` object in any program that requires a date—such as a payroll program, a personnel program, or an airline reservation program.

tip

When determining an object's attributes, it is helpful to consider how you would describe the object. A date, for example, typically is described in terms of a month, day, and year. The month, day, and year items, therefore, are the attributes of a `Date` object and need to be included in the `Date` class.

tip

The private members in a class can be directly accessed only by the member methods in the class.

Figure 14-2: Syntax and an example of the `class` **statement**

public and
private
keywords end
with a colon

class
statement
ends with a
semicolon

Syntax

```
class className
{
public:
    public attributes (data members)
    public behaviors (member methods)
private:
    private attributes (data members)
    private behaviors (member methods)
};
```

Example

method
prototypes

variables

```
//declaration section
class Date
{
public:
    //initializes variables
    Date();
    //assigns program values to variables
    void AssignDate(string, string, string);
    //returns formatted date
    string GetFormattedDate();
private:
    string month;
    string day;
    string year;
};
```

The C++ `class` statement begins with the keyword `class`, followed by the name of the class. The name of the class shown in Figure 14-2 is `Date`. Although it is not required by the C++ syntax, most C++ programmers capitalize the first letter in a class name to distinguish it from the name of a variable, which typically begins with a lowercase letter. You will use this naming convention for the classes you create in this book.

As Figure 14-2 indicates, you enclose in braces the attributes and behaviors that define the class, and you end the `class` statement with a semicolon. The attributes, called **data members**, are represented by variables within the `class` statement. The behaviors, called **member methods**, are represented by method prototypes. The `Date` class shown in Figure 14-2, for example, contains three variables named `month`, `day`, and `year`. Each variable is associated with an attribute of a `Date` object. The `Date` class also contains the prototypes for three methods: `Date()`, `AssignDate()`, and `GetFormattedDate()`. Each prototype represents a task that a `Date` object can perform. Here again, although it is not required by the C++ syntax, the convention is to capitalize the first letter in the method's name and the first letter of each subsequent word in the name. This helps to distinguish a method name from a function name, which typically begins with a lowercase letter.

As Figure 14-2 shows, the members of a class can be either public members or private members. You record the public members below the keyword `public` in the `class` statement, and you record the private members below the keyword `private`. In the `Date` class example shown in Figure 14-2, the method prototypes, which represent the object's behaviors, are listed below the keyword `public` in the `class` statement, while the statements that declare the variables are listed below the keyword `private`. Notice that each variable declaration statement specifies the variable's data type and name, but not its initial value; this is because you cannot initialize variables within the `class` statement. You can, however, use special methods, called constructors, to perform the initialization task when an object is created from the class. The method prototype `Date( )`, which appears below the keyword `public` in the `class` statement, is the name of a constructor. You learn more about constructors later in this lesson.

When you use a class to create an object in a program, only the public members of the class are exposed (made available) to the program; the private members are hidden. In most classes, you expose the member methods and you hide the data members. In other words, you list the method prototypes below the keyword `public` in the `class` statement, and you list the variable declarations below the keyword `private`, as shown in Figure 14-2. You expose the member methods to allow the program to use the service each method provides. You hide the data members to protect their contents from being changed incorrectly by the program.

When a program needs to assign data to a private data member, it must use a public member method to do so. It is the public member method's responsibility to validate the data, then either assign the data to the private data member (if the data is valid) or reject the data (if the data is not valid). Keep in mind that a program does not have direct access to the private members of a class. Rather, it must access the private members indirectly, through a public member method.

MINI-QUIZ

Mini-Quiz 2

1) A program cannot access a public member method directly.
    a. True
    b. False

2) In C++, you enter the `class` statement in the _____ section of a class definition.

3) The data members (attributes) are represented by _____ in a class definition.
    a. constants
    b. member methods
    c. public data members
    d. variables

4) A private data member can be accessed directly by a public member method.
    a. True
    b. False

Next, you learn about the implementation section of the class definition.

The Implementation Section of the Class Definition

Each method listed in the declaration section must be defined in the **implementation section** of the class definition. The implementation section of the `Date` class definition is shown in Figure 14-3.

tip

As you do with functions, you list the data type of the formal parameters, separated by commas, within the parentheses following the method's name in the method prototype. You list both the data type and name of the formal parameters, separated by commas, within the parentheses following the method's name in the method header.

Figure 14-3: Implementation section shown in the `Date` **class definition**

declaration section

implementation section

```
//declaration section
class Date
{
public:
    //initializes variables
    Date();
    //assigns program values to variables
    void AssignDate(string, string, string);
    //returns formatted date
    string GetFormattedDate();
private:
    string month;
    string day;
    string year;
};

//implementation section
Date::Date()
{
    month = "0";
    day   = "0";
    year  = "0";
} //end of default constructor

void Date::AssignDate(string m, string d, string y)
{
    month = m;
    day = d;
    year = y;
}   //end of AssignDate method

string Date::GetFormattedDate()
{
    string separator = "/";
    return month + separator + day + separator + year;
}   //end of GetFormattedDate method
```

The implementation section shown in Figure 14-3 contains the definitions for three methods. Notice that each definition corresponds to a method prototype listed in the declaration section. The first definition recorded in the implementation section, as well as the first prototype listed in the declaration section, pertains to the default constructor.

The Default Constructor

A **constructor** is a member method whose instructions are processed, automatically, each time you use the class to create—or in OOP terms, **instantiate**—an object. The sole purpose of a constructor is to initialize the class's variables. Every class should have at least one constructor. Each constructor included in a class must have the same name as the class, but its formal parameters (if any) must be different from any other constructor in the class. A constructor that has no formal parameters is called the **default constructor**.

You list each constructor's prototype below the keyword `public` in the declaration section of the class definition; you define each constructor in the implementation section. Unlike other prototypes and definitions, a constructor's prototype and definition do not begin with a data type. Because the sole purpose of a constructor is to initialize the class's variables, a constructor never returns a value, so no data type—not even **void**—is included in the prototype or definition.

The **Date** class shown in Figure 14-3 has one constructor, **Date()**. Because the constructor has no formal parameters, it is the default constructor for the **Date** class. Notice that the default constructor's header contains the name of the class—**Date**—and the name of the constructor—**Date()**. As you learned in Chapter 13, the two colons (**::**) that appear between the class name and method name are called the scope resolution operator and indicate that the method to the right of the operator is contained in the class whose name appears to the left of the operator. In this case, the scope resolution operator indicates that the **Date()** constructor belongs to the **Date** class.

Recall that a program does not have direct access to the private members of a class. Rather, it must access the private members through a public member method.

Public Member Methods

The public member methods in a class define the tasks that an object can perform. You already have learned about one public member method: a constructor. Recall that a constructor automatically initializes an object's private data members when the object is created in a program.

In addition to one or more constructors, most classes also contain public member methods that programs can use to assign new values to an object's private data members and also view the contents of the private data members. For example, a program can use the **Date** class's **AssignDate()** method to assign new values to a **Date** object's private **month**, **day**, and **year** variables. A program can use the **Date** class's **GetFormattedDate()** method, on the other hand, to view the contents of a **Date** object's private variables.

As Figure 14-3 indicates, the **AssignDate()** method is a void method, and the **GetFormattedDate()** method is a value-returning method. Notice that the **AssignDate()** method receives three **string** values from the program that calls it. The first value represents the month number, the second value the day number, and the third value the year number. The **AssignDate()** method assigns these values to the three variables listed in the **private** area of the class. Unlike the **AssignDate()** method, the **GetFormattedDate()** method does not receive any information from the program that calls it. The method simply returns the contents of the **month**, **day**, and **year** variables separated by a slash (/).

Next, you learn how to use a class to create an object in a program.

Using the Class in a Program

Once a class is defined, you then can create an instance of it—in other words, an object—in a program. You create an object using the syntax *className objectName*;, where *className* is the name of the class, and *objectName* is the name of the object. For example, to create a **Date** object named **hireDate**, you use the statement **Date hireDate;**.

You call (invoke) a public member method using the syntax *objectName.methodName* (*[argumentlist]*). In the syntax, *objectName* is the name of the object, and *methodName* is the name of the method. The *argumentlist* section in the syntax specifies one or more arguments to pass to the method. Notice that the *argumentlist* section is optional. To call the **hireDate** object's **GetFormattedDate()** method, you use **hireDate .GetFormattedDate()**. However, you use **hireDate.AssignDate(10, 24, 2004)** to call the **hireDate** object's **AssignDate()** method, passing the method the month, day, and year arguments.

The hire date program shown in Figure 14-4 uses the Date class to create a Date object. The statement that creates the Date object, as well as the statements that call the public member methods, are shaded in the figure.

Figure 14-4: Hire date program

tip

Typically, the class definition code is entered in a header file rather than in the program itself. You learn how to enter a class definition in a header file in Lab 14.3 in the Application lesson.

```cpp
#include <iostream>
#include <string>

using std::cout;
using std::cin;
using std::endl;
using std::string;

//declaration section
class Date
{
public:
        //initializes variables
        Date();
        //assigns program values to variables
        void AssignDate(string, string, string);
        //returns formatted date
        string GetFormattedDate();
private:
        string month;
        string day;
        string year;
};

//implementation section
Date::Date()
{
        month = "0";
        day   = "0";
        year  = "0";
} //end of default constructor

void Date::AssignDate(string m, string d, string y)
{
        month = m;
        day = d;
        year = y;
}   //end of AssignDate method

string Date::GetFormattedDate()
{
        string separator = "/";
        return month + separator + day + separator + year;
}   //end of GetFormattedDate method
```

Figure 14-4: Hire date program (continued)

```cpp
int main()
{
    //create Date object
    Date hireDate;

    //declare variables
    string hireMonth = "";
    string hireDay   = "";
    string hireYear  = "";

    //get month, day, and year
    cout << "Enter the month number: ";
    cin >> hireMonth;
    cout << "Enter the day number: ";
    cin >> hireDay;
    cout << "Enter the year number: ";
    cin >> hireYear;

    //use the Date object to set the date
    hireDate.AssignDate(hireMonth, hireDay, hireYear);

    //display the formatted date
    cout << "Employee hire date: "
        << hireDate.GetFormattedDate() << endl;

    return 0;
}   //end of main function
```

Study closely the **main()** function's code shown in Figure 14-4. When the hire date program is executed, the **Date hireDate;** statement creates a **Date** object named **hireDate**. After the object is created, the default constructor is called, automatically, to initialize the private data members. In this case, the default constructor initializes the **month**, **day**, and **year** variables to the empty string. The next three statements in the **main()** function create and initialize three **string** variables named **hireMonth**, **hireDay**, and **hireYear**. The user then is prompted to enter the month, day, and year that the employee was hired. The program assigns the user's responses to the **hireMonth**, **hireDay**, and **hireYear** variables.

Next, the program calls the **Date** class's **AssignDate()** method, passing it the hire date information. Recall that the **AssignDate()** method is a public member of the **Date** class. The **AssignDate()** method assigns the hire date information to the private data members of the **Date** class. In this case, the private data members are the **month**, **day**, and **year** variables. The program then calls the **GetFormattedDate()** method to return the contents of the **month**, **day**, and **year** variables separated by a slash (/). The program displays the returned information on the screen.

The last statement processed is the **return 0;** statement, which returns the number 0 to the operating system to indicate that the program ended normally.

Mini-Quiz 3

1) The scope resolution operator is _____.

2) Write the default constructor's prototype for a class named `Item`.

3) Assume the `Item` class in Question 2 contains two private data members: a `char` variable named `code` and an `int` variable named `price`. Write the definition for the default constructor.

You now have completed Chapter 14's Concept lesson. You can either take a break or complete the end-of-lesson questions and exercises before moving on to the Application lesson.

SUMMARY

A class is a pattern for creating one or more instances of the class—in other words, one or more objects. A class encapsulates all of an object's attributes and behaviors. An object's attributes are the characteristics that describe the object, and its behaviors are the operations (actions) that the object can perform.

The OOP term *abstraction* refers to the hiding of an object's internal details from the user; this is done to prevent the user from making inadvertent changes to the object. The idea behind abstraction is to expose to the user only the attributes and behaviors that are necessary to use the object and to hide everything else. In most classes, you expose an object's behaviors (member methods) and you hide its attributes (data members).

Polymorphism is the object-oriented feature that allows the same instruction to be carried out differently depending on the object.

You can use a constructor to initialize the data members in a class when an object is created. A class can have more than one constructor. Each constructor has the same name, but its formal parameters (if any) must be different from any other constructor. A constructor that has no formal parameters is called the default constructor. A constructor does not have a data type, because it cannot return a value.

You create an object using the syntax *className objectName;*, where *className* is the name of the class and *objectName* is the name of the object. You call (invoke) a public member method using the syntax *objectName.methodName(*[*argumentlist*]*)*, where *objectName* is the name of the object and *methodName* is the name of the method. In the optional *argumentlist* section, you enter any arguments you want passed to the method.

ANSWERS TO MINI-QUIZZES

Mini-Quiz 1

1) object-oriented programming

2) b. False

3) b. an instance of the class

4) behaviors

Mini-Quiz 2

1) b. False

2) declaration

3) d. variables

4) a. True

Mini-Quiz 3

1) :: (two colons)

2) Item();

3)
```
Item::Item()
{
    code = ' ';
    price = 0;
} //end of default constructor
```

QUESTIONS

1) A blueprint for creating an object in C++ is called _____.
   A. a class
   B. an instance
   C. a map
   D. a pattern

2) Which of the following statements is false?
   A. An example of an attribute is the `minutes` variable in a `Time` class.
   B. An example of a behavior is the `SetTime()` method in a `Time` class.
   C. An object created from a class is referred to as an instance of the class.
   D. A class is considered an object.

3) You hide a member of a class by recording the member below the _____ keyword in the `class` statement.
   A. `confidential`
   B. `hidden`
   C. `private`
   D. `restricted`

4) You expose a member of a class by recording the member below the _____ keyword in the `class` statement.
   A. `common`
   B. `exposed`
   C. `public`
   D. `unrestricted`

5) A program can access the private members of a class _____.
   A. directly
   B. only through the public members of the class
   C. only through other private members of the class
   D. none of the above—the program cannot access the private members of a class in any way

6) In most classes, you expose the _____ and hide the _____.

A. attributes, data members

B. data members, member methods

C. member methods, data members

D. variables, member methods

7) The method definitions for a class are entered in the _____ section in the class definition.

A. declaration

B. implementation

C. method

D. program-defined

8) Which of the following is the scope resolution operator?

A. ::   (two colons)

B. *   (asterisk)

C. .   (period)

D. ->   (hyphen and a greater than symbol)

9) The name of the constructor method for a class named `Animal` is _____.

A. `Animal()`

B. `AnimalConstructor()`

C. `ConstAnimal()`

D. any of the above could be used as the name of the constructor method

10) Which of the following statements is false?

A. You typically use a public member method to change the value stored in a private data member.

B. Because the constructor does not return a value, you place the keyword `void` before the constructor's name.

C. The public member methods in a class can be accessed by any program that uses an object created from the class.

D. An instance of a class is considered an object.

11) Which of the following creates an `Animal` object named `dog`?

A. `Animal dog;`

B. `Animal "dog";`

C. `dog = "Animal";`

D. `dog Animal();`

12) Assume a program creates an `Animal` object named `dog`. Which of the following calls the `DisplayBreed()` method, which is a public member method contained in the `Animal` class?

A. `Animal::DisplayBreed()`

B. `DisplayBreed()`

C. `dog::DisplayBreed()`

D. `dog.DisplayBreed()`

Look For These
Symbols

Debugging

Discovery

EXERCISES

1) In this exercise, you create the hire date program you viewed in the lesson.

   A. If necessary, start Visual Studio .NET. Open the Ch14ConE01 Solution (Ch14ConE01 Solution.sln) file, which is contained in the Cpp\Chap14\ Ch14ConE01 Solution folder.

   B. Enter the hire date program shown in Figure 14-4.

   C. Save and then build the solution.

   D. Execute the program. Test the program by entering the number 4 as the month, the number 23 as the day, and the number 2004 as the year. The program should display the formatted date 4/23/2004 in the Command Prompt window. Close the Command Prompt window.

   E. When the program is working correctly, close the Output window, then use the File menu to close the solution.

2) Write the class definition for a class named **Employee**. The class should include data members for an employee object's name and salary. (The salary may contain a decimal place.) The class should contain two member methods: the default constructor and a method that allows a program to assign values to the data members.

3) Add two member methods to the **Employee** class you created in Exercise 2. One member method should allow any program using an **Employee** object to view the contents of the salary data member. The other member method should allow the program to view the contents of the employee name data member. (*Hint*: Have the member method simply return the contents of the appropriate data member.)

4) Add another member method to the **Employee** class you modified in Exercise 3. The member method should calculate an **Employee** object's new salary, based on a raise percentage provided by the program using the object. Before making the calculation, the member method should verify that the raise percentage is greater than or equal to 0. If the raise percentage is less than 0, the member method should assign the number 0.00 as the new salary.

5) In this exercise, you use the **Employee** class from Exercise 4 to create an object in a program.

   A. If necessary, start Visual Studio .NET. Open the Ch14ConE05 Solution (Ch14ConE05 Solution.sln) file, which is contained in the Cpp\Chap14\ Ch14ConE05 Solution folder.

   B. Enter the class definition from Exercise 4.

   C. The instructions to create an **Employee** object, assign values to the object, display the name and current salary, calculate the new salary, and display the new salary are missing from the program. Complete the program, using the comments as a guide.

   D. Save and then build the solution.

   E. Execute the program. Test the program by entering your name, a current salary amount of 54000, and a raise rate of .1. The program should display your name, the number 54000, and the number 59400. Close the Command Prompt window.

   F. When the program is working correctly, close the Output window, then use the File menu to close the solution.

6) In this exercise, you modify the program you created in Exercise 1. The modified program will allow the user to display the formatted date using either slashes (/) or hyphens (-).

A. If necessary, start Visual Studio .NET. Open the Ch14ConE06 Solution (Ch14ConE06 Solution.sln) file, which is contained in the Cpp\Chap14\ Ch14ConE06 Solution folder.

B. Open the Ch14ConE01.cpp file, which is contained in the Cpp\Chap14\ Ch14ConE01 Solution\Ch14ConE01 Project folder.

C. Copy the instructions in the Ch14ConE01.cpp file to the clipboard, then close the Ch14ConE01.cpp window. Click the Ch14ConE06.cpp tab, then paste the instructions into the Ch14Cone06.cpp file.

D. The `GetFormattedDate()` method should receive a string that indicates whether the program wants slashes (/) or hyphens (-) in the date. Modify the program's code accordingly.

E. Save and then build the solution.

F. Execute the program. Test the program by entering 12 as the month, 5 as the day, 2005 as the year, and a - (hyphen) as the separator. The formatted date, 12-5-2005, should appear in the Command Prompt window. Close the Command Prompt window.

G. Execute the program again. This time, enter 9 as the month, 30 as the day, 2004 as the year, and a / (slash) as the separator. The formatted date, 9/30/2004, should appear in the Command Prompt window. Close the Command Prompt window.

H. When the program is working correctly, close the Output window, then use the File menu to close the solution.

7) In this exercise, you modify the **Date** class created in this lesson. The modified class will allow the program to view the contents of the private data members, individually.

A. If necessary, start Visual Studio .NET. Open the Ch14ConE07 Solution (Ch14ConE07 Solution.sln) file, which is contained in the Cpp\Chap14\ Ch14ConE07 Solution folder.

B. Add three member methods to the class. Each method should allow a program to view the contents of one of the three private data members.

C. Complete the three statements that display the month, day, and year, using the member methods you created in Step B.

D. Save and then build the solution.

E. Execute the program. Test the program by entering 3 as the month, 7 as the day, and 2005 as the year. The formatted date, month, day, and year should appear on separate lines in the Command Prompt window. Close the Command Prompt window.

F. When the program is working correctly, close the Output window, then use the File menu to close the solution.

8)   Correct the errors in the **Item** class shown in Figure 14-5.

Figure 14-5

```
class Item
{
private:
     item();
     void AssignItem(string, double);
public:
     string name;
     double price;
}

Item()
{
     name = "";
     price = 0.0;
}   //end of default constructor

void AssignItem(string n, double p)
{
     name = n;
     price = p;
}   //end of AssignItem method
```

Application Lesson

Using Classes and Objects in a C++ Program

Lab 14.1 - Stop and Analyze If necessary, start Visual Studio .NET. Open the Ch14Lab1 Solution (Ch14Lab1 Solution.sln) file contained in the Cpp\Chap14\Ch14Lab1 Solution folder. Figure 14-6 shows the code entered in the Ch14Lab1.cpp file. (The line numbers are included in the figure only.) Study the code, then answer the questions.

Figure 14-6: C++ instructions entered in the Ch14Lab1.cpp file

```cpp
1  //Ch14Lab1.cpp - increases and displays a price
2  //Created/revised by <your name> on <current date>
3
4  #include <iostream>
5  #include <string>
6
7  using std::cout;
8  using std::cin;
9  using std::endl;
10 using std::string;
11
12 //declaration section
13 class Item
14 {
15 public:
16     //initializes variables
17     Item();
18     //assigns program values to variables
19     void AssignData(string, double);
20     //returns the increased price
21     double GetIncreasedPrice(double);
22 private:
23     string id;
24     double price;
25 };
26
27 //implementation section
28 Item::Item()
29 {
30     id    = "";
31     price = 0.0;
32 } //end of default constructor
33
34 void Item::AssignData(string idNum, double p)
35 {
36     id = idNum;
37     price = p;
38 } //end of AssignData method
39
40 double Item::GetIncreasedPrice(double rate)
41 {
```

Figure 14-6: C++ instructions entered in the Ch14Lab1.cpp file (continued)

```
42      if (rate > 1.0)
43          rate = rate / 100.0;
44      //end if
45      return price + price * rate;
46 }    //end of GetIncreasedPrice method
47
48
49 int main()
50 {
51      //create Item object
52      Item computer;
53
54      //declare variables
55      string computerId    = "";
56      double computerPrice = 0.0;
57      double incRate       = 0.0;
58
59      //get computer ID
60      cout << "Enter the computer ID (X to end): ";
61      cin >> computerId;
62      while (computerId != "X" && computerId != "x")
63      {
64          //get price and increase
65          cout << "Enter the price: ";
66          cin >> computerPrice;
67          cout << "Enter the increase rate: ";
68          cin >> incRate;
69
70          //use the Item object to assign the ID and price
71
72
73          //display the increased price
74          cout << "The new price of computer " << computerId << " is $";
75
76
77          //get computer ID
78          cout << "Enter the computer ID (X to end): ";
79          cin >> computerId;
80      }   //end while
81
82      return 0;
83 }    //end of main function
```

Questions

1. What are the names of the private member variables in the **Item** class?
2. What is the name and purpose of the default constructor?
3. What is the purpose of the **AssignData()** method?
4. What is the purpose of the **GetIncreasedPrice()** method?
5. What statement is missing from Line 71? Enter the missing statement in the program.
6. What statement is missing from Line 75? Enter the missing statement in the program.
7. Save and then build the solution.
8. Execute the program. Enter AB34 as the ID, 455 as the price, and .15 as the rate. What is the new price for the computer? Close the Command Prompt window, then close the Output window.
9. Use the File menu to close the solution.

Lab 14.2 The owners of two small businesses want you to create programs for them. Sharon Terney of Terney Landscaping wants a program that the salespeople can use to estimate the cost of laying sod. Jack Sysmanski, the owner of All-Around Fence Company, wants a program that he can use to calculate the cost of installing a fence. In this lab, you will create the Terney Landscaping program. You will create the All-Around Fence Company program in Exercise 1 at the end of this lesson.

While analyzing the Terney Landscaping and All-Around Fence Company problems, you notice that each involves a rectangular shape. For example, in the Terney Landscaping program, you need to find the area of a rectangle on which the sod is to be laid. In the All-Around Fence Company program, on the other hand, you need to find the perimeter of the rectangle around which a fence is to be constructed. To save time, you decide to create a **Rectangle** class that contains the attributes and behaviors of a rectangle. You will use the **Rectangle** class to create a **Rectangle** object in the Terney Landscaping and All-Around Fence Company programs.

Before you can create a **Rectangle** object in a program, you first must create a class that specifies a **Rectangle** object's attributes and behaviors. When determining an object's attributes, it is helpful to consider how you would describe the object. Rectangles, for example, typically are described in terms of two dimensions: length and width. The length and width dimensions are the attributes of a **Rectangle** object. You will include both attributes as private data members in the **Rectangle** class, using the **double** variables **length** and **width**.

Next, you determine the object's behaviors, which are the tasks that the object can perform. To be useful in both the Terney Landscaping and All-Around Fence Company programs, a **Rectangle** object must be capable of performing the four tasks shown in Figure 14-7.

Figure 14-7: Tasks a Rectangle **object should be capable of performing**

Tasks
1. initialize the private data members (default constructor)   2. assign values to the private data members   3. calculate and return the area of the object   4. calculate and return the perimeter of the object

As Figure 14-7 indicates, a **Rectangle** object will need to initialize its private data members; you will include a default constructor in the class for this purpose. A **Rectangle** object also will need to provide a means for the program to assign values to the private data members. This task will be handled by a void member method named **SetDimensions()**. You will use two value-returning member methods named **CalcArea()** and **CalcPerimeter()** to perform the third and fourth tasks listed in Figure 14-7, which are to calculate and return the area and perimeter of a **Rectangle** object. Figure 14-8 shows the completed class definition for the **Rectangle** class.

Figure 14-8: Completed class definition for the `Rectangle` **class**

```
//declaration section
class Rectangle
{
public:
    Rectangle();
    void SetDimensions(double, double);
    double CalcArea();
    double CalcPerimeter();
private:
    double length;
    double width;
};

//implementation section
Rectangle::Rectangle()
{
    length = 0.0;
    width  = 0.0;
}   //end of default constructor

void Rectangle::SetDimensions(double len, double wid)
{
    //assigns length and width to private data members
    if (len > 0.0 && wid > 0.0)
    {
        length = len;
        width = wid;
    }   //end if
}   //end of SetDimensions method

double Rectangle::CalcArea()
{
    return length * width;
}   //end of CalcArea method

double Rectangle::CalcPerimeter()
{
    return (length + width) * 2.0;
}   //end of CalcPerimeter method
```

Now that you have defined the `Rectangle` class, you can begin creating the Terney Landscaping program, which will use the class to create a `Rectangle` object. Figure 14-9 shows the IPO chart and C++ instructions for the Terney Landscaping program.

Figure 14-9: IPO chart for the Terney Landscaping program

IPO chart information	C++ instructions

Input
  length in feet
  width in feet
  sod price per square yard
	`double lawnLength = 0.0;`
	`double lawnWidth = 0.0;`
	`double priceSqYd = 0.0;`

Processing Rectangle object	`Rectangle lawn;`

Output
  area
  total price
	`double lawnArea = 0.0;`
	`double totalPrice = 0.0;`

Algorithm
1. enter length in feet,
  width in feet, and sod
  price per square yard
	`cout << "Length (in feet): ";`
	`cin >> lawnLength;`
	`cout << "Width (in feet): ";`
	`cin >> lawnWidth;`
	`cout << "Sod price (in square yards): ";`
	`cin >> priceSqYd;`

2. use the Rectangle object's
  SetDimensions() method to
  assign the length and width
  to the Rectangle object
	`lawn.SetDimensions(lawnLength, lawnWidth);`

3. use the Rectangle object's
  CalcArea() method to calculate
  the area in square feet, then
  divide the result by 9 to get
  the area in square yards
	`lawnArea = lawn.CalcArea() / 9.0;`

4. calculate the total price by
  multiplying the area in square
  yards by the sod price per
  square yard
	`totalPrice = lawnArea * priceSqYd;`

5. display the area in square
  yards and the total price
	`cout << setiosflags(ios::fixed) << setprecision(2);`
	`cout << "Square yards: " << lawnArea << endl;`
	`cout << "Total price: " << totalPrice << endl;`

The IPO chart in Figure 14-9 shows that the output is the area (in square yards) and the total price. The input is the length and width of the rectangle (both in feet), and the price of a square yard of sod. Notice that a `Rectangle` object is used as a processing item in the program.

As the algorithm indicates, the program first gets the length, width, and price information from the user. The program passes the length and width information to the `Rectangle` object's `SetDimensions()` method, which assigns the values (assuming that both are greater than 0) to the `Rectangle` object's private data members.

Step 3 in the algorithm is to calculate the area of the `Rectangle` object in square yards. To do so, the program first calls the `Rectangle` object's `CalcArea()` method to calculate the area in square feet. It then converts the value returned by the `CalcArea()` method from square feet to square yards by dividing the return value by the number 9, which is the number of square feet in a square yard.

Step 4 in the algorithm is to calculate the total price by multiplying the number of square yards by the price per square yard of sod. The last step in the algorithm is to display the area (in square yards) and the total price on the screen. Notice that, although the `Rectangle` object also is capable of calculating its perimeter, the current program does not require the object to perform that task.

Activity for Lab 14.2

In this activity, you enter the C++ instructions shown in Figures 14-8 and 14-9 into the computer. You then test the program to verify that it is working correctly.

To create the Terney Landscaping program, then test the program:

1. If necessary, start Visual Studio .NET. Create a blank solution named Ch14Lab2 Solution. Save the solution in the Cpp\Chap14 folder.

2. Add an empty C++ Win32 Console Project to the solution. Name the project Ch14Lab2 Project.

3. Add a new C++ source file to the project. Name the source file Ch14Lab2.

4. Type **//Ch14Lab2.cpp – calculates and displays the cost of laying sod** and press **Enter**.

5. Type **//Created/revised by <*your name*> on <*current date*>**, replacing <*your name*> and <*current date*> with your name and the current date, respectively. Press **Enter** twice.

6. Type the following two #include directives, then press **Enter** twice:

   #include <iostream>
   #include <iomanip>

7. Type the following six using statements, then press **Enter** twice:

   using std::cout;
   using std::cin;
   using std::endl;
   using std::setprecision;
   using std::ios;
   using std::setiosflags;

8. Complete the program by entering the Rectangle class definition and main() function, which are shaded in Figure 14-10.

Figure 14-10: Terney Landscaping program

```
//Ch14Lab2.cpp - calculates and displays the cost of laying sod
//Created/revised by <your name> on <current date>

#include <iostream>
#include <iomanip>

using std::cout;
using std::cin;
using std::endl;
using std::setprecision;
using std::ios;
using std::setiosflags;

//declaration section
class Rectangle
{
```

Figure 14-10: Terney Landscaping program (continued)

```cpp
public:
    Rectangle();
    void SetDimensions(double, double);
    double CalcArea();
    double CalcPerimeter();
private:
    double length;
    double width;
};

//implementation section
Rectangle::Rectangle()
{
    length = 0.0;
    width  = 0.0;
}   //end of default constructor

void Rectangle::SetDimensions(double len, double wid)
{
    //assigns length and width to private data members
    if (len > 0.0 && wid > 0.0)
    {
        length = len;
        width = wid;
    }   //end if
}   //end of SetDimensions method

double Rectangle::CalcArea()
{
    return length * width;
}   //end of CalcArea method

double Rectangle::CalcPerimeter()
{
    return (length + width) * 2.0;
}   //end of CalcPerimeter method

int main()
{
    //create Rectangle object
    Rectangle lawn;

    //declare variables
    double lawnLength = 0.0;
    double lawnWidth = 0.0;
    double priceSqYd = 0.0;
    double lawnArea = 0.0;
    double totalPrice = 0.0;

    //get length, width, and sod price
    cout << "Length (in feet): ";
    cin >> lawnLength;
    cout << "Width (in feet): ";
    cin >> lawnWidth;
    cout << "Sod price (in square yards): ";
    cin >> priceSqYd;
```

Figure 14-10: Terney Landscaping program (continued)

Figure 14-10: Terney Landscaping program (continued)

```
    //assign input to Rectangle object
    lawn.SetDimensions(lawnLength, lawnWidth);

    //calculate area and total price
    lawnArea = lawn.CalcArea() / 9.0;
    totalPrice = lawnArea * priceSqYd;

    //display area and total price
    cout << setiosflags(ios::fixed) << setprecision(2);
    cout << "Square yards: " << lawnArea << endl;
    cout << "Total price: $" << totalPrice << endl;

    return 0;
}    //end of main function
```

9. Save and then build the solution. Verify that the program generated no warnings.

10. Execute the program. When prompted to enter the length, type **120** and press **Enter**. When prompted to enter the width, type **75** and press **Enter**. When prompted to enter the price per square yard of sod, type **1.55** and press **Enter**. The Command Prompt window shows that the area in square yards is 1000.00 and the total price is $1550.00, as shown in Figure 14-11.

Figure 14-11: Result of processing the Terney Landscaping program

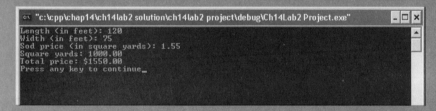

11. Close the Command Prompt window.

12. Close the Output window, then use the File menu to close the solution.

Lab 14.3 In this lab, you modify the program you created in Lab 14.2. More specifically, you will enter the `Rectangle` class definition in a header file, then include the header file in the Terney Landscaping program.

Activity for Lab 14.3

Before modifying the program created in Lab 14.2, you copy the instructions contained in the Ch14Lab2.cpp file to a new solution.

To copy the instructions contained in the Ch14Lab2.cpp file to a new solution:

1. If necessary, start Visual Studio .NET. Create a blank solution named **Ch14Lab3 Solution**. Save the solution in the Cpp\Chap14 folder.

2. Add an empty C++ Win32 Console Project to the solution. Name the project **Ch14Lab3 Project**.

3. Add a new C++ source file to the project. Name the source file **Ch14Lab3**.

4. Use the File menu to open the Ch14Lab2.cpp file contained in the Cpp\Chap14\Ch14Lab2 Solution\Ch14Lab2 Project folder. Select the contents of the file, then copy the contents to the clipboard.

5. Close the Ch14Lab2.cpp window.

6. Click the **Ch14Lab3.cpp** tab, then paste the instructions from the clipboard into the Ch14Lab3.cpp window.

7. Change the filename in the first program comment to **Ch14Lab3.cpp**. If necessary, change the date in the second comment.

First you will add a header file to the solution. You then will move the Rectangle class definition to the header file.

To add a header file to the solution, then move the class definition into the header file:

1. Click **File** on the menu bar, point to **New**, and then click **File**. The New File dialog box opens.

2. If necessary, click **Visual C++** in the Categories list box.

3. Click **Header file (.h)** in the Templates list box. See Figure 14-12.

Figure 14-12: New File dialog box

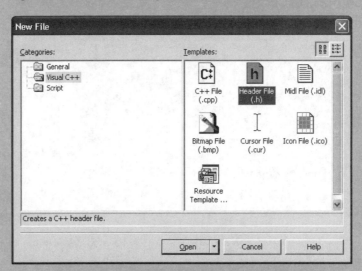

4. Click the **Open** button. An empty header file appears in the Header1 window.

   Before entering any text in the header file, you will save the file, using the name RectangleClass.

5. Click **File** on the menu bar, then click **Save Header1 As**. The Save File As dialog box opens.

   Typically, header files are saved in a separate folder, because they usually are used in more than one solution. In this case, you will save the RectangleClass header file in the MyClasses folder.

6. Locate and then open the Cpp\MyClasses folder.

7. In the Save File As dialog box, type **RectangleClass** in the File name text box, then click the **Save** button. The window tab indicates that the header file's name is RectangleClass.h. (The ".h" stands for "header".)

8. Click the **Ch14Lab3.cpp** tab. Select (highlight) the Rectangle class definition. Click **Edit** on the menu bar, and then click **Cut**. Click the **RectangleClass.h** tab, then click **Edit**, and then click **Paste**.

9. Enter the comments shaded in Figure 14-13, replacing the <your name> and <current date> text with your name and the current date.

Figure 14-13: Comments entered in the header file

```cpp
//RectangleClass.h - Rectangle class definition
//Created/revised by <your name> on <current date>

//declaration section
class Rectangle
{
public:
    Rectangle();
    void SetDimensions(double, double);
    double CalcArea();
    double CalcPerimeter();
private:
    double length;
    double width;
};

//implementation section
Rectangle::Rectangle()
{
    length = 0.0;
    width  = 0.0;
}   //end of default constructor

void Rectangle::SetDimensions(double len, double wid)
{
    //assigns length and width to private data members
    if (len > 0.0 && wid > 0.0)
    {
        length = len;
        width = wid;
    }   //end if
}   //end of SetDimensions method

double Rectangle::CalcArea()
{
    return length * width;
}   //end of CalcArea method

double Rectangle::CalcPerimeter()
{
    return (length + width) * 2.0;
}   //end of CalcPerimeter method
```

10. Click **File** on the menu bar, and then click **Save RectangleClass.h**.

11. Close the RectangleClass.h window.

For a program to use a class defined in a header file, the program must contain a `#include` directive whose syntax is **#include** *headerFilename*. As you learned in Chapter 3, a `#include` directive tells the C++ compiler to include the contents of another file—in this case, a header file—in the current program. The `#include` directive provides a convenient way to merge the source code from one file with the source code in another file, without having to retype the code.

To include the RectangleClass.h header file in the Terney Landscaping program:

1. Position the insertion point below the `#include <iomanip>` directive in the Ch14Lab3.cpp window.

2. Type **#include "C:\Cpp\MyClasses\RectangleClass.h"** and press **Enter**. (If necessary, change the `#include` directive to reflect the location of the RectangleClass.h header file on your system.)

3. Save and then build the solution. Verify that the program generated no warnings.

4. Execute the program. When prompted to enter the length, type **120** and press **Enter**. When prompted to enter the width, type **75** and press **Enter**. When prompted to enter the price per square yard of sod, type **1.55** and press **Enter**. The Command Prompt window shows that the area in square yards is 1000.00 and the total price is $1550.00.

5. Close the Command Prompt window.

6. Close the Output window, then use the File menu to close the solution.

You now have completed Chapter 14's Application lesson. You can either take a break or complete the end-of-lesson exercises.

ANSWERS TO LABS

Lab 14.1

1. The names of the private member variables are `id` and `price`.

2. The name of the default constructor is `Item()`. The constructor's purpose is to initialize the private member variables in the class.

3. The purpose of the `AssignData()` method is to assign the program values to the private member variables in the class.

4. The purpose of the `GetIncreasedPrice()` method is to calculate and return the new price of the item, given the current price and the increase rate.

5. The `computer.AssignData(computerId, computerPrice);` statement is missing from Line 71.

6. The `cout << computer.GetIncreasedPrice(incRate) << endl;` statement is missing from Line 75.

8. The new price is $523.25.

Lab 14.2

No answer required.

Lab 14.3

No answer required.

Look For These
Symbols

Debugging

Discovery

EXERCISES

1) In this exercise, you use the **Rectangle** class that you saved to a header file in Lab 14.3 to declare a **Rectangle** object in the All-Around Fence program. (Recall that the **Rectangle** class is defined in the Cpp\MyClasses\ RectangleClass.h file on your computer's hard disk.)

A. If necessary, start Visual Studio .NET. Open the Ch14AppE01 Solution (Ch14AppE01 Solution.sln) file, which is contained in the Cpp\Chap14\ Ch14AppE01 Solution folder.

B. Click File on the menu bar, then click Add Existing Item. Open the Cpp\MyClasses folder. If necessary, click RectangleClass.h in the list of file-names. Click the Open button to add the header file to the current solution.

C. Enter the appropriate #include directive to include the contents of the RectangleClass.h header file in the program.

D. Jack Sysmanski, the owner of All-Around Fence Company, wants a program that he can use to calculate the cost of installing a fence. Use the IPO chart shown in Figure 14-14 to complete the program. Display the perimeter as an integer. Display the total price with a dollar sign and two decimal places.

Figure 14-14

Input	Processing	Output
length in feet width in feet fence cost per linear foot	Processing items: Rectangle object Algorithm: 1. enter length in feet, width in feet, and fence cost per linear foot 2. use the Rectangle object's SetDimensions() method to assign the length and width to the Rectangle object 3. use the Rectangle object's CalcPerimeter() method to calculate the perimeter 4. calculate the total price by multiplying the perimeter by the fence cost per linear foot 5. display the perimeter and total price	perimeter total price

E. Save and then build the solution.

F. Execute the program. Test the program using 120 as the length, 75 as the width, and 10 as the cost per linear foot. The program should display 390 as the perimeter and $3900.00 as the total price.

G. When the program is working correctly, close the Output window, then use the File menu to close the solution.

2) In this exercise, you modify the `Rectangle` class that you created in Lab 14.2 so that it allows the program to view the contents of the `length` and `width` data members. You also modify the Terney Landscaping program so that it displays the length and width measurements.

A. If necessary, start Visual Studio .NET. Create a blank solution named Ch14AppE02 Solution. Save the solution in the Cpp\Chap14 folder. Add an empty C++ Win32 Console Project to the solution. Name the project Ch14AppE02 Project. Add a new C++ source file to the project. Name the source file Ch14AppE02.

B. Use the File menu to open the Ch14Lab2.cpp file contained in the Cpp\Chap14\ Ch14Lab2 Solution\Ch14Lab2 Project folder. Select the contents of the file, then copy the contents to the clipboard. Close the Ch14Lab2.cpp window. Click the Ch14AppE02.cpp tab, then paste the instructions from the clipboard into the Ch14AppE02.cpp window.

C. Change the filename in the first program comment to Ch14AppE02.cpp. If necessary, change the date in the second comment.

D. Add two value-returning methods to the class. Each method should return the value of one of the attributes.

E. Modify the program so that it displays the length and width of the rectangle, in addition to the area and total price. (Use the methods you created in Step D.)

F. Save and then build the solution.

G. Execute the program. Test the program using 120 feet as the length, 75 feet as the width, and 1.55 as the price. The program should display 120.00 as the length, 75.00 as the width, 1000.00 as the area in square yards, and $1550.00 as the total price.

H. When the program is working correctly, close the Output window, then use the File menu to close the solution.

3) In this exercise, you modify the `Rectangle` class that you created in Lab 14.2 so that its `SetDimensions()` method returns a value. You also modify the Terney Landscaping program.

A. If necessary, start Visual Studio .NET. Create a blank solution named Ch14AppE03 Solution. Save the solution in the Cpp\Chap14 folder. Add an empty C++ Win32 Console Project to the solution. Name the project Ch14AppE03 Project. Add a new C++ source file to the project. Name the source file Ch14AppE03.

B. Use the File menu to open the Ch14Lab2.cpp file contained in the Cpp\Chap14\ Ch14Lab2 Solution\Ch14Lab2 Project folder. Select the contents of the file, then copy the contents to the clipboard. Close the Ch14Lab2.cpp window. Click the Ch14AppE03.cpp tab, then paste the instructions from the clipboard into the Ch14AppE03.cpp window.

C. Change the filename in the first program comment to Ch14AppE03.cpp. If necessary, change the date in the second comment.

D. Modify the `SetDimensions()` method so that it returns a value that indicates whether the length and width dimensions passed to the method are greater than 0.

E. If the `SetDimensions()` method indicates that the length and width dimensions are greater than 0, the program should calculate and display both the area and the total price; otherwise, it should display an error message. Modify the program appropriately.

F. Save and then build the solution.

G. Execute the program. Test the program using 120 feet as the length, 75 feet as the width, and 1.55 as the price. The program should display 1000.00 as the area in square yards and $1550.00 as the total price. Close the Command Prompt window.

H. Execute the program again. Enter −5 as the length, 6 as the width, and 3 as the price. The program should display an error message, because the length dimension is less than 0. Close the Command Prompt window.

I. When the program is working correctly, close the Output window, then use the File menu to close the solution.

4) In this exercise, you create a **Triangle** class. You also complete a program that uses the **Triangle** class to create a **Triangle** object.

A. If necessary, start Visual Studio .NET. Open the Ch14AppE04 Solution (Ch14AppE04 Solution.sln) file, which is contained in the Cpp\Chap14\ Ch14AppE04 Solution folder.

B. Create a **Triangle** class. The class should include a void method that allows the program to set the triangle's dimensions. The method should verify that all of the dimensions are greater than 0 before assigning the values to the private data members. The class also should include two value-returning methods. One value-returning method should calculate the area of a triangle, and the other should calculate the perimeter of a triangle. The formula for calculating the area of a triangle is 1/2 * b * h, where b is the base and h is the height. The formula for calculating the perimeter of a triangle is a + b + c, where a, b, and c are the lengths of the sides. Determine the appropriate variables to include in the class. Be sure to include a default constructor that initializes the variables.

C. Declare a **Triangle** object. Prompt the user for the triangle's dimensions, then display the triangle's area and perimeter amounts. Display the amounts with zero decimal places.

D. Save and then build the solution.

E. Execute the program. Test the program appropriately.

F. When the program is working correctly, close the Output window, then use the File menu to close the solution.

5) In this exercise, you modify an existing header file.

A. If necessary, start Visual Studio .NET. Click File on the menu bar, point to Open, and then click File. Open the MyDateClass.h header file, which is contained in the Cpp\MyClasses folder. The header file defines a class named **MyDate**. Study the code, then close the header file.

B. Open the Ch14AppE05 Solution (Ch14AppE05 Solution.sln) file, which is contained in the Cpp\Chap14\Ch14AppE05 Solution folder.

C. Add the MyDateClass.h header file to the solution.

D. Enter the appropriate #include directive to include the contents of the MyDateClass.h header file in the program.

The program uses the **MyDate** class to create an object named **today**. Study the code. Notice that the program prompts the user to enter the month, day, and year. It then uses the **MyDate** class's public methods—**SetDate()** and **DisplayDate()**—to set and display the date entered by the user. The program also uses a public method named **UpdateDate()** to increase the day by 1. It then displays the new date on the screen.

E. Save and then build the solution.

F. Execute the program. Enter 3 as the month, 15 as the day, and 2005 as the year. The Command Prompt window shows that today is 3/15/2005 and tomorrow is 3/16/2005, which is correct. Close the Command Prompt window.

G. Execute the program again. Enter 3 as the month, 31 as the day, and 2004 as the year. The Command Prompt window shows that today is 3/31/2004 and tomorrow is 3/32/2004, which is incorrect. Close the Command Prompt window.

H. Open the Solution Explorer window, then open the Header Files folder. Right-click MyDateClass.h, then click Open. Modify the **UpdateDate()** method so that it updates the date correctly. For example, if today is 3/31/2005, then tomorrow is 4/1/2005. If today is 12/31/2005, then tomorrow is 1/1/2006. You do not have to worry about leap years; treat February as though it always has 28 days.

I. Save the header file, then close the MyDateClass.h window.

J. Build the solution, then execute the program. Test the program four times, using the following dates: 3/15/2004, 4/30/2005, 2/28/2004, and 12/31/2005. The Command Prompt window should show that tomorrow's dates are 3/16/2004, 5/1/2005, 3/1/2004, and 1/1/2006.

K. When the program is working correctly, close the Output window, then use the File menu to close the solution.

6) In this exercise, you modify the Terney Landscaping program that you created in Lab 14.2 so that it passes an object to a function.

A. If necessary, start Visual Studio .NET. Create a blank solution named Ch14AppE06 Solution. Save the solution in the Cpp\Chap14 folder. Add an empty C++ Win32 Console Project to the solution. Name the project Ch14AppE06 Project. Add a new C++ source file to the project. Name the source file Ch14AppE06.

B. Use the File menu to open the Ch14Lab2.cpp file contained in the Cpp\Chap14\ Ch14Lab2 Solution\Ch14Lab2 Project folder. Select the contents of the file, then copy the contents to the clipboard. Close the Ch14Lab2.cpp window. Click the Ch14AppE06.cpp tab, then paste the instructions from the clipboard into the Ch14AppE06.cpp window.

C. Change the filename in the first program comment to Ch14AppE06.cpp. If necessary, change the date in the second comment.

D. Modify the program so that it uses a function named **calcAndDisplay()** to calculate and display the area and the total price. Pass the **Rectangle** object and the price per square yard to the function.

E. Save and then build the solution.

F. Execute the program. Test the program using 120 feet as the length, 75 feet as the width, and 1.55 as the price. The program should display 1000.00 as the area in square yards and $1550.00 as the total price. Close the Command Prompt window.

G. When the program is working correctly, close the Output window, then use the File menu to close the solution.

7) In this exercise, you learn how to overload a method.

A. If necessary, start Visual Studio .NET. Click File on the menu bar, point to Open, and then click File. Open the DiscRecClass.h header file, which is contained in the Cpp\MyClasses folder.

Pool-Time, which sells in-ground pools, wants a program that its salespeople can use to determine the number of gallons of water required to fill an in-ground pool—a question commonly asked by customers. To calculate the number of gallons, you need to find the volume of the pool. The volume formula is length * width * depth.

B. Modify the `Rectangle` class appropriately. You will need to include an additional private data member and an additional public method. You also will need to modify the default constructor and the `SetDimensions()` method. Be sure to verify that the depth value is greater than 0 before assigning the value to the private data member.

C. Save and then close the header file.

D. Open the Ch14AppE07A Solution (Ch14AppE07A Solution.sln) file, which is contained in the Cpp\Chap14\Ch14AppE07A Solution folder.

E. Add the DiscRecClass.h header file to the solution.

F. Enter the appropriate `#include` directive to include the contents of the DiscRecClass.h header file in the program.

G. Complete the program, using the IPO chart shown in Figure 14-15. Display the volume and number of gallons amounts with two decimal places.

Figure 14-15

Input	Processing	Output
length in feet width in feet depth in feet	Processing items: Rectangle object Algorithm: 1. enter length in feet, width in feet, of water and depth in feet 2. use the Rectangle object's SetDimensions() method to assign the length, width, and depth to the Rectangle object 3. use the Rectangle object's CalcVolume() method to calculate the volume in cubic feet 4. calculate the number of gallons of water by dividing the volume by .13368 5. display the volume in cubic feet and the number of gallons of water	volume in cubic feet number of gallons

H. Save and then build the solution.

I. Execute the program. Use 25 feet as the length, 15 feet as the width, and 6.5 feet as the depth. The program should display 2437.50 as the volume and 18233.84 as the number of gallons. Close the Command Prompt window.

J. When the program is working correctly, close the Output window, then use the File menu to close the solution.

Now observe what happens when you use the modified `Rectangle` class in the Terney Landscaping program that you created in the lesson.

K. Open the Ch14AppE07B Solution (Ch14AppE07B Solution.sln) file, which is contained in the Cpp\Chap14\Ch14AppE07B Solution folder.

L. Add the DiscRecClass.h header file to the solution.

M. Enter the appropriate `#include` directive to include the contents of the DiscRecClass.h header file in the program.

N. Study the program's code. Notice that the program passes two actual arguments to the `SetDimensions()` method. Save and then build the solution. The C++ compiler displays an error message indicating that the `SetDimensions()` method does not take two parameters.

In C++, you can assign the same name to more than one method, so long as each method has a different set of formal parameters. To use the `Rectangle` class in both the Terney Landscaping and Pool-Time programs, for example, you will provide two `SetDimensions()` methods in the `Rectangle` class: one having two formal parameters (for the Terney Landscaping program) and the other having three formal parameters (for the Pool-Time program). When two methods have the same name but different parameters, the methods are said to be *overloaded*.

O. Open the Solution Explorer window, then open the Header Files folder. Right-click DiscRecClass.h, then click Open. Enter the prototype and definition for a `SetDimensions()` method that first accepts two **double** values, then verifies that the values are greater than 0, and then assigns the values to the private data members.

P. Save and then close the header file.

Q. Save and then build the solution. Execute the program. Enter 120 as the length, 75 as the width, and 1.55 as the price per square yard of sod. The program displays 1000.00 as the area in square yards and $1550.00 as the total price. Close the Command Prompt window.

R. When the program is working correctly, close the Output window, then use the File menu to close the solution.

 8)   In this exercise, you debug a C++ program.

A. If necessary, start Visual Studio .NET. Open the Ch14AppE08 Solution (Ch14AppE08 Solution.sln) file, which is contained in the Cpp\Chap14\ Ch14AppE08 Solution folder. The program prompts the user to enter an item name and the amount of the item in inventory. It then displays the name and amount on the screen.

B. Save and then build the solution. Correct any errors in the program, then save and build the solution.

C. Execute the program. Enter Chair as the item name and 10 as the amount. The program should display "Name: Chair" and "Amount: 10" in the Command Prompt window. Close the Command Prompt window. If necessary, correct any errors in the program.

D. When the program is working correctly, close the Output window, then use the File menu to close the solution.

 Please visit the Testing Center at www.course.com/testingcenter for more practice on the topics covered in this chapter.

ASCII Codes

Character	ASCII	Binary	Character	ASCII	Binary	Character	ASCII	Binary
SPACE	32	00100000	B	66	01000010	d	100	01100100
!	33	00100001	C	67	01000011	e	101	01100101
"	34	00100010	D	68	01000100	f	102	01100110
#	35	00100011	E	69	01000101	g	103	01100111
$	36	00100100	F	70	01000110	h	104	01101000
%	37	00100101	G	71	01000111	i	105	01101001
&	38	00100110	H	72	01001000	j	106	01101010
'	39	00100111	I	73	01001001	k	107	01101011
(	40	00101000	J	74	01001010	l	108	01101100
)	41	00101001	K	75	01001011	m	109	01101101
*	42	00101010	L	76	01001100	n	110	01101110
+	43	00101011	M	77	01001101	o	111	01101111
,	44	00101100	N	78	01001110	p	112	01110000
–	45	00101101	O	79	01001111	q	113	01110001
.	46	00101110	P	80	01010000	r	114	01110010
/	47	00101111	Q	81	01010001	s	115	01110011
0	48	00110000	R	82	01010010	t	116	01110100
1	49	00110001	S	83	01010011	u	117	01110101
2	50	00110010	T	84	01010100	v	118	01110110
3	51	00110011	U	85	01010101	w	119	01110111
4	52	00110100	V	86	01010110	x	120	01111000
5	53	00110101	W	87	01010111	y	121	01111001
6	54	00110110	X	88	01011000	z	122	01111010
7	55	00110111	Y	89	01011001	{	123	01111011
8	56	00111000	Z	90	01011010			124	01111100
9	57	00111001	[	91	01011011	}	125	01111101
:	58	00111010	\	92	01011100	~	126	01111110
;	59	00111011	]	93	01011101	DELETE	127	01111111
<	60	00111100	^	94	01011110			
=	61	00111101	_	95	01011111			
>	62	00111110	`	96	01100000			
?	63	00111111	a	97	01100001			
@	64	01000000	b	98	01100010			
A	65	01000001	c	99	01100011			

C-Strings

Declaring and Using C-Strings

As you learned in Chapter 4, the `string` data type is added to the C++ language through the use of the `string` class, which comes with Visual C++ .NET. Rather than using the `string` class to create a `string` variable or `string` named constant, you also can use an array of `char` variables. Such an array is referred to as a C-string, because this is how C programmers created strings before the `string` class was available.

Figure B-1 shows the syntax of a C-string and includes several examples of using the syntax to create C-string variables and C-string named constants.

Figure B-1: Syntax and examples of creating a C-string

Syntax
char *variablename*[*x*] = *initialvalue*;

Examples and results
`char petName[5] = "Spot";`
creates a C-string variable named **petName** and initializes it to the string "Spot" plus the null character; the variable can store four characters plus the null character
`char petName[5] = "";`
creates a C-string variable named **petName** and initializes it to the empty string plus the null character; the variable can store four characters plus the null character
`char partNo[] = "ABC356";`
creates a C-string variable named **partNo** and initializes it to the string "ABC356" plus the null character; the variable can store six characters plus the null character
`char partNo[] = {'A', 'B', 'C', '3', '5', '6', '\0'};`
creates a C-string variable named **partNo** and initializes it to the characters 'A', 'B', 'C', '3', '5', '6', and '\0' (which is the null character); the variable can store six characters plus the null character
`const char title[11] = "HP Company";`
creates a C-string variable named title and initializes it to the string "HP Company" plus the null character; the variable can store 10 characters plus the null character

Notice that the syntax includes [*x*] after the *variablename*. The *x* value, which must be enclosed in square brackets, is a number that is one more than the maximum number of characters you want to store in the variable. For example, to store 10 characters in a C-string variable, you use the number 11 as the *x* value. This is because C++ appends an additional character, referred to as the null character, to the end of a C-string variable. The **null character** marks the end of the **char** array in the computer's internal memory.

Study closely the examples shown in Figure B-1. The `char petName[5] = "Spot";` statement shown in the first example creates a C-string variable named **petName** that is composed of five **char** variables. The first **char** variable contains the letter S, the second the letter p, the third the letter o, the fourth the letter t, and the fifth the null character, which is designated by a backslash and the number 0, enclosed in single quotation marks, like this: '\0'. Figure B-2 illustrates the **petName** variable in the computer's internal memory.

Figure B-2: Illustration of the `petName` variable in memory

```
S
p
o
t
\0
```

The char petName[5] = ""; statement in the second example creates a five-element C-string variable named petName. The petName variable can store four characters plus the null character. The statement initializes the first four elements in the variable to the empty string, then stores the null character in the fifth element.

The char partNo[] = "ABC356"; statement in the third example in Figure B-1 creates a seven-element C-string variable named partNo. The statement initializes the first six elements to the string "ABC356", then stores the null character in the seventh element. Notice that the x value is optional when creating a C-string; however, the square brackets are not optional. When you do not provide the x value, the computer uses the *initialvalue* section to determine the number of elements to reserve in memory.

Because a C-string is simply an array of char variables, you also could create and initialize the partNo variable using the statement char partNo[] = {'A', 'B', 'C', '3', '5', '6', '\0'};, as shown in the fourth example. However, it is more common to use a string enclosed in double quotation marks to initialize a C-string.

The const char title[11] = "HP Company"; statement in the fifth example creates a C-string named constant named title. The statement assigns the string "HP Company" and the null character to the named constant.

You can use various methods to assign data to an existing C-string variable.

Assigning Data to a C-String Variable

Figure B-3 shows examples of assigning data to an existing C-string variable.

Figure B-3: Examples of assigning data to a C-string variable

Examples and results
`strcpy(petName, "Tess");` assigns the string "Tess" and the null character to the petName variable
`strcpy(petName, myPetName);` assigns the contents of the myPetName variable, including the null character, to the petName variable
`cin >> partNo;` assigns the characters entered at the keyboard, plus the null character, to the partNo variable
`cin >> setw(7) >> partNo;` assigns a maximum of six characters entered at the keyboard, plus the null character, to the partNo variable
`cin.getline(partNo, 7);` assigns a maximum of six characters entered at the keyboard, plus the null character, to the partNo variable

Unlike other variables, C-string variables cannot be assigned a new value from an assignment statement. Rather, you use the C++ strcpy() function to assign a new value to a C-string variable, as shown in the first and second examples in Figure B-3. (`strcpy` stands for *string copy*.) The syntax of the `strcopy()` function is **strcpy(***variablename***,** *string***);**. In the syntax, *variablename* is the name of a C-string variable, and *string* can be either zero or more characters enclosed in double quotation marks, or the name of another C-string variable. The `strcpy(petName, "Tess");` statement in the first example assigns the string "Tess" and the null character to the `petName` variable. The `strcopy(petName, myPetName);` statement in the second example assigns the contents of the `myPetName` variable, including the null character, to the `petName` variable.

You also can use the extraction operator (`>>`) to assign to a C-string variable the data entered at the computer keyboard. For example, you can use the `cin >> partNo;` statement shown in the third example in Figure B-3 to assign the keyboard input to the `partNo` variable. However, there is one problem that you should be aware of when using the `>>` operator to enter information into a C-string variable: If the user enters more characters than the variable can store, the computer stores the additional characters in memory locations adjacent to, but not reserved for, the variable. Storing the additional characters in these unreserved locations may write over some important information in memory, perhaps crashing either the program or your system.

You can use the C++ `setw` stream manipulator to ensure that the string read into the C-string variable does not exceed the variable's size; this is demonstrated in the fourth example in Figure B-3. (`setw` stands for *set width*.) The syntax of the `setw` stream manipulator is **setw(***size***)**, where *size* is an integer that indicates the size of the C-string variable. In other words, it indicates the total number of characters, including the null character, that the variable can store. As the fourth example in the figure indicates, you use the `cin >> setw(7) >> partNo;` statement to store a maximum of six characters entered at the keyboard, plus the null character, in the `partNo` variable. To use the `setw` stream manipulator in a program, the program must contain the `#include <iomanip>` directive and the `#using std::setw;` statement.

You also can use the `getline()` function to assign keyboard input to a C-string variable. Recall that you use the `getline()` function rather than the `>>` operator when the input may contain a space character. When using the `getline()` function to assign data to a C-string variable, you use the syntax **cin.getline(***variablename***,** *size***);**. In the syntax, *variablename* is the name of a C-string variable, and *size* is an integer that indicates the total number of characters, including the null character, that the variable can store. The `getline()` function stops reading characters from the keyboard either when it encounters the newline character in the input or when the number of characters read is one less than the *size* of the C-string variable. As the last example in Figure B-3 indicates, you use the `cin.getline(partNo, 7);` statement to assign a maximum of six characters entered at the keyboard, plus the null character, to the `partNo` variable.

Next, you learn how to compare C-strings.

Comparing C-Strings

You use either the `strcmp()` function or the `stricmp()` function to compare C-strings in C++. The `strcmp()` function performs a case-sensitive comparison, while the `stricmp()` function performs a case-insensitive comparison. (`strcmp` stands for *string compare*, and `stricmp` stands for *string, ignore case, compare*.) Figure B-4 shows the syntax of each function and includes examples of using each function.

tip

As you learned in Chapter 4, the newline character represents the Enter key.

Figure B-4: Syntax and examples of the `strcmp()` and `stricmp()` functions

Syntax
strcmp(_string1_, _string2_**)**   **stricmp(**_string1_, _string2_**)**   Both functions return 0 if _string1_ is equal to _string2_. They return 1 if _string1_ is greater than _string2_, and return −1 if _string1_ is less than _string2_.

Examples and results
`strcmp("Kelly", "Kelly")`   returns 0 because both strings are equal
`stricmp("Kelly", "KELLY")`   returns 0 because, ignoring case, both strings are equal
`strcmp("Kelly", "Kate")`   returns 1 because the e in Kelly (_string1_) is greater than the a in Kate (_string2_)
`strcmp("KELLY", "Kelly")`   returns −1 because the E in KELLY (_string1_) is less than the e in Kelly (_string2_)
`strcmp("Kelly", "KYLE")`   returns 1 because the e in Kelly (_string1_) is greater than the Y in KYLE (_string2_)
`stricmp("Kelly", "KYLE")`   returns −1 because, ignoring case, the e in Kelly (_string1_) is less than the Y in KYLE (_string2_)
`strcmp("Mary", firstName)`   assuming the `firstName` variable contains the string "Paul", returns −1 because the M in Mary (_string1_) is less than the P in Paul (_string2_)
`stricmp(first, firstName)`   assuming the `first` variable contains the string "MARY", and the `firstName` variable contains the string "Mary", returns 0 because, ignoring case, both strings are equal

As Figure B-4 indicates, if _string1_ is equal to _string2_, both functions return the number 0. For instance, the `strcmp("Kelly", "Kelly")` function shown in the first example in Figure B-4 returns the number 0 because both strings are equal. The `stricmp("Kelly", "KELLY")` function shown in the second example also returns the number 0 because, ignoring case, both strings are equal.

If _string1_ is greater than _string2_, the `strcmp()` and `stricmp()` functions return the number 1. An example of a function that returns the number 1 is `strcmp("Kelly", "Kate")`, which is shown in the third example in the figure. The number 1 is returned because the e in Kelly is greater than the a in Kate.

If *string1* is less than *string2*, the `strcmp()` and `stricmp()` functions return the number –1. An example of a function that returns the number –1 is `strcmp("KELLY", "Kelly")`, which is shown in the fourth example in Figure B-4. The number –1 is returned because the E in KELLY is less than the e in Kelly.

In the fifth example, the `strcmp("Kelly", "KYLE")` function returns the number 1 because the e in Kelly is greater than the Y in KYLE. In the sixth example, the `stricmp("Kelly", "KYLE")` statement returns the number –1 because, ignoring case, the e in Kelly is less than the Y in KYLE.

Assuming the `firstName` variable contains the string "Paul", the `strcmp("Mary", firstName)` statement in the seventh example returns the number –1, because the M in Mary is less than the P in Paul.

Assuming the `first` variable contains the string "MARY", and the `firstName` variable contains the string "Mary", the `stricmp(first, firstName)` statement shown in the last example in Figure B-4 returns the number 0 because, ignoring case, both strings are equal.

Figure B-5 shows a C++ program that demonstrates most of the concepts you learned in this appendix.

Figure B-5: Program containing a C-string variable

```cpp
#include <iostream>
#include <iomanip>

using std::cout;
using std::cin;
using std::endl;
using std:: setw;

int main()
{
    //declare variable
    char id[4] = "";

    //enter input
    cout << "Enter a three-character ID: ";
    cin >> setw(4) >> id;

    //display output
    if (stricmp(id, "MSN") == 0)
        cout << "Microsoft Network" << endl;
    else
        cout << "Other network" << endl;
    //end if

    return 0;
} //end of main function
```

You now have completed Appendix B.

Pointers

Using Pointer Variables

As you learned in Chapter 4, a variable is a location (within the computer's internal memory) where a program can temporarily store data. The data may be entered by the user at the keyboard, or it may be read from a file, or it may be the result of a calculation made by the computer.

A **pointer variable**, referred to simply as a **pointer**, is a special type of variable. Rather than storing a value, a pointer stores the memory address of a variable that contains data. In other words, a pointer tells the computer where the data is located in the computer's internal memory. As you will learn later in this appendix, you can use a pointer to access the data stored in the variable to which it points.

Although the concept of a pointer may sound confusing, pointers are really nothing new to you; you have been using pointers since you were in elementary school. Think about the last time you looked up a topic in the index of a book. Once you found the topic, you used the page number that appeared next to the topic to locate the information in the book. In essence, the page number is a pointer to the information.

Before you can use a pointer, you must declare it. As with all variables, you also should initialize the pointer variables you create.

Declaring and Initializing a Pointer

Figure C-1 shows the syntax you use to declare and initialize a pointer in C++. It also includes examples of using the syntax.

Figure C-1: Syntax and examples of declaring and initializing a pointer

Syntax
datatype ***** *pointername* **=** *initialvalue*;
Examples and results
`int *numPtr = NULL;`
creates a pointer named `numPtr` and initializes it to `NULL`; the pointer can store the address of an `int` variable
`double *salesPtr = NULL;`
creates a pointer named `salesPtr` and initializes it to `NULL`; the pointer can store the address of a `double` variable
`char *idPtr = NULL;`
creates a pointer named `idPtr` and initializes it to `NULL`; the pointer can store the address of a `char` variable

In the syntax, *datatype* is the type of data stored in the variable to which the pointer points. For example, if the pointer points to a `double` variable, then the pointer's *datatype* should be `double`. Similarly, a pointer that points to an `int` variable should be declared as `int`. If you attempt to store in a pointer the address of a variable that has a different datatype—for example, if you try to store the address of an `int` variable in a `double` pointer—the C++ compiler will display an error message.

Pointername in the syntax is the name of the pointer. The name should follow the same naming rules as for variables. The asterisk (*) that appears before the *pointername* is called the **indirection operator** and it indicates that the variable being created is a pointer. The term *indirection* refers to the fact that the pointer can be used to refer, indirectly, to the variable to which it points.

Initialvalue in the syntax is the beginning value for the pointer. As with an uninitialized variable, an uninitialized pointer contains an arbitrary number that could refer to a crucial location in memory. If your program changes the value stored at that location, your system could be corrupted and subsequently crash. To prevent this from happening, you always should initialize a pointer when it is created. Pointers typically are initialized to the NULL value. **NULL** is a named constant built into C++. When a pointer contains the NULL value, the pointer is pointing to nothing in memory, so the program cannot destroy, inadvertently, a critical memory location.

The names of the pointers created by the statements shown in Figure C-1 are `numPtr`, `salesPtr`, and `idPtr`. In other words, the asterisk is not part of the name; rather, it tells the computer that the name that follows it is the name of a pointer. Notice that the names of the pointers in Figure C-1 end with the three characters *Ptr*, which stand for *pointer*. Although the C++ syntax does not require pointer names to end with *Ptr*, doing so makes it clear that the name refers to a pointer (which contains the address of a variable) rather than to a variable (which contains data).

After you declare and initialize a pointer, you then can assign the address of a variable to it.

Assigning an Address to a Pointer

Figure C-2 shows the syntax of an assignment statement that assigns an address to a pointer. The figure also includes examples of using the syntax.

Figure C-2: Syntax and examples of assignment statements that assign an address to a pointer

Syntax
pointername = **&***variablename*;
Examples and results
`numPtr = &number;` assigns the address of the **number** variable to the **numPtr** pointer
`salesPtr = &qtrSales;` assigns the address of the **qtrSales** variable to the **salesPtr** pointer
`idPtr = &initial;` assigns the address of the **initial** variable to the **idPtr** pointer

In the syntax, *pointername* is the name of a pointer, and *variablename* is the name of the variable whose address you want to assign to the pointer. Notice that the syntax uses the address-of operator (&) to assign the variable's address to the pointer. (You learned about the address-of operator in Chapter 10.)

After assigning the address of a variable to a pointer, you then can use the pointer to access the value stored in the variable.

Using a Pointer to Access the Value Stored in a Variable

Assume that a program declares an `int` variable named `number` and initializes it to the number 5. The program also declares a pointer named `numPtr`, to which it assigns the address of the `number` variable, as shown in Figure C-3.

Figure C-3: Contents of the `numPtr` **pointer and** `number` **variable**

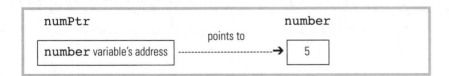

Notice that the **number** variable contains the number 5, and the **numPtr** variable contains the address of the **number** variable. The **numPtr** variable tells the computer where the **number** variable is located in memory. In other words, it tells the computer where the number 5 is stored.

Now assume that you want to display the contents of the **number** variable on the computer screen. You can display the contents of a variable by referring to the variable either directly or indirectly. You refer to a variable directly by using the variable's name in a statement. For example, the **cout << number << endl;** statement displays the contents of the **number** variable on the screen. This method of referring to a variable is called **direct reference** because the statement uses the variable's name to directly access its contents.

You also can use a pointer to indirectly access the contents of a variable. You do so using the indirection operator (*) followed by the pointer's name in a statement. For example, you could use the **cout << *numPtr << endl;** statement to display the contents of the **number** variable on the screen. This method of referring to a variable is called **indirect reference** because, rather than using the variable's name to access its contents, the statement uses the address stored in its associated pointer.

Figure C-4 shows examples of referring to the **number** variable both directly and indirectly.

Figure C-4: Examples of referring to a variable directly and indirectly

Reference	Statement	Result
Direct Indirect	`cout << number << endl;` `cout << *numPtr << endl;`	Either statement can be used to display the contents of the **number** variable
Direct Indirect	`number = 3;` `*numPtr = 3;`	Either statement can be used to assign the number 3 to the **number** variable
Direct Indirect	`cin >> number;` `cin >> *numPtr;`	Either statement can be used to store the value entered at the keyboard to the **number** variable
Direct Indirect	`number = number * 2;` `*numPtr = *numPtr * 2;`	Either statement can be used to multiply the contents of the **number** variable by 2, then store the result in the **number** variable

Notice that you can accomplish the same result using either direct or indirect referencing. For example, you can use either the **number = 3;** statement or the ***numPtr = 3;** statement to assign the number 3 to the **number** variable. The ***numPtr = 3;** statement tells the computer to assign the number 3 to the variable whose address is stored in **numPtr**. In this case, **numPtr** contains the address of the **number** variable.

When referencing a variable indirectly, be sure to include the indirection operator before the pointer's name. If you omit the indirection operator, the computer will use the pointer itself rather than the variable to which the pointer points. For example, the **cout << numPtr << endl;** statement will display the address contained in the **numPtr** pointer rather than the value contained in the **number** variable.

Figure C-5 shows a program that uses a pointer, and Figure C-6 shows a sample run of the program.

Figure C-5: Pointer demo program

```cpp
#include <iostream>

using std::cout;
using std::endl;

int main()
{
    //declare variable
    int number = 5;

    //declare pointer
    int *numPtr = NULL;

    //assign variable's address to pointer
    numPtr = &number;

    //use the pointer to assign a value to the
    //number variable
    *numPtr = 3;

    //use the pointer to display the contents
    //of the number variable
    cout << "The number variable contains the number: "
        << *numPtr << endl;

    //display the contents of the pointer
    cout << "The numPtr pointer contains the address: "
        << numPtr << endl;

    return 0;
}   //end of main function
```

Figure C-6: Sample run of the pointer demo program

```
"c:\cpp\appc\pointer demo solution\pointer demo project\debug\Pointer Demo Project.exe"

The number variable contains the number: 3
The numPtr pointer contains the address: 0012FED4
Press any key to continue_
```

Do not be concerned if the memory address shown in Figure C-6 looks confusing. Addresses in memory are specified using the hexadecimal (base 16) system rather than the decimal (base 10) system. In the decimal system, all numbers are formed using one or more of the ten digits from 0 through 9. For example, the number 125 is a combination of the digits 1, 2, and 5. In the hexadecimal system, all numbers are formed using one or more of the following sixteen digits and letters: 0, 1, 2, 3, 4, 5, 6, 7, 8, 9, A, B, C, D, E, and F. In the hexadecimal system, the letter A is equivalent to the number 10 in the decimal system. The letter B is equivalent to the number 11, and so on.

Next, you learn how to pass a pointer to a function.

Passing a Pointer to a Function

Jerod Antiques needs a program that the store clerks can use to increase by 10% the price of each item in inventory. Figure C-7 shows a program that can be used to accomplish this task, and Figure C-8 shows a sample run of the program.

Figure C-7: Jerod Antiques program

indirection operator

indirection operator

```
#include <iostream>
#include <iomanip>

using std::cout;
using std::cin;
using std::endl;
using std::setprecision;
using std::ios;
using std::setiosflags;

//function prototype
void calcNewPrice(double *);

int main()
{
    //declare variable
    double price = 0.0;

    //declare pointer
    double *pricePtr = NULL;

    //assign variable's address to pointer
    pricePtr = &price;

    //get the old price
    cout << "Enter the old price: ";
    cin >> *pricePtr;

    //call function to calculate the new price
    calcNewPrice(pricePtr);

    //display the new price
    cout << setiosflags(ios::fixed) << setprecision(2);
    cout << "New price: " << *pricePtr << endl;

    return 0;
}   //end of main function

//*****function definitions*****
void calcNewPrice(double *num)
{
    *num = *num * 1.1;
}   //end of calcNewPrice function
```

Figure C-8: Sample run of the Jerod Antiques program

The `main()` function shown in Figure C-7 declares and initializes a `double` variable named `price`. The `main()` function needs to pass the `price` variable to the `calcNewPrice()` function, whose task is to calculate the new price, then replace the old price stored in the `price` variable with the new price. For the `calcNewPrice()` function to change the contents of the `price` variable, the `main()` function must pass the variable's address to the function. You can pass the address using either the address-of operator or the pointer that contains the variable's address. The `main()` function shown in Figure C-7 passes the `pricePtr` pointer to the `calcNewPrice()` function. Notice that, when passing a pointer to a function, you include the indirection operator (*) in the function's prototype and header.

You now have completed Appendix C.

Index

C

N

O